North-East Asia
on a shoestring

Robert Storey
Geoff Crowther & Choe Hyung Pun
Joe Cummings
Robert Strauss
Chris Taylor
Tony Wheeler

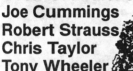

North-East Asia on a shoestring

3rd edition

Published by
Lonely Planet Publications
Head Office: PO Box 617, Hawthorn, Vic 3122, Australia
Branches: PO Box 2001A, Berkeley, CA 94702, USA and London, UK

Printed by
Singapore National Printers Ltd, Singapore

Photographs by
Front cover: Doorknocker in old temple–Canton, China
© Auschromes, photograph by Roy Bisson

First Published
August 1985

This Edition
March 1992

Although the authors and publisher have tried to make the information as accurate as possible, they accept no responsibility for any loss, injury or inconvenience sustained by any person using this book.

National Library of Australia Cataloguing in Publication Data

Robert Storey
North-East Asia on a shoestring.

3rd ed.
Includes index.
ISBN 0 86442 135 4.

1. East Asia – Description and travel – Guide-books.
I. Title.

915.04429

Robert Storey

Devoted mountain climber and computer hacker, Robert has had a number of distinguished careers, including monkeykeeper at a zoo and slot machine repairman in a Las Vegas casino. After running out of money in Taiwan, Robert finally got a decent job, learned Chinese, wrote Lonely Planet's *Taiwan - a travel survival kit* and became a pillar of the community. He updated two other Lonely Planet books – *China* and *Hong Kong, Macau & Canton* – before updating this edition.

Tony Wheeler

Tony was born in England but spent his youth in places like Pakistan, the West Indies and the US. A degree in engineering and an MBA did nothing to settle him down and he dropped out on the Asian overland trail with his wife Maureen. *Across Asia on the Cheap* was their first book, and they've been travelling, writing and publishing guidebooks ever since, setting up Lonely Planet in the mid-70s.

Robert Strauss

In the early '70s Robert took the overland route to Nepal and then studied, taught and edited in England, Germany, Portugal and Hong Kong. For Lonely Planet Robert has worked on the China and Tibet travel survival kits. For Bradt Publications he wrote *The Trans-Siberian Rail Guide*. He has contributed photos and articles to other books, magazines and newspapers in the USA, Australia and Asia.

Joe Cummings

Joe has travelled extensively in Asia. Before travel writing became a full-time job, he was a Peace Corps volunteer in Thailand, a translator/interpreter in San Francisco, a graduate student in Asian Studies (MA 1981) at the University of California (Berkeley), a columnist for the *Asia Record*, an East-West Center Scholar in Hawaii (MA 1985), a university lecturer in Malaysia and an educational consultant in the US and Taiwan. Joe is also author or co-author of Lonely

Planet guides to Thailand, Laos, Burma, Malaysia, Singapore and Indonesia. He is now living in northern California.

Chris Taylor

Originally hailing from Bristol, England, Chris's vocational training includes a stint as a student psychiatric nurse, an eventful year as a clerk in the public service, a protracted period of neglect and grinding poverty while posing as a singer/songwriter, and a year serving as a cultural missionary teaching English in Japan. Numerous trips around Asia and a BA later, Chris joined the Lonely Planet team to edit our phrasebooks. He is currently based in Taiwan.

Geoff Crowther & Choe Hyung Pun

Geoff was born in Yorkshire, England, and started his travelling days as a teenage hitchhiker. Later he got involved with the London underground information centre BIT, helping to put together their first tatty, duplicated overland guides. Geoff has written or collaborated on guides to South America, Malaysia, East and North Africa, India and Korea. He lives with Hyung Pun, who he met in Korea, and their son Ashley, in the rainforests near the New South Wales/Queensland border.

This Book

Lonely Planet's shoestring guides are designed with the budget traveller in mind and give compact, essential information on the countries of a particular region. This guide was compiled from research gathered for our series of *travel survival kits*, which give in-depth coverage of a single country for a range of budgets.

North-East Asia on a shoestring combines the talents of a battalion of Lonely Planet authors. The first edition was put together by Alan Samalgalski and Michael Buckley (China), Tony Wheeler (Hong Kong and Macau), Ian McQueen (Japan) and Geoff Crowther (Korea). The second edition was assembled by Laurie Fullerton, with new research by the same team plus Robert Strauss (China) and Robert Storey (Taiwan). Robert Storey went back to the region to update this third edition – including a completely new chapter on Mongolia – and he also condensed the work of Tony Wheeler, Robert Strauss & Chris Taylor (Japan), Joe Cummings (China) and Geoff Crowther & Choe Hyung Pun (South Korea).

We are deeply grateful to a number of local residents whose assistance in this mammoth project greatly enhanced the quality of the book. With apologies to any who were left out, special thanks go to David & Kil-sup Mason (Korea), Han Nam-sung (Korea), Youn Joung-won & Joung-son (Korea), Jason Gau (Taiwan), John & Jennifer Bryce (Taiwan), Stanley Mo (Hong Kong), Andre & Patrick De Smet (Hong Kong), Galtmaa & Batbaatar (Mongolia).

Many others out there on the road took the time and trouble to write to Lonely Planet with new information. We'd like to thank the following people:

Palmer Acheson (C), Michael Agelasto, Stephen Bailey (UK), Elizabeth Bluntzer (UK), Pam Bowers (UK), Simon Braham (Aus), T Clifford (C), Dave Connolly (Ire), Scott Cooper (USA), H Dammerboer (D), Susanna Dunk (USA), Richard Ganter (UK), Henry Genthe (USA), Ron Gluckman (HK), Joe Gonzales (USA), Jeff & Lois Gunn (Aus), Paul Hagmen (USA), Stephan Hammond (USA), Howard Hattersley (UK), Geert Henau (Bel), Paul Key, Spencer Lane (UK), Christy Lanzl, Randy Levitch (USA), Patton Maclean, David A Mason (Kor), Galen Moore (USA), M & R Pick (Aus), Susanne Randecker (D), Alexandra Rathbone (UK), Tomas Rohlin (Sw), Sumner Rosen (USA), Mark Rosenfeld, Ron Slamowicz (Aus), Anne & Lorenzo Walker (USA), James Wilcox (C)

Aus - Australia, Bel - Belgium, C - Canada, D - Germany, HK - Hong Kong, Ire - Ireland, Kor - Korea, UK - United Kingdom, USA - United States of America, Sw - Sweden

From the Publisher

This edition was edited by Caroline Williamson and proofread by Kay Waters. The maps were updated by Trudi Canavan and the book was designed and laid out by Valerie Tellini. Many thanks also to Tom Smallman for his patient support, to Sharon Wertheim for the index, to Greg Herriman for last-minute bits and pieces, and to Peter Morris for out-of-hours work beyond the call of duty.

Warning & Request

Things change – prices go up, schedules change, good places go bad and bad places go bankrupt – nothing stays the same. So if you find things better or worse, recently opened or long since closed, please write and tell us and help make the next edition better!

Your letters will be used to help update future editions and, where possible, important changes will also be included as a Stop Press section in reprints.

All information is greatly appreciated and the best letters will receive a free copy of the next edition, or any other Lonely Planet book of your choice.

Contents

Map Legend

BOUNDARIES

—·—·—·—	International Boundary
—··—··—	Internal Boundary
+++++++++	National Park or Reserve
— — — — —	The Equator
················	The Tropics

SYMBOLS

◉ NEW DELHI	National Capital
● BOMBAY	Provincial or State Capital
● Pune	Major Town
● Borsi	Minor Town
■	Places to Stay
▼	Places to Eat
☰	Post Office
✈	Airport
i	Tourist Information
⊖	Bus Station or Terminal
66	Highway Route Number
☽ ✝ ☨	Mosque, Church, Cathedral
∴	Temple or Ruin
✚	Hospital
☀	Lookout
⚊	Camping Area
⊓	Picnic Area
⌂	Hut or Chalet
▲	Mountain or Hill
	Railway Station
	Road Bridge
	Railway Bridge
	Road Tunnel
	Railway Tunnel
	Escarpment or Cliff
	Pass
	Ancient or Historic Wall

ROUTES

——————	Major Road or Highway
- - - - - - - -	Unsealed Major Road
——————	Sealed Road
- - - - - - - -	Unsealed Road or Track
═══════	City Street
+++++++++	Railway
—●—	Subway
············	Walking Track
- - - - - - - -	Ferry Route
+H+H+H+H+	Cable Car or Chair Lift

HYDROGRAPHIC FEATURES

	River or Creek
	Intermittent Stream
	Lake, Intermittent Lake
	Coast Line
	Spring
	Waterfall
	Swamp
	Salt Lake or Reef
	Glacier

OTHER FEATURES

	Park, Garden or National Park
	Built Up Area
	Market or Pedestrian Mall
	Plaza or Town Square
	Cemetery

Note: not all symbols displayed above appear in this book

Introduction

North-East Asia is many different and contrasting things: high-energy Hong Kong, a British colony nervously watching the countdown for its return to China; tiny Macau, a curious and colourful colonial relic; Japan, the economic powerhouse of the world, with a myriad glimpses of a picture-postcard rural side still to be found; Mongolia, once the world's largest empire but now one of Asia's least visited backwaters; Korea, exotic and dynamic but split into two violently opposed halves; Taiwan, another dynamic economy but also uneasy about the intentions of its huge would-be parent; and finally China, ancient, vast, varied and stumbling towards modernisation.

Hong Kong, with its superb natural harbour, is the key to this whole region, the centre from which to explore other parts of North-East Asia. This over-populated city-state, offset by beautiful and sparsely populated islands, wins this role through its central position and its reputation as an office for issuing visas and a supermarket for cheap air fares.

Just an hour away by jetfoil is Macau, the oldest European settlement in the East and an interesting contrast to the bustle of Hong Kong. Yet it offers one form of modernisation that Hong Kong lacks – casino gambling.

Individual travel in China will provide you with a host of impressions: a giant statue of Mickey Mouse (adored by the Chinese), the ancient splendour of the Forbidden City and the Great Wall, or the hackwork that is creating modern China. And every so often China throws up something that takes you completely by surprise – like a village lifted lock, stock and barrel out of Switzerland and grafted onto a Chinese mountaintop.

In Japan, despite overwhelming modernisation, you can still find the traditional way of life. In Tohoku in northern Honshu there are towns with old thatched-roof buildings that have survived earthquakes and wars. Despite its comprehensive transport system, Japan is still a country of heavily beaten highways and barely visited back roads.

Taiwan also remains a land of sharp contrasts – heavy industrialisation has taken its toll on the urban environment, yet the rural areas remain amazingly unspoilt. The island is extremely mountainous and offers some of the best hiking opportunities in the region. Traditional Chinese culture flourishes, and is in fact better preserved in Taiwan than on the Chinese mainland.

Although parts of North-East Asia are the most advanced and developed in the whole of Asia, others are as backward as you'll come across. Travellers have been beating a shoestring path across Hong Kong and China for years, but South Korea and Taiwan are relatively little known. Tales of high costs have scared many travellers away from Japan, while Mongolia and North Korea have until recently been about as isolated as the South Pole. North-East Asia is waiting for you to explore it.

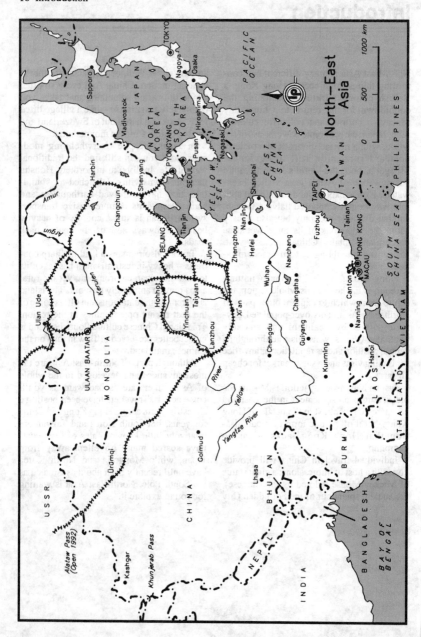

Facts for the Visitor

PLANNING
When, How Much & How Long?

The lunar new year is a week-long holiday falling roughly in late January or February – it's a time to avoid! Nothing exciting happens at this time, but it's a family holiday so everything is closed and public transport is jam-packed. If you have to stay in North-East Asia at this time, stock up with food and reading matter and wait for the chaos to end. Lunar new year falls on 24 January in 1993; 11 February in 1994; 31 January in 1995; and 19 February in 1996. A similar but less severe week of chaos occurs during the Chinese Easter, known as the Qing Ming Festival or Tomb Sweep Day. This usually falls in early April.

The season that most travellers try to avoid is winter. The northernmost regions of China, Mongolia, Korea and Japan experience frigid temperatures, as low as minus 45°C. On the other hand, northern winters are very dry and the snow makes for good

scenery, but as you move south towards central China and southern Japan, winters tend to be chilly and rainy. The only places in North-East Asia that have pleasant winters are south-west Taiwan, the southern half of China's Hainan Island and Yunnan Province in south-west China.

The spring brings moderate temperatures but the weather is fickle – the temperature can plunge suddenly whenever the monsoonal winds blow in from Siberia. Spring is the time to see the various cherry-blossom festivals in Japan, South Korea and Taiwan. Unfortunately, the flowering season only lasts a few weeks and varies from year to year, so it isn't wise to plan your trip around this elusive phenomenon.

Summer is hot throughout the region except high in the mountains. High humidity and rains plague the regions near the Pacific Ocean, but it's much drier as one travels north-west. Indeed, much of north-west China and Mongolia is desert. Summer is

Comparative Costs in North-East Asia
(All prices in US$)

	China	Hong Kong & Macau	Japan	South Korea	Taiwan
100 km by bus	1.50		11.20	1.80	5.75
100 km by train	1.40		11.60	2.00	7.10
Big Mac		1.15	2.95	2.80	2.40
Cheap hotel	9.30	19.00	38.50	10.75	19.20
Cheap restaurant	1.50	2.60	7.70	2.00	1.35
Glass of beer	0.40	3.20	3.50	1.00	3.10
Hostel	2.80	5.20	14.70	8.00	5.75
Loaf of bread	0.40	0.60	1.25	1.75	1.00
Local phone call	0.02	0.13	0.08	0.03	0.04
One litre of petrol		1.05	1.10	0.70	0.70
Time magazine	3.10	3.20	5.40	3.20	3.85

Mongolia
With budget accommodation and no tour, as low as $5 per day. With tours, up to $100 per day

North Korea
$100 to $180 per person per day

also the beginning of typhoon season, but this won't affect you if you keep at least 200 km inland.

The autumn is the best season for the entire region. Temperatures tend to be mild and the weather is dry.

Sporting enthusiasts may have different ideas about what is ideal weather. If you're a skier, January and February are the best months for a visit to the far north. Trekkers have a longer season – spring through autumn. Beach lovers should of course aim for the summer. Other than that, plan your trip according to the most comfortable seasons and your available funds.

What Kind of Trip?

Your finances and commitments are likely to affect what kind of trip you have. Those who are working full-time will most likely have to make a mad dash or even settle for a tour. Travelling this way will of course only allow you to catch a glimpse of a foreign culture. Some travellers compensate for this by concentrating on a special interest, such as skiing, mountain climbing or temple viewing.

Most travellers using this book will have more time than money. If you fall into this category, you're part of a time-honoured tradition. Spending more time in one place is preferable to a mad dash, but if finances become a problem, you might have to either cut the trip short or turn your journey into a working holiday.

What to Bring

If you own more than you can carry on your back, it will own you. The point is, bring as little as possible – but not so little that you have to scrounge off others as some of the 'super lightweight' travellers do. It's better to start with too little rather than too much – you may surprise yourself with how little you need.

A backpack is still the most popular carrying container as it is commodious and the only way to go if you have to do any walking.

On the debit side a backpack is awkward to load on and off buses and trains and doesn't offer much protection for your valuables.

An alternative is a combination backpack and shoulder bag, whose straps zip away inside when not in use. They're not really suitable for long hiking trips but they're much easier to carry than a bag. In either case get some tabs sewn on so you can semi-thief-proof it with small padlocks. Forget suit cases.

Inside? Lightweight and compact are two words that should be etched in your mind when you're deciding what to bring. Saw the handle off your toothbrush if you have to – anything to keep the weight down! You only need two sets of clothes – one to wear and one to wash. You will, no doubt, be buying clothes along the way – except for Japan and possibly Taiwan, clothing is cheap in Asia, and you can find some real bargains in Hong Kong and China. However, don't believe sizes – 'large' in Asia is often equivalent to 'medium' in the West. Asian clothing manufacturers would be wise to visit a Western tourist hotel to see what 'large' really means.

Nylon running or sports shoes are best – comfortable, washable and lightweight. If you're going to be in cold weather, buy them oversized and wear with heavy wool socks – it's better than carrying a pair of boots. Of course, if you're going to be in really bitter cold weather, you'll need insulated shoes or boots, but get something lightweight. A pair of thongs (flip-flop sandals) are useful footwear for indoors and shower rooms.

A Swiss army knife (even if not made in Switzerland) comes in handy, but you don't need one with 27 separate functions. Basically, you need one small sharp blade, a can opener and bottle opener – a built-in magnifying glass or backscratcher isn't necessary.

It's wise to bring a few recent passport-size photos (5x5 cm) just in case your passport gets nicked. In some countries (Mongolia, for example) getting these photos is difficult or time-consuming. You will also need visa photos. See the Visas section for explanation.

The secret of successful packing is plastic

bags or 'stuff bags' – they keep things not only separate and clean but also dry.

The following is a checklist of things you might consider packing, but don't feel obliged to pack everything on this list – you can skip the overcoat and long underwear in summer.

Passport, money, air ticket, address book, business cards, visa photos, passport photos, Swiss army knife, electric immersion coil (for making hot water), cup, padlock, camera & accessories, sunglasses, alarm clock, leakproof water bottle, torch (flashlight) with batteries, comb, compass, daypack, long pants, short pants, long shirt, T-shirt, nylon jacket, overcoat, sweater, woollen stocking cap, mittens, raincover for backpack, rainsuit or poncho, razor, razor blades, shaving cream, sewing kit, spoon, sunhat, sunscreen, toilet paper, tampons, toothbrush, toothpaste, dental floss, deodorant, shampoo, underwear, long underwear, socks, thongs, nail clipper, tweezers, mosquito repellent, vitamins, painkillers, laxative, anti-diarrhoeal drugs, contraceptives (including condoms) and any special medications you use plus a copy of the prescription.

The padlock will lock your bag to a train or bus luggage rack and will also fortify your hotel room – which often has a place to attach the padlock. It comes in handy at some youth hostels which have lockers. You'll need a medium-sized padlock – a heavy-duty one will not fit through the latches usually provided.

A final thought: airlines do lose bags from time to time – you've got a much better chance of it not being yours if it is tagged with your name and address *inside* the bag as well as outside. Other tags can always fall off or be removed.

Appearances & Conduct

Although Asians expect madness from foreigners and will make allowances, there are certain standards of dress and behaviour which are expected. Knowing some of these common courtesies will make your trip smoother.

Fitting in rates higher among Asians than standing out – children who are naturally left-handed are taught to use the right hand just to avoid being 'odd'! Western notions about individuality can cause offence in the Orient – a punk haircut and tattered jeans will not win you any points with most Asians, especially immigration officers and other sombre figures of authority.

Wearing shorts is OK in all the countries of this book except Korea and Mongolia, but long trousers are more acceptable. People dress more formally in big cities than in the countryside. Very short shorts, miniskirts and see-through clothing can easily cause offence except maybe in ultra-fashionable Hong Kong. Public nudity is simply not on, unless you want to see the inside of an Asian police station or gaol.

Thongs should never be worn outdoors in public places, but a regular sandal with a strap across the back of the ankle is OK. This is somewhat less true in Taiwan, but even there you may not be allowed to enter restaurants or theatres if your feet aren't 'strapped-in'.

Abrasive Western reactions to incompetence, delays, mistakes and dishonesty are totally unpalatable to Asians, who are acutely aware of loss of face. Should this occur in front of others it can have a devastating effect. You'll get a lot further with government officials, ticket agents and hotel clerks if you keep smiling and bowing – even when you hate them. Bear this in mind whilst you are in Asia – if you have a sharp tongue, keep it in check.

When handing a piece of paper, a business card, or a gift to someone, always use both hands – this shows respect. If you must use one hand, be sure it's the right hand.

When you want to set down a pair of chopsticks, place them horizontally across the top of your bowl. Never leave a pair of chopsticks sticking vertically in your food. This resembles two sticks of incense placed vertically in an incense burner – a universal death sign in most countries of the Orient.

If you write a letter or note to anyone, avoid writing in red ink. A note written in red is considered unfriendly, and in many countries it signifies that the writer is going to die soon. If you get stuck and must write something in red, be sure to apologise to the person receiving the note, explaining that your other pen stopped working.

In Japan, Korea and Taiwan, it's considered rude to eat something while walking on the street. It's OK to eat something while standing next to a foodstall or sitting on a park bench, but not while walking. The Japanese are particularly strict about this, although they seem to make an exception for ice-cream cones, to which they are thoroughly addicted.

Death, divorce and other such negative matters are not suitable topics for discussion except with close friends and relatives. Asians will often ask if you're married – if you're divorced or widowed, just say you're not married and let it go at that.

When you meet people for the first time, give them a business card – if you don't have any, get some made and always carry them. Except in very poor places like rural China or Mongolia, most people have business cards and hand them out like confetti. Even if your last job was working the counter at McDonald's, try to come up with something impressive – *Joe Smith, Customer Relations Specialist*. Business cards can be printed in Asia easily enough, but be sure to check the spelling after they've done the typesetting – mistakes when typing English are very common. Hong Kong has business card machines in some of the major train and ferry terminals.

One quaint sign in Korea said, 'Please don't wear shoes in this room – thank you very big'. Bad English or not, the point to remember is that in Japan, Korea and Taiwan, shoes are generally not worn in homes or some hotel rooms, especially where the floor is carpeted or covered with tatami mats. If you see shoes piled up next to the doorway, that's a sure sign that you should remove yours too.

Lastly, there is a special etiquette concerning toilets because the plumbing systems in much of Asia cannot handle toilet paper. If you see a wastebasket right next to the toilet, in most cases this is where the used toilet paper goes. In some hotels the owners will be quite angry if you flush paper down the toilet and jam up the system.

The Top 10
Nara, Japan, where deer will eat out of your hand; Sorak-san National Park, South Korea, but only when the kids are in school; the Ice Lantern Festival in Harbin, China; the Forbidden City in Beijing; the Turpan oasis in China's Xinjiang Province; Dali in China's Yunnan Province; the walk up Hohuanshan in Taiwan; Hong Kong's Victoria Peak at night; winning big in a Macau casino; Chinese food.

The Bottom 10
Thumbs Down Awards go to: the Lunar New Year, Hong Kong's money-grubbing shopkeepers, Taiwan's Window On China, Japan's Beppu Hot Springs, the China International Travel Service (CITS), nightlife in North Korea, South Korea's immigration office, losing big in a Macau casino, Japanese prices and Mongolian department stores.

VISAS
Visas can be annoying, expensive and time-consuming pieces of red tape. Many countries do not require a visa for short stays – see the section on visas under the individual countries in this book.

Effectively, a visa is a permit to enter a country. Normally, these are stamped in your passport, though occasionally issued on separate pieces of paper. You can either get them before you go or along the way. The advantage of pre-departure collection is that it doesn't waste travelling time; the post office can do the legwork, and occasionally 'difficult' embassies are less difficult in your own country. The two main drawbacks are that some countries may not even be represented in your own country, and often visas have a limited lifespan – it is no good getting a visa that will expire in three months if you are not going to be in the country until four months later.

You can always get a visa at an embassy or a consulate in a neighbouring or nearby country, and sometimes it is available at the border or at the airport on arrival. It is often cheaper to get them in neighbouring countries. Be aware that embassies and consulates are notorious for using the flimsiest excuse to take a day off: during all local holidays, holidays 'back home' (wherever that is), during the ambassador's birthday or when the moon is full. Some embassies are better than others, but at many the workers start late, go home early, take long lunch hours, enjoy numerous coffee breaks and need three days to process your visa application even though they could easily do it in 10 minutes. You need to pay attention to these details – if you buy an air ticket for next day departure, you may find yourself out of luck if you require a visa straight away.

You normally need a photograph of yourself to apply for a visa – some countries even require three photos for one visa. Almost all countries will accept cheapie prints you can get from a machine, but at least one country (South Korea) wants passport-quality photos (5x5 cm). To save time, it would be prudent to keep about 10 cheapie and three passport-quality photos with you while travelling – you can always get more made along the way.

Some visas are issued free while others will cost you money. There may be other requirements too, like having a certain amount of money or travellers' cheques. You may have to provide the dreaded 'ticket out' – which means before you can obtain a visa to enter the country you must have a ticket to leave it. This can often be a real nuisance if you should want to leave by some obscure method for which tickets are only available within the country, or want to keep your travel plans flexible. In fact, few countries in North-East Asia require a ticket out unless you stay too long, return too many times or hold a passport from a Third World country. If you fall into these categories, the answer is to get the cheapest ticket out with a reputable airline and have it refunded later.

There are many types of visas – tourist, transit, business, student, working, resident, etc. In most cases, you should apply for a tourist visa. There are also single-entry versus multiple-entry visas. Multiple-entry visas are usually easier to obtain in your home country than once you're abroad, and some are valid for up to five years. These are worthwhile getting if you plan a long trip with a lot of zigging and zagging across Asia rather than a straight through quick journey. Some countries don't care if you work or study on a tourist visa, but others are very strict. South Korea, for example, has become really sticky – even if you have a working visa, they will not allow you to enrol in a language course because that requires a student visa. Furthermore, these rules are enforced with hefty fines and occasional prison sentences. Regulations do change periodically – when in doubt, check with the immigration authorities.

DOCUMENTS

A passport is essential, and if yours is within a few months of expiry, get a new one now – many countries will not issue a visa if your passport has less than six months of validity remaining. Also, be sure it has plenty of space for visas and entry and exit stamps. It could be embarrassing to run out of blank pages when you are too far away from an embassy to get a new passport issued or extra pages added.

Losing your passport is very bad news – getting a new one takes time and money. It helps if you have a separate record of passport number, issue date, and a photocopy of your birth certificate. While you're compiling that info, add the serial numbers of your travellers' cheques, details of health insurance and US$100 or so as emergency cash – and keep all that material totally separate from your passport, cheques and other cash.

If your passport is stolen, you'll need to make your way to the nearest embassy or consulate representing your country. Don't expect much help beyond replacing your passport – usually, they leave travellers twisting in the wind.

If you plan to be driving abroad get an International Driving Permit from your local automobile association. They are valid for one year only. Even if you're on a tight budget, there are a few areas where you might want to rent or buy a motorcycle – Taiwan and Japan are likely places for motorcycle touring.

An International Youth Hostel Federation (IYHF) card can be useful in Japan, Korea and Hong Kong. Although some Asian hostels don't require that you belong to the IYHF, they will sometimes charge less if you're a card-carrying member.

If you plan to pick up some cash by teaching, photocopies of university diplomas, transcripts and letters of recommendation could prove helpful. If you're travelling with your spouse, a photocopy of your marriage licence just might come in handy should you become involved with the law, hospitals or other bureaucratic authorities. Useful (though not essential) is an International Health Certificate – see Vaccinations for more details.

The International Student Identity Card (ISIC) can perform all sorts of miracles, such as getting you a discount on some international and domestic flights, as well as discounts at museums, parks, etc. Small wonder there is a worldwide trade in fake cards, but the authorities have tightened up on the abuse of student cards in several ways. You may be required to provide additional proof of student status – such as 'student' in your passport or a letter from your university or college stating that you are a student. Additionally, there are now maximum age limits (usually 26) for some concessions, and the fake-card dealers have been clamped down on. Nevertheless fake cards are still widely available and usable, but some are quite poor quality.

Remember that a student is a very respectable thing to be, and if your passport has a blank space for occupation you are much better off having 'student' there than something unpleasant like 'journalist' or 'photographer'.

MONEY

Estimate how much money you think you'll need, then multiply by three. You should have some money in hard cash (US dollars are the favourite) but most should be in travellers' cheques. American Express or Thomas Cook travellers' cheques are probably the best to carry because of their 'instant replacement' policies. The main idea of carrying cheques rather than cash is the protection they offer from theft, but it doesn't do a lot of good if you have to go back home first to get the refund. Amex has offices in many big cities in the region, but the replacement is not always as instant as the adverts would have you think. Keeping a record of the cheque numbers is vitally important, and it's very helpful to have the initial purchase receipts. Without these you may well find that 'instant' takes a very long time indeed.

Credit cards are accepted easily in some places (Hong Kong), but in others (Mongolia) they are only just gaining acceptance so they may not be of much use to you. In Japan they tend to be accepted only by the more expensive shops.

Travellers' cheques, including American Express, are often available in yen – if you're going to spend long in Japan they might be a good idea. Travellers' cheques are available in Hong Kong dollars but these are generally *not* a good idea, except in Hong Kong.

Taiwanese and South Korean money can be changed in Hong Kong but can be difficult to get rid of elsewhere. North Korean and Mongolian currency isn't worth the paper it's printed on once you leave those countries. Chinese money is also a problem, but it is possible to unload it in Hong Kong and Macau.

When exchanging money for local currency remember to keep your transaction receipts as you will need these to convert the local currency back to hard currency, especially in China, Korea and Taiwan. There are no restrictions on money-changing in Hong Kong and Macau.

The Hong Kong dollar is as readily accepted as the Macau dollar in Macau, but the Macau pataca is difficult to unload in Hong Kong – only a few banks will do it.

How should you carry your money? Take

some travellers' cheques, some hard cash, some local currency and carry it safely in a money belt. Carry some cheques in small denominations for last-minute conversions. As you may be charged a service fee for each cheque, don't have it all in small amounts. It is often worth checking around a couple of banks – exchange rates do vary and there are those hidden extras like service fees. Most airports are good for changing money, except Hong Kong airport where the exchange rate is terrible. Banks are usually your best bet.

Cash is very useful for emergency non-bank transactions you have to make from time to time, but forget about black market money-changing – it's virtually disappeared in North-East Asia, except Mongolia where *everybody* does it.

The only safe place to carry all this money is next to your skin. A money belt or pouch or an extra pocket inside your jeans will help to keep things with their rightful owner. Remember that if you lose cash you have lost it forever, so don't go overboard on the convenience of cash over cheques. Try to have a totally separate emergency stash for use if everything else disappears.

Your budget will depend on how you live and travel. If you're moving around fast, going to lots of places and spending time in the big cities, then your day-to-day living costs are going to be quite high, and sometimes there is no alternative to paying up – being too tight with your money can spoil your trip as much as being robbed can.

If you have to have money sent to you, ask your home bank to send you a telegraphic transfer and specify the city and the bank you want the money transferred to. If your bank prefers to nominate its own correspondent bank, ask it to advise you of the address. Hong Kong, for example, seems to have banks on every street corner, and tracking down the one with your money could take a long time.

Money sent by telegraphic transfer should reach you in a couple of days, but some countries (China) are horribly slow – just what they do with the money while you're waiting is anybody's guess. Cheques sent by mail could take a month or more to clear. When you finally get the cash you can usually have it in US dollar travellers' cheques or converted into local currency – foreign currency is not often available. Hong Kong is exceptional – it's the banking centre of Asia and you can be paid in everything from Swiss francs to Indonesian rupiah.

ELECTRICITY

In Asia, electric power comes in a variety of voltages and different plug designs. Try to avoid dealing with it – life will be simpler if you can manage without your electric hair dryer or rechargeable Walkman batteries. Unfortunately, there are some of us – travel book writers for example – who can't live without their laptop computers, modems and other hi-tech toys. See the individual country chapters of this book for voltages and illustrations of the types of plugs required.

HEALTH

Health and fitness while travelling depend on two things – your predeparture protection (immunisations) and your day-to-day health on the road. North-East Asia is generally quite a healthy region to travel in and it's unlikely you'll have any serious problems if you exercise proper precautions. Plan your immunisations ahead – some must be spaced out over a course of several months.

Predeparture Preparations

Health Insurance Although not absolutely necessary, it is a good idea to take out travellers' health insurance. The policies are usually available from travel agents. If you purchase an International Student Identity Card (ISIC) or Teacher Card (ISTC), you may be automatically covered depending on which country you purchased the card in. Check with the student travel office to be sure. If you're neither a student nor a teacher, but you're between the ages of 15 and 25, you can purchase an International Youth Identity Card (YIEE) which entitles you to the same benefits. Some student travel offices also sell insurance to others who don't hold these cards.

Some policies specifically exclude 'dangerous activities' which may include motorcycling, scuba diving and even hiking. Obviously, you'll want a policy that covers you in all circumstances you're likely to find yourself in.

Hopefully you won't need medical care, but do keep in mind that any health insurance policy you have at home is probably not valid outside your country. The usual procedure with travellers' health insurance is that you pay in cash first for services rendered and then later present the receipts to the insurance company for reimbursement after you return home. Other policies stipulate that you make a reverse-charge call to a centre in your home country where an immediate assessment of your problem is made.

The best policies cover the expense of flying you home in a dire emergency.

Medical Kit Carry a small, straightforward medical kit with any necessary medicines, anti-diarrhoeal drugs (Lomotil, Imodium), a laxative, tweezers (for removing splinters), plasters, antiseptic, paracetamol (Panadol, Tylenol, etc) and a thermometer. Rehydration kits can be useful if you suffer from severe diarrhoea. In South Korea, Taiwan and China, you'll usually find that if a medicine is available at all it will generally be available over the counter and it will be much cheaper than in the West.

Vaccinations Some countries require vaccinations against cholera if you arrive within five days of leaving an infected area – ditto for yellow fever.

Though not required, some vaccinations which might prove useful include influenza, tetanus, hepatitis B, tuberculosis, and (for Tibet) rabies. If you're bringing children, be sure they've had all the usual childhood vaccines such as polio, diphtheria, whooping cough, measles, mumps, rubella, etc.

As proof of all these scratches, jabs and punctures, you'd be wise to get an International Health Certificate to be signed and stamped by your doctor and local health authority. Although you'll seldom be asked to show it, if you pass through an epidemic area it might suddenly become compulsory. In some countries (Australia, the UK, many countries in Asia) immunisations are available from airport or government health centres. Travel agents or airline offices will tell you where. In Japan the least expensive place for vaccinations is the Tokyo Port Authority or the health facility at Narita Airport.

Basic Rules
Most food in North-East Asia is pretty healthy. The main thing to look out for is the cleanliness of the utensils – disposable chopsticks are widely available throughout the region and it would be wise to use them or carry your own.

Take care about what you eat – make sure food is well cooked and hasn't been sitting around. Make sure fresh food has been properly cleaned.

Water poses a bigger problem than food. In Japan and Hong Kong there is no problem at all. Korea is also pretty safe, Taiwan is marginal and in China water should definitely be boiled. Uncooked food is also a problem in China – avoid salads and always peel fruit before eating. Freezing things doesn't kill germs, so don't trust ice cubes. Bottled water, beer and soft drinks should be safe. Hotels do provide vacuum flasks of boiled water for guests so finding something to drink is not too difficult. Water purification tablets could be worth taking for emergencies, but you probably won't have trouble finding boiled water or bottled drinks anywhere.

It is best to bring your spectacle prescription with you, though in many Asian countries you get a free eye examination when you buy spectacles. If you need glasses you can get them made up cheaply and efficiently in Hong Kong, but avoid the eyeglass shops in tourist-trap ghettoes like Tsimshatsui.

Do yourself a favour and get your teeth checked before you depart. Dental problems in remote areas are no fun.

Medical Problems & Treatment

If you're going to get sick in North-East Asia, you're probably best advised to do it in Taiwan where medical care is excellent and reasonably priced. South Korea probably comes in second place. Of course, Japan has outstanding health facilities charging outstanding prices. Hong Kong has modern facilities and moderate prices, but as the 1997 deadline for China's takeover approaches, qualified health care professionals are emigrating in droves. Macau isn't too bad, though not recommended for major surgery. China's hospitals are fine if you don't mind 1950s technology. Mongolia is not a good place to get sick, while North Korea remains a big unknown. All of the above applies to dental care too, except that Hong Kong is unusually expensive.

If you need medical help your embassy or consulate can usually advise on a good place to go, but don't count on it – just getting through the layers of bureaucrats and security guards to talk to somebody can make you sick. Your best bet for advice on hospitals and clinics is usually your hotel, or else the local English-speaking tourist bureau.

Tetanus & Typhoid Both are serious illnesses best treated by a doctor. Prevention is the best option – there are three types of vaccinations available: plain typhoid protection; TAB, which protects against typhoid and paratyphoid A and B; and TABT, which protects you against the lot and also against tetanus. TABT lasts for three years.

Diarrhoea Intestinal upsets are usually due simply to a change of diet or a system unused to spicy food. Many times, however, contaminated food or water is the problem. If prevention fails and you do get a stomach upset, the simplest treatment is to do nothing. If your system can fight off the invaders naturally you'll probably build up some immunity. Eat lightly, and stick to hot water or herb tea – regular tea, coffee, cola or anything else containing caffeine may increase diarrhoea. Your diet should be as free as possible of roughage and spices – if

you start eating beans with hot sauce, you're going to regret it. If you do decide to resort to modern medicines don't do so too readily – don't overdo them – and if you start a course of antibiotics follow it through to the end.

There are various over-the-counter cures like the popular Lomotil. The name indicates that it 'lowers motility'; it simply slows your system down and lets it work things out. Imodium is also effective, but even plain codeine will often do as well. Antibiotics will actually attack the bacterial invaders, but also kill off friendly bacteria as well – which is why you shouldn't resort to them at the first sign of illness.

Dysentery The word 'dysentery' is used far too loosely by many travellers. If you've just got loose movements you've got diarrhoea. If blood or pus are also present then you probably have dysentery. If on top of that you have a fever then it's probably bacillary dysentery and you need an antibiotic like tetracycline or ampicillin. If there is no fever, then it could be amoebic dysentery, a serious illness which must be treated with an anti-amoebic drug like metronidazole (Flagyl). If you take Flagyl, do not under any circumstances consume alcohol at the same time – not a drop! Similar to amoebic dysentery – but not as serious – is giardia, which is also treated with Flagyl.

Whether you just have travellers' diarrhoea or something worse, it's important to keep your fluid and salt intake up to avoid dehydration.

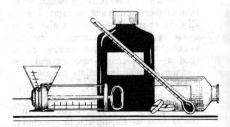

Constipation Ironically, some travellers are afflicted with the opposite problem, constipation. This is especially true when visiting northern Asia in the winter when fresh fruits, vegetables and other high-fibre foods are scarce. Obviously, the best solution is to try and eat more fibre – carry some bran if you have this problem. Having a laxative in your first-aid kit wouldn't be a bad idea, though these can easily be bought along the way if you can communicate your needs to a local pharmacist. Failing that, strong coffee and tea often have a mildly laxative effect on many people.

Some travellers speculate that you can cure constipation by eating at the dirtiest, scuzziest restaurant or street stall you can find, thus inducing diarrhoea. Although the theory sounds logical, this is generally *not* a good idea.

Hepatitis The hep comes in two varieties – A and B. No true vaccine exists for hepatitis A. However, there is gamma-globulin – an antibody made from human blood which is effective for just a few months. Most people don't consider it worthwhile because its effectiveness is so transitory. The best preventive measures are to eat food that is clean and well cooked, and to use disposable chopsticks. If you should be so unfortunate as to get the dreaded hepatitis the only real cure is good food, no alcohol and rest.

Hepatitis B is usually transmitted the same three ways the AIDS virus spreads: by sexual intercourse; contaminated needles; or inherited by an infant from an infected mother. For reasons unknown, infection rates are very high in China, Hong Kong and Taiwan, but it is probably a case of being passed down from mother to child and then spread sexually. In recent years, it has also been spreading rapidly in developed countries due to casual sex and drug use. Innocent use of needles – ear piercing, tattooing and acupuncture – can also spread the disease.

There is a very effective vaccine for hepatitis B, but it must be given before you've been exposed. Once you've got the virus, you're a carrier for life and the vaccine is useless. Therefore you need a blood test before the vaccine is administered to determine whether you're a carrier. The vaccine requires three injections each given a month apart. Unfortunately, the vaccine is expensive.

Rabies It's very rare, but rabies is such a deadly disease that it's worthy of your attention. You're probably most at risk of catching it in Tibet, where packs of wild dogs roam the streets of major towns and villages. Other mammals, such as monkeys and rats, can also transmit the rabies virus to humans. If you are bitten by a rabid animal, try to get the wound flushed out and scrubbed immediately with soapy water and then alcohol. It would be prudent to seek professional treatment since rabies carries a 100% fatality rate if it reaches the brain. How long you have from the time of being bitten until it's too late varies – anywhere from 10 days to a year depending on where the bite occurred. Those bitten around the face and upper part of the body are in the most immediate danger. Don't wait for symptoms to occur – if you think there's good chance that you've been bitten by a rabid animal, get medical attention promptly even if it means cancelling your trip.

A vaccine for rabies exists though few people bother to get it because the risk of infection is so low. The vaccine will not give you 100% immunity, but will extend the time you have for seeking treatment, and the treatment will not need to be nearly so extensive.

Tuberculosis Tuberculosis (TB) bacteria are transmitted by inhalation. Coughing spreads infectious droplets into the air. In closed, crowded spaces with poor ventilation (like a train compartment), the air can remain contaminated for some time. Especially in overcrowded China – where the custom is to cough and spit in every direction – it's not hard to see why infection rates remain high.

Many carriers of tuberculosis experience no symptoms. The disease is opportunistic – the patient feels fine, but the disease suddenly becomes active when the body is weakened by other factors such as injury, poor nutrition, surgery or old age. People who are in good health are less likely to catch the disease. Tuberculosis strikes at the lungs and the fatality rate is about 10%.

There are good drugs to treat tuberculosis, but prevention is the best cure. If you're only travelling for a short time there is no need to be overly worried. Tuberculosis is usually contracted after repeated exposures.

The effective vaccine for tuberculosis is called BCG and is most often given to school children because it must be taken before infection occurs. Once you have TB, you carry it for life. If you want to be vaccinated, you first must be tested to see if you're a carrier – if you are, the vaccination will do no good. The only disadvantage of the vaccine is that, once given, the recipient will always test positive with the TB skin test. Even if you never travel, the tuberculosis vaccine could be useful – the disease is increasing worldwide.

Skin Problems Hot, humid weather can lead to fungal infections of the skin. Bathe twice daily and thoroughly dry yourself before getting dressed. Standing in front of the electric fan is a good way to get thoroughly dry. Apply an anti-fungal ointment or powder (ointments are better) to the affected area – popular brand names are Desenex, Tinactin or Mycota, all available in Hong Kong. The Chinese have equivalent medications but you may have a hard time getting this across to a pharmacist who doesn't speak English. Wear light cotton underwear or very thin nylon that is 'breathable' – maybe even no underwear at all if the condition gets serious. Wear the lightest and loosest outer clothing possible when the weather is really hot and humid. For athlete's foot, wearing open-toed sandals will often solve the problem without further treatment. It also helps to clean between the toes with warm soapy water and an old toothbrush.

Influenza & Bronchitis You may have heard of the 'Shanghai flu', but it's a lot more than just a case of the sniffles. China is one vast reservoir of influenza viruses and many travellers find it impossible to get well until they leave the country. After a week of the flu you may well be left with bronchitis, which is characterised by almost constant coughing which brings up large quantities of thick phlegm. The Chinese have made a national sport of spitting this gob in every direction which helps spread the disease.

Bronchitis can be very distressing – it is usually worse at night, making it impossible to sleep. You can attack the virus with antibiotics, but unpleasant side effects may result, so it's wise to first try more conservative treatments. Drinking hot fluids helps, as does keeping warm and resting in bed. Keep your head elevated at night with pillows – otherwise, the phlegm tends to creep up into the throat and set off a coughing fit. Cigarette smoke is a disaster – keep away from it. If all this fails, give your battered lungs a vacation – a warm beach in Thailand may be what you need.

Vaccinations for influenza are often hard to come by – different strains appear annually. Vaccines are usually available in the autumn only from public health services in Western countries and the shot is good for no more than a year.

Sexually Transmitted Diseases Sexual contact with an infected partner spreads these diseases, and while abstinence is the only 100% preventative, use of a condom is also effective. Gonorrhea and syphilis are the commonest, and sores, blisters or rashes around the genitals, discharges, or pain when urinating are common symptoms. Symptoms may be less marked or not observed at all in women. The symptoms of syphilis eventually disappear completely but the disease continues and can cause severe problems in later years. Treatment of gonorrhea and syphilis is by antibiotics.

There are numerous other sexually transmitted diseases for most of which effective treatment is available. There is no cure for herpes and there is also currently no cure for AIDS, which up till now has largely spread in the West through male homosexual activity and intravenous drug use. It is common among heterosexuals in parts of Africa, Thailand and the Philippines. The Chinese acknowledged in 1991 that there were 500 HIV-positive drug users in Yunnan. Always carry condoms when you're travelling, and avoid any sexual practice that involves the exchange of body fluids.

AIDS can be spread through infected blood transfusions (most developing countries cannot afford to screen blood for transfusions) or by dirty needles – vaccinations, acupuncture and tattooing are as dangerous as intravenous drug use if the equipment is not clean. If you do need an injection it may be a good idea to buy a new syringe from a pharmacy and ask the doctor to use it.

Malaria Malarial mosquitoes are found in parts of North-East Asia, especially in rural parts of southern China. The problem is most serious in the summer. Prevention consists of weekly doses of chloroquine or daily doses of paludrine which you start taking some time before your trip and continue taking for some time after it. Doctors differ on which is better, and travellers differ on which is easier to remember to take. There are chloroquine-resistant strains of malaria around so enquire before you depart whether chloroquine alone is adequate in the areas you intend to visit. Should you be so unfortunate as to catch malaria the same tablets in much greater doses are also the cure. Don't take chances; once you have had malaria, even if cured, there is a fair chance of it recurring later and it is not a pleasant experience. Where there are mosquitoes around, mosquito nets and/or mosquito coils offer some protection.

Dengue Fever This is a mosquito-borne disease which resembles malaria, but is not fatal and doesn't recur once the illness has passed unless you're bitten again. It's found in the southernmost parts of China and there have been summer outbreaks in Taiwan.

A high fever, severe headache and pains in the joints are the usual symptoms – the aches are so bad that the disease is also called breakbone fever. The fever usually lasts two to three days, then subsides, then comes back again and takes several weeks to pass. Only the symptoms can be treated, usually with complete bed rest, aspirin, codeine and an intravenous drip. There is no means of prevention other than to avoid getting bitten by mosquitoes, but once you've had dengue fever, you're immune for about a year. The patient should be kept under a mosquito net until after the fever passes – otherwise there is the risk of infecting others.

Women's Health

Gynaecological Problems An inadequate diet, lowered resistance due to the use of antibiotics for stomach upsets and even contraceptive pills can lead to vaginal infections when travelling in hot climates. Keeping the genital area clean and wearing skirts or loose-fitting trousers and cotton underwear will help to prevent infections.

Yeast infections, characterised by a rash, itch and discharge, can be treated with a vinegar or even lemon-juice douche or with yoghurt. Nystatin suppositories are the usual medical prescription – these can be hard to find in China or Mongolia, so bring them. Trichomonas is a more serious infection; symptoms are a discharge and a burning sensation when urinating. Male sexual partners must also be treated. If a vinegar-water douche is not effective medical attention should be sought. Flagyl is the prescribed drug.

Pregnancy Most miscarriages occur during the first three months of pregnancy, so this is the most risky time to travel as far as your own health is concerned. The last three months should also be spent within reasonable distance of good medical care, as quite serious problems can develop at this time, and a baby born after as little as 24 weeks of pregnancy stands a chance of survival in a good modern hospital. Pregnant women should avoid all unnecessary medication, but vaccinations should still be taken where possible. Additional care should be taken to prevent illness and particular attention should be paid to diet and nutrition. Alcohol and nicotine are dangerous to the foetus, particularly in the first four months of pregnancy.

DANGERS & ANNOYANCES
Theft
The situation has gotten worse in recent years. Places like South Korea and Taiwan – once perfectly safe – have become increasingly dangerous, though nowhere near as bad as China. Theft in North-East Asia is rarely violent – the biggest threat comes from pickpockets and bag slashers.

The most important things to avoid getting stolen are your passport, papers, tickets and money. It's best always to carry these next to your skin or in a sturdy leather pouch on your belt. Be especially careful on buses and trains and even in hotels – don't leave valuables lying around in your room. Be a little wary of your fellow travellers too – unfortunately not everybody on the road is scrupulously honest.

Dope
It is around, both in its light and heavy varieties, and everybody, including the authorities, knows about it. In North-East Asia cannabis is not part of the local culture in the way it is in other parts of Asia, and nowhere in the region is it legal. Although enforcement is sporadic, occasionally the authorities decide to 'make an example' out of some traveller. If you want to do first-hand research on the human rights situation in Asian prisons, using and selling drugs is one way to do it.

Mosquitoes
Aside from being annoying, some types of mosquitoes spread malaria and dengue fever. Mosquito incense coils are widely available in Asia, and these not only scare off mosquitoes, but actually kill them. Unfortunately, the smoke is not particularly good for your lungs, so if you're going to resort to chemical weapons, at least keep a window open.

A safer alternative is insect repellent, especially if it contains the magic ingredient

diethyl toluamide, commonly known as 'deet'. Nothing is more effective. Autan is a popular brand widely available in Western countries and in Hong Kong. In areas where malaria is common, it wouldn't hurt to use both incense coils and insect repellent simultaneously. The Chinese cure-all Tiger Balm is widely available throughout North-East Asia, and makes a reasonable substitute for mosquito repellent – and once bitten you can use it to stop the itching.

A mosquito net is too bulky to carry, and is of no use unless you have a way to suspend it over your bed. Some hotels supply mosquito nets, but this is rare.

Snakes
We speak here not of Hong Kong shopkeepers, but of the kind that crawl around on their bellies and make hissing noises. Asia has a fairly thorough assortment of poisonous snakes, most commonly in subtropical regions such as south-east China, Taiwan and the southernmost islands of Japan.

There are several poisonous species such as the cobra, habu and bamboo snake. All sea snakes are poisonous and are readily identified by their flat tails. Taiwan has an interesting snake called the '100 pacer', so called because if it bites, you can expect to walk about 100 paces before dropping dead.

Fortunately, you probably won't get to see many poisonous snakes in North-East Asia, except on the dinner plate in Canton's exotic Snake Restaurant. Snakes tend to be shy, and – contrary to popular rumour – do not eat people. Most snake-bite victims are people who accidentally step on a snake. Be careful about walking through subtropical areas with a lot of undergrowth. Wearing boots gives a little more protection than running shoes.

Should you be so unfortunate as to get bitten, try to remain calm (sounds easier than it really is) and not run around. The conventional wisdom is to rest and allow the poison to be absorbed slowly. Tying a rag or towel around the limb to apply pressure slows down the poison, but the use of tourniquets is not advisable because it can cut off circulation and cause gangrene. Cutting the skin and sucking out the poison has also been widely discredited. Immersion in cold water is also considered useless.

Treatment in a hospital with an antivenin would be ideal. However, getting the victim to a hospital is only half the battle – you will also need to identify the snake. In this particular case, it might be worthwhile to kill the snake and take its body along, but don't attempt that if it means getting bitten again. Try to transport the victim on a makeshift stretcher.

All this may sound discouraging, but the simple fact is that there is very little first-aid treatment you can give which will do much good. Fortunately, snake bite is rare and the vast majority of the victims survive even without medical treatment.

ACTIVITIES
Surfing
Surfing is possible in most countries mentioned in this book, though you can forget it in North Korea. China is also pretty hopeless for renting equipment, and Mongolia lacks an ocean. Overall, surfing is not popular in this part of the world and you may well have the waves to yourself.

Skiing
Downhill skiing is popular in Japan and catching on in South Korea – costs are slightly lower than in the West. It's cheaper in north-east China though the facilities leave much to be desired. As long as you don't have enormous feet, equipment rentals should not be a problem, but devoted skiers might want to bring their own boots.

Cross-country skiing is not well known in Asia even though there are some good places for pursuing this hobby – bringing your own equipment is strongly advised.

Hiking
Local hiking clubs are active in Japan, South Korea and Taiwan. Most trips are day hikes, though overnight backpacks are possible in the more remote regions of these small countries. Hiking, backpacking and rock climbing equipment is widely available, and is quite cheap in South Korea and Taiwan.

Given the tiny land area and urban congestion, Hong Kong has a surprisingly large number of hiking enthusiasts. Hong Kong is fairly mountainous, though you'd be hard pressed to find a rural area for an overnight trip.

Hiking in China is a mixed bag. There are undoubtedly unlimited possibilities for trekking through some of the most ruggedly beautiful and remote territory on earth. The problem is that the best areas (Tibet for example) are mostly closed to foreigners except those on expensive packaged tours. There are no local hiking clubs that foreigners can join, and you won't find the sort of free trekking that is so popular in Nepal. For most travellers, hiking in China means climbing some of the 'sacred mountains' which are criss-crossed with stone steps and dotted with temples, pavilions and statues. These hikes are worth doing, but they're not exactly a wilderness experience.

From all appearances, Mongolia has great potential for hiking, but this option has been little explored since the country has only just started opening up to the outside world.

Whitewater Rafting
A quick glance at the map of North-East Asia makes it obvious that China has what whitewater enthusiasts crave – high mountains cut by long rivers, most of which have not yet been damned by dams. Indeed, China offers some of the most challenging whitewater runs in the world, and Western river runners have been beating a path to the People's Republic ever since it opened up to the outside world.

Sad to say, success has spoiled China's rafting and kayaking scene. Not that the rivers have become jam-packed with paddle-toting tourists – far from it. The problem is that greedy Chinese officials were quick to sense the lunacy of well-moneyed thrill-seekers, and now charge outrageous fees for the privilege of floating downstream. Certain popular venues like the Yangtze River are pretty much off limits to all but millionaires. To add insult to injury, there are plans to dam China's unspoilt rivers, including the Yangtze.

There are a few commercial whitewater outfitters in Japan, and even fewer in Taiwan – all equipment is supplied. In South Korea, a few hardy souls have been exploring the remaining meagre unspoilt rivers on the east coast. The problem is that all these countries are small and their rivers have either been dammed or are too short to offer more than a few hours of excitement. Needless to say, it's mostly a summer activity though Taiwan's rafting season is a little longer than most other countries in the region.

Courses

Language courses have been attracting a steady stream of devotees to Japan, China, Taiwan and South Korea, and the flow has increased along with the growing economic importance of North-East Asia. However, there are other regional specialities in the Orient which are worth investigating. Martial arts enthusiasts have for years been flocking to Japan and South Korea. Now that China has opened up, curious Westerners have come to study acupuncture, herbal medicine, calligraphy and Chinese watercolour painting.

WORK

It is possible to work in North-East Asia, and a few countries (Japan, South Korea and Taiwan) pay good salaries for teaching English. Some of these jobs are advertised in the English-language newspapers in various Asian countries. Many other jobs can be got through word of mouth – youth hostels are the likely place to enquire.

The big hurdle is the immigration authorities. Most teaching jobs are illegal and you could get fined or deported. Enforcement varies – South Korea has clamped down with an iron fist. Taiwan, Japan and Hong Kong are tightening up, but it is still possible to work for a few months before your visa expires. Once your visa expires you may have a hard time renewing it – the authorities probably won't believe you want to be a

tourist for six months or a year. You can often get around this by becoming a student in a legally-recognised language school, but you'll have to pay tuition and actually attend class. Still, teaching English and studying an Asian language is not a bad thing to do if you want the experience of living in a foreign culture.

Under some circumstances, you can get a visa to teach English legally, even in South Korea. This often takes a few months to arrange and may require you to sign a one-year contract and pay income tax, but salaries are generally high enough to make it worthwhile. The main question is whether or not you're willing to make a long-term commitment to this line of work.

Teaching English in China is feasible, but salaries are very low by Western standards, though still much higher than what a Chinese teacher would get for doing the same job. Enquire at Chinese embassies or universities if interested.

It's possible to teach English in Hong Kong, but the large number of expatriates keeps salaries low.

Attractive Western women can pick up good money working as bar hostesses or cocktail waitresses. In most cases, this is a legitimate (though illegal) job and does not involve prostitution. Nevertheless, any woman entering the hostess profession should have it made clear from the outset just exactly what is expected of her.

If you have a special skill (accountant, computer programmer) you may find it easy to land a good legal job with a big company on a long-term contract – most budget travellers do not fall into this category.

Busking is a possibility for the desperate in Japan, Taiwan and Hong Kong. Others try selling paintings on the street – this seems to work best in Japan, assuming of course that you actually have artistic talent.

Some travellers reckon that they can earn a living buying and selling. That is, they buy something in a country where it's cheap and resell it in a country where it's more expensive. A nice theory, but it seldom works in practice. Whenever you find two neighbouring countries with widely differing prices for goods – Hong Kong and China, for instance – the locals quickly latch on to the idea and set up their own smuggling operations, and do not welcome foreign competition.

ACCOMMODATION

Accommodation in North-East Asia is generally not as straightforward nor as cheap as in other parts of Asia. In China the places where Westerners can stay are strictly defined and limited and while not horrendously expensive they're not as cheap as places travellers head for in South-East Asia or West Asia. There are, however, dormitories in many hotels although getting into them can involve some ingenuity.

In Hong Kong there are cheap guesthouses, almost all of them in one convenient location, plus various hostels. In Japan if you're trying to travel on a shoestring you're going to have to stay in the youth hostels, of which there is an extensive and well-organised chain. Other cheaper possibilities are the traditional *ryokan* and *minshuku*.

In South Korea cheap accommodation can be found at the traditional *yogwan* and *yoinsuk* where you sleep on the floor. In Taiwan, hotels are generally fairly expensive, but there are youth hostels and many hotels in rural areas have dormitory-style *tatami* rooms.

More details about the budget hotel scene is provided in the individual country chapters of this book.

FOOD

One of the great treats of travelling in Asia is the quality and variety of food. It's also reasonably cheap in most of the countries in this book except Japan, where you pay the earth for stingy portions. In general, Chinese and Korean food continues to get rave reviews; opinions about Japanese food are decidedly mixed; Mongolian food comes out on bottom when you buy it in Mongolia, though Mongolian hotpot is a favourite dish throughout the region. Another problem is that Mongolia currently suffers from a food shortage.

If you're on a tight budget, look for cheap food stalls along major streets and back alleys. There are times when you may break down and head for Western fast-food restaurants – after months of rice and noodles, a Big Mac can suddenly look like exotic, foreign cuisine.

Self-catering is a distinct possibility, and is probably the only way you can afford to eat in Japan. Peanut butter makes good backpacking food – stock up before heading into China or Mongolia where it's a rare commodity.

Getting There & Away

AIR

Most travellers in the region start in Hong Kong, the gateway to China and Macau, and a good place to buy cheap air tickets to just about anywhere else. Hong Kong is also a good place to pick up visas.

It's useful to see what's available and become familiar with airline ticketing jargon. One of the best sources of information is the monthly magazine *Business Traveller* which is available in a British and Hong Kong version. They're available from newsstands in most developed countries, or direct from 60/61 Fleet St, London EC4Y 1LA, UK, and from 13th floor, 200 Lockhart Rd, Hong Kong.

Airline Tickets

Remember to reconfirm your departing flight whenever you arrive in another country – just because your ticket shows a definite departure date does not mean that they'll hold your seat. The most convenient place for reconfirming is right in the airport – you can do it the day you arrive.

Fares will vary according to your point of departure, the time of year, how direct the flight is and how flexible you can be. You are almost always better off buying tickets from travel agents rather than the airlines themselves – airlines do not usually offer discounts but agents do.

You will have to choose between buying a ticket to Hong Kong only and then making other arrangements when you arrive, and buying a ticket allowing various stopovers around North-East Asia.

Normal Economy-Class Tickets Despite the name, these are usually not the most economical way to go though they do give you maximum flexibility and the tickets are valid for 12 months. Also, if you don't use them they are fully refundable, as are unused sectors of a multiple ticket.

Bucket Shop Tickets At certain times of year and/or on certain sectors, many airlines fly with empty seats. This isn't profitable. It's more cost-effective for them to fly full even if that means having to sell a certain number of tickets which have been drastically discounted. They do this by off-loading them onto certain agents which are commonly known as 'bucket shops'. The agents, in turn, sell them to the public at reduced prices. These tickets are often the cheapest you will find. You cannot buy them from the airlines themselves. Their availability varies widely and you not only have to be flexible in your travel plans but you have to be quick off the mark once the advertisements for them appear in the press.

Most of the bucket shops are reputable organisations but there will always be the occasional fly-by-night operator who sets up shop, takes your money and then either disappears or issues you with an invalid or unusable ticket. Be sure to check what you are buying before you hand over the money.

These agents advertise in newspapers and magazines. There's a lot of competition and different routes available so it's best to telephone first before rushing round there. Naturally, they'll advertise the cheapest available tickets, but by the time you get there those for the date on which you want to leave may be sold and you might be looking at something slightly more expensive if you cannot wait.

APEX Tickets APEX (Advance Purchase Excursion) tickets are sold at a discount but will lock you into a rigid schedule. Such tickets must be purchased two or three weeks ahead of departure, do not permit stopovers and may have minimum and maximum stays as well as fixed departure and return dates. Unless you definitely must return at a certain time, it's best to purchase APEX tickets on a one-way basis only. There are stiff cancellation fees if you decide not to use your APEX ticket.

Round-the-World Tickets These are usually offered by an airline or combination of airlines, and let you take your time (six months to a year) moving from point to point on their routes for the price of one ticket. The main restriction is that you have to keep moving in the same direction; a drawback is that because you are usually booking individual flights as you go, and can't switch carriers, you can get caught out by flight availabilities, and have to spend more or less time in a place than you want.

Student Discounts Some airlines offer student discounts on their tickets of between 20 to 25% to student card holders. The same often applies to anyone under the age of 26. These discounts are generally only available on ordinary economy-class fares. You wouldn't get one, for instance, on an APEX or a Round-the-World ticket since these are already discounted.

Children's Fares Airlines usually carry babies up to two years of age at 10% of the relevant adult fare, a few may carry them free of charge. Reputable international airlines usually provide nappies (diapers), tissues, talcum and all the other paraphernalia needed to keep babies clean, dry and half-happy. For children between the ages of four and 12 the fare on international flights is usually 50% of the regular fare or 67% of a discounted fare. These days most fares are likely to be discounted.

Back-to-Front Tickets Avoid these! A back-to-front ticket is best explained by example – if you want to fly from Japan (where tickets are expensive) to Hong Kong (where tickets are cheap) you can have a friend or travel agent in Hong Kong mail the ticket to you. The problem is that the airlines have computers and will know that the ticket was issued in Hong Kong rather than Japan, and they will refuse to honour it. Consumer groups have filed lawsuits over this practice with mixed results, but in most countries the law protects the airlines, not consumers. In short, you must be physically present in the country where the ticket was issued.

To/From the USA

There are some very good open tickets which remain valid for six months or one year (opt for the latter), but don't lock you into any fixed dates of departure. For example, there are cheap tickets between the US west coast and Hong Kong with stopoffs in Japan, Korea and Taiwan for very little extra money – the departure dates can be changed and you have one year to complete the journey. However, be careful during the peak season (summer and Chinese New Year) because seats will be hard to come by unless reserved months in advance.

Usually, and not surprisingly, the cheapest fare to whatever country is offered by a bucket shop owned by someone of that particular ethnic origin. San Francisco is the bucket shop capital of the USA, though some good deals can be found in Los Angeles, New York and other cities. Bucket shops can be found through the Yellow Pages or the major daily newspapers. Those listed in both Roman and oriental scripts are invariably discounters. A more direct way is to wander around San Francisco's Chinatown where most of the shops are – especially in the Clay St and Waverly Place area. Many of these are staffed by recent arrivals from Hong Kong and Taiwan who speak little English. Enquiries are best made in person.

It's not advisable to send money (even cheques) through the post unless the agent is very well established – some travellers have reported being ripped off by fly-by-night mail order ticket agents.

Council Travel is the largest student travel organisation, and though you don't have to be a student to use them, they do have specially discounted student tickets. Council Travel has an extensive network in all major US cities and is listed in the telephone book.

One of the cheapest and most reliable travel agents on the west coast is Overseas Tours (☎ (800) 3238777 in California, (800)

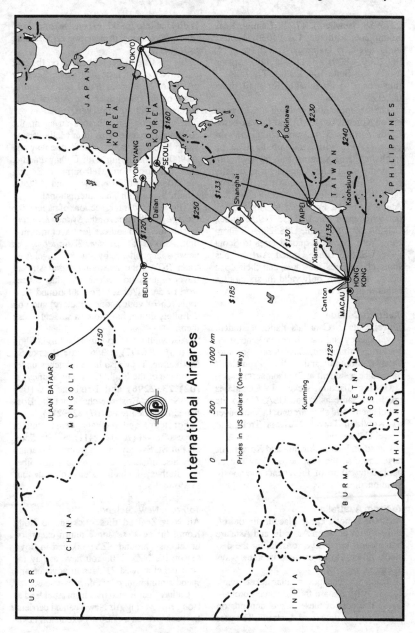

International Airfares

Prices in US Dollars (One-Way)

0   500   1000 km

2275988 elsewhere), 475 El Camino Real, Room 206, Millbrae, CA 94030. Another good agent is Gateway Travel (☎ (214) 9602000, (800) 4411183), 4201 Spring Valley Rd, Suite 104, Dallas, TX 75244 – they seem to be reliable for mail order tickets.

The cheapest fares through these agents are on Korean Air (KAL), the Taiwan-based China Airlines (CAL) and Philippine Airlines (PAL), which cut up to 30% on published APEX fares and 60% on full economy-class fares. One-way trips usually cost 35% less than a round trip. Discount fares on KAL quoted in 1991 from either Los Angeles or San Francisco to Hong Kong one-way/return were US$458/719; to Taipei, US$398/697; to Seoul, US$527/817. From New York, cheapest quoted fares to Seoul were US$685/1062. United Airlines has some cheap fares, but note that their open tickets are usually only valid for six months rather than one year.

To/From Canada

Travel Cuts is Canada's national student travel agency and has offices in Vancouver, Victoria, Edmonton, Saskatoon, Toronto, Ottawa, Montreal and Halifax. You don't have to be a student to use their services.

Getting discount tickets in Canada is much the same as in the USA. Go to the travel agents and shop around. In Vancouver try Kowloon Travel, Westcan Treks and Travel Cuts.

Canadian Pacific Airlines and Korean Air have some of the best deals. They can be booked by some of the agents previously mentioned.

To/From Australia

Australia is not a cheap place to fly out of, and air fares between Australia and Asia are ridiculously expensive considering the distances flown. However, there are a few ways of cutting the cost.

Among the cheapest regular tickets available in Australia are the Advance Purchase fares. The cost of these tickets depends on your departure date from Australia. The year

is divided into 'peak' (expensive) and 'low' (cheaper) seasons; peak season is December to January.

It's possible to get reductions on the cost of Advance Purchase and other fares by going to the student travel offices and/or some of the travel agents in Australia that specialise in cheap air tickets.

If you book through such an agent, the Advance Purchase fares from Melbourne to Hong Kong are around A$500 one way and A$900 return, flying with Cathay Pacific. Discount fares from Melbourne to Beijing are around A$1000 one way and A$1500 return, flying with Thai International.

The weekend travel sections of papers like the *Age* (Melbourne) or the *Sydney Morning Herald* are good sources for travel information. Also look at *Student Traveller*, a free newspaper published by Student Travel Australia (STA), the Australian-based student travel organisation which now has offices worldwide. STA has offices all around Australia (check your phone directory) and you definitely do not have to be a student to use them.

Also well worth trying is the Flight Shop (☎ (03) 6700477) at 386 Little Bourke St, Melbourne. They also have branches under the name of the Flight Centre in Sydney (☎ (02) 2332296) and Brisbane (☎ (07) 2299958). In Brisbane check out the Brisbane Flight Centre (☎ (07) 2299211).

For tours and package deals contact Access Travel (☎ (02) 2411128), 5th floor, 58 Pitt St, Sydney. Apart from China tours they also organise tours on the Trans-Siberian Railway, including a possible side tour to Mongolia.

To/From New Zealand

Air New Zealand flies Auckland to Hong Kong. In 'peak' season a return excursion ticket costs around NZ$1900, and in 'low' season it's NZ$1550. You have to pay for your ticket at least 21 days in advance and spend a minimum of six days overseas.

Cathay Pacific also flies from Auckland to Hong Kong using Air New Zealand carriers. In 'peak' season a one-way excursion ticket from Auckland to Hong Kong is around NZ$1500. An Advance Purchase return excursion ticket is around NZ$1900. As with the Air New Zealand excursion ticket, a minimum of six days must be spent overseas.

There are now weekly flights between Auckland and Taipei.

To/From the UK

British Airways, British Caledonian, Cathay Pacific and other airlines fly London-Hong Kong. Air-ticket discounting is a long-running business in the UK and it's wide open. The various agents advertise their fares and there is nothing under-the-counter about it at all. To find out what's going, there are a number of magazines in the UK which have good information about flights and agents. These include: *Trailfinder*, free from the Trailfinders Travel Centre in Earls Court; and *Time Out* and *City Limits*, the London weekly entertainment guides widely available in the UK.

Discount tickets are almost exclusively available in London. You won't find your friendly travel agent out in the country offering cheap deals. The danger with discounted tickets in the UK is that some of the bucket shops are unsound. Sometimes the back-stairs over-the-shop travel agents fold up and disappear after you've handed over the money and before you've got the tickets. Get the tickets before you hand over the cash.

Two reliable London bucket shops are Trailfinders in Earls Court, and STA with several offices.

You can expect a one-way London-Hong Kong ticket to cost from around £250, and a return ticket around £450. London ticket discounters can also offer interesting one-way fares to Australia with a Hong Kong stopover from around £520.

A standard-price one-way ticket with CAAC from Beijing to London will cost Y3284.

To/From Europe

The Netherlands, Brussels and Antwerp are good places for buying discount air tickets. In Antwerp, WATS has been recommended.

In Zurich try SOF Travel and Sindbad. In Geneva try Stohl Travel. In the Netherlands, NBBS is a reputable agency.

CAAC (also called Air China) has flights between Beijing and Belgrade, Bucharest, Frankfurt, London, Moscow, Paris, Athens and Zurich. However, there are very few, if any, cut-rate fares on CAAC. Much better deals can be had on the Soviet airline Aeroflot, the Polish airline LOT and the Rumanian airline Tarom. Be aware that most East European airlines have a reputation for poor safety and lost luggage.

To/From Other Asian Countries

To/From Singapore There are direct flights between Singapore and Hong Kong. A good place for buying cheap air tickets in Singapore is Airmaster Travel Centre. Also try Student Travel Australia. Other agents advertise in the *Straits Times* classified columns.

To/From Indonesia Garuda Airlines has direct flights from Jakarta to Hong Kong, and from Denpasar to Hong Kong via Jakarta. Cheap discount air tickets out of Indonesia can be bought from travel agents in Kuta Beach in Bali and in Jakarta. There are numerous airline ticket discounters around Kuta Beach – several on the main strip, Jalan Legian. You can also buy discount tickets in Kuta for departure from Jakarta. In Jakarta cheapest tickets are available from Seabreeze Travel (☎ 326675).

To/From Thailand In Bangkok, Student Travel in the Thai Hotel is helpful and efficient. There is a very popular once-weekly flight from Bangkok to Kunming, China.

To/From Nepal There are direct flights between Kathmandu and Lhasa twice weekly for about US$180 one way, but you have to book through an expensive CITS tour.

To/From the Philippines Manila is well connected with Hong Kong, Taipei and Tokyo. CAAC runs direct flights to China; a twice-weekly flight to Beijing and four flights weekly to Xiamen.

To/From Myanmar (Burma) There is a once-weekly flight from Rangoon to Kunming. Your stay in Myanmar (formerly known as Burma) is limited to two weeks and you usually must have an air ticket out of the country before they'll issue you a visa. At the time of this writing, Myanmar was experiencing serious political chaos and civil unrest, so visits to that country are an uncertain proposition.

To/From Hong Kong Adam Smith would be pleased by the freewheeling capitalist competition which keeps ticket prices in Hong Kong among the lowest in the world. Recommended agents include Traveller Services (☎ 3674127), Room 704, Metropole Building, 57 Peking Rd, Tsimshatsui, Kowloon; Travel Expert (☎ 5432770), Room 708, Haleson Building, 1 Jubilee St, Central; and Phoenix Services (☎ 7227378), Room B, 6th floor, Milton Mansion, 96 Nathan Rd, Tsimshatsui, Kowloon.

TRAIN

The ever-popular Trans-Siberian Railway is a great way to start or finish your trip to Asia. Compared with the cost of a boring old flight, the train ride is competitively priced and infinitely more interesting. However, at the time of writing the former Soviet republics were busy establishing their own visa requirements etc, so travellers will have their own research to do. Some of the information that follows will be out of date by the time you read it.

For the latest information, contact specialist agencies or national tourist agencies such as Intourist (USSR). For more depth, there's the *Trans-Siberian Rail Guide* (Bradt Publications, UK, 1987) by Robert Strauss, and the *Trans-Siberian Handbook* (Trailblazer, The Old Manse, Tower Rd, Hindhead, Surrey, GU26 6SU, UK) by Bryn Thomas.

It can be hard to book this trip during the summer peak season. Travel agents in Europe say that it's even difficult to get a September booking in April! Off-season shouldn't be a problem, but plan as far ahead as possible.

Which direction you go makes a big difference. Because of lower demand, it's much cheaper and easier to book this trip from China to Europe than vice versa.

It's a long haul. There are three main routes, but travellers to China normally use only the Trans-Mongolian and Trans-Manchurian lines.

Trans-Siberian (Moscow-Khabarovsk-Nakhodka)

This is the route for those heading for Japan; from the Soviet port of Nakhodka near Vladivostok there is a boat to Yokohama and there is also one to Hong Kong. The boat only runs from May through October. Allow about seven days for the Nakhodka-Hong Kong boat journey. Your Intourist rail ticket will be timed to connect with the specific sailing. The *Rossia* express departs Moscow's Yaroslavsky Station daily in the morning and the trip to Nakhodka takes about 8½ days. It is also possible to travel part of the route by air, stopping at Novosibirsk, Irtutsk or Khabarovsk, where you usually stay overnight before picking up the train connection to Nakhodka and Japan.

Prices for the complete rail/ship journey from Moscow to Yokohama start from 400 roubles (about US$640) for a 2nd-class sleeper on the train and a four-berth cabin on the ship. Intourist recommends a minimum of four weeks' notice to take care of visas, hotel bookings and train reservations. Further details are available in a special Intourist folder, 'Independent Travel to the USSR – The Trans-Siberian Railway'.

Trans-Manchurian (Moscow-Manzhouli-Beijing)

This is the Russian service which bypasses Mongolia. The trip takes six days, departing Moscow on Fridays late at night, and arriving in Beijing the following Friday, early in the morning. Prices on this route from Moscow to Beijing start at about US$530 for a 2nd-class sleeper in a four-berth compartment.

Trans-Mongolian
(Moscow-Ulaan Baatar-Beijing)

This is the Chinese train which passes through Mongolia and takes 5½ days. Trains depart Moscow every Tuesday in the afternoon and arrive in Beijing the following Monday in the afternoon. Prices on this route from Moscow to Beijing start at about US$530 for a 2nd-class sleeper in a four-berth compartment.

Visas

The average time required to complete the visa and ticket hurdles is about one month if you're coming from Europe, but it only takes seven to 10 days from Beijing (off-peak season). A Mongolian visa is unnecessary if you take the Trans-Manchurian or Trans-Siberian.

In Beijing, if you didn't bring visa photos with you they can be obtained quickly at the CITIC building next to the Friendship Store.

China Try the Chinese Embassy in whatever country you happen to be in, or branches of the China International Travel Service. The Chinese Embassy in Moscow has also been issuing visas to travellers on their way through to China, but it takes two weeks. In Hong Kong or Macau, you can obtain tourist visas in 24 hours.

Mongolia Mongolian visas can be issued from their Embassy in London in 48 hours – they want to know the exact date you plan to enter. Mongolian visas can also be obtained in Budapest, from the Mongolian Embassy, X 11 Istenhedyi UT-59-61, Budapest (☎ 15-14-12, 15-50-87). They can be issued in 24 hours in Irkutsk at the Mongolian Consulate, ulitsa Lapina 11. Bring passport, photos and onward ticket. At the time of writing they cost US$17 cash, but price hikes are frequent.

In Beijing, you'll find the Mongolian Embassy (☎ 5321203) at 2 Xiushui Beijie, Jianguomenwai Compound. Hours are

Monday, Tuesday and Friday from 8.30 to 11.30 am. You can get a visa in one day or pick it up the next day even if the visa section is closed. Prices for visas depend on nationality – most foreigners pay US$20, but UK citizens are charged US$28. For visas issued on the spot, the fee rises to US$24, or US$36 for the British. It is possible to break your journey in Ulaan Baatar for one or two days if you book a room in advance by telex and pay a hefty ransom – enquire at the Embassy. If you're taking the Trans-Manchurian train then you will not of course require a Mongolian visa.

USSR There is a very big difference between a tourist visa and a transit visa. The Trans-Siberian only requires a transit visa, and that is your best bet if you want to save time and money. It is normally possible to arrange a stopover in Moscow for up to three days on a transit visa, and extend it after you arrive there. It's easy to extend your visa if you're staying at a legitimate hotel (as opposed to an illegal hostel). The hotel 'service bureau' will do it for you through Intourist – with hotel bookings, of course.

With a tourist visa, you can stay much longer, but you will pay heavily for the privilege. All hotels must be booked in advance through the official Soviet travel agency, Intourist. Their attitude is to milk travellers for every cent they can get (who said they aren't capitalists?). For a two-star hotel, expect to pay around US$65 outside Moscow, and US$135 a day in Moscow.

The hotel bookings must be confirmed by telex (which you will also have to pay for) and the whole bureaucratic procedure takes about three weeks. On a transit visa, you can sleep in the station or in some of the rapidly proliferating cheap private hostels.

In Beijing, the USSR Embassy (☎ 5322051) is just off Dongzhimen, Beizhongjie 4, west of the Sanlitun Embassy Compound. Hours are Monday, Wednesday and Friday from 9 am to 1 pm (the Embassy is closed on 7 and 8 November, New Year's Day, 8 March, 1 and 9 May, and 7 October). Transit visas are valid for a maximum of 10 days and tourist visas are required if the journey is broken. In practice, you can stay in Moscow for three days on a transit visa and apply for an extension when you arrive.

A transit visa can be issued the same day or take three to seven days depending on how much you pay and how busy they are. There are two fees you must pay: a visa application fee and a bizarre 'consular fee'. Visa application fees are US$15 for a visa issued in seven days; US$18 if issued in three days; and US$27 if issued the same day. The consular fee varies according to nationality. French citizens pay only US$11, but those with a passport from the Netherlands pay US$81! Three photos are required. The Embassy does not keep your passport, so you are free to travel while your application is being processed. Someone can apply for the visa on your behalf and use a photocopy of your passport (all relevant pages must be included). You can avoid the long queues at the Beijing Embassy if you apply at the Soviet Consulate in Shanghai, but it's only open on Tuesday and Thursday from 10 to 11.30 am.

If you are taking the Trans-Mongolian from Beijing, then your Soviet visa can – if you wish – be issued for the day *after* departure from Beijing, thus giving you an extra day in the USSR since the train takes a day to go through Mongolia.

If you arrive in Moscow on a transit visa, you can sleep for free in the waiting hall of Belorussky Station (not Yaroslavsky Station), but lock up your bags in the luggage lockers near the hall. Furthermore, many illegal youth hostels have sprung up in Moscow. Basically, people are turning their apartments into youth hostels and soliciting travellers who arrive off the Trans-Siberian. Costs are low – around US$5 or less per night.

The Soviet Consulate in Budapest is at Nepkoztarsasag utca 104 (open Monday, Wednesday and Friday from 10 am to 1 pm).

Poland In Beijing, the Embassy (☎ 5321235) is at 1 Ritan Lu, Jianguomenwai

Compound. Hours are Monday to Friday, 8.30 to 2 pm. If you apply after 11 am you might have to come back the next morning to pick it up. Express visa service costs an additional Y48. You can get a discount with an ISIC card. Two photos are needed.

In China, you can also get visas at the Polish Consulate on Shamian Island, Canton, near the White Swan Hotel. This office issues visas in just 10 minutes. For some reason, visas issued in Canton give you 48 hours to transit Poland, while those issued in Beijing are valid only for 24 hours. Apparently the visa can also be obtained, more expensively, on the train at the Polish-Soviet border, but this is risky – some travellers have been sent back.

Hungary Tourist or transit visas are US$20 for next-day service, or US$28 for visas issued the same day. Two photos are needed. In Beijing, the Embassy (☎ 5321431) is at 10 Dongzhimenwai Dajie, open 9 am to noon. The visas are *not* needed by most Western nationalities. People still requiring visas include Greeks, Portuguese, New Zealanders and Australians. Those with passports from Third World countries may have to wait over four weeks.

Tickets

Intourist provides an excellent timetable of the international passenger routes with rail prices. The most expensive section is usually the connection between Europe and Moscow, so you may want to save money by starting your trip close to Eastern Europe. You could also book an itinerary starting from Berlin or Helsinki, or you could fly to Moscow and continue from there by rail.

If coming from Budapest, you can buy tickets from Star Tours (☎ 137062, 334728), 1085 Budapest, József krt 45. Daily train services from Budapest to Moscow depart Budapest at night – it's about a 33 to 35-hour trip to Moscow. Two trains depart each night, and the earlier one is usually certain to catch the connection to Beijing – reservations for this train should also be made well in advance.

In China, tickets can be obtained from the China International Travel Service (CITS) office in Beijing, which is in the Beijing Tourist Tower (☎ 5158844), 28 Jianguomenwai – the large building just behind the New Otani Hotel which is opposite the Friendship Store. CITS is open from 8.30 am to 11 am and 2 to 4.30 pm. There is another, smaller CITS (☎ 5120510) in the Beijing International Hotel. Book your seat on the train before you start getting your visas. Once you have the visas, return to CITS and pay for your ticket. Tickets are sold in three classes, 'hard', 'soft' and 'deluxe', but even 'hard' is reasonably comfortable.

CITS prices in US dollars from Beijing are as follows:

Destination	Hard	Soft	Deluxe
Bucharest	254	372	411
Moscow	193	271	310
Prague	271	387	426
Sofia	283	417	455
Ulaan Baatar	60	83	96
Warsaw	232	335	373

At the time of this writing, seats to Berlin and Budapest were impossible to book and CITS could not quote prices. This situation is likely to change in the future.

Black Market Tickets

Up until 1990, you could buy black market tickets for as little as US$30. These tickets were usually issued in Hungary but had no reservation – you had to book the reservation separately. Sad to say, these 'open tickets' are now worthless. If you buy a ticket without a confirmed booking, then you might as well use it for toilet paper, because that's all the ticket will be good for. A booking has to be made through Intourist, CITS or one of their authorised agents, and they will not book a black market ticket. The only 'black market' tickets that still exist are return portions of legitimate tickets that travellers have already bought but decided not to use, so they want to sell them. Since tickets do not have a name on them, you can use these, but make absolutely certain that the ticket carries a booking and is not one of the old worthless open tickets.

Travel Agents

Several readers have recommended Scandinavian Student Travel Service (SSTS), 117 Hauchsvej, 1825 Copenhagen V, Denmark. This organisation has branch offices in Europe and North America, and provides a range of basic tours for student or budget travellers (mostly in the summer). Prices start at US$1095 for a 20-day trip from Helsinki to Yokohama via Leningrad, Moscow, Novosibirsk, Irkutsk, Khabarovsk and Nakhodka.

In Hong Kong, the specialist in the Trans-Siberian route is the staff at Monkey Business (☎ 7231376), 4th floor, E-Block, Flat 6E, Chungking Mansions, Tsimshatsui, Kowloon. Officially, their name is Moonsky Star Ltd, but they earned the name Monkey Business back in the days when black market ticket dealing was possible. They make all arrangements, charge reasonable prices, and seem to be able to get tickets even during the high season when no one else has them. A lot of travellers have had good things to say about this company.

Monkey Business also maintains an office in Beijing at the Qiaoyuan Hotel (new building), room 716 (☎ 3012244, ext 716), but it's best to book through their Hong Kong office (as far in advance as possible). Hong Kong is a good place to stock up on cash US dollars in small denominations, visa photos and any foods you crave for the Siberian crossing.

Also in Hong Kong is Wallem Travel (☎ 5286514), 46th floor, Hopewell Centre, 183 Queen's Rd East, Wanchai, specialising in travel to the USSR and other Eastern European countries.

Hong Kong Student Travel Bureau or HKSTB (☎ 7213269), Room 1021, 10th floor, Star House, Salisbury Rd, Tsimshatsui, Kowloon, also arranges Trans-Siberian travel. Their prices tend to be on the high side. Get there at opening time or be prepared for a long wait.

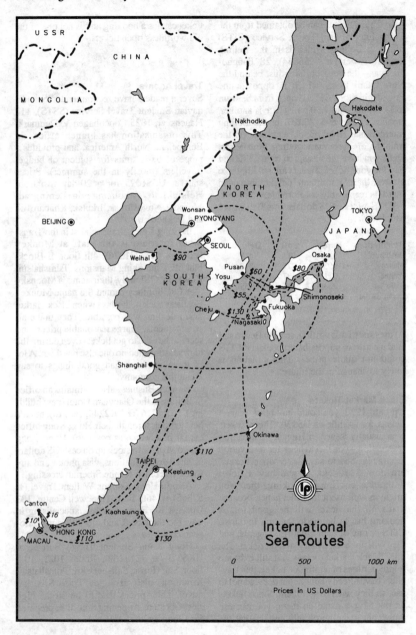

International Sea Routes

0   500   1000 km

Prices in US Dollars

Predeparture Tips

US dollars in small denominations are essential. Food in the Chinese and Russian trains is not bad, but abysmal in Mongolia – stock up in advance. Alcohol is not sold on the Russian portion of the Trans-Siberian, but you can buy it on the train within China and Mongolia.

Arrival in Moscow

Coming from China, the train usually gets into Moscow's Yaroslavsky Station late – very late if you have encountered blizzards. For those who booked a hotel room the Intourist official will be waiting with a transfer taxi usually included in the hotel price. If you haven't booked, you could try sharing with someone who has. If you want to hire a taxi they are notoriously scarce (although foreign currency helps) and drivers are renowned for stinging the unwary with extravagant prices. Make sure you get the price straight first; US dollars have been known to work wonders.

The metro (underground) is another choice, providing you obtain some coins. The metro is baffling without help, but with a few words in Cyrillic written down by Intourist staff, you can find your way from Komsomolskaya Metro Station (beside Yaroslavsky Station) three stops along to Belorusskaya Station, which is beside Belorussky Station (for all trains to the West) – take Koltsevaya Linia (Circle Line). There is an Intourist office at Belorussky Station (open 9 am to 8 pm) where you can buy tickets to the West. You can sleep on the seats in the huge waiting hall but do not forget to use the luggage lockers, as cameras and other desirable consumer durables often disappear. You can sleep in a bed on an empty train if one happens to be in the station. Check in between 10 pm and midnight – prices are very low.

Getting Around

AIR

Air services are very well developed in North-East Asia, except for a few blank spots. Macau does not have an airport yet, but one is under construction. There is still no direct air service between China and Taiwan or China and South Korea. Except for the flight to Beijing, North Korea is cut off from the world. Mongolia is nearly as isolated, with just five flights weekly from Ulaan Baatar to Beijing.

Elsewhere in the region, air services are frequent, fast and comfortable. They're also reasonably cheap, except for air tickets bought in Japan. China and Taiwan are also not very cheap places to buy tickets, but much better than Japan. Hong Kong – where travel agents compete fiercely – is still cheapest.

Within the countries of the region there are all sorts of possibilities for travel. See the individual country chapters for more details.

SEA

There are daily regular ferries between Japan and South Korea. Between Hong Kong and Macau, there is a steady stream of ferries, hydrofoils, jetfoils, hovercraft and so on. Ferries running the Hong Kong-China and Macau-China routes are also frequent. Less frequent are ferries plying the Japan-China, China-South Korea, Okinawa-Taiwan and Taiwan-Macau routes.

LAND

Within the region there are only a few places where you can cross borders by land – China to Hong Kong, Macau, Mongolia or North Korea. Don't even think about crossing the border between the two Koreas.

China

After being shut down for repairs for 30 years, China flung open its doors to tourism in 1981. Prior to that time, individuals could travel to the People's Republic of China (PRC) by invitation only, but now visas are being issued to all and sundry. China is not always an easy country for the individual to travel in. Although most of the country is now accessible, foreigners may be inconvenienced by the Chinese government's bureaucracy and absurd restrictions. But after centuries of isolation, the Middle Kingdom is trying to modernise and catch up with the West, and the present open-door policy offers a wonderful opportunity to see a fascinating land.

Facts about the Country

HISTORY
Early China
The first Chinese dynasty, the Xia, was formed about 4000 years ago; it was followed by the Shang dynasty from the 16th to 11th centuries BC, which established the area around the Yellow River as the cradle of Chinese civilisation. During the Zhou dynasty of the 11th to 5th centuries BC, the most enduring feature of Chinese thinking was formulated: the concept of the 'mandate of heaven', linking the emperor directly to the firmament. As the Zhou dynasty declined the Warring States period began. Confucius lived in this era, around 500 BC, and his response to turmoil was to advocate a return to what he saw as the dependable ways of the past.

In the 3rd century BC the short-lived Qin dynasty, marked by the extreme cruelty of its emperor, laid the foundations for a unified empire. A network of roads was constructed; writing, coinage, weights and measures were standardised; and the fortifications of feudal states were destroyed.

Under the succeeding Han dynasty, which ruled until 220 AD, the empire reached its zenith and Confucianism became the basis of education and admission to the Chinese civil service for almost the next 2000 years. In the period of disunity that followed the collapse of the Han dynasty, Buddhism spread throughout China. In the 6th century AD, the country was reunited under the short-lived Sui dynasty, which was succeeded in 618 AD by the Tang dynasty. This is now regarded as China's golden age. The capital at Chang'an (today's Xi'an) was one of the greatest cities in the world, and canals and roads linked the boundaries of the empire as China became a centre of international trade with a large foreign community.

In 1211, Mongol tribes under Genghis Khan swept over the Great Wall and by 1279 Genghis' grandson Kublai controlled southern China and had founded the Yuan dynasty. It was to the China of the Mongols that Europeans like Marco Polo came – and their books revealed the splendours of Asia to an amazed Europe. After Kublai died in 1294, the Mongol hold on China disintegrated, and the Ming dynasty came to power. Buddhism and Taoism were made state religions. The Ming emperors, who saw China as both culturally superior to the outside world and economically self-sufficient, closed the doors to Europe just when the Europeans were entering their most dynamic phase since the Roman Empire.

In 1628 a famine and ensuing turmoil led the Manchus to invade China and found the Qing dynasty. The period from 1663 to 1796 was a time of prosperity: the throne was occupied by some of China's most able rulers; China, Mongolia and Tibet were brought under Manchu rule; taxation was reduced and flood-control and irrigation projects were undertaken.

The Impact of the West
Meanwhile, the Europeans were about to

expand their power on a scale undreamt of by the isolated Chinese. The Portuguese arrived in China in 1516, and in 1557 set up a trading base in Macau. In the next century the British, Dutch, French and Spanish all landed in China. Trade flourished – mainly in China's favour until 1773, when the British began to redress the balance by exchanging Indian opium for Chinese silver. This eventually led to the first round of the Opium Wars when the British attacked Canton in 1839. The Chinese lost each round, and were forced to sign a series of 'unequal treaties', resulting in more ports being opened to foreign trade.

In the mid-19th century, the Western powers assisted the now hopelessly corrupt Qing government to put down the Taiping Rebellion. That accomplished, the foreign powers returned to the task of carving up China; but in the last few years of the 19th century, the Boxer Rebellion brought relations between China and the West to crisis point. It was crushed, but laid the seeds for many secret anti-dynastic societies within China and abroad. In 1905 several of these groups banded together into the Alliance for the Chinese Revolution; in 1911 an army uprising spread from Wuhan and the Manchu Dynasty crumbled; in 1912 Sun Yatsen became the first president of the Republic of China.

The Kuomintang

The establishment of a republic was no panacea. The country was racked internally by warlordism and looting; externally the greatest threat came from Japan. In a search for solutions to China's crises, Sun Yatsen revived the Nationalist Party, or Kuomintang (KMT), which had emerged as the dominant political force after the abdication of the Manchus, and based it in Canton in 1917. Meanwhile Marxist study groups and societies – led by Mao Zedong, Zhou Enlai, Lin Biao and others – sprang up all around China. The Chinese Communist Party was founded in 1921, but a year later Moscow urged the CCP to join the KMT to strengthen China against outside intervention, particularly from Japan.

Having established a secure political base in Canton, the KMT began training its National Revolutionary Army (NRA), but the death of Sun Yatsen in 1925 robbed the faction-ridden KMT of his unifying influence. In 1926 the 'Northern Expedition' under Chiang Kaishek brought the northern warlords under control. In Shanghai the plan called for an uprising of workers who would take over key installations while the KMT armies advanced upon the city. The plan worked, but the KMT – supported by Shanghai industrialists and foreigners – betrayed the CCP and unleashed a massacre against the Communists and their supporters.

By mid-1928 Chiang Kaishek had reached Beijing and established a national government, but his corrupt government wished to maintain a privileged elite rather than relieve the misery of the ordinary Chinese. Although the first CCP attempt at insurrection in 1927 was a failure, it led to the founding of the Red Army. After a power struggle within the CCP, Mao Zedong and his supporters emerged as leaders, and they quickly moved the power-base of the revolution to the countryside and the peasants.

A policy of guerrilla warfare was adopted; by 1930 Mao's band of peasants had grown to an army of 40,000, posing a threat to Chiang Kaishek, who staged several 'extermination' campaigns against the Communists. In October 1934, when the Communists were on the brink of defeat, a decision was made to march out of Jiangxi to join up with other Communist forces. On the way, supreme command of the Red Army was conceded to Mao. The famed Long March began with 90,000 troops. In July 1935 they linked up with other Red Army units in Sichuan, and in October the survivors – just 20,000 – finally reached Shaanxi. The march had taken over a year, covered 8000 km of inhospitable terrain, and proved that the peasants would fight if they were given organisation, leadership, hope and weapons.

In 1931 the Japanese invaded Manchuria.

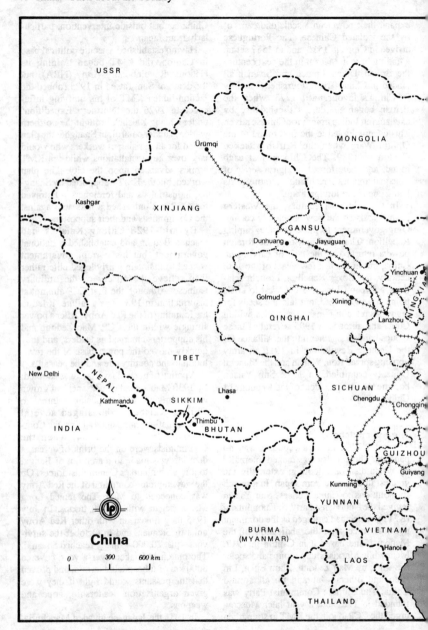

China

0   300   600 km

The Communists wanted to form a united front with the KMT against this common enemy, but Chiang Kaishek had other plans. In 1936 Chiang went to Xi'an to launch another extermination campaign, but was taken prisoner by his own troops and forced to form an alliance with the Communists.

In 1937 the Japanese launched an all-out invasion of China, and by 1939 controlled all of eastern China, in spite of fierce resistance from the Chinese, who were supported initially by the Soviet Union and later by the USA, the UK and France. The KMT and Communists scrambled for position after the Japanese surrendered in 1945. US-trained and equipped KMT forces went to battle with the Red Army which, together with its support-units, had grown to several million.

The turning-point came between 1948 and 1949 when whole divisions of the KMT went over to the Communist side. On 1 October 1949 Mao Zedong proclaimed the formation of the People's Republic of China while the KMT fled to Taiwan with about 1½ million supporters, the country's gold, its art treasures and what was left of the KMT air force and navy.

Communist China

The People's Republic began as a bankrupt nation decimated by war. Yet the Communists recall the 1950s as a successful period – because of the elation of victory, the reconstruction of the country and because they fought the Americans to a standstill in the Korean War. By 1953 inflation had been halted, industrial production restored to pre-war levels and land redistributed to peasants. But the desire to fulfil speedily the promise of the revolution led to the ill-fated Great Leap Forward in the mid-1950s. Peasants were set to work on small-scale industrial projects like 'backyard' steel furnaces, and gigantic rural communes were established; the resulting misdirected agricultural and industrial output caused a disastrous slump in useful production. Floods and drought ruined the harvests of 1959 and 1960, resulting in widespread famine. Political disputes

with the Russians led to the withdrawal of Soviet aid and advisers in 1960.

The power of Liu Shaoqi, Deng Xiaoping and their supporters, who held pragmatic economic views, increased at Mao's expense. Incentives much like those being tried today were instituted, and by 1965 the economy had recovered some of its equilibrium and the hardship of 1959 to 1962 had passed. For Mao these policies reeked of capitalism and by 1964 he had launched the 'Socialist Education Movement', which denounced those taking the 'capitalist road'.

In 1966 the Party Central Committee launched the Cultural Revolution 'to struggle against and crush those persons in authority who are taking the capitalist road'. Many of Mao's opponents (including Deng Xiaoping) were purged, but the whole exercise soon turned into an unprecedented disaster. Mao was quick to recognise the disruptive potential of the Red Guards who materialised in 1966. Millions of teenagers were suddenly given the opportunity to attack and humiliate teachers, scientists and other 'stinking intellectuals'. People were beaten, imprisoned and killed for playing a musical instrument, possessing a stamp collection or having a relative living abroad. It wasn't long before Red Guard factions battled each other and the country moved towards civil war. In 1967, Mao had to call in the army to put down the Red Guards, but not before they had destroyed or vandalised anything that was a physical reminder of China's past or 'evil foreign influence'. By this time, Mao was raised to a god-like status and anyone who wanted to stay healthy quoted frequently from his Little Red Book.

In 1972 it was suddenly announced that Lin Biao had been killed in a plane crash the previous year allegedly whilst fleeing China after an assassination attempt upon Mao. His removal cleared the path for Zhou Enlai to assume the number two position in China – and with the health of Mao (aged 79) declining, it was Zhou (73) who soon took over the reins and began to steer a more pragmatic and rational course. Fear of the Soviet Union prompted a reconciliation with the USA, and in 1973, with the Chinese leadership split into opposing 'Maoists' ('leftists') and 'moderates', Zhou Enlai managed to return to power none other than Deng Xiaoping, who had been vilified during the Cultural Revolution.

Zhou died in early 1976 and Deng disappeared from public view. In March came the Tiananmen Riots, which occurred after wreaths in honour of Zhou were placed in Tiananmen Square. The wreaths were torn down on 5 April and those who tried to prevent their removal were arrested. Later that day, tens of thousands of protesters were dispersed by members of the Workers' Militia. Deng Xiaoping was blamed for the riots, and on 7 April was stripped of all his offices. The next month Mao slipped out of public view. He died on 9 September 1976 and a month later the 'Gang of Four' were arrested. Nicknamed 'little bottle' as a pun on his name and for his uncanny ability to bob back up to the top, Deng Xiaoping was once more returned to power in mid-1977 and China embarked on its path of modernisation.

The 1980s saw a decade of progress and rapid economic liberalisation, but it ended on a bitter note. The death of former Party General Secretary Hu Yaobang (considered a liberal) served to rally 'pro-democracy' demonstrators in the latter half of April 1989. The demonstrations quickly grew into a full-scale movement involving over half a million people who marched through the streets of Beijing and camped out in Tiananmen Square. While vehemently denouncing the demonstrations, Communist Party leaders showed surprising restraint for a while, but martial law was declared on 20 May. Then Party General Secretary Zhao Ziyang openly sided with the student demonstrators. On 4 June, tanks and troops moved into Tiananmen Square and crushed the pro-democracy movement. Estimates of the death toll ranged from several hundred to several thousand. Zhao Ziyang was arrested along with thousands of others accused of 'counter-revolutionary crimes'. Foreign tourism collapsed and many Western coun-

tries – disgusted by China's disregard for human rights – imposed economic sanctions. Although the situation is slowly getting back to normal, China's brutal crackdown has left many wondering if much has changed since the last emperor was dethroned.

GEOGRAPHY

China is the third largest country in the world, after the Soviet Union and Canada. The government also regards Taiwan, Hong Kong and Macau as territory belonging to the People's Republic.

The land surface of China is a bit like a descending staircase. To the west are the high plateaus of Tibet and Qinghai, 4500 metres above sea level. On the eastern rim of these plateaus, the terrain drops abruptly to 1000 to 2000 metres above sea level. The east is dominated by plains – the most important agricultural areas of the country and heavily populated. The north-west region of the country is a sparsely inhabited desert.

The environment has taken a heavy beating in some parts of the country – chimneys belching out thick, black smoke are not an uncommon sight. However, poverty is China's ecological salvation – the agricultural economy and the relative lack of industrialisation has kept much of the countryside well preserved.

CLIMATE

China gets a lot of it. Spread over such a vast area, the country is subject to the worst extremes of temperature, from bitterly cold to sizzling hot.

In the north, December to March is a period of incredibly cold and windy weather. Beijing's temperature doesn't rise above 0°C though it is generally dry and sunny. North of the Great Wall and into Inner Mongolia and Heilongjiang the temperature can drop to as low as minus 44°C. Summer in the north is from May to August and temperatures can rise to 38°C or more. July and August are also the rainy months in the eastern region, but the west is a vast desert and humidity is never a problem. Spring and autumn are the best

Beijing Temperatures & Rainfall

	Jan	Feb	Mar	Apr	May	Jun	Jul	Aug	Sep	Oct	Nov	Dec
Temp (°C)	-4.7	-1.9	4.8	13.7	20.1	24.7	26.1	24.9	19.9	12.8	3.8	-2.7
Rain (mm)	4	5	8	17	35	78	243	147	58	16	11	3

Shanghai Temperatures & Rainfall

	Jan	Feb	Mar	Apr	May	Jun	Jul	Aug	Sep	Oct	Nov	Dec
Temp (°C)	3.4	4.3	8.2	13.7	18.9	23.1	27.1	27.2	23	17.7	11.6	5.9
Rain (mm)	49	62	85	91	96	177	148	139	132	74	53	38

Canton Temperatures & Rainfall

	Jan	Feb	Mar	Apr	May	Jun	Jul	Aug	Sep	Oct	Nov	Dec
Temp (°C)	13.6	14.2	17.2	21.6	25.6	27.3	28.8	28.2	27.2	24	19.7	15.7
Rain (mm)	27	65	101	185	256	292	264	248	149	49	51	34

times for visiting the north, with temperatures in the 20° to 30°C range.

In the central region (including Shanghai) summers are long, hot and humid – the area is known as China's oven. Winters are short and cold, but the weather can also be wet and miserable at any time other than summer.

In the south, April to September is a hot, humid period and the temperature can rise up to 38°C. Heavy rains are common, and typhoons are liable to hit the south-eastern coast between July and September. The short winter from January to March is nowhere near as bad as in the north, but bring some warm clothes anyway.

GOVERNMENT
Every revolution evaporates, leaving behind only the slime of a new bureaucracy.
Franz Kafka

Highest authority rests with the 25-member Standing Committee of the Communist Party Politburo (often just called the Politburo). Below it is the 210-member Central Committee. The Party's chain of command moves down through different layers right down to universities, government offices and industries, thus ensuring strict central control.

The Politburo still retains supreme power but its members are now accorded a hodgepodge of titles. Foremost on the Standing Committee is general secretary Jiang Zemin. Octogenarian Deng Xiaoping no longer holds any official government posts, yet remains the most powerful man in China. Another member of the Standing Committee is the relatively youthful (in his 60s) Premier Li Peng.

The day-to-day running of the country lies with the State Council, which is directly under the control of the Communist Party. The State Council is headed by the Premier. Rubber-stamping the decisions of the Communist Party leadership is the National People's Congress (NPC).

If the NPC is a white elephant, then the great stumbling block of the Chinese political system is the bureaucracy. There are 24 ranks on the ladder, each accorded its own particular privileges. The term 'cadre' is usually applied to all bureaucrats, but it's unclear who this includes.

At grass-roots level the basic unit of social organisation outside the family is the work unit (*dānwèi*). Every Chinese is a member of one. Many Westerners may admire the co-operative spirit this system is supposed to engender, but they would cringe if their own lives were so intricately controlled. Nothing can proceed without the work unit. It issues ration coupons, decides if a couple may marry or divorce and when they can have a child. It assigns housing, sets salaries, handles mail, recruits Party members, keeps files on each unit member, arranges transfers to other jobs or other parts of the country, and gives permission to travel abroad. The work unit's control extends into every part of the individual's life.

The role of the army should also not be forgotten. Mao held that 'political power grows out of the barrel of a gun'. Pro-democracy demonstrators in 1989 were pointedly reminded of this fact.

ECONOMY

Mao feared economic ties with other countries would bring dependency, and China under his rule became economically isolated. Since his death, however, this approach has been radically altered. The present economic policies are usually dubbed the 'Four Modernisations' – those of industry, agriculture, defence and science and technology – and the intention is to transform China into a modern state by the year 2000. Today, the PRC's centrally planned economy has become a three-tier system. On the first rung is the state, which continues to control consumer staples and industrial and raw materials. On the second rung are private purchases or sales of services and commodities within a price range set by the state. On the third rung is the rural and urban 'free market', where prices are established between buyer and seller, with the state stepping in to correct 'unfair practices'. The last loophole is sometimes used to quash entrepreneurs who are giving inefficient state-run enterprises too much competition or not paying sufficient bribes to local officials.

POPULATION & PEOPLE

China has a population of more than a billion people. Of that total, 93% is Han Chinese and the rest is composed of China's 55 or so minority groups. A quarter of the population is illiterate and there are a mere 4.4 million university graduates, so the country has scant scientific and technical expertise to draw upon for its modernisation programmes.

China's birth control policies are the strictest in the world – every couple is only allowed one child. This policy is strongly enforced in the cities, but in rural areas – where 80% of the people live – enforcement is much less effective. Although the rate of increase is slowing, China's population continues to grow and is expected to hit 1.25 billion by the year 2000.

ARTS

Calligraphy – writing Chinese characters with brush pens and ink – is one of China's ancient art forms. Closely related is Chinese watercolour painting – the basic tools are those of calligraphy, which influenced painting in both technique and theory. Pottery, bronze vessels and funerary objects also have a long history in China.

Taijiquan (slow-motion shadow boxing) has in recent years become quite trendy in Western countries – it has been popular in China for centuries. *Gongfu* (previously known as kungfu) differs from taijiquan in that the former is performed at much higher speed and with the intention of doing bodily harm. Gongfu also often employs weapons.

Then there is *qigong* – not easily described in Western terms but it's rather like faith healing. *Qi* represents life's vital energy, and *gong* is from *gongfu* – one form of Chinese martial arts. Qigong can be thought of as energy management and healing. Practitioners try to project their qi to perform various miracles, including driving nails through boards as well as healing others.

One of the highlights of a visit to China is to see a Peking opera – obviously, most easily accomplished in Beijing.

Traditional Chinese music performed with flutes, piccolos, zithers, along with ceremonial trumpets and gongs, can often been seen and heard in Chinese movies and operas. China's first concert featuring a foreign rock group was in 1985, when the British group Wham! was allowed to perform. Music fans who dared to get up and dance in the aisles were hauled off by Public Security. Since then, things have become more liberal and China has produced some notable home-grown bands.

Disco music is big with the hip young urban Chinese; love songs and soft rock from Taiwan and Hong Kong are in vogue in Canton; in Beijing, tastes run more towards heavy metal and punk. In an attempt to show that the geriatric leadership is also hip, government officials have authorised a disco version of 'The East is Red'. A few young Chinese have even caught on to Brazil's erotic dance, the 'lambada'. Exactly where all this is leading no-one knows.

CULTURE

The usual standards of Asian decorum apply, but in some ways China is a relief after fashion-conscious Tokyo, Seoul and Hong Kong. In other words, you can get away with being a slob in China – backpackers will fit right in!

The Chinese place little importance on what foreigners wear, as long as it's within acceptable levels of modesty. While shorts are less acceptable for women, plenty of Chinese women wear them. Skirts and dresses are frequently worn in big cities – in Beijing, miniskirts are in vogue and many young women have started wearing skin-hugging tights. However, bikinis have still not made their debut in China, and public nudity is absolutely taboo (though the Chinese would love to see it).

RELIGION

Traditional Chinese religions – Taoism, Buddhism and Confucianism – are in a dismal state. During the Cultural Revolution, rampaging Red Guards swept through China like a laxative, purging the People's Republic of religion and its practitioners. Temples and monasteries were ransacked and often levelled, and monks and priests were imprisoned, murdered or sent to the countryside to labour in the fields. In Tibet, for example, the theocracy which had ruled the country for 1000 years was wiped out virtually overnight. Muslims were often given the job of raising pigs. The present Chinese government professes atheism and considers religion to be a superstition, but religious freedom is guaranteed under the Chinese constitution and worshippers seem to be on the increase. On the other hand, those who hold allegiance to a church, mosque or temple are not permitted to join the Communist Party.

These days, the people who still practise their religion sincerely in China are mainly ethnic minorities such as the Muslim Uigurs in Xinjiang, or Lama Buddhists in Tibet. There's a growing minority of Christians, but their numbers are small. While China is dotted with ancient Taoist and Buddhist temples, they have a distinctly empty appearance. The last few years have seen many of these temples restored, but they function mainly as tourist attractions for foreigners and Overseas Chinese. If you really want to see traditional Chinese religion in practice, you'd do better in Taiwan or Hong Kong.

LANGUAGE

The official language is the Beijing dialect, known as Mandarin in the West and as *putonghua* or 'common speech' in China. About 70% of the population speaks Mandarin but there are many other Chinese dialects.

Chinese is a tonal language. One word can mean several different things depending on its intonation. Written Chinese has something like 50,000 characters – but only about 5000 are in common use and about 1500 are needed to read a newspaper easily. The Communist government has simplified the written script – about 50% of the strokes were eliminated, which also makes it simpler to learn and much faster to write. However, the simplified characters differ significantly from those used in Taiwan and Hong Kong, and any serious student of Chinese now must learn both systems.

In 1958 the Chinese officially adopted a system known as *pinyin* to enable them to write using the Roman alphabet, but don't expect all literate Chinese to know pinyin. Howwever, it's commonly used on shop fronts, street signs and advertising billboards. Basically the sounds are pronounced as in English, with a few exceptions:

Vowels

a	like the 'a' in 'father'
ai	like the 'i' in 'I'
ao	like the 'ow' in 'cow'
e	like the 'u' in 'blur'
ei	like the 'ei' in 'weigh'
i	like the 'ee' in 'meet' or the 'oo' in 'book'*
ian	like in 'yen'
ie	like the English word 'yeah'
o	like the 'o' in 'or'
ou	like the 'oa' in 'boat'
u	like the 'u' in 'flute'
ui	like 'way'
uo	like 'w' followed by an 'o' like in 'or'
yu	like German umlaut 'ü' or French 'u' in 'union'
ü	like German umlaut 'ü'

Consonants

c	like the 'ts' in 'bits'
ch	like in English, but with the tongue curled back
h	like in English, but articulated from the throat
q	like the 'ch' in 'chicken'
r	like the 's' in 'pleasure'
sh	like in English, but with the tongue curled back
x	like the 'sh' in 'shine'
z	like the 'ds' in 'suds'
zh	like the 'j' in 'judge' but with the tongue curled back

*The letter i is pronounced like the 'oo' in 'book' when it occurs after c, ch, r, s, sh, z, zh.

Consonants can never appear at the end of a syllable except for **n, ng** and **r**.

In pinyin, apostrophes are occasionally used to separate syllables. So, you can write *ping'an* to prevent the word being pronounced as *pin'gan*.

Tones

Their are four basic tones used in Mandarin Chinese, while other dialects such as Cantonese can have as many as nine. For example, in Mandarin Chinese the word *ma* can have four distinct meanings depending on which tone is used:

high tone *mā* is mother
rising tone *má* is hemp or numb
falling-rising tone *mǎ* is horse
falling tone *mà* is to scold or swear

There are many people in China who study English, which makes life a little easier for travellers. In the tourist hotels and at the CITS offices there is nearly always someone around who speaks a little English. In many universities, there are 'English corners' where the students go to practice – foreigners are enthusiastically welcomed. Phrase books are invaluable – you may want to pick up Lonely Planet's *China Phrasebook*. A small dictionary in English, pinyin and Chinese characters will come in handy – these are readily available from the Xinhua Bookstore which has branches all over China.

Greetings & Civilities

Hello
  nǐ hǎo   你好
Goodbye
  zàijiàn   再见
Thank you
  xièxie   谢谢
You're welcome
  bùkèqì   不客气
no, don't have
  méiyǒu   没有
no, not so
  bù shì   不是
Excuse me
  duìbuqǐ   对不起

Getting Around

I want to go to...
wǒ yào qù... 我要去 ...

bicycle
zìxíngchē 自行车

bus
gōnggòngqìchē 公共汽车

train
huǒchē 火车

hard-seat
yìngxí, yìngzuò 硬席，硬座

soft-seat
ruǎnxí, ruǎnzuò 软席，软座

hard-sleeper
yìngwò 硬卧

soft-sleeper
ruǎnwò 软卧

ferry pier
mǎtóu 码头

taxi
chūzū chē 出租车

ticket
piào 票

station
zhàn 站

entrance
rùkǒu 入口

exit
chūkǒu 出口

information
wènxúnchù 问询处

open/closed (for shops and restaurants only)
kāishǐ yíngyé/tíngzhǐ yíngyé
开始营业 / 停止营业

prohibited
jìnzhǐ 禁止

toilets
cèsuǒ 厕所

Accommodation

tourist hotel
bīnguǎn, fàndiàn, jiǔdiàn
宾馆，饭店，酒店

dormitory
duō rén fáng 多人房

Could you write down the address for me, please?
nǐ néngbunéng bǎ dìzhǐ xiěxiàlai gěi wǒ?
你能不能把地址写下来给我？

Do you have a...available?
nǐmen yǒumeiyǒu... 你们有没有 ...

single room
dān rén fáng 单人房

double room
shuāng rén fáng 双人房

How much is it?
yào duōshǎo qián? 要多少钱

bathtowel
yùjīn 浴巾

hotel namecard
lǚguan de míngpiàn 旅馆的名片

Around Town

Where is the...?
...zài nǎr? ....在哪儿？

China International Travel Service (CITS)
zhōngguó guójì lǚxíngshè
中国国际旅行社

Bank of China
zhōngguó yínháng 中国银行

Public Security Bureau
gōng'ān jú 公安局

Foreign Affairs Branch
wài shì kē 外事科

CAAC
zhōngguó mínháng 中国民航

city centre
shì zhōngxīn 市中心

Food

Food stall
xiǎochīdiàn 小吃店

Restaurant
fànguǎn 饭馆

I'm vegetarian.
wǒ chī sù 我吃素

How much is it?
duōshao qián? 多少钱

Time & Dates

When
shénme shíhou 什么时候

today
jīntiān 今天

tomorrow
míngtiān 明天

the day after tomorrow
hòutiān 后天

three days ahead		
dà hòutiān	大后天	
in the morning		
zǎochén	早晨	
afternoon		
xiàwǔ	下午	
night, evening		
wǎnshàng	晚上	

Numbers

0	*líng*	零
1	*yī, yāo*	一，一
2	*èr, liǎng*	二，两
3	*sān*	三
4	*sì*	四
5	*wǔ*	五
6	*liù*	六
7	*qī*	七
8	*bā*	八
9	*jiǔ*	九
10	*shí*	十
11	*shíyī*	十一

Emergencies

Help!
  jiùmìng a! 救命啊！
Go away!
  zǒu kāi! 走开
Call a doctor!
  qǐng jiào yíwèi yīshēng!
请叫一位医生！
Call the police!
  qǐng jiào jǐngchá! 叫警察！
I'm allergic to...
  wǒ duì...guòmǐn 我对....过敏
penicillin
  qīngméisù 青霉素
antibiotics
  kàngjūnsù 抗菌素
I'm diabetic.
  wǒ yǒu tángniào bìng. 我有糖尿病

Facts for the Visitor

VISAS & EMBASSIES

Visas for individual travel are readily available from many agents in Hong Kong and can be issued the same day for an extra fee. Two photos are required and there must be a blank page in your passport. The visa length is normally one month from date of issue, *not* from date of entry, so don't get a visa too far in advance. Visa extensions are handled by the Foreign Affairs Section of the local Public Security Bureaus (the police force).

The cost of the visa ranges from HK$90 to HK$250, depending on how quickly you want it and where you get it. More expensive are the two-entry visas. Multiple-entry visas are expensive (HK$700), and you can stay for just 30 days at a time (no extensions permitted), but the visa remains valid for six months. It will only be issued if you've already been to China at least once and have stamps in your passport to prove it. The following Hong Kong agencies are good for visas:

Visa Office of the Ministry of Foreign Affairs of the People's Republic of China
  5th floor, Low Block, China Resources Building, 26 Harbour Rd, Wanchai, Hong Kong Island (☎ 8939812). Open Monday to Friday, 9 am to 12.30 pm and 2 to 5 pm, Saturday 9 am to 12.30 pm. This place issues the cheapest visas. A three-month visa issued in two days costs HK$90.
Phoenix Services
  Room B, 6th floor, Milton Mansion, 96 Nathan Rd, Tsimshatsui, Kowloon (☎ 7227378)
Traveller Services
  Room 704, Metropole Building, 57 Peking Rd, Tsimshatsui, Kowloon (☎ 3674127)

In Macau, you can get Chinese visas at China Travel Service (☎ 388922), Hotel Beverly Plaza, Avenida do Dr Rodrigo Rodrigues.

Chinese Embassies

Following are the addresses of Chinese embassies in major cities around the world.

Australia
  247 Federal Highway, Watson, Canberra, 2602 ACT
Canada
  411-415 Andrews St, Ottawa, Ontario KIN 5H3
Japan
  15-30 Minami-Azabu, 4-Chome, Minato-ku, Tokyo

New Zealand
   2-6 Glenmore St, Kelburr, Wellington
Switzerland
   Kalecheggweg 10, Berne
UK
   31 Portland Place, London WIN 3AG
USA
   2300 Connecticut Ave NW, Washington, DC
   20008. Consulates: 3417 Montrose Blvd,
   Houston, TX 77006; 104 South Michigan Ave,
   Suite 1200, Chicago, IL 60603; 1450 Laguna St,
   San Francisco, CA 94115; 520 12th Ave, New
   York, NY 10036

Foreign Embassies in China

Embassies and consulates are concentrated in the two compounds of Jianguomenwai and Sanlitun in Beijing. The Jianguomenwai Compound is in the vicinity of the Friendship Store. Some embassies located here are:

Bulgaria
   4 Xiushui Beijie (☎ 5322232)
Czechoslovakia
   Ritan Lu (☎ 5321531)
Ireland
   3 Ritan Donglu (☎ 5322691)
Japan
   7 Ritan Lu (☎ 5322361)
Mongolia
   2 Xiushui Beijie (☎ 5321203)
New Zealand
   1 Ritan Dong 2-Jie (☎ 5322731)
Philippines
   23 Xiushui Beijie (☎ 5322451)
Poland
   1 Ritan Lu, Jianguomenwai (☎ 5321235)
Romania
   corner of Ritan Dong 2-Jie and Ritan Donglu
   (☎ 5323315)
Thailand
   40 Guanghua Lu (☎ 5321903)
UK
   11 Guanghua Lu (☎ 5321961)
USA
   Embassy: 3 Xiushui Beijie (☎ 5323831).
   Consulate: 2 Xiushui Dongjie
Vietnam
   32 Guanghua Lu (☎ 5321125)

The Sanlitun Compound is several km northeast of Jianguomenwai, near the Agricultural Exhibition Hall:

Australia
   15 Dongzhimenwai Dajie (☎ 5322331)

Burma (Myanmar)
   6 Dongzhimenwai Dajie (☎ 5321584)
Canada
   10 Sanlitun Lu (☎ 5323031)
Hungary
   10 Dongzhimenwai Dajie (☎ 5321431)
Nepal
   1 Sanlitun Xi 6-Jie (☎ 5321795)
Pakistan
   1 Dongzhimenwai Dajie (☎ 5322504)
USSR
   4 Dongzhimen Beizhongjie, west of the Sanlitun
   Compound in a separate compound (☎ 5322051)

In Canton, there are consulates for Japan, Poland, Thailand and the USA. In Shanghai, there are consulates for Australia, Belgium, France, Germany, Hungary, Japan, Poland, the UK, the USA and the USSR.

DOCUMENTS

To travel to closed places like Tibet, you require an official 'Alien's Travel Permit' obtainable from the Foreign Affairs Office of the Public Security Bureau (the police). If you get a permit to visit an unusual destination, the best strategy is to go there as fast as you can (by plane if possible). Other PSBs don't have to honour the permit and can cancel it and send you back. Transit points, at which you can usually stay overnight, generally don't require a permit.

CUSTOMS

Customs is pretty much a formality these days, but you must declare cameras, electronics and other high-tech goodies so that you cannot sell them in China or give them away as presents. Try not to lose the declaration form as you are supposed to account for these items when you leave. Should your camera get stolen in China, have Public Security make out a loss report which you can show Customs when you depart.

You can take in 600 cigarettes, two litres of alcohol, approximately half a litre of perfume and 72 rolls of film. 'Subversive literature' (literature that makes the Chinese government look bad) cannot be brought in. Customs will also seize pornography (which the officers will probably take home to share with their friends).

When you leave China, antiques (or things which look antique) may be confiscated unless you have an official receipt. Some herbs are also prohibited exports.

MONEY
Currency

The basic unit of Chinese currency is the *yuan* (Y), which is divided into *jiao* and *fen*. Ten fen make up one jiao (pronounced *mao*), and 10 jiao make up one yuan.

China has an absurd dual-currency system. *Renminbi* (people's money or RMB) are for the masses. Foreign Exchange Certificates (tourist money or FEC) are for the use of foreigners, including Overseas Chinese. Foreigners are supposed to pay for hotels and travel fares in FEC – in practice, you can sometimes use RMB in places that normally require payment in FEC. Having two currencies is a real pain because people will often demand FEC and give change in RMB, which means you can easily wind up with excess RMB – you'll have to make an effort to spend it. To make things worse, you cannot legally exchange RMB at the border when you leave China.

Foreign currency and travellers' cheques can be changed at the main centres of the Bank of China, at branch offices in the tourist hotels and some Friendship Stores. You can usually swap FEC for RMB with local Chinese, sometimes at a premium. RMB are useful for street stalls, restaurants and markets. Credit cards are now becoming accepted in the big cities, but don't rely on plastic – most places don't have machines to process cards.

When you leave China you can convert FEC (not RMB) back to foreign currency, but you *must* have your exchange receipts with you to prove that you changed foreign currency in the first place. You are only permitted to exchange *half* the total amount indicated on your receipts. If you find yourself with leftover RMB, you can usually unload it in Hong Kong at some of the hostels because many travellers are heading for China.

Exchange Rates

A$1	=	Y4.20
C$1	=	Y4.75
HK$1	=	Y0.70
NZ$1	=	Y3.00
UK£1	=	Y9.40
US$1	=	Y5.40
Y100	=	Y4.20

Costs

Next to Mongolia, China is certainly the cheapest country covered in this book, but that statement needs to be qualified. It's not going to be as cheap as India, the Philippines or many other places in Asia, because the Chinese government has made it a policy to milk every dollar it can from foreigners. With the cooperation of the police, foreigners are usually forced to stay in the most expensive accommodation and charged

double or more for train and plane tickets. In the restaurant at Shanghai's airport, foreigners were being told that they must order from the 'Western menu' which has prices five times higher than the 'Chinese menu'. For admission to Beijing's Forbidden City, foreigners have the privilege of paying Y30 (US$5.70) – which would be several days' wages for a Chinese worker.

Costs per day start at around US$10 (Y53), assuming you live in dormitories, take hard-seat trains, pay Chinese prices for tickets, eat at street stalls etc. Figure two or three times that if you want to have a comfortable double room, eat well and occasionally take a CAAC flight. You *can* travel cheaply in China, but it's continuous combat – you versus the authorities. On the other hand, your journey can be a miserable experience if you're constantly worried about how far the money is going to stretch and if you force yourself to live in perpetual discomfort. Good luck.

Tipping

Tipping is not normally a custom. Bribery is another matter. Don't be blatant about it, but if you need some special service, it's customary to offer someone a cigarette and just tell him/her 'Go ahead and keep the pack – I'm trying to quit'. In China, a 'tip' is given before you receive the service, not after.

Bargaining

There's a lot of room to bargain in China – for hotel rooms, in private stores (not government-owned) and even with the police if you are fined. Always be polite and smiling when bargaining – nastiness will cause the other party to lose face, in which case they'll dig their heels in and you'll come out the loser.

WHAT TO BRING

A medical kit is important. This is discussed in detail in this book in the introductory Health section.

Sunglasses are needed for the Xinjiang desert or the high altitudes of Tibet. Ditto UV (sunblock) lotion. If you wear contact lenses,

bring your own cleaning solution, eye drops and other accessories.

A water bottle can be a lifesaver during summer. Make sure you get one that doesn't leak.

Shaving cream and good razor blades are rare items. Mosquito repellent guards against malaria – a good brand available in Hong Kong is *Autan*. Chinese nail clippers are poor quality and deodorant is unknown. Chinese toothbrushes are usually too hard – more suitable for removing rust than cleaning your teeth. Dental floss is hard to find in China and tampons are unavailable. Condoms are widely available but not always reliable.

An alarm clock is essential for catching early-morning trains. A lightweight digital model is best – make sure the battery is OK because you'll have trouble finding replacements in China.

Good batteries are hard to come by in China – bring what you need for your camera and consider rechargeable batteries and a recharger (220 volts) if you can't live without your Walkman.

A gluestick is convenient for sealing envelopes and pasting on stamps. The Chinese equivalent is a leaky bottle of glue.

Having something to read will help preserve your sanity as well as pass the time.

Chinese tea is sold everywhere – if you need the Indian variety, you'll have to bring it.

Chinese cigarettes have the gentle eastern aroma of old socks. Foreign-made cigarettes (and imitations) and alcohol are available from hawkers, small shops, hotel shops and Friendship Stores all over China.

If you want to give someone a gift, English books and magazines are much in demand. Many Chinese people are avid stamp-collectors, and also desire foreign postcards (including photos of Hong Kong). Pictures of you and your family also make good gifts.

TOURIST OFFICES
Local Tourist Offices

CITS China International Travel Service organises travel arrangements and is supposed to speak English. CITS is known for poor service and high prices, and foreigners have suggested they change their name to GUYMAGTHO – 'Give us your money and get the hell out'. CITS usually has an office in the major tourist hotel of each city in China.

CTS China Travel Service is set up for Overseas Chinese. They usually don't speak English and therefore seldom deal with Western tourists, but you can use them in Hong Kong to book trains, planes, hovercraft, etc to China.

Overseas Reps
China International Travel Service The main office of CITS in Hong Kong has a particularly good collection of pamphlets about China, all in English. Outside of China and Hong Kong, CITS is usually known as China National Tourist Office.

Australia
 China National Tourist Office, 11th floor, 55 Clarence St, Sydney NSW 2000 (☎ (02) 29 4057, fax 290 1958)
France
 China National Tourist Office, 51 Rue Saint-Anne, 75002, Paris (☎ 4296 9548, fax 4261 5468)
Germany
 China National Tourist Office, Eschenheimer Anlage 28, D-6000 Frankfurt am Main-1 (☎ (069) 55 5292, fax 597 3412)
Hong Kong
 Main Office, 6th Floor, Tower Two, South Seas Centre, 75 Mody Rd, Tsimshatsui East, Kowloon (☎ 732 5888, fax 721 7154)
 Central Branch, Room 1018, Swire House, 11 Chater Rd, Central (☎ 810 4282, fax 868 1657)
 Mongkok Branch, Room 1102-1104, Bank Centre, 636 Nathan Rd, Mongkok, Kowloon (☎ 388 1619, fax 385 6157)
 Causeway Bay Branch, Room 1104, Causeway Bay Plaza, 489 Hennessy Rd, Causeway Bay (☎ 836 3485, fax 591 0849)
Japan
 China National Tourist Office, 6F Hachidal Hamamatsu-cho Building, 1-27-13 Hamamatsu-cho Minato-ku, Tokyo (☎ (03) 3433 1461, fax 3433 8653)
UK
 China National Tourist Office, 4 Glentworth St, London NW1 (☎ (071) 935 9427, fax 487 5842)

USA
 China National Tourist Office, Los Angeles Branch, 333 West Broadway, Suite 201, Glendale CA 91204 (☎ (818) 545 7505, fax 545 7506)
 New York Branch, Lincoln Building, 60E, 42nd St, Suite 3126, New York, NY 10165 (☎ (212) 867 0271, fax 599 2892)

China Travel Service In Hong Kong, the Kowloon and Mongkok branch offices of CTS are open on Sundays and public holidays.

Australia
 Ground floor, 757-759 George St, Sydney, NSW 2000 (☎ (02) 211 2633, fax 281 3595)
Canada
 PO Box 17, Main Floor, 999 West Hastings St, Vancouver, BC V6C 2W2 (☎ (604) 684 8787, fax 684 3321)
France
 10 Rue De Rome, 75008, Paris (☎ (1) 4522 9272, fax 4522 9279)
Hong Kong
 Central Branch, China Travel Building, 77 Queens Rd, Central, Hong Kong Island (☎ 521 7163, fax 525 5525)
 Kowloon Branch, 1st Floor, Alpha House, 27-33 Nathan Rd, Tsimshatsui (☎ 721 4481, fax 721 6251)
 Mongkok Branch, 2nd floor, 62-72 Sai Yee St, Mongkok (☎ 789 5970, fax 390 5001)
Japan
 Nihombashi-Settsu Building, 2-2-4, Nihombashi, Chuo-ku, Tokyo (☎ (03) 3273 5512, fax 3273 2667)
Macau
 2nd floor, Hotel Beverly Plaza, Avenida do Dr Rodrigo Rodrigues (☎ 38 8922, HK 540 6333)
Philippines
 489 San Fernando St, Binondo, Manila (☎ 047-41-87, fax 40-78-34)
Singapore
 Ground Floor, Sia Building, 77 Robinson Rd, Singapore 0106, (☎ 224 0550, fax 224 5009)
Thailand
 460/2-3 Surawong Rd, Bangkok 10500 (☎ (2) 233 2895, fax 236 5511)
UK
 24 Cambridge Circus, London WC2H 8HD (☎ (01) 836 9911, fax 836 3121)
USA
 2nd Floor, 212 Sutter St, San Francisco, CA 94108 (☎ (415) 398 6627, fax 398 6669)
 Los Angeles Branch, Suite 138, 233E, Garvey Ave, Monterey Park, CA 91754 (☎ (818) 288 8222, fax 288 3464)

USEFUL ORGANISATIONS

Public Security Bureau (PSB) is the name given to China's police force. In any large city, the PSB has a Foreign Affairs Office at their headquarters. This office issues visa extensions and Alien's Travel Permits.

BUSINESS HOURS & HOLIDAYS

In China, no-one moves slower than a government employee, except a dead government employee. As a rough guide only, government offices are open Monday to Saturday – they open around 8 to 9 am, close for two hours around noon, and then re-open until 5 or 6 pm. Sunday is a public holiday, but some businesses are open Sunday morning and make up for this by closing on Wednesday afternoons.

Government restaurants are open for early morning breakfast (sometimes as early as 5.30) until about 7.30 am, then open for lunch and again for dinner. The Chinese eat early and go home early. Privately run restaurants are usually open all day, and often late into the night especially around railway stations.

Long-distance bus stations and railway stations open their ticket offices around 5 or 5.30 am before the first trains and buses pull out. Apart from a one or two-hour break in the middle of the day, they often stay open until late at night.

The People's Republic has nine national holidays during the year, as follows: New Year's Day, 1 January; Chinese Lunar New Year, usually in February – sheer chaos for one week (avoid it); International Working Women's Day, 8 March; International Labour Day, 1 May; Youth Day, 4 May; Children's Day, 1 June; Anniversary of the founding of the Communist Party of China; 1 July; Anniversary of the founding of the People's Liberation Army, 1 August; National Day, 1 October.

CULTURAL EVENTS

The ice festival is magnificent in the north-eastern city of Harbin during January and February – so long as you're prepared for temperatures of minus 40° C.

The birthday of Confucius (28 September) would be the best time to visit the Confucius Temple in the great sage's home town of Qufu, Shandong Province.

POST & TELECOMMUNICATIONS
Postal Rates

International surface mail costs Y1.50 up to 20 g, and Y3 above 20 g and up to 50 g. Air-mail letters are an additional Y0.50 for every 10 g or fraction thereof. Postcards are Y1.10 by surface mail and Y1.60 by air mail. Aerograms are Y1.90 to anywhere in the world. There are discounts for printed matter, small packets and parcels.

Sending Mail

Some have reported their outgoing mail has been opened and read. This seems to affect tourists less, although letters with enclosures will almost certainly be opened. Your mail is less likely to be opened if it's sent from cities that handle high volumes of mail, like Beijing.

Receiving Mail

It's worth noting that some foreigners living in China have had their mail opened or parcels pilfered before receipt. Officially, the People's Republic prohibits several items from being mailed to it, including books, magazines, notes and manuscripts.

Poste restante seems to work, but they haven't discovered alphabetical order. In large cities, the GPO will assign numbers to letters as they are received and post the number and names on a noticeboard. You have to find your name and write down the number(s) of your letters, then tell the clerk at the counter. We've seen some strange names on the noticeboards – 'Par Avion', 'General Delivery', and 'Hold Until Arrival'.

Telephones

Public pay phones are a rare breed. Direct dialling for international calls is gradually being introduced at top hotels in the major cities, but prices are high. Rates for station-to-station calls to most countries in the world are Y18 per minute. Hong Kong is slightly cheaper at Y12 per minute. There is a minimum charge of three minutes. Reverse-charge calls are cheaper than calls paid for in China. The country code for calling China is 86.

Telephone cards are available, in denominations of Y20, Y50, Y100 and Y200.

If you are expecting a call, advise the caller of your hotel room number. The operators frequently have difficulty understanding Western names, and the hotel receptionist may not be able to find you.

Fax, Telex & Telegraph

Big hotels that have international telephone service usually also have fax machines. Telegrams and telexes can be sent from the central telecommunication offices in major cities.

TIME

As ridiculous as it may seem, China is one big time zone – Greenwich Mean Time plus eight hours.

When it is noon in China it is also noon in Singapore, Hong Kong, Taiwan and Perth; 2 pm in Sydney; 8 pm the previous day in Los Angeles; 11 pm the previous day in New York; and 4 am in London.

Daylight savings time is in effect from the first Sunday of the second 10 days of April until the first Sunday of the second 10 days of September.

Daylight savings time causes massive confusion in China. Bus companies and the airlines put all their flights ahead one hour, thus eliminating the benefits of the change. The trains stick to the old schedule. Some cities, especially those near Hong Kong, still refuse to follow daylight savings time.

LAUNDRY

Almost all tourist hotels have a laundry service, but tend to be expensive. If the hotel doesn't have a laundry, they can usually direct you to one. Expensive garments have a tendency to disappear.

WEIGHTS & MEASURES

China uses the metric system, but some traditional measures can still be found.

Metric		Chinese		Imperial
1 metre	=	3 chi	=	3.28 feet
1 km	=	2 li	=	0.62 miles
1 hectare	=	15 mu	=	2.47 acres
1 litre	=	1 gongsheng	=	0.22 gallons
1 kg	=	2 jin	=	2.20 pounds

ELECTRICITY

Electricity is 220 V, 50 cycles AC. Power blackouts are frequent during summer.

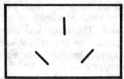

BOOKS & MAPS

Lonely Planet's *China – a travel survival kit* gives a complete rundown on the country and how to get around it on your own. Lonely Planet's *Tibet – a travel survival kit* covers all of Tibet.

The Soong Dynasty by Sterling Seagrave (Sidgwick & Jackson) is one of the most popular books on the corrupt Kuomintang period. The classic book on the Chinese revolution is *Red Star Over China* by Edgar Snow, an idealistic account by a Western journalist who visited the Red Army and its leaders during the 1930s.

Fox Butterfield's *China – Alive in the*

Bitter Sea (Coronet, 1983) is one of the biggest sellers – a harshly critical account. A chilling best seller about the Cultural Revolution is *Life and Death in Shanghai* by Nien Cheng (Grafton). Franz Kafka's *The Trial* wasn't written with China in mind, yet his book is a potent reminder of the helplessness of individuals against the all-powerful state bureaucracy.

Chinese Lives by Zhang Xinxin and Sang Ye (Penguin) was written by two Chinese journalists who interviewed Chinese people at all levels of society. A lively and informative book is *Cycling to Xian* by Michael Buckley (ITMB, 736A Granville St, Vancouver, BC V6Z 1G3, Canada).

The most useful map of China is published by Cartographic Publishing House in Beijing and is called the 'Map of the People's Republic of China (Zhonghua Renmin Gongheguo Ditu)'.

MEDIA

Newspapers & Magazines

The *China Daily* is the only English-language daily newspaper. The *Beijing Review* is a weekly magazine on political and current affairs. *China Today* is a monthly magazine founded in 1952, previously called *China Reconstructs*. The name was changed in 1989 because – as one official said – '37 years is a hell of a long time to be reconstructing your country'.

Foreign magazines can be found in major hotels in large cities – elsewhere, forget it. If you need something to read, bring it yourself.

Radio & TV

If you want to keep up with foreign news, bring a short-wave radio.

There are some imported English-language shows, but the majority are in Chinese. Many shows are designed to guide the public's moral education. Movies and soap operas urge the people to be good citizens, work and study hard, not to lie, cheat, slash foreigners' backpacks, etc. Most Chinese find their public television so boring, it's no wonder they stare at foreigners

– cheap entertainment. Those who have access to video tape players consume Western movies with a passion.

FILM & PHOTOGRAPHY

Colour print film is readily available, but slide film is hard to get and often out of date when you find it. Film is significantly more expensive in China than in Hong Kong. The quality of photoprocessing facilities varies, and they sometimes 'lose' controversial photos.

Obviously, don't film anything that looks like it has a military function.

In Tibetan temples, photography is often prohibited (ask if not sure) – some of those monks can rip film out of a camera so fast you'll swear they must possess special martial arts skills.

HEALTH

Vaccinations against cholera are required if you arrive within five days of leaving an infected area. They're recommended in any case, required or not. Yellow fever vaccinations are required if you're arriving within six days of leaving an infected area. China is starting to ask for HIV (AIDS) certificates before granting work permits. (The government has acknowledged that there are 500 HIV-positive drug users in Yunnan.) It may be a good idea to have a tetanus injection before you leave to guard against infection from cuts. There is a risk of malaria in the southern and south-eastern provinces and taking malaria tablets is a good idea in summer. There is also a danger of hepatitis because of poor sanitation. Immunisation against tuberculosis wouldn't hurt. Rabies and giardia exist in Tibet. Bring your own condoms; the local product is unreliable.

More details about health are included in the Facts for the Visitor chapter.

WOMEN TRAVELLERS

Women report relatively little sexual harassment except in Muslim areas like Xinjiang, where it is best to dress very conservatively.

Women may need to take special precautions with their health. For example, if you're prone to yeast infections, bring your own medication (Nystatin suppositories). Tampons are not available and Chinese sanitary pads are big and bulky.

DANGERS & ANNOYANCES

China is the most dangerous country in this book in terms of theft. Be especially wary of pickpockets in crowded areas. Thieves often slash backpacks with razor blades in order to get at valuables. Report thefts of items listed on your declaration form to the Public Security Bureau. They will issue a loss report which should clear you with Customs on departure.

To less sophisticated Chinese people, staring at a foreigner is better than television. Staring squads are everywhere in China, and staring back doesn't seem to help – indeed, the crowd will love it. The best bet is to keep moving so a crowd of enthusiastic onlookers can't get organised.

Foreign men should avoid situations in which they are alone in a room with a closed door with a Chinese woman – even if nothing is going on but polite conversation. There have been cases of the police bursting into a foreign man's hotel room, accusing him of performing 'indecent activities with a Chinese woman' and then hauling him down to the police station to pay a huge fine. Foreigners who have found themselves in this situation suspect they have been set up, the real purpose being to extort money from them.

WORK

There are opportunities to teach English and other languages, or even other technical skills. The pay is generally poor. The main reason to do it is to experience living and working in China. If interested, contact a Chinese embassy or the universities directly.

ACTIVITIES
Hiking

China is somewhat disappointing for hiking and camping. Those areas which would be most interesting – like Tibet – are closed to independent travellers. Those areas which are open tend to be intensively cultivated. Probably your best bet is to climb some of the 'sacred mountains' like Emeishan and Taishan.

Skiing

Don't expect to find another Aspen or St Moritz, but you can pursue the art of sliding downhill in China. Westerners may have trouble renting ski boots which are large enough. In north-east China, 20 km from Jilin town (Jilin Province) are the Songhua Lake skifields. A more advanced skifield is at Tonghua. The best skifields are near Harbin in Heilongjiang Province.

Courses
Language Studying Chinese is indeed possible, though many come to the conclusion that Taiwan is better because it's easier to make friends with individual Chinese there. Studying in China might also not be as cheap as you expect. One place to contact is the Beijing Language Institute (yŭyán xúeyùan).

Traditional Medicine China is undoubtedly the best place to study herbal medicine and acupuncture. One popular place for this activity is the Traditional Chinese Medicine Hospital (zhōngyī yīyùan) on Zhuji Lu in Canton.

HIGHLIGHTS

Opinions differ, but Yunnan Province probably rates first for the sheer number of scenic wonders and pleasant people. Some popular places in Yunnan include Dali and Xishuangbanna.

Jiuzhaigou National Park in Sichuan could well be the most beautiful place in China, but is difficult to get to.

The nation's capital – Beijing – is also China's cultural capital. The Forbidden City is just as fascinating now as it was 500 years ago.

Remote Xinjiang in China's rugged north-west offers unique scenery and culture. Highlights of this region include Turpan and

Kashgar, plus the trip to Pakistan over Khunjerab Pass (4800 metres).

Tibet remains one of China's greatest wonders, but getting there currently requires that you sign up for an expensive tour.

ACCOMMODATION

Hotels are a source of contant frustration in China. There are plenty of cheap places to stay for the Chinese, but Public Security has placed most of them off limits to foreigners. Consequently, you may be forced to pay for luxury you don't really need or want.

Segregation is not universally enforced, and there are times when you will be able to stay in a 'Chinese-only' hotel. In very small towns, for example, there may only be one hotel so everyone stays there. In many hotels, there is a Chinese section and a for-eigners section.

Generally foreigners will pay double what a Chinese would pay for the same room, and foreigners usually have to pay in FEC. The price of rooms varies enormously and often illogically – sometimes you pay exorbitant rates for a dump, and at other times you bask in luxury at rock-bottom prices. You *can* bargain the price for a room in many hotels, but do so politely. Dormitory accommodation *(dūo rén fáng)* is often available – standards vary wildly from first-rate to Third World. In some places you still have to battle to get into a dormitory – politely insist that you're a student and can't afford a double room.

FOOD

Chinese food comes in a wide variety of styles, depending in part on which region of the country it originated in. Probably most familiar to foreigners is the Cantonese variety, prevalent in Hong Kong and Guangdong Province. The emphasis is on steaming, pot boiling and stir frying, with lots of vegetables, roast pork, chicken, steamed fish and fried rice. The Cantonese are famous for their ability to eat almost anything, including snake, monkey, pango-lin (an armadillo-like creature), bear, giant salamander and raccoon, not to mention more mundane dog, cat and rat dishes. Some other Cantonese specialities include shark's fin soup, roast pig and pigeon. You may also see 'thousand-year eggs', which are black in colour and made by soaking in horses' urine.

Beijing (Peking) and Shandong food orig-inated in one of the coldest parts of China and use heaps of spices to warm the body. Bread and noodles are often used instead of rice. The chief speciality is Peking duck, of which the crisp skin is the prized part. Another speciality is a Mongolian barbecue – assorted barbecued meats and vegetables mixed in a hotpot.

Sichuan (Szechuan) food is the hottest of the categories and is characterised by the heavy use of spices and peppers. The *mapo doufu* or spicy bean curd, is a Sichuan classic. Sichuan food also features noodles and beautiful, warm bread.

Shanghai cuisine uses lots of chilli and spices, and is heavier and oilier than either Beijing or Cantonese food. Given the fact

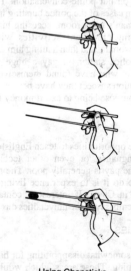

Using Chopsticks

that Shanghai is a main port, it's not surprising that seafood plays an important role. Eels are popular, as is drunken chicken – the bird is cooked in *shaoshing*, a potent Chinese wine which tastes a bit like warm sherry. The big speciality of Shanghai food is the strange, hairy crab which arrives in September or October and keeps the gourmets happy for three months or so. The crabs are eaten for the roes and are beyond the price of most shoestring travellers.

Chaozhou *Chiu Chow* originated in the port of Shantou in south-eastern China. Seafood figures prominently, especially steamed lobster, deep-fried shrimp balls, crab meat balls and steamed eel, all served with lots of vegetables.

Incidentally, you do not find fortune cookies in China – they are a foreign invention.

Quality and standards of cleanliness vary enormously. Food quality is also affected by region and by the seasons – fresh fruits and vegetables can be scarce during the winter in many parts of China. However, Chinese food is generally good – just be prepared for the occasional disappointment.

Always ask the price of what you're ordering before you eat it. There have been horror stories of foreigners ordering food without first asking the price, and then being presented with an outrageous bill. It happens even in government-run restaurants.

If you visit the dining rooms of luxury hotels, you'll often have the chance to see government officials gorging themselves at expensive banquets – literally feeding at the public trough. In a daring denunciation of cadre corruption, Chinese rock star Cui Jian wrote the 'Official Banquet Song':

I'm a big official, so I eat and drink, eat and drink;
To the Mongolian restaurant we go for hotpot;
To Quanjude for Peking duck;
Anyway, it's not my money;
So eat and drink and all be merry!

DRINKS

Green tea is the most common drink. Coffee and Indian tea are not generally available.

The top-brand Chinese beer, Tsingtao (Qingdao), is great stuff – but it's really a German beer, since the brewery dates back to the days of the foreign concessions. Local beers of varying but generally good quality are found all over China. Stronger brews have the exquisite, subtle flavour of rocket-fuel.

ENTERTAINMENT

Chinese nightlife is a dead loss. Some of the big hotels have expensive discos catering to Hong Kongers, but most Westerners don't find it very exciting.

Visitors to China try to create their own nightlife. In places where foreigners are numerous, there are sometimes late-night restaurants where travellers congregate to sip beer or Cokes and swap yarns – that's about as thrilling as it gets.

THINGS TO BUY

Chinese department stores can be fascinating. Many consumer items still use 1950s technology (treadle sewing machines, 'Brownie' box cameras), but prices are low and quality is often surprisingly good. Clothing is a bargain – check out the down jackets. Good deals can be had on tools, clocks and other appliances, but always test the goods to be sure they are working – defective merchandise does exist. When buying anything electric, remember that China uses 220 volts.

'Friendship Stores' – which cater to tourists – can be good for finding arts & crafts. The Beijing Friendship Store is exceptionally well stocked. Branches of the Xinhua Bookstore not only sell books, but also maps, art supplies and posters. Copies of the Little Red Book and Mao caps are available on the free market.

Getting There & Away

AIR

CAAC (Civil Aviation Administration of China, also known as Air China) is China's domestic and international carrier. CAAC has a well-deserved reputation for poor service, cancelled flights and accidents. In an attempt to spur competition and polish its tarnished image, CAAC has been 'broken up' into a number of other airlines – Shanghai Airlines, Xinjiang Airlines, etc. It hasn't made a bit of difference – they still print 'CAAC' on the tickets, all flights are listed in the CAAC timetable, and the traditional cancellations and occasional crashes continue. 'CAAC-Survivor!' T-shirts are available in Hong Kong. Interestingly, the shirts are made in China.

Basically, there are two main ways of entering China – directly or via Hong Kong. Most independent travellers prefer to arrive from Hong Kong – it's cheaper and Hong Kong is a major transport hub for all of east Asia. Hong Kongers like to visit relatives in China when they have time off, so weekend and holiday border crossings should be avoided if possible. If you're determined to enter China directly by air from some place other than Hong Kong, it can be done but it's going to cost you.

To/From Hong Kong

You'll save considerably if you go to Canton overland and then take a domestic flight to your destination in China. However, direct flights from Hong Kong are faster and safer.

CAAC operates direct flights between Hong Kong and Canton. The fare is around HK$300 (Y150 in the other direction), and the flight takes about 35 minutes.

There are also daily flights to Beijing (around HK$1700, Y1155); flights six days a week to Shanghai (HK$1200, Y815); and flights twice a week to Kunming (HK$1100, Y747).

There are frequent charter flights between Hong Kong and popular tourist destinations such as Xi'an and Sanya (Hainan Island). Check with CTS or CAAC.

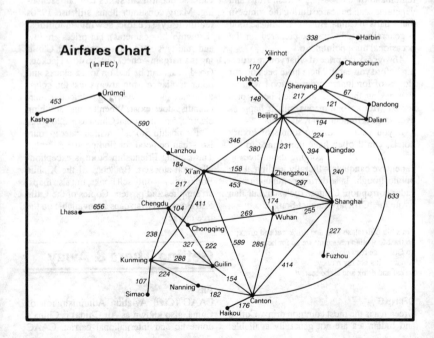

In Hong Kong flights can be booked at the CAAC office on the ground floor of Gloucester Tower, des Voeux Rd, Central, Hong Kong Island (☎ 5216416). There is another CAAC office on the ground floor, Hankow Centre, 4 Ashley Rd, Tsimshatsui, Kowloon (☎ 7390022).

To/From Japan

You can fly directly from Tokyo to Beijing, Shanghai or Dalian. There are also flights from Osaka and Nagasaki.

Obscure Flights in Asia

If you're booked on a tour, you can fly from Kathmandu, Nepal, to Lhasa in Tibet. There are CAAC flights connecting Beijing to Ulaan Baatar, Mongolia and Pyongyang, North Korea. From the obscure outpost of Ürümqi in Xinjiang, there are flights to Istanbul, Turkey, and Alma-Ata in the USSR. There are CAAC flights between Kunming and Bangkok or Rangoon.

To/From the USA & Canada

For direct flights from the USA to China the general route is from San Francisco (with connections from New York, Los Angeles and Vancouver) to Tokyo, Shanghai and Beijing. A round-trip excursion fare from San Francisco to Hong Kong is likely to cost from US$1000, and to Beijing from $1250.

To/From Europe

CAAC has flights from Beijing to Belgrade, Bucharest, Frankfurt, London, Moscow, Paris, Athens, Istanbul and Zurich. Other international airlines operate flights out of Beijing but there are very few, if any, cut-rate fares from the Chinese end. Try the Soviet airline Aeroflot and the Romanian airline Tarrom.

To/From Australia & New Zealand

There are direct flights from Melbourne to Beijing, but you should get a cheaper fare if you fly to Hong Kong first – from about A$650 (A$1100 return).

From Auckland to Hong Kong will set you back around NZ$1750 return, and to Beijing around NZ$2550 return.

LAND

To/From Hong Kong

The express train between Hong Kong and Canton is fast and comfortable. The adult fare is HK$190 one way. Timetables change, so check departure times. There are usually three or four express trains daily, and the whole trip takes a bit less than three hours.

In Hong Kong, tickets can be booked up to seven days before departure at CTS. On the day of departure, tickets can be bought from Hunghom Railway Station. Return tickets are also sold, but only between seven and 30 days before departure. Bicycles can be carried in the freight car.

A cheaper alternative to the express train is the local train. The trains start running early in the morning, and the border stays open until 10 pm (11 pm daylight savings time in China). You can take it from the Hunghom Station (Kowloon) to the Hong Kong/China border at Lo Wu, then walk across the border bridge to Shenzhen and pick up the local train to Canton. The fare from Kowloon to Lo Wu is HK$35 ordinary class.

There are about a dozen local trains a day between Shenzhen and Canton. Tourist-price hard-seat is Y35, soft-seat Y65. The Shenzhen-Canton journey takes about 2½ to 3½ hours.

To/From Macau

Macau is just over the border from China's Special Economic Zone of Zhuhai. The border post is at Gongbei. The Macau-Gongbei border is open from 7 am to 9 pm. Cyclists can ride across. There are buses from the long-distance bus station in Canton to Gongbei (Y10, five hours). There is also an express bus service from Macau (see the Macau chapter).

To/From the USSR

A great way to start or finish your China trip is to travel on the Trans-Siberian Railway.

More information on this journey is provided in the Getting There & Away chapter.

Some time within the lifespan of this book, a new railway line is supposed to be opened between the USSR and Xinjiang in north-west China via the Alataw Pass. If it really happens, it will provide a fascinating alternative to the Trans-Siberian.

To/From Mongolia

The Trans-Siberian takes 1½ days to reach Ulaan Baatar – see the Mongolia chapter for details.

To/From Pakistan

The journey between Pakistan and Kashgar in China's north-west takes you through Khunjerab Pass in the spectacular Karakoram Mountains. This trip is only possible during the warm months, and the Chinese have at times closed the route because of anti-government rioting in Kashgar.

To/From Nepal

The road between Nepal and Tibet has been periodically closed due to landslides and political earthquakes. Due to political earthquakes, it is currently closed again, but could reopen if the Chinese authorities feel sufficiently confident that they've crushed Tibetan nationalism.

SEA

To/From Hong Kong

There are two boats which sail between Hong Kong and Shanghai. The trip is very popular, especially for the return journey. You can get tickets in Hong Kong from CTS or the China Merchants Steam Navigation Company (☎ 5440558 or 5430945) on the 18th floor, 152-155 Connaught Rd, Central, Hong Kong Island. In Shanghai, tickets can be bought from the office of the China Ocean Shipping Agency (☎ 216327 ext 79) at 255 Jiangxi Rd.

The Hong Kong-Canton ship receives rave reviews from travellers. The trip takes about 10 hours, and the boats leave at 9 pm from the China Ferry Terminal in Kowloon,

and from the Zhoutouzui Wharf in Canton. The boats are large, clean and very comfortable, but have very aggressive air-conditioning. Fares range from HK\$180 for a two-person cabin, to HK\$120 for a dormitory. Children under five accompanied by an adult are admitted free.

There are also a couple of boats which go to Chinese ports on the south-east coast. Boats run between Hong Kong and Shantou, Xiamen or Zhanjiang.

Much faster than the ferries are the hovercraft which can do the Hong Kong-Canton run in about three hours. In Hong Kong the hovercraft leaves from China Ferry Terminal in Kowloon for Zhoutouzui Wharf in Canton. The fare from Hong Kong is HK\$160.

Tickets can be bought at the China Travel Service offices in Hong Kong, or at the China Ferry Terminal. In Canton tickets can be bought at Zhoutouzui Wharf.

There are also hovercraft running from China Ferry Terminal to Shekou – the port of the Chinese Shenzhen Special Economic Zone on the peninsula to the north-west of Hong Kong's New Territories.

There is a direct hovercraft from Hong Kong to Wuzhou, which leaves from China Ferry Terminal on even-numbered dates at 7.20 am.

To/From Japan

There is a ferry between Shanghai and Osaka/Kobe. It leaves once weekly, one week to Osaka and the next to Kobe, and takes two days. The fare is US\$120.

To/From Macau

There is a daily ferry between Canton and Macau – see the Macau chapter for details.

To/From South Korea

Also useful is the boat between the South Korean port of Inchon and Weihai in China's Shandong Province. The cost is US\$90 in economy class, US\$110 (2nd class), US\$130 (1st class) and US\$150 (special 1st class). In China, tickets are available from Weihai China International Travel Service (CITS).

In South Korea, tickets are sold by Universal Travel Service (UTS) just behind City Hall in Seoul (near the Tourist Information Centre).

If you're going from South Korea to China, getting the Chinese visa is tricky because there is no Chinese embassy in South Korea. UTS can get the visa for you, but charges US$100 for the service. If you get it before coming to South Korea, you'll save considerably; but note that Chinese visas are only valid for one month from date of issue, though they can be easily extended in China. You can't get a South Korean visa in China, but most Western nationals can stay in South Korea for two weeks without one. However, this can't be extended after arrival.

LEAVING CHINA
Airport departure tax is Y40. There is no departure tax if you leave by ship.

Getting Around

AIR
CAAC publishes a combined English and Chinese timetable each year in April and November. It's best to get a copy from the CAAC office in Hong Kong, though they can be obtained in China.

Foreigners pay a surcharge of 30% of the fare charged local Chinese. For planes, unlike trains, there is no way past this CAAC regulation. If you have a Chinese student ID card, you can pay in RMB, but that's the only concession you'll get. If you do somehow happen to get the Chinese price and it's discovered, your ticket will be confiscated and no refund given. Children over 12 are charged adult fare.

Cancellation fees vary depending on how long before departure you cancel. If you cancel 24 hours beforehand on domestic flights you lose 10% of the fare; if you cancel between two and 24 hours before the flight you lose 20%; and if you cancel less than two hours before the flight you lose 50%. If you

don't show up for a domestic flight, your ticket is cancelled and there is no refund.

BUS
The long-distance bus service in China is reasonably good, although the roads are like washboards and accidents are an effective method of population control. The price of a bus seat is comparable to a hard-seat on a train. The seats are numbered and tickets are bought at long-distance bus stations. There is very little room on the bus, certainly not enough for a bulky backpack, so travel light.

There are now some night buses, but rides can be reckless and uncomfortable with gongfu videos blaring all through the night.

TRAIN
Trains are the best way of getting around in reasonable speed and comfort. Food is available on trains or from vendors at stations. You can get boiled water at the end of each carriage but on long runs they sometimes run out.

Classes
There are no classes as such on the trains, but there are hard-seat, soft-seat, hard-sleeper and soft-sleeper designations. A hard-seat is actually padded, but you'll get no sleep; the carriages are crowded and uncomfortable. Soft-seats are cleaner and less crowded and cost the same as hard-sleepers. Soft-seats are usually only available for short journeys, never on overnight trips.

Hard-sleepers are comfortable, doorless compartments with six bunks in three tiers. Sheets, pillows and blankets are provided. Go for a middle bunk, as the top ones can be near loudspeakers and the bottom ones get taken over by people wanting to sit. Soft-sleepers are the luxury class; closed compartments with four bunks, lace curtains, pot plants and often air-conditioning. You can even turn the loudspeakers off.

Fares
Calculating prices is a complex business and depends on many rational and irrational factors. Foreigners are usually charged twice

as much as locals, but it is often possible to get a Chinese-priced ticket. At many stations they will sell you a Chinese-priced ticket as long as you pay with RMB. Of course, there will be no problem if a Chinese person buys the ticket for you.

You can always get local prices by using an official PRC student card. However, the proliferation of fake student cards has made railway workers suspicious to the point where they sometimes reject legimate student cards. If you manage to buy a cheap ticket at the station, the conductor may still ask you to make up the difference on the train though this rarely happens. It used to be possible to use a Taiwan student card (Taiwan is officially considered part of China), but this trick usually no longer works.

As a rough guide, a 1000-km train ride will cost between Y74 (hard-seat) and Y228 (soft-sleeper).

Reservations

Tickets can be bought one to four days in advance at CTS or CITS, usually found in major tourist hotels. They charge for this service and they are often slow. You can do it yourself faster at the railway station either on the day of departure or the night before. However, CITS can often get sleeping berths even when they are 'sold out'.

Stations in large cities often have notoriously long queues (more like riots), but there is often a special ticket window for foreigners. Indeed, you may be forced to use it – the other windows will probably be Chinese-only. Although you'll have to pay in FEC at the usual 100% markup, the foreigner's window allows you to avoid the horrors of the queues.

Depending on the distance to the destination, hard-seat tickets are valid for from one to seven days. This system enables you to break your journey and board the next day without booking again or claiming refunds. Ticket validity is: 250 km – one day; 500 km – two days; 1000 km – three days; 2000 km – six days; 2200 km – about seven days. On some lines this system is not followed.

BOAT

The most famous boat trip in China is the three-day ride down the Yangtze River from Chongqing to Wuhan. Although the trip itself is a bit dull, it's a great way to get from Chongqing to Wuhan and makes a change from trains. You can travel all the way to Shanghai this way if you want to.

There is a very popular route from Canton upriver to Wuzhou, where you can catch a bus to Guilin or Yangshuo.

LOCAL TRANSPORT

Around the cities buses are the most common means of transport apart from bicycles. Walking is often not practicable as Chinese cities are usually very spread out, but you may find yourself doing a lot of legwork anyway.

Streets are sometimes split into sectors. Each sector is given a number or (more usually) labelled according to its position relative to the other sectors and to the points of the compass. For example *Zhongshan Lu* (Zhongshan Rd) might be split into an east and a west sector. The east sector will be designated *Zhongshan Donglu* and the west will be *Zhongshan Xilu*.

Bus

These are almost universally horribly crowded and somewhat slow, but you rarely pay more than two jiao per trip unless you get your pocket picked. Good maps of Chinese cities, complete with bus routes, are generally available.

Minibus

These are an excellent alternative to the horrors of Chinese buses. Minibuses cost about 10 times more, but are still reasonable at around Y2 per journey. They generally follow the major bus routes.

Taxi

These are widely available in major cities but scarce in small cities and the countryside. You can always find taxis around large hotels and railway stations.

Auto-Rickshaws

Trishaws and three-wheel motorised scooters (auto-rickshaws) congregate outside train and bus stations, and sometimes outside tourist hotels. Agree on a price before you set out in order to avoid furious arguments at your destination.

Bicycle

This is the main mode of private transport in China. It is possible to rent a bike for around Y6 per day and rental places usually want a deposit or a passport for security. Check that the bike is in good working order, has brakes and that the tyres are well pumped up. Bicycles can be left in bicycle parks for a small charge. Otherwise they could be towed away. Around 9 pm, when bicycle parks close down, the proprietor stores the bike until you come to claim it – a hassle best avoided! Chain locks with keys are sold at department stores and are highly recommended.

TOURS

CITS and CTS always have tours but these are usually expensive. Much cheaper is to go with a local Chinese tour group. There are such one-day tours to the Great Wall and other major attractions.

Beijing 北京

China revolves around Beijing; all Chinese time is set to Beijing time and putonghua, the Beijing dialect, is spoken throughout the land. From here the great monolith is controlled.

All cities in China are equal, but some are more equal than others. Beijing (*běijīng*) has the best of everything: food, hotels, education and temples. And yet it is a city which lacks a soul – the drab government buildings may leave you uninspired. If Beijing is all you see of China, you will probably be convinced that the Chinese are living pretty high. For a more realistic impression of China, go down to Beijing Railway Station

where newly arrived poor peasants from the countryside squat on the pavement, wondering what their next move should be. Or better still, get out into the countryside yourself.

Orientation

The independently administered Beijing zone sprawls about 80 km from the city centre. Although it might not seem like it in the chaos of arrival, Beijing is a city of very orderly design with long straight boulevards. Streets in the central area end with the suffix *nei* meaning 'inner' (ie Jianguomennei). Moving further afield, the suffix becomes *wai* meaning 'outer' (ie Jianguomenwai). Unfortunately, the name of a major boulevard may change six or eight times along its length.

Information

CITS There are two offices. One is in the Beijing Tourist Tower (☎ 5158844), 28 Jianguomenwai – the large building just behind the New Otani Hotel. The other one (☎ 5120510) is in the Beijing International Hotel (*guójì fàndiàn*) on Jianguomennei, the large tower just one block north of the Beijing railway station.

Public Security Bureau This office (☎ 553102) is at 85 Beichizi Dajie. It is open from 8.30 to 11.30 am and 1 to 5 pm on Monday to Friday, and from 8.30 to 11.30 am on Saturday. It's closed on Sundays.

Money Hotels change money, and the main branch of the Bank of China is on Fuchengmennei Dajie near the intersection with Fuchengmennan Dajie. This is the largest bank in the country – bus No 103 from the railway station goes there. On request they will cash US$ travellers' cheques and give you US$ cash. Another bank which does this is CITIC, International Building, 19 Jianguomenwai which is across from the Friendship Store. Another useful Bank of China is at 32 Dengshikou Xilu near the Beijing Hotel.

Post & Telecommunications You'll find

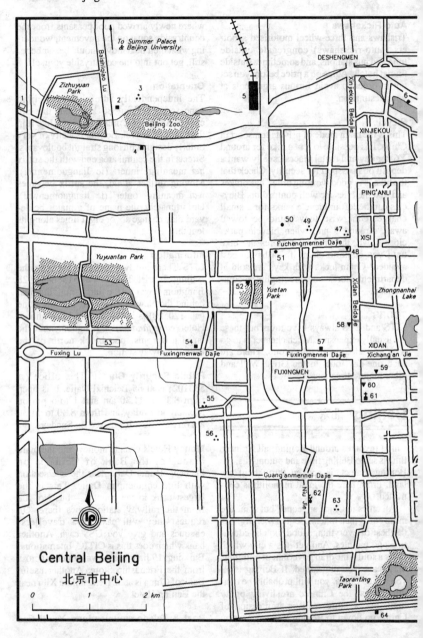

To Summer Palace
& Beijing University

DESHENGMEN

Zizhuyuan
Park

Beijing Zoo

XINJIEKOU

PING'ANLI

50 49

47

XISI

Fuchengmennei Dajie
48

Yuyuantan Park

51

52

Yuetan
Park

Zhongnanhai
Lake

58

53

XIDAN

54

57

Fuxing Lu   Fuxingmenwai Dajie   Fuxingmennei Dajie   Xichang'an Jie

59

FUXINGMEN

60

61

55

56

Guang'anmennei Dajie

62   63

Niu Jie

Central Beijing
北京市中心

0   1   2 km

Taoranting
Park

64

Baishiqiao Lu

Xinjiekou Beidajie

Xidan Beidajie

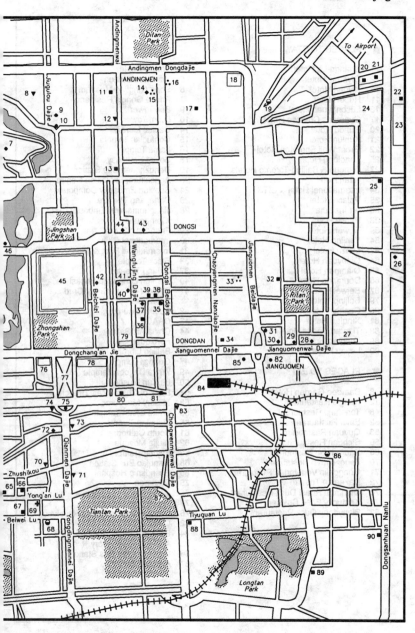

■ PLACES TO STAY

1   Shangri-La Hotel
2   Olympic Hotel
4   Xiyuan Hotel
11   Hebei Hotel
13   Lüsongyuan Hotel
17   Overseas Chinese Hotel
20   Huadu Hotel
21   Kunlun Hotel
22   Great Wall Sheraton Hotel
25   Zhaolong Hotel
27   Jianguo & Beijing-Toronto Hotels
32   Ritan Hotel
34   International Hotel & CITS
35   Palace Hotel
36   Art Institute
38   Peace Hotel
39   Taiwan Hotel
54   Yanjing Hotel
57   Minzu Hotel
64   Qiaoyuan Hotel
65   Qianmen Hotel
66   Dongfang Hotel
67   Beiwei Hotel
79   Beijing Hotel
80   Capital Hotel
81   Xinqiao Hotel
88   Tiantan Sports Hotel
89   Longtan Hotel
90   Leyou Hotel

▼ PLACES TO EAT

8   Bamboo Garden Hotel
12   Kangle Restaurant
48   Tongheju Restaurant
52   Emei Restaurant
58   Quyuan Restaurant
59   Sichuan Restaurant
60   Kaorouwan Restaurant
70   Fengzeyuan Restaurant
71   Gongdelin Vegetarian Restaurant
72   Dazhalan Theatre
73   Qianmen Roast Duck Restaurant
74   Kentucky Fried Chicken
83   Bianyifang Duck Restaurant

OTHER

3   Wuta Temple
5   Xizhimen Station
6   Song Qingling Museum
7   Prince Gong's Residence
9   Bell Tower
10   Drum Tower
14   Capital Library
15   Confucian Temple
16   Lama Temple
18   Soviet Embassy
19   Dongzhimen Bus Station
23   Agricultural Exhibition Centre
24   Sanlitun Embassy Compound
26   Chaoyang Theatre
28   Jianguomenwai Embassy
      Compound
29   Friendship Store
30   International Club
31   International Post & Telecom Office
33   Black Temple
37   Jixiang Theatre
40   Foreign Language Bookstore
41   Bank of China (Credit Card
      Advances)
42   Public Security
43   CAAC
44   China Art Gallery
45   Forbidden City
46   Beijing Library
47   Guangji Temple
49   White Dagoba Temple
50   Lu Xun Museum
51   Bank of China (Main Branch)
53   Military Museum
55   White Cloud Temple
56   Tianning Temple
61   South Cathedral
62   Niujie Mosque
63   Fayuan Temple
68   Tianqiao Bus Station
69   Friendship Hospital
75   Qianmen
76   Great Hall of the People
77   Tiananmen Square
78   History Museum of the Revolution
82   CITS
84   Beijing Railway Station
85   Ancient Observatory
86   Guangqumen Bus Station
87   Antique Market

■ **PLACES TO STAY**

1 香格里拉大饭店
2 奥林匹克饭店
4 西苑饭店
11 河北饭店
13 侣松园宾馆
17 华侨饭店
20 华都饭店
21 昆仑饭店
22 长城饭店
25 兆龙饭店
27 建国和京伦饭店
32 日坛宾馆
34 国际饭店
35 王府饭店
36 美术学院
38 和平宾馆
39 台湾饭店
54 燕京饭店
57 民族饭店
64 侨园饭店
65 前门饭店
66 东方饭店
67 北纬饭店
79 北京饭店
80 首都宾馆
81 新侨饭店
88 天坛体育宾馆
89 龙潭公园
90 乐游饭店

▼ **PLACES TO EAT**

8 竹园宾馆
12 康乐餐厅
48 同和居饭店
52 峨嵋饭店
58 曲园酒楼
59 四川饭店
60 烤肉宛饭庄
70 丰泽园饭庄
71 功德林素菜馆
72 大栅栏戏院
73 前门全聚德烤鸭店
74 肯德基炸鸡
83 便宜坊烤鸭店

OTHER

3 五塔寺
5 西直门站
6 宋庆玲故居
7 恭王府
9 钟楼
10 鼓楼
14 首都图书馆
15 孔庙
16 雍和宫
18 苏联大使馆
19 东直门汽车站
23 全国农业展览馆
24 三里屯使馆区
26 朝阳戏院
28 建国门外使馆区
29 友谊商店

30 国际俱乐部
31 国际邮电局
33 智化寺
37 吉祥戏院
40 外文书店
41 中国银行
42 公安局外事科
43 中国民航
44 中国美术馆
45 紫禁城
46 北京图书馆
47 广济寺
49 白塔寺
50 鲁迅博物馆
51 中国银行
53 军事博物馆
55 白云观
56 天宁寺
61 南堂
62 牛街礼拜寺
63 法源寺
68 天桥汽车站
69 友谊医院
75 前门
76 人民大会堂
77 天安门广场
78 中国革命历史博物馆
82 中国国际旅行社
84 北京火车站
85 古观象台
86 广渠门汽车总站
87 古文市场

the International Post & Telecommunications Building on Jianguomen Beidajie, not far from the Friendship Store. Hours are 8 am to 7 pm. Large tourist hotels offer the same service for the same price.

Foreign Embassies These are listed in the Facts for the Visitor section.

Bookshops The Friendship Store is a gold mine of US, British and European magazines, newspapers, books and other saddle-bag material. Also try the Beijing Hotel, other tourist hotels and the Foreign Language Bookstore near the Beijing Hotel. On Wangfujing there is a huge Xinhua Bookstore.

Emergency The clinic at the Friendship Hospital (☎ 338671) at 95 Yongan Lu, on the western side of the Temple of Heaven in the Tianqiao area, caters for foreigners.

Things to See

Tiananmen Square (tiān'ānmén guǎngchǎng) This enormous open space is Mao's creation in the heart of Beijing. It has been the centre of many of China's political events, but you can see people relaxing here, flying colourful kites if the weather allows. Surrounding the square are other monuments to Chinese history.

Tiananmen (Gate of Heavenly Peace) is at the north end of the square. It was built in the 15th century. There are five doors to the gate and seven bridges spanning a stream in front of it. In earlier times only the emperor could enter through the central gate. It was here that Mao proclaimed the People's Republic of China in 1949.

History Museum & Museum of the Revolution (zhōngguó gémìng lìshǐ bówùguǎn) These are housed in the same building on the east side of Tiananmen Square.

Mao Zedong Memorial Mausoleum (máo zhǔxí jìniàn táng) This is behind the Monument to the People's Heroes, on the southern side of Tiananmen. It was built to house the body of the Chairman.

Xu Beihong Museum (xú běihóng bówùguǎn) This is the gallery to visit for traditional Chinese paintings, oils, gouaches and sketches. Reproductions and Chinese stationery are on sale. It's at 53 Xinjiekou Beidajie, Xicheng District; it is open from 9 am to 5 pm except on Mondays.

Beihai Park (běihǎi gōngyúan) The former playground of the emperors and of Mao's wife Jiang Qing, No 1 of the 'Gang of Four', is just north-west of the Forbidden City. It covers 68 hectares, half of which is a lake which freezes up in winter.

Tiantan Park (tiāntán gōngyúan) The Temple of Heaven, a perfect example of Ming architecture, is here. It appears in endless advertisements and as a brand name for a wide range of products. Set in the 267-hectare park, it has four gates at the compass points and walls to the north and east. The five-metre-high Round Altar was built in 1530 and rebuilt in 1740. The main structure is the Hall of Prayer for Good Harvests. It was burnt to the ground in 1889, but reconstructed in 1890.

Lama Temple (yōnghégōng) This beautiful Tibetan temple features lovely gardens, stunning frescoes and tapestries and incredible carpentry. Open daily, except Mondays, from 9 am to 4.30 pm, the temple is in active use again. Prayers are held early in the morning, but are not public. However, if you enquire discreetly the head lama may let you return to view the praying the following morning. It's off Dongsi Beidajie to the north-east of the city centre.

Forbidden City (zǐjìnchéng) The best sight in Beijing, this is the largest and best-preserved cluster of ancient buildings in China. It was the home of the emperors of the Ming and Qing dynasties and off limits for 500 years. It is open daily from 8.30 am to 5 pm, except on Mondays. The admission price is

Y30. Just inside the gate, for Y20 you can rent a cassette tape player and tape for a self-guided tour – this requires a Y100 deposit. According to recent travellers, the tape looks like becoming compulsory!

Activities

CITS does a brief tour of the Underground City, a former system of bomb shelters now housing restaurants, hotels, clinics, shops and factories. The tour costs Y10.

Places to Stay

For many years, low-budget headquarters has been the *Qiaoyuan Hotel* (☎ 338861) *(qiáoyúan fàndiàn)* on Dongbinhe Lu near the Yongdingmen Railway Station. Dorm beds are Y11, double rooms Y36 to Y60 with shower, triples Y40. To get there take bus Nos 20 or 54 from the main Beijing station to the terminus (Yongdingmen); walk for about 10 minutes along the canal to the hotel. Or from just north of the Chongwenmen Hotel take trolley bus No 106 to the terminus. Warning: some travellers have complained about dirt, rudeness from the staff, and noise from thoughtless fellow-travellers.

Increasingly popular with budget travellers is the *Jingtai Hotel* (☎ 764675) *(jǐngtài bīnguǎn)*, 65 Yongwai Jingtaixi, a small alley running off of Anlelin Lu south of Tiantan Park. Dorm beds cost Y10, doubles Y40 and triples Y50. Bus No 45 will drop you off at the intersection of Yongdingmennei Jie and Anlelin Lu, a 10-minute walk from the hotel. Bus No 25 goes right down Anlelin Lu and will drop you off near the hotel – this bus both terminates and starts at the Anlelin Lu's east end. Another way to get there from the railway station is to take bus No 39 to the first stop after it crosses the canal – the name of the bus stop is *Puhuangyu*. From there, you've got a 15-minute walk west on Anlelin Lu.

Just a two-minute walk from the Jingtai Hotel is the *Yongdingmen Hotel (yǒngdìngmén fàndiàn)*, another budget place, once popular but now rapidly falling apart. It's right on Anlelin Lu. Triple rooms cost Y30

to Y50. Both the Jingtai and Yongdingmen will (reluctantly) accept RMB.

Tiantan Sports Hotel (☎ 752831) *(tiāntán tǐyù bīnguǎn)*, 10 Tiyuguan Lu falls in the mid-range. Singles are Y85 and doubles Y100 – a good place to stay if you want something comfortable but not ridiculously expensive. Take the subway one stop from Beijing Main Station to Chongwenmen then bus Nos 39, 41 or 43.

Another budget place rapidly gaining in popularity is the Longtan Hotel *(lóngtán fàndiàn)*, which has good clean dorms for Y30, friendly staff and a cheap restaurant. The hotel is opposite Longtan Park in the south of the city, close to a hospital. Bus No 51 (to the last stop) lets you out near the hotel.

University dorms are another possibility, but be on your best behaviour because they don't have to accept you. Typical prices are Y20 for dormitories, Y40 for double rooms. Most of these places have no beds – just Japanese-style tatami mats – but they're reasonably comfortable. The staff is only on duty from around 8 am to 5 pm with the usual two-hour lunch break and few speak English. The school with the most central location (and therefore often full) is the *Art Institute* (☎ 55473) *(měishù xúeyùan)*, in an alley off of Wangfujing near the Beijing Hotel. The second best place to stay is *Beijing University (běidà)*, far out in the north-west part of the city. Bus Nos 331 and 332 stop near the campus. It's relatively easy to get into here.

The *Qianmen* (☎ 3016688, 336556) *(qiánmén fàndiàn)*, at the corner of Yong'an Lu and Hufang Lu, south-west of Qianmen gate, has singles from Y170 to Y190, but a few foreigners claim to have bargained them down to Y90.

Places to Eat

There used to be 10,000 snack bars and restaurants in Beijing in 1949 before the Communists decided that these were a symbol of bourgeois decadence. Although restaurants dwindled to 700 by 1976, they have now staged a comeback.

Most styles of Chinese cooking are represented. Northern cuisine specialities are Beijing duck, Mongolian hotpot, Muslim barbecue and imperial food. Imperial cuisine is very expensive and available around Beihai Park and the Summer Palace, but you could try some of the cheaper snacks. Muslim barbecues use lamb and have a Chinese Muslim influence; at the *Kaorouwan Restaurant* south of Xidan intersection you can sometimes grill your own. Beijing duck is a delicacy. The duck is first force-fed with soya bean paste and grain. During cooking the fat duck is lacquered with molasses, pumped with air, filled with boiling water, dried and roasted over a fruitwood fire.

The *Qianmen Roast Duck* (☎ 7011379) *(qiánmén qùanjùdé kǎoyādiàn)* at 32 Qianmen, on the eastern side near the Qianmen subway, has a cheap section where you can get a whole duck for Y12 which will sate two very greedy Westerners. The cheap section is crowded so get there by 6 pm. Dishes in the expensive section start at Y20. Language is not a problem, as one basic dish is served in various delicious stages.

The *Bianyifang Duck Restaurant* (☎ 750505) *(biànyìfāng kǎoyādiàn)* at 2 Chongwenmenwai Dajie, is just east of CITS and has been in business for years.

For superb Sichuan-style dishes and great decor try the *Sichuan Restaurant* (☎ 336356) *(sìchūan fàndiàn)*. To get there go south from Xidan intersection, turn left into a *hutong* (alley) marked by traffic lights and a police box and continue until you find a grey wall entrance at No 51 Rongxian Hutong. You need to bring drinks to cool yourself down; and yoghurt is also a good idea. In the more expensive parts of the restaurant you get more variety, but the back dining room will do just fine. This restaurant is highly recommended.

One of the best restaurants in Beijing is the *Gongdelin Vegetarian* *(gōngdélín sùcàiguǎn)* at 158 Qianmen Lu. It serves some wonderful veggie food at low prices.

A favourite haunt for travellers is the *Emei Restaurant* (☎ 863068) *(éméi fàndiàn)* on Yuetan Beilu. It serves very cheap, spicy Sichuanese food.

For something different, try the *Moscow Restaurant* (☎ 894454) *(mòsīkē cāntīng)* on the west side of the Soviet-designed Exhibition Centre. Foreigners are shuffled off into a side room overlooking the Beijing Zoo (makes you wonder about those meat dishes). Grab the English menu and rush back to the central section for borscht, cream prawns au gratin or chicken à la Kiev.

For Western breakfasts the place to put one together is the *Friendship Store (yǒuyí shāngdiàn)*. Alternatively, try the *Beijing Hotel* but don't expect budget prices. Other venues for Western meals at greater than Western prices include the *Xinqiao, Minzu* and *Jianguo* hotels.

Entertainment

Beijing goes to bed early – most cultural events start around 7 pm and finish by 9.30 pm (when transport becomes infrequent). Buses which run after 11 pm are Nos 200, 201, 202, 203 and 204.

The *China Daily* lists the cultural events recommended for foreigners: concerts, theatre, minority dance events and some cinema. You can pick up tickets at CITS.

Beijing Opera For the height of Chinese culture, try a night (or at least an hour or so) at the opera. Most performances start around 7 or 7.30 pm.

The best bets are the Dazhalan Theatre *(dàzhàlán xìyùan)* on Dazhalan Jie; the Jixiang 14 Jinyu Hutong, off Wangfujing; and Chaoyang *(cháoyáng xìyùan)*, at Dongsanhuan Beilu and Chaoyang Beilu out in the east part of the city.

Some others that might be worth a try include the Chang'an theatre at 126 Xi Chang'an Jie, just east of the intersection with Xuanwumennei Dajie; the Erqi on Fuxingmenwai Dajie; the Tianqiao at 30 Beiwei Lu near the Temple of Heaven; the Renmin on Huguosi Dajie. The oldest in Beijing is the Guanghe at 24-26 Qianmen Lu – it's actually down an alleyway leading off Qianmen.

Acrobatics Besides the acrobatics you have to go through buying a train ticket or getting information from CITS, there are genuine shows which are popular with foreigners. For authentic atmosphere, try the Acrobat Rehearsal Hall on Dazhalan, once the major theatre location in Beijing. CITS and the Qiaoyuan Hotel sell tickets for around Y15 but you can usually roll up, roll in and get a seat for Y3. The show starts at 7.15 pm and acts change nightly. The shows sometimes cancel, and the place is always closed on Saturdays. Dazhalan is a hutong off the subway end of Qianmen Dajie.

Getting There & Away
Air The CAAC booking office (☎ 558861 for enquiries) is at 155 Dongsi Xidajie. There is also a booking office in the Beijing Hotel.

Enquiries for all airlines can be made at Beijing International Airport (☎ 552515). The individual offices of airlines are at:

Aeroflot Soviet Airlines
  Hotel Beijing-Toronto (☎ 5002412)
Air France
  2716 China World Trade Centre, 1 Jianguomenwai (☎ 5051818)
All Nippon Airways
  West Building, Beijing Hotel (☎ 5125551)
British Airways
  Room 210, 2nd floor, SCITE Tower, 22 Jianguomenwai (☎ 5124070)
Canadian Airlines
  China World Trade Centre, 1 Jianguomenwai (☎ 5001956)
Cathay Pacific
  Room 152, Jianguo Hotel (☎ 5003339)
Finnair
  18-5 CITIC Building, 19 Jianguomenwai (☎ 5127180)
Japan Airlines
  Room 2279, Hotel Beijing-Toronto (☎ 5002221)
JAT Yugoslav Airlines
  Room 427, Kunlun Hotel (☎ 5003388 ext 426)
LOT Polish Airlines
  Room 139, Jianguo Hotel (☎ 5002233)
Lufthansa
  SCITE Tower, 22 Jianguomenwai (☎ 5123535)
Northwest Airlines
  Room 101-103, Jianguo Hotel (☎ 5004529)
Pakistan International
  Diplomatic Apartments, 12-43 Jianguomenwai (☎ 5323274)
Philippine Airlines
  12-53 Jianguomenwai (☎ 5323992)
Qantas
  5th floor, Beijing Fortune Building, 5 Dongsanhuan Beilu, Chaoyangqu (☎ 5002481)
Romanian Air Transport
  Romanian Embassy Compound, Ritan Lu, Dong 2-Jie, Jianguomenwai (☎ 5323552)
SAS-Scandinavian Airlines
  18th floor, SCITE Tower, 22 Jianguomenwai (☎ 5120575)
Singapore Airlines
  (☎ 5044138), 1-2 CITIC Building, 19 Jianguomenwai
Swissair
  Room 201, SCITE Tower, 22 Jianguomenwai (☎ 5123555)
Thai International
  Room 204, SCITE Tower, 22 Jianguomenwai (☎ 5123881)
United Airlines
  Room 204, SCITE Tower, 22 Jianguomenwai (☎ 5128888)

Bus Long-distance bus depots in Beijing are on the city perimeter: at Dongzhimen (north-east), Tianqiao (near the theatre on the west side of the Temple of Heaven) and at Guangqumen (south-east).

Train There's a Foreigners' Ticketing Office at the main railway station (Beijing Zhan), to the left and through a door at the back of the main entrance hall. Look for the sign saying 'International Passenger Booking Office'. It's open daily from 5.30 to 7.30 am, 8 to 11.30 am, 1 to 5.30 pm and 7 pm to 12.30 am. Tickets can be booked several days in advance, which greatly improves your chances of getting a sleeper. Book international trains through CITS.

Getting Around
To/From the Airport You can take the unreliable CAAC bus (Y2.50) which leaves the city centre office at irregular times – likewise coming from the airport to Beijing.

If you can get yourself to Dongzhimen (north-east part of the city) there are frequent local buses to the airport.

Alternatively take a taxi. Split between a maximum of four passengers, the fare is not too bad; plus the taxi leaves from your hotel

Beijing Subway Stations

Dots indicate the location of stops underground, not the exits.

北京地铁站

(Map labels:) To Friendship Hotel, Beijing University, Summer Palace; To Badaling Ming Tombs; To Five Pagoda Temple; Bashiqao Lu; Zizhuyuan Park; Zoo; Xizhimenwai Dajie; Xizhimennei Dajie; Chegongzhuang Dajie; Fuchengmenwai Dajie; Fuchengmennei Dajie; Yuetan Park; Yuetan Dajie; Fuxingmennei Dajie; Xizhimen Railway Station; Xinjiekouwai Dajie; Xinjiekou; Xinjiekou Nandajie; Beidajie; Di'anmen; Xisi Beidajie; Wenjin; Xidan Beidajie; Telegraph Building; Xichang'an

(Station labels:) D, C, B, A, 9, 10, 11, 12, 13, 14, 15, 16

– an important consideration if your plane leaves at 6 am. The journey takes half an hour.

Bus One or two-digit buses are city central, series 100 are trolley buses, and series 300 are suburban lines. If you can work out how to combine subways and buses (get a bus map) you will speed things up considerably.

There are also privately operated minibuses with fixed fees, about Y2 minimum.

Underground Better than the buses, the subway is less crowded as trains run every four minutes during peak hour and there are about 200 trains a day. Platform signs are in English and the fare is two jiao regardless of distance. The east-west line is 24 km and has 17 stops, while the 16-km circle line, which loops the city and has 13 stations, is very useful for sightseeing. The subway is open from 5 am to 11 pm.

Taxi They usually have a sticker on the window indicating their per-km charge. If you don't get one with a meter, be sure to negotiate the fare in advance. You can

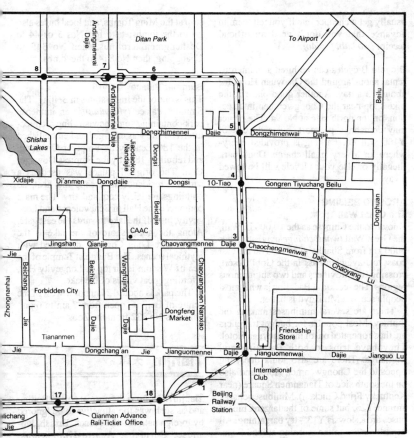

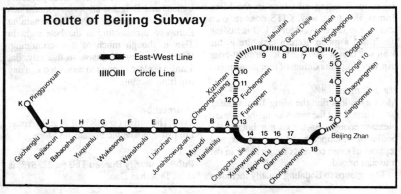

usually get a cheaper rate if you tell them in advance that you don't need an official receipt *(wǒ bùbì fāpiào)*.

Bicycle Bicycles can be hired at numerous rental shops around the Qiaoyuan Hotel for about Y3 a day. Another good place is the bike shop near the Chongwenmen intersection, on the north side at No 94. The owner may demand a passport, but a deposit of Y100 will do. Parking is provided everywhere for a very small charge. Don't park illegally or else your bicycle will be towed away.

AROUND BEIJING
The Great Wall 长城
Known to the Chinese as the 10,000 Li Wall, the Great Wall *(wànlǐ chángchéng)* stretches 6000 km from Shanhaiguan Pass on the east coast to Jiayuguan Pass in the Gobi Desert, crossing five provinces and two autonomous regions. The section at Badaling is what most people see, but Mutianyu is better.

There are several minibuses making the journey. Most popular for budget travellers are those operated out of the Qiaoyuan Hotel. They have trips to both Badaling and Mutianyu. There are also tours departing opposite the Chongwenmen Hotel and also on the south side of Tiananmen Square (near Kentucky Fried Chicken). Minibuses charge around Y25, but some of the larger Chinese buses are as low as Y13 – try bargaining. All departures are in the morning around 8 am. Tours to Badaling also take in the Ming Tombs along the way. CITS does its own tour to the Great Wall for Y130 including lunch and a guide. Return taxi hire to the Wall will cost at least Y200 for an eight-hour trip, carrying a maximum of four passengers.

Ming Tombs 明陵
Most travellers find the Ming Tombs *(míng líng)* boring, but the views along the way are pleasant enough. Each rock pile housed the bodies of an emperor and his consorts, and replicas of tomb contents are on show in the museum outside.

Tour groups to Badaling usually include a stop at the Ming Tombs, and local buses also go to the tombs; take bus Nos 5 or 44 to Deshengmen terminus, then No 345 to Changping, then No 314 to the tombs.

Summer Palace 颐和园
This is one of the finest sights in Beijing. The Summer Palace *(yíhéyúan)* is an immense park containing some newish Qing architecture. The site was enlarged and embellished in the 18th century by Emperor Qianlong, and rebuilt in 1888 by the Empress Dowager Cixi. The original palace was used as a summer residence to escape the heat, so buildings are fairly cool and airy. The main complex is the Hall of Benevolence and Longevity, just off the lake towards the east gate. Along the north shore of the lake is the 7228-metre Long Corridor, decorated with mythical scenes. The Buddhist Temple of the Sea of Wisdom is on top of Longevity Hill, affording great views of the lake.

The park is about 12 km north-west of the centre of Beijing, open from 7 am to 6 pm. Take bus No 332 from the Zoo.

Tianjin 天津

Tianjin *(tiānjīn)* is the nearest port to Beijing and as such was too attractive to be ignored by foreign nations. The French, British, Japanese, Germans, Austro-Hungarians, Italians and Belgians all set up concessions here around 1895 to 1900. The remaining European architecture is the best sight in Tianjin, though much of it is crumbling. Hotels are very expensive in this city, but Tianjin is close enough to be visited as a day trip from Beijing.

Information
CITS The office (☎ 318550) is at 20 Youyi Lu, just opposite the Friendship Store.

Public Security Bureau This (☎ 223613) is at 30 Tangshan Dao.

Money The Bank of China (☎ 312020) is at 80 Jiefang Beilu.

Post & Telecommunications The International Post Office is the Dongzhan Post Office, next to the main railway station; overseas parcels can be mailed and long-distance phone calls can be made here.

Places to Stay
Cheapest is the huge *Tianjin Grand Hotel* (☎ 319000) *(tiānjīn bīnguǎn)* which is on Youyi Lu, Hexi District. Doubles cost from Y90. Take bus No 13 from the main railway station.

The *Tianjin No 1 Hotel (tiānjīn dìyī fàndiàn)* (☎ 316438) is at 198 Jiefang Beilu, directly opposite the Hyatt Hotel. Doubles are Y160. Take bus No 13 three stops from the main railway station and walk south.

Getting There & Away
Air CAAC (☎ 701224) is at 242 Heping Lu. There are daily international flights to Hong Kong. Other useful flights include Beijing, Canton, Shanghai, Wuhan and Zhengzhou.

Bus Bus trips to Beijing take about three hours. Departures are from in front of the Tianjin main railway station. Buses don't leave until full.

Train The main Tianjin railway station has frequent trains to Beijing. The express train takes two hours.

Hebei 河北

The province is often viewed as an extension of Beijing and Tianjin – and they do take up a fair slice of the pie. Tianjin used to be the state capital, but is now central administration, and Shijiazhuang has replaced it. To the north of Hebei *(héběi)* is mountain tableland, where the Great Wall runs; in the south is a monotonous agricultural plain. The weather is scorching and humid in summer and freezing in winter, with dust fallout in spring and heavy rains in July and August.

BEIDAIHE 北戴河
This seaside resort is part of the Beidaihe, Qinhuangdao and Shanhaiguan districts which stretch 35 km along the coast. Bikinis have not made their debut but bare thighs are now in vogue. High-ranking officials gather here in summer for 'meetings' at government expense. There are shark nets – it's questionable whether sharks can live off this coast, so maybe they're submarine nets. Beidaihe *(běidàihé)* has large numbers of sanatoriums where patients can get away from the noise of the city – if you've been in China any length of time, you may wish to join them.

That's about all you need to know about Beidaihe. The Chinese have tried to categorise the rocks and decide whether they're shaped like dragons, tigers or steamed bread, and immortalise the place where Mao sat and wrote lines about fishing boats disappearing. Nobody gives a damn – they come for the beaches and so should you.

Places to Stay
There are only two places that accept foreigners. The *Guesthouse for Diplomatic Missions (wàijiāo rényúan bīnguǎn)* has triples for Y45.

Up market there's the spotless *Jinshan Guesthouse* (☎ 441678) *(jīnshān bīnguǎn)* by the shorefront on Zhonghaitan Lu. Doubles cost Y165.

Places to Eat
There's plenty of seafood in season at the restaurants. Try the *Beihai Fandian* near the markets and the *Haibin Fandian* near the Bank of China.

Near the Guesthouse for Diplomatic Missions is *Kiesslings (qǐshìlín cāntīng)*, which operates from June to August.

Getting There & Away
Train The three railway stations of Beidaihe, Qinhuangdao and Shanhaiguan are all accessible by train from Beijing, Tianjin or Shengyang. The trains are frequent but don't

always stop at all three stations. The usual stop is Shanhaiguan; several skip Beidaihe.

Beidaihe is the best place to stay but the hotel at Shanhaiguan is within walking distance of the railway station, whereas at Beidaihe the nearest hotel is at least 10 km from the station. If you arrive during daylight there are plenty of minibuses that meet incoming trains at Beidaihe Station. If you're going to arrive in the dead of night, it's better to do it at Shanhaiguan.

SHANHAIGUAN 山海关

Shanhaiguan (shānhǎiguān), where the Great Wall meets the sea, is worth a visit. The main attraction is the **First Pass Under Heaven**, also known as the East Gate. The Great Wall meets the sea at **Old Dragon Head** (lǎo lóng tóu). The original wall has long since crumbled away but a portion has recently been reconstructed here. It's a four-km hike or taxi ride from the centre of Shanhaiguan.

Places to Stay

The cheapest place is the *North Street Hotel* (běijiē zhāodàisuǒ) where dorms cost Y14 and doubles are Y60 with a little bargaining. The hotel is right near the First Pass (East Gate).

Also in the same neighbourhood is the up-market *Jingshan Hotel* (☎ 551130) (jīngshān bīnguǎn) where doubles are Y80.

Liaoning 辽宁

Liaoning (liáoníng), Jilin and Heilongjiang provinces comprise what used to be called Manchuria. Overall, travellers tend to find the north-east disappointing. There are a couple of scenic natural areas, but mostly it's prairies, farms, oil wells and petrochemical plants. To add insult to injury, this part of China has the most expensive accommodation.

SHENYANG 沈阳

Shenyang (shěnyáng) became the capital of the Manchu empire by the 17th century. With the Manchu conquest of Beijing in 1644, Shenyang became a secondary capital under the Manchu name of Mukden, and a centre of the ginseng trade.

Shenyang is the centre of Liaoning's industrial effort but there are a couple of things worth seeing in the city.

Information

CITS This office (☎ 466953) is at 113 Huanghe Nandajie which is south of the Liaoning Mansions.

Public Security Bureau You'll find them just off the traffic circle on Zhongshan Rd near the Mao statue.

Money The Bank of China is at 75 Heping Beidajie.

Post The main post office is at 32 Zhongshan Rd, Section 1.

Foreign Consulates Odd as it might seem, Shenyang has a US Consulate (☎ 290035), 40 Lane 4 Section 5, Sanjing Jie, Hepingqu.

Things to See

The **Mao Statue** in Zhongshan Square is one of the largest monuments to the follies of the Cultural Revolution still remaining in China.

The **North Tomb** (běilíng) is the finest sight in Shenyang. Set in a magnificent park, the North Tomb is the burial place of Huang Taiji (1592-1643), who founded the Qing dynasty. Take bus No 220 from the railway station.

The **Imperial Palace** (gùgōng) is a much scaled-down version of Beijing's Forbidden City. The main structures were started by Nurhachi, leader of the Manchus, and completed in 1636 by his son, Huang Taiji. You can take bus No 213 from the North Tomb or bus No 10 from the railway station.

Places to Stay

The *Hua Sha Hotel* (húaxià fàndiàn) is near the railway station at No 3 Zhongshan Lu.

Singles/doubles are Y70/130. CTS is located here.

The *Dongbei Hotel* (☎ 368120) *(dōngběi fàndiàn)* is at 100 Tianjin Beijie – one block south of Taiyuan Beijie, the main shopping street. It's also known as the Dongning Hotel. Singles/doubles are Y70/85.

Getting There & Away

Air CAAC (☎ 363705) is at 31 Zhonghua Lu, Section 3. Useful flights include those to Beijing, Canton, Chengdu, Kunming, Mudanjiang, Shanghai, Wuhan, Xi'an, Xiamen and Yanji.

Train All major train services connect here.

DALIAN 大连

Dalian *(dàlián)* is a major port. The city itself is remarkably clean and orderly – it has wide avenues and attractive architecture (a rarity in China).

Dalian is actually a health resort of a kind, so beaches with their attached parks are the main attraction. The beaches are a fair way

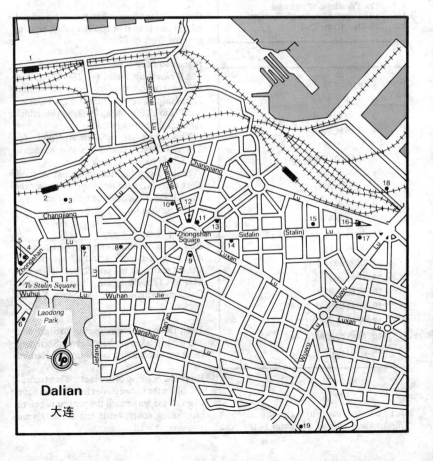

Dalian

大连

1	North Railway Station
2	Dalian Railway Station
3	Holiday Inn
4	CAAC
5	Civil Aviation Hotel
6	CITS
7	Long-distance Bus Station
8	Dong Fang Hotel
9	Dalian Hotel (Binguan)
10	Dalian Hotel (Fandian)
11	Post Office
12	Bank of China
13	Public Security Bureau
14	International Hotel
15	Furama Hotel
16	International Seamen's Club
17	Friendship Store/Hotel
18	Harbour Passenger Terminal
19	Nanshan Hotel

1	大连北站
2	大连火车站
3	九州假日酒店
4	中国民航
5	民航大厦
6	中国国际旅行社
7	往丹东汽车
8	东方饭店
9	大连宾馆
10	大连饭店
11	邮局
12	中国银行
13	公安局外事科
14	国际大酒店
15	富丽华酒店
16	海员俱乐部
17	友谊商店/宾馆
18	海港客运站
19	南山宾馆

out of town. Fujiazhuang Beach (*fùjiāzhuāng hǎishuǐ yùchǎng*) is the best,

but it's not easy to get to – take bus No 102 and then change to bus No 5.

Information
CITS This office (☎ 335795) is on the 4th floor, 1 Changtong Jie, on the west side of Laodong Park and opposite the Civil Aviation Hotel and CAAC.

Public Security Bureau This is just to the north-east of Zhongshan Square (see map).

Money The Bank of China (☎ 235167) is at 9 Zhongshan Square.

Post & Telecommunications The post and telephone office is at 10 Zhongshan Square, near the Bank of China.

Places to Stay & Eat
The *Friendship Hotel* (☎ 234121) (*yǒuyí bīnguǎn*) is on the 3rd floor above the Friendship Store at 137 Sidalin Lu. Doubles are Y72 to Y100 – cheap for Dalian but rather far from the railway station.

The seven-storey *Dalian Hotel* (☎ 233171) (*dàlián fàndiàn*) is at 6 Shanghai Lu. Single rooms go for Y96.

Seafood is a big deal in Dalian. A good place to try is the *Haiwei Seafood Restaurant* (*hǎiwèi fàndiàn*), near the railway station at 85 Zhongshan Lu.

Getting There & Away
Bus The government-run long-distance bus station is one block south of the railway station, and there is a private bus station just next to CITS. Buses run along the coast to Dandong which is on the North Korean border.

Train There are nine trains daily to Shenyang and the trip takes six hours. From Shenyang there are direct trains to Beijing and Harbin.

Boat The booking office is at the boat terminal. Since the railway lines from Dalian have to go all the way round the peninsula before proceeding south, boats can actually save you time as well as money.

There are boats to Yantai or Shanghai daily; to Qingdao every other day; and to Canton every four to six days.

Jilin 吉林

CHANGCHUN 长春
Changchun (chángchūn), capital of Jilin Province (jílín), has little of interest but makes a useful transit point for trips to Tianchi, the one outstanding scenic spot in north-east China.

Information
CITS The office (☎ 882401) is directly behind Changbaishan Hotel in the Bank of China Building (this Bank of China does not change money).

Public Security Bureau This is on the south-west corner of Renmin Square (rénmín guǎngchǎng) near the Bank of China.

Money The Bank of China is on the north-west corner of Renmin Square, on the corner of Xi'an Dalu and Sidalin Dajie.

Post The post office is on Sidalin Dajie, two blocks south of the railway station.

Places to Stay & Eat
The Chunyi Guesthouse (☎ 35951) (chūnyí bīnguǎn), 2 Sidalin Dajie, is one block south of the railway station. They charge Y100 for big, beautiful double rooms with private bath. There are no dormitories.

The main tourist joint is the Changbaishan Hotel (☎ 883551) (chángbáishān bīnguǎn). Doubles cost Y140. CITS is located here. It's nine km from the railway station – take trolley Nos 62 or 63. The Chinese restaurant in this hotel is excellent.

Getting There & Away
Air CAAC (☎ 39772) is at 2 Liaoning Lu. There are daily flights to Beijing and Canton.

Train The advance railway ticket office is one block east of the railway station on the 2nd floor. You can pay in RMB.

There are frequent trains heading north to Harbin (four hours) and south to Shenyang (five hours). There is an overnight train for Yanji (depart 6.40 pm, arrive 6.30 am), which is the route you take to Tianchi.

TIANCHI 天池
Tianchi (tiānchí) – the Lake of Heaven – is in the Changbaishan (Ever-White Mountains) Nature Reserve. The reserve is China's largest, covering 210,000 hectares of dense virgin forest.

Tianchi is one of China's prime scenic spots. It's a volcanic crater lake at an elevation of 2194 metres. Three rivers run off the lake, and a roaring 68-metre waterfall is the source of the Songhua and Tumen rivers. Hiking at the lake is limited by sharp and dangerous peaks and surrounding rocky debris, and also because the lake overlaps China's border with North Korea.

The only unpleasant aspect of Tianchi is the Chinese habit of filling up the volcanic crater with rubbish.

Places to Stay
The Birch Hotel (yùehúa lóu) has doubles for Y110. Some cheaper alternatives include the Nature Reserve Bureau Hotel (bǎohù jú bīnguǎn) for Y80 and the Meilinsong Guesthouse (měilínsōng bīnguǎn) for Y90. The largest hostel is the Tianchi Hotel (tiānchí fàndiàn) where doubles cost Y120. Expect hand-to-hand combat if you want a cheap dormitory bed. If you have a sleeping bag, you might consider camping.

Getting There & Away
The Changbaishan area is remote, and a journey there somewhat expeditionary. The only season in terms of transport access is late June to September. The transit point is the town of Baihe – 40 km and two hours by bus from Tianchi.

Antu Route There are trains to Antu from Changchun – the trip takes 10 hours. The

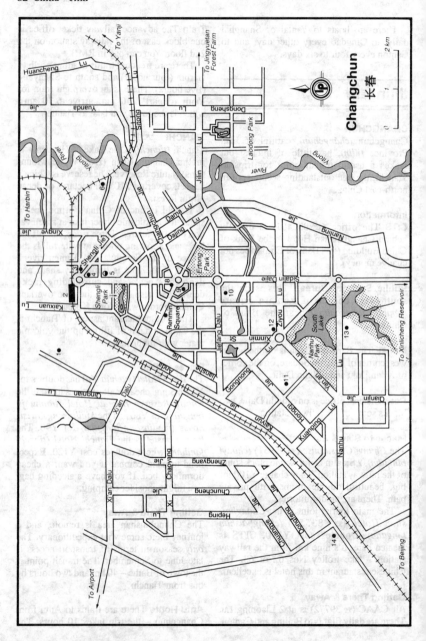

Changchun 长春

1 Railway Carriage Factory
2 Railway Station
3 Advance Rail Ticket Office
4 Chunyi Guesthouse
5 Post Office
6 Puppet Emperor's Palace & Exhibition Hall
7 Changchun Hotel
8 Bank of China
9 Public Security Bureau
10 Jixiang Hotel
11 Film Studio
12 Changbaishan Hotel & CITS
13 Nanhu Guesthouse
14 No 1 Automobile Factory

1 客车工厂
2 火车站
3 火车售票处
4 春谊宾馆
5 邮局
6 傀儡帝宫殿和展览馆
7 长春宾馆
8 中国银行
9 公安局外事科
10 吉香宾馆
11 电影制造厂
12 长白山宾馆
13 南湖宾馆
14 第一汽车制造厂

evening train departs from Changchun at 6.40 pm. There are sleepers but you might have to book them all the way to Yanji. There is a small hotel in Antu. Buses for Baihe depart from 7.20 to 10.30 am. You can also get buses to Baihe from Yanji (further down the rail line) but then you'll have to backtrack. From Antu it takes five hours to travel the 125 km. Unless you arrive early in Baihe, you may find yourself waiting till the next morning for transport to Tianchi. Special tourist buses run from Antu to the Changbaishan Hot Springs area in July and August but they may be crowded.

Tonghua Route The morning train leaves Shenyang at 6.30 am for Tonghua; from Dandong, there are buses to Tonghua departing at 6.30 am. Tonghua to Baihe is 277 km or about 10 hours by train. The two daily trains between Tonghua and Baihe have no sleepers, and soft-seat is highly recommended. The soft-seat waiting-room at Tonghua Station is the lap of luxury.

Heilongjiang 黑龙江

HARBIN 哈尔宾
This city is known for its freezing winters, but also hosts the dazzling Ice Lantern Festival. These days there are many tourists from the USSR in Harbin – a Soviet consulate is planned. Harbin (hā'ěrbīn) makes a possible start or finish for travellers taking the Trans-Siberian Railway.

Information
CITS The office (☎ 221088) is next to the Swan Hotel (tiān'é fàndiàn), which is on the bus No 3 route.

Public Security Bureau This is on Zhongyang Dajie.

Money The Bank of China is on Honglun Jie near the International Hotel.

Post & Telecommunications The post office is at the corner of Dongda Zhijie and Fendou Lu. The telephone company is also on Fendou Lu, two blocks from the post office.

Things to See
If you don't mind the cold then try not to miss Harbin's No 1 drawcard, the **Ice Lantern Festival** (bīngdōng jié) held from 1 January to early March (Lunar New Year) in Zhaolin Park.

Down by the river, **Stalin Park** *(sīdàlín gōngyúan)* is a tacky strip stacked with statues. The sandy banks of the Songhua take on a beach atmosphere in summer. CITS has a boat tour along the Songhua River which lasts 2½ hours and costs Y15 per head. During winter the Songhua is a road of ice – the perfect venue for hockey, skating, ice-sailing, sledding and sleighing. The ice toys can be rented.

Crumbling Soviet architecture is still much in evidence in Harbin, with spires, cupolas and scalloped turreting. The area known as **Daoliqu** – near Zhongyang Lu – is especially good to investigate.

The **Japanese Germ Warfare Experimental Base** *(rìběn xìjūn shíyàn jīdì)* is not for the faint of heart. In 1939 the Japanese army set up a top-secret, germ warfare research centre here with horrific results. Take bus No 338 from the main railway station to the terminus, which is close to Pingfangqu.

Places to Stay

The only budget place to stay is the *Harbin Institute of Technology* (☎ 228383, ext 4673) *(hā'ěrbīn gōngyè dàxúe)*. It's for foreign teachers but you might be able to talk your way in. Dormitory No 6 is on Hanguang Jie – rooms go for Y25.

The *International Hotel* (☎ 31441) *(gúojì fàndiàn)* is at the intersection of Xida Zhijie and Honglun Jie, less than one km from the railway station. Singles/doubles are Y96/120. It's run down and overpriced – only the location is good.

The *Swan Hotel* (☎ 220201) *(tiān'é fàndiàn)*, 73 Zhongshan Lu, is good but far from the railway station. Doubles range from Y98 to Y120. CITS is in the same compound and CAAC is nearby. There are minibuses running down Zhongshan Lu that can take you here for Y1.

The *Modern Hotel* (☎ 465842) *(mǎdié'ěr bīnguǎn)* is on Zhongyang Dajie. Doubles range from Y80 to Y120. Beware – some people have been overcharged in the hotel's restaurant.

Places to Eat

There are a couple of places around Stalin Park. On the edge of Zhaolin Park at 113 Shangzhi Lu is the *Beilaishun Restaurant* (☎ 49027) *(běiláishùn fàndiàn)* serving Muslim beef and mutton dishes upstairs and hotpot in winter. The *Futailou Restaurant* (☎ 417598) *(fútàilóu fàndiàn)* at 19 Xi Shisan-dao Jie serves Beijing roast duck and other dishes.

Getting There & Away

Air CAAC (☎ 52334) has its office at 87 Zhongshan Lu close to the Swan Hotel. There are flights to Beijing, Canton, Chengdu, Shanghai and Xi'an.

Bus There is a long-distance bus station near Sankeshu Railway Station which takes care of a large proportion of bus departures. Other buses depart from the main railway station.

Train Connections to Beijing are excellent. Connections to other parts of Heilongjiang Province are sporadic.

JINGBO LAKE   镜泊湖

The name means Mirror Lake *(jìngbó hú)*, and it's probably the most impressive sight in Heilongjiang. The area includes forests, hills, streams, pools and cliffs around the lake and there is a lava cave in the area. Peak season (July and August) is crowded – autumn is nice when the leaves are turning. Get out on the lake in a rowing boat – loads of stars at night. Slightly to the north of Jingbo Villa, Diaoshuilou Waterfall offers an opportunity to jump off into the pools below and amaze the Chinese.

Places to Stay

The centre of operations is *Jingbo Villa (jìngbó shānzhuāng)*, at the north end of the lake. Double rooms start from Y50 – dormitories exist but it will be a battle to get into one. There are other, cheaper hotels around the lake but they aren't allowed to take foreigners.

Getting There & Away

The best approach is by rail from Harbin. Take a train to Dongjing *(dōngjīng)*. From there, it's one hour by minibus to the lake.

Some trains only go as far as Mudanjiang, a city of 700,000. If you get off at Mudanjiang, it's three hours by bus to Jingbo Lake. Buses depart between 6 and 7 am from the square in front of Mudanjiang Station, summer only (June to September).

Shanxi 山西

Shanxi *(shānxī)* counts for about a third of China's known coal deposits, and cities such as Datong and Taiyuan are major industrial centres. But the province's greatest wealth lies in its history. It was one of the earliest centres of Chinese civilisation, and is still a gold mine of temples, cave-temples and monasteries. The main attraction is the Yungang Buddhist Caves at Datong.

TAIYUAN 太原

Taiyuan *(tàiyúan)* was first settled about 2500 years ago and was a prosperous city by the time Marco Polo saw it. These days it's the drab provincial capital of Shanxi, but many travellers pass through on the way to Datong and the Shuanglin Monastery.

Information

CITS This office (☎ 441155 ext 679) is in the building adjacent to Yingze Hotel.

Money The Bank of China (☎ 666637) is on Yingze Dajie west of Xinjian Lu. The tourist hotels also change money.

Post & Telecommunications There's a post office in the Yingze Guesthouse and a telephone office next door.

Things to See

The No 1 attraction is the **Jinci Temple** *(jìncí)*, an ancient Buddhist complex beside Xuanwang Hill at the source of the Jin River, 25 km south of Taiyuan. The temple proba-

bly dates back 1000 years or more. Buses to the temple leave from the city centre. Walk one block east past May 1st Square, turn left and the bus station is at the end of that street. Take bus No 8 to the temple.

Chongshan Monastery *(chóngshàn sì)* is on a side street west of Jianshe Beilu. The interior of the main hall is really worth seeing. It contains three large statues including the 1000-armed Goddess of Mercy, Guanyin, and beautifully decorated and illustrated book covers showing scenes from the life of Buddha. You'll have to tag on to a tour group to see them as the temple doesn't seem to be open at any other time.

The entrance to **Yingze Park** *(yíngzé gōngyúan)* is on the opposite side of the road and to the west of the Yingze Guesthouse. The Ming Library is an ornate building in Yingze Park and is worth a look.

Places to Stay

The *Yingze Hotel* (☎ 443211) *(yíngzé bīnguǎn)*, 51 Yingze Dajie, is two km from the railway station – take bus No 1. The arrogant and lazy staff are notorious for claiming that they're 'all full', but CITS is in the same compound and a call from them will magically produce rooms. Singles/doubles are Y87/130.

The *Bingzhou Hotel* (☎ 442111) *(bìngzhōu fàndiàn)*, 32 Yingze Dajie, has doubles for Y90. It's a little closer to the railway station than the Yingze Hotel.

Getting There & Away

Air CAAC (☎ 442903) is at 38 Yingze Dong Dajie. Flight connections include Beijing, Shanghai and Xi'an.

Train Taiyuan is connected northwards by rail to Beijing via Datong. There are also direct trains to Xi'an.

SHUANGLIN MONASTERY 双林寺

This fine monastery *(shuānglín sì)* is 97 km south of Taiyuan and is well worth the effort of getting there – you can do it as a day trip out of Taiyuan if you go early.

Take a train from Taiyuan to Pingyao,

which is on the train line heading south-west from Taiyuan. The 2½-hour journey costs a few yuan, hard-seat. When you arrive at Pingyao you can get a pedicab from the railway station to the temple, a half-hour ride.

DATONG 大同

The Northern Wei dynasty established its capital here. Now Datong *(dàtóng)* is a grotty town but it's also the site of the outstanding Yungang Buddhist Caves.

Information

CITS The office (☎ 522265) is in the Yungang Hotel on Yingbin Xilu.

Public Security Bureau This is next to the large department store on Xinjian Beilu.

Money Try the exchange counter in the Yungang Hotel.

Post & Telecommunications There is a post office in the Yungang Hotel. The main post and telephone office is the large building with the clock tower facing the square in the city centre.

Things to See

Datong Locomotive Factory *(dàtóng jīchē chǎng)* This factory was the last one in China making engines for the main railway lines. In 1989 they finally switched over to the production of diesel and electric engines, but the factory still maintains a museum with about seven old steam engine locomotives. To visit, you must arrange a tour with CITS. You can only go if there's a spare seat on one of the tour buses or if you can get a group together.

Yungang Caves *(yúngāng shíkū)* This is the reason for coming to Datong. These fine caves are cut into the southern cliffs of Wuzhou Mountain 16 km west of Datong next to the pass leading to Inner Mongolia. The caves contain over 50,000 statues and stretch for about one km east to west.

Take bus No 17 to the terminus and then

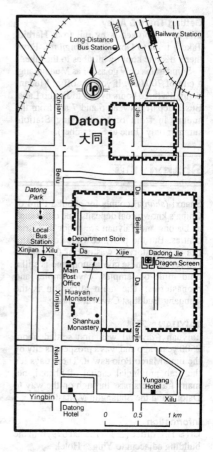

hop onto bus No 3. After boarding bus No 3, it's about another 30 minutes to the caves. Another route – take bus No 6 (just outside and turn right from Datong Hotel) and let the conductor know you want bus No 3. They'll drop you off by the bus No 3 stop.

Places to Stay & Eat

The cheapest accommodation is at the *Datong Hotel (dàtóng bīnguǎn)* where dorms are Y10. Double rooms are available from Y75.

More pleasant is the *Yungang Hotel (yúngāng bīnguǎn)*. Double rooms are

Y108. Though they hate to admit it, they have a small dormitory for Y15.

Food stalls around the railway station rate about 85 on the vomit meter. The grocery stores might be your best bet, or you could eat at the Yungang Hotel.

Getting There & Away
There are daily express trains to Taiyuan (seven to nine hours), Beijing (seven to 8½ hours) and Hohhot (five to six hours).

HANGING MONASTERY 悬空寺
Perched on Jinlong Canyon in the mountains 75 km from Datong is the peculiar Hanging Monastery (*xúankōng sì*). It's more than 1400 years old but has been rebuilt several times.

The easiest way to get there is with a Chinese tour bus from the long-distance bus station at the corner of Xinjian Beilu and Xinhua Jie in Datong. Tickets are Y8. You only get 30 minutes at the monastery. Many of the tours also include a stop at the Wooden Tower.

There are also minibuses, either from the railway station or sometimes right from the hotel car park. Try to make arrangements the day before. Cost is Y8 (depending on the number of passengers). It takes 1½ hours to reach the monastery. Departures are usually early, often before 7 am.

Shaanxi 陕西

Shaanxi (*shǎnxī*) was the political heart of China until the 9th century AD. The great Sui and Tang dynasty capital of Chang'an (modern-day Xi'an) was built there, and the province was a crossroads on the trading routes from eastern China to central Asia. Its history over the next thousand years, however, was punctuated by famines and rebellions, and by the 1920s the Shaanxi peasants were ready to give enthusiastic support to the Communists, who established their base in the remote town of Yan'an, at the end of the Long March.

The north of the province is a loess plateau, deeply eroded, with ravines and almost vertical cliff faces. In the far north is the Great Wall, beyond which human existence was always precarious. The south is mountainous but comparatively lush, with a mild climate.

XI'AN 西安
Known as Chang'an in ancient times, Xi'an (*xī'ān*) was once the gateway to the Silk Road and was one of the greatest cities in the world, rivalling Rome and Constantinople. These days it attracts a steady stream of travellers who come to marvel at the thousands of terracotta soldiers who guard the tomb of Qin Shihuang, the first emperor of unified China.

Orientation
Xi'an retains the rectangular shape of old Chang'an. The centre of town is the enormous Bell Tower and from here run Xi'an's four main streets: Bei, Nan, Xi and Dong Dajie. The famous terracotta warriors and the Neolithic village of Banpo are on the plain which surrounds Xi'an.

Information
CITS The office (☎ 713329) is on the 2nd floor of the Jiefang Hotel, right near the railway station.

Public Security Bureau This (☎ 25121) is at 138 Xi Dajie, a 10-minute walk west of the Bell Tower.

Money The Bank of China (☎ 716931) is at 223 Jiefang Lu near the corner with Dong 6-Lu. Business hours are daily from 9 am to 12 noon, and 2.30 to 5.30 pm. It's closed on Wednesday and Sunday afternoons.

Things to See
In the south of Xi'an is **Big Goose Pagoda** (*dà yàn tǎ*), originally built in 652 AD. It's an impressive, fortress-like building of wood and brick which rises 64 metres out of the surrounding wheat fields. It was built to house the Buddhist scriptures brought back

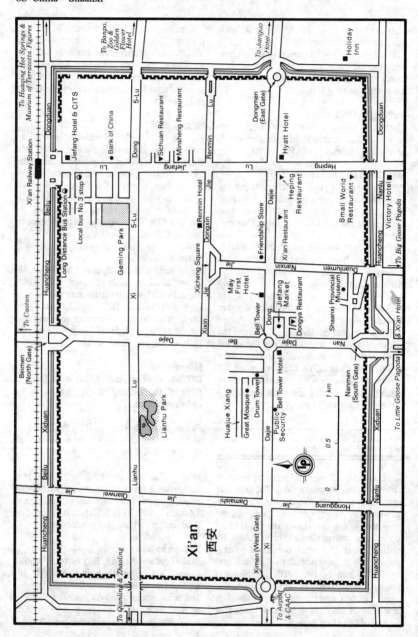

Xi'an
西安

To Huaqing Hot Springs & Museum of Terracotta Figures

To Banpo, Zoo & Golden Flower Hotel

To Jianguo Hotel

Holiday Inn

Xi'an Railway Station

Dongduan

Jiefang Hotel & CITS

Bank of China

5-Lu

Sichuan Restaurant

Minsheng Restaurant

Renmin Lu

Dong Lu

Jiefang Lu

Dongmen (East Gate)

Hyatt Hotel

Heping

Dongduan

Huancheng

Long Distance Bus Station

Local bus No 3 stop

Geming Park

5-Lu

Xi

Renmin Hotel

Dongxin Jie

Jie

Friendship Store

Xicheng Square

Xi'an Restaurant

Heping Restaurant

Small World Restaurant ▼

Victory Hotel

Nanlu

Bellu

Beimen (North Gate)

To Caotan

Xinxin Jie

Xi Jie

May First Hotel

Bell Tower

Bei

Dong

Dajie

Jiefang Market

Dongya Restaurant

Nanxin

Duanlumen

Nan

Shaanxi Provincial Museum

Huancheng

To Big Goose Pagoda

To Little Goose Pagoda

Huajue Xiang

Great Mosque

Drum Tower

Bell Tower Hotel ●

Public Security

Lianhu Park

Lianhu Lu

Dajie

Nanmen (South Gate)

Nanlu

& Xi'an Hotel

Xi'an Hotel

To Qianling & Zhaoling

Beilu

Xiduan

Qianwei Jie

Jie

Lianhu

Damaishi

Xi Jie

Hongguang Jie

Ximen (West Gate)

Xiduan

Huancheng

To Airport & CAAC

1 km

0.5

0

N

from India by the travelling monk Xuan Zang, who then set about translating them into 1335 Chinese volumes. The pagoda is at the end of Yanta Lu. Take bus No 5 down Jiefang Lu to the end of Yanta Lu and get off before it turns right into Xiaozhai Donglu.

The **Bell Tower** (*zhōnglóu*) is a huge structure at the centre of Xi'an. The **Drum Tower** (*gǔlóu*) is a smaller structure to the west of the Bell Tower and it marks the Muslim quarter of Xi'an.

The **Great Mosque** (*qīngzhēn dà sì*) in Xi'an is one of the largest in China. Still an active place of worship, the mosque holds several prayer services each day. It stands north-west of the Drum Tower.

The **Shaanxi Provincial Museum** (*shănxī bówùguǎn*) was once the temple of Confucius and houses a large collection of relics from the Zhou, Qin, Han, Sui and Tang dynasties, including a collection of rare relics unearthed in Shaanxi Province. The 'Forest of Steles' is an extraordinary exhibit of engraved stone tablets spanning 2000 years. The 'rare relics' exhibition is in another building and includes a gold-plated bronze horse from the Western Han dynasty. The museum is open daily, except Mondays, from 8.30 am to 6 pm.

The main reason to come to Xi'an is to see the terracotta warriors at the **Tomb of Qin Shihuang** (*qín shǐhúang líng*). When the Emperor took the throne, work on his tomb began immediately and continued for 36 years, until the year before his death. The tomb is one km north of Mt Lishan and most of it has not been excavated. The 2nd-century BC historian Sima Qian wrote in his *Historical Records* that the tomb contains palaces and pavilions filled with rare gems and other treasures, and crossbows which automatically shoot at intruders.

Just how far the necropolis extends is anybody's guess. In 1974 an underground vault containing 6000 terracotta figures was discovered 1500 metres from the site. The life-size figures represented an army of warriors and their horses in battle formation. They can be found 30 km east of the present city of Xi'an. Admission to see the Qin ter-

racotta army is Y12 plus an additional Y10 for the museum. It's forbidden to take photos and your film will be confiscated if you get caught (helps prop up the postcard industry). The tomb is near the town of Lintong – 30 km east of Xi'an. To reach Lintong, take a bus from the eastern side of the Xi'an railway station. Some trains also stop in Lintong. From Lintong take another bus an additional five km to the Tomb of Qin Shihuang.

Tours run by the Jiefang and Victory hotels only cost Y10 but give you just 30 minutes each at the Qin Tomb, Huaqing Pool and Banpo. The guides only speak Chinese. CITS does a grand tour for Y98.

The **Banpo Neolithic Village** (*bànpǒ bówùguǎn*) is the second best sight in Xi'an after the terracotta warriors. The ruins of this 6000-year-old settlement are the earliest signs of human habitation around Xi'an. There's a museum at the site, which displays the artefacts excavated from the village, and a book on sale entitled *Neolithic Site at Banpo Near Xi'an*, which describes the objects on display. The site is open daily from 8.30 to 11.30 am and from 2 to 5 pm. Tours to see the terracotta warriors take in a stop at Banpo. To get there on public transport, take bus No 8 from the stop on Dong Dajie immediately to the east of the Bell Tower. This bus stops short of the village. About five minutes walk up the road is the stop for trolley bus No 5, which will take you the last stretch to the village. Alternatively, take trolley bus No 5 from the stop on Bei Dajie just north of the Bell Tower. This bus goes past the village. Or take bus No 11 from the railway station.

Places to Stay

The *Victory Hotel* (☎ 713184) (*shènglì fàndiàn*) has become the main backpackers' haunt though it's inconveniently located just outside the city walls south of Heping Gate. It's also very dirty. Dorm beds cost Y13 and doubles are Y30. Bicycle rentals are Y5 per day. Bus No 5 from the railway station will take you there.

The *Jiefang Hotel* (☎ 713417) (*jiĕfàng fàndiàn*) is on Jiefang Lu, diagonally opposite the railway station. The 'dormitories' are simply double rooms, but they find a room-mate for you if you're not travelling with someone else. They ask Y40 for this arrange-ment and can be bargained to Y35. Double rooms are exactly double, Y80.

The *May First Hotel* (☎ 710804) *(wŭyī fàndiàn)* is at 351 Dong Dajie, near the corner with Nanxin Jie near the Bell Tower. Doubles cost Y42.

Places to Eat
Budget travellers staying at the Victory Hotel will no doubt want to try the line-up of restaurants catering to the backpacker trade. On Heping Lu just inside the city wall you can find the *Small World*, *He Sheng*, *Olympic Games* and *East* restaurants. All have English menus, decent food and reasonable prices.

The restaurant on the 2nd floor of the Jiefang Hotel is good, though prices are slightly higher than you'll find outside.

For Muslim food try the stalls along Sajinqiao Lu in the Muslim quarter near the Great Mosque.

The *May First Restaurant (wŭyī fàndiàn)* is at 351 Dong Dajie, near the corner with Nanxin Jie and next to the Foreign Language Bookstore. Highly recommended.

The *Dongya Restaurant (dōngyà fàndiàn)* serves possibly the best food in Xi'an. The restaurant is south-east of the Bell Tower on Luoma Shi, a small street which runs off Dong Dajie.

Getting There & Away
Xi'an is well served by train and plane, with connections to and from all major destina-tions.

Air CAAC (☎ 42861) is on the south-east corner of Xiguan Zhengjie and Laodong Lu, 1½ km to the west of the West Gate and only one km from the airport. You may find it more convenient to buy air tickets from CITS.

There are direct flights to Beijing, Canton, Chengdu, Guilin, Lanzhou, Shanghai, Taiyuan, Ürümqi and other destinations.

There are direct flights between Xi'an and Hong Kong (three times weekly, fare Y990).

Bus There's a daily bus from Xi'an to Lanzhou at 5.40 am from the bus station near the railway station.

Train To reach Guilin by train, change at Wuhan. There are direct trains to Beijing, Shanghai and Ürümqi.

Getting Around
To/From the Airport It's a hassle by bus. You can take a bus to the CAAC office (which is just outside the airport), then take the CAAC bus to the airport. From the railway station, a taxi to the airport charges around Y20.

Bus Transport around the city is mostly by bus or minibus (about Y2).

HUASHAN 华山
Huashan *(húashān)*, one of the sacred moun-tains of China, is 2200 metres high. It lies just south of the Xi'an-Luoyang railway line. There's only one route to the top, a north-south path about 15 km long.

Places to Stay & Eat
The *Twelve Caves Inn (shí èr dòng lǔshè)* is good, and run by monks from the adjacent Buddhist temple.

Getting There & Away
Bus Xi'an is a good jumping off point. There is a direct bus to Huashan.

Train You can take a train from Xi'an to Huashan Station (two hours). However, few trains stop there, so you may have to take a train to Mengyuan, which is one station further down the line, and from there get a bus to Huashan.

YAN'AN 延安
North of Xi'an, Yan'an *(yán'ān)* was the Communist headquarters from 1936 to 1947. The Long March from Jiangxi ended in 1936, when the Communists reached the

northern Shaanxi town of Wuqi. The following year they moved their base to Yan'an.

Places to Stay

The *Yan'an Hotel* charges Y40 for a good, clean double room with television and bathroom. The hotel restaurant is cheap.

Getting There & Away

There are flights from Xi'an twice a week. There are daily buses but it's a rough ride.

Henan 河南

The unruly Yellow River snakes its way across the north of Henan *(hénán)*, where it all began. About 3500 years ago the Chinese were turning their primitive settlements into an urban-centred civilisation governed by the Shang dynasty. Zhengzhou was their capital for a while, and the ancient city walls are still visible.

Today the province is heavily populated and Zhengzhou is a major industrial centre. The biggest drawcard for travellers is the Longmen Caves near Luoyang.

ZHENGZHOU 郑州

The modern-day provincial capital *(zhèngzhōu)* is basically a dump – its main interest to travellers is as a transit point between Luoyang and Kaifeng.

Places to Stay

Opposite Zhengzhou Railway Station is the cavernous *Zhongyuan Mansion (zhōngyuán dàxià)*. Doubles are Y18 without private bath, Y40 with bath, assuming the plumbing is working, which often is not the case. Some cheerless dungeons are available for Y10.

Getting There & Away

Air Some useful air connections include Beijing, Canton, Xi'an, Shanghai, Tianjin and Wuhan.

Bus The long-distance bus station is opposite the railway station. Buses also leave from the square in front of the railway station. There are frequent buses to Kaifeng (two hours) and Luoyang (4½ hours).

Train Zhengzhou is on the main Beijing-Canton line. It's a major railway junction and you may have to stop here overnight to change trains. There are direct trains to Beijing (12 hours); Shanghai (14 hours); Xi'an (12 hours); Canton (23 hours); Luoyang (four hours). There are also trains to Taiyuan and Datong.

KAIFENG 开封

Kaifeng *(kāifēng)* was once the imperial capital of China. This honour came to an end in 1127 when the Song dynasty fled south. These days, travellers come here as a stopover on the route between Qufu and Luoyang.

Chief among the sights is the **Xiangguo Monastery** *(xiànggúo sì)* in the centre of town, originally founded in 555 AD but completely destroyed in 1644. The present buildings date from 1766. Other sights include the **Iron Pagoda** *(tiě tǎ)* and **Longting Park** *(lóngtíng gōngyuán)*.

Places to Stay

The Chinese hotels here seem to accept foreigners, and private hotels send runners to meet incoming trains.

Among the government hotels, one of the best is *Bianliang Hotel (biànliáng lǚshè)* where doubles are Y15. It's is on Zhongshan Lu, about 100 metres to your left as you leave the railway station. Across the street is the *Dongfeng Hotel (dōngfēng lǚshè)* which charges similar prices. Further down the street is the privately run *Zhongshan Hotel (zhōngshān lǚshè)* which charges Y12.

Foreign tour groups usually put up at the *Kaifeng Guesthouse (kāifēng bīnguǎn)* on Ziyou Lu where doubles are Y80. Take bus No 3 from the railway station and get off at the third stop. Another expensive alternative is the *Songdu Guesthouse (sòngdū bīnguǎn)* near Bianjing Park. Doubles are Y50.

LUOYANG 洛阳

Founded in 1200 BC, Luoyang *(lùoyáng)* was the capital of 10 dynasties, until the 10th century when the Jin emperor moved the capital to Kaifeng. The main attraction here is the Longmen Cave Temples.

Things to See

The magnificent **Longmen Cave Temples** *(lóngmén shíkū)* are among the best in China. Work began on the cave temples from 494 AD onwards, and over the next 200 years or so more than 100,000 images and statues of Buddha and his disciples were carved into cliff walls on the banks of the Yi River, 16 km south of the city. They represent one of the high points of Buddhist cave art.

From the Luoyang railway station area, bus No 81 goes to the Longmen Caves. From the Friendship Guesthouse, take bus No 60 – it leaves from the far side of the small park opposite the hotel. Bus No 53 from the old town west gate also runs past the caves. Many of the hotels put on tour buses to the caves too.

Places to Stay & Eat

The cheapest place in town is the *Luoyang Hotel* (☎ 35181) *(lùoyáng lǔshè)* where doubles cost Y30. It's right across the street from the train and bus stations, which means it can be incredibly noisy. Try to get a room at the back.

Just around the corner on Jingguyuan Lu is the *Tianxiang Hotel* (☎ 37846) *(tiānxiāng lǔshè)* where doubles are Y68 to Y100. It's a huge place. The restaurant serves good, cheap meals.

The *Friendship Guesthouse* (☎ 22111) *(yǒuyí bīnguǎn)* at 6 Xiyuan Lu is the high-class tourist joint. A bed in an air-con triple room in the new wing is Y150, slightly cheaper in the old wing. It is difficult to get to, and you'll probably have to take a taxi from the railway station (Y15).

Getting There & Away

Air There are flights twice weekly to Canton (Y463), Shanghai (Y319) and Ürümqi.

There are flights six days a week to Xi'an (Y117).

Bus The long-distance bus station is opposite Luoyang West Railway Station. Regular buses run to Zhengzhou (Y4.50, 4½ to five hours). There's one bus daily from Luoyang to Xi'an at 6 am (Y12).

Train From Luoyang there are direct trains to Beijing via Zhengzhou (16 hours); to Shanghai (18 hours); and to Xi'an (eight hours). There are some direct trains north to Taiyuan and south to Xiangfan and Yichang. Yichang is a port on the Yangtze River where you can pick up the Chongqing-Wuhan ferry.

Shandong 山东

Shandong *(shāndōng)* is overpopulated and poor, and plagued by the rotten Yellow River, which has changed direction 26 times in its history. In the late 19th century the Boxers arose out of Shandong and their rebellion set all of China ablaze.

Travellers tend to gloss over this province, which is a shame since it has much to offer: the coastal ports of Qingdao and Yantai, Qufu and Taishan which are packed with sights, and unknowns like the Shengli Oilfield and Zibo.

QINGDAO 青岛

Qingdao *(qīngdǎo)* is a remarkable replica of a Bavarian village dropped onto the coast of China. The crumbling colonial presence lingers in Qingdao in the town's famous beer, in the villas built along the beaches and in the railway station, with its vintage clocks. It's best visited in summer when you can enjoy its white, sandy beaches.

CITS The office (☎ 270695) is behind the Huiquan Dynasty Hotel at 9 Nanhai Lu, but they're geared mostly to tour groups.

Public Security Bureau This is at 29 Hubei

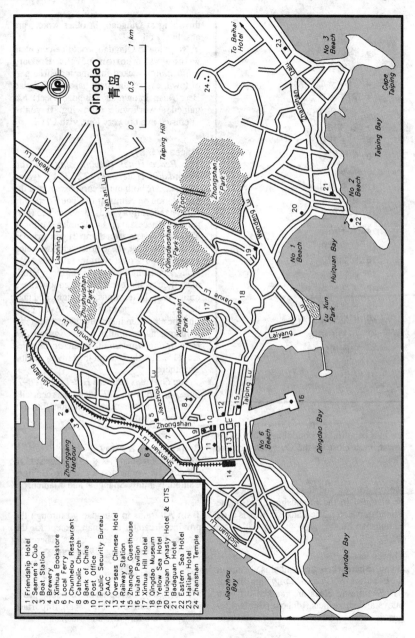

Qingdao 青岛

1 Friendship Hotel
2 Seamen's Club
3 Boat Station
4 Brewery
5 Xinhua Bookstore
6 Local Ferry
7 Chunhelou Restaurant
8 Catholic Church
9 Bank of China
10 Post Office
11 Public Security Bureau
12 CAAC
13 Overseas Chinese Hotel
14 Railway Station
15 Zhanqiao Guesthouse
16 Huilan Pavilion
17 Xinhua Hill Hotel
18 Qingdao Museum
19 Yellow Sea Hotel
20 Huiquan Dynasty Hotel & CITS
21 Badaguan Hotel
22 Eastern Sea Hotel
23 Haitian Hotel
24 Zhanshan Temple

1	友谊饭店
2	海员俱乐部
3	海港客运站
4	青岛啤酒厂
5	新华书店
6	小港码头
7	春和楼
8	天主教堂
9	中国银行
10	邮局
11	公安局外事科
12	中国民航
13	华侨饭店
14	火车站
15	栈桥宾馆
16	回澜阁
17	迎宾馆
18	青岛博物馆
19	黄海饭店
20	汇泉王朝大酒泉
21	八大关宾馆
22	东海饭店
23	海天大酒店
24	湛山寺

Lu in a beautiful old building with a clock tower, very close to the Overseas Chinese Hotel.

Money Money and travellers' cheques can be changed in the Friendship Store in the Friendship Hotel. The Bank of China is at 62 Zhongshan Lu.

Things to See
If you're here when the weather is warm, put the **beaches** (hǎishuǐ yùchǎng) high on your list. Swimming areas are marked off with buoys and shark nets, lifeboat patrols, lifeguards and medical stations. Your chances of

drowning at Qingdao, in other words, are absolutely nil.

No guide to Qingdao would be complete without a mention of the **Brewery** (píjiǔchǎng), tucked into the industrial part of town, east of the main harbour. Tsingtao Beer (also known as Qingdao Beer) has gained a worldwide following. If you're interested in a brewery tour, visit CITS.

Places to Stay
The *Peace Hotel (hépíng bīnguǎn)* and *Friendship Hotel* (☎ 223231) *(yǒuyí bīnguǎn)* are both in the complex around the boat station on Xinjiang Lu. The Friendship Hotel has dormitory beds for about Y15 (bargaining is necessary), and doubles starting at Y30. Both hotels are a dump. If you arrive in Qingdao by boat, these hotels are just a step away. If you arrive by train, take bus No 6 along Zhongshan Lu to the northern terminus, then walk back under an overhead bridge near the terminus, turn right, and take bus No 21 for one stop north. If you can't find the stop then just walk the last stretch.

Increasingly popular is the *Eastern Sea Hotel (dōnghǎi fàndiàn)* where dormitories are Y15. Bus No 26 from the railway station goes there.

The *Overseas Chinese Hotel* (☎ 279092) *(húaqiáo fàndiàn)*, 72 Hunan Lu, is centrally situated near the railway station, but it's often full. Doubles are Y150.

Getting There & Away
Air CAAC (☎ 88047) is at 29 Zhongshan Lu. Qingdao is connected by air to Beijing, Canton, Nanjing, Shanghai and Xiamen.

Train All trains to Qingdao go through the provincial capital of Ji'nan, except for the direct Qingdao to Yantai trains. There are direct trains to Beijing (17 hours).

JI'NAN 济南
Ji'nan (jìnán), the capital of Shandong Province, is a dull city but is an important transport hub for Qufu and Taishan.

TAISHAN 泰山

Taishan *(tàishān)* is the most revered of the five sacred mountains of China, adopted in turn by Taoists, Buddhists, Confucians and Maoists. From its summit, imperial sacrifices to heaven and earth were offered. Taishan does not offer the mountain-climbing you might expect, and its scenic beauty is not outstanding, but it's an engrossing experience and certainly worthwhile. The town of Tai'an lies at the foot of Taishan and is the gateway to the mountain.

Information

CITS The office (☎ 7020, 3259) is on the 2nd floor, 46 Hongmen Lu, which is just next to the Taishan Guesthouse in Tai'an.

Things to See

Before climbing Taishan, check out the **Dai Temple** *(dài miào)* at the foot of the mountain south of the Taishan Guesthouse.

The biggest attraction is climbing **Taishan**. Allow at least eight hours up and down at the minimum. The mountain is 1545 metres above sea level, with a climbing distance of 7.5 km from base to summit on the central route. You can also cheat your way to the top – minibuses run from the Tai'an railway station to Zhongtianmen, halfway up Taishan, with several departures each morning. From Zhongtianmen there is a cable car to the summit.

Places to Stay

Most popular is the *Taishan Guesthouse (tàishān bīnguǎn)*. Dormitory beds are Y18. Doubles cost from Y60 but can be bargained down to Y40 in the off season. The hotel is four km from the railway station and just a short walk from the start of the central route up Taishan. Take bus No 3 from the railway station to the second-to-last stop.

Somewhat less convenient is the *Overseas Chinese Hotel* (☎ 8122) *(húaqiáo dàxià)* on Dongyue Dajie. Doubles are Y160 in the low season, Y180 during peak times. The only other place in Tai'an that takes foreigners is the *Taishan Grand Hotel* on Daizhong Dajie where doubles are Y120.

On Taishan itself, you can stay at *Zhongtianmen Guesthouse* midway up or the *Daiding Guesthouse* on the summit.

Getting There & Away

Buses connect Tai'an to Qufu and there are trains to Ji'nan.

QUFU 曲阜

Qufu *(qūfù)* is the birthplace of Confucius who began and ended his life here (551 to 479 BC). His impact was not felt in his own lifetime and he spent his years in abject poverty – but his descendants, the Kong family, fared considerably better.

In 1948 Confucius' direct heir, the first-born son of the 77th generation of the Kong family, fled to Taiwan, breaking a 2500-year tradition of Kong residence in Qufu.

During the Cultural Revolution Confucian teachings were out of favour (to put it mildly), and in the 1960s a contingent of Red Guards came on a mission of destruction. The leader of the ransacking guards, Tan Houlan, was jailed in 1978 and tried in 1982. Confucian ethics have made a comeback, and respect and obedience are being promoted to instil civic-mindedness. In 1979 the Qufu temples were renovated and reopened.

Information

CITS This is on the 2nd floor of the Lüyou Binguan, near the bus station. There isn't much for them to do in a small place like Qufu, but they could help you buy a bus ticket.

Things to See

The **Confucius Temple** *(kǒng miào)* takes up one-fifth of Qufu. It is more than one km long and the entrance, Star Gate, is at the south. The dominant features are clusters of twisted pines and cypresses, and the rows of steles – with more than 1000 in the temple grounds.

Confucius Mansions *(kǒng fǔ)* is a maze of 450 rooms. The town of Qufu grew around the mansions and was an autonomous estate administered by the Kongs.

The **Confucian Forest** *(kǒng lín)* north of

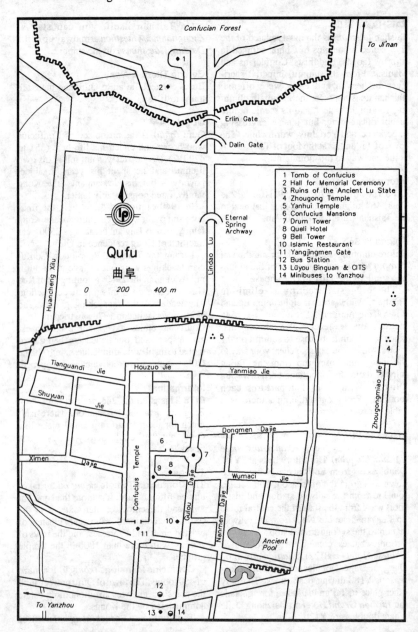

Confucian Forest

To Ji'nan

Erlin Gate

Dalin Gate

Eternal
Spring
Archway

Qufu
曲阜

0   200   400 m

1 Tomb of Confucius
2 Hall for Memorial Ceremony
3 Ruins of the Ancient Lu State
4 Zhougong Temple
5 Yanhui Temple
6 Confucius Mansions
7 Drum Tower
8 Queli Hotel
9 Bell Tower
10 Islamic Restaurant
11 Yangjingmen Gate
12 Bus Station
13 Lüyou Binguan & CITS
14 Minibuses to Yanzhou

Huancheng Xilu

Tianguandi Jie

Shuyuan Jie

Houzuo Jie

Yanmiao Jie

Lindao Jie

Zhougongmiao Jie

Confucius Temple

Ximen   Dajie

Dongmen Dajie

Wumaci Jie

Gulou Dajie

Nannen Dajie

Ancient
Pool

To Yanzhou

12

13   14

1 孔墓	8 阙里宾舍
2 祭奠堂	9 钟楼
3 鲁国址	10 回民饭店
4 周公庙	11 仰经门
5 颜庙	12 汽车站
6 孔府	13 旅游宾馆
7 鼓楼	14 往兗州小公共汽车

Confucius Mansions, about 2½ km along Gulou Dajie, is the largest artificial park and best-preserved cemetery in China. A time-worn route, it has a kind of 'spirit-way' lined with ancient cypresses. It takes about 40 minutes to walk, 10 minutes by auto-rickshaw.

Places to Stay & Eat

Many travellers stay right in Confucius Mansions itself at the *Confucius Mansions Hotel* (☎ 412374, 412686). It's got genuine classical architecture but it's falling apart and the rooms are dirty. There are three standards, all with private bath. Prices for doubles are Y25 (shared room), Y60 and Y160. The food here is easily forgotten.

The up-market place in town is the *Queli Hotel (qùelǐ bīnshé)* (☎ 411300), 1 Queli St, where singles/doubles cost Y100/130 – the height of luxury.

Aside from the usual dirt-cheap noodle stands near the bus station, there is a good *Islamic Restaurant* on Gulou Dajie with a sign in English.

Getting There & Away

Bus There are frequent minibuses from Qufu to Yanzhou and direct buses to Tai'an and Ji'nan.

Train There are no trains in Qufu; the nearest tracks go to Yanzhou, 13 km away. Yanzhou is on the Beijing to Shanghai line. You can also pick up trains in Ji'nan.

Jiangsu 江苏

The southern part of Jiangsu *(jiāngsū)* lies in the rich Yangtze Basin – a beautiful tapestry of greens, yellows and blues offset with whitewashed farm buildings. Jiangsu is the most populated province, with the highest land productivity and an above-average educational level. It also has the third highest industrial output in the land, after Shanghai and Liaoning. North of the Yangtze is a complete contrast, however: decayed and backward.

Summers are hot and humid; winters can touch freezing point. It rains a lot, but it's a nice rain, adding a misty soft touch to the landscape.

THE GRAND CANAL 大运河

The original Grand Canal *(dà yùnhé)* was a series of interlocking projects from different eras. The canal runs from north to south, providing China with a major water transport route – the longest canal in the world.

Kublai Khan extended the canal to Beijing, but this section has been silted up. Gradually trains displaced water transport, and the canal fell into disrepair, reduced to one-third of its original length due to silting, floods, and poorly planned dams, watergates and irrigation systems.

In 1980 the canal suddenly became a tourist attraction, and work was done on it to enable flat-bottomed cruisers to make week-long trips all the way from Yangzhou to Suzhou.

The CITS in Wuxi sells tickets on the Dragon Boat – a replica of an imperial barge. The canal trip gives glimpses of everyday Chinese life, like oil slicks, sewage and women pounding their washing to a pulp. As one traveller wrote, the canal journey was 'the highlight of our trip...a filthy but picturesque slice of life in China'.

Travellers who have taken the route from Hangzhou to Suzhou on overnight passenger boats (with sleeping berths) or on daytime 150-seat ferries, report that the boats are dirty, uncomfortable and crowded. It is also still difficult to get on a passenger boat. The Chinese worry about the condition of the boats, and prefer travellers to take the train, or one of the Dragon Boat cruises. Trips are slow – estimated times for sections south of the Yangtze are:

Hangzhou to Suzhou
    14 hours, overnight berth or day boat
Suzhou to Wuxi
    Five to six hours, early morning day boat
Wuxi to Changzhou
    Four to five hours
Changzhou to Zhenjiang
    Eight to nine hours (possible break in Danyang)

It's also possible to break the Hangzhou to Suzhou journey around the halfway mark at the final canal town of Jiaxing. Jiaxing is also linked by rail to Shanghai and Hangzhou.

SUZHOU 杨州

Travellers from Marco Polo onwards have rated this as one of the finest places in China. Marco Polo's Suzhou (*sūzhōu*) was inhabited by beautiful maidens, rich merchants, artists, artisans and magicians. It has been variously dubbed the 'Venice of the East' and the 'Garden City', and seems to have survived the Cultural Revolution well.

Sericulture – raising silkworms – has been the town's major industry since time immemorial and is largely responsible for its continued prosperity. About 600,000 people live here.

CITS This office (☎ 223063) is in a separate building in the Suzhou Hotel compound, 115 Shiquan Jie.

Public Security Bureau This (☎ 5661) is at 7 Dashitou Lane.

Money The Bank of China is at 490 Renmin Lu. All major hotels change money.

Things to See

Suzhou is a great place to walk around, particularly along the bridges over the main moat to the west of the Grand Canal. The best preserved city gate, **Panmen**, is next to the **Wumen Bridge** which is the largest single-arched stone bridge in Suzhou.

At the northern end of Renmin Lu is the **North Temple Pagoda** (*běi sì*), a nine-storey structure dating from the 17th century. You can climb to the top for a superb aerial view of the town and surrounding farmland.

Some blocks east is the **Suzhou Museum** (*sūzhōu bówùguǎn*), once the residence of the Taiping leader Li Xiucheng. It is open daily from 8 am to 5 pm.

The area surrounding Guanqian Lu – the **Suzhou Bazaar** (*sūzhōu shāngchǎng*) – has numerous restaurants, theatres, speciality shops, street vendors, hairdressing salons, noodle dispensaries, silk merchants and sweet shops. At the heart of the bazaar is the Taoist **Temple of Mystery** (*xuánmiàoguān*), founded in the 3rd century AD.

Suzhou's gardens are looked upon as works of art. The gardens are usually open from early morning to dusk (7.30 am to 5 pm) and there is a small admission charge.

The **Humble Administrator's Garden** (*zhuózhèng yuán*) in northern Suzhou was built in the 1500s. In 1350 the monk Tian Ru built the **Lion Grove** (*shīzilín*) just up the street. The **Garden of Harmony** is off Renmin Lu, just south of Guanqian.

The smallest (but by far the nicest) garden is the **Master of the Nets** (*wǎngshīyuán*), laid out in the 12th century and restored in the 18th. It may be hard to find, as the entrance is a narrow alley just west of the Suzhou Hotel.

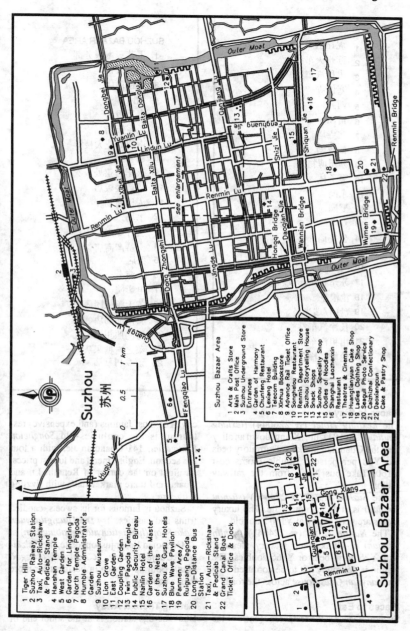

Suzhou 苏州

1 Tiger Hill
2 Suzhou Railway Station
3 Taxi, Auto-Rickshaw & Pedicab Stand
4 Hanshan Temple
5 West Garden
6 Garden for Lingering In
7 North Temple Pagoda
8 Humble Administrator's Garden
9 Suzhou Museum
10 Lion Grove
11 East Garden
12 Coupling Garden
13 Twin Pagoda Temple
14 Public Security Bureau
15 Nanlin Hotel
16 Garden of the Master of the Nets
17 Suzhou & Gusu Hotels
18 Blue Wave Pavilion
19 Panmen Area/ Ruiguang Pagoda
20 Long-Distance Bus Station
21 Taxi, Auto-Rickshaw & Pedicab Stand
22 Grand Canal Boat Ticket Office & Dock

Suzhou Bazaar Area

1 Arts & Crafts Store
2 Main Post Office
3 Suzhou Underground Store
   Entrances
4 Garden of Harmony
5 Chunfeng Restaurant
6 Lexiang Hotel
7 Telecom Building
8 Xinhua Bookstore
9 Advance Rail Ticket Office
10 Songhelou Restaurant
11 Renmin Department Store
12 Suzhou Storytelling House
13 Snack Shops
14 Suzhou Specialty Shop
15 Oodles of Noodles
16 Shanghai Laozhenxin Restaurant
17 Theatres & Cinemas
18 Huanglianyuan Cake Shop
19 Ladies Clothing Shop
20 Seagull Photo Service
21 Caizhizhai Confectionary
22 Daoxiangcun Cake & Pastry Shop

Suzhou Bazaar Area

1	虎丘山
2	苏州火车站
3	出租汽车站
4	寒山寺
5	西园
6	留园
7	北寺塔
8	拙政园
9	苏州博物馆
10	狮子林
11	东园
12	娶园
13	双塔
14	公安局外事科
15	南林饭店
16	网师园
17	苏州和姑苏饭店
18	沧浪亭
19	盘门/瑞光塔
20	长途汽车站
21	出租汽车站
22	轮船运输公司

SUZHOU BAZAAR AREA

1	工艺美术服务部
2	邮电大楼
3	展销商店
4	怡园
5	春风饭店
6	乐乡饭店
7	南门商业大楼
8	新华书店
9	火车售票处
10	松鹤楼饭店
11	人民商场
12	书场
13	玄外观点心店
14	土特产商店
15	面店
16	上海老正兴菜馆
17	电影院
18	黄天源糕团店
19	女用品商店
20	海鸥照相馆
21	菜之斋糖果店
22	道乡村糕店

Places to Stay

The *Lexiang Hotel* (☎ 226044) *(léxiāng fàndiàn)* is at 18 Dajing Xiang, down an alley near the Guanqian markets. Dormitory beds are Y20 per person. Double rooms cost Y160. Take bus No 1 from the railway station.

The *Suzhou Hotel* (☎ 224646) *(sūzhōu fàndiàn)* is at 115 Shiquan Jie. The luxury rooms are very pricey at Y110 a double.

The *Nanlin Hotel* (☎ 224641) *(nánlín fàndiàn)* at Gunxiufang is very pleasant, with Y25 dorm beds or Y166 doubles. The Nanlin is definitely not to be confused with the *Nanyuan Guesthouse* across the road.

Places to Eat

Suzhou Bazaar is the restaurant centre of the city. The most famous (and expensive) restaurant is the centuries-old *Songhelou Restaurant*, 141 Guanqian Jie, with a tour bus section, English menu and tourist prices. At night on the corner of Renmin Lu and Guanqian Lu are market stalls with sizzling tasty fare.

Suzhou is famous for its sweets, candied fruits and pastries. Try the *Huangtianyuan Cake Shop (huángtiānyuán gāobǐngdiàn)* at 38 Guanqian Jie, or just opposite, the *Caizhizhai Confectionary (cǎizhīzhāi tángguǒ diàn)*. Both have been in business for more than a century.

Getting There & Away

Bus The bus station is at the south end of

Renmin Lu. There are good connections to Shanghai, Hangzhou, Wuxi and Changzhou.

Train Suzhou is on the Nanjing-Shanghai line, and there are frequent express services.

Boat Along the Grand Canal it's six hours to Wuxi and 14 hours to Hangzhou.

WUXI 无锡

Wuxi (wúxī), a largely industrial town just up the line from Suzhou, is divided into two sections. There are few historical relics or sights – the main attraction is Lake Tai, just outside town.

CTS This office (which is not CITS) is conveniently placed in a building facing the square in front of the main railway station. Several people here speak English.

Things to See

Lake Tai (tàihú) is a freshwater lake with a total area of 2200 sq km and an average depth of two metres. There are about 90 islands scattered across the lake, and the entire area is referred to as 'the land of fish and rice' because of its fertile soil, mild climate and abundant rainfall.

Places to Stay

In Wuxi there's the *Liangxi Hotel* (☎ 226812) (liángxī fàndiàn) on Zhongshan Nanlu. Doubles are Y90, but bargain. Take bus No 12 from the railway station. The tourist hotels are by the lake. The *Taihu Hotel* (☎ 667901) (tàihú fàndiàn) has relatively cheap rooms in the old building. Singles/doubles are Y40/90. Take bus No 2 to the terminus, walk for 20 minutes, and you're there.

Places to Eat

The *China Restaurant* (zhōngguó fàndiàn) is one of the better ones. Walk directly from the railway station and across the bridge; it's on your left, second block down, on the ground floor of the China Hotel. Eating places can also be found in the markets off Renmin Lu and along Zhongshan Lu. Try the *Jiangnan*

Restaurant (jiāngnán càiguǎn) at 435 Zhongshan Lu.

On Lake Tai food is available in the hotel dining rooms, or from the stalls and teahouses scattered throughout the town.

Getting There & Away

The advance ticket office for boat, bus and train in Wuxi is at 224 Renmin Lu.

Bus There are long-distance buses to Nanjing, Shanghai and Suzhou.

Train Wuxi is on the Beijing-Shanghai line with a frequent service.

Boat From Wuxi there are at least 10 boat routes along smaller canals to outlying counties, as well as boats across Lake Tai and along the Grand Canal. Since Wuxi covers an area of 400 sq km and is open to travellers without a permit, day tripping along the canals is not legally out of bounds. A variety of motorboats ply these routes including two-deck motor barges with air-conditioning, 100 soft-seats and restaurants.

Getting Around

There are about 15 local bus lines. Bus No 2 runs from the railway station to the Taihu Hotel. Bus No 1 starts at the Wuxi Hotel for the Liyuan Gardens. There are plenty of auto-rickshaws at the railway station.

CHANGZHOU 常州

Although often overlooked, Changzhou (chángzhōu) is a delightful mixture of old and new. It's a back-alley town on a skein of canals. If you want to avoid the crush at Wuxi or Suzhou, Changzhou is a good place to go.

The *Changzhou Hotel (Chang Chow Guesthouse)* (☎ 600713) (chángzhōu bīnguǎn) is central, well off the street and quiet. Reception asks Y150 for a double but they have a few doubles with shared bath for only Y40.

NANJING 南京

Nanjing (nánjīng) means 'southern capital'. It was China's capital under the first Ming emperor, and also under the Kuomintang. In fact, maps produced in Taiwan still show this as China's capital city. Beijing (northern capital) is not recognised by the Kuomintang, which chooses to call it 'Beiping', or 'northern plain'.

Nanjing lies on the eastern bank of the Yangtze River. Most things to see are to the east of Nanjing, in or around Purple Mountain (Zijinshan).

Information
CITS This office (☎ 639013) is at 202 Zhongshan Beilu.

Money The Bank of China is near the central traffic circle at 3 Zhongshan Donglu. There is also a money-exchange counter at the Jinling Hotel.

Post The main post office is at 19 Zhongshan Lu, around the corner from the Jinling Hotel. Most large hotels have a postal service.

Things to See
Before picking over the remnants of 3000 years of history, go and see Nanjing's prime tourist attraction, the **Jinling Hotel** (*jīnlíng fàndiàn*).

The **Ming City Wall** is the longest city wall ever built in the world, measuring over 33 km. Some of the original 13 **Ming City Gates** remain, including Heping Gate in the north and Zhonghua Gate in the south.

Built in 1382, the **Drum Tower** (*gǔlóu*) is in the city centre in the middle of a traffic circle on Beijing Xilu. Drums were usually beaten to give directions for the change of the night watches and in rare instances to warn the populace of impending danger. North-east of the Drum Tower, the **Bell Tower** houses an enormous bell dating from 1388. The bell was originally in a pavilion on the west side of the Drum Tower. The present tower dates from 1889.

The **Tomb of Hong Wu** (*míngxiàolíng*) lies east of the city on the southern slope of Purple Mountain. Hong Wu was the first emperor of the Ming dynasty (1368-1644).

Sun Yatsen, the man regarded as the father of modern China (by both the Communists and the Kuomintang) died in Beijing in 1925 and wished to be buried in Nanjing. Less than a year after his death construction of the immense **Sun Yatsen Mausoleum** (*zhōngshānlíng*) began at the southern foot of Purple Mountain. No doubt he would have preferred greater simplicity than the Ming-style tomb which his successors built for him.

To the east of the city by Purple Mountain is **Linggu Park** (*línggǔ*) with an assortment of sights. A road leads either side of the **Beamless Hall** and up two flights of steps to the **Pine Wind Pavilion**, originally dedicated to the Goddess of Mercy as part of the Linggu Temple. The **Linggu Temple** and its memorial hall to Xuan Zang is close by. After you pass through the Beamless Hall, turn right and follow the pathway. Xuan Zang was the Buddhist monk who travelled to India and brought back the Buddhist scriptures. Close by is the **Linggu Pagoda**, which was built in the 1930s under the direction of an American architect. It's an octagonal building 60 metres high and has nine storeys.

Places to Stay
It's difficult to find anything really cheap. Best bet is *Nanjing University* (*nánjīng dàxué*), off Zhongshan Lu before Beijing Lu traffic circle. Doubles in the foreign students dorm cost Y12; if it's full, the staff might find you somewhere else to stay on campus. Bus No 3 from the bus station/railway station area will pass just north of the campus.

The *Shuangmenlou Hotel* (☎ 685961) (*shuāngménlóu bīnguǎn*) at 185 Huju Beilu has doubles in the old wing for Y85. Bus No 21 from Nanjing West Railway Station stops right in front of the hotel.

Places to Eat
Dasanyuan (☎ 641027) (*dàsānyuán jiǔjiā*) at 40 Zhongshan Lu has good, cheap dishes downstairs – fancier fare is available upstairs. The *Laoguangdong* (*lǎoguǎngdōng*

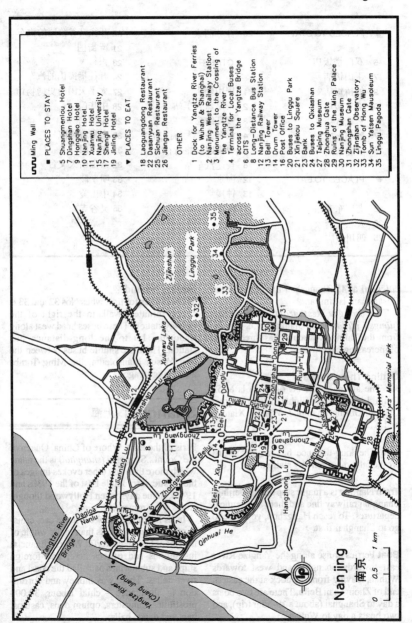

Nan jing
南京

PLACES TO STAY
5 Shuangmenlou Hotel
7 Dingshan Hotel
9 Hongqiao Hotel
10 Nanjing Hotel
11 Xuanwu Hotel
15 Nanjing University
17 Shengli Hotel
19 Jinling Hotel

PLACES TO EAT
18 Laoguangdong Restaurant
22 Dasanyuan Restaurant
25 Sichuan Restaurant
26 Jiangsu Restaurant

OTHER
1 Dock for Yangtze River Ferries (to Wuhan & Shanghai)
2 Nanjing West Railway Station
3 Monument to the Crossing of the Yangtze River
4 Terminal for Local Buses across the Yangtze Bridge
6 CITS
8 Long-Distance Bus Station
12 Nanjing Railway Station
13 Bell Tower
14 Drum Tower
16 Post Office
20 Buses to Linggu Park
21 Xinjekou Square
23 Bank
24 Buses to Qixiashan
27 Taiping Museum
28 Zhonghua Gate
29 Ruins of the Ming Palace
30 Nanjing Museum
31 Zhongshan Gate
32 Zijinshan Observatory
33 Tomb of Hong Wu
34 Sun Yatsen Mausoleum
35 Linggu Pagoda

■ PLACES TO STAY	26 江苏酒家	20 开往灵谷公园的汽车
		21 新街口
5 双门楼饭店	OTHER	23 银行
7 丁山饭店		24 开往栖霞山的汽车
9 虹桥饭店	1 中山码头	27 太平天国历史博物馆
10 南京饭店	2 南京西火车站	28 中华门
11 玄武饭店	3 渡江纪念碑	29 牛朝门
17 胜利饭店	4 汽车站（大桥南路）	30 南京博物院
19 金陵饭店	6 中国国际旅行社	31 中山门
	8 长途汽车站	32 紫金山天文台
▼ PLACES TO EAT	12 南京火车站	33 明孝陵
	13 钟楼	34 中山陵
18 老广东菜馆	14 鼓楼	35 灵谷寺
22 大三元酒家	15 南京大学	
25 四川饭店	16 邮局	

càiguǎn) at 45 Zhongshan Lu, opposite the Dasanyuan, is similar.

The *Jiangsu Restaurant* (☎ 623698) (*jiāngsū jiǔjiā*) at 26 Jiankang Lu, not far from the Taiping Museum, has three floors of increasing excellence.

Getting There & Away

Air The airline office (☎ 643378) is at 52 Ruijin Lu. Important flights include Beijing, Canton, Guilin, Shanghai, Wuhan, Xiamen and Xi'an.

Bus The long-distance bus station is just west of the main railway station.

Train Nanjing is a major stop on the Beijing-Shanghai railway line and there are frequent departures. To reach Hangzhou, you have to go to Shanghai first.

Boat Ferries cruise along the Yangtze River east towards Shanghai and west towards Wuhan, leaving from the dock at the eastern end of Zhongshan Beilu. There are two boats a day to Shanghai (about a 19-hour trip), and two boats a day to Wuhan.

Getting Around

The terminus for trolleybus Nos 32 and 33 is a few minutes' walk to the right of the railway station. These buses head west along Shaoshan Lu to the long-distance bus station. There are shuttle buses between the Sun Yatsen Mausoleum, the Ming Tombs and Linggu Pagoda.

Shanghai 上海

Paris of the East, Whore of China, Queen of the Orient...Shanghai (*shànghǎi*) is the name which more than any other evokes images of the mystic, inscrutable East of the 1930s and 1940s, in the days when Hollywood thought slums were romantic.

In its heyday, there were more cars cruising the Shanghai streets than in the whole of the rest of China; powerful Western financial institutions had offices here; and foreign ships and submarines patrolled the coast and river deltas. There was money and corruption in abundance – child labour, 30,000 prostitutes, gangsters, opium dens, casinos, bars and dance halls.

Under the Communists the opium dens and brothels quickly disappeared, but the city still has a certain 1930s appearance about it.

Orientation

There are four main areas of interest in Shanghai: the Bund (Zhongshan Donglu) from the Friendship Store to the Dongfeng Hotel; Nanjing Donglu from the Peace to the Park Hotels; Frenchtown, the strip of Huaihai Zhonglu from Shaanxi Nanlu to Chongqing Nanlu marked by the colossal wings of the Jinjiang Hotel; and the Jade Buddha Temple and the side strip along Suzhou Creek.

Information

CITS This office (☎ 3217200) is on the ground floor of the Peace Hotel. Tickets for domestic travel and tours can be booked here. CITS will book tickets on the Trans-Siberian Railway to Europe; and they can arrange tours of factories, schools and film studios – also tickets for theatre, opera, etc.

Public Security Bureau This is at 210 Hankou Lu.

Money There are money-exchange counters on the premises of the larger tourist hotels. Credit cards are more readily accepted in Shanghai than in other parts of China. The Bank of China branch right next to the Peace Hotel on the Bund will change foreign cash and travellers' cheques.

Post & Telecommunications Letters and parcels can be received if addressed to the Peace Hotel, where they are held at the counter. The express mail service and poste restante are at 276 Bei Suzhou Lu. You can make long-distance calls from hotel rooms, or from the international telegraph office, next to the Peace Hotel on Nanjing Donglu.

Foreign Consulates It's possible to get your visas here for the Trans-Siberian journey though Beijing is better. The consul-ates can also replace passports if you're unfortunate enough to have lost one.

Australia
    17 Fuxing Xilu (☎ 4334604)
Hungary
    Room 1810 Union Building, 100 Yan'an Donglu
    (☎ 3261815)
Japan
    1517 Huaihai Zhonglu (☎ 4336639)
Poland
    618 Jianguo Xilu (☎ 4370952)
UK
    244 Yongfu Lu (☎ 4330508)
USA
    1469 Huaihai Zhonglu (☎ 4336880)
USSR
    20 Huangpu Lu (☎ 3242682)

Emergency Shanghai is credited with the best medical facilities and the most advanced medical knowledge in China. Foreigners are referred to Shanghai No 1 People's Hospital (☎ 240100) at 190 Bei Suzhou Lu. Western medicines are sold at the Shanghai No 8 Drugstore at 951 Huaihai Zhonglu.

Things to See

Shanghai starts as early as 5 am, with people exercising in the streets or concentrating on their taijiquan and other martial arts. Markets abound. The atmosphere in Shanghai in the early hours is enjoyable, before its millions begin to crowd the streets.

The Bund is an Anglo-Indian term for the embankment of a muddy waterfront. It's called *wàitān* in Chinese and Zhongshan Donglu on the map. It's Shanghai's most scenic street and a popular hangout for locals and foreigners.

The facades of the buildings along the Bund are a mix of neo-classical 1930s Chicago with a hint of Egyptian. They were used as trading houses, hotels, residences and clubs – and some still are.

Huangpu Park, at the north-western end of the Bund, was originally the British Public Gardens – at that time a notorious sign by the gate said 'No Dogs or Chinese Allowed'. You can also visit the **Dongfeng Hotel**. It has a sumptuous interior and was originally

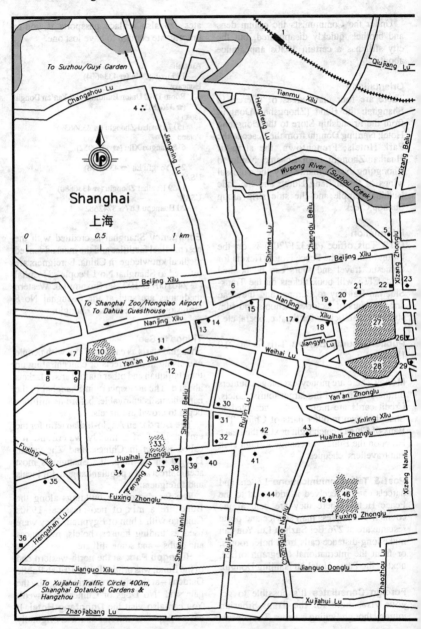

To Suzhou/Guyi Garden

Changshou Lu

Tianmu Xilu

Hengfeng Lu

Qiujiang Lu

Xizang Beilu

4

Jiangning Lu

Wusong River (Suzhou Creek)

Shanghai
上海

0   0.5   1 km

Shimen Lu

Chengdu Beilu

Beijing Xilu

5

Beijing Xilu

6

21   22

23

Nanjing

19   20

To Shanghai Zoo/Hongqiao Airport
To Dahua Guesthouse

15

Nanjing Xilu

17

Xilu

18

27

13   14

Jiangyin
Lu

26

11

Weihai Lu

7

10

28

Yan'an Xilu

29

8   9

12

Shaanxi Beilu

Ruijin Lu

Yan'an Zhonglu

30

Jinling Xilu

31

Xizang Nanlu

42

43

32

Huaihai Zhonglu

Fuxing Xilu

33

Huaihai Zhonglu

41

34

37   38

39   40

Tenyang Lu

35

44

45   46

Fuxing Zhonglu

Fuxing Zhonglu

Hengshan Lu

36

Shaanxi Nanlu

Ruijin Lu

Chongqing Nanlu

Zhaozhou

Jianguo Xilu

Jianguo Donglu

To Xujiahui Traffic Circle 400m,
Shanghai Botanical Gardens &
Hangzhou

Zhaojiabang Lu

Xujiahui Lu

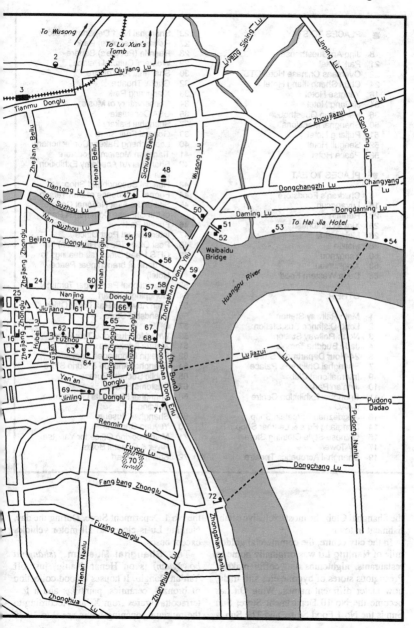

■ PLACES TO STAY

8	Jing An Guesthouse
21	Park Hotel
22	Overseas Chinese Hotel/CTS
24	Chun Sheng Jiang Hotel
16	Yangtse Hotel
31	Jinjiang Hotel
36	Hengshan Guesthouse
50	Shanghai Mansions
51	Pujiang Hotel
52	Seagull Hotel
58	Peace Hotel

▼ PLACES TO EAT

6	Children's Foodstore
18	Luyangcun
20	Renmin
25	Xinya Cantonese
26	Meiweizhai
38	Meixin
60	Yangzhou
63	Xinghualou
66	Deda Western Food

OTHER

1	Main Railway Station
2	Long-Distance Bus Station
3	North Railway Station
4	Jade Buddha Temple
5	24-Hour Department Store
7	Shanghai Children's Palace
9	International Club
10	Jing'an Park
11	Shanghai Exhibition Centre
12	CAAC
13	Jingdezhen Porcelain Shop
14	Dongfang Furs & Leather Shop
15	Chinese-Style Clothing Store
17	TV Tower
19	Shanghai Acrobatics Theatre
23	Shanghai No 1 Department Store
27	Renmin (People's) Park
28	Renmin (People's) Square
29	Workers' Cultural Palace
30	Shanghai Art Theatre
32	Guotai Theatre
33	Xiangyang Park
34	Conservatory of Music
35	USA Consulate
37	Shanghai Bakery
39	Gongtai Fruit Store
40	Laodacheng Bakery/Confectionery
41	Tianshan Moslem Foodstore
42	Shanghai Art Academy Exhibition Hall
43	Huaihai Secondhand Shop
44	Former Residence of Sun Yatsen
45	Site of the First National Congress of the Chinese Communist Party
46	Fuxing Park
47	International Post Office
48	Post Office (Poste Restante)
49	CITS Head Office (all dealings to be done at branch near Peace Hotel)
53	International Passenger Terminal
54	Gongpinglu Wharf
55	Main Advance Rail Ticket Office
56	Friendship Store
57	CITS
59	Wharf for Huangpu Tour Boats
61	Xinhua Bookstore
62	Foreign Languages Bookstore
64	Shanghai Antique & Curio Store
65	Public Security Bureau
67	Customs House
68	Shanghai Municipal Government Building
69	Shanghai Museum
70	Yuyuan Gardens
71	Main Booking Office for Yangtse River & Coastal Boats
72	Shiliupu Wharf

the Shanghai Club, the most exclusive establishment in town.

In the city centre, the commercial golden mile of **Nanjing Lu** was originally home to restaurants, nightclubs and coffin makers. Prestigious stores of bygone eras still trade, now under different names. Wing On has become the No 10 Department Store; Sun Sun is the No 1 Food Store; and The Sun is the No 1 Department Store. During the day, Nanjing Lu is closed to all motor vehicles except buses.

The **Shanghai Museum** (*shànghǎi bówùguǎn*) is on Henan Nanlu, just off Yan'an Donglu. It houses a good collection of bronzes, ceramics, paintings and a few terracotta figures from Xi'an. According to the museum, opening hours are 9 to 10.30

■ PLACES TO STAY	OTHER	39 公泰水果店
		40 老大昌食品店
8 静安饭店	1 火车总站	41 天山回民食品店
21 国际饭店	2 长途汽车站	42 画院美术馆
22 华侨饭店	3 火车北站	43 淮海旧货商店
24 春申江宾馆	4 玉佛寺	44 孙中山故居
16 长江宾馆	5 二十四时百货商店	45 中共一大会址
31 锦江饭店	7 少年宫	46 富兴公园
36 衡山宾馆	9 国际俱乐部	47 国际邮局
50 上海大厦	10 静安公园	48 总邮局
51 浦江饭店	11 上海展览馆	49 国际旅行总局
52 海鸥饭店	12 中国民航	53 国际客运站
58 和平饭店	13 景德镇艺术瓷器服务部	54 公平路码头
	14 东方毛服装厂	55 火车售票处
▼ PLACES TO EAT	15 龙风中式服装厂	56 友谊商店
	17 电视楼	57 中国国际旅行社
6 儿童食品店	19 杂技场	59 浦江游航码头
18 绿扬村酒家	23 第一百货商店	61 新华书店
20 人民饭店	27 人民公园	62 外文书店
25 斯雅粤菜饭店	28 人民广场	64 文物商店
26 美味宅	29 工人文化宫	65 公安局外事科
38 美心酒家	30 艺术剧院	67 海关楼
60 扬州饭店	32 国泰剧院	68 上海市人民政府
63 杏花楼	33 香扬公园	69 博物馆
66 德西餐社	34 音乐学校	70 豫园
	35 美国领事馆	71 轮船售票处（长江）
	37 上海食品店	72 十六浦码头

am (closing at 11.45 am) and 1 to 3.30 pm (closing at 4.45 pm). The museum is closed on Sundays.

The **Arts & Crafts Research Institute** (*gōngyì měishùpǐn yànjiūsuǒ*) is at 79 Fenyang Lu, in a villa of the bourgeois French style. The institute has 15 specialities, and acts as technical adviser to specialist factories around Shanghai.

Some of the best views of Shanghai are seen from the water. **River tour boats** depart from the dock on the Bund, slightly north of the Peace Hotel. There are several decks on the boat, but prices for foreigners are Y33 (special class A) and Y17 (special class B). Departure times are 8.30 am and 1.30 pm, with possible extra departures in the summer and on Sundays. The schedule may become more erratic in winter due to bad weather. Tickets can be purchased in advance from CITS at the Peace Hotel (there's a small surcharge), or at the boat dock – but there's no real need if you're taking upper deck since it is unlikely to be full.

Yuyuan Bazaar (*yùyúan shāngchǎng*), in the Yuyuan gardens at the north-eastern end of the old Chinese city, is a place where hundreds of thousands of people come to look at each other, stroll and eat. The Yu Gardens were built by the Pan family from 1559 to 1577. There you can see the Temple of the Town Gods, the main hall of which was rebuilt in 1926.

Central to the district is the **Wuxingting Teahouse** *(wǔxíng cháguǎn)*, a pentagon set in a pond and surrounded by zigzag bridges. A hundred small shops surround the teahouse. The maze of alleys is best explored in the early morning.

If you want to visit the famous **Jade Buddha Temple** *(yùfó sì)*, bus No 16 from the Yuyuan Bazaar takes you there, travelling across half of Shanghai. There are 70 monks in residence and the centrepiece is a white-jade buddha almost two metres high, which was brought from Burma in 1882. Photographs are not allowed. The temple is open daily from 8 am to 5 pm.

Places to Stay

There are some cheap Chinese hotels near the railway station, but no foreigners are allowed. The established backpacker dormitory in Shanghai is at the *Pujiang Hotel* (☎ 246388) *(pǔjiāng fàndiàn)* at 15 Huangpu Lu. Beds are Y20, including breakfast. There are also four-bed rooms for Y126, triples for Y109, and doubles for Y97.

If the Pujiang's full, you can almost always get a bed at the *Hai Jia Hotel* (☎ 3411440) at 1001 Jiangpu Lu. Beds are only Y12 per person in five-bed rooms with communal bath. Three-bed rooms are also available for Y18 per person and doubles with air-con and private bath are Y100.

Another place to try is the *Conservatory of Music* (☎ 4370137) *(yīnyuè xuéxiào)* at 20 Fenyang Lu off Huaihai Zhonglu in the French Concession area. The foreign student dorm will take non-students when there's room (best bet is during the summer) and costs Y20 per person in a comfortable double. To find it, take the first left after passing through the main gate, then another immediate left past the buildings on the left; the dorm will be on your right.

Just bridging the gap between budget and medium-priced accommodation is the *Chung Shen Jiang Hotel* (☎ 3205710) *(zhōngshēn jiāng)* at 626 Nanjing Donglu. Large doubles with air-con, phone, TV, and hot water are a bargain Y90. The front desk can be hopeless about bookings, however, since they don't seem to know when they're full and when they're not – if they say it's full, check with the floor maids to see if they can locate an empty room.

The *Seagull Hotel (hǎiōu bīnguǎn)* is on the waterfront and a minute's walk from the Pujiang Hotel. Clean doubles cost from Y145. A moderately priced restaurant on the 2nd floor serves Chinese and European dishes with generous helpings.

Places to Eat

Shanghai is noted for its seafood. Lunch is usually served from 11.30 am to 2 pm and dinner from 5 to 7 pm. The major restaurants are very crowded.

Not to be missed in Shanghai is the ease and delight of snack-eating. You get waylaid for hours trying to make it along the length of Nanjing Lu, stumbling from one pastry shop to another, wiping off the smudges of lemon meringue pie, chocolate and cream, only to fall immediately into the sweet store next door.

Along Nanjing Donglu there are several places of interest. The *Sichuan* (☎ 221965) *(sìchuān fàndiàn)* at No 457 has hot and spicy food, including camphor-tea duck. The *Xinya* (☎ 223636) *(xīnyǎ fàndiàn)* at No 719 has foreigners' cubicles and Cantonese food on the 3rd floor.

Nanjing Xilu is also good for various restaurants. The *Wangjiasha* at No 805 is good for snacks, including chicken, shrimp in soup, and dumplings.

Fuzhou Lu is the best street for low-cost food. For example the *Xinghualou* (☎ 282747) *(xìnghuālóu)* at No 343 has all sorts of snacks and Cantonese food upstairs. The *Meiweizhai* (☎ 221705) at No 600, serves Suzhou and Wuxi food.

In the old French Concession area try the *Shanghai Western Restaurant* (☎ 374902) *(shànghǎi xīcāntīng)* at 845 Huaihai Zhonglu. Along the Huailai Zhonglu are also a string of confectioners worth trying. The *Tianshan Moslem Foodstore* at No 671 has Muslim delicacies. The *Laodacheng Bakery and Confectionary (lǎodàchēng shípǐndiàn)* at No 875 has a downstairs bakery with superb ice cream in season. The *Shanghai Bakery (shànghǎi shípǐndiàn)* at No 979 has French bread, wholemeal bread and chocolate.

Vegetarians are catered for in Shanghai with an array of fare including beans, dried mushrooms, fungus and seaweed. The *Gongdelin* (☎ 580218) *(gōngdélín sùcàiguǎn)* at 43 Huanghe Lu has mock crab, other mock seafood, mock duck and roasted bran-dough. The *Sanjiaodi Vegetable Market* is at 250 Tanggu Lu in the Hongkou district north of the Bund, and it has a huge selection of raw and cooked goods.

Entertainment

Shanghai has quietened down a lot since the 1920s and 1930s. The missionaries had a go at reducing the nightlife, but it was the Communists who finally succeeded. The Chinese, who get up at 6 am, usually like to go to bed by 10 pm. Foreigners, on the other hand, may want to rage on until midnight.

A quest for decadence could lead to the Peace Hotel Jazz Bar, open from 8 to 11 pm. The cover charge will pay for renditions of 'Tea for Two', etc. Waiters armed with starched napkins serve Manhattans, Russian Bears and Shanghai Cocktails (a mixture of gin and Chinese white wine).

Each of the elite Euro-American-style hotels, eg the Sheraton Hua Ting, Shanghai Hilton and Yangtze New World, has at least one international nightclub where businesspeople and tech reps shake it as best they can.

You can also see first-class travelling troupes specialising in acrobatics, music, ballet, puppets, opera, burlesque, etc. The Shanghai Art Theatre is down the road from the Jinjiang Club. The Conservatory of Music (☎ 4370137) *(yīnyuè xuéxiào)* is at 20 Fenyang Lu, off Huaihai Lu in Frenchtown.

Performances take place on Sunday evenings at 7 pm and are a treat – they feature child prodigies. Tickets are available at CITS or the theatre.

Acrobats are China's speciality. The Shenyang Acrobatic Troupe has toured the world to great acclaim. The Shanghai Acrobatics Dome on Nanjing Xilu has spectacular performances most evenings, occasionally introducing a tiger or a panda into the act – but not at the same time! CITS will book seats (for a fee) or try the office next to the Dome.

Getting There & Away

Air Not surprisingly, Shanghai is well connected to almost every city in China, and there are international flights to Hong Kong, Japan, France, Canada and the USA. Flights depart from Hongqiao Airport, 15 km from the central district. CAAC has an office at 789 Yan'an Zhonglu but you can also buy tickets from CITS.

Several international airlines maintain Shanghai offices:

Alitalia (☎ 2553957)
 Room 824-5, Shanghai Hilton
 250 Huashan Lu
Canadian Airlines International (☎ 2582582)
 Room 109, Jinjiang Hotel
 59 Maoming Nanlu
Cathay Pacific (☎ 4336435)
 Room 123, Jinjiang Hotel
 59 Maoming Nanlu
Dragon Air (☎ 4336435)
 Room 123, Jinjiang Hotel
 59 Maoming Nanlu
Japan Air Lines (☎ 4336337)
 Ruijin Building
 205 Maoming Lu
 1202 Huaihai Zhonglu
Northwest Airlines (☎ 2582582)
 Room 127, Jinjiang Hotel
 59 Maoming Nanlu
Singapore Airlines (☎ 4330517)
 Room 1341, 3/F, Jinjiang Hotel
 59 Maoming Lu
United Airlines (☎ 2553333)
 Shanghai Hilton Shopping Arcade
 250 Huashan Lu

Bus The long-distance bus station is on

Qiujiang Lu to the north of the North Railway Station. There are several buses a day to Hangzhou, Wuxi and Changzhou.

Train Many parts of the country can be reached by direct train from Shanghai. If you need a sleeper, your best bet is to buy a ticket from CITS. Although you'll have to pay tourist price, the advantage is that you avoid the enormous queues. If hard-seat will do, just go to the station and dive into the crowd.

Boat One of the cheapest and best ways of getting to or leaving Shanghai is by boat. Tickets to Hong Kong are available through CITS, but they charge a commission. There are several classes.

Special class
    Two-berth cabin, HK$939 to HK$1018 per person
First class
    One-berth cabin, HK$782
    Three-berth cabin, HK$861 per person
Second class
    Four, three and two-berth cabins, HK$679-739 per person
Third class
    Two and four-berth cabins, HK$565-622 per person
General class
    Large dormitory with upper and lower berths and lights that stay on all night, around HK$479 per person, not recommended

There are also boats along the Yangtze River. The main destinations are Nantong, Nanjing, Wuhu, Guichi, Jiujiang and Wuhan. Tickets for all domestic passenger shipping out of Shanghai can be bought from CITS or the main booking office at 1 Jinling Donglu.

Getting Around

To/From the Airport China Eastern Airlines has a bus from the CAAC Yan'an Lu office to the airport which costs Y1.80. The trip takes about half an hour. The Jinjiang Hotel has an airport shuttle that costs Y8.

Bus Shanghai's buses are about the most crowded in China, but if you don't get crushed they'll get you where you want to go.

There are trolley buses (Nos 1 to 30), and city buses (Nos 31 to 99). Nos 201 to 220 are peak-hour city buses, and Nos 301 to 321 are all-night buses.

No 18 runs north-south from the front of the North Railway Station to the Huangpu River. No 65 goes to the Bund.

No 49 from Public Security goes west along Yan'an Lu.

No 11 travels the ring road of the old Chinese city.

No 16 runs from the Jade Buddha Temple to Yuyuan Bazaar, then on to a ferry hop over the Huangpu River.

Anhui 安徽

Northern Anhui (*ānhuī*) forms part of the North China Plain, where the Han Chinese settled in large numbers during the Han dynasty. The southern area, below the Yangtze, was not settled until the 7th and 8th centuries AD. Most of the tourist attractions are in the south, and are more easily accessible from Hangzhou or Shanghai than from the provincial capital of Hefei. The Yangtze River ports of Guichi and Wuhu are convenient jumping-off points for the spectacular Huangshan mountains.

HEFEI 合肥

A nondescript industrial town, the capital of Anhui is not really worth a visit. The only real attraction is the local Provincial Museum whose prize possession is a 2000-year-old burial suit made of jade pieces held together with silver thread.

Hefei (*héféi*) is connected by train with Ji'nan, Beijing and Zhengzhou, with the Yangtze River port of Wuhu to the south, and with Xi'an to the west.

HUANGSHAN 黄山

Huangshan (*huángshān*) – or 'Yellow Mountain' – is the collective name of a range of 72 peaks in the south of Anhui Province,

280 km west of Hangzhou. The highest is the Lotus Flower Peak at 1800 metres, followed by the slightly smaller Bright Summit and Heavenly Capital peaks.

Buses pull into the base camp at the foot of the range, an overgrown tourist resort with a couple of hotels, a hot-spring public bath and two Friendship Stores. From here there are two ways of getting to the top of the mountain: long or short.

For the shorter eastern route, take the bus to the Yonguzhi Hostel from the Hot Spring Guesthouse. Bus tickets are Y0.80. Near the hostel there is a steep flight of steps to the top. It's a 7½-km climb, and takes two to three hours depending on how energetic you are. There's little to see on the way up.

At the top of the mountain is the Beihai Guesthouse, and a very long, steep descent. This is the (longer) western route. The western path has some spectacular scenery, and leads you to the Yupinglou Hostel and the mid-level monastery, and eventually back to base camp. You can comfortably do the round trip in 10 hours. Guides aren't necessary, as there are paths, steps and people everywhere.

Places to Stay & Eat
The *Beihai Guesthouse* (☎ 2555) *(běihǎi bīnguǎn)* at the summit of the mountain charges Y60 per person in single or double rooms but is almost always full – it's best to call ahead. Dorms for Y10 exist but are Chinese only. Outside is a canteen where you can get basic Chinese meals for a few yuan.

The *Yupinlou Hotel (yùpínglóu bīnguǎn)* has basic accommodation for Y30 and a restaurant – it's halfway down the mountain on the western side.

More expensive hotels are near the hot springs bathhouse and CITS office. The big *Tao Yuan Hotel* (☎ 2295, 2381) *(táoyuán bīnguǎn)* costs Y120 for a double – rooms in the annexe are Y80. CITS runs the Tao Yuan and does a poor job of it. Across the bridge from the Tao Yuan is the better *Huangshan Wenquan Hotel* (☎ 2196) *(huángshān wénquán bīnguǎn)* – rooms are Y76 to Y140

with advance booking or Y100 to Y160 walk-in.

Getting There & Away
Air CAAC has flights from the nearby airport at Tunxi to Beijing, Canton, Hangzhou, Hefei, Nanjing, Shanghai and Xiamen.

Bus There are buses between the Huangshan base camp and numerous cities, including Hangzhou, Shanghai and Nanjing.

Zhejiang 浙江

North of Hangzhou, Zhejiang Province *(zhéjiāng)* is part of the lush Yangtze River delta, similar to southern Jiangsu. The land has been intensively farmed for a thousand years, and the plain has a dense network of waterways, canals and irrigation channels. To the south, the province is mountainous.

Hangzhou, Ningbo and Shaoxing have been important trading centres and ports since the 8th century AD. Today Zhejiang is known as 'the land of silk', producing a third of China's raw silk, brocade and satin.

HANGZHOU 杭州
Hangzhou *(hángzhōu)* is the provincial capital and famous in China for its West Lake, a large freshwater lake set in hills and gardens, its banks dotted with pavilions and temples.

Orientation
To the south of Hangzhou is the Qiantang River, and to the west a range of hills. West Lake is between the hills and the urban area.

Information
CITS This office (☎ 27160) is on the ground floor of the Hangzhou Shangri-La Hotel on the north side of the lake. CTS is in the Overseas Chinese Hotel on Hubin Lu.

Public Security Bureau This is at the junction of Dingan Lu and Huimin Lu.

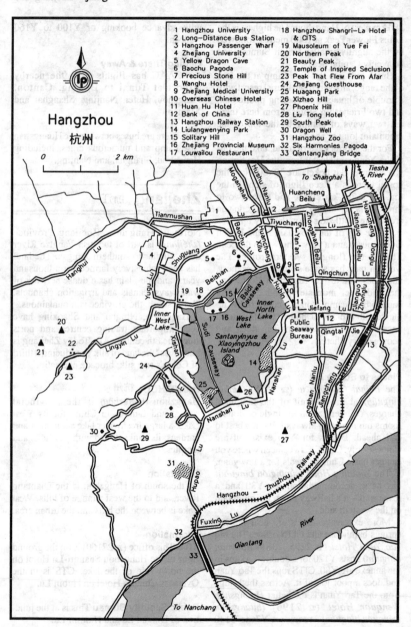

Hangzhou 杭州

0   1   2 km

1 Hangzhou University
2 Long-Distance Bus Station
3 Hangzhou Passenger Wharf
4 Zhejiang University
5 Yellow Dragon Cave
6 Baochu Pagoda
7 Precious Stone Hill
8 Wanghu Hotel
9 Zhejiang Medical University
10 Overseas Chinese Hotel
11 Huan Hu Hotel
12 Bank of China
13 Hangzhou Railway Station
14 Liulangwenying Park
15 Solitary Hill
16 Zhejiang Provincial Museum
17 Louwailou Restaurant
18 Hangzhou Shangri-La Hotel & CITS
19 Mausoleum of Yue Fei
20 Northern Peak
21 Beauty Peak
22 Temple of Inspired Seclusion
23 Peak That Flew From Afar
24 Zhejiang Guesthouse
25 Huagang Park
26 Xizhao Hill
27 Phoenix Hill
28 Liu Tong Hotel
29 South Peak
30 Dragon Well
31 Hangzhou Zoo
32 Six Harmonies Pagoda
33 Qiantangjiang Bridge

1	杭大	12	中国银行	23	飞来峰
2	长途汽车站	13	杭州火车站	24	浙江宾馆
3	杭州客运码头	14	柳浪闻莺	25	花港公园
4	浙江大学	15	孤山	26	夕照山
5	黄龙洞	16	浙江省博物馆	27	凤凰山
6	保俶塔	17	楼外楼饭馆	28	六通宾馆
7	宝石山	18	杭州饭店	29	南高峰
8	王湖宾馆	19	岳飞墓	30	龙井
9	浙江医学院	20	北高峰	31	杭州动物园
10	华侨饭店	21	美高峰	32	六和塔
11	环湖饭店	22	灵隐寺	33	钱塘江桥

Money You can change money at the Hangzhou Shangri-La Hotel and Zhejiang Guesthouse. The Bank of China is at 140 Yan'an Beilu.

Post There is a post office in the Hangzhou Shangri-La Hotel.

Things to See
The main attraction in Hangzhou is the **Temple of Inspired Seclusion** (*língyǐn sì*). It dates from 326 AD, but has been restored 16 times since then. At the front of the temple is the Hall of the Four Main Guardians. A statue of Buddha sits in the middle on a platform flanked by two dragons. Behind the hall there's the Great Hall, where the 20-metre-high statue of Siddhartha Gautama sits, with 150 small figures behind him. To get there take bus No 7 to the terminus at the foot of the hills west of Hangzhou.

The **Peak that Flew from Afar** (*fēilái fēng*) is so named because it is identical to a mountain in India. Its sides are covered in sculptures dating from 951 AD.

Northern Peak (*běi fēng*) faces the Temple of Inspired Seclusion and is reached by a cable car. You can get a good view across the lake to the city below.

The **Mausoleum of General Yue Fei** (*yuèwáng miào*), commemorating a soldier hero, was ransacked during the Cultural Revolution but has been restored. It's in a compound surrounded by a large brick wall, just a few minutes' walk west of the Hangzhou Shangri-La Hotel.

Six Harmonies Pagoda (*liùhé tǎ*) is in the south-west of the city close to the railway bridge, which spans the Qiantang River. The pagoda was built in 970 AD as a lighthouse tower, and escaped demolition during the Cultural Revolution because of its sheer size.

West Lake (*xī hú*), upon which Hangzhou is built, is about three km long and wide, and split into sections by two causeways. In the middle of the lake are some islands; the largest is Solitary Hill, where you'll find the Provincial Museum, the Louwailou Restaurant and Zhongshan Park. There are a couple of places around the lake where you can hire paddle boats.

The interesting **Zhejiang Provincial Museum** (*zhèjiāng bówùguǎn*), on Solitary Hill Island in West Lake, features the preserved bodies of a man and a woman excavated from a tomb in Xinjiang.

Places to Stay
The *Zhejiang Guesthouse* (☎ 777988) (*zhéjiāng bīnguǎn*) at 68 Santaishan Lu is the best place to stay, though rather isolated and on the outskirts of Hangzhou. Dorm beds cost Y18, doubles from Y100. Take bus No 28 from near the long-distance bus station; get off where bus No 28 route intersects the bus No 27 route, and take bus No 27 the rest

of the way. South of the Zhejiang a bit is the similar garden-style *Liu Tong Hotel* (☎ 773376) *(liùtōng bīnguǎn)* with dorms for Y15, doubles for Y74.

The *Overseas Chinese Hotel* (☎ 23401) *(huáqiáo bīnguǎn)* on Hubin Lu has doubles for Y147. Take bus No 7 from the railway station.

Places to Eat

There's a vegetarian restaurant on You Dian Lu, just east of the intersection with Yan'an Lu. The *Louwailou (lóuwài lòu)* on Solitary Hill (Gushan) Island has good, cheap food.

Getting There & Away

Air CAAC (☎ 24259) is at 304 Tiyuchang Lu, but they refer foreigners to CITS! Useful connections include flights to Beijing, Canton, Guilin, Huangshan, Xiamen and Xi'an. There are international flights to Hong Kong.

Bus The long-distance bus station is on Hushu Nanlu just north of the intersection with Huancheng Lu. Here buses leave for Shanghai, Huangshan, Tunxi, Hefei and Tiantaishan.

Train There are trains to Fuzhou, Nanchang, Shanghai and Canton, and east to the small towns of Shaoxing and Ningbo. For trains to the north you must first go to Shanghai.

Boat You can travel by boat up the Grand Canal to Suzhou. The boat leaves from the dock near the corner of Huancheng Lu and Changzheng Lu in the northern part of town. Departures are twice daily at 5.30 am and 5.50 pm and the trip takes 12 hours.

TIANTAISHAN 天台山

One of the sacred mountains of China, Tiantaishan *(tiāntáishān)* is notable for its scenery and its lack of Chinese sightseers. The Buddhist monastery dates back to the 6th century. From Tiantaishan it's a three-km hike to Gougingsi Monastery at the foot of the mountain. There are buses available from Hangzhou, Shaoxing, Ningbo and Wenzhou.

Fujian 福建

Fujian Province *(fújiàn)* is lush and attractive, and its lively and prosperous port towns on the narrow coastal strip are open to foreigners. The rugged interior is said to be very poor, and over the centuries the Fujianese have emigrated in great numbers.

XIAMEN 厦门

Formerly called Amoy, Xiamen *(xiàmén)* is an important port on the south-east coast. European influence has been heavy and this is reflected in the interesting architecture.

Xiamen was opened to the tourist trade in 1980, and became a Special Economic Zone in 1981. Fishing boats from Taiwan do a good deal of smuggling around here, and if the trade is ever legalised Xiamen's fortunes could rise once again.

Orientation

Xiamen is connected to the mainland by a long causeway. The railway station is in the far eastern part of town and the long-distance bus station is in the north. Zhongshan Lu is the main street and starts at the pier where you board the ferry to Gulangyu Island.

Information

CITS They have a ticketing counter (☎ 22922) in the Lujiang Hotel.

CTS They have an office (☎ 25602) in the Overseas Chinese Building, 70-74 Xinhua Lu, but they speak little English. Good luck!

Public Security Bureau This is near the Overseas Chinese Building. Across from the hotel is a red-brick building – the wide footpath on the right side leads to the gateway of the office.

Money The Bank of China is at 10 Zhongshan Lu, near the Lujiang Hotel.

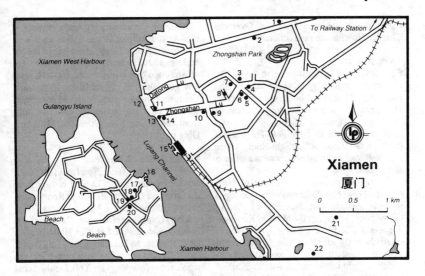

1	Long-Distance Bus Station		12	Ferry Pier (Mainland-Gulangyu)
2	Bus No 3 Stop		13	Bus No 2 Stop
3	Public Security Bureau		14	Bank of China
4	Bus No 1 Stop		15	Xiamen-Hong Kong Ferry Pier
5	Overseas Chinese Building		16	Ferry Pier (Gulangyu-Mainland)
6	Xin Qiao Hotel		17	Post Office
7	Post Office		18	Ke Le Restaurant
8	Xiaxi Market		19	Gulangyu Restaurant
9	Food Stalls		20	Gulangyu Tourist Hotel
10	Ludao Restaurant		21	Nanputuo Temple
11	Lujiang Hotel		22	Xiamen University

1	长途汽车站	10	绿岛饭店	16	渡船码头
2	第三汽车站	11	鹭江大厦		（鼓浪屿→大陆）
3	公安局外事科	12	渡船码头	17	邮局
4	第一汽车站		（大陆→鼓浪屿）	18	可乐饭馆
5	华侨旅社	13	第二汽车站	19	鼓浪屿饭馆
6	新侨饭店	14	银行	20	鼓浪屿旅行社
7	邮局	15	渡船码头	21	南普陀
8	市场		（厦门→香港）	22	厦大
9	小吃部				

Post Across the road from the Overseas Chinese Hotel is the post office.

Things to See

First developed by Westerners in the 1840s, **Gulangyu Island** *(gǔlàngyǔ)* retains the charming old colonial buildings. A ferry to Gulangyu leaves from the pier just north of the Lujiang Hotel in Xiamen. Ferries run from about 5 am to midnight. The highest point on the island is Sunlight Rock. There are steps leading to an observation platform and a great view.

Zheng Chenggong Memorial Hall *(zhèng chénggōng jìniànguǎn)* on Gulangyu is dedicated to the memory of Zheng Chenggong, known in the West as Koxinga. A general allied to the Ming dynasty, he is credited with ousting the Dutch from Taiwan. He used Xiamen as a base from which to fight the Manchu. Although allied to the imperial Ming, Zheng Chenggong is regarded as a national hero. The captions to the exhibits which commemorate the Dutch and the victory over them are all in Chinese, but the museum is worth a look. It is open daily from 8 to 11 am and 2 to 5 pm.

Nanputuo Temple *(nánpǔtuó sì)*, on the southern outskirts of Xiamen, is a Buddhist temple originally built during the Tang dynasty more than 1000 years ago. Here you can see the Maitreya, the fat buddha, in Tian Wang Hall. In front of the courtyard is the Great Heroic Treasure Hall, housing three buddhas representing Sakyamuni in his past, present and future lives. On the lotus-flower base of the buddha figure is carved the biography of Sakyamuni and the story of Xuan Zang, the monk who made the pilgrimage to India to bring back the Buddhist scriptures. The Great Compassion Hall contains four bodhisattvas, a multi-armed standing figure and three seated figures. Worshippers throw divining sticks at the statues' feet to obtain heavenly guidance.

To get to the temple take bus No 1 from the stop outside the Overseas Chinese Hotel, or bus No 2 from the intersection of Zhongshan Lu and Lujiangdao. Both stop outside the temple.

Xiamen University *(xiàmén dàxué)* is next to the temple. It was established with Overseas Chinese funds, and some of the old buildings have a certain charm. The Museum of Anthropology is on the campus – it houses a large collection of prehistoric stones and Chinese, Taiwanese and Malayan pottery, as well as clothing, sculpture and paintings from the Shang through to the Ming and Qing dynasties.

Places to Stay & Eat

Cheapest is the *Xiaxi Hotel* next to Xiaxi Market by Zhongshan Lu and not far from the Overseas Chinese Building. Rooms with shared bath are Y20.

The *Overseas Chinese Building* (☎ 25606) *(huáqiáo dàshà)* is at 70-74 Xinhua Lu at the east end of Zhongshan Lu. Triples are Y22 per person or you can book the whole room *(bāofáng)* for Y66. Doubles cost Y110. Just next door is the *Xin Qiao Hotel* (☎ 38388) where singles are Y125 to Y165, doubles Y190. Take bus No 1 from the railway station – from the bus station walk (20 minutes) or take a pedicab.

The *Lujiang Hotel* (☎ 22922) *(lùjiāng bīnguǎn)* is at 54 Lujiang Lu near the Gulangyu ferry pier. Singles cost Y145 to Y160, doubles Y160 to Y225. It's often full.

There's also the *Floating Hotel*, converted from a Danish cruise ship, moored in the harbour, with double rooms for Y12. A free launch connects the boat with the mainland, and operates three times per hour from 5 am to midnight. The ship has been highly recommended by travellers.

Xiamen has many seafood restaurants along Zhongshan Lu and its side streets. On Gulangyu, try upstairs (downstairs is dirty) at the *Gulangyu Restaurant* for seafood with generous servings.

Getting There & Away

Air There are flights to Beijing, Canton, Shanghai and Xi'an. There are international flights to Manila and Singapore, and charter flights to Hong Kong.

Bus From the long-distance bus station there

are buses which leave in the early morning (6 am onwards) for Fuzhou, Quanzhou and Shantou. There are express buses to Canton and Shenzhen.

Train The railway line from Xiamen heads north and connects the city with the main Shanghai-Canton line at Yingtan junction. There are also direct lines to Zhengzhou, Yingtan, Shanghai and Fuzhou.

Boat Boats depart for Hong Kong on Tuesdays and Fridays at 12 noon from the Passenger Station of Amoy Port Administration on Tongwen Lu.

Getting Around
Bus No 3 runs from the railway station and long-distance bus station to the Lujiang Hotel. Walking around town is certainly possible, and on Gulangyu no motor vehicles are allowed.

QUANZHOU 泉州
To the north-east of Xiamen is Quanzhou (*quánzhōu*), the site of the 14th-century port city of Zaiton. When Marco Polo came here it was one of the world's greatest ports, exporting silk, satin, sugar and spices to India, Arabia and West Asia. Although no longer so glorious, it is still a lively little town radiating an air of prosperity.

The main street of Quanzhou, Zhongshan Lu, divides the town. Most facilities are on this street.

Information
CTS They have an office (☎ 2366) – not to be confused with CITS – on the ground floor of the Overseas Chinese Hotel.

Public Security Bureau This is at 334-336 Dong Jie, east of the intersection with Zhongshan Lu.

Money The Bank of China is at the corner of Jiuyi Lu and Zhongshan Lu, just north of the Overseas Chinese Hotel.

Things to See
The **Kaiyuan Temple** (*kāiyuǎn sì*) is the main attraction of Quanzhou. Founded in the 7th century during the Tang dynasty, it eventually housed 1000 monks during the Song dynasty. Five large golden buddhas are in the main hall, behind which stands the Guanyin Temple, with its thousand-armed buddha and his guardians. In the grounds of the temple is the **Museum of Overseas Communications History** which contains the enormous hull of a Song dynasty sea-going junk. The temple is on Xi Lu in the northwest part of the town.

Places to Stay & Eat
The *Overseas Chinese Hotel* (☎ 22192) (*huáqiáo lǚxíngshè*) is close to Zhongshan Lu – a 15-minute walk from the bus station. A bed in a three-bed dorm costs Y20. Singles/doubles are Y75/100. There are plenty of great seafood restaurants near the hotel.

Getting There & Away
Air There are no flights from Quanzhou but there are plans to build an airport. At the moment, the nearest flights are from Xiamen.

Bus The long-distance bus station is in the south-eastern part of town. Buses to Xiamen take 2½ hours; there are about a dozen buses a day. Buses to Fuzhou take six hours and depart several times a day.

Train The nearest railheads are at Xiamen and Fuzhou.

Jiangxi 江西

Jiangxi (*jiāngxī*) was sparsely populated until the 8th century AD, when the Grand Canal opened it up as a trade route from Guangdong. It declined in the 19th century, with the opening of coastal ports to foreign shipping. The province was one of the most famous Communist guerrilla bases; the

Kuomintang took several years to drive them out onto the Long March to Shaanxi.

LUSHAN 庐山

Imagine a Swiss village grafted onto the side of a Chinese mountain! Lushan (*lúshān*), in the very north of Jiangxi Province, is regarded as one of the most beautiful mountains in China. The hill resort here was established by Europeans in the 19th century and features European-style hotels, churches and stone cottages. The panoramic views from the bus are spectacular – there are sheer drops to the Jiangxi plains below.

Orientation

The main hill station is at Guling, a village scattered over the mountainside. The restaurants, shops, long-distance bus station and Lushan Hotel are all within walking distance.

Information

CITS This office (☎ 2275) is at the Lushan Hotel.

Places to Stay & Eat

The *Lushan Hotel* (*lúshān bīnguǎn*), in an old colonial building, is the main tourist hotel. There are double rooms only. Walk from the bus station for 15 minutes, turn right opposite a long flight of steps, and it's 10 minutes away on the right-hand side.

The *Lulin Fandian* is by beautiful Luling Lake. There are restaurants at the hotels and along Guling's main street.

Getting There & Away

There are daily buses for Nanchang and Jiujiang, but book in advance – they are always crowded!

Getting Around

Walking is the best way to see the town; Guling is compact, and there are well-defined tracks everywhere. A bus tour goes to Jiujiang, taking in some of the sights of Lushan on the way.

Hubei 湖北

Eastern Hubei is a low plain drained by the Yangtze. To the west are mountains with small cultivated valleys, which divide Hubei from Sichuan. The province was settled by the Han Chinese 3000 years ago. In the 19th century it was the first inland province to industrialise. Today it is still one of China's most important provinces.

WUHAN 武汉

Wuhan (*wǔhàn*) is one of the largest cities in China. The terminus for Yangtze ferries from Chongqing, it is a transit point for many travellers.

Orientation

Wuhan is divided by the Yangtze River: Wuchang lies on the eastern bank, Hankou is the centre of things, while Hanyang is on the western bank, south of Hankou. The main road is Zhongshan Dadao, parallel to the Yangtze River.

Information

CITS The office (☎ 511049) is at 89 Yanjiang Dadao, near the Yangtze ferry terminal. It's not very useful for individual travellers.

Public Security Bureau The office (☎ 25129) is at 206 Shengli Jie.

Money The Bank of China is on the corner of Zhongshan Dadao and Jianghan Lu.

Things to See

Since Hankou was a foreign concession area, there are quite a few European-style buildings, particularly along Yanjiang Dadao.

Guiyuan Temple (*guīyuǎn sì*) is across the river in Hanyang. This Buddhist temple dates from the late Ming dynasty, and is slowly being restored. The chief attraction is the main hall, featuring numerous seated statues of Buddha's disciples (often in comical poses).

Wuhan's **Yangtze Bridge** (*wǔhàn*

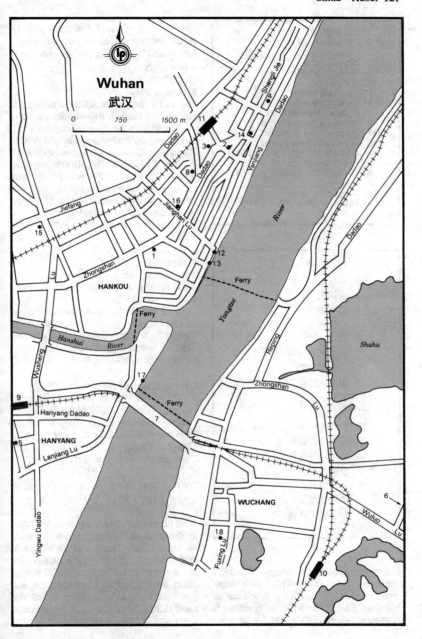

Wuhan
武汉

0   750   1500 m

HANKOU

HANYANG

WUCHANG

Shahu

Yangtze River

Hanshui River

Ferry

Ferry

Ferry

Shengli Jie

Yanjiang Dadao

Dadao

Dadao

Jiefang

Jianghan Lu

Zhongshan Lu

Wusheng

Hanyang Dadao

Lanjiang Lu

Yingwu Dadao

Fuxing Lu

Zhongshan Lu

Heping

Wuluo Lu

1	Fun Palace
2	Jianghan Hotel
3	Aiguo Hotel
4	Shengli Hotel
5	Guiyuan Temple
6	Hongshan
7	Wuchang Bridge
8	Laotongcheng Restaurant
9	Hanyang Railway Station
10	Wuchang Railway Station
11	Hankou Railway Station
12	Dock for Yangtse Ferries
13	Booking Office for Yangtse Ferries
14	Public Security Bureau
15	CAAC
16	Bank of China
17	Qing Chuan Hotel
18	Hubei Province Military Region Hotel

1	民众乐园
2	江汉饭店
3	爱国旅行社
4	胜利饭店
5	归元禅寺
6	洪山
7	武汉长江大桥
8	老通城酒楼
9	汉阳火车站
10	武昌火车站
11	汉口站
12	长航客运站
13	港务局售票处
14	公安局外事科
15	中国民航
16	中国银行
17	晴川宾馆
18	湖北省军区招待所

chángjiāng dàqiáo) was completed in 1957 and is regarded as a symbol of China's industrial progress. It connects Wuchang to Hanyang. East of the bridge in Wuchang is **Hongshan** (Red Hill), noted for its nine-storey, 1000-year-old Buddhist pagoda. **Hubei Provincial Museum** *(húběishěng bówùguǎn)* is a must if you're interested in archaeology.

Places to Stay

The tourist hotels are within walking distance of the Hankou Railway Station. Take bus No 30 from the Yangtze ferry dock.

The *Aiguo Hotel (àiguó lǚxíngshè)* is on Zhongshan Dadao, a 10-minute walk from Hankou Railway Station. Dorms are from Y10 to Y16, doubles Y40 with private bath.

The *Jianghan Hotel* (☎ 23998) *(jiānghàn fàndiàn)* at 245 Shengli Jie, a 15-minute walk from Hankou Railway Station, is nice but expensive. Double rooms with bath cost Y120.

Places to Eat

The *Laotongcheng Restaurant* (☎ 24559) *(lǎotōngchéng dòupí guǎn)* is at 1 Dazhi Lu at Zhongshan Dadao.

Or try the *Jinghan Canguan* on Chezhan Lu (the road leading south from the railway station) for Wuchang fish from Wuhan's East Lake – it has an English menu and provides enormous servings.

Getting There & Away

Air CAAC (☎ 357186) is at 209 Liji Beilu, Hankou. There are daily flights to Canton, Beijing, Nanchang, Nanjing, Shanghai, Tianjin and Xi'an. Less frequent flights to Chengdu, Chongqing, Fuzhou and Xiamen. There are charter flights to Hong Kong.

Train Wuhan is on the main Beijing to Canton railway line.

Boat Ferries travel the Yangtze from Wuhan to Shanghai via Nanjing, a trip which takes 48 hours in all. Tickets can be bought in Wuhan at the CITS office, the booking office at the river port or the tourist hotel service desks. Fourth class is a 16-person room, and you have to argue to get them to sell you these tickets. Third class is an eight-person room, and 2nd class a two-person cabin.

Yangtze Ferries from Wuhan				
destination	2nd class	3rd class	4th class	duration
Jiujiang	49	19	12	1 night
Wuhu	88	41	31	30 hours
Nanjing	101	47	35	36 hours
Shanghai	149	69	53	48 hours
Chongqing	227	105	80	5 days

The first major town in Jiangxi is Jiujiang, the departure point for nearby Lushan. The first large city in Jiangsu Province is Nanjing, followed by Zhenjiang and the port of Nantong, at the confluence of the Tongyang and Tonglu canals. The ferry proceeds down the Yangtze, then down the Huangpu to Shanghai.

Hunan 湖南

Hunan Province (húnán) – birthplace of Mao Zedong – lies on some of the richest agricultural land in China; under the Ming and Qing dynasties it was one of the empire's granaries. By the 19th century, however, it was suffering from land shortage and landlordism, and the increasingly desperate economic situation led to the massive Taiping Rebellion of the 1850s and 1860s. The Communists took refuge on the mountainous Hunan-Jiangxi border in 1927.

Hill-dwelling minorities can be found in the border regions of the province. They include the Miao, Tujia, Dong (a Thai people) and Yao – and, oddly enough, a pocket of Uigurs.

SHAOSHAN 韶山
This village is so small that it's not shown even on many large-scale maps, but Mao Zedong was born here in 1893. He was the son of poor peasants who made their way in the world to become rich peasants. Mao went to school and worked on his father's farm here. He also witnessed peasant resentment – sometimes directed against his father.

Things to See
Although Shaoshan (sháoshān) is a national shrine, a trip here is really an excuse to see some of the Chinese countryside. Shaoshan is set in a beautiful valley amidst sleepy little villages. The principal shrine is **Mao Zedong's House** (máo zédōng jiùjū).

More information about the life of Mao can be found in the **Mao Zedong Exhibition Hall** (máo zédōng zhǎnlǎnguǎn), which features paintings, photos, books and statues.

Places to Stay & Eat
The Shaoshan Guesthouse (shāoshān bīnguǎn) is a pleasant place surrounded by trees. Doubles are Y30. Meals are Y6 each, and beer Y1.30 a bottle. The guesthouse is a five-minute walk up from the bus station.

Getting There & Away
Bus There is a bus from Changsha.

Train The train from Changsha arrives at 10.42 am and departs at 4.30 pm. The trip takes about 3½ hours. A bus to the village meets the daily train from Changsha.

CHANGSHA 长沙
Changsha's prosperity is due to its position by the Xiang River on the fertile Hunan plains. Large numbers of Europeans and Americans came to live here in the early part of this century, building factories, churches and schools.

Today Changsha (chángshā) is the capital of Hunan Province and has a population of 2.6 million people.

It was here that Mao studied at the Teachers' Training College and set up the 'New People's Study Society' with a group of 70 or 80 students, among them Liu Shaoqi and Xiao Chen. It was in Changsha in 1927 that Mao organised the 'Autumn Harvest Uprising' with troops drawn from the peasantry, the Hengyang miners and rebel Kuomintang soldiers.

Orientation
Most of Changsha and most of the tourist sites are on the eastern bank of the Xiang

River. The New Railway Station is at the far east of the city, and the main road, Wuyi Lu, leads from here to the river.

Information
CITS The office (☎ 27356) is at the Lotus Hotel, 9 Wuyi Donglu. The Xiangjiang Hotel can assist with transport bookings as well.

Money The Bank of China is located next to the CAAC office on Wuyi Lu. You can also change money at the Xiangjiang Hotel, the Lotus Hotel, or the Civil Aviation Hotel.

Post & Telecommunications The post and telecommunications office is at the corner of Wuyi Lu and Cai'e Lu. There's a post office in the Xiangjiang Hotel.

Things to See
Apart from lots of Mao-bilia, it is worth seeing the mummified remains of a Han dynasty woman in the **Hunan Provincial Museum** *(húnán bówùguǎn)*. She has been excavated from a tomb 2100 years old. Other finds in the tomb include a silk painting of the underworld (on display) and silks, clothing, pottery and lacquerware.

Maoist pilgrimage spots are scattered around the city and include the **Hunan No 1 Teachers' Training College** *(dìyī shīfàn xuéxiào)*. You can get to it on bus No 1 from the Xiangjiang Guesthouse. There is also the **Museum of the Former Office of the Hunan (Xiang District) Communist Party Committee** *(zhōngguó gòngchǎndǎng zǎoqī huódòngde dìfang)*. Most of these places feature photographs and historical items from the 1920s.

Places to Stay
The *Xiangjiang Hotel* (☎ 26261) *(xiāngjiāng bīnguǎn)* is at 2 Zhongshan Lu. Take bus No 1 from the New Railway Station. Singles/doubles are Y70/100, and dormitory beds Y15 to Y27.

Very close to the railway station is the *Civil Aviation Hotel*, part of the CAAC office. A good, clean hotel with dorms for Y20 per person, doubles for Y70. Close by

at 9 Wuyi Donglu is the *Lotus Hotel* (☎ 26246) with singles/doubles for Y70/100.

Places to Eat
Hunan food is spicy. Chillies are a favourite here, as in neighbouring Sichuan. There are many small restaurants in the vicinity of the Xiangjiang Hotel. The much-touted *Youyicun (Yu Yi Tsun) Restaurant* (☎ 22797) *(yǒuyìcūn)* at 116 Zhongshan Lu, is worth trying.

Getting There & Away
Air CAAC (☎ 23820) is at 5 Wuyi Donglu near the railway station. Useful flights include those to Beijing, Canton, Chengdu, Kunming, Shanghai and Xi'an.

Bus There are three buses to Shaoshan, which leave from the long-distance bus station.

Train There are direct trains to Guilin, and Changsha is on the main Beijing-Canton railway line. The train for Shaoshan departs at 7.35 am.

Guangdong 广东

Guangdong *(guǎngdōng)* is the wealthiest and most progressive province in China. The main force behind this development is neighbouring Hong Kong from which flow investment, tourism, capitalist ideas and various other 'corrupting' influences.

SHENZHEN 深圳经济特区
Stretching from the northern border of Hong Kong, from Daya Bay (site of China's new nuclear power plant) in the east to the Pearl River in the west, is China's most important Special Economic Zone (SEZ) *(jīngjì tèqū)*. The SEZs were set up with reduced taxation schemes, low wages and operating costs to encourage investment. The Shenzhen SEZ, chosen for its proximity to Hong Kong, was established in 1979. Shenzhen *(shēnzhèn)* is reached after a quick train ride from Hong

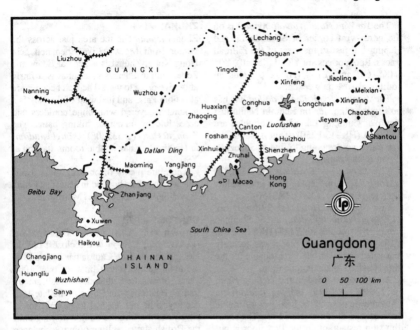

Guangdong
广东

0   50 100 km

Kong followed by a sometimes long wait in immigration queues.

Most travellers don't take any time to look around Shenzhen – a pity, even though this isn't the 'real China'. The small city of Shenzhen is a semi-successful attempt to clone Hong Kong. In the outlying areas are some luxury resort hotels catering to Hong Kongers. These are sights in themselves – equipped with discos, saunas, castles, monorails and Disneyland decor.

Orientation

A 'Tourist Service' booth near the railway station exit distributes hotel brochures and can make hotel bookings. The staff are friendly but speak little English. Many of the high-rise hotels in Shenzhen can be seen from the station.

Also next to the railway station are the taxi stand and bus terminal.

Information

CITS The office (☎ 238411) is at 2 Chuanbu Jie, Heping Lu, just north of the railway station.

Places to Stay

Shenzhen has no dormitories or dirt cheap hotels. 'Bottom-end' means any hotel costing under Y100 for a double.

The *Fenghua Hotel* (☎ 351168) *(fēnghúa jǐu diàn)* is on a small side street called Nanji Lu, but there is a large sign in English that says 'FH'. Doubles range from Y75 to Y98. It's a rather run-down place and not especially recommended.

The *Binjiang Hotel (bīnjiāng dàjǐudiàn)* on Hongling Lu looks like an American-style motel. Double rooms start at Y83 (but an absurd HK$168!), and go up to Y123 (HK$198) and Y150 (HK$300). As long as you're paying in Chinese money, it's good value.

The *Yat Wah Hotel (rìhúa bīnguǎn)* is on the north-west corner of Shennan Lu and Heping Lu, just to the west of the railroad tracks. Room prices are Y85 (HK$140), Y95 (HK$160) and Y130 (HK$210), plus an additional 10% on weekends.

The *Jinghu Hotel (jīnghú dàjiǔdiàn)* has no English sign. It's on Renmin Nanlu just south of Cunfeng Lu. Singles/doubles are Y88/170 (HK$130/250). This is about the best value you're going to find in Shenzhen if you're by yourself.

The *Shen Tieh Building (☎ 234248) (shēntiě dàxià)* on Heping Lu is good value. Double rooms are Y100 (HK$150).

The *Shenzhen Hotel (☎ 238000, fax 222284) (shēnzhèn jiǔdiàn)* at 156 Shennan Donglu has doubles for Y118 (HK$198) and Y158 (HK$258). This place was recently renovated and is certainly reasonable for the high standard of accommodation.

Also recommended is the *Heping Hotel (☎ 228151, 228149) (hépíng jiǔdiàn)* on Chuanbu Jie near CITS. Really comfortable doubles start at Y120 (HK$190). The small dim sum restaurant on the first floor is not bad at all.

The *Jing Peng Hotel (☎ 227190) (jīngpéng bīnguǎn)* is a elegant-looking place that offers good value for the money. Doubles with twin beds are Y115 (HK$170) and Y120 (HK$180). The hotel has its own billiard room, restaurant, gift shop and karaoke bar.

Getting There & Away

Bus Outside Shenzhen Railway Station you can get minibuses to Canton. There are also buses to towns on the south-east coast including Shantou, Fuzhou, Xiamen, Zhengzhou and Quanzhou.

Train There are about a dozen local trains a day between Canton and Shenzhen. Tourist-price tickets are HK$35 hard-seat, HK$65 soft-seat. The trip takes 3½ hours.

At Shenzhen you pass through Customs and catch the train to Kowloon. The border closes at 10 pm (11 pm daylight savings time).

ZHUHAI 珠海

Zhuhai *(zhūhǎi)* is the area just across the border from Macau. Like Shenzhen near Hong Kong, Zhuhai is a Special Economic Zone. Unlike Shenzhen, Zhuhai is a fairly attractive place to visit. The best beaches are at Haibin Park, and just west of the park is a mountain covered with huge boulders and accessible by numerous hiking paths. The *Zhonglü Hotel (☎ 332208) (zhōnglǚ jiǔdiàn)* in Haibin Park has double rooms starting at Y90.

There are plenty of one-day tours available which can be booked in Macau at China Travel Service in the Hotel Metropole.

CANTON 广州

Known in China as Guangzhou *(guǎngzhōu)*, Canton is the closest city to Hong Kong. In fact, Canton has been one of the main gateways to China for over 1000 years. It was here that the British set up trading relations with China in the late 18th century. Silk and tea had to be paid for in silver, and the Chinese bought nothing until the British started selling opium to balance the trade. Chinese attempts to ban the drug trade and seize the opium led to the Opium Wars.

Today five million people live in Canton, and it's the most prosperous city in China. Most travellers come here first before plunging into the heart of the People's Republic.

Orientation

Canton owes its existence to the Pearl River which flows through the city. Everything of interest to travellers is on the north bank, except for the Zhoutouzui liner terminal.

Information

CITS The office (☎ 6662447) is at 179 Huanshi Lu next to the main railway station. Foreigners must book all train tickets out of Canton at CITS.

Public Security Bureau The office (☎ 3331060) is at 863 Jiefang Beilu, opposite the road which leads up to the Zhenhai Tower.

Money It's easiest to change money at the tourist hotels. On Shamian Island, the black market is controlled by a large gang – almost without exception, every foreigner who changes money on the streets of Shamian Island gets ripped off. The only way to avoid this is to change money in some of the small shops. There are several shops on or near Shamian Island that will do this.

Post & Telecommunications Just about all the major tourist hotels have post offices where you can send letters and packets containing printed matter.

The telecommunications office is near the railway station on the south-east corner of Jiefang Beilu and Huanshi Zhonglu. The tourist hotels have fax, telex and long-distance telephone facilities. Most large hotels have cheap direct-dial service to Hong Kong.

Foreign Consulates The US Consulate (☎ 6669900, ext 1000) is in the Dongfang Hotel, on the 11th floor of the old wing. The Japanese Consulate (☎ 3338999) is in the Garden Hotel. The Thai Consulate (☎ 8886968, ext 3310) is in room 310 of the White Swan Hotel. The Polish Consulate is on Shamian Island near the White Swan Hotel – useful if you need a visa for the Trans-Siberian.

Emergency If you get sick you can go to one of the hospitals or to the medical clinic for foreigners – Guangzhou No 1 People's Hospital (☎ 3333090) *(dìyī rénmín yīyùan)*, 602 Renmin Beilu.

Dangers & Annoyances In terms of theft, Canton is the most dangerous city in China. Be especially wary of black market moneychangers – most are crooks. Thieves can be violent here – many taxi drivers have been knifed in the back. As a result, taxis have a wire screen separating rear-seat passengers from the driver – only women are allowed to sit in the front. The railway station is a haven for pickpockets, bag slashers and purse snatchers.

Things to See

The **Sun Yatsen Memorial Hall** *(sūn zhōngshān jìniàn táng)* on Dongfeng Lu was built in honour of Sun Yatsen, with donations from Overseas Chinese and from Canton citizens.

There are a number of interesting temples in Canton. The **Temple of the Six Banyan Trees** *(liù róng sì huā tǎ)* is the most significant. It was rebuilt at the end of the 10th century after being destroyed by fire. Within the temple compound is the octagonal-shaped Flower Pagoda built in the 6th century, the oldest and tallest pagoda in the city.

The **Bright Filial Piety Temple** *(guangxiào sì)* is near the Temple of the Six Banyan Trees, and was founded in the 4th century AD. Two iron pagodas at the entrance were presented to the monastery in 951 AD. In each are a thousand representations of Buddha.

The present buildings of **Five Genies Temple** *(wǔ xiān guan)* are comparatively recent. Stone tablets flanking the courtyard commemorate the various restorations the temple has undergone. The large hollow in the rock in the courtyard is said to be the impression of a genie's foot, and one of Canton's 'eight great sights'. The temple is at the back of a lane off Xianyang Lu.

Qingping Market *(qīngpíng shìchǎng)* – near the north side of Shamian Island with an entrance from Liu'ersan Lu – is one of the most interesting sights in Canton. As you wander further in, the market starts to resemble a take-away zoo featuring owls, pigeons, pangolins, dogs, rats, monkeys and raccoons.

Yuexiu Park *(yùexiù gōngyúan)* is the biggest park in Canton. It contains the Zhenhai Tower which is the only part of the city wall that remains. The tower, which provides good views, also houses the City Museum. South of the tower is Sun Yatsen's Monument, which is also good for views. The park also features a roller-coaster and three artificial lakes where boats can be hired – you have to leave a small deposit.

The **Nanyue Museum** *(nányùe wáng*

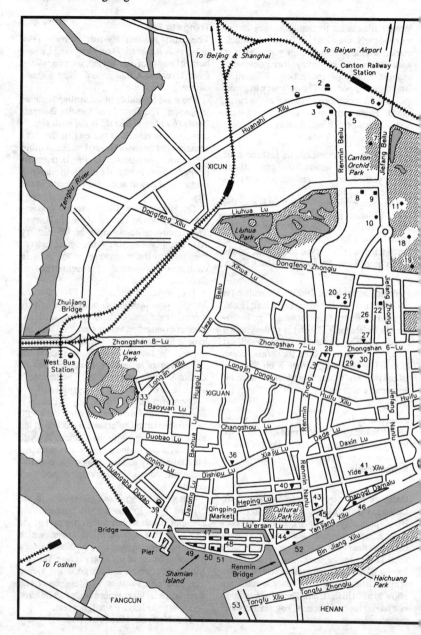

To Beijing & Shanghai
To Baiyun Airport
Canton Railway Station

Huanshi Xilu
Renmin Beilu
Jiefang Beilu
Canton Orchid Park
XICUN
Dongfeng Xilu
Zengbu River
Liuhua Lu
Liuhua Park
Dongfeng Zhonglu
Xihua Lu
Jiefang Zhong Lu
Liwan Beilu
Zhuijiang Bridge
Zhongshan 8-Lu
Zhongshan 7-Lu
Zhongshan 6-Lu
West Bus Station
Liwan Park
Longjin Xilu
Longjin Donglu
Huifu Xilu
Huifu
XIGUAN
Renmin Zhong Lu
Dade Lu
Jiefang Nanlu
Baoyuan Lu
Huagui Lu
Changshou Lu
Daxin Lu
Baohua Lu
Duobao Lu
Xiajiu Lu
Yide Xilu
Enning Lu
Dishipu Lu
Renmin Nanlu
Changdi Damalu
Heping Lu
Daxong Lu
Qingping Market
Cultural Park
Liu'ersan Lu
Yanjiang Xilu
Bridge
Shamian Island
Renmin Bridge
Bin Jiang Xilu
Pier
To Foshan
FANGCUN
Tongfu Xilu
Tongfu Zhonglu
Haichuang Park
HENAN
Huangsha Dadao

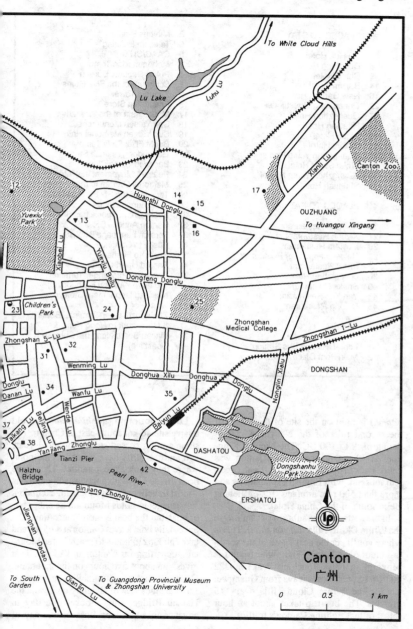

To White Cloud Hills

Lu Lake

Luhu Lu

Canton Zoo

Xianli Lu

Yuexiu Park

12

Huanshi Donglu

14
15
16

17

OUZHUANG

To Huangpu Xingang

Xiaobei Lu

Yuexiu Beilu

13

Dongfeng Donglu

25

Zhongshan Medical College

Children's Park

23

24

Zhongshan 1-Lu

DONGSHAN

Zhongshan 5-Lu

32

31

Wenming Lu

Donghua Xilu   Donghua

Nonglin Xilu

Dongshan
Dongwu

Dongwu

Dongfeng

34

Wanfu Lu

Wende Lu

Danan Lu

Donglu

35

Baiyun Lu

37

Beijing Lu

Taikang Lu

38

Yanjiang   Zhonglu

DASHATOU

Dongshanhu Park

Haizhu Bridge

Tianzi Pier

Pearl River

42

ERSHATOU

Binjiang Zhonglu

Jiangnan Dadao

Canton
广州

To South Garden

Qianjin Lu

To Guangdong Provincial Museum
& Zhongshan University

0   0.5   1 km

■ PLACES TO STAY

4	Liu Hua Hotel
8	Dongfang Hotel
9	China Hotel
14	Baiyun Hotel
16	New Garden Hotel
22	Guangdong Guesthouse
37	Guangzhou Hotel
38	Huaqiao Hotel
46	Aiqun Hotel
47	Victory Hotel
48	Guangdong Youth Hostel
49	White Swan Hotel
50	Guangzhou Youth Hostel
51	Shamian Hotel

▼ PLACES TO EAT

13	Beiyuan Restaurant
27	Xiyuan Restaurant
28	Moslem Restaurant
29	Caigenxiang (Veg) Restaurant
33	Banxi Restaurant
36	Guangzhou Restaurant
40	Snake Restaurant
43	Yan Yan Restaurant
45	Datong Restaurant

OTHER

1	Long-Distance Bus Station
2	Main Post Office
3	Minibus Station
5	Telecom Building
6	CAAC/CITS
7	Mohammedan Tomb
10	Public Security Bureau
11	Sculpture of the Five Rams
12	Zhenhai Tower
15	Friendship Store
17	Mausoleum of the 72 Martyrs
18	Sun Yatsen Monument
19	Sun Yatsen Memorial Hall
20	Bright Filial Piety Temple
21	Guangdong Antique Store
23	Buses to White Cloud Hills
24	Peasant Movement Institute
25	Memorial Garden to the Martyrs
26	Temple of the Six Banyan Trees
30	Huaisheng Mosque
31	South China Specialties Store
32	Canton Antique Store
34	Foreign Language Bookstore
35	Buses to Conghua
39	Buses to Foshan
41	Sacred Heart Church
42	Dashatou Passenger Terminal (Boats to Wuzhou & Zhaoqing)
44	Nanfang Department Store
52	No 1 Pier
53	Zhoutouzui Liner Terminal (Boats & Hovercraft to Hong Kong & Macau/Boats along the Chinese Coastline)

hànmù) is built on the site of the palace of the second ruler of the Nanyue Kingdom dating back to 100 BC. The Nanyue Kingdom is what the area around Canton was called back in the Han Dynasty. It's an excellent museum with English explanations and more than 500 rare artefacts. It's on Jiefang Beilu south of the China Hotel.

In the north-eastern suburbs of Canton are the **White Cloud Hills** (*báiyún shān*). This is where you'll get the best views of the seething metropolis below. The highest point is Moxingling (Star Touching Peak) at 382 metres. Express buses leave from Guangwei Lu for the White Cloud Hills every 15 minutes. The bus trip takes about an hour (most of that fighting Canton's traffic).

Lotus Mountain (*liánhūa shān*) is a old quarry site 46 km south-east of Canton. The stone cutting ceased several hundred years ago and the cliffs have eroded to the point where they look almost natural. They have been dressed up with pagodas and pavilions – most travellers find it a pleasant excursion. You can get to Lotus Mountain by either bus or boat, but the boat is more interesting. The once-daily boat leaves Canton at 8.45 am and takes about 2½ hours to reach Lotus Mountain, departing for Canton at 4.15 pm. That gives you about five hours on the mountain. Departures are from Tianzi Pier on Yanjiang Lu, one block east of Haizhu Square and the Haizhu Bridge. Buy a ticket one day in advance to avoid long lines on the day of

■ PLACES TO STAY	28 回民饭店	18 孙中山纪念碑
	29 菜根香素菜馆	19 孙中山纪念堂
4 流花宾馆	33 洋溪酒家	20 光孝寺
8 东方宾馆	36 广州酒家	21 广东古玩店
9 中国大酒店	40 蛇餐馆	23 开往白云山的汽车
14 白云宾馆	43 人人菜馆	24 农民运动讲习所旧址
16 花园宾馆	45 大同饭馆	25 广州起义烈士陵园
22 广东迎宾馆		26 六榕寺花塔
37 广州宾馆	OTHER	30 怀圣寺光塔
38 华侨大厦		31 华东特产商店
46 爱群大厦	1 广东省汽车客运站	32 广州古玩店
47 胜利宾馆	2 邮政总局	34 外文书店
48 广东青年招待所	3 小汽车出租点	35 开往从化的汽车
49 白天鹅宾馆	5 电信局	39 开往佛山的汽车
50 广州青年招待所	6 中国民航/国际旅行社	41 石室
51 沙面宾馆	7 穆罕默德墓	42 大沙头码头
	10 公安局	44 南方大厦
▼ PLACES TO EAT	11 五羊塑象	52 一号码头
	12 镇海楼	53 洲头嘴码头
13 北园酒家	15 友谊商店	
27 西园饭店	17 黄花岗七十二烈士墓	

departure. Buses depart from the railway station area in Canton but are no faster than the boat.

Places to Stay

Near the massive White Swan Hotel is the *Guangzhou Youth Hostel* (☎ 8884298) *(guǎngzhōu qīngnián zhāodàisǔo)* at 2 Shamian 4-Jie. Dormitory beds are Y10 to Y14 and double rooms Y40.

Also on Shamian Island is the *Guangdong Youth Hostel* (☎ 8887617) *(guǎngdōng qīngnián lǔshè)*, 26 Shamian Dajie. Dorms cost Y10 to Y14 and doubles are Y40. It's very clean and nice.

The *Shamian Hotel* (☎ 8888124) *(shāmiàn bīnguǎn)* is only about five moneychangers east of the Guangzhou

Youth Hostel on Shamian Island. Doubles start at Y87.

The *Aiqun Hotel* (☎ 6661445) *(aìqún dàjiǔdiàn)* at 113 Yanjiang Xilu (at the corner with Changdi Damalu) is right on the river front. Singles/doubles are Y70/110, a bargain for the high standard of accommodation. Some travellers have even managed to pay RMB. Take bus No 31 from the railway station; get off when you come to the river, turn left and walk up Yanjiang Lu for about 10 minutes.

The *White Palace Hotel* (☎ 8882313) *(báigōng jiǔdiàn)* is a good place to stay though the staff speak little English. It's near the river at 17 Renmin Nanlu and doubles cost Y80.

The *Guangzhou Hotel* (☎ 3338168)

(guǎngzhōu bīnguǎn) is at Haizhu (Sea Pearl) Square, east of the Aiqun Hotel. Singles/doubles are Y135/150. Bus No 29 from Huanshi Xilu near the railway station goes past the hotel. Haizhu Square is a big roundabout with a giant statue in the middle – you can't miss it.

The *Airport Hotel* (☎ 6661700) *(báiyún jīchǎng bīnguǎn)* – right next to the main terminal – is an excellent place to stay if you're catching a morning flight. In a nine-bed dorm, beds are Y20; Y35 in a three-bed dorm; Y65 for a single and Y85 for a double. All rooms are air-conditioned and reasonably clean.

Places to Eat

On Shamian Island, the *Pearl Inn (yèmíngzhū jiǔdiàn)* is just to your right as you face the Shamian Hotel on Shamian Nanjie. They have good and cheap dim sum on the ground floor restaurant. There is also a coffee shop serving Western breakfasts.

Also on Shamian Island is the *Victory Restaurant*, attached to the Victory Hotel. Prices are amazingly reasonable for such a high standard of service, but seafood is expensive. An English menu is available.

There are a couple of good places close to the river front. Foremost is the *Datong* (☎ 8888988) *(dàtóng jiǔjiā)* at 63 Yanjiang Xilu, just around the corner from Renmin Lu. The restaurant occupies all of an eight-storey building by the river and is a great place for morning dim sum.

The *Aiqun Hotel* has a fine restaurant on the 14th floor overlooking the river.

Getting There & Away

Canton is a major transport hub with connections to almost every city in China.

Air The CAAC office (☎ 662969) is at 181 Huanshi Lu, to your left as you come out of the railway station. You can also book tickets in the White Swan Hotel and China Hotel.

Canton's Baiyun Airport is in the northern suburbs, 12 km from the city centre. There are daily flights to Beijing, Guilin, Kunming, Shanghai, Nanjing, Haikou (Hainan Island) and Xi'an. There are also daily flights to Hong Kong and a few odd flights to Thailand, Singapore and Australia.

Bus The long-distance bus station is on Huanshi Xilu, a 10-minute walk west of the railway station. From there you can get buses to many places in and beyond Guangdong Province. The first major town on the route up the south-east coast is Shantou. There are also buses to Quanzhou, Xiamen and Fuzhou. West of Canton there's Zhanjiang, where you can get a bus/boat connection to Haikou on Hainan Island. There is a direct bus to Guilin, which has an overnight stop in Wuzhou. There are also around eight or nine departures a day to Gongbei, the border town with Macau.

Train The fastest express to Beijing takes about 33 hours. Tourist-price fares from Canton to Beijing are Y140 hard-seat, Y233 hard-sleeper and Y444 soft-sleeper.

The express trip to Shanghai takes about 24 hours. There is a direct train from Canton to Guilin. Alternatively, take a train to Hengyang and then change. The entire trip takes around 24 hours either way but most travellers take the boat.

Boat Canton has two main wharves – Zhoutouzui and Dashatou – and a harbour, Huangpu (formerly Whampoa), 25 km east. The ticket office for ferries and hovercraft to Hong Kong and Macau is at the gateway of Zhoutouzui.

Boats and hovercraft to Hong Kong, and boats to Hainan Island and Macau, leave from Zhoutouzui on the south side of the Pearl River.

Boats to Wuzhou leave from Dashatou on Yanjiang Donglu, in eastern Canton. From Wuzhou you can continue by bus to Yangshuo or Guilin. This is a very popular route.

Getting Around

Bus Good bus maps in Chinese are sold by hawkers outside the railway station and at most tourist hotel bookshops. Bus No 31 runs along Hongde Lu, across Renmin Bridge and straight up Renmin Lu to the main railway station.

Bus No 30 runs from the main railway station, passing both the Baiyun Hotel and the New Garden Hotel.

Bus No 5 takes a route similar to bus No 31, but goes along Liu'ersan Lu on the north side of the canal which separates the city from Shamian Island. Get off here and walk across the small bridge to the island.

Bicycle There is a bicycle rental on Shamian Island directly across the street from the Guangzhou Youth Hostel.

FOSHAN 佛山

Foshan *(fóshān)* is worth a day trip if you have the time – it's just 28 km south-west of Canton. It's been a centre for handicrafts since the 10th century, and Foshan paper-cuts are sold throughout China.

Orientation
The railway starts in Canton, passes through Foshan and heads west about 60 km to Hekou.

The first stop for the bus is Foshan Railway Station, after which it crosses the narrow Fen River and stops at the long-distance bus station a few minutes down the road.

Information
CITS The office is at 64 Zumiao Lu (☎ 87923 or 85775).

Things to See
Originally built in the 11th century, the **Ancestor Temple** *(zǔ miào)* is at the southern end of Zumiao Lu. After being destroyed by fire it was rebuilt at the end of the 13th century by the Ming emperor Hong Wu, who converted it into a Taoist temple. The main hall contains a statue of a god known as Beidi (the Northern Emperor) as well as an interesting collection of ornate weapons used on ceremonial occasions during imperial days. The **Foshan Museum** is in the temple grounds, as is the Foshan Antique Store. The

temple is open daily from 8.30 am to 4.30 pm.

Zhongshan Park is on the north side of the Fen River and is a good place to relax.

Places to Stay
The *Pearl River Hotel* (☎ 287512) *(zhūjiāng dà jiǔdiàn)* is on Chenren Lu. Double rooms begin at Y45. Around the corner is the *Overseas Chinese Building (húaqiáo dàxià)* (☎ 223828), 14 Zumiao Lu, where singles/doubles are Y75/100. Just across the street is the *Rotating Palace Hotel* (☎ 85622) *(xúangōng jiǔdiàn)* where doubles start at Y130.

Places to Eat
On Zumiao Lu near the Ancestor Temple are two good dim sum places, the plebeian *Rose* and its classier cousin, *Fok Lam*. There are also several decent pastry shops in this vicinity.

Getting There & Away
The bus for Canton leaves from the Foshan Bus Terminal and there are also frequent private minibuses.

SHANTOU 汕头

Shantou *(shāntóu)* is the chief port of eastern Guangdong Province and now one of China's Special Economic Zones. It is a rather colourful and lively place. Shantou is the first major stop on the long haul along the coast road from Canton to Fujian. Shantou lies on a peninsula separated from the mainland in the west and north by a river and canals.

Information
CITS The office (☎ 235226) is in the Peninsula Hotel on Jinsha Lu. They sell bus tickets to Canton and Shenzhen, and boat tickets to Canton.

Public Security Bureau This is on Yuejin Lu, near the corner with Nanmai Lu.

Money The Bank of China is on Jinsha Donglu.

Places to Stay

The *Overseas Chinese Hotel (huáqiáo dàshà)* is on Shanzhang Lu; it has no single rooms, doubles are Y40 and dorm beds Y12. To get there take bus No 3 from the traffic circle left of the long-distance bus station, and get off at the stop outside the CAAC office.

The *Swatow Peninsula Hotel* (☎ 230046) *(bàndǎo bīnguǎn)* on Jinsha Lu is around the corner from Shanzhang Lu – no relation to the Hong Kong Peninsula but it's a very civilised place; doubles cost Y30 to Y40, 'standard' rooms are Y50 to Y84 and 'superior' rooms go for Y116 to Y180.

Places to Eat

The best places to eat in Shantou are the street markets. 'Food Street' is a small street near the Overseas Chinese Hotel which has many evening seafood stalls.

Getting There & Away

Air CAAC (☎ 251915) is at 46 Shanzhang Lu. There are daily flights to Canton and less frequent flights to Beijing, Kunming and Shanghai. There are international flights to Bangkok and charters to Hong Kong.

Bus From the long-distance bus station there are daily buses to Canton, Shenzhen, Chaozhou and Xiamen.

Boat There are boats to Canton and Hong Kong.

ZHANJIANG 湛江

Zhanjiang *(zhànjiāng)* is the largest Chinese port west of Canton, and a naval base and part of China's southern defences against the Vietnamese. The trip from Canton is spectacular, but Zhanjiang itself is rather drab. You are most likely to come to Zhanjiang if you're on your way from Canton or Nanning to Hainan Island.

Places to Stay

The *Canton Bay Overseas Chinese Hotel* (☎ 224996) is in the southern part of town at 22 Renmin Dadao. Double rooms start at Y70.

The *Haibin Hotel* (☎ 223555) *(hǎibīn bīnguǎn)*, 32 Haibin 2-Lu is a Hong Kong-China joint venture on the southern outskirts of Zhanjiang. Double rooms are Y120 in the new wing and Y82 in the old wing.

Getting There & Away

Air There are daily flights from Zhanjiang to Canton. There are three charter flights weekly to Hong Kong.

Bus There are buses to Canton from both the north and south bus stations. The trip takes about 13½ hours.

Train From Zhanjiang South Railway Station trains depart for Guilin (a 13-hour trip), and for Nanning (9½ hours).

Boat A combined bus-and-boat trip leaves from Zhanjiang to a port on the Leizhou Peninsula and to Hainan Island. There's also a fast vessel (resembling a Hong Kong jetfoil) from Leizhou Peninsula to Hainan Island which takes 45 minutes.

Hainan 海南岛

China's tropical island province, Hainan *(hǎinán dǎo)* is also a Special Economic Zone. The beaches on the southern shore of the island are a popular winter retreat for busy Hong Kongers, weary travellers and cadres attending 'meetings' at government expense.

HAIKOU 海口

The capital of Hainan Island, Haikou *(hǎikǒu)* is split into three sections: the port area in the west, the centre in the north, and the urban area in the south.

Information

CITS The office (☎ 72187) is in Room 301 of the HTSO Building, Sanjiachi. CTS is in the Overseas Chinese Hotel.

Money The Bank of China (☎ 22851) is at 16 Datong Lu.

Places to Stay

The *Overseas Chinese Hotel* (*húaqiáo dàxià*) is at 17 Datong Lu near the Bank of China. Double rooms are Y36, dorm beds are Y10.

Up-market accommodation is at the *Haikou Hotel* (☎ 72266), 4 Haifu Dadao.

Places to Eat

The *Pau Tau Restaurant* (*băodăo cāntīng*) sells Chinese, Malaysian and Western food – turn left outside the gates of the Overseas Chinese Hotel and walk 50 metres towards the park.

The *Cafe de Rosa* is a fast food restaurant which appears to be a Hong Kong joint venture. Turn right out of the Overseas Chinese Hotel and walk down the road until you reach the traffic circle marked by a small obelisk. Turn right again and you're there.

Getting There & Away

Air CITS operates an airline ticket office (☎ 72266) in the Haikou Hotel. There are daily flights to Canton and Shanghai. There are less frequent flights to Beijing, Chengdu and Kunming. CITS sells tickets on charter flights to Hong Kong.

Bus There are buses to Sanya and other points on the island.

Boat Boats leave Haikou at 11.30 am and 12.30 and 1.30 pm for the 1½-hour trip to the Leizhou Peninsula, where you catch a connecting bus to Zhanjiang. There are direct boats to Canton and Hong Kong. Tickets can be bought from the booking office on the ground floor of the Overseas Chinese Hotel.

SANYA 三亚

Sanya (*sānyă*) is a busy port and tourist resort on the southern tip of Hainan Island. It's one of the few places in China that has a tropical climate. The most popular beaches are at Dadonghai (*dàdōnghăi*), Luhuitou

Peninsula (*lùhuítóu*) and Tianya Haijiao (*tiānyà hăijiăo*).

Places to Stay & Eat

The *Luhuitou Hotel* (*lùhuítóu lŭguăn*) is three km out of town on its own peninsula. Room rates range from Y7 to Y20 per person. The more expensive rooms have bath, air-con and separate sitting room. The restaurant at the hotel is excellent. Various set meals are available from Y3 to Y5.

Just outside the back entrance of the Luhuitou Hotel is *Charlie's Kangaroo Club* which offers lobster, crab, prawns and squid. It's best to order seafood in advance; it is then weighed in the kitchen and cooked as you wish.

Getting There & Away

Air There are four flights a week to Canton via Haikou and charter flights to Hong Kong. Book plane tickets at the Dadonghai Binguan reception desk.

Bus From Sanya Bus Station there are frequent buses and minibuses to most parts of Hainan.

Boat Boats leave Sanya twice a month for Hong Kong. Prices range from Y65 to Y148. There is a weekly boat connection between Sanya and Canton. Buy tickets from the ticket office close to the harbour.

Guangxi 广西

Guangxi Province (*guăngxī*) was first occupied by the Han Chinese in 214 BC, but it was never firmly under Chinese control. The east and south were ruled directly, but in the west there was a system of indirect rule through chieftains of the aboriginal Zhuang people. There was continuous trouble with the hill tribes.

The province has always been comparatively poor. It's famous for its bizarre landscape. The largest minority – the Zhuang – is virtually indistinguishable from the Han

Chinese, but the province is also home to smaller numbers of the Dong, Maonan, Mulao, Gin and Yi peoples.

WUZHOU 梧州

Wuzhou *(wúzhōu)* is basically just a stopover between Canton and Guilin/Yangshuo. Its only claim to fame is its large snake depositories. A million snakes a year are sent here from all over China for transport to the restaurants of Hong Kong and Macau.

Places to Stay

Along Xijiang Yilu, which parallels the Xijiang River waterfront, are several inexpensive, adequate hotels.

The gloomy *Xinxi Hotel (xīnxī fàndiàn)*, two blocks west of the bus station on Xijiang Yilu, has somewhat dingy rooms for Y15 to Y25. A bit farther west along Xijiang Yilu on the right is the better *Yuan Jiang Hotel (yuānjiāng fàndiàn)*, with basic doubles for Y10 to Y25 per person with private bath, Y8 in a triple with communal bath.

In the opposite direction on Xijiang Lu, east from the bus station/dock area, is the somewhat nicer *Baiyun (White Cloud) Hotel* (☎ 26683) *(báiyún fàndiàn)*, where triples are Y58, doubles Y70 to Y120.

Alternatively, there's the *Hebin Hotel (hébīn fàndiàn)*, across the Gui River near the bridge. Doubles cost around Y50 a night, but it's a bit of a concrete hulk.

Getting There & Away

From Wuzhou's long-distance bus station there are two buses a day to Yangshuo and Guilin, plus daily buses to Nanning and Canton.

GUILIN 桂林

One of the great drawcards of China and the No 1 attraction of Guangxi Province is Guilin *(guìlín)*. It is famous for its landscape of high karsts (limestone peaks).

The town of Guilin is surrounded by huge limestone pinnacles jutting out of the rice fields. There are lots of travellers' hangouts, coffee shops and bicycle rental places.

Travellers' coffee shops, bicycle rentals, a substantial black market and one or two fledgling discount-tour-ticket operators got off to an early start here. Guilin was, and still is, a great place to learn about capitalism!

If Guilin is too crowded you can break away to Yangshuo – a couple of hours down the Li River – and enjoy similar scenery without the tourist hype.

Orientation

Most of Guilin lies on the west bank of the Li River and the main road, Zhongshan Lu, runs parallel to the river from Guilin South Railway Station.

Information

CITS The office (☎ 2648) is at 14 Ronghu Beilu on the northern bank of Banyan Lake.

Public Security Bureau This office (☎ 3202) is on Sanduo Lu which runs west off Zhongshan Lu; it is open daily from 8 am to 5 pm.

Money All tourist hotels change money. The Bank of China is on Jiefang Lu.

Post & Telecommunications The Post & Telecommunications Building is on Zhongshan Lu. Another post and telecommunications office is by the large square in front of the railway station. Some large hotels also have post offices.

Things to See

In the centre of town is **Duxiu Feng** (Solitary Beauty) *(dúxiùfēng)*, a 152-metre-high pinnacle. At its foot is the gate of a palace built in the 14th century. Bus Nos 1 and 2 from the Guilin South Railway Station go past the peak.

The best scenery lies outside the town, and good views of the area can be seen from the top of the Li River Hotel.

Fubo Hill (Whirlpool Hill) *(fúbōshān)*, on the west bank of the nearby river, offers a good view and has two caves worth seeing. **Huanzhu Dong** (Returned Pearl Cave) takes its name from a local legend, and **Qianfo Dong** (Thousand Buddhas Cave) houses over 300 statues dating back to the Tang and Song dynasties. Bus No 2 takes you there.

North of Solitary Beauty is **Diecai Hill** (Folded Brocade Hill) *(diécǎishān)*. Climb the stone pathway which takes you through the Wind Cave, with walls decked with inscriptions and Buddhist sculptures. Bus No 1 runs past the hill.

Ludi Yan (Reed Flute Cave) *(lúdíyán)* has some extraordinary scenery. The grottoes were once used as air-raid shelters – one large chamber, the Crystal Palace of the Dragon King, can hold about 1000 people. Take bus No 3 from the railway station. Reed Flute Cave is the last stop.

Places to Stay

Public Security requires foreigners to stay at 'one-star' hotels or higher, which means you have to pay more. Close to the Guilin South Railway Station is the *Hidden Hill Hotel (yǐnshān fàndiàn)*. Hidden Hill charges Y15 per person in a triple, Y20 to Y25 for a single room and Y35 to Y40 for a double, all with private bath. The place is becoming run-down and there is speculation it will be placed off limits to foreigners.

The *Hubin Hotel (húbīn fàndiàn)*, on Ronghu Beilu facing Banyan Lake, is in a similar position to the Hidden Hill – just hanging on to its licence and charging Y30 to Y50 per room. The *Rongshuluo Hotel*, just round the corner from CITS, has similarly priced rooms. Yet a fourth in the 'one-star' category is the *South Hotel (nánfāng jiǔdiàn)* on Wu Mei Lu, just off Zhongshan Lu. Same rates, same conditions.

In the 'two-star' category you have to pay at least Y60 to Y80, often double that. One such place is the *Taihe Hotel* (☎ 33504) *(tàihé fàndiàn)*, next to the long-distance bus station on Zhongshan Nanlu.

The *Osmanthus Hotel (dānguì fàndiàn)*, just before the first bridge on Zhongshan Lu, has doubles from Y65 to Y99 in the old wing, Y180 in the new 'international' wing. The *Yu Gui Hotel (yùguì fàndiàn)* on Nanhuan Lu near the Li River costs Y80 for a double.

The *Grand Hotel* (☎ 335831) *(jǐnguì fàndiàn)*, 15 Zhishan Lu, has rooms for Y70 to Y100 and is good value for the relatively high standard of accommodation. Another good deal is the *Guilin Overseas Chinese Mansion* (☎ 33573) *(guìlín huáqiáo dàshà)* at 29 Zhongshan Nanlu, a few minutes south of the railway station. Doubles with shared bath and fan are only Y38, more luxurious doubles with air-con, hot water, phone and TV are Y70. Even better doubles/triples cost Y112/141.

Places to Eat

The food in Guilin is basically Cantonese, serving traditional delicacies such as snake soup, wild-cat and bamboo-rat dishes, not to mention anteaters, owls and other endangered species. Introduce yourself to your dinner at the cages outside the restaurant before you go in. Generally the most exotic stuff you should come across is eels, catfish, pigeons, dog, rat, snake, monkey, bear and pangolins (a Chinese armadillo).

Beware of overcharging! Settle on the price before you eat or be prepared for indigestion later.

There are numerous cheap restaurants along Zhongshan Lu and Zhishan Lu. Just north of the Osmanthus Hotel on Zhongshan Lu is *Beer Street*, a half-indoor, half-outdoor place with a good variety of Chinese dishes and cold beer at fair prices.

The Guilin Overseas Chinese Mansion has a good, reasonably priced coffee shop, and just next door is a small restaurant with cheap Western breakfasts. The Chinese restaurant in the Grand Hotel has excellent dim sum.

Getting There & Away

Air Flying isn't a bad idea as train and bus connections are not very good. The CAAC office (☎ 3063) is at 144 Zhongshan Lu. Useful air connections include those to Beijing, Canton, Chengdu, Kunming, Shanghai and Xi'an.

Bus The long-distance bus station is on Zhongshan Lu near the South Railway Station. There are a dozen buses daily from

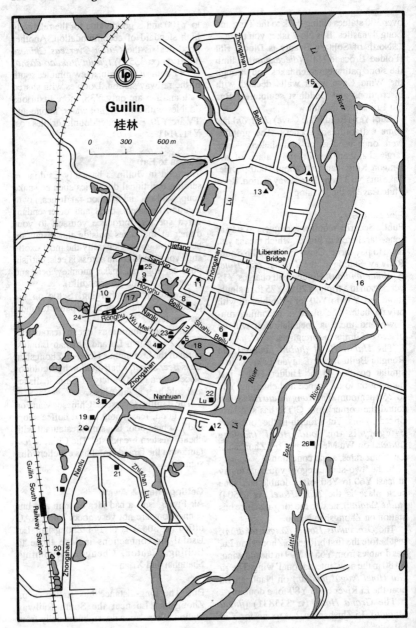

Guilin
桂林

0   300   600 m

1	Hidden Hill Hotel
2	Long-Distance Bus Station
3	Osmanthus Hotel
4	South Hotel
5	CAAC
6	Li River Hotel
7	Pier for Tour-Boats down the Li River
8	Hubin Hotel
9	CITS
10	Ronghu Hotel
11	Public Security Bureau
12	Elephant Trunk Hill
13	Solitary Beauty Peak
14	Whirlpool Hill
15	Folded Brocade Hill
16	Seven Star Park
17	Banyan Lake
18	Fir Lake
19	Taihe Hotel
20	Guilin Overseas Chinese Mansion
21	Grand Hotel
22	Yu Gui Hotel
23	Post Office
24	Holiday Inn Guilin (North Side of Ronghu Nanlu)
25	Rongshuluo Hotel
26	Guishan Hotel

1	隐山饭店
2	长途汽车站
3	丹桂饭店
4	南方酒店
5	中国民用航空总局
6	漓江饭店
7	游船码头
8	湖宾饭店
9	旅行社
10	榕湖饭店
11	公安局
12	象鼻山
13	独秀峰
14	伏波山
15	叠采山
16	七星山
17	榕湖
18	杉湖
19	大喜宾馆
20	桂林华侨大厦
21	锦桂饭店
22	Yu Gui Hotel
23	邮局
24	假日桂宾馆
25	Rongshuluo Hotel
26	桂山酒店

Guilin to Yangshuo, and to Wuzhou where you can pick up a boat or bus to Canton.

Daily buses to Canton take two days with an overnight stopover in Wuzhou.

Train There are useful train connections to Guilin, but some tend to involve hauls in incredibly crowded carriages. Guilin Railway Station has a separate ticket office for foreigners, which means you'll have to pay tourist prices.

Boat There is a boat trip from Guilin down the Li River to Yangshuo, but tickets cost an outrageous Y132 return. There is a bus/boat combination ticket which takes you by bus to Wuzhou and then by boat to Canton.

Getting Around
Bicycles are definitely the best way to get around Guilin. Just look around Zhongshan Lu for bike-hire shop signs; most of them charge between Y0.50 and Y0.60 an hour.

YANGSHUO 阳朔
Yangshuo (*yángshuò*) is a tiny town on the west bank of the Li River, 80 km south of Guilin. You can explore the limestone peaks and small villages from Yangshuo and avoid the tourist rush-hour at Guilin.

Information
CITS The office (☎ 2256) is on the grounds of the Yangshuo Hotel. They have some very useful maps.

Money The Bank of China is at 38 Xi Jie.

Things To See
The **Li River**, which connects Guilin to Yangshuo, has some spectacular scenery and is one of the area's main tourist attractions. The river trip takes six hours and most people find it drags towards the end. There are a couple of boats a day to Fuli from Yangshuo (Y8) – you can take a bicycle and pedal back.

Green Lotus Peak (bìlián fēng) is the main peak in Yangshuo and stands next to the Li River in the south-eastern corner of town.

Moon Hill (yuèliangshān), south of the Jingbao River, just west of the highway towards Guilin, is a limestone pinnacle with a moon-shaped hole in the centre. Cycle down the main road out of town towards the river and turn right on the road before you actually reach the river, then continue for about 50 minutes.

Places to Stay
Only four hotels in town accept foreigners. Cheapest is the *Xilang Shan Hotel (xīláng-shān fàndiàn)* where beds in a three or four-bed room are Y8; simple doubles with shared bath are Y14. Also basic is the *Zhu Yang Hotel (zhūyáng fàndiàn)* where dorm beds/doubles are Y10/25.

The *Sihai Hotel (sìhǎi fàndiàn)* is on Xi Jie in the town centre and has beds for Y10 per person.

The *Yangshuo Hotel (yángshuò fàndiàn)* has singles/doubles with attached bathroom for Y25/50. Beds for Y10 per person in a triple are possible.

Getting There & Away
Bus There are over a dozen buses daily to and from Guilin; the first departs Yangshuo about 8 am and the last about 6.30 pm. The fare is Y2 to Y4.

Boat You can bus to Wuzhou and then take a boat to Canton.

Getting Around
Bicycle The town itself is small enough to walk around, but hire a bicycle to go further afield. Just look for rows of bikes and signs. The charge is about Y2 per day.

Boat CITS has half-day and full-day river trips for Y5 to Y12. Check signs near the boat dock to see what's available.

Guizhou 贵州

Guizhou *(guìzhōu)* has always been one of the most backward and sparsely populated provinces of China. Some development took place during the war with Japan, when the Kuomintang retreated to the south-west; and the building of railways has improved communications under Communism, but the province remains poor.

About 75% of the population is Han and the rest a flamboyant mixture of minorities. Between them they celebrate nearly 1000 festivals a year. The province's most famous export is the fiery Maotai liquor.

GUIYANG 贵阳
Guiyang *(guìyáng)* is the provincial capital, and the only reason to come here is to change trains or visit Huangguoshu Falls.

Places to Stay & Eat
The *Dujuan Hotel (dùjuān fàndiàn)* between Yan'an Lu and Huancheng Lu is very close to the bus station and has dormitories for Y10 and doubles for Y40. The *Jinqiao Hotel (☎ 25872) (jīnqiǎo bīnguǎn)* at 34 Ruijin Zhonglu (on the bus No 1 route) offers doubles for Y80. At the north end of town is the *Yunyan Hotel (☎ 23324) (yúnyán bīnguǎn)*, 68 Beijing Lu, with rooms from Y50 to Y100.

Getting There & Away
Bus Buses to Huangguoshu Falls (Anshun) depart from the long-distance bus station in the north-west of the city. A bus (usually bus No 103) leaves Guiyang at 7 am.

Train Direct trains run to Kunming, Guilin, Chongqing and Nanning.

HUANGGUOSHU FALLS
黄果树大瀑布

Huangguoshu Falls *(huángguǒshù dàpùbù)*, 155 km west of Guiyang, is China's premier cataract. About 50 metres wide, it has a 70-metre drop, and hiking nearby is superb. At the edge of the falls is the Water Curtain Cave where you can view the rushing water from the inside of the waterfall. One km above Huangguoshu Falls in this huge falls, karst and cave area, is Doupo (the Steep Slope Falls), while eight km below Huangguoshu is the Star Bridge Falls. In all there are about 18 falls, four subterranean rivers and 100 caves in the area.

The region is also homeland of the Bouyei, the 'aboriginals of Guizhou'. Of Thai origin, the Bouyei are related to the Zhuang of Guangxi.

There are food stalls at the bus park near the falls, and the *Huangguoshu Guesthouse (huángguǒshù bīnguǎn)* is also nearby. Clean rooms with bathrooms start at Y20 per person and set meals are available for Y4. Just before the bridge on the way into town from Anshun is the *Tianxing Hotel* with beds for Y10 per person.

ANSHUN 安顺

Once an opium-trading centre, Anshun *(ānshùn)* remains the commercial hub of western Guizhou and is now known for its batiks. The town lies on the Guiyang-Kunming railway line, a two-hour ride from Guiyang, and is probably the best place to stop en route to Huangguoshu Falls.

Places to Stay & Eat

Near the bus station are several hotels. The *Xixiushan Hotel (xīxiushān bīnguǎn)* opposite the station has dorm beds (expect to fight for them) but also has doubles for Y40. The *Minzu Hotel (mínzú fàndiàn)* on Tashan Donglu (east side of town) has doubles for Y40 to Y50. The *Hongshan Hotel (☎ 23454) (hóngshān bīnguǎn)*, 39 Baihong Lu, is the up-market place and home of CITS, but is inconveniently located three km from the railway station. The hotel minibus charges Y5 for the run to the station.

Getting There & Away

Buses depart at 7.40 am and noon, and leave the Falls at 10.30 am and 2, 3, 4 and 4.30 pm.

Yunnan 云南

Geographically, Yunnan *(yúnnán)* is the most varied of all China's provinces, with terrain ranging from tropical rainforest to icy Tibetan highlands. It is the home of a third of all China's ethnic minorities, and it harbours half of all China's plant and animal species.

After 15 centuries of resistance to northern rule, Yunnan was integrated into the empire in the mid-13th century. For many years, however, it continued to be an isolated frontier region, with scattered Chinese garrisons and valley settlements. Its chief attraction is those pockets that have successfully resisted Chinese influence and retain their strong local identities.

KUNMING 昆明

In the tropics but at 1890 metres above sea level, the city has a mild climate all year round. Kunming *(kūnmíng)* is the provincial capital and has fine scenery, but it's also the starting point for fascinating trips further afield.

Information

CITS You'll find them (☎ 23922) on the ground floor of the Kunming Hotel and you can buy railway tickets here. About four days' notice is generally required. Otherwise try to buy a ticket the night before departure at the railway station.

Public Security Bureau This is at 525 Beijing Lu. It's a tiny office with a small plaque in English on the wall outside.

Post The main post office is on the east side of Beijing Lu between Tuodong Lu and Huancheng Nanlu.

Emergency The Yan'an Hospital *(yán'ān*

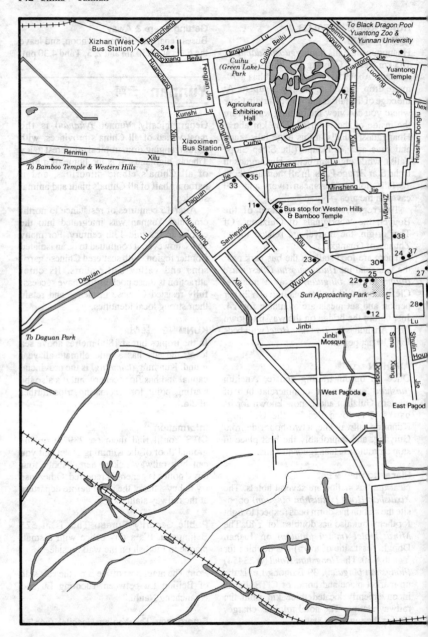

To Black Dragon Pool
Yuantong Zoo &
Yunnan University

Beimen Lu
Qingyun Jie
Cuihu Beilu
Yuantong Jie
Yuantong Temple
Yuantong Jie
Luofeng Jie
Jiexi

Xizhan (West
Bus Station)
34

Huancheng
Qingyun Lu
Cuihu Beilu
Qingyun Jie

Yuanfeng
Yuantong Temple

Fenglian Jie
Kunshi Lu
Dongfeng
Beilu
Loaoxiang Beilu
Huancheng

Cuihu
(Green Lake)
Park

Huashan
17

Huashan Donglu

Agricultural
Exhibition
Hall

Nanlu
Xilu

Xiaoximen
Bus Station

Cuihu

Wucheng

Renmin   Xilu
To Bamboo Temple & Western Hills

Wucheng Lu
Wuyi
Lu

Minsheng Jie

Zhengyi Lu

35
33

Daguan Lu
11

2   Bus stop for Western Hills
& Bamboo Temple

38

Sanheying
Xilu

24   37
30

Huancheng

Daguan Lu

23
22   6
25

27

To Daguan Park

Wuyi Lu

Sun Approaching Park
Lu

28

12

Jinbi

Jinbi
Mosque

Sima
Xiang

Shulin
Hou

Dongsi Jie

West Pagoda

East Pagod

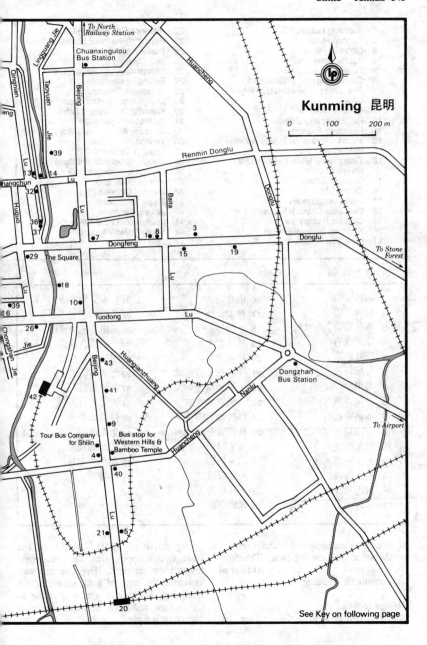

Kunming 昆明

0   100   200 m

1	Kunming Hotel/CITS	22	Advance Rail Booking Office
2	Yunnan Hotel	23	Kunming Provincial Museum
3	Camellia Hotel	24	Poster Shop
4	Kunhu Hotel	25	Tour Operators
5	Three Leaves Hotel	26	Guanshengyuan Restaurant
6	Chuncheng Hotel/Restaurant	27	Beijing Restaurant
7	Post Office & Telecom Building	28	Chuanwei Restaurant
8	CAAC	29	Gongnongbing Restaurant
9	Dianchi Cinema	30	Kunming Department Store
10	Public Security Bureau	31	Yunnan Antique Store
11	Hongxing Theatre	32	Kunming Arts & Crafts Store
12	Yunnan Across the Bridge Noodles Restaurant	33	Yunnan Arts & Crafts Store
13	Yingjianglou Muslim Restaurant	34	Zhengyi Department Store
14	Riverside Cafe	35	Dongfeng Department Store
15	Cooking School	36	Foreign Languages Bookstore
16	Coffee Shop	37	Xinhua Bookstore
17	Cuihu Guesthouse	38	Zhengyi Chinese Pharmacy
18	Overseas Chinese Restaurant	39	Three Teahouses
19	Olympic Restaurant	40	Jinlong Fandian
20	Kunming Railway Station	41	International Post Office
21	Main Bus Station	42	South Railway Station
		43	Liu's Cafe

1	昆明饭店	16	咖啡店	31	云南文物商店
2	云南饭店	17	翠湖宾馆	32	昆明工艺美术服务部
3	茶花宾馆	18	华侨饭店	33	云南工艺美术服务部
4	昆湖饭店	19	奥林匹克饭店	34	三招百货商店
5	三叶饭店	20	昆明火车站	35	东风百货商店
6	春城饭店	21	昆明汽车客运站	36	外文书店
7	邮电局	22	火车售票处	37	新华书店
8	中国民航	23	云南省博物馆	38	正义中药店
9	滇池电影院	24	广告画商店	39	桃源街茶馆
10	公安局外事科	25	旅游服务处	40	金龙饭店
11	红星剧院	26	冠生园饭店	41	国际邮局
12	云南过桥米线	27	北京饭店	42	明南火车站
13	映江楼饭店	28	川味饭店	43	咖啡馆
14	河边的饭店	29	工农兵饭店		
15	学厨饭店	30	百货商店		

yīyùan) is on Jiaosanqiao Lu, about one km north-east of the Kunming Hotel. The clinic for foreigners (☎ 2184) is on the 1st floor of the outpatients' building.

Things to See

Kunming is a great place for walking. Try going north along Huguo Lu to the Changchun shopping area. Then head west towards the teahouse. Here you can start exploring the cobbled back streets of old Kunming. Eventually you may come to Cuihu Park, and from there continue on to Yuantong Temple.

Yuantong Temple *(yuántōng sì)*, the largest Buddhist complex in Kunming, is to the north-west of the Kunming Hotel. It is more than 1000 years old and has been renovated many times.

Kunming Provincial Museum *(kūnmíng bówùguǎn)* on Wuyi Lu houses an exhibition on China's minority groups, as well as a collection of artefacts from the tomb excavations near Lake Dian.

The ramshackle 400-year-old **Ancient Mosque** *(qīngzhēn sì)* in the city centre was turned into a factory during the Cultural Revolution. It was reopened in 1977. A dozen households still live in its courtyard, and it's in need of repair.

The **Golden Temple** *(jīndiàn)* is seven km north-east of Kunming and dates from the Ming dynasty. It was the summer residence of General Wu Sangui, the rebel warlord who turned against the Manchu. In the courtyard are ancient camellia trees. Take bus Nos 3 or 23 to the Chuangxingulou terminal, and change to bus No 10 for the temple.

The **Bamboo Temple** *(qióngzhú sì)* is 12 km north-west of Kunming and dates from the Tang dynasty. Burned down and rebuilt in the 15th century, it was restored from 1883 to 1890 when the abbot employed the master Sichuan sculptor Li Guangxiu and his apprentices to fashion 500 arhats. The sculptures are so vivid and accurate that they could serve as an anthropological record of the time. The easiest way to get there is to take an express bus from the Yunnan Hotel, directly to the temple. From the Kunming Hotel, take bus No 5 to Xizhan (West Bus Station) where there's a direct bus to the temple.

Lake Dian *(diānchí)*, to the south of Kunming, is dotted with settlements, farms and fisheries. The western side is hilly and the eastern is flat. The lake covers 300 sq km and is 150 km in circumference and 40 km long. *Fanchuan*, pirate-sized junks, ply the waters.

At the northernmost tip of Lake Dian is the 60-hectare **Daguan Park**, three km south-west of the city. The Daguan Tower provides a vantage point over Lake Dian. At the north-eastern end of the park is a dock where boats leave at 8 am for Haikou. The one-way trip takes four hours. From Haikou you can catch bus No 15 back to the Xiaoximen terminal in Kunming.

The **Western Hills** *(xīshān)* spread out across a long wedge of parkland on the western side of Lake Dian. From Kunming to the Western Hills, the most convenient connection is the express bus which runs direct to Sanqingge Temple, which is high among the peaks.

Places to Stay

The *Three Leaves Hotel (sānyè fàndiàn)* is a short walk from Kunming Main Railway Station. Doubles cost Y40, a bed in a triple costs Y10.

The *Camellia Hotel* (☎ 23000) *(cháhuā bīnguǎn)* is about 100 metres east of the Kunming Hotel. Doubles are around Y72 and dorm beds are Y10 per bed. The hotel is on the bus No 5 route.

The *Kunhu Hotel* (☎ 27732) *(kūnhú fàndiàn)* is on Beijing Lu close to Kunming South Railway Station. Doubles are Y14 with shared bath or Y40 with private facilities. Dorm beds are only Y4 each. Bus tickets to Dali are sold at reception. The hotel is two stops from the station on bus Nos 3, 23 or 25.

The *Kunming Hotel* (☎ 22063) *(kūnmíng fàndiàn)* at 145 Dongfeng Donglu is split into two wings: a squat older building and a 15-storey high-rise. Doubles run from Y75 to Y108.

Places to Eat

Kunming's regional specialities include ginger chicken cooked in an earthenware pot, Yunnan duck and ham, 'across-the-bridge noodles' and Muslim beef and mutton dishes. Western fare is also available.

The *Cooking School* on Dongfeng Lu has an English menu but is somewhat overrated as a place to eat. The *Olympic Restaurant (àolínpīkè fàndiàn)* nearby is also popular with travellers, and has an English menu that includes chicken steampot, toasted goat cheese, French toast and potato salad.

The *Worker-Peasant-Soldier Restaurant*

(☎ 25679) (gōngnóngbīng fàndiàn) at 262 Huguo Lu has awful decor but nice food. Buy a ticket and select from cauldrons on the ground floor.

The *Yingjianglou Muslim Restaurant* (☎ 5198) (yìngjiānglóu fàndiàn) nearby is at 360 Changchun Lu. It has the best Hui food (mutton and beef) in Kunming.

Near Yunnan University's main gate is the highly recommended *Tong Da Li Restaurant*. Coming out of the Yunnan University gate, go left on the main road and then take the first left onto a small back street; Tong Da Li is the first restaurant on the right.

Low prices, Spartan decor, but filling meals are found at the *Shanghai* (☎ 22987) (shànghǎi fàndiàn) at 73 Dongfeng Xilu, in a yellow-fronted building.

Getting There & Away
Air The CAAC office (☎ 4270) is at 146 Dongfeng Donglu. There are flights to Beijing, Canton, Changsha, Chengdu, Chongqing, Guilin, Guiyang, Nanning, Shanghai and Xi'an. There are also international flights to Hong Kong, Bangkok and Rangoon (Yangon).

Bus The two most useful bus stations are the main bus station (chēzhàn) close to the main railway station and the west bus station (xīzhàn). Tickets to Xiaguan (where you connect for Dali) are sold at the main bus station, west bus station and Kunhu Hotel.

Train There are only two rail approaches to Kunming, via Guiyang or Chengdu. There are trains to Shanghai via Guilin and direct trains to Beijing.

Getting Around
Bus Local transport is awkward, crowded and time-consuming. There are tour buses to the sights, but these are expensive. Try the Kunming Bus Service Company at the Sun-Approaching Tower, or the Yunnan Tourist Bus Co at the Kunming Hotel. You can schedule a three-day itinerary which includes all the Kunming sights and the Stone Forest.

Bicycle Bikes are OK for getting around town. Liu's Cafe on Beijing Lu hires out bikes for Y0.50 per hour or Y5 per day. The Kunming Hotel has relatively expensive bike hire at Y10 per day.

THE STONE FOREST 石林
The Stone Forest (shílín) is an exotic collection of grey limestone pillars, fissured by rainwater and eroded into their present fanciful forms. The tallest are about 30 metres high. The whole area is a giant rock garden with pavilions and pathways.

The section open to foreigners covers about 80 hectares. Stone Forest is in Lunan County, home of the Sani branch of the Yi tribespeople whose craftwork is sold at the entrance to the Stone Forest.

Places to Stay & Eat
The *Shilin Hotel* (shílín bīnguǎn) is a villa near the main entrance to the forest with singles/doubles for Y60/100. The *Yunlin Hotel* (yúnlín fàndiàn), which is off the road that forks to the right in front of the entrance, charges similar prices.

Some hotels near the bus terminal have singles for around Y10 – basic but cheap.

The Shilin Hotel and Yunlin Hotel have set meals that are OK – the Yunlin Hotel's meals are a better deal. There are several restaurants near the bus terminal and food vendors near the entrance to the Stone Forest.

Getting There & Away
It takes about 3½ hours to get to the Stone Forest from Kunming. Buses leave Kunming between 7 and 8 am. The regular long-distance bus costs Y5.50 one way or Y11 return and leaves the Kunming bus station at 8.30 am and 2.30 pm. The Kunming Hotel runs a tour bus for the same price but you must return the same day.

DALI 大理
Dali (dàlǐ) lies on the western edge of Erhai Lake, with the imposing Cangshan mountain range behind it. The main inhabitants of the region are the Bai people, who number about

1.1 million in Yunnan. The Chinese claim this region as none other than China's Switzerland. Foreigners sometimes call it the 'new Kathmandu'. Dali can't as yet match the sophistication of these places but it's already a haven for foreigners who want to slow down and relax in one of China's most peaceful spots.

The Third Moon Street Fair (*sān yùe jié*) begins on the 15th day of the third lunar month (usually April) and ends on the 21st day. The fair attracts thousands of people from all over Yunnan.

Orientation

Dali is a tiny city with cobbled streets and traditional stone architecture behind its old walls. It takes about half an hour to walk across town from the southern to the northern gate.

Things To See

The **Three Pagodas** (*sān tǎ*) stand on the hillside behind Dali and look particularly beautiful reflected in the nearby lake.

Erhai Lake (*érhǎi*) is a 40-minute walk from town where you can watch the large sailing junks or the smaller boats with their captive cormorants.

Another thing to see is **Shaping Market**, which operates every Monday at Shaping, 30 km north of Dali. The colourful costumes of the local Bai minority provide the main attraction. The minibus ride from Dali costs Y2.

Places to Stay & Eat

Most budget travellers prefer the *No 2 Guesthouse (dì èr zhāodàisuǒ)* on Huguo Lu in the town centre. Doubles are Y12 to Y24, and dorm beds cost Y5.

The only other show in town is the *Dali Hotel (dì yī zhāodàisuǒ)* off Fuxing Lu where doubles cost Y40 to Y60 and dorm beds are Y6.

Some favourite restaurants include *Jim's Peace Cafe*, the *Yin Yang Cafe* (also called the *Tibetan Cafe*), the *Coca-Cola Restaurant*, *Happy Restaurant* and the *Teahouse Restaurant*.

Getting There & Away

Buses to Lijiang leave at 7.20 am from the Dali Hotel. Private minibuses make the run faster – buy tickets from the office next to the No 2 Guesthouse. Modern Polish buses to Kunming leave the bus station opposite the post office at 6.20 am – the trip takes 11 hours.

LIJIANG 丽江

North of Dali, bordering Tibet, is the town of Lijiang (*lìjiāng*) with its spectacular mountain backdrop. Lijiang is the home of the Naxi minority. The Naxi (also spelt Nakhi) are descended from Tibetan nomads and lived until recently in a matriarchal society. Women still seem to run the show, certainly in the old part of town.

Orientation

Lijiang is divided into a boring Chinese section and an old town full of character, cobbled streets and market life. The approximate line of division is a hill topped with a radio mast. Everything west of the hill is the new town, and everything east of the hill is the old town.

Information

Public Security Bureau This is across from the Lijiang Guesthouse.

Money The Bank of China is next to the bridge on the main road in the old town.

Things to See

Crisscrossed by canals and a maze of cobbled streets, the **old town** is not to be missed. Arrive by mid-morning to see the market square full of Naxi women in traditional dress.

Also check out **Black Dragon Pool Park** (*hēilóng tán gōngyúan*) on the northern edge of town; it has a pond and pavilion, all set against the distant backdrop of snow-peaked Jade Dragon Mountain (*yùlóngshān*).

The small village of **Baisha** (*báishā*) on the plain north of Lijiang is a lovely stop on the way to **Yufeng Monastery** (*yùfēngsì*). The latter provides a magnificent view across the valley to Lijiang, and it also houses a famous 500-year-old camellia tree.

Places to Stay

The *No 2 Guesthouse (dì èr zhāodàisuǒ)* is very basic but cheap at Y6 per person for room with shared bath or Y24 for a double (private bath).

The *Lijiang Guesthouse (No 1 Hotel) (dì yī zhāodàisuǒ)* is higher standard with dorm beds for Y5. Doubles with shared bath cost Y24; with private bath, Y48.

Getting There & Away

Buses run daily between Lijiang and Dali. There is a connection between Lijiang and Jinjiang, a town on the Chengdu-Kunming railway line. The bus trip to the railway takes nine hours from Lijiang.

HUYAOXIA 虎越峡

Huyaoxia (Tiger Leap Gorge) is a 15-km gorge on the Yangtze where cliffs drop nearly 300 metres to the river below. A narrow path clings to vertical walls at a height of over 3900 metres above sea level. To reach Huyaoxia, 94 km from Lijiang, you can either hire a jeep or take local transport.

XISHUANGBANNA 西双版纳

In the deep south of Yunnan Province, next to the Burmese and Laotian borders, is the region of Xishuangbanna *(xīshuāngbǎnnà)*. The Han Chinese and the Dai people make up a third of the population, the rest are a hotchpotch of minorities including the Miao, Zhuang, Yao and lesser-known hill tribes.

JINGHONG 景洪

Jinghong *(jǐnghóng)*, the capital of Xishuangbanna prefecture, is beside the Mekong River (Lancangjiang).

Information

CITS The office (☎ 2708) is on the Banna Hotel grounds opposite reception – enter via the stairs on the left.

Public Security Bureau This is opposite Peacock Park in the centre of town.

Money The Bank of China is on Galan Lu south of the big traffic circle. The Banna Hotel also changes money.

Places to Stay & Eat

The *Banna Hotel (bǎnnà bīnguǎn)* close to the centre of town has double rooms with a view of the Mekong River for Y12 to Y40. Dorm beds are Y8.

Along Manting Lu are numerous Dai homes that double as restaurants and guesthouses. Basic rooms cost Y3 to Y4 per person – facilities are primitive.

The *Dai Minority Guesthouse (dǎizú fànguǎn)* has great food.

Getting There & Away

There are flights to Kunming, but Jinghong is difficult to fly into or out of – seats are booked up a week in advance. Buses leave daily for Kunming (Y40) – the trip takes two days and the road is beautiful but dangerous. Buses can be booked at the Three Leaves Hotel.

MENGHAN

Menghan is a village on the Mekong south of Jinghong, and the main reason for coming here is the ride on the ferry.

MENGHAI 勐海

This uninspiring place serves as a centre for trips to surrounding areas such as the Sunday market at Menghun and Nannuoshan (Mt Nannuo).

Places to Stay & Eat

There are a couple of drab hotels (Y3 per bed); one is at the main bus station.

MENGLONG 勐龙

Menglong *(měnglóng)* is 70 km south of Jinghong, a few km from the Burmese border. There are many temples and stupas in the area, including the **Manfeilong Pagoda**, which has nine stupas and was built in 1204.

Sichuan 四川

Sichuan *(sìchuān)* supports 100 million people and is the largest and most heavily populated province in China. The eastern region, the great Chengdu Plain, has one of the densest rural populations in the world, while the regions to the west are mountainous, remote and populated mainly by Tibetans.

CHENGDU 成都
This city *(chéngdū)* is the capital of Sichuan and the stepping stone to the rest of the province.

Orientation
The best navigational landmark is the colossal statue of Mao outside the Sichuan Exhibition Centre; if there were any pigeons left in Chengdu, they would probably use it to take their bearings – apart from putting the statue to other uses.

Information
CITS This office (☎ 28731) is in the Jinjiang Hotel, 180 Renmin Nanlu, but is almost useless. The front desk staff of the hotel speak better English.

Public Security Bureau The office (☎ 6577) is on Xinhua Donglu, east of the intersection with Renmin Lu.

Money Most hotels have foreign exchange services.

Post The GPO is on the corner of Huaxinzhen Jie and Shuwa Beijie. Poste restante is at the window marked 'International Post'.

Foreign Consulates The US Consulate (☎ 51912, 52791) is in the Jin Jiang Hotel.

Things to See
There are all manner of markets scattered throughout the city, from butcher to bird markets, from indoor to tinker and tailor markets. A spot near the Chengdu Restaurant is a local mecca for clothing and on-the-spot tailoring.

Renmin Park *(rénmín gōngyuán)* is one of the great parks in China. Near the entrance is a candyman who makes butterflies, birds and fish from melted sugar. The teahouse here is excellent.

Some distance from the Jinjiang Hotel are a number of temple parks.

Du Fu Cottage *(dù fǔ cǎotáng)* is the thatched cottage of the celebrated poet Du Fu (712 to 770 AD). The present grounds are larger than the original, and include tranquil tea gardens, which are popular for strolling through.

The **Temple of Wuhou** *(wǔhòu sì)* in Nanjiao Park was named after a famous military strategist of the Three Kingdoms period (220 to 265 AD). He was the prime minister of the state of Shu when Chengdu was the capital.

Wenshu is the God of Wisdom, and so revered that the **Wenshu Monastery** *(wénshū yuàn)* is overcrowded with worshippers and best avoided at weekends. The monastery's Buddhist statue was made in Tibet. The monastery, on an alley running eastwards off Renmin Zhonglu, is open from 8 am to 8 pm.

Chengdu Zoo *(chéngdū dòngwùyuán)* is the best place in China to see pandas. It's open from 8 am to 6 pm daily and is at the end of the bus No 302 route, six km from the city.

Places to Stay
The *Jiaotong Hotel* (☎ 52814) *(jiāotōng fàndiàn)* next to Xinnanmen Bus Terminal is most popular with budget travellers. Dorm beds start at Y4; a bed in a triple is Y14 and doubles go for Y28.

Even cheaper but not as nice is the *Binjiang Hotel* (☎ 24451) on Binjiang Lu, across the river from the Jiaotong toward Renmin Lu. Dorm beds go for Y9 to Y11; doubles with bath and air-con are Y25 to Y43.

The *Black Coffee Hotel* *(hēi kāfēi fàndiàn)*, a few minutes' walk east of the

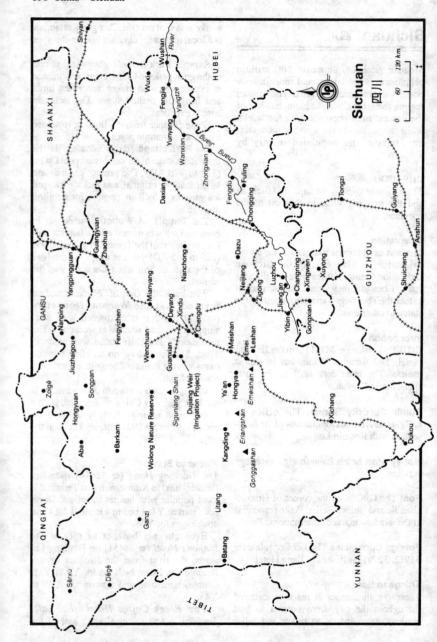

Sichuan 四川

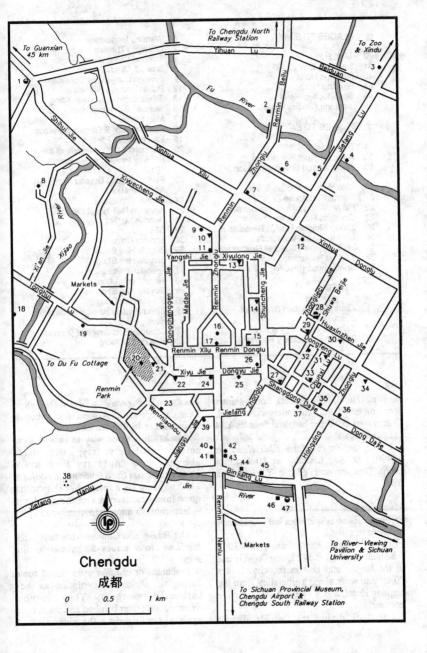

Chengdu
成都

0   0.5   1 km

■ PLACES TO STAY

2	Tibet Hotel
41	Jin Jiang Hotel/CITS
43	Minshan Hotel
44	Binjiang Hotel
45	Black Coffee Hotel
46	Jiaotong (Traffic) Hotel

▼ PLACES TO EAT

4	Teahouse
10	Rong Le Yuan Restaurant
13	Pock-marked Grandma's Bean Curd
14	Xiao Yuan Teahouse & Bar
21	Renmin Teahouse
22	Fat Mr Wang's Duck Restaurant
27	Chengdu Restaurant
29	Zhong Shuijiao Ravioli Restaurant
30	Shi Mei Xuan Restaurant
31	Lai Tangyuan Rice-Ball Restaurant
33	Yaohua Restaurant
34	Snackshops (Sweets)

OTHER

1	Ximen Bus Station (Buses for Guanxian)
3	Bamboo Weaving Factory
5	Sichuan Embroidery Factory

6	Wenshu Monastery
7	Chengdu Theatre
8	Tomb of Wang Jiang
9	Drum & Cymbal Shop
11	Foreign Languages Bookstore
12	Public Security Bureau
15	Telecommunications Building
16	Sichuan Exhibition Hall
17	Mao Statue
18	Cultural Park & Qingyang Palace
19	Lacquerware Factory
20	Monument to the Martyrs of the Railway Protecting Movement 1911
23	Public Security Bureau (Exit/Entry Administration)
24	Xinhua Bookstore
25	Advance Rail Ticket Office
26	Renmin Market
28	GPO
32	Bank of China
35	Bicycle Hire Shop
36	Bicycle Hire Shop
37	Friendship Store
38	Temple of Wuhou
39	Bicycle Hire Shop
40	Bicycle Hire Shop
42	China Southwest Airlines/Blue Sky Hotel
47	Chengdu Bus Terminal (Xinnanmen Bus Station)

Binjiang Hotel, is a former bomb-shelter now converted into an underground hotel. Dorms start at Y5 per bed, and doubles Y14 per person.

In the mid-range is the *Tibet Hotel* (☎ 334001) *(xīzàng fàndiàn)* at 10 Renmin Beilu. Doubles cost Y88 to Y110; triples Y54.

Places to Eat

Sichuan cuisine is spicy hot but snacks may be sweet or salty.

The *Chengdu Restaurant* (☎ 7301) *(chéngdū cāntīng)* at 642 Dong Dajie is one of the largest and best in the city. It is a 20-minute walk along a side alley from the Jinjiang Hotel, and it's a good idea to arrive here early.

For duck dishes try *Fat Mr Wang's*

Duckshop (wángpàng yādiàn) at the foot of Dongchenggen Jie. A great duck shop is *Weiyuelou* at 46 Renmin Zhonglu.

Snacks are a good way to sample local cuisine in all its variety; snack places abound. You could try *Pock-marked Grandma's Bean Curd (chén mápó dòufu)* at 113 Xi Yulong Jie, a small white shop with a green front which serves a mean mapo doufu – beancurd simmered in numb-and-spicy sauce.

The *Tai Bai Lou* Chinese restaurant in the *Minshan Hotel* serves Sichuan-style dim sum.

Teahouses or *chádiǎn* were closed down during the Cultural Revolution as they harboured insurgents. They are now reopened with their bamboo armchairs once again sprawling over the sidewalks. A favourite haunt is the *Renmin Teahouse* in Renmin Park with a great outdoor location by a lake.

Getting There & Away

Air In Chengdu CAAC disguises itself as 'China Southwest Airlines' but still offers the same sloppy service. Its office is diagonally across the street from the Jinjiang Hotel. Popular flights include those to Beijing, Canton, Chongqing, Guilin, Kunming, Lhasa, Shanghai, Ürümqi and Xi'an. There is a charter flight to Hong Kong.

Bus The main bus station is Xinnanmen, conveniently next to the Jiaotong Hotel, with departures for Emei, Baoguo, Leshan, Dazu, Kangding, etc. The Ximen Bus Station, in the north-east of the city, runs buses to Guanxian and places on the Jiuzhaigou route.

Train Most trains leave from Chengdu Main (North) Station. There are direct trains to Emei, Leshan, Kunming, Chongqing and Xi'an, as well as to Lanzhou, Hefei and Beijing.

Getting Around

Bus Bus No 16, which runs from the North Railway Station to the South Railway Station, is the most useful for getting around.

Bicycle Cheapest bike hire is at shops along Dong Dajie. For more money, you can hire bicycles at the Jinjiang Hotel.

XINDU

Xindu is a small town 18 km north of Chengdu. The **Temple of Divine Light** (*bǎoguāng sì*) is an active Buddhist monastery in the north of Xindu County. It comprises five halls and 16 courtyards surrounded by bamboo. The temple was founded in the 9th century and reconstructed in the 17th. The temple is rich in artefacts, and the Arhat Hall contains 500 two-metre-high clay figurines.

Getting There & Away

Bus Buses from the traffic circle at Chengdu take 40 minutes to get to Xindu. On the way back, the bus can drop you off at the Chengdu Zoo.

Bicycle It takes about four hours to pedal the 18 km from Chengdu to Xindu on a Chinese bike.

EMEISHAN 峨眉山

One of China's four famous mountains (the others are Putuo, Wutai and Jiuhua), Emeishan (éméishān) is the site of annual pilgrimages for young and old. Unfortunately many of the monasteries built on the mountainside and summit were burnt down or looted during successive wars with local and foreign aggressors. Since 1976 the remnants of temples destroyed during the Cultural Revolution have been renovated and access to the mountain has been improved.

The hiking is spectacular – craggy rocks, dense fir forest, azaleas, butterflies, rain and fog. The goal is to view sunrise or sunset over the sea of clouds at the summit; and in the afternoon you can sometimes see a phenomenon known as 'Buddha's Aureole' – rainbow rings.

The best time to visit is from May to October. You should be prepared for sudden changes in weather, as Emeishan is 3099 metres high. There is no heating or insulation in the monasteries, although blankets are provided. You will also need a good pair of rough-soled shoes, as the going becomes slippery higher up the mountain.

Places to Stay & Eat

Two to three days on the mountain is enough. The old monasteries provide food and shelter but they often ask ridiculous prices for foreigners – bargain! Prices should range from Y0.80 for a bed in a very large dormitory to Y10 for a single room. If you leave food lying around you may get a nocturnal visit from rats. At the foot of Emeishan is the *Hongzhushan Hotel (hóngzhūshān bīnguǎn)* with accommodation for Y15 per person.

Getting There & Away

Public transport links Emeishan to Baoguo village and Emei town, which has markets and a cheap dormitory in the *Emei Hotel*. From Emei Station you can take a minibus to Baoguo. There are buses from Baoguo to Emei and you can also travel from Baoguo to Leshan and Chengdu. Emei Railway Station is on the Chengdu-to-Kunming railway line. Luggage can be left at Emei Station, at the Hongzhushan Hotel or at one of the monasteries.

Baoguo village is the key transport junction. From here you can take a bus to Wannian and Qingyin. Most people start their ascent at the Wannian Si temple and finish at the Qingyin Ge pavilion. Buses from Baoguo to Wannian Si temple leave at 7.10, 9, and 11 am and at 1 and 2.10 pm.

The route is:

Wannian Si; 15 km to Xixiang Chi; 15 km to Jinding; 3.5 km to Wanfo Ding; 3.5 km to Jinding; 15 km to Xixiang Chi; 12.5 km to Xianfeng Si; 15 km to Hongchunping; 6 km to Qingyin Ge; 12.5 km to Leiyin Si; 1.5 km to Fuhu Si; 1 km to Baoguo Si.

LESHAN 乐山

Apart from providing an insight into village life in China, Leshan (lèshān) is the home of the Grand Buddha, Dafu (dàfó), 71 metres high and carved from the cliff face overlooking the confluence of the Dadu and Min rivers. It's the largest buddha in the world. You can climb to the top or descend to the foot, or float past the front of the statue in the boat that leaves Leshan pier every 40 minutes until 5.30 pm.

First stop on the boat after passing the buddha is the Wulong Temple, which contains calligraphy, painting and artefacts. You can get off here and walk to the Grand Buddha Temple near the buddha's head. To get back to Leshan, walk south to the small ferry going directly across the Min River. The entire trip takes about 1½ hours.

Places to Stay & Eat

The grandest place is the *Jiazhou Hotel (jiāzhōu bīnguǎn)*, with deluxe rooms at Y40 and dorm beds at Y15. Amazing dinners at Y8 a head are served from 6 to 7 pm but for hotel guests only with advance orders.

Near the Wuyou Monastery is the *Da Du He Hotel (dàdù hé fàndiàn)* with beds for Y5 to Y10.

In the town centre is the *Leshan Educational Research Centre* (☎ 22964) *(lèshān jiàoyù yánjiūsuǒ)* at 156 Liren, around the corner from the bus station. Doubles are Y20, triples Y10 to Y15 per person.

Getting There & Away

Bus There are five buses daily to Chengdu, 165 km and more than five hours away. Emeishan is 30 km away. There's a soft-seat coach daily at 7 am to Chongqing. The trip takes 12 hours and costs Y29.

Boat There is a boat to Chongqing departing Leshan at 5.30 and 7.30 am every few days but it's difficult to get on. The trip takes 36 hours and costs Y40 in 3rd class.

CHONGQING 重庆

This big city is heavily industrialised, but Chongqing retains vestiges of old China – neighbourhoods of ancient stone steps and alleys, crumbling tiled rooftops.

For many travellers, the main attraction here is that Chongqing *(chóngqìng)* is the starting point for the boat trip down China's greatest river, the Yangtze.

Information

CITS There is an office (☎ 51449) in the Renmin Hotel compound.

Public Security Bureau The office (☎ 43973) is on Linjiang Lu. Bus No 13 from the front of the Renmin Hotel will take you there.

Money The Bank of China is on Xinhua Lu,

diagonally opposite the Chung King Hotel. Major hotels also change money.

Things to See

Chongqing is best seen by simply walking around. There are great views from some of the hills. Walk up Xinhua Lu past the booking hall for the Yangtze boats, and turn onto Minzu Lu. From here continue up to Cangbai Lu, where you can catch the cable car across the Jialing River.

Red Cliff Village *(hóngyán cūn)* just outside Chongqing was used as the offices and living quarters of Communist representatives during the tenuous alliance between the Communists and the Kuomintang. Take bus No 16 four stops from the station on Liziba Lu.

The **Northern Hot Springs** *(běi wēnquán gōngyuán)* are on the site of a 5th-century AD Buddhist temple in the large park overlooking the Jialing River to the north-east of the city. There is a large public pool plus private rooms with large hot baths. Swimsuits can be rented.

Places to Stay

The *Renmin Hotel (rénmín bīnguǎn)* is one of the most incredible hotels in China. Inspired by Beijing's Temple of Heaven, the hotel is made up of two wings separated by an enormous circular concert hall. The rooms themselves are pretty basic but not cheap. The cheapest singles are Y147 and doubles run from Y209 to Y297. Take bus No 1 from the railway station on Zhongshan 3-Lu as far as the first traffic circle. Then walk or take bus Nos 13 or 15 to the hotel.

The *Huixianlou Hotel (huíxiān bīnguǎn)*, close to the Liberation Monument, has a dorm (Y15 per bed) with magnificent views.

The relatively new *Chung King Hotel* (☎ 49301) *(chóngqìng fàndiàn)* is on Xinhua Lu near the Chaotianmen pier area. Singles are Y95 and doubles are Y160 to Y200.

Places to Eat

The business district in the eastern part of the city near the docks has numerous small restaurants and street vendors. The noodle

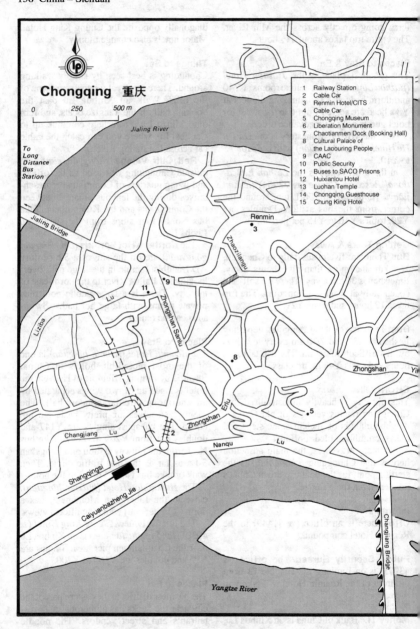

Chongqing 重庆

0   250   500 m

Jialing River

To
Long
Distance
Bus
Station

Jialing Bridge

1	Railway Station
2	Cable Car
3	Renmin Hotel/CITS
4	Cable Car
5	Chongqing Museum
6	Liberation Monument
7	Chaotianmen Dock (Booking Hall)
8	Cultural Palace of the Laoouring People
9	CAAC
10	Public Security
11	Buses to SACO Prisons
12	Huixianlou Hotel
13	Luohan Temple
14	Chongqing Guesthouse
15	Chung King Hotel

Renmin
•3

Zhaozijiangsu

•9
•11

Lu

Liziba

Zhongshan Sanlu

Zhongshan

Yi

•8

Zhongshan

•5

Ertu

Changjiang   Lu

Zhongshan

•2

Nanqu   Lu

Lu

Shangqingsi

1

Caiyuanbazheng Jie

Changjiang Bridge

Yangtze River

1 火车站
2 缆车铁道
3 人民宾馆
4 嘉陵缆车铁道
5 博物馆
6 解放碑
7 朝天门码头（售票处）
8 劳动人民文化宫
9 中国民船
10 公安局外事科
11 至中美合作所汽车站
12 会仙楼宾馆
13 罗汉寺
14 重庆宾馆
15 重庆饭店

shops are around Xinhua Lu and Shaanxi Lu towards Chaotianmen. There are night markets behind the Huixianlou Hotel near the Luohan Temple.

The *Chung King Hotel* has a good restaurant, and next door is the famous *Chung King Restaurant (chóngqìng fàndiàn)*.

Getting There & Away

Air CAAC (☎ 52970 or 52643) can be found at 190 Zhongshan 3-Lu, or you can buy tickets at the Chung King Hotel. There are flights to Beijing, Canton, Changsha, Chengdu, Guilin, Kunming, Nanjing, Shanghai, Wuhan and Xi'an.

Bus The long-distance bus station is on the northern side of the Jialing River, across the Jialing Bridge.

Train There are direct trains to Beijing, Chengdu, and Guiyang. Change at Chengdu for Kunming and at Guiyang for Guilin.

Boat You can take a boat trip from Chongqing to Wuhan down the Yangtze River – an interesting break from the trains.

Getting Around

Buses are very slow. There are no bicycles, but taxis can be hired from CITS or the reception desk of the Renmin Hotel. There is a cable car that lifts passengers over the Yangtze River from Xinhua Lu.

DOWN RIVER ON THE YANGTZE

The Yangtze is 6300 km long and the third longest river in the world, flowing from the Tanggulashan mountains to the East China Sea. The three gorges between Fengjie and Yichang provide some of the most exciting scenery. Enjoy it while you can – the government has plans to build a dam and flood these gorges to generate hydroelectric power.

The trip from Chongqing to Wuhan takes three days and two nights but the trip the other way takes five days. It's possible to leave the boat at Yichang, and take the train north to Xiangfan and Luoyang, or at

Yueyang, where you can catch the train to Canton.

Tickets are available at CITS or the booking office at the Chaotianmen Dock. You usually have to book two or three days in advance. Second class is a two-berth cabin, 3rd class a four to eight-berth cabin and 4th class a 24-bed cabin with communal showers and toilet. There is no 1st class.

The boat departs Chongqing at approximately 7 am from Chaotianmen Dock. You can sleep on the boat the night before departure for Y8 – easier than rushing to the dock in the morning.

If you want to go further down the Yangtze to Nanjing or Shanghai, you must change boats at Wuhan.

There are restaurants on each boat, but it's not a bad idea to bring some food – just make sure it's in *rat-proof* containers!

Most boats leave Chongqing at 7 am and arrive at Fuling at 11.30 am. A huge rock called the **Baihe Ridge** in the middle of the river has ancient carvings called 'stone fish' on one side.

In the afternoon the boat passes by **Shibaozhai** (Stone Treasure Stronghold), a 30-metre-high rock with an impressive red wooden temple. At 7 pm the boat docks at Wanxian for the night.

On the second day, the boat leaves Wanxian at about 4 am. It arrives at Fengjie soon afterwards. A few km away is **Baidicheng**, at the entrance to Sanxia and the three gorges of **Qutang, Wuxia** and **Xiling**, which stretch ahead for the next 200 km. The gorges vary from 300 metres wide at their widest section to 100 metres wide at their narrowest.

The last gorge, Xiling, is the largest of the three and 80 km long. At the end of the gorge the boat passes through the locks of the huge **Gezhouba Dam**. The boat reaches Yichang at 3 pm, and after leaving Yichang passes under the immense **Changjiang Bridge** at the town of Zhicheng.

There is absolutely nothing to see on the third day. The river is wide and the plains are flat. If the boat is on time you arrive at Wuhan around 5 pm.

Yangtze Ferry Fares from Chongqing			
	2nd class	3rd class	4th class
Wanxian	189	88	67
Yichang	345	160	122
Shashi	388	180	130
Wuhan (Hankou)	510	237	181

DAZU 大足

The grotto art of Dazu *(dàzú)* County, 160 km north-west of Chongqing, is among the best in China. The main groupings of rock carvings and cave paintings are at Beishan (North Hill) and the more interesting Baoding. They date from the Tang dynasty (9th century) to the Song dynasty (13th century).

JIUZHAIGOU 九寨沟

Jiuzhaigou *(jiǔzhàigōu)* in northern Sichuan Province has several Tibetan settlements and a number of dazzling features. It's a spectacular nature reserve with mountains, forests and pristine lakes. You should calculate between a week and 10 days for the round trip by road. The rainy season is from June to August, but there are tours available at this time. Such tours are booked out of Chengdu, but be very careful – some of these tour companies have acquired a reputation for overcharging, outright rip-offs and/or rotten service.

The road is dangerous and accidents are frequent. The bus company in Chengdu now requires that foreigners present a PICC (People's Insurance Company of China) card certifying that they're insured against accidents in northern Sichuan (also in parts of Gansu Province to the north). The card costs Y20 from the PICC office on Renmin Donglu in Chengdu.

Inner Mongolia 内蒙古

The nomadic Mongol tribes were united by Genghis Khan in 1206, and they went on under his leadership to conquer China and most of the known world. The Mongol Yuan dynasty lasted until 1368, after which the tribes went back to their roaming way of life.

The Qing emperors took control of the area in the 18th century, and the Russian empire set up a protectorate over the northern part of Mongolia. These divisions were set in concrete in the 1940s and the Chinese region is known as Inner Mongolia *(nèi měnggǔ)*.

Much of the region is natural grazing land. The economy is based on the stock breeding of cattle, sheep, horses and camels; timber comes from the mountains; and there are important mineral deposits. The border with the Soviet Union is of course militarily very sensitive.

HOHHOT 呼和浩特

Hohhot *(hūhéhàotè)* became the capital of Inner Mongolia in 1952. The name means 'green city' in Mongolian, and although it can be bleak in the dead of winter, it's reasonably green in summer and is certainly one of China's more pleasant cities.

Information

CITS The office (☎ 24494) is in the Inner Mongolia Hotel.

Public Security Bureau This is in the vicinity of the Renmin Park, near the corner of Zhongshan Lu and Xilin Guole Lu.

Money Most convenient for changing money are the Bank of China branches inside the Inner Mongolia Hotel and Zhaojun Hotel. You'll find the main branch is on Xinhua Dajie.

Things to See

The biggest attraction in town is the **Inner Mongolia Museum** *(nèi měnggǔ bówùguǎn)*, 1 Xinhua Dajie. The museum includes a large mammoth skeleton, Mongolian costumery and other traditional artefacts, archery equipment, saddles and a yurt.

The **Five Pagoda Temple** *(wǔtǎ sì)* dates

back to 1740 but is now bereft of its temple, leaving the Five Pagodas standing on a rectangular block. The Five Pagodas are on the bus No 1 route. The Great Mosque *(qīngzhēn dà sì)* is not so great and is in sad shape. It dates back to the Qing dynasty, with later expansions.

Places to Stay

Most popular is the *Xincheng Hotel* *(xīnchéng bīnguǎn)* (☎ 27231), with nice dorms with three beds each for Y10. Double rooms with private bath go for Y60. It's two km from the railway station. You can take bus No 5 two stops from the station to get within 10 minutes' walking distance of the hotel.

Just next door is the *Inner Mongolia Hotel* *(nèi měnggǔ fàndiàn)*. Doubles cost Y80 and there are some so-so dormitories for Y15 in the old wing.

The *Hohhot Hotel (hūhéhàotè bīnguǎn)* is near the railway station and has dorms for Y13 to Y18. Doubles are Y36.

Places to Eat

The Chinese restaurant in the *Inner Mongolia Hotel* is very cheap and very good. The *Malaqin* (horseman) restaurant is really great – they have both Chinese and Mongolian food. *Yikesai* is yet another good restaurant.

Getting There & Away

Air CAAC (☎ 42722) is on Xilin Guole Lu. There are useful flights to Beijing, Canton, Shanghai, Xi'an and Xilinhot.

Bus There are sporadic bus connections between Hohhot, Datong and Baotou.

Train Hohhot is on the Beijing to Lanzhou railway line that cuts a long loop through Inner Mongolia.

THE GRASSLANDS 草原

At present there are three officially open grasslands *(cǎoyuán)* that can be approached from Hohhot, but you are forced to go on a tour organised by Hohhot CITS. Tour prices range from Y79 for a one-day tour to Y715 for a three-day tour – prices will of course depend on the size of your group, the number of days and which grassland you want to visit.

Overall impression – the tours are not really worth the cost or effort since you can see much the same thing at Dongsheng and even stay there in a yurt for a fraction of what CITS charges. Or, of course, you can go to Mongolia itself.

DONGSHENG 东胜

Dongsheng *(dōngshèng)* lies south-west of Hohhot and serves as a staging post for Ejin Horo Qi *(yǐjīn huòluò qí)*, the site of **Genghis Khan's Mausoleum** *(chéngjí sīhàn língyuán)* – built as recently as 1954, when his supposed ashes were brought from Qinghai, where they had been taken to keep them from the invading Japanese. The area also affords a fascinating glimpse of Mongol culture.

Getting There & Away

There is a bus directly from Hohhot – departs at 7.30 am, takes six hours and costs Y21. After spending a night in Dongsheng, most travellers head for the mausoleum. Buses leave Dongsheng Bus Station at 7 am and take one hour to get to Ejin Horo Qi *(yǐjīn huòluò qí)*, which is 25 km from the Genghis Khan Mausoleum. The fare is Y1.20. Some of these buses continue all the way to the mausoleum, others will only drop you off in Ejin Horo Qi from where you take a minibus (30 minutes, Y3) to the mausoleum. Buy tickets the day before – the bus to Ejin Horo Qi is usually packed solid by departure time, and even more passengers are added en route.

Ningxia 宁夏

Much of Ningxia *(níngxià)* is populated by a few hardy nomads who make their living grazing sheep and goats. Winters are hard and cold; blistering summers make irrigation necessary. The Yellow River is Ningxia's lifeline. Most of the population live near it or the irrigation channels that run off it.

About a third of the population are Hui – the Muslim descendants of Arab traders who travelled to China during the Tang dynasty and of later immigrants from Central Asia.

YINCHUAN 银川

Yinchuan (yínchuān) was once the capital of the Western Xia, a mysterious kingdom founded during the 11th century. Today it's the capital of tiny Ningxia Province.

Orientation

Yinchuan is divided into two parts: a new industrial section close to the railway station, and the old town about four km away. The railway station is in the new town – everything worth seeing and the hotels are in the old town.

Information

CITS There is an office (☎ 22131) in room 129 of the Ningxia Hotel. The main CITS office (☎ 33720, 33466) is inside the Bank of China on the 4th floor, 150 Jiefang Xijie.

Public Security Bureau This is on Jiefang Xijie in a white building called Gong'an Ting.

Money The Bank of China is at 150 Jiefang Xijie.

Post & Telecommunications The post and telephone office is right in the centre of town at the corner of Minzu Jie and Jiefang Jie.

Things to See

The **North Pagoda** (běi tǎ) is easy to spot – standing like a stone spaceship to the north of town. There is no public transport – other than walking, you can reach the pagoda by bicycle or taxi. The distance from the Oasis Hotel is 2½ km. The **West Pagoda** (xī tǎ) is in the south-west part of the city. The **Drum Tower** (gǔlóu) is similar to other drum towers you find in China – this one is in good condition. Just to the east of the Drum Tower

is the **Yuhuang Pavilion** (yùhúang gé) – 400 years old but has been restored.

The **South Gate** (nánmén) is a mini-model of Tiananmen gate in Beijing, complete with Mao portrait. Close to the South Gate is the **Mosque** (qīngzhēn sì) which features a huge water fountain in the front.

Places to Stay

The *Ningxia Hotel (níngxià bīnguǎn)* is a classy place with prices starting at Y60 for a double. The restaurant is only for the famished or the desperate.

The *Oasis Hotel (lǜzhōu fàndiàn)* is on Jiefang Xijie and easily distinguished by the 'rocket ship' on the roof. Singles without private bath are Y30; doubles without bath Y40; doubles with bath are Y60. There's a good shop in the lobby for picking up snacks. There's a good restaurant upstairs.

Getting There & Away

There are flights to Beijing and Xi'an.

Buses connect Yinchuan with major towns such as Zhongwei, Tongxin and Guyuan. The bus station is in the south-east part of town near Nanmen Square.

Yinchuan lies on the Lanzhou-Beijing railway which runs through Baotou, Hohhot and Datong.

Getting Around

Bus Buses and minibuses connect the old town to the railway station.

Bicycle Bikes are available at the No 2 Guesthouse (dì èr zhāodàisǔo). Turn right outside the Ningxia Hotel, then right again at the next junction and continue about 70 metres down the road, looking for a gate.

Gansu 甘肃

Gansu (gānsù) is a barren province – mostly mountains and deserts. But through this impoverished region ran the Silk Road, along which camel caravans carried goods in and out of China. The Great Wall ends here. Traditionally towns were established in the oases where agriculture was possible; some industrial development and mining has now taken place.

Apart from the Hui minority, you will also find Mongols, Tibetans, Kazakhs and others.

LANZHOU 兰州

Lanzhou (lánzhōu), the capital and only city in Gansu, has been an important garrison town and transport centre since ancient times.

Orientation

Lanzhou stretches for 20 km along the the Yellow River. The eastern segment of town harbours the railway station and most of the tourist facilities.

Information

CITS The office (☎ 26798, 26181) is in a building in the walled-in compound of the Jincheng Hotel.

Public Security Bureau This is on Wudu Lu in a large compound with no English sign.

Money The Bank of China (☎ 418044) is at 70 Donggang Lu, just west of the Lanzhou Hotel.

Things to See

You'll find three mosques, two pagodas, numerous pavilions and a large, white Buddhist shrine at **White Pagoda Hill** (báitǎ shān). Bus No 7 from the railway station goes there. You have to cross a bridge, but there is also an occasional ferry. Admission is Y3 for foreigners.

The **Bingling Si Caves** are a remarkable sight. The Victory Hotel (shènglì bīnguǎn) runs minibuses (maximum 10 passengers) to the caves. Tickets are best booked in advance. The price per person is Y45 – student discounts available. There is an additional Y3 charge to enter the site. Show up at 7.30 am to board the bus at 8 am. You can also arrange to have the bus pick you up at

your hotel. The trip takes all day and is well worth it.

Places to Stay

The Lanzhou Hotel (☎ 22131) (lánzhōu fàndiàn), 204 Donggang Xilu, has doubles with shared bath for Y30 – with private bath the price jumps to Y120. The hotel is a 20-minute walk from the railway station or you can take bus No 1 two stops. Lots of minibuses ply this route – fare is Y2.

Just next door is the plush Jincheng Hotel (☎ 27931) (jīnchéng fàndiàn) at 363 Tianshui Lu. Doubles cost from Y95 to Y158 – dorms are Y12 but aren't particularly nice.

The Friendship Hotel (☎ 33051) (yǒuyí fàndiàn), 14 Xijin Xilu, has excellent dormitories for Y10. Doubles are Y92 to Y114. It's far from the railway station but close to the bus station for Xiahe.

Places to Eat

The Jincheng Hotel has a reasonably good Chinese restaurant with English menu. The Lanzhou Hotel restaurant is awful.

Getting There & Away

Air CAAC (☎ 23431/2) is at 46 Donggang Xilu, a five-minute walk west of the Lanzhou Hotel. There are flights to Beijing, Canton, Chengdu, Dunhuang, Xi'an and Ürümqi.

Bus The west bus station handles departures to Linxia and Xiahe.

Train Trains run from Ürümqi to Beijing, Xi'an and Shanghai.

Getting Around

Apart from the buses, there are heaps of minibuses plying the main streets. Fares run from Y1 to Y5 depending on distance. Ask at the Victory Hotel about bike hire.

XIAHE 夏河

If you don't visit Tibet, at least visit Xiahe (xiàhé). This is one of the most enchanting places in China. The town is dominated by **Labrang Monastery**, which appears to be one of the most active Tibetan communities

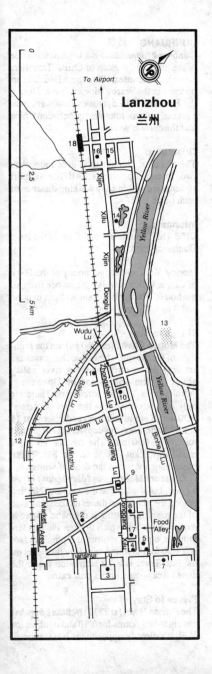

1 Main Railway Station
2 Post Office
3 Lanzhou University
4 Lanzhou Hotel
5 CITS
6 Jincheng Hotel
7 Ningwozhuang Guesthouse
8 Bank of China
9 The East is Red Square
10 Public Security Bureau
11 Victory Hotel
12 Five Springs Park
13 White Pagoda Hill & Park
14 West Bus Station
15 Friendship Hotel
16 Gansu Museum
17 CAAC
18 West Railway Station

1 火车总站
2 邮局
3 兰州大学
4 兰州饭店
5 中国国际旅行社
6 金城饭店
7 宁卧庄宾馆
8 中国银行
9 东方红广场
10 公安局外事科
11 胜利宾馆
12 五泉公园
13 白塔山公园
14 汽车西站
15 友谊饭店
16 甘肃省博物馆
17 中国民航
18 火车西站

in existence. Admission tickets cost Y6 per person and are sold at a kiosk to the right of a large yard – from the Minzu Fandian it's a two-km walk.

Xiahe is a great place for hiking amidst mountains, temples and grazing land. Be careful of dogs which run loose all over the town – carrying a large stick is advised.

Places to Stay

The up-market place to stay is the *Xiahe Binguan (xiàhé bīnguǎn)*. It's a long way from the bus station – 45 minutes by foot or negotiate a 'bicycle taxi'. Dorms cost Y10 to Y13. The hotel has hot showers.

Much closer to the bus station and less expensive is the *Minzu Fandian (mínzú fàndiàn)*. Dorm beds are Y6 to Y10, single rooms cost Y12. It's not very attractive and there is no place to bathe, but you're best off staying here the night before departure if you want to catch the 6.30 am bus.

Getting There & Away

You might have trouble. At the time of this writing, the bus company in Lanzhou was refusing to sell tickets to foreigners because 'buses are too dangerous'.

You have three options. One is to get a Chinese person to buy your ticket. Another is to just get on the bus and then buy your ticket – this sometimes works. If both these methods fail, you can also round up a group of foreigners at the bus station (usually easy to do) and negotiate a price for a minibus to take you to Linxia. Many minibus drivers hang around the station looking for customers. Cost is about Y15 per person depending on the size of the group. In Linxia, you can switch to the public bus to Xiahe (it stops there for a lunch break).

The place to get buses in Lanzhou is the west bus station *(qìchē xīzhàn)*. Buses run from around 6.30 am until about 2 pm as far as Linxia, but take the earlier buses if you want to make it to Xiahe in one day. To Linxia takes three to four hours – double that to Xiahe.

Your final alternative is to take a pricey CITS tour.

DUNHUANG 敦煌

Dunhuang *(dūnhúang)* is a large oasis in one of the most arid regions of China. Travellers come here because of the superb Buddhist art on view in the nearby Mogao Caves. During the Han and Tang dynasties Dunhuang was a pivotal point of interchange between China and the outside world.

Orientation

The centre of Dunhuang is little more than two intersecting roads. All life-support systems are within easy walking distance of each other.

Information

CITS This is on the second floor of the large Dunhuang Hotel.

Money You can change money at the Bank of China, which is walking distance from all the hotels. The bank is open 9.15 am to noon and 3 to 5.30 pm.

Things to See

The **Mogao Caves** *(mògāo kū)* are the highlight of Dunhuang. These Buddhist caves are set into desert cliffs above a river valley about 25 km south-east of Dunhuang. Admission is Y16 for foreigners. There are only two buses daily – the first departs at 7.30 am (8 am in summer) and returns at 11 am. The afternoon bus departs at 1.30 pm and returns at 4.30 pm. The cost is Y3 for a round-trip ticket – sold on the bus. These buses may not run in the dead of winter.

Crescent Moon Lake *(yùeyáqúan)* is just a pond, but it's well worth visiting. Nestled among the giant sand dunes on the south side of the oasis, the setting is dramatic. There is a once-daily bus which departs the bus terminal at 6 pm and returns at 8 pm. The fare is Y1.50 for the round-trip. Buy the ticket on the bus. There is a Y2 admission fee to the dunes area – camel rides cost extra.

Places to Stay

The *Feitian Hotel* (☎ 2337) *(fēitiān bīnguǎn)* has eight-bed dorms for Y10 and doubles for Y39. It's directly opposite the bus station.

There are two Dunhuang Hotels (their Chinese names are different). The large Dunhuang Hotel *(dūnhúang bīnguǎn)* is an up-market place but has dorms for Y15 in the old building and Y20 in the new building. Doubles are Y90 (old building) and Y116 (new building). There are student discounts on the double rooms.

Places to Eat
Food at the large *Dunhuang Hotel* is good and reasonably cheap. During summer evenings, the best place to eat is around the traffic circle by the post office. Literally hundreds of tables are set up here.

Getting There & Away
Air You can book at CITS in the Dunhuang Hotel or walk across the street and book yourself at the CAAC office (☎ 2389). There are flights to Jiayuguan and Lanzhou, but service is irregular.

Bus Buses to Liuyuan (130 km) depart eight times daily from the bus station between 7.30 am and 6 pm. The fare is Y6 and the trip takes about 2½ hours.

Buses to Golmud leave at 6.30 am (7.30 in summer). The fare is Y24 and the trip takes 13 hours.

Train Liuyuan (on the Lanzhou-Ürümqi line) is the jumping-off point for Dunhuang.

Xinjiang 新疆

Xinjiang *(xīnjiāng)* is divided by the east-west Tianshan range into two major regions. To the south of the range is the Tarim Basin, and to the north is the Junggar Basin. To the east is the huge salt marsh and lake of Lop Nur – almost uninhabited and used by the Chinese for nuclear weapons tests. The climate tends towards extremes – sizzling summers and frigid winters. The population used to be mostly Uigur, but with large-scale Chinese immigration to the north, the Uigurs now number less than half the total, plus Kirghiz, Kazakhs and other minorities.

TURPAN 吐鲁番
When you first arrive at Turpan Station, you'll wonder if you haven't landed on another planet. After exploring the town, you'll begin to wonder what century it is. Turpan *(tǔlǔfān)* is unique – a stronghold of one of China's most interesting minorities, the Turkish-speaking Muslim Uigurs. They are not Chinese at all and could easily pass for southern Europeans or Arabs. Donkey carts, grapevines, mosques, two ancient ruined cities and numerous other sights make Turpan an exotic place to visit.

If the culture is exotic, the geography is bizarre – Turpan is an oasis situated in a basin 154 metres below sea level. It's the lowest spot in China and the second lowest depression in the world. It's also the hottest place in China, with a record temperature of 49.6°C. Yet this barren desert is a rich agricultural region thanks to melting snow from the nearby mountains. Don't miss it!

Orientation
The centre of the Turpan oasis is little more than a few main roads and a couple of side streets. The centre is called Old City *(lǎochéng)* and the western part is New City *(xīnchéng)*. Most of the sights are scattered on the outskirts of the oasis or in the surrounding desert.

Information
CITS The office (☎ 22768) is at the Oasis Hotel.

Public Security Bureau This is one block west of the Bank of China.

Money The most convenient place to change money is the Oasis Hotel. There is also a Bank of China about a 10-minute walk from the hotel.

Post The post office is right near the bus station and the market. More convenient is the post office inside the Oasis Hotel – they can even handle parcels.

Things to See

The **Bazaar** is one of the most fascinating markets in China. It's just opposite the bus station.

CITS puts on a traditional Uigur **Song & Dance Show** almost every night during the summer in the courtyard of the Turpan Guesthouse at 10 pm. Tour groups usually put up the money (Y400) but most travellers get to watch for free.

Most of the best sights are around Turpan and you need to book a minibus tour to see them. This requires a full day. You won't have to find the minibuses – they'll find you. Drivers typically ask Y110 to Y150 for the bus (bargain!) for a whole day. Since a minibus holds six to eight people, you can split the cost. A typical trip should include the **Atsana Graves** (*āsītǎnà gǔmù qū*), **Gaochang Ruins** (*gāochāng gùchéng*), **Bezeklik Caves** (*bózīkèlǐ qiānfó dòng*), **Grape Valley** (*pútáo gōu*), **Emin Minaret** (*émǐn tǎ*), **Underground Irrigation Channels** (*dì xià shuǐ*) and **Jiaohe Ruins** (*jiāohé gùchéng*) (usually in that order).

Places to Stay

The *Turpan Guesthouse* (*tǔlǔfān bīnguǎn*) is still the most popular hotel in Turpan, and it's also one of the best in China. Sit under the vine trellis and try their watermelon juice. Rates are Y7 for a dormitory bed and Y86 for a double in the new wing.

The *Oasis Hotel* (*lǜzhōu bīnguǎn*) is the modern tourist place in town, but has cheap dorms in the old wing for Y13. Doubles in the new wing are Y90. All rooms, including dorms, have air-con.

The *Jiaotong Hotel* (*jiāotōng bīnguǎn*) is right next to the bus station and market – a busy, noisy place. Dorms are Y10 and doubles cost Y57.

Places to Eat

The *Turpan Guesthouse* is the best place to eat – the food is excellent and cheap. Food at the *Oasis Hotel* is outstanding but expen-sive – figure about Y40 per meal per person. Right across the street from the entrance to the Oasis Hotel is the *Silk Road Restaurant* (*sīlù jiǔjiā*) – good cheap food and ice-cold drinks.

Getting There & Away

Bus There are bus connections between Turpan and Ürümqi or Daheyan. In Turpan, the bus station is near the market. Make sure you get to the station an hour before depar-ture, because there is invariably a long queue for tickets.

There are at least four buses daily to Ürümqi plus private minibuses about once every hour. In Turpan, the public buses want FEC!

Train The nearest railway line is the Ürümqi-Lanzhou line north of Turpan. The nearest railway station is at Daheyan. There are four buses daily between Daheyan and Turpan. There are six trains daily in both directions.

ÜRÜMQI 乌鲁木齐

Ürümqi (*wūlǔmùqí*) is Xinjiang's capital and basically a Chinese city though there is a considerable Uigur presence. It's an interest-ing place to visit but the best sights are in the surrounding areas.

Information

Tourist Offices The CITS office (☎ 25794) is in a compound on the east side of Renmin Square and has a reputation for avarice and incompetence. Somewhat better is the Xinjiang Overseas Tourist Corporation (☎ 78691) (*xīnjiāng hǎiwài lǚyóu zǒng gōngsī*), 32 Xinhua Nanlu. Also worth trying is the CTS office in the Overseas Chinese Hotel.

Public Security Bureau This is a 10-minute walk from the CITS office, in a large govern-ment building just to the north-west of Renmin Square.

Money The Bank of China is at 343 Jiefang Lu close to Renmin Square.

Post The main post office is a big Corin-

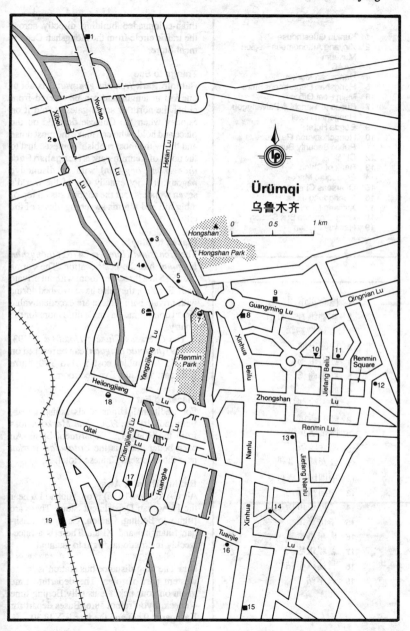

Ürümqi
乌鲁木齐

1 Kunlun Guesthouse
2 Xinjiang Autonomous Region Museum
3 CAAC
4 Hongshan Market
5 Hongshan Department Store
6 Main Post Office
7 Buses to Tianchi & Baiyanggou
8 Hongshan Hotel
9 Bogda Hotel
10 Hongchunyuan Restaurants
11 Public Security Bureau
12 CITS
13 Bank of China
14 Erdaoqiao Market
15 Overseas Chinese Hotel
16 Guangdong Jiujia
17 Xinjiang Hotel
18 Long-Distance Bus Station
19 Railway Station

1 昆仑宾馆
2 新疆维吾尔自治区博物馆
3 中国民航
4 红山市场
5 红山商场
6 邮局
7 往天池/白扬沟汽车
8 红山宾馆
9 博格达宾馆
10 鸿春园饭店
11 公安局外事科
12 中国国际旅行社
13 中国银行
14 二道桥市场
15 华侨宾馆
16 广东酒家
17 新疆饭店
18 长途汽车站
19 火车站

thian-colonnaded building directly across the traffic circle from the Hongshan Department Store.

Things to See

Renmin Park (*rénmín gōngyúan*) is about one km in length and can be entered from either the north or south gates. Avoid it on Sunday when the Chinese descend on the place and hold 'who can make the most noise and throw the most rubbish' contests. Just to the north of Renmin Park is **Hongshan Park** (*hóngshān gōngyúan*) with its distinctive pagoda. It's not exactly one of the world's seven wonders, but the pagoda sits on top of a big hill and affords sweeping views of the city.

Places to Stay

The *Hongshan Hotel* (☎ 24761) (*hóngshān bīnguǎn*) has the best location. The dorms cost Y15 in a three-bed room without private bath. For Y25, they also have two-bed dorms with private bath – these are excellent value if you don't mind paying a little more for the luxury.

The *Overseas Chinese Hotel* (☎ 77793, 70529) (*húaqiáo bīnguǎn*) can be reached on bus No 7. Doubles cost Y70 to Y90; dorm beds cost Y20 in a five-bed room.

Places to Eat

For traditional Uigur foods (shish kebab, flatbread), try the *Hongshan Market* across from the Hongshan Department Store. An even better place is the *Erdaoqiao Market* near the Overseas Chinese Hotel.

Getting There & Away

Air CAAC (☎ 41536) is on Youhao Lu near the Hongshan Department Store. There are flights to Beijing, Canton, Chengdu, Kashgar, Shanghai and Xi'an. There is a once-weekly international flight to Istanbul.

Bus The long-distance bus station is in the western part of town. The departure time given on your ticket is usually Beijing time – check if you're not sure. Buses depart for Kashgar at 9 am and the fare is Y38.30.

Train From Ürümqi there are eastbound trains at least six times daily.

TIANCHI 天池

Tianchi (Lake of Heaven) *(tiānchí)* is a sight you'll never forget. Halfway up a mountain in the middle of a desert, it looks like a chunk of Switzerland or Canada that's been exiled to western China.

The lake is 115 km east of Ürümqi at an elevation of 1900 metres. Horses are also offered at Y40 to Y60 per day for a trek to the snow line. The trek to the snow line and back takes 10 hours. There's a hotel at the lake that has dorms for Y10 and there are also yurts for rent (Y8).

Getting There & Away

Buses leave Ürümqi at around 8 am from both the north and south gates of Renmin Park – the north side is more convenient if you're staying at the Hongshan Hotel. Departures are from where the sign says in English 'Taxi Service'. A one-way ticket costs Y11. Buy your ticket about 30 minutes ahead of time to assure getting a seat. The trip takes over three hours. The bus will probably drop you off at the end of the lake – from there it's a 20-minute walk to the hotel on the banks.

KASHGAR 喀什

Kashgar *(kāshí)* is a giant oasis and one of those bizarre end-of-the-earth sort of places like Timbuktu where time seems frozen in a different age. The culture is heavily Muslim and relations between the Uigur majority and the Han rulers are very tense. In 1990, ethnic riots broke out and the city was closed to foreigners. It is gradually opening again, but this situation could change – hopefully for the better.

Information

CITS The office (☎ 3156) is just off of Jiefang Beilu.

Money The Bank of China (☎ 2461) is on Renmin Xilu near the post office. The money-changing brigade will pursue you all over Kashgar. US dollars are snapped up for Sino-Pakistani trade and by Kashgaris preparing for pilgrimage to Mecca.

Things to See

The focus of activity is the bazaar and the **Id Kah Mosque** *(ài tí gǎ ér qīngzhēn sì)*.

The **Abakh Hoja Tomb** *(xiāngfēi mù)* is a strange construction in the eastern part of the oasis. It looks something like a stubby, multi-coloured miniature of the Taj Mahal. The tomb is the burial place of Hidajetulla Hoja, a Muslim missionary and saint. It's an hour's walk from the Kashgar Guesthouse, but you should be able to hitch a lift on a donkey cart.

You should not miss the **Sunday Market** *(jiàrì jíshì)* on the eastern fringe of town. Hundreds of donkey carts, horsemen, pedestrians and animals thunder into town for a bargaining extravaganza.

Places to Stay

The *Seman Hotel* (☎ 2129, 2060) *(sèmǎn bīnguǎn)* is on the western edge of town. A double with bath costs Y35 – check the plumbing. A bed in the dormitory costs Y10.

The *Kashgar Guesthouse* (☎ 2367/8) *(kāshí gě'ěr bīnguǎn)* is the top-rated hotel but far from the town centre – the main intersection is a good hour's walk away, and there's no bus. You can usually wave down a jeep or hitch a lift on a donkey cart. Double rooms with private bath go for Y100. Dorm beds cost Y12.

Places to Eat

For a wide variety of Uigur foods, pop into the food market close to the Id Kah Mosque. There you can try shish kebab, rice and mutton. Whatever you buy, pay for it when you get it and take it with you – there have been reports of travellers eating first and then being overcharged (and physically threatened if they didn't pay up).

The *Kashgar Guesthouse* serves Chinese meals for Y25 each.

Getting There & Away

Air CAAC (☎ 2113) is on Jiefang Beilu north of the Id Kah Mosque. There are daily flights

Kashgar
喀什

0   0.5   1 km

1 Oasis Hotel
2 Seman Hotel
3 Friendship Hotel
4 Public Security Bureau
5 Chini Bagh Hotel
6 CAAC
7 Id Kah Mosque
8 CITS
9 Bank of China
10 Post Office
11 Mao Statue
12 Local Bus station
13 Long-Distance Bus Station
14 Renmin Park & Zoo
15 Abakh Hoja Tomb
16 Kashgar Guesthouse
17 Saytalasrahan's Tomb

1 绿洲宾馆	10 邮局
2 色满宾馆	11 毛泽东塑像
3 友谊宾馆	12 市公共汽车站
4 公安局外事科	13 长途汽车站
5 其尼巴合宾馆	14 人民公园
6 中国民航	15 香妃墓
7 艾提尔清真寺	16 喀什噶尔宾馆
8 中国国际旅行社	17 赛衣提艾里艾斯拉罕墓
9 中国银行	

from Kashgar to Ürümqi and the fare is Y435.

Bus At the time of this writing, CITS was saying foreigners can only go to Kashgar by air. However, if you manage to get into Kashgar, it's possible that you can still depart by bus, at least to Ürümqi. There is a daily bus to Ürümqi via Aksu, Korla and Toksun. Tickets for the bus can only be bought one day before departure and the bus is scheduled to depart Kashgar at 8 am. The trip takes three days.

Getting Around

The city buses are of no use; to get around you have to walk or hire a bike, donkey cart or jeep.

KARAKORAM HIGHWAY 中巴公路

This highway (zhōngbā gōnglù) over Khunjerab Pass (4800 metres) was opened to foreigners in May 1986 – it closed again in April 1990. The official excuse was landslides, but the real reason was ethnic rioting in Kashgar. It could be open again by the time you read this. Take warm clothing, food and drink on board with you – once stowed on the roof of the bus your baggage is not easily accessible.

The rough section between Kashgar and the Pakistan border still needs a few more years before it can be called a road, but facilities are being steadily improved.

If the route is open, you can go from Kashgar as far as Pirali just for the trip (or some hiking en route) without crossing the border.

Information

For information or advice, contact the Pakistan Tourism Development Corporation, H-2, St. 61, F-7/4, Islamabad, Pakistan. CITS in Ürümqi has no maps, no knowledge of the highway and no interest other than to sell you an outrageously expensive tour.

A separate guide, *The Karakoram Highway – a travel survival kit* (Lonely Planet Publications), is available.

Tibet 西藏

Most of Tibet *(xīzàng)* is an immense plateau which lies at an altitude of 4000 to 5000 metres, broken by a series of east-west mountain ranges. It's completely barren apart from some poor grasslands to the south-east. The Qamdo region to the east is lower, wetter and warmer; some agriculture is possible here, and most of the population lives here. The Chinese can't understand why anyone would want to go to the forgotten end of their Middle Kingdom, but Westerners have been captivated by Tibet's extraordinary isolation and its fascinating culture.

LHASA 拉萨

Lhasa *(lāsà)* has long been the capital of Tibet and remains the political centre, the most important city and the showpiece of the region. The Chinese officially opened the Roof of the World to foreigners in late 1984. In late 1987 the situation changed dramatically when Tibetans in Lhasa gave vent to their feelings about the Chinese and their policies. A series of demonstrations became a virtual uprising. Tibet is closed once more except for tour groups, but perhaps things will have changed by the time you read this.

Orientation

The city lies 3683 metres above sea level. Towering above Lhasa is the Potala Palace and forming the nucleus of the Tibetan part of the city is the Jokhang Temple.

Information

CITS The office is at the Lhasa Holiday Inn.

Public Security Bureau This is behind the Potala.

Money The Bank of China is close to the PSB, just behind the Potala. Hours are 10 am to 1.30 pm and 4 to 6.30 pm, Monday to Saturday; closed Sunday. The Lhasa Holiday Inn also has a bank which can be snooty about serving those who are not staying at the hotel.

Foreign Consulates The Nepalese Consulate General (☎ 22880) is at 13 Norbulingka Lu.

Things to See

The most imposing attraction of Lhasa is the **Potala Palace** *(bùdǎlāgōng)*, once the centre of the Tibetan government and the winter residence of the Dalai Lama. One of the architectural wonders of the world, this huge 17th-century edifice was built on the site of its 7th-century forerunner and contains thousands of rooms, shrines and statues. The Potala is open daily except Sunday.

The golden-roofed **Jokhang Temple** *(dàzhāo sì)* is 1300 years old and one of Tibet's holiest shrines. It was built in commemoration of the marriage of the Tang princess Wen Cheng to King Songsten Gampo, and houses a pure gold statue of the Buddha Sakyamuni, brought to Tibet by the princess. The Jokhang is east of the Potala and best visited early in the morning.

Around the periphery of the Jokhang is the **Barkhor Market**, always a hive of activity.

About three km west of the Potala is the **Norbu Lingka** *(luóbù línkǎ)*, once the summer residence of the Dalai Lama. The gardens are a favourite picnic spot for the Tibetans.

Places to Stay

At the time of this writing, foreigners were being forced to stay at the *Lhasa Holiday Inn* (☎ 2221) *(lāsà fàndiàn)* as part of an all-inclusive tour package. Doubles start at Y214 per room. The hotel has everything from a souvenir shop to a wrestling arena (want to go a few rounds with CITS?). The other place open to tour groups is the *Tibet Hotel (xīzàng bīnguǎn)* a few metres up the road from the Holiday Inn. Doubles start at Y173 in the high season, Y117 in the low.

On the optimistic assumption that Lhasa will open again to individual travellers, the following hotels should accept foreigners.

The *Snowlands* (☎ 23687) *(xuěyù lǚguǎn)*, close to the Jokhang Temple, has dorm beds for Y10; the *Banak Shol* (☎ 23829) *(bālángxuě lǚshè)* on Xingfu Donglu near the Barkhor has dorms/doubles for Y10/22; and the *Kirey Hotel (jírì lǚguǎn)*, close to the Banak Shol, has dorms/doubles for Y10/12.

Places to Eat

The *Lhasa Holiday Inn* has a Chinese restaurant and a coffee shop which serves Western food such as hamburgers, French fries and club sandwiches.

The *Banak Shol* restaurant operates a choose-your-own ingredients system. It deserves reverence as the probable birthplace of the yakburger.

Getting There & Away

Tours At the time of this writing, you had little choice but to sign up for a tour. These are readily booked by CITS in either Chengdu or Golmud. They are determined to milk the cash cow (foreign tourists) for all they can get. Prices begin at Y3000 (after bargaining) for three days in Lhasa; the trip might be extendable once you are there (talk to Lhasa CITS about this). A minimum group size of three is required. It's possible to enter one way and depart by another route, even by way of Nepal.

Air CAAC (☎ 22417) is at 88 Jiefang Lu. There are flights to Chengdu. International flights to Kathmandu can be booked even as part of a tour package.

Bus Lhasa has two bus stations. The old bus station is in the centre of town, close to the main post office. The new bus station is a monstrosity four km out of town, near the Norbulingka.

Road Although there are five major road routes to Lhasa, foreigners are officially allowed to use only the Nepal and Qinghai (Golmud) routes. On the Nepal road, you can visit the historic and attractive towns of Shigatse, Gyantse and Sakya.

YARLONG VALLEY 雅鲁流域

About 190 km east of Lhasa, the Yarlong Valley (yǎlǔ liúyù) is considered to be the birthplace of Tibetan culture. Within a radius of the adjacent towns of Zêtang and Nedong, which form the administrative centre of the region, are several sites of religious importance: the Samye Monastery, Yumbu Lhakang (the legendary first building in Tibet, recently renovated) and the Tombs of the Kings.

SHIGATSE 日喀则

The second-largest urban centre in Tibet is Shigatse (rìkāzé). This is the seat of the Panchen Lama, a reincarnation of Amitabha (Buddha of Infinite Light), who ranks close to the Dalai Lama. The most recent Panchen, the 10th, was taken to Beijing during the 1960s, and lived a largely puppet existence there, visiting Tibet only occasionally. He died recently.

GYANTSE 江孜

Gyantse (jiāngzī) is one of southern Tibet's chief centres, although its scale is that of a small village which retains some Tibetan charm.

SAKYA 萨迦

Sakya (sàjiā) is 152 km west of Shigatse and about 25 km south of the main road. The huge, brooding monastery at Sakya was Tibet's most powerful 700 years ago and once the centre for the Sakyapa sect which was founded in the 11th century. The monastery probably contains the finest collection of Tibetan religious relics remaining in Tibet – but the monks may restrict you to a couple of halls.

Qinghai 青海

Historically Qinghai (qīnghǎi) was part of Tibet – its separate existence is one of the great cartographical constructions of our time. Today it's a sort of Chinese Siberia, where common criminals as well as political prisoners are incarcerated. The people of the province include Kazakhs, Mongols, Hui and Tibetans, with Han settlers concentrated around Xining.

XINING 西宁

Xining (xīníng) is the only large city in Qinghai and is the capital of the province. It serves as a stopover for foreigners following the route between Qinghai and Tibet.

Information

CITS There is an office (☎ 45901 ext 1109) in the front building of the Xining Guesthouse (xīníng bīnguǎn).

Public Security Bureau This is on Bei Dajie near the Xining Guesthouse.

Things to See

Xining has nothing exceptional to see, but it is a convenient point for visiting Ta'er Lamasery and Qinghai Lake.

The **Great Mosque** (qīngzhēn dà sì) is on Dongguan Dajie. The **Beishan Temple** (běishān sì) is about a 45-minute walk up the mountainside west of the Xining Hotel. The hike is pleasant and there's a good view over Xining from the temple.

Places to Stay

Xining Hotel (☎ 23901) (xīníng bīnguǎn) is the most popular place for budget travellers. The rear building contains the reception desk. Dorms cost Y8, doubles are Y11 to Y65. Take bus No 9 from opposite the railway station – it's five km.

Xining Daxia is a basic hotel but it's close to the station. A bed in a four-bed room costs Y6. Take bus No 1 from the station and get off at the second stop.

Places to Eat

The market near the West Gate (xīmén) is the best sight in town as well as the best place to eat and is also reasonably clean.

A good place for Chinese food is the Peace Restaurant (☎ 48069) (hépíng jiǔjiā) on Dong Dajie.

Getting There & Away

Air There are flights from Xining to Beijing (Y597), Lanzhou (Y56) and Taiyuan (Y422). The airport is being expanded and there are plans to add flights soon to Golmud and Xi'an.

Bus The main bus station, opposite the railway station, has daily departures in the morning for Heimahe (near Qinghai Lake) and Golmud (1½ days).

Train Xining has frequent rail connections to Lanzhou (4½ hours). There are two trains to Golmud; one leaves daily and one leaves every other day.

TA'ER LAMASERY   塔尔寺

This is a large Tibetan monastery (tǎ'ěr sì), one of the six great monasteries of the Yellow Hat sect of Tibetan Buddhism, located in the town of Huangzhong about 25 km south-east of Xining.

Places to Stay & Eat

The monastery has a couple of buildings which have been converted from monks' quarters into tourist accommodation. A bed in a three-bed room costs Y10.

The Ta'er Hotel (tǎ'ěr sì bīnguǎn) is just opposite the Tibetan hospital and charges Y60 for a double.

The food at the monastery is good. For a change, take a wander down the hill towards town and try some noodles in a Muslim restaurant. Stalls on the approach road to the monastery sell great yoghurt and peaches.

Getting There & Away

Buses to Huangzhong leave Ximen Station in Xining about every 10 minutes between 7 am and 6.30 pm. The 45-minute ride costs Y2. Minibuses also do the trip faster for a fare of Y5.

Catch your return bus or minibus to Xining from the square in Huangzhong.

QINGHAI LAKE   青海湖

Qinghai Lake (qīnghǎi hú), known as the 'Western Sea' in ancient times, is a some-what surreal-looking saline lake lying 300 km west of Xining and 3200 metres above sea level. It's the largest lake in China and produces copious quantities of fish.

The main attraction is **Bird Island** (niǎo dǎo), a breeding ground for all manner of species. You will only see birds in any quantity during the mating and breeding season between March and early June.

Getting There & Away

It's a hassle. The north shore is accessible by train, but Bird Island (on the south shore) has no public transport. Every Sunday during the summer months only, there is a day trip from Xining to Bird Island for only Y40. Buses depart at 7 am from Ximen Bus Station (xīmén qìchē zhàn) and return at 9 pm. The passengers are mostly Chinese, so don't expect a tranquil nature experience – you may want to bring earplugs.

If you can get together a group, it is possible to rent minibuses through the Peace Restaurant (☎ 48069) (hépíng jiǔjiā). Go to the 3rd floor to enquire.

CITS organises a three-day trip to Bird Island which costs Y80 FEC based on a minimum of 10 passengers. This price is for the bus only – meals and accommodation are an additional Y60 per day.

GOLMUD   格尔木

Golmud (gé ěr mù) is a town on the high, desolate plateau of central Qinghai. The residents will be the first to tell you that from here to hell is a local call, but the moonscape is scenic in its own eerie way. The town owes its existence to the potash mining industry. Golmud is the main overland gateway to Tibet assuming you can get in.

Information

CITS The office (☎ 2001 ext 254) is in the Golmud Hotel. They can arrange three-day tours to Lhasa.

Public Security Bureau This is in the Golmud Hotel.

Money The Bank of China is on the corner of Kunlun Lu and Chaidaimu Lu.

Post The post office is on the corner of Chaidamu Lu and Jiangyuan Lu.

Places to Stay
There's only one place accepting foreigners, the *Golmud Hotel* (☎ 2001) *(gé ěr mù bīnguǎn)*. Dorms in the old building cost Y10, doubles are Y40. Not a bad place but the showers seldom work. From the railway station to the hotel costs Y1 on the minibus. Walking takes about 35 minutes.

Places to Eat
Just outside the gate of the Golmud Hotel is the *Golmud Hotel Restaurant*. Right next door is *The Best Cafe* – good, friendly and has an English menu.

Getting There & Away
Air There are no flights at present, but there are plans to begin service between Xining and Golmud. CAAC estimates the airfare will be Y235.

Bus The bus station is opposite the railway station. Golmud to Dunhuang takes 13 hours, departs 6.30 am (7.30 am during summer), and costs Y24. Foreigners must pay in FEC! Buy your ticket a day in advance. The bus departs from behind the station, not in front, and no-one will bother to tell you this.

As for Tibet, the bus company will not sell tickets to foreigners but perhaps this will change. There are daily departures for Lhasa. It's essential to take enough food, drink and warm clothing to survive the long, icy night in the bus.

There is also a deluxe Japanese bus going to Lhasa. These buses depart from the Xizang Lhasa Yunshu Gongsi which is on the road which heads out of town in the direction of Lhasa.

Train From Xining, there are two trains, one express and one local. The local runs daily, the express every other day. Xining to Golmud costs Y130 in hard-sleeper, Y66 for a hard-seat. Be careful of luggage thefts at night – it's best to chain your bag to the luggage racks.

Hong Kong

Precariously perched on the edge of China, Hong Kong is a curious anomaly. It's an energetic paragon of the virtues of capitalism but nevertheless gets the unofficial blessing of the largest Communist country in the world – on which it is dependent for its very existence. The countdown to 1997, when Hong Kong is due to be handed back to the People's Republic, has made it an even more volatile and interesting enigma.

For most visitors its reputation as a shopping centre eclipses almost everything else, but it's also a fascinating city-state where you can see glimpses of rural China in the New Territories and on some of the relatively untouched islands. These days it is also the major jumping-off point for travel to China.

Facts about the Country

HISTORY

Hong Kong must stand as one of the more successful results of dope running. The dope was opium and the runners were backed by the UK government. European trade with China goes back over 400 years, but as the trade mushroomed during the 18th century, and European demand for Chinese tea and silk grew, the balance of trade became more and more unfavourable to the Europeans – until they started to run opium, grown in Bengal under the control of the British East India Company, into the country.

The Middle Kingdom finally grew tired of the barbarians and their 'foreign mud', as opium was known, and attempted to throw the chief offenders, the British, out – but not too far out, as their money if not their opium was still wanted. Unfortunately the war of words ended when, in true British fashion, the gunboats were sent in; there were only two of them, but they managed to demolish a Chinese fleet of 29 ships. The ensuing First Opium War went much the same way and at its close in 1842 the island of Hong Kong was ceded to the British.

Following the Second Opium War in 1860, the UK took possession of the Kowloon peninsula, adding another 11 sq km to the 78 sq km of the island. Finally in 1898 a 99-year lease was granted on the 948 sq km of the New Territories. What would happen after the lease ended on 1 July 1997 was the subject of considerable speculation. Although the UK supposedly had possession of Hong Kong Island and the Kowloon Peninsula for all eternity, it was pretty clear that if they handed back the New Territories China would want the rest as well. In any case the People's Republic does not recognise any pre-1949 agreements.

In late 1984 an agreement was finally reached that China would take over the entire colony lock, stock and skyscrapers, but that Hong Kong's unique free enterprise economy would be maintained for at least 50 years. It would be a tiny enclave of all-out capitalism within the Chinese empire. China has issued an invitation to Taiwan to return to the motherland under similar conditions. But many Hong Kongers – well aware of China's broken promises and erratic policies of the past – aren't buying it. The emigration queues at the embassies of Australia, Canada, New Zealand and the USA grow longer all the time.

The reality of the situation has always been, of course, that China could reclaim not only the New Territories, but all the rest of Hong Kong any time it wanted to. Hong Kong has survived so long already simply because it's useful. Conveniently situated, it acts as a funnel for Chinese goods to the West and for Western goods into China and as a source of foreign exchange and information, without the need for China to let corrupting foreign influences across the borders.

The upheavals during the Cultural Revolution, the China-inspired riots that had the colony in turmoil, and the relaxation of border controls that allowed a flood of Chinese into Hong Kong, all served as a flexing of the mainland muscles...just to show where the power was.

Acting as an intermediary hasn't been Hong Kong's only function. During the Korean War the USA placed an embargo on Chinese goods, which threatened to strangle the colony economically. To survive it developed extremely vigorous manufacturing, banking and insurance industries instead.

Part of the reason for the boundless energy of Hong Kong is that it is a capitalist's dream: lax controls and a maximum tax rate of 18%. Fortunes could be made; and were usually made fast because who knew what tomorrow would bring. Even with less than six years to go to the handover, fortunes are still being made, new skyscrapers are still being hurled up, new BMWs and Mercedes are still pouring out of the showrooms. You can smell the money in the air.

GEOGRAPHY

Hong Kong's 1070 sq km is divided into four main areas – Kowloon, Hong Kong Island, the New Territories and the Outer Islands.

Hong Kong Island is the heart of the colony, but covers only 78 sq km or just 7% of Hong Kong's land area. Kowloon is the densely populated peninsula to the north. The New Territories, which include the outlying islands, occupy 980 sq km, or 91% of Hong Kong's land area. Much of it is rural but tourists seldom visit this scenic part of Hong Kong.

CLIMATE

Although it never gets really cold, even in the middle of winter (January and February),

Hong Kong is certainly colder than South-East Asia. If you're flying here in winter from Bangkok, Manila or Singapore, be prepared. Summer is hot and humid, and thunderstorms often send visitors scampering for cover. From June to October Hong Kong is occasionally hit by typhoons. Spring and autumn are the pleasantest times of the year.

GOVERNMENT

Hong Kong is not a democracy, and China seems determined to make sure it doesn't become one. At the moment, Hong Kong is a UK colony.

Heading Hong Kong's administration is a governor who presides over meetings of both the Executive Council (EXCO) and the Legislative Council (LEGCO). The Urban Council is in charge of the day-to-day running of services in Hong Kong Island and Kowloon. This council is concerned with street cleaning, garbage collection and the like. In the New Territories, the Regional Council has much the same function as the Urban Council.

Staff in all government departments and other areas of administration are under the umbrella of the Hong Kong Civil Service which employs 173,000 people, of whom about 3500 are UK expatriates filling nearly all the top policy-making positions.

ECONOMY

Trade with both the West and China, as well as the flourishing duty-free tourist trade, has always been the cornerstone of the Hong Kong economy; but now there are other important elements. There is a thriving light-industrial sector and Hong Kong is a major

| **Hong Kong Temperatures & Rainfall** | | | | | | | | | | | |
	Jan	Feb	Mar	Apr	May	Jun	Jul	Aug	Sep	Oct	Nov	Dec
Temp (°C)	15.8	15.9	18.5	22.2	25.9	27.8	28.8	28.4	27.6	25.2	21.4	17.6
Rain (mm)	23	48	67	162	317	376	324	391	300	145	35	27

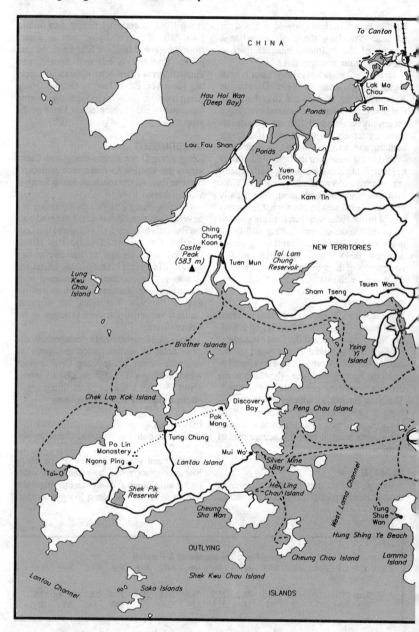

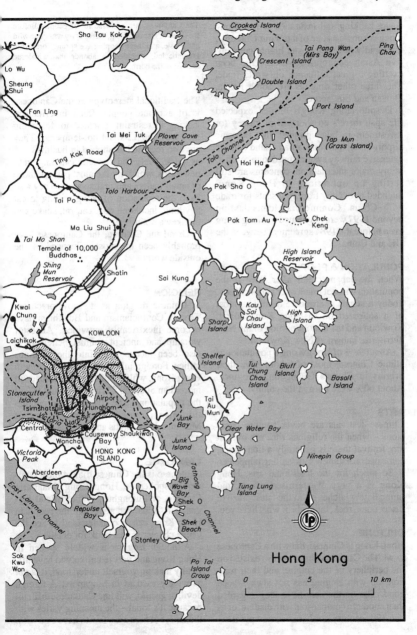

Hong Kong

Asian banking and insurance centre. Hong Kong is known as one of the 'Four Dragons', the rapidly developing and highly competitive Asian economies which have been exerting a great influence on world trade. The three other dragons are South Korea, Taiwan and Singapore.

Despite Hong Kong's limited expected life span there's no shortage of money for investment in huge projects like the new airport being built on Lantau Island and the extensive railway system needed to reach it. Many major international concerns are still setting up operations in Hong Kong, intended to occupy front row seats for trade with China. Commercial loans lasting beyond 1997 were negotiated in Hong Kong even before the 1984 agreement between the UK and China.

POPULATION & PEOPLE

When the Japanese left after WW II the population was not much over half a million. Today it stands at around 5.8 million, most of it squeezed on to Hong Kong Island, Kowloon and the bottom portion of the New Territories known as New Kowloon.

About 98% of Hong Kong's population is ethnic Chinese, most of whom have their origins in China's Guangdong Province. About 60% were born in the colony.

ARTS

Chinese festivals are never sombre occasions – when the religious rites are over at any festival there is generally a lion dance, some opera or a show by a visiting puppeteer.

So much for the traditional arts. Hong Kong is a very Westernised place, and immediately latches on to the latest craze in disco, punk, rock, lambada or what have you.

CULTURE

Hong Kong is Chinese, but with a Cantonese twist. The Cantonese have always existed on the periphery of the empire, and their relationship with Beijing has not always been good. The northerners have long regarded their southern compatriots with disdain, or as one 19th-century northern account put it:

The Cantonese...are a coarse set of people...Before the times of Han and Tang, this country was quite wild and waste, and these people have sprung forth from unconnected, unsettled vagabonds that wandered here from the north.

The traditional stereotype of the Cantonese is of a proud people, frank in criticism, lacking in restraint, oriented to defending their own interests and hot-tempered. They are also regarded as shrewd in business and as quick, lively and clever in catching on to new skills, which for the most part are those of small traders and craftspeople. They also have the reputation of being willing to eat anything, including dog, cat, rat, snake and monkey's brain.

Of all the Chinese, the Cantonese have probably been the most influenced by the outside world.

RELIGION

In Chinese religion as it's now practised, Taoism, Confucianism and Buddhism have become inextricably entwined. Ancestor worship and ancient animist beliefs have also been incorporated into the religious milieu. Foreign influence has been heavy in Hong Kong, which explains the presence of more than 500,000 Christians (about 9% of the population). The cosmopolitan population also incorporates a smattering of Muslims, Jews, Sikhs and Hindus.

LANGUAGE

Cantonese is the Chinese dialect most commonly spoken in Hong Kong. Mandarin Chinese, or Putonghua, is the official language in China, and about half the people in Hong Kong can also understand it. See the China chapter in this book for details.

Although English is widely spoken in Hong Kong and you're unlikely to have difficulty making yourself understood, it is not as widely used as in Singapore. A foreign devil, or *gwailo*, will find Cantonese difficult because it's tonal – the meaning varies with the tone; but here are a few to have a go with.

How much?	*gay doa cheen?*
Too expensive.	*tie goo-why*
Waiter, the bill.	*fo-kay, my don*
Go away!	*jaaw hoy!*

Facts for the Visitor

VISAS & EMBASSIES

For most non-Communist nationalities there are no visa requirements. UK passport holders are permitted to stay for 12 months, citizens of UK territories and all the Commonwealth countries can stay for three months, citizens of the USA and certain Western European and South American nations can stay for one month.

Enquire at the Immigration Department (☎ 8246111), 2nd floor, Wanchai Tower Two, 7 Gloucester Rd, Wanchai. In general, they do not like to grant extensions unless there are special circumstances – cancelled flights, illness, registration in a legitimate course of study, legal employment, marriage to a local, etc.

China is now wide open; see the chapter on China in this book or *China – a travel survival kit* (Lonely Planet) for the full story. Visas for individual travel in China are readily available in Hong Kong and once in the Middle Kingdom you can go almost anywhere you please.

Visas are more quickly and conveniently obtained by travel agents, but at higher cost. Most single-entry visas are valid for 90 days. More expensive are the two-entry visas. Multiple-entry visas are not only expensive, but you can stay for just 30 days at a time (no extensions permitted) but the visa remains valid for six months. Multiple-entry visas are only issued if you've already been to China at least once and have stamps in your passport to prove it.

Foreign Consulates in Hong Kong

Australia
    23rd & 24th floor, Harbour Centre, 25 Harbour Rd, Wanchai (☎ 5731881)

Canada
    11th-14th floor, Tower One, Exchange Square, 8 Connaught Place, Central (☎ 8104321)

China
    Visa Office of the Ministry of Foreign Affairs, 5th floor, Lower Block, 26 Harbour Rd, Wanchai (☎ 8353794)

Japan
    24th floor, Bank of America Tower, 12 Harcourt Rd, Central (☎ 5221184)

Korea (South)
    5th floor, Far East Finance Centre, 16 Harcourt Rd, Central (☎ 5294141)

New Zealand
    Room 3414, Jardine House, Connaught Rd, Central (☎ 5255044)

Philippines
    21st floor, Wah Kwong Regent Centre, 88 Queen's Rd, Central (☎ 8100183)

Taiwan
    Chung Hwa Travel Service, 4th floor, East Tower, Bond Centre, 3 Queensway, Central (☎ 5258315)

Thailand
    8th floor, Fairmont House, 8 Cotton Tree Drive, Central (☎ 5216481)

USA
    26 Garden Rd, Central (☎ 5239011)

DOCUMENTS

You're advised to carry some form of identification on you at all times in Hong Kong. Something with a photo will do.

CUSTOMS

Even though Hong Kong is a duty-free port, there are still a few items on which duty is charged. The duty-free allowance for visitors is 200 cigarettes (one carton), one litre of alcohol, 60 ml of perfume and 250 ml of toilet water. It's not allowed to bring in fireworks, which is why Hong Kongers returning from China are so vigorously searched but foreigners are seldom hassled.

MONEY
Currency

Hong Kong's unit of currency is the Hong Kong dollar, divided into 100 cents. There are different banknote designs in circulation, although the notes are interchangeable.

Bills are issued in denominations of $10 (green), $50 (blue), $100 (red), $500 (brown) and $1000 (yellow). Coins are issued in denominations of $5, $2, $1, 50 cents, 20 cents and 10 cents.

Changing Money

Hong Kong is a dream come true for changing money. Any major trading currency, and even many insignificant currencies, can be exchanged. All major international credit cards are accepted.

Banks give the best exchange rates by far, but it varies from bank to bank. One of the best is Wing Lung Bank, 4 Carnarvon Rd, Tsimshatsui, next to the New Astor Hotel. Another good bank for changing money is Hang Seng Bank which has numerous branches all over the city. The main Tsimshatsui branch of Hang Seng Bank is at 18 Carnarvon Rd. The small branches in the Mass Transit Railway (MTR) stations do not change money.

The Hongkong Bank gives relatively poor rates for a bank, and in addition tacks on a HK$20 service charge for each transaction.

Bank hours are 9 am to 4 pm Monday to Friday, and 9 am to 12 noon or 1 pm on Saturday. Standard Chartered opens 9 am to 6 pm Monday to Friday.

Licensed moneychangers in the tourist districts operate 24 hours a day, but give relatively poor exchange rates which are clearly posted. However, you can almost always get a much better rate by bargaining!

Try not to change any money at the airport – the exchange rate there is pathetic though you can try bargaining.

Exchange Rates

A$1	=	HK$6.00
C$1	=	HK$6.80
NZ$1	=	HK$4.40
UK£1	=	HK$13.80
US$1	=	HK$7.80
Y100	=	HK$6.00

Costs

Hong Kong is certainly not cheap – it's a result of the continuing economic boom and the ever-increasing cost of land. You can still find dorm beds for around HK$40 but it takes effort to find a double room for less than HK$100 these days.

On the other hand food is reasonably priced, transport is cheap and amazingly efficient and Hong Kong is still a great place to shop. Keep on your toes though, plenty of people in Hong Kong are after the faster dollar and 'never give a sucker an even break' is often the motto of the day.

The main way to cut costs is to control yourself – shopping in Hong Kong can be addictive.

Tipping

A 10% service charge is added to most res-

taurant bills; if you're not sure if it's included ask. In taxis you should round the fare up to the nearest 50c or even dollar.

Bargaining

If you shop for cameras, Walkmans, and other big ticket items in the tourist ghetto of Tsimshatsui, bargaining is essential. However, bargaining is *not* the norm in Hong Kong. It's only normal in places where tourists congregate. Out in the shopping malls like Cityplaza where the Chinese shop, everything has a price tag and there is little or no scope for bargaining.

TOURIST OFFICES
Local Tourist Offices

The enterprising Hong Kong Tourist Association (HKTA) has desks at the airport, on the Kowloon side of the Star Ferry run, and in Central, Hong Kong Island. The one at the Kowloon Star Ferry pier is open 8 am to 6 pm Monday to Friday, and from 9 am to 5 pm weekends and holidays. The office on Hong Kong Island is in Shop 8, Basement, Jardine House, 1 Connaught Place, Central – open 8 am to 6 pm weekdays, and 8 am to 1 pm on Saturdays and closed on Sundays and holidays. The desks at Kai Tak Airport are open 8 am to 10.30 pm daily, and only provide information for arriving passengers.

You can call the HKTA hotline (☎ 8017177) from 8 am to 6 pm daily. Shopping advice and enquiries on HKTA members can be obtained by phone (☎ 8017278), 9 am to 5 pm Monday to Friday, and 9 am to 12.45 pm on Saturdays.

HKTA Offices Overseas

Australia
Level 5, 55 Harrington St, The Rocks, Sydney (☎ (02) 2512855, outside Sydney (008) 251071)
Canada
347 Bay St, Suite 909, Toronto, Ontario M5H 2R7 (☎ (416) 3662389)
Japan
4th floor, Toho Twin Tower Building, 1-5-2 Yurakucho, Chiyoda-ku, Tokyo 100 (☎ (03) 35030735)
4th floor, Hong Kong & Shanghai Bank Building, 6-1 Awaji-machi 3-chome, Chuo-ku, Osaka 541 (☎ (06) 2299240)

New Zealand
PO Box 2120, Auckland (☎ (09) 5213167)
Singapore
10 Collyer Quay, 13th floor, 13-08 Ocean Building, Singapore 0104 (☎ 5323668)
UK
5th floor, 125 Pall Mall, London, SW1Y 5EA (☎ (071) 9304775)
USA
333 North Michigan Ave, Suite 2400, Chicago, Illinois 60601-3966 (☎ (312) 7823872)
5th floor, 590 Fifth Ave, New York, New York 10036-4706 (☎ 212 8695008)
10940 Wilshire Blvd, Suite 1220, Los Angeles, California 90024 (☎ (213) 2084582)
360 Post St, Suite 404, San Francisco, California 94108 (☎ (415) 7814582)

USEFUL ORGANISATIONS

Since the likelihood of getting ripped off by shopkeepers is high, it's good to know about the the Hong Kong Consumer Council (☎ 7363322). The main office is in China Hong Kong City, Canton Rd, Tsimshatsui, Kowloon. It has a complaints and advice hot line (☎ 7363636) and an Advice Centre (☎ 5411422) at 38 Pier Rd, Central, near the Outlying Islands ferry pier.

BUSINESS HOURS & HOLIDAYS

Office hours are Monday to Friday from 9 am to 5 pm, and on Saturday from 9 am to noon. Lunch hour is from 1 pm to 2 pm and many offices simply shut down and lock the door at this time. Banks are open Monday to Friday from 9 am to 4.30 pm and do not close for lunch – on Saturday they are open from 9 am to 12.30 pm.

Stores and restaurants that cater to the tourist trade keep longer hours, but almost nothing opens before 9 am. Even tourist-related businesses shut down by 9 or 10 pm, and many will close for major holidays, especially Chinese New Year.

Western and Chinese culture combine to create an interesting mix of holidays. The first day of the first moon (late January or early February) is Chinese New Year (see the introductory Facts for the Visitor chapter for dates). Only the first three days of this are a public holiday, but everything pretty much shuts down for a week and all flights out of

Hong Kong are booked solid for nearly three weeks.

The other big public holiday to avoid is Ching Ming (visits to ancestors' graves) which falls around Easter time. Transport at this time is also a problem.

The last public holidays are Christmas (25 December) and Boxing Day (26 December), when the lights of Hong Kong are bright and the streets are packed.

CULTURAL EVENTS

There are literally hundreds of cultural events throughout the year, but the exact dates vary. The Hong Kong Tourist Association publishes a complete schedule every month. If you want to time your visit to Hong Kong to coincide with a particular event, it would be wise to contact the HKTA beforehand. Some colourful non-public holidays include the birthdays of Tin Hau (the goddess of fisherfolk), Tam Kung (another patron saint of boat people) and Lord Buddha. The Cheung Chau Bun Festival features raucous fun on Cheung Chau island. Then there's the Yue Lan Festival of Hungry Ghosts (late August or September) which is a great time to visit Taoist temples. A brief rundown of important annual events includes:

HK Arts Festival.
    An assortment of exhibitions and shows usually held in January.
HK Festival Fringe.
    The Fringe Club supports upcoming artists and performers from Hong Kong and elsewhere. This three-week festival occurs from late January to February.
Orienteering Competition.
    Sponsored by the Urban Council, this event is usually staged in January in Tai Tam Country Park.
HK International Marathon.
    Organised by the Hong Kong Amateur Athletic Association, this major event is held in Shatin, usually in March.
HK Food Festival.
    Sponsored by the HKTA and usually held in March.
HK International Film Festival.
    Organised by the Urban Council, this event usually occurs in March or April.

International Dragon Boat Festival.
    Usually falling in June, the international festival is usually held the week after the Chinese dragon boat races.
International Arts Carnival.
    This unusual summer festival promotes performances by children's groups. The carnival usually falls in July or August.
Asian Regatta.
    Organised by the Hong Kong Yachting Association, this event usually occurs in October.
Mid-Autumn Festival.
    Moon cakes are eaten around the time of the 15th night of the 8th moon.
Festival of Asian Arts.
    This is one of Asia's major international events, attracting performers from Australia as well as nearby countries. This festival usually occurs in October or November.

Cultural Centres

The main venue for cultural events is the shiny new Hong Kong Cultural Centre (☎ 7342009), 10 Salisbury Rd, Tsimshatsui, Kowloon. The Philharmonic Orchestra and Chinese Orchestra, among others, have regular performances here.

Big events such as rock concerts and the like are held at the Hong Kong Coliseum (☎ 7659234), 9 Cheoung Wan Rd, Hunghom, Kowloon, a 12,500-seat indoor concert hall very close to the Kowloon Canton Railway Station.

On Hong Kong Island, the main centre for cultural events is the Hong Kong Academy for the Performing Arts (☎ 8231505), 1 Gloucester Rd, Wanchai. Just across the street is the Hong Kong Arts Centre (☎ 8230230), 2 Harbour Rd, Wanchai.

Some groups book performances at City Hall Theatre (☎ 5233800), right next to the Star Ferry Terminal in Central. The Queen Elizabeth Stadium (☎ 5756793), 18 Oi Kwan Rd, Wanchai, is the site for a wide range of events, including sporting events and concerts.

There are three big cultural centres in the New Territories: Shatin Town Hall (☎ 6942503), 1 Yuen Ho Rd, Shatin; Tuen Mun Town Hall (☎ 4527308), 3 Tuen Hi Rd, Tuen Mun; Tsuen Wan Town Hall (☎ 4939143), 72 Tai Ho Rd, Tsuen Wan.

POST & TELECOMMUNICATIONS

Postal Rates

The Hong Kong postal service divides the world into two distinct zones. Zone 1 is China, Japan, Taiwan, South Korea, South-East Asia, Indonesia and India. Zone 2 is everywhere else. Postcards are HK$1.80 to Zone 1 and HK$2.30 to Zone 2; the prices are the same for letters up to the first 10g, plus HK$1.00/1.10 for each additional 10g.

A local letter weighing under 30g costs HK$0.80.

Sending Mail

All post offices are open from Monday to Saturday from 8 am to 6 pm, and are closed on Sunday and public holidays. On the Kowloon side, one of the most convenient post offices is at 10 Middle Rd, east of Nathan Rd, Tsimshatsui.

Receiving Mail

The GPO with poste restante service is beside the Star Ferry Terminal in Hong Kong Central.

Telephones

If you want to phone overseas, it's cheapest to use an IDD (International Direct Dialling) telephone. You can place an IDD call from most phone boxes, but you'll need a stack of HK$5 coins handy if your call is going to be anything but very brief. An alternative is to buy a 'Phonecard', which comes in denominations of HK$50, HK$100 or HK$250. You can find Cardphones in shops, on the street or at a Hongkong Telecom office. There's a Hongkong Telecom at 10 Middle Rd in Tsimshatsui and another at Exchange Square in Central.

For calls to countries that do not have IDD service, you can call from a Hongkong Telecom office – first pay a deposit and they will hook you up (minimum three minutes) and give you your change after the call is completed.

To make an IDD call from Hong Kong, first dial 001, then the country code, area code and number. If calling to Hong Kong from abroad, the country code is 852.

Dial 108 for directory inquiries. To check the time and temperature, dial 1852.

Fax, Telex & Telegraph

All your communication needs can be taken care of at Hongkong Telecom. To send a one-page (A4 size) fax, they charge HK$10 within Hong Kong; HK$30 for South-East Asia; HK$35 to Australia, New Zealand, Canada, USA and UK; and HK$45 to all other countries. For HK$10 per page, you can also receive a fax here.

You can also send or receive a fax from many hotels, but check the cost first – a few hotels charge ridiculous prices for this service.

TIME

The time in Hong Kong is Greenwich Mean Time plus eight hours. When it is noon in Hong Kong it is also noon in Singapore and Perth; 2 pm in Sydney; 8 pm the previous day in Los Angeles; 11 pm the previous day in

New York; and 4 am in London. Daylight savings time is not observed.

LAUNDRY

Many hotels, even the cheap youth hostels, have a laundry service. If they don't, just ask where one is. Prices are normally HK$22 for three kg. If less than three kg, you still pay the same, so you might want to throw your clothes together with a friend's.

Two convenient laundry services in Tsimshatsui are Carlye Steam Laundry, Golden Crown Court, 66-70 Nathan Rd, and Purity Laundry, 25 Chungking Arcade, Chungking Mansions, 30 Nathan Rd.

WEIGHTS & MEASURES

The international metric system is in official use in Hong Kong. In practice, traditional Chinese weights and measures are still common.

If you want to shop in the local markets, become familiar with Chinese units of weight. Things are sold by the *leung*, which is equivalent to 37.5 grams, or in *catty*, where one catty is about 600 grams. There are 16 leung to the catty.

ELECTRICITY

The standard is 200 V, 50 Hz (cycles) AC.

BOOKS & MAPS

The Government's annual report is entitled *Hong Kong 1990, Hong Kong 1991*, etc. In addition to the excellent photographs, the text is a gold mine of information about the government, politics, economy, history, arts and just about any other topic relevant to Hong Kong.

A good antidote to the government's upbeat version of history is *The Other Hong Kong Report* (Chinese University Press). It's a fascinating and somewhat cynical rebuttal.

Maurice Collin's *Foreign Mud* (Faber & Faber, UK, 1946) tells the sordid story of the Opium Wars.

Borrowed Place, Borrowed Time is the book to read on Hong Kong's birth and development. It was written by the late Richard Hughes, one of the real 'old China hands'. Novels to dip into include the readable (and highly dramatic) *Tai-pan* by James Clavell, which is (very) loosely based on the Jardine-Matheson organisation in its early days. Richard Mason's *The World of Suzie Wong* is also interesting – after all she was Hong Kong's best-known citizen.

If you want more information on Hong Kong and the surrounding area, look for the Lonely Planet guidebook *Hong Kong, Macau & Canton*. Lonely Planet also publishes *China – a travel survival kit*.

The giveaway maps provided by the HKTA are adequate for finding your way around most places in Kowloon or the city part of Hong Kong Island.

MEDIA
Newspapers & Magazines

The two main newspapers produced in Hong Kong are the *South China Morning Post* and the *Hong Kong Standard*.

Hong Kong is the home of the *Far Eastern Economic Review*, one of the most authoritative magazines covering Asian events.

Radio & TV

Radio Television Hong Kong (RTHK) operates three stations: RTHK (Radio 3) at AM 567 kHz and 1584 kHz, and FM 97.9 mHz and 106.8 mHz; RTHK (Radio 4) at 97.6 mHz and 98.9 mHz FM; RTHK (Radio 6) with the BBC World Service relay at AM 675 kHz. Commercial Radio (CR) is at AM 864 kHz. The British Forces Broadcasting Service (BFBS) is at FM 93.1, 96.6, 102 and 104.8 mHz.

Hong Kong's TV stations are run by two companies, Television Broadcasts Ltd (TVB) and Asia Television Ltd (ATV). Each company operates one English-language and one Cantonese-language channel. The two

English stations are TVB Pearl and ATV World.

The programme schedules for radio & TV are listed daily in the English-language newspapers.

FILM & PHOTOGRAPHY

Everything you could possibly need in the way of film, camera and photographic accessories is available in Hong Kong, usually at cheaper prices than you'd pay at home.

HEALTH

Hong Kong is a very healthy place. You can drink water straight from the tap, and even the street markets are reasonably clean despite their dubious appearance.

Public hospitals charge reasonable fees, but Hong Kong residents pay less than foreign visitors. Public hospitals include: *Queen Elizabeth Hospital* (☎ 7102111), Wylie Rd, Yaumati, Kowloon; *Princess Margaret Hospital* (☎ 7427111), Lai Chi Kok, Kowloon; *Queen Mary Hospital* (☎ 8179463), Pokfulam Rd.

Private doctors usually charge reasonable fees, but it pays to make some enquiries first. Most large hotels have resident doctors.

Hong Kong has a shortage of dentists and fees are consequently very high. If the next stop on your itinerary is Taiwan, you might want to wait because the cost for dental treatment is much lower there.

Most pharmacies in Hong Kong are open 9 am to 6 pm, with some until 8 pm.

WOMEN TRAVELLERS

While Hong Kong poses no special dangers for women, unpleasant incidents can occur. And like anything else in Hong Kong, sex is a business. One woman traveller had this to report:

A young Chinese man came to the Travellers Hostel looking for an English girl who was after some modelling work. He asked me if I wanted some extra money, offering me escort/film work. I replied 'No' as I was returning home shortly and didn't need money. However, as he persisted and offered me HK$1000 for an evening solely as an escort, I agreed, with another girl, to meet him the next evening. He turned out to be working as a pimp for Chinese 'high-class' customers. OK, I should have known better. I left as soon as possible amid threats from him and an Indian boss, and quite frankly I was really frightened. My friend who was interested in modelling stayed, but soon found out that the entire business was just to find European girls to have sex with Chinese men.

DANGERS & ANNOYANCES

In a form of poetic Chinese justice, the colony's initial opium-based founding has rebounded and Hong Kong has a serious dope problem. Like elsewhere, addicts turn to crime to finance their habit. For the most part, it's non-violent crime: pickpocketing, burglaries and (in the case of women addicts) prostitution. However, muggings do occasionally occur, though seldom in tourist areas since these are heavily patrolled by the police.

More visitors have been ripped off by their fellow travellers than by Hong Kong residents. Especially if you're staying in a dormitory, be careful with your valuables.

The biggest annoyance of life in Hong Kong is the appalling rudeness of shopkeepers. The Hong Kong Tourist Association is aware of the problem, and has attempted to educate sales clerks not to bite the tourists. They've tried all sorts of catchy slogans: 'Smile at our foreign friends', etc. Unfortunately, most shopkeepers prefer the motto 'Give us your money and get the hell out!'

WORK

Some travellers do find short-term work in Hong Kong (mostly illegal). English teaching pays around HK$50 an hour, but we've had warnings from people who have been ripped off by English-teaching schools. Other possibilities are bar and waitressing jobs, modelling and babysitting. Some travellers turn to busking, but this doesn't seem to be very profitable in Hong Kong.

If you have a special technical skill, you might find it very easy to get work in Hong Kong. In that case, your only real problem will be obtaining a work visa. UK citizens can work in the colony without legal hassles, but other nationalities require a work visa.

There are severe penalties for employers who hire workers illegally. Applications for employment visas can be made to any UK embassy or UK consular or diplomatic office. If you arrive in Hong Kong as a visitor and get a job, you will have to leave the colony, apply for a visa and return when it is obtained.

ACTIVITIES

Anyone who is serious about sports should contact the *South China Athletic Association* (☎ 5776932), Caroline Hill Rd, Causeway Bay, Hong Kong Island. The SCAA has numerous indoor facilities such as bowling, tennis, ping pong tables, an exercise room, yoga classes, karate classes and others. Membership costs HK$40, but visitors can join for HK$10 per month.

Cycling

There are bicycle paths in the New Territories mostly around Tolo Harbour. The paths run from Shatin to Tai Po and continue up to Tai Mei Tuk. You can rent cycles in these three places, but it's very crowded on weekends. On a weekday you may have the paths to yourself.

Horse Racing

The racing season is from late September to June. Normally, races at Shatin are held on Saturdays from 1 to 6 pm. At Happy Valley, races are normally on Wednesday evenings from about 7 to 11 pm.

Hiking

Hong Kong has some excellent walks. Practically everyone does the walk around Victoria Peak. The MacLehose Trail in the New Territories is 100 km long and goes over the summit of Hong Kong's highest peak, Tai Mo Shan. Almost equally challenging is the 70-km Lantau Trail on Lantau Island.

HIGHLIGHTS

The trip on the Peak Tram to Victoria Peak has been practically mandatory for visitors since it opened in 1888. A 30-minute ride on a sampan through Aberdeen Harbour is equally exciting. Lunch at a good dim sum restaurant is one of the great pleasures of the Orient; and of course, shopping is what Hong Kong is all about. For those who prefer a less frantic pace, a pleasant time can be spent exploring quiet backwaters in the Outlying Islands such as Lantau's Po Lin Monastery.

ACCOMMODATION

The cost of accommodation is the major expense in visiting Hong Kong, although you can still get by reasonably cheaply with a little effort. There are a number of youth hostels and similarly oriented places with dormitory accommodation; or you can head for the guesthouses which are clustered in Chungking Mansions.

The prices at guesthouses are variable with supply and demand and also with the length of your stay. If you're in Hong Kong during a low-season period or you plan to stay for an extended time it's definitely worth bargaining over the price.

The majority of cheap accommodation is on the Kowloon side. With a few exceptions the places on Hong Kong Island are expensive 'international' hotels. You can, however, find some interesting cheap accommodation out on the islands or in the New Territories, at least on weekdays. At weekends, prices on the islands escalate dramatically, though you can often get cheap deals if you rent by the week or month. At the airport there is a hotel reservation desk, but they generally only deal with the more expensive hotels.

You can get as much as a 40% discount at mid-range and luxury hotels if you book through certain travel agents. One agent offering this service is *Traveller Services* (☎ 3674127, fax 3110387), 7th floor, 57 Peking Rd, Tsimshatsui.

FOOD

Hong Kong has just about every dining possibility you can think of from McDonald's to Mexican or Sichuan to spaghetti. It's not a fantastically cheap food trip like Singapore but you can still eat well at a fairly low cost. If you're really economising, however, you might find yourself eating more Big Macs than you might have expected.

DRINKS

You can drink as much tea as you like usually free of charge in any Chinese restaurant. On the other hand, coffee is seldom available except in Western restaurants or coffee shops, and is never free.

There are three main types of tea: green or unfermented; *bolay* fermented, also known as black tea; and oolong, which is semi-fermented. There are many varieties of tea. Jasmine tea *(heung ping)* is a blend of tea and flowers which is always drunk straight, without milk or sugar.

Beer is extremely popular among the Chinese. The brands made in China are excellent, the most popular being *Tsingtao*, now a major export. It's actually a German beer – the town where it is made, Tsingtao (Qingdao), was once a German concession. The Chinese inherited the brewery when the Germans were kicked out.

ENTERTAINMENT

Pubs & Bars

Apart from a scattering of girlie bars, topless bars, hostess bars and god-knows-what-else bars around Tsimshatsui and Wanchai, Hong Kong also has lots of straightforward places where you can get a reasonably priced beer in pleasant surroundings. Many of them are English or Australian in their flavour.

A beer typically costs HK$25 in these bars but in the early evening 'happy hours' you can get drinks at half price or two for the price of one. At some big hotels not only are the drinks cheap but there are lots of snacks and nibbles on offer under the heading of 'small chow'.

THINGS TO BUY

Oh yeah, shopping – some people do come to Hong Kong for that. Well, a lot of the same things apply as in Singapore: shop around, try and find out what the 'real' retail price is before you believe the discounts, make sure guarantees are international and – most important – don't go on a buying binge. It's

very easy in Hong Kong to decide suddenly you need all sorts of consumer goods you don't really need at all.

It's hard to say just how Hong Kong and Singapore really compare in price or choice – they're probably pretty similar. The HKTA has a shopping guide booklet which lists approved shops, but that old story, caveat emptor (let the buyer beware), applies as strongly as ever.

The worst neighbourhood for shopping happens to be the place where most tourists shop. Tsimshatsui, the tourist ghetto of Kowloon, is the most likely place for tourists to be cheated. Notice that none of the cameras or other big ticket items have price tags. This is *not* common practice elsewhere in Hong Kong. If you go out to the Chinese neighbourhoods where the locals shop, you'll find price tags on everything. Furthermore, the non-touristy shops seldom bargain. Their prices, however, are still lower than what you can bargain for in Tsimshatsui

If you're staying in Kowloon, Mongkok is a much better neighbourhood for shopping. On Hong Kong Island, Central and Causeway Bay are the tourist trap zones. You'll often do better by heading out to Cityplaza, a shopping mall in Quarry Bay. Take the MTR to the Tai Koo Station.

If possible, try not to be in a hurry. Shop around a little bit and be sure you understand the prices. Of course, shops realise that tourists do this, so they have other clever methods for cheating you. The most common trick is to offer you a good price on a camera and then rip you off on the accessories like filters, neckstrap, camera case, batteries, etc.

More diabolical tricks include selling second-hand equipment as new, selling goods without proper guarantees, selling grey-market equipment (ie imported by somebody other than the official local agent), passing off superseded models as new ones, persuading you that standard equipment actually costs extra, and on and on! Yet another ploy is to deliberately sell you electronic equipment of the wrong voltage. When you discover the mistake later and bring it back, they refuse to exchange unless you pay more.

You should be especially wary if they want to take the goods into the back room to 'box it up'. This provides ample opportunity to remove essential items that you have already paid for.

There is really no reason to put a deposit on anything unless it is being custom-made for you, like a fitted suit or a pair of eye-glasses.

If buying film you get a better price buying in bulk, say 10 or 12 rolls at a time.

Hong Kong's reputation for made-to-measure clothes is not what it was – prices have escalated so they're no longer really cheap. You'd do better to check out some of the places that sell ready-made clothes as Hong Kong is becoming very fashion conscious. It's a good cheap place to buy jeans and other denim clothes.

Buying jade or antiques is more for the knowledgeable purchaser, and authenticity depends on buying from reputable dealers. Antique shops on Hollywood Rd (up from Central) are interesting to wander around. If you're into 'instant oil paintings' they're available very cheaply around Kowloon. Glasses and contact lenses are cheap and well made.

Check out the People's Republic emporium Chinese Arts and Crafts where you'll find many unusual items, often of good quality and (sometimes) low prices. An excellent emporium is Yue Hwa Chinese Products at the corner of Nathan and Jordan roads.

BOOKSHOPS

There are several excellent bookshops in Hong Kong. One of the biggest and best is Swindon Books, 13 Lock Rd, Tsimshatsui.

Times Books gives its address as Shop C, 96 Nathan Rd, but the entrance is around the corner on Granville Rd in Tsimshatsui. It's also large and has another branch (☎ 7226583) in Tsimshatsui East in Houston Centre, lower ground floor, Shop No LG-23. Another Times Books (☎ 5258797) is at

Hutchison House, Shop G-31, Central, Hong Kong Island. Hutchison House is at the corner of Murray Rd and Lambeth Walk.

Wanderlust Books, 30 Hollywood Rd, Central, Hong Kong Island, is well worth visiting for its collections of travel books, maps and books about Hong Kong. The staff are extremely helpful and friendly, a rarity in Hong Kong bookshops. It's at the corner of Hollywood Rd and Shelley St.

There is a South China Morning Post Bookshop is at the Star Ferry Terminal on Hong Kong Island. They have another branch on the 3rd floor, Ocean Terminal in Tsimshatsui.

Peace Book Company, 35 Kimberly Rd, Tsimshatsui, is an excellent store and has many books about China.

Not to be overlooked is the Government Publications Centre in the GPO building next to the Star Ferry.

LIBRARIES

The main library is at City Hall, City Hall High Block, Central, just a block to the east of the Star Ferry Terminal. However, they will not let you make photocopies of anything which is copyright (which means just about everything). As a result, most of their reference books have pages ripped out of them by frustrated students.

The American Library (☎ 5299661), 1st floor, United Centre, 95 Queensway, Admiralty, has good research facilities and *does* allow you to make photocopies.

EMERGENCY

The emergency telephone number for fire, police or ambulance is ☎ 999.

Getting There & Away

AIR

For most of us the normal arrival point will be Kai Tak Airport – with its runway sticking out from Kowloon into the harbour it makes a pretty dramatic entrance.

See the introductory Getting There &

Away chapter for details of air fares to Hong Kong from Australia, Europe or North America. If you are going anywhere in the north-east Asian region (Japan, Korea, Taiwan, China) or to the Philippines or Sabah in Borneo then Hong Kong is one of the best gateways to the region.

Hong Kong is a popular place for shopping for discounted airline tickets. Typical one-way fares include: Auckland HK$3350, Bangkok HK$1400, Beijing HK$1450, Canton HK$300, Honolulu HK$2150, Kathmandu HK$2000, Kuala Lumpur HK$2250, London HK$2500, Manila HK$1350, New York HK$2850, Perth HK$2500, San Francisco HK$2480, Seoul HK$1900, Singapore HK$1250, Sydney HK$2750, Taipei HK$1050, Tokyo HK$1250, Toronto HK$3500 and Vancouver HK$3150. These are special fares and will have various restrictions upon their use.

Travel Agencies

A major contender in the budget ticket business is Shoestring Travel (☎ 7232306), Flat A, 4th floor, Alpha House, 27-33 Nathan Rd, Tsimshatsui.

Travel Expert (☎ 5432770), Room 708, Haleson Building, 1 Jubilee St, Central, has about the cheapest fares we've seen anywhere.

Traveller Services (☎ 3674127), Room 704, Metropole Bulding, 57 Peking Rd, Tsimshatsui, is fast, cheap and reliable.

Equally good is Phoenix Services (☎ 7227378) in Room B, 6th floor, Milton Mansion, 96 Nathan Rd, Tsimshatsui, Kowloon. Many travellers have spoken very highly of this place.

The Hong Kong Student Travel Bureau (☎ 7303269) is in Room 1021, 10th floor, Star House, Tsimshatsui.

LAND

If you just want a brief guided visit to the People's Republic you can do that quite easily. There are plenty of one-day cross-the-border jaunts available from Hong Kong or Macau and slightly longer 'Canton Quickies' which give you a few days in the neighbouring city.

A train to Lo Wu at the border will cost you just HK$35. You walk across the border to the city of Shenzhen, and from there you can take a local train to Canton (Guangzhou) and beyond.

Alternatively you can take an express train straight through from Hunghom Station in Kowloon to Canton (Guangzhou) for HK$180.

SEA

Hong Kong has one of the most spectacular harbours in the world so it's kind of a shame that there's not much of a chance of arriving by boat – unless you're rich and on a cruise liner. It may still be possible though for budget travellers, if you want to take a boat from China. The Shanghai to Hong Kong ferry is very popular with travellers, and it's a great way to leave China.

You can go to China by hovercraft from the China Hong Kong City ferry terminal in Tsimshatsui. Perhaps cheapest (HK$120) and most pleasant is to take the overnight ferry from Kowloon to Canton; you sleep in dormitory beds and save one night's accommodation charge at a hotel.

LEAVING HONG KONG
Departure Tax

Airport departure tax is now a hefty HK$150, but you don't have to pay if you can persuade them you're aged under 12. If departing by ship to Macau or China, departure tax is included in the price of the ticket.

Getting Around

Hong Kong has a varied and frequent public transport system, but there are two advance words of warning. Before setting out to travel anywhere by bus ensure you have a good pocketful of small change – the exact fare normally must be deposited in a cash box and nobody has change. The second warning is that on weekends everybody, plus

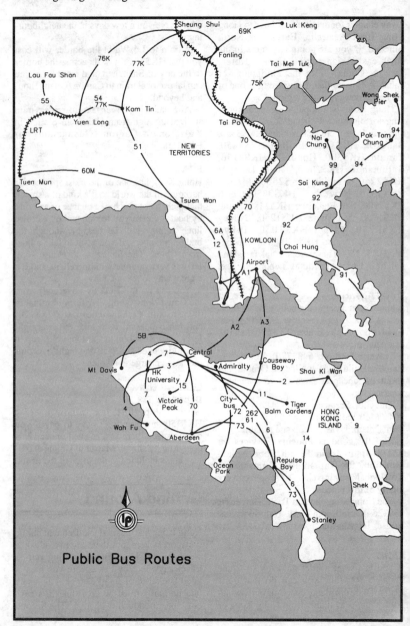

Public Bus Routes

his/her brother, sister and boy/girlfriend, sets out to go somewhere. Particularly on Sundays you must be prepared for it to take much longer getting anywhere, to pay more on certain ferries, and even to miss the odd overfull bus. Plus everybody (and their etc) will be taking photographs of everybody else so take care you don't appear in too many family portraits.

TO/FROM THE AIRPORT

There's a variety of ways of getting to and from the airport, the easiest of which is by taxi (fares to most hotels are listed at the airport). To most places in the Tsimshatsui area it should cost in the HK$35 to HK$40 range. It'll cost rather more to places on Hong Kong Island since taxis are entitled to charge an additional HK$20 to cover the toll for the Cross-Harbour Tunnel going both ways. During rush hour the tunnel can get very clogged up – so allow sufficient time and be prepared for a higher fare at those times. Usually the fare from the airport should be HK$55 to HK$60 to Causeway Bay or HK$65 to HK$71 to Central. The only other addition to the fare should be a charge of HK$2 per bag.

The Airbus airport bus services are very convenient and are significantly cheaper than taxis. There are three services – the A1 to Tsimshatsui (HK$8), the A2 to Wanchai, Central and the Macau Ferry Terminal (HK$12) and the A3 to Causeway Bay (also HK$12). The buses operate every 15 minutes from 7 am to midnight and depart from right outside the arrival area. There's plenty of luggage space on board and they go past most of the major hotels.

The A1 service to Tsimshatsui in Kowloon goes down Nathan Rd right in front of Chungking Mansions, then turns around at the Star Ferry and heads back. They have an Airbus brochure at the departure area with a map showing the bus route. The Airbuses also stop at regular signposted bus stops.

BUS

There are plenty of buses with fares starting at HK$1.80 and going up to HK$9 for the longest ride you can take in the New Territories. You pay the fare as you enter the bus so

Buses in Hong Kong

Hong Kong Island

bus	from	to	every (mins)	trip (mins)	cost
tram	Central	Sai Wan Ho	2-7	40	HK$1.00
6	Central	Stanley	10-20	40	HK$4.50
7	Aberdeen	Central	6-10	30	HK$3.00
14	Sai Wan Ho	Stanley	20-30	40	HK$4.50
70	Central	Aberdeen	4-10	25	HK$2.80
73	Stanley	Aberdeen	15-30	30	HK$4.50

New Territories

bus	from	to	every (mins)	trip (mins)	cost
51	Tsuen Wan	Kam Tin	15-25	50	HK$3.60
54	Yuen Long	Kam Tin	7-12	20	HK$1.40
60M	Tsuen Wan	Tuen Mun	7-15	36	HK$3.60
75K	Tai Po	Tai Mei Tuk	12-30	26	HK$2.40
77K	Kam Tim	Sheung Shui	12-20	25	HK$3.00
92	Choi Hung	Sai Kung	6-15	38	HK$2.60

make sure you have the exact change ready. The double-decker buses are blue and cream on Hong Kong Island (operated by China Motor Bus) or red and cream in Kowloon (operated by Kowloon Motor Bus).

Most services stop around 11 pm or 12 midnight but the 121 and 122 are 'Cross Harbour Recreation Routes' which operate through the Cross-Harbour Tunnel every 15 minutes from 12.45 to 5 am. Bus No 121 runs from Macau Ferry Terminal on Hong Kong Island, then through the tunnel to Chatham Rd in Tsimshatsui East before continuing on to Choi Hung on the east side of the airport. Bus No 122 runs from North Point on Hong Kong Island, through the Cross-Harbour Tunnel, Chatham Rd in Tsimshatsui East, the northern part of Nathan Rd and on to Laichikok in the north-west part of Kowloon.

Minibus

The small red-and-yellow minibuses supplement the regular bus services. They are a little more expensive (generally HK$2 to HK$6) and the prices often go up during the rush hour or in rainy weather! They generally don't run such regular routes but you can get on or off almost anywhere. If you know where you are going and where they are going, you may well find them fast and convenient.

Maxicabs are just like minibuses except they are green and yellow and they do run regular routes. Two popular ones are from the carpark in front of the Star Ferry in Central to Ocean Park or from HMS Tamar (east of the Star Ferry) to the Peak. Fares are around HK$1 to HK$5.

TRAIN

The Kowloon-Canton Railway (KCR) runs right up to the border where visitors to China used to have to walk across the bridge and change trains. There are also four express trains daily which run right through to Canton. Apart from being one of the best ways of entering China it's also an excellent alternative to buses for getting into the New Territories. The last stop before China is Lo

Wu but you can only go there if you have a visa for China.

The trains operate every 10 to 15 minutes. There are two classes, first and ordinary. It's a scenic and interesting trip out to the New Territories. Tai Po Market and Fanling are interesting places to stop for a look around.

Mass Transit Railway

Opened in 1979-80, the Mass Transit Railway (MTR) operates from Central across the harbour and up the Kowloon Peninsula. This ultramodern, high-speed subway system has been quite a hit with office commuters. Fares vary from HK$3 to HK$7 one way. The ticket machines do not give change and the tickets are valid only for the day they are purchased. Once you pass through the turnstile, you must complete the journey within 90 minutes or the ticket becomes invalid. Crossing the harbour costs HK$5. The MTR operates from 6 am to 1 am.

If you use the MTR frequently, it's very useful to buy a Common Stored Value Ticket for either HK$50 or HK$100. These can also be used on the Kowloon-Canton Railway except for the Lo Wu Station on the China border. The MTR Tourist Ticket is a rip-off at HK$25 because it gives you only HK$20 worth of fares!

Smoking, eating and drinking are not permitted in the MTR stations or on the trains (makes you wonder about all those Maxim Cake Shops in the stations!). The fine for eating or drinking is HK$1000, while smoking will set you back HK$2000. Busking, selling and soliciting are also prohibited activities. There are no toilets in the MTR stations.

TRAM

There is just one tram line, but it is a long one – all the way from Kennedy Town (to the west of Central) to Shaukiwan (at the eastern end of the island) and it also runs right through the middle of Central. As well as being ridiculously picturesque and fun to travel on, the tram is quite a bargain at HK$1 for any distance. You pay on leaving.

Some of the trams diverge off the regular route to go to Happy Valley and some of them don't run all the way to the end of the line but basically you can just get on any tram that comes by. They pass frequently and there always seem to be half a dozen trams actually in sight.

TAXI

The minimum charge is HK$8 and then it's 90c for each 250 metres. There's an additional charge of HK$2 for each bag carried. In the New Territories or on Lantau Island the charges are lower. If you're taking a taxi through the harbour tunnel, taxi drivers are entitled to charge an additional HK$20 to cover return toll costs.

Taxi drivers can cover Kowloon or Hong Kong Island but in practice they tend to stick to one side or the other. It can be difficult to get taxis around shift change time (4 pm), and just like anywhere else in the world taxis disappear when rain comes down. Saturday afternoons or Wednesday evenings are also bad times to find taxis because that's when the horse races are held!

If you have a complaint about a taxi driver, get the licence number and call the police hotline (☎ 5277177).

BOAT
Star Ferries

The Star Ferries shuttle back and forth across the harbour every few minutes for a mere HK$1 (lower deck) or HK$1.20 (upper deck) – a real travel bargain. It's often said that this is one of the most picturesque public transport journeys in the world. The crossing takes less than 10 minutes and the ferries operate from 6.30 am to 11.30 pm.

Once upon a time you had to rent a sampan (*walla walla*) for after-hours crossings but these days there are all-night buses and taxis through the tunnel. The Star Ferry Terminals are right at the end of Tsimshatsui on the Kowloon Peninsula and right in the middle of Central on Hong Kong Island.

There is a second Star Ferry service which operates between Wanchai and Tsimshatsui. Yet another boat operates from the Star Ferry pier in Central to Hunghom on the Kowloon side. If you're on your way to China by train this is a good way of getting to the railway station.

Other Harbour Ferries

There are other ferries making longer trips across the harbour – from Wanchai to Tsimshatsui for example. The Central to Tuen Mun (New Territories) hoverferry takes 30 minutes and is one of the longest rides you can take through the harbour. You can also get a ferry to or from Hunghom (the other side of the railway station in Kowloon) to North Point on Hong Kong Island (an interesting trip back through Causeway Bay and Wanchai). Out on the harbour there seems to be a nonstop procession of ferries ploughing back and forth.

Island Ferries

The HKTA can supply you with a schedule for these ferries. There are more services on Sundays and holidays when the fares also go up and the boats are very crowded. From Central most ferries go from the Outer Island Terminal between the Star Ferry and Macau Ferry terminals. Fares range from about HK$6 on weekdays but can jump as much as 50% on weekends.

Lantau Island Most services go via Peng Chau Island to Silver Mine Bay (Mui Wo). There are about 19 services a day. There are two boats daily on Saturdays, Sundays and holidays to Tai O on the other end of the island.

Cheung Chau Island There are about 19 services a day, each taking just over an hour.

Lamma Island There are separate services to Sok Kwu Wan (seven a day) and Yung Shue Wan (12 a day).

Tolo Harbour There are just two ferries a day running out from Ma Liu Shui to Tap Mun (Grass Island) with lots of stops en route.

Ping Chau Island This isolated island gets only one ferry every weekend, departing on Saturday and returning on Sunday.

BICYCLE

Bike riding in Kowloon or Central would be suicidal, but in quiet areas of the New Territories or on the islands a bike can be quite a nice way of getting around. The bike rental places tend to run out early on weekends.

RICKSHAW

These are really only for photographs – would you want to ride in one? Count on HK$10 to HK$20 just to take a picture, HK$50 for a short ride. Prices are subject to bargaining. The old guys who operate these rickshaws are very pushy and may try to take you for a round-the-block ride even if you don't want it.

TOURS

There are so many tours available it's impossible to list them all. You can get one to just about anywhere in Hong Kong. Some popular destinations include the Sung Dynasty Village, Ocean Park, Stanley, the outer islands or the duck farms in the New Territories.

Tours can be booked through the HKTA, travel agents, large tourist hotels or directly from the tour company. If you're a student, the HKSTB offers discounts of HK$10 or HK$20 on the cost of the tours. Here's a sample of what's on:

Watertours. There are more than a dozen of these popular tours, covering such diverse places as Victoria Harbour and Cheung Chau Island. Book these trips through a travel agent or call Watertours (☎ 5254808). Costs vary enormously according to which tour you take.

Harbour Cruises. These are offered by the Star Ferry Company, and you book at the Star Ferry Pier. There are both day and evening cruises. Cost: HK$80 to HK$120 for adults, HK$60 for children.

Tram Dim Sum Tours. You ride a tram, sample dim sum and explore the city. Book at the Star Ferry Pier. Cost: HK$97 for adults, HK$80 for children.

Come Horseracing Tour. You get to sit in the Visitors' Box of the Members' Enclosure of the Royal Hong Kong Jockey Club. A Western lunch or dinner is thrown in. The tour follows the racing season, and you must be 18 or older to participate. Cost: HK$350. Tour conducted by the HKTA.

Cultural Diversions Tour. Held at the Hong Kong Cultural Centre, the tour covers Chinese acrobatics, folk dances, songs and magic shows, and ends with an eight-course banquet. Cost: HK$290 for adults, HK$240 children aged six to 15. Tour conducted by the HKTA.

Heritage Tour. This covers major historical sights, including Lei Cheng Uk, a 2000-year-old burial chamber. Cost: HK$250. Tour conducted by the HKTA.

Housing Tour & Home Visit. You visit two public housing estates and see how the people live. You get to visit a family's apartment, a rest home and a large Taoist temple. Cost: HK$180 for adults, HK$140 for children under 16. Tour conducted by the HKTA.

Land Between Tour. This popular tour covers the New Territories. Cost: HK$260 for adults, HK$210 for children under 16. Tour conducted by the HKTA.

Sports & Recreation Tour. You get to use the facilities at the Clearwater Bay Golf & Country Club. This include the golf course, jacuzzi, swimming pool, sauna, tennis courts, etc. A free meal is thrown in. Cost: HK$260 for the tour, plus HK$600 for use of the facilities. Tour conducted by the HKTA.

Yum Sing Night on the Town. This self-guided tour has two options. The Grand Package costs HK$130, and you receive a coupon for drinks at a pub, bar or nightclub, and one coupon for a drink at a disco. All cover charges are waived. The Deluxe Package costs HK$380 and includes a drink and an hour of chatting with a hostess at a high-class girlie bar. This tour is sponsored by the HKTA.

Around the Country

Hong Kong is conveniently divided into four parts. First there is Hong Kong Island, the original part of the colony on which stands Hong Kong Central, the 'city' of Hong Kong. A short ferry ride across the harbour from the island is the Kowloon Peninsula which is also totally 'city'. These are the two parts which were originally conceded to the UK and are not due to be handed back to

China until 1997. The southern tip of the peninsula is Tsimshatsui, the tourist heart of Kowloon. Most of Hong Kong's hotels are in Central or in Tsimshatsui. People speak of 'Hong Kong side' and 'Kowloon side'. Hong Kong Island can be further subdivided into the 'northside' (also called 'harbourside') and 'southside'.

Kai Tak Airport is also in Kowloon, although its runway juts out into the harbour. Beyond Kowloon you move into the New Territories, the rural area that runs up to the Chinese border. The New Territories get progressively less rural each year as Kowloon sprawls further and further out.

The islands that dot the area to the west of Hong Kong Island, the fourth part of the colony, are really just more of the New Territories (except for tiny Stonecutter's Island) since they are also part of the 99-year lease package. Largest of the islands is sparsely populated Lantau, which is much larger than Hong Kong Island itself. The islands are relatively undeveloped and in some ways the most surprising and enjoyable part of Hong Kong.

KOWLOON

Kowloon, the peninsula pointing out towards Hong Kong Island, is packed with shops, hotels, bars, restaurants, nightclubs and tourists. Nathan Rd, which runs through Kowloon like a spine, has plenty of all. Some of the ritziest shops are in the Ocean Terminal beside the Star Ferry. There always seems to be one ocean liner full of millionaire geriatrics moored here.

The tip of the peninsula, the area most popular with tourists, is known as Tsimshatsui. If you continue north up Nathan Rd you come into the tightly packed Chinese residential areas of Yaumati and Mongkok. Streets like Shanghai St, Saigon St, Battery St and Reclamation St are fascinating places to wander and gawk at the shops and stalls... everything from herbalists and snake dealers to streetside barbers and coffin makers. The Yaumati typhoon shelter is an equally congested home for the water people (the Tanka) and their sampans.

Things to See

The **Museum of History**, in Kowloon Park on Haiphong Rd (10 minutes' walk from the Star Ferry), has a good collection of early photographs of Hong Kong and some excellent models of the various types of junks and their fishing methods. (Open daily except Friday, 10 am to 6 pm, Sunday 1 to 6 pm, admission free.)

Adjacent to the Star Ferry Pier is the **Cultural Centre**, one of the city's landmarks. The **Planetarium & Space Museum** are right next door. Admission to the Exhibition Hall and Hall of Solar Sciences is free but the planetarium show costs HK$20. The museum is open from 10.30 am on Sundays, from 2 pm on Mondays, Wednesdays, Thursdays and Fridays, and from 1 pm on Saturdays. Closing time is 9.30 pm but it's closed all day on Tuesdays. Shows in the Space Theatre are all in Cantonese but headphones offering a simultaneous English translation are available free of charge.

The **Hong Kong Science Museum** is in Tsimshatsui East at the corner of Chatham Rd and Granville Rd. This multi-level complex houses over 500 exhibits. Admission costs HK$25 for adults, HK$15 for students and seniors. Operating hours are 1 to 9 pm Tuesday to Friday, and 10 am to 9 pm on weekends and holidays. The museum is closed on Mondays.

The tomb of Lei Cheng Uk was discovered during excavations for one of Hong Kong's resettlement projects. The late Han dynasty (25 to 220 AD) tomb and its contents can be examined at the **Lei Cheng Uk Museum**; it's open daily, except Thursday, from 10 am to 1 pm, 2 to 6 pm. Admission is 10c. To get there take a No 2 bus from the Star Ferry to Tonkin St and walk east to No 41 almost at the end of the street. This area of Shamshuipo is rarely visited by tourists so it's interesting in other respects as well.

Sung Dynasty Village in Laichikok in North Kowloon is a modern recreation of a Chinese village of the Sung (Song) dynasty (960 to 1279 AD). The village is big with tour groups, but individuals are admitted from 10 am to 8.30 pm daily. Admission

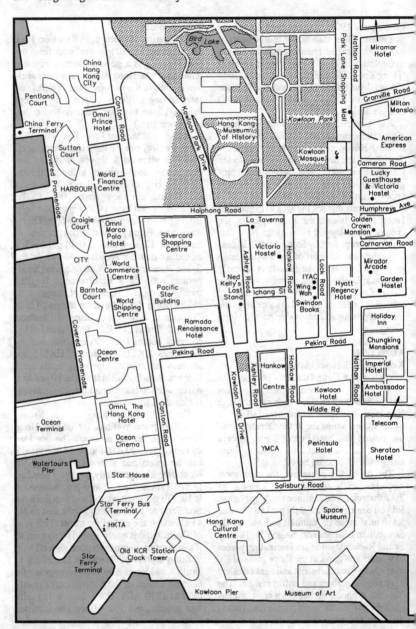

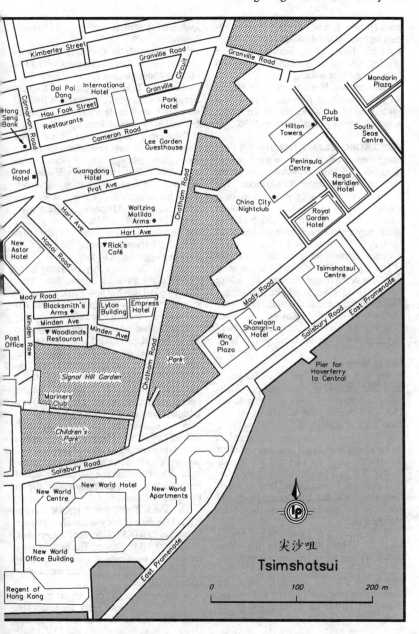

尖沙咀
Tsimshatsui

0   100   200 m

costs HK$95. It drops to HK$75 on weekends and public holidays between 12.30 pm and 5 pm. Take a 6A bus from the Kowloon Star Ferry Terminal or a tunnel bus No 105 from Hong Kong Island.

The **Kowloon Mosque** stands on Nathan Rd at the corner of Kowloon Park. It was opened in 1984 on the site of an earlier mosque originally constructed in 1896.

HONG KONG ISLAND, NORTHSIDE

Hong Kong Central is only a small part of Hong Kong Island, crowded close to the harbour looking across to Kowloon. The island is steep and rugged which gives it much of its appeal – buildings cling to the hillsides and you start climbing steeply uphill only a block back from the middle of Central.

Central is the banking and business centre of Hong Kong. Des Voeux Rd is the main street and down it runs the tram line; a long ride on Hong Kong's delightfully ancient double-decker trams is one of the best introductions to the city. Moving east from Central you come to Wanchai and Causeway Bay, both virtually continuous with Central.

Things to See

If you walk west up Des Voeux Rd you'll soon find yourself in one of the most interesting and colourful areas of Hong Kong. There are markets and streets for almost every kind of goods – the HKTA's walking tour of this area is an excellent introduction. As the streets head up the hills many of them become too steep for cars and the famous Ladder St is well named! Unfortunately Cat St (Upper and Lower Lascar Row to which Ladder St leads) has been redeveloped and much of the picturesqueness has been ploughed under.

At the junction of Ladder St and Hollywood Rd is **Man Mo Temple**, the oldest temple in Hong Kong. Next door is the building used as Suzie Wong's hotel in the film. **Hollywood Rd** is a wonderful street for window shopping as it's packed with antique shops. The further up the road you go the more bizarre the odds and ends you see. The

high quality stuff is further down towards Central.

The **Tiger Balm Gardens** were constructed by the Haw Par brothers with a few of the millions gleaned from the Tiger Balm medicament. It is two hectares of Chinese imagination run wild. Admission is free and it's open from 9 am to 4 pm daily. A No 11 bus will get you there from Central.

Causeway Bay, east of Hong Kong Central, is a touristy shopping and amusement centre, though not as ridiculous as Tsimshatsui. Wander Jardine's Bazaar and Jardine's Crescent – busy shopping streets today but reminders that this was the area where the Jardine-Matheson company operated in its early days. The noonday gun, by the waterfront across from the Excelsior Hotel, is a daily reminder of those pioneering days in Hong Kong's history.

Between Causeway Bay and Hong Kong Central is the girlie bar centre, **Wanchai** – full of topless bars but now a pale shadow of its peak of activity during the Vietnam War and not very exciting to wander around.

Take the famous Peak Tram from Garden Rd, up behind the Hilton Hotel, to the top of **Victoria Peak**. As you climb higher up the hill the houses and apartment blocks get steadily flashier and more expensive. Don't just admire the view from the top – wander up Mt Austin Rd to the old **Governor's Lodge** (demolished by the Japanese during WW II) or take the more leisurely stroll around Lugard and Harlech Rds – together they make a complete circuit of the peak. You can walk right down to Aberdeen on the south side of the island or you can try the Old Peak Rd for a couple of km return trip to Hong Kong Central.

The Peak Tram costs HK$8 (return HK$14) to the top, but you can also get there by bus No 15 (HK$3.80) or the Peak minibus No 1 from HMS *Tamar*. The peak is very crowded on weekends. It's worth repeating the peak trip at night – the illuminated view is something else.

In the evenings the cars depart from the car park by the Macau Ferry Terminal. The stalls and vendors move in and the area is renamed the **Poor Man's Nightclub**. It's bright, noisy and good fun – an excellent place for a cheap meal while you watch the action.

There are pleasant walks and views in the **Zoological & Botanical Gardens** on Robinson Rd overlooking Hong Kong Central. Come early in the morning to see people practising *taijiquan* – traditional Chinese shadow boxing. Entry is free to the **Hong Kong Museum of Art** in the City Hall (closed Thursdays), and the **Fung Ping Shan Museum** in Hong Kong University (closed Sundays) is also free.

Hong Kong Park is just behind the city's tallest skyscraper, the Bank of China. It's a very unusual park, not at all natural but beautiful in its own weird way. Within the park is the **Flagstaff House Museum**, the oldest Western-style building still standing in Hong Kong. Inside, you'll find the Museum of Teaware. Admission is free.

Some of the new office buildings and hotels are spectacular. The Bond Building between Central and Wanchai is all lumps and bumps and ominously mirrored glass. Nearby is the wonderful Hongkong & Shanghai Bank Building which looks like one of those clear plastic models built so you can see how everything works inside. You can see the lifts go up and down, the chains wind round under the escalators, even the fire escape stairways are all on view.

The very tall building in Central with the spikes on top is the Bank of China Building and it's reputed to have terrible *fung shui*. Before any building can be put up in Hong Kong a fung shui expert has to be called in to ensure the design, position and alignment don't bring bad luck, or even worse. Well, the Bank of China's fung shui is bad news, but not for the Bank of China, for the buildings around it. Reportedly the Bank of China Building positively radiates bad vibes (all those sharp corners of course) and some neighbouring buildings have had to actually seal up windows or cover them over in order to keep the harmful influence out. China, the lease, 1997 and all that, it's hardly surprising say the local cynics.

HONG KONG ISLAND, SOUTHSIDE

For HK$12 in fares you can make an interesting circuit of Hong Kong Island. Start in Central. You have a choice of hopping on bus No 6 at the Exchange Square Bus Terminal and going directly to Stanley, or taking a tram first to Shaukiwan and changing to a bus. The bus is easier and faster, but the tram is more fun. The tram takes you through hustling Wanchai and bustling Causeway Bay to the Sai Wan Ho Ferry Pier at Shaukiwan. Look for the trams marked 'Shaukiwan' and hop off just before the end of the line. You then hop on bus No 14 which takes you up and over the central hills; look for the cemetery off to your left that is terraced up the hills. You'll also pass a popular rowing boat hire spot before terminating at **Stanley**. Many Europeans working in Hong Kong live in Stanley which is a small and pleasant fishing port with a nice beach and many junks anchored offshore. It also has a maximum security prison.

From Stanley, catch bus No 73 which takes you along the coast, by beautiful **Repulse Bay** (stop off here if you wish) and Deep Water Bay, to the floating town of **Aberdeen**. There used to be 20,000 people living on the thousands of sampans that literally packed the harbour area, but most of them have been rehoused on dry land. There will generally be a few sampans ready to take you on a half-hour tour of this floating city for about HK$40 per person, but be sure to bargain. Floating regally amid the confusion are the Tai Pak, the Sea Palace and the even larger and appropriately named Jumbo Restaurant. This floating behemoth has huge dragons coiled at the entrance – with eyes that glow red in the dark. You get a free Aberdeen tour by taking the Jumbo's pickup boat out to the restaurant, walking around it (it's worth seeing) and then riding back. From Aberdeen a final short ride on bus No 7 takes you back to your starting point, via the Hong Kong University.

Things to See

The spectacular aquarium and funfair at **Ocean Park** is on the south side of Hong

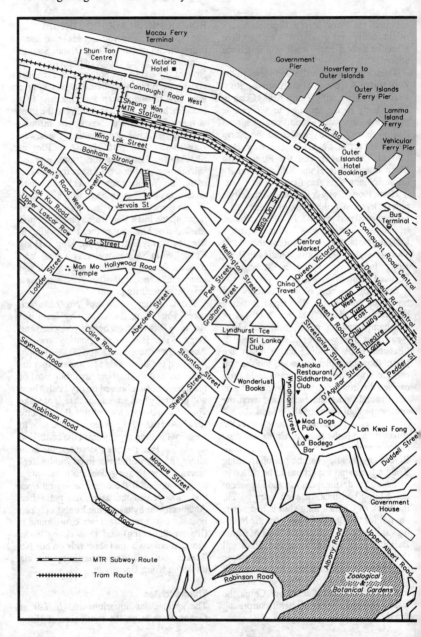

MTR Subway Route

Tram Route

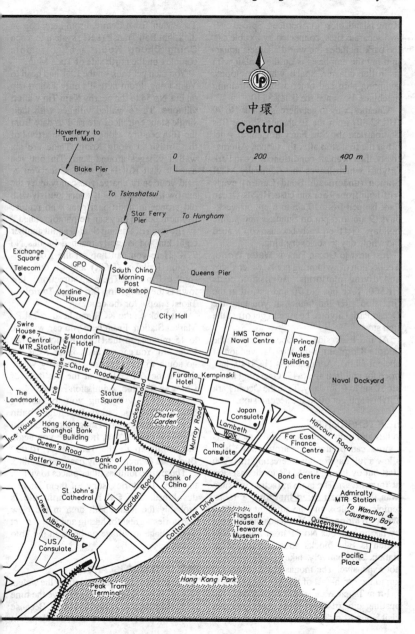

中環
Central

Hoverferry to Tuen Mun
Blake Pier

To Tsimshatsui
Star Ferry Pier
To Hunghom

Exchange Square
Telecom
GPO
South China Morning Post Bookshop
Queens Pier

Jardine House
City Hall

Swire House
Central MTR Station
Mandarin Hotel
HMS Tamar Naval Centre
Prince of Wales Building

The Landmark
Chater Road
Furama Kempinski Hotel
Naval Dockyard

Statue Square
Chater Garden
Japan Consulate

Hong Kong & Shanghai Bank Building
Lambeth Walk
Far East Finance Centre

Queen's Road
Thai Consulate

Battery Path
Bank of China
Hilton
Bond Centre

St John's Cathedral
Bank of China
Admiralty MTR Station
To Wanchai & Causeway Bay

Lower Albert Road
Garden Road
Flagstaff House & Teaware Museum
Queensway

US Consulate
Cotton Tree Drive
Pacific Place

Peak Tram Terminal
Hong Kong Park

Ice House Street
Jackson Road
Murray Road
Harcourt Road

Kong Island, close to Aberdeen. Spread over two separate sites, connected by a cable car, the park includes the world's largest aquarium but the emphasis is on the funfair with its roller coaster, space wheel, octopus, swinging ship and other astronaut-training machines. Entrance fee is HK$140.

Cheapest way to get there is on bus No 70 (HK$2.80) from the Exchange Square Bus Station near the Star Ferry in Central – get off at the first stop after the tunnel. Alternatively, there's an air-conditioned Ocean Park Citybus which leaves the Admiralty MTR Station (underneath Bond Centre) every half-hour from 9 am and costs HK$8. Ocean Park is open from 10 am to 6 pm on weekdays, 9 am to 6 pm on Sundays and public holidays. Get there early because you'll need the whole day to see everything.

Just next to Ocean Park is **Water World**, a collection of swimming pools, water slides and diving platforms. Admission costs HK$60. Take bus No 70 and get off at the first stop after the tunnel. If you take the Ocean Park Citybus, be sure to get off at the first stop.

At the back side of Ocean Park is the **Middle Kingdom**, a modern-day version of ancient China. Admission is HK$140, half price for children age 6-17. Operating hours are 10 am to 6 pm daily. Take the Ocean Park Citybus and get off at the second stop.

NEW TERRITORIES

A bus and train exploration of the New Territories can be done for around HK$20 – allow a full day for this interesting trip. You start out by taking the MTR to the last stop at **Tsuen Wan**. The main attraction in Tsuen Wan is the **Yuen Yuen Institute**, a Taoist temple complex, and the adjacent Buddhist **Western Monastery**. You reach the institute by taking minibus No 81 from Shiu Wo St which is two blocks south of the MTR station. Alternatively, take a taxi, which is not expensive. The monastery is about 1.5 km to the north-east of the MTR station.

From Tsuen Wan, take bus No 60M to the bustling city of **Tuen Mun**. Here you can visit Hong Kong's largest shopping mall, the Tuen Mun Town Centre. From here, hop on the Light Rail Transit (LRT) system to reach **Ching Chung Koon**, a huge temple complex on the north side of Tuen Mun.

You then get back on the LRT and head to Yuen Long. From here it's only a short trip on bus No 54 to the nearby **Kam Tin walled villages**. These walled villages with their single stout entrances are said to date from the 16th century – long before the arrival of the British in Hong Kong. There are six walled villages around Kam Tin but you usually visit Kut Hing Wei. Once you've paid your entry charge you can wander the narrow little lanes, but it's very touristy with old crones in traditional gear who require payment before they can be photographed.

The town of Sheung Shui is about another eight km and is easily reached by bus No 77K. Here you can hop on the Kowloon-Canton Railway (KCR) and go one stop south to Fan Ling. The main attraction in this town is the **Fung Ying Sin Kwun Temple**, a Taoist temple for the dead.

Get back on the KCR and head to Tai Po Market Station. From here you can walk 10 to 15 minutes to the **Hong Kong Railway Museum**. You can get back on the KCR and go south to the Chinese University where there's the Art Gallery at the **Institute of Chinese Studies**. Admission is free.

The KCR will bring you to bustling Shatin, where you can visit the huge **Shatin Town Centre**, one of Hong Kong's biggest shopping malls. Also, from here you begin the climb up to the **Temple of 10,000 Buddhas** (which actually has over 12,000).

There are countless other places to visit in the New Territories, some of them far less developed. The **Sai Kung Peninsula** is probably the least spoilt area in the New Territories – great for hiking and you can get from village to village on boats in the Tolo Harbour.

THE OUTLYING ISLANDS

There are over 200 islands dotting the waters around Hong Kong and if you have the time several are definitely worth visiting. Because they are part of the leased land, development has been slower than the frantic pace of Hong Kong Island and Kowloon, although some of them are almost commuter suburbs. There are frequent ferries to the islands but they're very crowded on weekends.

Cheung Chau Island

This dumbbell-shaped island has become very popular for Western residents who can't afford Hong Kong's sky-high rentals. It's a pleasant little place with a Mediterranean air to it. Were it not for the Chinese signs and people, you might think you were in some Greek island village.

The town sprawls across the narrow bar connecting the two ends of the island. You'll see junks being built on slips up from the beach and at the north end of the town the old **Pak Tai Temple** built in 1783. At the southern tip of the island is the hideaway cave of notorious pirate Cheung Po Tsai. There are some pleasant beaches, and each May there is the frantic Bun Festival, when seekers of good fortune scramble up a 20-metre-high tower of sugar buns to get the topmost (and luckiest) one.

Cheung Chau has one expensive hotel, the *Cheung Chau Warwick Hotel* (☎ 9810081) where doubles cost a mere HK$805 on a weekday and HK$1127 on a weekend, plus a 10% service charge and 5% tax. The best cheap place to stay is the *Star House Motel* (☎ 9812186) at 149 Tai Sun Bak St. Double rooms start at HK$120 on weekdays and run to between HK$600 and HK$700 a night on weekends.

The big gwailo nightlife spot is the Garden Cafe/Pub (☎ 9814610), 84 Tung Wan Rd in the centre of the island.

Peng Chau Island

This is another small island with a similarly Mediterranean-looking town and an old temple (Tin Hau – 1792). If you're going to Lantau it's worth stopping for a look around.

Lantau Island

This is the largest of the islands and the most sparsely populated – it's almost twice the size of Hong Kong Island but the population is only 20,000. It's definitely worth spending a couple of days here as there are some excellent walking trails and you can get a bit of a feel for rural Chinese life in some relatively untouched parts of the island.

Mui Wo (Silver Mine Bay) is the normal arrival point for ferries, but there's a more interesting way of getting there. Take a ferry from HK Central bound for Mui Wo, but get off at Peng Chau. A small sampan (it meets every ferry) will shuttle you across the narrow stretch of water to Lantau Island, and if you follow the trail up the hill you'll find yourself at a Trappist Monastery. Keep walking up and over the hill (fine views from the top), and you'll soon see Silvermine Bay down below. On the descent you pass a deserted building that looks like it would make a fine little hotel – Balinese losmen style. There are some good cheap eating places just before you reach Mui Wo and you can get a cold drink right at the bottom of the hill when you arrive at the beach.

From Mui Wo if you have the time you can take a long (four to five-hour) walk right across the island to Tung Chung. The trail passes through a whole series of relatively unspoilt settlements including Pak Mong, a very fine example of an old walled village. At Tung Chung there is a fort and ferries run from here to Castle Peak, from where you can bus into Kowloon.

From Tung Chung you can follow a paved footpath up an interminable hill for a couple of hours finally passing through a tea plantation and arriving at the spectacularly ornate Po Lin (Precious Lotus) Monastery.

It's a relatively recent construction and almost as much a tourist attraction as a religious centre. Just outside the monastery is the world's largest outdoor statue of Buddha, built at a total cost of HK$60 million. It's possible to have a vegetarian lunch at the monastery dining hall or even spend the night in the dormitories for HK$150 which includes three meals – lights out early and the beds are distinctly hard. For HK$25 you can stay at the S G Davis Youth Hostel (YHA card required). Next day you can take a bus back to Mui Wo and thus complete a fairly in-depth look at the island.

It's a lot of walking to do in one day, so if you intend to do the whole circuit it might be better to start off by going straight from Central to Mui Wo and leave the Trappist monastery and Peng Chau till day two, catching the ferry back from Peng Chau to Hong Kong Central. You can also bus straight from Mui Wo to Po Lin if you're not keen on walking at all. Alternatively you can continue right down to the end of the island at Tai O, from where ferries also operate back to Central.

Apart from the monastery you can stay in Silver Mine Bay (Mui Wo) at the Silver Mine Bay Beach Hotel (☎ 9848295) or the somewhat cheaper Sea House (☎ 9847757).

Lamma Island

Another fairly large island, Lamma has good beaches and a very relaxed pace on weekdays, but on weekends it's mobbed like anywhere else. Ferries run to Yung Shue Wan or Sok Kwu Wan on the island.

There are several places to stay on Lamma – the cheapest is the Wing Yuen Hostel (☎ 9820222) at Hung Shing Ye beach where rooms are HK$160 on weekdays, or HK$330 on weekends. Right by the ferry pier in Yung Shue Wan is the Man Lai Wah Hotel (☎ 9820220) where rooms on weekdays cost HK$250. There's a solid row of good seafood restaurants in Yung Shue Wan and Sok Kwu Wan. The Corner Bar is a lively place for nightlife, starting from around 6 pm.

BEACHES

Hong Kong has many excellent beaches both on the south side of Hong Kong Island and in the New Territories and on the outer islands. On Hong Kong Island, Repulse Bay is the best known beach, but others worth checking out in the summer include Big Wave Bay and Shek O. Best beaches in the New Territories are in the east around the Sai Kung Peninsula, including Clear Water Bay. Cheung Sha Wan on Lantau Island is Hong Kong's longest beach, but Cheung Chau and

Lamma Island also have good but small beaches.

PLACES TO STAY
Hostels

Many of the guesthouses have dorm beds as well as rooms, particularly the ones that go out of their way to cater for backpackers. The Travellers' Hostel in Chungking Mansions is a particularly popular example but there are a couple of other popular hostels in Kowloon and a number of youth hostels which are members of the International Youth Hostel Federation.

Victoria Hostel (☎ 3120621), 1st floor, 33 Hankow Rd, Tsimshatsui, is one of the nicest hostels in Hong Kong. There are several dormitories. The cheaper ones have no air-conditioning and cost HK$40. The air-conditioned dorms are HK$51. On the 3rd floor of the same building is Lucky Guest House (☎ 3670342), a very popular place with travellers. Dormitory beds cost HK$38 a night.

The International Youth Accommodation Centre (☎ 3663419) is on the 6th floor at 21A Lock Rd. It's a little bit anonymous but quite easy to find, directly behind the Hyatt Hotel. It's another good information source and beds in the air-conditioned dorm cost HK$40.

Around the corner from Chungking Mansions is the Garden Hostel (☎ 7218567). It's in Mirador Mansion, 58 Nathan Rd, but it's easier to find if you enter from Mody Rd. Turn right as you come out of the main entrance to Chungking and then right at the first street (Mody Rd). On the left side of the street you see an obvious sign. Enter the stairwell and go to the 3rd floor. Accommodation costs HK$38 a night in an air-conditioned dormitory. This place is getting a bit tattered, but is certainly popular.

The STB Hostel (☎ 3321073), operated by the Hong Kong Student Travel Bureau, costs HK$50 in the dormitory, HK$250 to HK$300 for twins. Clean and well-managed, it's on the second floor at Great Eastern Mansion, 255-261 Reclamation St, Mongkok, on the corner of Reclamation and

Dundas Sts, just to the west of the Yaumati MTR Station. Its chief disadvantage is that it's some distance from the Tsimshatsui area of Kowloon. From the airport, buses 1A, 9 or 13 will get you there.

Club Hostel (☎ 3800782) is a new place and highly recommended. It's on the 3rd floor of 714 Shanghai St, Mongkok. A dormitory bed will set you back HK$45; private rooms start at HK$90.

YHA Hostels Apart from these independent youth hostels there are also a number of real YHA places. The YHA representative is the Hong Kong Youth Hostels Association (☎ 7881638), Room 225, Block 19, Shek Kip Mei Estate, Kowloon. The hostels are closed between 10 am and 4 pm, you must be a IYHA member to use them and lights-out is at 11 pm. If you're not already a member the annual subscription is HK$60 in Hong Kong. The hostels are usually located in remote areas and it's generally a good idea (or even required at some of the hostels) to book in advance. At some of the hostels it's possible to camp.

Ma Wui Hall (☎ 8175715) on top of Mt Davis on Hong Kong Island is beautifully situated, very popular and the most centrally located of the YHA hostels. To get there take a 5B bus to the end of the line, walk back 100 metres and look for the YHA sign. You've then got a 20 to 30-minute climb up the hill! There are 112 beds here and the nightly cost is HK$25.

There are four other YHA hostels, but they are located in remote areas of the New Territories or Outlying Islands.

Sze Lok Yuen (☎ 4888188) is on Tai Mo Shan Rd. Beds cost HK$25 and tent camping is permitted. Take the No 51 bus (Tsuen Wan Ferry Pier – Kam Tin) at Tsuen Wan MTR Station and alight at Tai Mo Shan Rd. Follow Tai Mo Shan Rd for about 45 minutes, then turn on to a small concrete path on the right-hand side which leads directly to the hostel. This is a good place from which to climb Tai Mo Shan, Hong Kong's highest peak. Because of the high elevation, it can get amazingly cold at night, so be prepared.

Wayfoong Hall is another YHA hostel. It was being rebuilt at the time of this writing, so currently has no telephone number. The name might also be changed in the future. The hostel is at the base of Plover Cove Reservoir on Ting Kok Rd, just a few hundred metres south of Tai Mei Tuk. Take the Kowloon-Canton Railway (KCR) train to Tai Po Railway Station, then take bus No 75K to Tai Mei Tuk and follow the access road with the sea on your right side.

Pak Sha O Hostel (☎ 3282327) charges HK$25 a bed and also permits tent camping. A YHA card is needed. Take bus No 92 from the Choi Hung Estate bus terminus and get off at the Sai Kung terminus. From Sai Kung, take Bus No 94 towards Wong Shek Pier, but get off at Ko Tong Village. From there, find Hoi Ha Rd and a road sign 30 metres ahead showing the way to Pak Sha O.

Also on the Sai Kung Peninsula is *Bradbury Hall* (☎ 3282458), in Chek Keng. From Choi Hung Estate bus terminus, take bus No 92 to the Sai Kung terminus. From Sai Kung, take bus No 94 to Yellow Stone Pier, but get off at Pak Tam Au. There's a footpath at the side of the road leading to Chek Keng Village. The hostel is right on the harbour just facing the Chek Keng ferry pier. An alternative route is to take the ferry from Ma Liu Shui (adjacent to the Chinese University Railway Station) to Chek Keng Pier.

For more help in finding these hostels, contact the YHA.

The Y's & other Possibilities

The *YMCA International House* (☎ 7719111), 23 Waterloo Rd, Yaumati, has some cheap rooms with shared bath for HK$125 for men only. The majority of their rooms are rented to both men and women, but these are expensive at HK$420 to HK$560. Get there on a bus No 1A or No 9 from the airport or a No 7 or No 7A from the Star Ferry. The Y has a Western and Chinese restaurant, the latter does very good dim sum.

The *YWCA* (☎ 7139211) is inconveniently located near Pui Ching Rd and Waterloo Rd in Mongkok. It's actually on Man Fuk Rd, up a hill behind a Caltex petrol station. Relatively cheap rooms for women only are HK$190. Other single rooms are HK$300, and twins cost HK$380 to HK$410.

The Salvation Army runs a place called *Booth Lodge* (☎ 7719266), 11 Wing Sing Lane, Yaumati, where doubles/twins are HK$374/462. Just around the corner is *Caritas Bianchi Lodge* (☎ 3881111), 4 Cliff Rd, Yaumati, where doubles range from HK$405 to HK$465.

Guesthouses

Chungking Mansions Next door to the Holiday Inn and across the road from the Hyatt on Nathan Rd, right in the centre of the Tsimshatsui area of Kowloon is Chungking Mansions – the magic word for cheap accommodation in Hong Kong. Down at the bottom of this multistorey block is Chungking Arcade, a rather dumpy shopping arcade. If you wander around you'll find a number of lifts labelled A to E and over the elevator doors are name plates for guesthouses. There are lots of them and the standards vary widely. The best policy is to pick a block and try a few. There's some concern in Hong Kong that Chungking Mansions is a potential fire risk.

In winter they'll be less crowded than in summer and at any time of year it's worth haggling over the price, particularly if you plan a longer stay. With effort you can find a double room for less than HK$100. You pay a little more for rooms with extras like attached bathrooms. Several of the guesthouses specialise in catering for backpackers and have dormitories with beds for about HK$40.

Some of the places are 'short-time' specialists – if you get an odd response it's likely that the place generally rents rooms by the hour. Others specialise in catering for visitors from India or Pakistan. If a place doesn't seem to want you just try another! The lifts can be a real problem since there are only two of them for all 16 floors of each block. At peak times you can have a long wait.

Walking down the steps of Chungking Mansions can be very depressing since they're extremely dirty and dismal. In between the guesthouses are offices, private apartments, Indian 'club messes' (actually open to anyone and with excellent Indian food), and lots of cottage industry – clothes making, semiprecious-stone grinding – a regular hotbed of Hong Kong enterprise.

There are far too many guesthouses in Chungking Mansions to make real recommendations. Although Chungking Mansions has a rough and ready reputation, in actual fact many of the guesthouses are very pleasant, friendly, well run and spotlessly clean. The rooms may be minute but that's a reflection of the price of real estate in Hong Kong. Many places operate on several floors or in different blocks or the same people may operate several different guesthouses. The names that follow are just a few ideas to begin with.

Block A, at the front, is the block with the heaviest concentration of guesthouses and here you'll find the *Travellers' Hostel* (☎ 3687710) on the 16th floor. It's a reasonably clean and well-run place. Equally important, the noticeboard is an an excellent information source. Dorm beds are HK$38 while rooms run HK$80 to HK$130. The same management also operates a cheap beachside hostel at Ting Kau in the New Territories – enquire if interested.

Park Guest House (☎ 3681689), 15th floor, has singles from HK$80 to HK$100 and doubles from HK$100 to HK$120. With an attached private bath, doubles are from HK$160 to HK$180. It's clean, air-conditioned and friendly.

Moving down there's the *New Grand* on the 14th floor and the *Ashoka Guest Houses* on the 13th. The 12th has the *Peking*. On the 11th floor there's the *Lucky* with clean but small singles for HK$130. On the same floor is the *New International* which has singles with shared/attached bath for HK$90/160.

Singles are HK$80 to HK$110 in the *New Asia* on the 8th floor, where you'll also find *Tom's*. The 7th floor has *Double Seven* and the popular *Welcome Guest House* which is clean and well kept and has a variety of rooms and prices. For HK$120 you can get a tiny single room with an even tinier attached bathroom – you sort of stand on the toilet to shower!

London Guest House (☎ 7245000) on the 6th floor is friendly and clean and has singles from HK$85 to HK$180 with TV and air-conditioning.

On the 5th and 4th floors, *Chungking House* (☎ 3665362) is one of the biggest and fanciest places in Chungking Mansions. Rooms here are HK$230 single or HK$320 double, all with attached bathrooms. The single rooms are really doubles since they have a double bed. Rooms at the front have a view of the Hyatt Hotel, across the road, which is often 'better than television'!

Sky Guest House, A Block, 3rd floor, won't win any contests for cleanliness but it's one of the cheapest places in Hong Kong with dormitory beds for HK$35.

That's just one of the blocks at Chungking Mansions although admittedly it's the block with the most guesthouses. In B block, the cheapest is the *Friendship Travellers House*, B Block, 6th floor, where beds are HK$35 a night. Moving slightly up-market, there's the *New Washington* on the 13th floor where clean doubles range from HK$100 to HK$160. *Harbour* on the 4th floor is clean, bright and friendly, and has doubles for HK$150 with attached private bath. Many people have good things to say about the *New Regent* on 16th floor, where singles cost HK$110, and large, bright double rooms are HK$160.

C block doesn't have as many places, but the big advantage is that there are seldom any queues for the lifts. It's also cleaner than the other blocks. *Tom's* on the 16th floor is clean and quiet and has singles for HK$80 and doubles for HK$120 to HK$130. *Berlin*, 14th floor, is small and comfortable and has singles/doubles for HK$70/110.

The *Garden* on the 7th floor is new and clean and charges HK$150 for a room with attached bath. *New Brother's*, 6th floor, is very clean and has singles for HK$120. *Centre Point Inn*, 3rd floor, is a Chungking Mansions classic with singles/doubles for HK$120/140 with shared bath.

There are some interconnecting walkways between C or E block and D block. In D block there's the *Four Seas Guest House* on the 15th floor, the *Broadway Inn* on the 10th, *New Shanghai* on the 8th, and the friendly *Princess* on the 3rd.

E block is another quiet backwater and seldom has queues for the lifts. On the 17th floor there's the *Shan-E-Punjab*. There's the *Far East Guest House* on the 14th and the up-market *Hometown* on the 10th. On the 3rd floor you'll find the *Sheraton* – no relation to another rather larger Sheraton establishment further down Nathan Rd.

Take a look down the lightwells off the D block stairs for a vision of hell, Chungking Mansions at its worst. They're dark, dirty, festooned with pipes and wires and covered in what looks like the debris of half a century. Why bother to put rubbish in the bin when it's so much easier to throw it out the window? Discarded plastic bags fall only halfway down before lodging on a ledge or drainpipe. Soon they're joined by old newspapers, used toilet paper, clothes fallen off lines, half-eaten apples, an expired rat (was it too dirty for him too?). All manner of garbage drapes and hangs down from above. It's a horrible sight. Occasionally you're forced onto the stairs when the wait for the lift becomes too interminable. A buzzer sounds when one too many people have clambered aboard the lifts and in one of them I spotted a sign which announced, 'The Irresponsible for Accident due to Overloading'.

Other Kowloon Guesthouses Guesthouses aren't restricted to Chungking Mansions although there are so many of them there. If you wander down the streets off Nathan Rd in Tsimshatsui you'll see signs for many other guesthouses. They will often be similar in character to the Chungking Mansions places but simply not being in Chungking Mansions can be a major advantage.

A short way up Nathan Rd at number 58 is Mirador Mansion, somewhat like a smaller and cleaner version of Chungking Mansions. The *First Class Guest House* on the 16th floor has singles starting from HK$100. The best deal seems to be the *Man Hing Lung Guest House* on the 14th, where beautiful singles with private bath go for HK$90. You can also try the *Mini Hotel* on the 7th floor.

At 66-70 Nathan Rd there's Golden Crown Court with the *London, Golden Crown* and *Wah Tat* guesthouses, all on the 5th floor. The Golden Crown has dormitory beds for HK$40 as well as more expensive private rooms.

The friendly *Lee Garden Guest House* (☎ 3672284) is on the 8th floor, D Block, 36 Cameron Rd, close to Chatham Rd. Doubles with shared/private bath cost HK$150/250.

The *Lyton Building*, 32-40 Mody Rd, has several good guesthouses. *Lyton House Inn* on the ground floor is very quiet and has small but clean rooms with an attached private bath. Doubles without air-con are HK$150. With air-con, it's HK$200. On the 6th floor of the north-east block is *Tourist House*, which has rooms with private baths for HK$180.

A definitely up-market but great place to stay is the *Star Guest House* (☎ 7238951), 6th floor, 21 Cameron Rd. Immaculately clean rooms with private bath and TV cost HK$250. The manager, Charlie Chan, is extremely helpful and friendly.

Hong Kong Island Guesthouses *Leishun Court*, at 116 Leighton Rd in Causeway Bay, is Hong Kong Island's answer to Chungking Mansions. The building houses a number of cheap guesthouses, mostly on the lower floors. *Fuji House*, 1st floor, charges HK$150 for a room with private bath. On the same floor is the *Villa Lisboa Hotel* and *Cannes House*.

An up-market guesthouse is *Noble Hostel* (☎ 5766148) at Flat C1, 7th floor, 37 Paterson St, Paterson Building, Causeway Bay, just above Daimaru Department Store. It's very clean and safe – they have locked metal gates and a security guard in the lobby. Singles/doubles are HK$190/240 with shared bath, and HK$290 with private bath. Highly recommended.

A rather interesting place is the *Phoenix Apartments*, 70 Lee Garden Hill Rd, Causeway Bay. This place houses a number of elegant and reasonably priced guesthouses,

but most are short-time hotels where rooms are rented by the hour. One hotel here proudly advertises 'Avoidance of Publicity & Reasonable Rates'. Nevertheless, as long as they've changed the sheets recently, it's not a bad place to stay. The *Sunrise Inn* on the 1st floor charges HK$128 for overnight or HK$58 for two hours. Moving up- market, the *Hoi Wan Guest House*, 1st floor, Flat C has plush rooms for HK$280, but you might be able to negotiate a cheaper rate for a longer term (or shorter term).

Mid-Range Hotels

Kowloon In Hong Kong middle certainly doesn't mean cheap – you can pay HK$100 in a Chungking Mansions guesthouse or HK$250 in an up-market guesthouse, whereas a middle-range hotel will cost you HK$350 to HK$600. Which is still a lot cheaper than the HK$1500 a night some of the five-star places ask. Count on another 15% for service and tax, however.

You can get as much as a 40% discount at mid-range and luxury hotels if you book through certain travel agents. One agent offering this service is *Traveller Services* (☎ 3674127, fax 3110387), 7th floor, 57 Peking Rd, Tsimshatsui. The *Mariner's Club* offers big discounts to sailors, in case you qualify.

Places in the mid-range category include the following:

Bangkok Royal, 2-12 Pilkem St, Yaumati (take MTR to Jordan Station), singles HK$350, twins HK$410 to HK$580 (☎ 7359181, fax 7302209)
Imperial, 30-34 Nathan Rd, Tsimshatsui, singles HK$500 to HK$620, doubles/twins HK$580/880 (☎ 3662201, fax 3112360)
International, 33 Cameron Rd, Tsimshatsui, singles HK$380 to HK$680, twins HK$500 to HK$880 (☎ 3663381, fax 3695381)
King's, 473-473A Nathan Rd, Yaumati, singles HK$340, doubles/twins HK$400/430 (☎ 7801281, fax 7821833)
Mariner's Club, 11 Middle Rd, Tsimshatsui, singles/doubles HK$330/390 (☎ 3688261)
Nathan, 378 Nathan Rd, Yaumati, singles HK$550, doubles/twins HK$600/700 (☎ 3885141, fax 7704262)
Shamrock, 223 Nathan Rd, Yaumati, singles HK$450 to HK$480, twins HK$520 to HK$700 (☎ 7352271, fax 7367354)

YMCA, 41 Salisbury Rd, Tsimshatsui, twins HK$560 (☎ 3692211, fax 7399315)

Hong Kong Island In terms of mid-range hotels, there's even less available on Hong Kong Island than in Kowloon. Figure on HK$450 at the minimum. Again, check with the Student Travel Bureau or other travel agents for discounts. Some places to check out include:

Bonham, 50-54 Bonham Strand East, Sheung Wan, twins HK$400 (☎ 5442882, fax 5443922)
China Merchants, 160-161 Connaught Rd West, Sheung Wan, singles HK$560 to HK$800, twins HK$620 to HK$850 (☎ 5596888, fax 5590038)
Emerald, 152 Connaught Rd West, Sheung Wan, singles HK$470, doubles/twins HK$570/690 (☎ 5468111, fax 5590255)
Garden View International House, 1 MacDonnell Rd, Central, twins HK$480 to HK$580 (☎ 8773737, fax 8456263)
Harbour View International, 4 Harbour Rd, Wanchai, doubles/twins HK$560/700 (☎ 5201111, fax 8656063)
Harbour, 116-122 Gloucester Rd, Wanchai, singles HK$460 to HK$620, twins HK$600 to HK$900 (☎ 5748211, fax 5722185)

PLACES TO EAT
Breakfast
Starting the day with dim sum is customary with Hong Kongers, but it's easy to get a Western-style breakfast as well. There are handy little bakeries and at breakfast time an apple or orange and a fresh bread roll or pastry makes an appetising and very economical start to the day. Fruit stall prices vary but even in touristy Tsimshatsui an apple will only cost around HK$3. *St Honore* is a chain of excellent bakeries around Hong Kong with the name written only in Chinese, but you'll soon recognise their ideogram. There's one at 221 Nathan Rd, Yaumati, and a much smaller one at 1A Hanoi Rd, Tsimshatsui.

The window of the *Wing Wah Restaurant* is always filled with great-looking cakes and pastries. It's at 21A Lock Rd near Swindon's Bookstore and the Hyatt Regency. Either take it away or sit down with some coffee. A very similar place is the nearby *Kam Fat Restaurant* at 11 Ashley Rd.

Oliver's has two stores in Tsimshatsui: one in Ocean Centre and another at China Hong Kong City on Canton Rd, the same place where you catch the ferries to China. It's a great place for breakfast – HK$10 for bacon, eggs and toast. The sandwiches are equally excellent, though it gets crowded at lunchtime.

Deep in the bowels of the MTR stations you can find *Maxim's Cake Shops*, but don't sink your teeth into the creamy delights until you're back on the street as it is prohibited to eat or drink anything in the MTR stations or on the trains – HK$1000 fine if you do.

Fast fooders can head for *McDonald's* and have hot cakes or the 'big' breakfast special.

Night Markets
Authentically Chinese fast food can be found at the *dai pai dongs* (street stalls) which set up at night from about 8 to 11 pm. You can get very good noodles for a couple of dollars and there's no language barrier, just point to whatever looks good. The largest night market is at the northern end of Temple St in Kowloon. A smaller night market called the *Poor Man's Nightclub* sets up in the car park on the west side of the Macau Ferry Terminal.

Fast Food
McDonald's has had quite an impact on Hong Kong and outlets have sprung up just about everywhere so you're never too far from a burger, French fries and a shake. They're just like back home (wherever that might be), probably in part because many of the components are imported anyway. A Big Mac will set you back HK$8.90, about the cheapest you'll find anywhere in the world.

Burger King, Kentucky Fried Chicken, Pizza Hut and other international chains also operate in Hong Kong. The local *Maxim's* chain has a number of outlets around town – burgers and similar snacks but not a bad place for a cheap breakfast.

Fairwood Fast Food is a Hong Kong chain, and if you don't throw up looking at the big plastic clown face on the door, it's a fine place to catch a quick meal. Prices are low and they do mixed Western and Chinese food. They have a branch at 6 Ashley Rd, Tsimshatsui.

Spaghetti House is a local chain with branches in a number of locations. In Tsimshatsui there's one at 3B Cameron Rd, over in Wanchai there's one on the corner of Hennessey and Luard roads, in Central there's one at 10-12 Stanley St. They have sandwiches, pizza, spaghetti and beer at low prices.

Dim Sum

One of the most popular ways of lunching (or even breakfasting) in Hong Kong is to **yum cha** or 'drink tea'. The name comes from the Chinese tea which is always consumed when eating dim sum. These restaurants are generally huge places with little old ladies circulating with trays or trolleys of dim sums. You take your chances, pick plates of anything that looks appetising.

You're issued a card which is stamped each time you choose a dish, and when you've had enough the bill is toted up from the number of stamps. This is a pretty economical way of eating, and often very crowded at lunch time when the office workers pack in. So arrive early if you want a seat and if you want the full variety of dim sum. Flip the lid over when you want the teapot refilled.

Dim sum restaurants can be a little difficult to locate as signs are rarely in English and will probably say something like 'Chinese Restaurant' or 'Seafood Restaurant'. This is because the same place which serves cheap dim sum by day is transformed at night into an expensive Cantonese restaurant. Try along Nathan Rd in Kowloon or Queens Rd in Central. There are also many in Causeway Bay. On Hong Kong Island you could try the *Asiania*, 1st floor, Asian House, 1 Hennessy Rd, Wanchai; *Diamond Restaurant*, at 265-75 Des Voeux

Some popular dim sum include:

har kau	淡水鮮蝦餃	shrimp dumpling
shiu mai	蟹黃干蒸卖	meat dumpling
pai kwat	豉汁蒸排骨	steamed spare ribs
ngau yuk mai	干蒸牛肉卖	steamed beef balls
tsing fun kuen	鸡丝蒸粉卷	steamed shredded chicken
kai bao tsai	香菇鸡飽仔	steamed chicken bun
cha siu bau	蚝油叉烧飽	steamed barbeque pork bun
tsing ngau yuk	荷叶蒸牛肉	steamed beef ball in lotus leaf
cha chun kuen	炸鸡丝春卷	fried spring roll
wook kok	蜂巢香芋角	fried taro vegetable puff
ham sui kok	软滑咸水角	fried dumplings
fun gwor	凤城蒸粉果	steamed dumplings filled with vegetables and shrimps
daan tart	千层鸡蛋挞	custard tart
ma tai go	炸马蹄糕条	fried water chestnut sticks
ma lai go	榄仁马拉糕	steamed sponge cake
ma yung bau	咸黄麻蓉飽	steamed sesame bun
yeh chup go	鲜奶椰汁糕	coconut pudding
shui tsung kau	雪耳水晶餃	white fungus sweet dumpling
chien tsang go	咸黄千层糕	1000 layer sweet cake with egg yolk filling
tse chup go	爽滑蔗汁糕	sugar cane juice roll

Rd, Central; or the *Broadway Seafood Restaurant*, Hay Wah Building, 73-85B Hennessy Rd, Wanchai.

Dim sum is also served at the *Jade Garden Restaurant*, which has premises on the 1st floor, Swire House, 9-25 Chater Rd, Central; and at Shop 5, lower ground floor, Jardine House, 1 Connaught Place, Central.

Other Hong Kong Island dim sum restaurants include the *Ruby*, 1st floor, Hong Kong Mansions, 1 Yee Wo St, Causeway Bay; *Tai Woo*, 15-19 Wellington St, Central; *Tsui Hang Village*, 2nd floor, New World Tower, 16-18 Queen's Rd, Central; *Tung Yuen Seafood*, 3rd floor, Tai Yau Building, 181 Johnston Rd, Wanchai; *Victoria City Seafood*, 2D, Sun Hung Kai Centre, 30 Harbour Rd, Wanchai.

In Kowloon, dim sum is served at the *Canton Court*, Guangdong Hotel, 18 Prat Ave, Tsimshatsui; *Dragon Feast Seafood*, 5th floor, Lifung Tower, China Hong Kong City, 33 Canton Rd, Tsimshatsui; *Fook Follow*, UG2, Chinachem Golden Plaza, 77 Mody Rd, Tsimshatsui East; *Harbour View Seafood*, 3rd floor, Tsimshatsui Centre, 66 Mody Rd, Tsimshatsui East; *Heichinrou Restaurant*, 2nd floor, Sun Plaza, 28 Canton Rd, Tsimshatsui; *International*, 3rd floor, Good Hope Building, 612 Nathan Rd, Mongkok; *Jade Garden*, 4th floor, Star House, 3 Salisbury Rd, Tsimshatsui.

Dim sum is also a popular way of having a long, leisurely Sunday brunch.

Other Chinese Restaurants

In the evening, the dim sum disappears and the same restaurants roll out more expensive Cantonese fare such as pigeon, snake and shark's fin soup. But Cantonese cuisine is not the only Chinese food around. If you like lots of dumplings, steamed bread, duck and noodles, try Beijing (Peking) food. Some Beijing-style restaurants include: *Beijing Restaurant*, 34-36 Granville Rd, Tsimshatsui; *Peking Garden*, 3rd floor, Star House, 3 Salisbury Rd.

In Causeway Bay *Food Street* is an artificial restaurant centre with a variety of places

to eat. It may be a bit plastic but some of the restaurants are quite good.

The heavier and oilier cuisine of Shanghai can be sampled in Kowloon at *Great Shanghai* at 26 Prat Ave, Tsimshatsui.

Lotus Pond (☎ 7308688), Shop 007, ground floor, Phase IV, Harbour City, 15 Canton Rd, Tsimshatsui, serves the type of spicy Sichuan (Szechuan) dish which brings tears to the eyes.

Vegetarian Restaurants

There are some good vegetarian places around like the traditional *Wishful Cottage* at 336 Lockhart Rd in Causeway Bay. There are several *Bodhi* vegetarian restaurants including one at 56 Cameron Rd in Tsimshatsui on Kowloon side and one at 388 Lockhart Rd in Causeway Bay on Hong Kong side.

Another vegetarian restaurant in Kowloon is the *Pak Bo Vegetarian Kitchen* at 106 Austin Rd, Yaumati. Over in Causeway Bay on Hong Kong side the *Vegi Food Restaurant* is at 8 Cleveland St, next to Food St.

Other Asian Cuisines

For good cheap subcontinent curries Chungking Mansions has some excellent Indian and Pakistani 'messes' between floors and a couple of bargain-priced ground floor places. At *Kashmir Fast Food* or *Lahore Fast Food* in the arcade you can get curried mutton or chicken with rice and chappatis for HK$20 and they start serving it out from early in the morning...if curry for breakfast is your ticket.

Upstairs in Chungking Mansions are many other places with better food and a more pleasant atmosphere. Prices are still low, with set meals from HK$28 to HK$35. Highly rated by travellers is *Kashmir Club* (☎ 3116308), 3rd floor, A Block. The *Taj Mahal Club Mess* (☎ 7225454), 3rd floor, B Block is pleasantly air-conditioned and very comfortable, plus the food is superb. On the 6th floor of B Block is the highly recommended *Centre Point Club* (☎ 3661086). Yet another cheap and good place is the *Delhi*

Club Mess (☎ 3681682) on the 3rd floor of C Block.

Behind Chungking Mansions at 8 Minden Ave is *Woodlands*, the name which is synonymous with southern Indian vegetarian food on the subcontinent. Go there to get your fingers into a good thali.

Over in Central *Club Sri Lanka* in the basement of 17 Hollywood Rd (almost at the Wyndham St end) has great Sri Lankan curries, their fixed price all-you-can-eat deal is a wonderful bargain. *Siddharth Club* at 57 Wyndham St has good Indian food, as well as the *Ashoka* next door.

There are a number of good Indonesian places like the *Indonesia Padang Restaurant*, 85 Percival St, Causeway Bay. With the Philippines so near it's hardly surprising there are some good Filipino places around like the *Mabuhay Restaurant*, 11 Minden Ave, Tsimshatsui.

Vietnamese immigrants flooded into Hong Kong after the end of the Vietnam war and brought their cuisine with them. There are several good places on Hillwood Rd in Kowloon. On the Hong Kong side you could try the small *Saigon Beach Restaurant* at 66 Lockhart Rd in Wanchai.

Korean, Singaporean, Malaysian, Japanese, Burmese and other regional cooking styles are also well represented in Hong Kong but Thai food has become the cuisine of the moment with some good places to try both in Kowloon and on Hong Kong Island. A reasonably priced and good Thai restaurant is *Royal Pattaya*, 9 Minden Ave, Tsimshatsui. Also good is *Sawadee*, 1 Hillwood Rd, Tsimshatsui.

Some of the most authentic and cheapest Thai food can be found out at the airport. If you're flying out at night it's worth checking in early and eating here before you depart. That is so long as you like your Thai food hot; at *Thai Wah* they spell HOT with capital letters. To get there take the footbridge from the terminal over the highway to the Regal Meridien Airport Hotel. Go through the hotel and out the back, turn left and at the corner take Kai Tak Rd, which bends back. Thai Wah is at number 24 and is so popular it often

spills out onto the pavement where you can sit and watch the 747s whistle in just overhead.

Set Meals & Western Food

Numerous places offer set meals at lunch time or in the evening where you can get a soup, main course, dessert and coffee at a knock-down price. The *Singapore Restaurant*, 23 Ashley Rd, Tsimshatsui, is a great bargain: excellent Malaysian, Chinese and Western food for about HK$45 for a set dinner. You might have to queue to get in.

In Tsimshatsui *Rick's Café* downstairs at 4 Hart Ave has oddly named sandwiches and Mexican snacks.

At 7B Hanoi Rd the *New Marseille* is good value with French/Chinese food and an inexpensive set dinner.

At the big hotels the buffets on offer at breakfast and lunch time can be a good deal if you're super-hungry. The *Holiday Inn* on Nathan Rd in Tsimshatsui is pretty good and the *Hilton* on Hong Kong side, just below the bottom station for the Peak Tram, has a particularly highly thought of buffet. You could try the rotating restaurant atop the *Furama Kempinski Hotel* for a night when you felt like a real splurge – terrific views and a not-too-expensive buffet.

Apart from the chain of *Spaghetti House* restaurants (see Fast Food) there are also several good Italian restaurants. On Kowloon side you could try *La Taverna* at 36-38 Ashley Rd in Tsimshatsui or on Hong Kong side there's the pleasantly relaxed *Rigoletto's* at 16 Fenwick St in Wanchai.

Pubs

A number of the bars and pubs mentioned under Entertainment have good food. They can be excellent places for a quiet break at lunch time. *Mad Dogs* at 33 Wyndham St in Central has good British-style pub food including pies and pasties for around HK$45 or sandwiches with salad and French fries. The *Jockey Pub*, Swire House, 11 Chater Rd, also does excellent sandwiches for HK$30 or so.

The *White Stag* at 72 Canton Rd in

Tsimshatsui and the various Aussie pubs also have pretty reasonable food.

Down the block from the Siddharth Club at No 31C is a tapas bar called *La Bodega*.

ENTERTAINMENT

Try the very popular *Ned Kelly's Last Stand* at 11A Ashley Rd in Kowloon. There's live jazz there most nights of the week and the food is pretty good too. Other places for a cold Fosters in Kowloon include the *Kangaroo Pub* at 11A Chatham Rd and *Harry's Bar* at 6-8A Prat Ave.

British-style pubs on the Kowloon side include the *Blacksmith's Arms*, at 16 Minden Ave, and the *White Stag* at 72 Canton Rd. Fancy a German beer? Then head to the *Biergarten* at 8 Hanoi Rd in the same area. A friendly atmosphere can be found at *Friar Tuck*, Room 053, World Shipping Centre, Harbour City, 7 Canton Rd, Tsimshatsui.

Over on Hong Kong Island there are dozens of great places. For good beer, visit

Schnurrbart in the Winner Building on D'Aguilar St, Central. *Joe Bananas*, 23 Luard Rd, Wanchai, has become a trendy nightspot and has no admission charge, but you may have to queue to get in. Happy hour is from 11.30 am until 9 pm when the disco party gets started. *DD II*, 38-44 D'Aguilar St, Central, is a trendy disco open from 10 pm to 4 am.

Wanchai has lots of bars too although many of them are of the topless variety. That still leaves plenty of straightforward pubs. Also in Wanchai at 54 Jaffe Rd, just west of Fenwick Rd, is the *Wanchai Folk Club* (also called *The Wanch*), a very pleasant little folk-music pub with beer and wine at regular prices.

If you want to spend more – well, you can lay out twice as much for a beer in the big hotel bars or head for the topless bars around Wanchai or Tsimshatsui East. Or you can simply go up the Peak for a free view of the nightlife down below. And don't forget you can always head for a cinema.

Japan

Japan is the most Westernised country in Asia, and certainly the richest. Although much of its traditional architecture has been lost to earthquakes, wartime bombing and 'development', Japan still retains its cultural traditions; and annual festivals from centuries ago and ritual visits to sacred temples remain an integral part of life.

To find the traditional Japan, it is necessary to travel away from the big cities into the countryside, to the towns and remote mountain regions where settlements are smaller. To understand the Japanese, consider a people still strictly governed by a social organisation and discipline that is hundreds of years old but who have managed to embrace 20th-century Western technology and culture as if it were their own. Indeed, many of Japan's young people are surprised to learn that McDonald's, Coca-Cola and Disneyland are not Japanese inventions.

Japan is expensive, but there are a few tricks to keeping costs down. For those who can afford the ticket, Japan is a rewarding travel experience.

Facts about the Country

HISTORY
Prehistory
Archaeological research suggests that the first settlement was at least 100,000 years ago, but the earliest civilisation that has been studied is the Jomon period, up to the 2nd century BC. The people may have had links with Polynesians and South-East Asians.

The Yayoi civilisation in the early centuries AD suggests closer relations with Korea. Bronze and iron appeared around this time. In the late 4th century, there was probably an invasion by nomadic, horse-riding warriors from Puyo (Korea) who had been displaced from Manchuria.

Early Rulers
An identifiable Japanese element appeared around the end of the 6th century, leading to the start of the Nara era (600 to 784 AD) when the first historical records were created. Under Prince Shotoku, Japan acquired a constitution, Buddhism and a system of state administration. The capital was at Nara, which prospered and grew to be much larger than the present city. Culture from Korea and China flowed into the country during this time. When the Buddhist temples became too powerful for a later ruler (Kammu) in 794, he moved the capital to Kyoto.

With this move began the Heian period (794 to 1192). It started off well with cultural delegations from China, conquest of the Ezo (Ainu aboriginal people) in Northern Honshū and the spread of Buddhism, but by the 12th century corruption under the Fujiwara family and then under the Taira family led to an overthrow by the Minamoto (better known as the Genji) in 1185.

Military Rule
This started the Kamakura era (1192 to 1333). The Genji made their headquarters at Kamakura (near present-day Tokyo) and began a period of military government under a *shogun* (or generalissimo) that continued until 1868. The imperial capital remained at Kyoto, but the emperor was a mere figurehead.

It was during this period that the Mongols under Kublai Khan tried in 1274 and 1281 to invade northern Kyūshū. The second attack was defeated with the help of a typhoon that destroyed the Mongol fleet. This divine intervention was said to be *kamikaze* or 'wind of the gods', a word that would be revived as part of Japan's war effort in the 1940s.

After this victory the military government did not satisfactorily reward the soldiers, unrest followed and Emperor Godaigo took

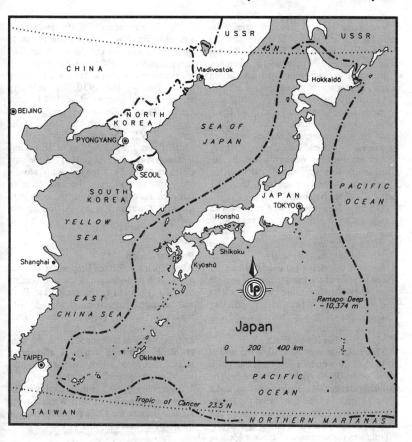

the opportunity to regain power for the imperial throne, for a brief period known as the Kammu restoration. But Godaigo over-indulged his courtiers and underpaid his warriors with the result that he was over-thrown by the Ashikaga clan, which restored the shogunate.

Then followed the Muromachi period (1336 to 1573). The new military govern-ment was set up in Kyoto, and for 57 years there were two royal courts, at Kyoto and Yoshino. The Muromachi era was a time of extravagance and luxury for Takauji Ashikaga, who built the Kinkakuji gold pavilion at Kyoto, but this was accompanied by poor administration and heavy taxes.

Civil war followed from 1467 until 1568, when Nobunaga Oda entered Kyoto, intend-ing to restore the shogunate. He was assassinated in 1582 and his efforts to control the country were taken over by Hideyoshi Toyotomi. The short Azuchi-Momoyama period (1573 to 1598) is named after the castles of these two leaders. Art and architec-ture flourished. Osaka Castle dates from this time.

The Edo period (1603 to 1867), or Toku-gawa era, began under Ieyasu Tokugawa, whose name became almost synonymous with the title of shogun. He set up a *bakufu* (military) government in Edo (now Tokyo) with a figurehead emperor still in Kyoto.

European contact with Japan had begun when a Portuguese ship ran aground in 1543. Subsequently the Japanese were introduced to gunpowder, Christianity and other European exports. However, under Tokugawa these growing foreign influences were seen as a threat to national stability, and virtually all contact with the Western world ceased. Christianity was suppressed and only the Dutch were allowed limited trade, through a small island off Nagasaki.

The only Japanese allowed contact with foreigners were prostitutes and merchants; this is probably why merchants were regarded as the lowest class in Tokugawa's rigidly class-structured society.

Japanese who left were executed on their return to prevent the introduction of outside ideas, and within Japan there were strict laws controlling every aspect of life. Military leaders expected instant obedience, and hesitation or expression of displeasure was likely to result in instant death.

This isolation continued until the arrival in 1853 of Commodore Perry and his 'black ships' of the US Navy, demanding trade. The British and other Westerners followed, and a show of force in 1864 convinced the Japanese that it was time to face the world. The Tokugawa shogunate lost power and imperial rule was restored under Emperor Meiji in 1868. He effectively abolished Buddhism and made Shinto the state religion, under which the emperor was to be revered as a living god.

Imperial Restoration

With the Meiji restoration began the Meiji era (1868 to 1912) and Japan's rapid transition from an isolated feudal agricultural nation to one of the world's major powers, with a strong military and industrial base. Western ways were widely adopted in many aspects of life and many traditional Japanese practices and relics were hastily discarded in the rush to modernisation.

The Taisho era (1912 to 1926) and Emperor Hirohito's Showa era (1926 to 1989) followed, with increased industrialisation and military confidence. Japan had been victorious over China in 1895 and Russia in 1905. During the 1930s the military increased their control and in 1937 invaded China. Then, following many years of strained relations with the USA, Japan entered WW II. The ultimate disaster of that conflict was the destruction of Hiroshima and Nagasaki – the first and (so far) the only cities ever to be attacked with atomic weapons. It was also the first time in recorded history that Japan had been conquered. Occupation by Allied forces followed.

Postwar Japan

After Japan's defeat the Emperor renounced any claims to divinity and the role became that of a symbol of the Japanese state. Postwar changes have been dramatic, with rejection of military values to such an extent that the armed forces are still held in low esteem. War was renounced in the new constitution, although Japan is allowed a self-defence force, which today is among the world's more powerful armed forces.

In January 1989 Hirohito died and the Showa era came to an end. When his son Akihito became the 125th emperor of Japan, the new Heisei era began.

GEOGRAPHY

There are four main islands – Honshū, Hokkaidō, Kyūshū and Shikoku – plus nearly 1000 small ones. Total area is 377,435 sq km, slightly larger than Great Britain, and 85% of the country is mountainous.

Japan is geologically young, and volcanic eruptions and earthquakes are an all too common occurrence. Mt Fuji last erupted in 1707. Tokyo is on the receiving end of a monster trembler about every 60 years. The last biggie measured 8.2 on the Richter scale and occurred in 1923, so another big one is overdue.

ECOLOGY

There's a low level of environmental concern in Japan, particularly when it comes to Japanese activities which do not affect life within Japan itself. The ivory trade has now stopped, but driftnet fishing, rainforest destruction and whaling continue. While materials such as glass are efficiently recycled, consumer goods are desperately over-packaged, and only the latest models are seen as desirable.

CLIMATE

Japan spans 22° of latitude, which means that climate varies considerably around the country. Winter is bitterly cold in the north but mild in the subtropical south. Summer is hot and humid everywhere except in high mountain areas. Typhoons can hit the southeast coast of Japan from August to the end of October. Spring temperatures are mild but the weather can be rainy and unstable. Autumn has the best combination of mild temperatures and blue skies.

GOVERNMENT

Japan's system of government is similar to the UK parliamentary system rather than the US presidential one. The Japanese Diet has two houses, the lower House of Representatives and the upper House of Councillors. The party that controls the majority of seats in the Diet is the party in power and has the right to appoint the prime minister, usually the party's president. The prime minister then appoints his cabinet, usually entirely constituted of Diet members.

Since its formation in 1955, the Liberal Democratic Party (LDP), the conservative party in Japanese politics, has been continuously in power. The LDP is riven with factions and has been plagued by major bribery scandals, but no other party has come close to offering a viable alternative. A healthy economy is of paramount importance to most Japanese voters, and so far the LDP has delivered the goods.

ECONOMY

The economic miracle of Japan is well known and needs little review. Even though Japan is an economic powerhouse, the economy has some surprising peculiarities. Despite high salaries, the exorbitant cost of living prevents most wage-earners from living well. Housing is a particularly serious problem: the cost of an apartment in Tokyo can easily exceed one's monthly salary, forcing Japanese workers to endure horribly long commutes to the less costly suburbs. Even there, a family will typically have to live in a tiny, overcrowded apartment of a kind which the Japanese themselves refer to as 'rabbit hutches'.

The situation might be somewhat ameliorated if both husband and wife worked, but this is seldom the case. Few Japanese women are expected to have any other career but 'homemaker'. A Japanese housewife will take care of all decisions related to domestic matters, and her husband will hand over his pay packet intact, receiving an allowance back from her for his daily needs. In public, however, he reigns supreme. The 'salaryman' is likely to spend far more of his waking hours with the firm he works for than with his family. If women's talents were ever put to wider use, Japan would leave the West even further behind.

POPULATION & PEOPLE

There are about 120 million people in Japan,

Tokyo Temperatures & Rainfall											
	Jan	Feb	Mar	Apr	May	Jun	Jul	Aug	Sep	Oct	Nov	Dec
Temp (°C)	3.7	4.3	7.6	13.1	7.6	21.1	25.1	26.4	22.8	16.7	11.3	6.1
Rain (mm)	48	73	101	135	131	182	146	147	217	220	101	62

with about 75% living in cities. Tokyo has over 11 million people.

The Japanese have ensured that only a small number of foreigners settle in their country. Less than 1% of the population are of non-Japanese origin, the vast majority of these being Koreans who were more or less abducted during WW II and taken to Japan to help the war effort. Koreans are an invisible minority – even the Japanese themselves have no way of knowing that someone is of Korean descent if he or she adopts a Japanese name. Nevertheless, Koreans born in Japan, who usually speak no other language than Japanese, are required to carry ID cards at all times and face discrimination in the workplace and other aspects of their daily lives. Being born in Japan does not automatically confer citizenship, unless one is of 'the Japanese race'. Thus, the ethnic Koreans living in Japan are not classified as citizens unless they become naturalised, which most have refused to do.

There is a tiny aboriginal population known as the Ainu (pronounced 'eyenoo'), whose language and culture bear no resemblance to those of other Japanese. And there is another group, a people ethnically Japanese, who were made outcasts in Japan's early history and have remained so ever since. Most Japanese will not let their children marry *burakumin* ('village people') as they are known.

ARTS
Music
Modern Japanese tastes in music range far and wide. At street level, pedestrians are often assaulted by gross electronic imitations of the sounds of nature – the evil apparatus which relentlessly spews out demented cuckoo sounds at street crossings is enough to drive one to vandalism.

Discos and live houses (live music venues) offer Jap rock, reggae, heavy metal, etc.

Sales of classical music recordings in Japan are among the highest in the world – another sound reason why Sony acquired CBS records in 1988.

Foreign jazz, pop and rock groups are continually jetting to and from Japan. The Japanese have also made a name for themselves in the field of synthesiser music.

The music from Okinawa has its own special sound. Japanese drumming is also worth a listen.

To find out what's happening in the music scene or to look for listings of events, you can consult newspapers, magazines such as *Tokyo Journal* or *Kansai Time Out* or call the Tourist Information Centre (TIC). Prices for concert tickets start at around Y3000; most cities have specialist ticket agencies giving discounts.

Painting
The techniques and materials used in the early stages of Japanese painting owed much to Chinese influence. Ink paintings by Chinese Zen artists were introduced to Japan during the Muromachi period and copied by Japanese artists who produced hanging pictures, scrolls and decorated screens and sliding doors.

Western techniques of painting, including the use of oils, were introduced during the 16th century by the Jesuits. Japanese painters who combined Western and Japanese styles sometimes produced interesting results: portraits of Westerners thoughtfully included an oriental incline to the eyes.

Another technique is the *ukiyo-e* woodblock print which caused great excitement when it was first introduced in the West. The biggest auctions of ukiyo-e are held not in Japan, but in New York and London. If you want to see the best and largest collection of ukiyo-e in the world, pay a visit to the Boston Museum of Fine Arts.

A more offbeat Japanese art form is the art of tattooing. In feudal times, the authorities tattooed criminals who then felt ashamed of the stigma of being 'branded'. Nowadays, many ordinary Japanese shun tattoos; it is a fair assumption that any Japanese you see flaunting tattoos are either *yakuza* (Japanese Mafia types) or have connections with the shady side of society.

Theatre

For many foreigners, the spectacular combinations of costume, make-up, scenery, action and music make *kabuki* the most enjoyable type of Japanese theatre. The acting portrays such roles as suicidal lovers, traitors, murderers, duellists, comics and female warriors.

Another form of theatre arts is called *Nō*. Each Nō performance normally consists of six plays.

Kyōgen is a type of farce developed mainly as an interlude for Nō plays. The subjects of its satire are often samurai, depraved priests and faithless women – the performers wear no masks and a chorus or chants are used.

Bunraku is traditional Japanese puppet theatre; some performances are full-length plays but others offer a medley from various plays.

Arts & Nature

Japanese gardens aim to imitate nature as opposed to the Western emphasis on reforming it.

Bonsai is the artificial dwarfing of trees or the miniaturisation of nature. *Ikebana* is the art of flower arranging – its schools have millions of students, including many eligible young ladies who view proficiency in the art as a means to improve their marriage prospects.

CULTURE

Traditional Lifestyle

Japan's formalised society has a number of strictly observed rules of behaviour. As a *gaijin* (foreigner) you won't necessarily be expected to follow these but it will enhance your visit if you do.

Avoiding Offence

Removing shoes is important when entering any private house or any tatami-matted place. House slippers are always supplied but don't wear these into the toilet; in private homes, youth hostels and other residential places, there will be a pair of slippers at the toilet entrance.

The Japanese bath, or *ofuro*, is an important part of life. It is hot and deep and meant for soaking, not washing. To get clean you soap and wash yourself at the tap, rinse off, and only then do you get in the ofuro. Don't add cold water, and never use soap in the bath.

Japanese avoid blowing their noses in public and retire to the toilet if possible to perform this highly personal bodily function. However, it is not uncommon for men to urinate in public, especially at night after a lot of beer.

The Japanese find it offensive to eat on the street, although they make an exception for ice-cream cones.

Sport

Sumō wrestling is a traditional Japanese sport with complicated rituals. However, the number one sport is baseball, and like so many exotic imports, most Japanese now think they invented it. *Kendo* (sword fighting) was the favourite of the samurai. *Karate* ('empty hand') originated in India, then spread through China and reached Okinawa in the 14th century. *Aikido* and *judo* are martial arts which originated in Japan.

RELIGION

Shinto (way of the gods) and Buddhism are both widely followed. Many people follow both beliefs with no conflict.

Shinto has no fixed ceremonies or scriptures and is basically an animistic belief concerned with obtaining the blessing of the gods for future events. It is quite common for a Shinto priest to be called to bless a building site before construction begins.

Shinto shrines, called *jinja*, *taisha* or *jingu*, are generally identifiable by a *torii* gate (two uprights and a double cross bar). There are normally carved stone *koma-inu* – guardian lions or dogs – at the entrance. The shrine is often a simple building although there are varied designs, each with its own symbolic importance.

Buddhism reached Japan from China in the 6th century, but Japanese modifications have meant that the faith in its present form is almost unrecognisable to most foreign Buddhists. There are numerous sects, some of quite recent origin. Japan has many beautiful Buddhist temples, especially in Kyoto.

Christians make up about 1% of the population although adherents are found in larger numbers in public life.

LANGUAGE

The language barrier can be a problem, as few people outside the main cities speak any English. If you learn some Japanese, it will probably be the Tokyo dialect, which is also used on television but not common in many rural areas.

If you want to learn the rudiments of the language, one of the best books is *Japanese Made Easy* by Monane, published by Tuttle. For a comprehensive study try *Beginning Japanese* by Jorden, published by Yale University Press. Lonely Planet's *Japanese Phrasebook* has most of the phrases you are likely to need while travelling in Japan.

Word order in Japanese is confusing to English speakers, but pronunciation is fairly easy and the language has no tones, unlike Chinese. The biggest problem is the writing system. Japanese uses three different scripts (four if you include the increasingly used Roman script, *romaji*). The most difficult of the three, for foreigners and Japanese alike, is *kanji*, the ideographic script developed by the Chinese.

Kanji works perfectly well for the Chinese language, but is less suitable to Japanese; any given character is likely to have a number of different pronunciations and meanings. It has been supplemented with an alphabet of syllables known as *hiragana* and also with a special script called *katakana* used mostly for foreign loan words such as *terebi* (television) and *femunisuto* (feminist).

Greetings & Civilities

Hello.
  (for during the day)
  konnichiwa   こんにちわ
  (for the evening)
  konbanwa   こんばんは
  (on the phone)
  moshimoshi   もしもし
Goodbye.
  sayōnara   さようなら
Please.
  (when presenting something)
  dōzo   どうぞ
  (when asking for something)
  onegai   おねがいします
Thank you.
  arigatō gozaimasu
  ありがとうございます
Yes.
  hai   はい
No.
  iie   いいえ
Excuse me.
  sumimasen   すみません

Getting Around

I want to go to...
  ...ni ikitai desu.
  ……に行きたいです
What time does...leave?
  nan ji ni shuppatsu shimasuka?
  何日に出発しますか？
What time does...arrive?
  nan ji ni tōchaku shimasuka?
  到着しますか？
bus/tram
  basu/toramu   バス/トラム
train
  densha   電車
boat/ferry
  bōto/ferī-bōto   ボート/フェリーボー
one-way (ticket)
  katamichi kippu   片道切符
return (ticket)
  ōfuku kippu   往復切符
station
  eki   駅
ticket
  kippu   切符
ticket office
  kippu uriba   切符売場
entrance
  iriguchi   入口
exit
  deguchi   出口

information
  annai　　　案内
open/closed
  kaiten chu/heiten
  開店中/閉店
prohibited
  kinshi　　　禁止
toilets
  otearai　　お手洗い

Accommodation
hotel
  hoteru　　　ホテル
inn
  ryokan　　　旅館
What is the address?
  gojūsho wa nan desuka?
  ご住所はなんですか？
Please write it down.
  kaite kudasai　　書いて下さい
Do you have a...available?
  ...wa arimasuka?
  ……はありますか？
bed
  futon　　　蒲団
cheap room
  yasui heya　安い部屋
How much is it per night?
  ippaku ikura desuka?/hitori　一泊
How much is it per person?
  hitori ikura desuka?
  一人いくらですか？

Around Town
Where is the/a...?
  ...wa doko desuka?
  ……はどこですか？
bank
  ginkō　　　銀行
city centre
  toshi no chūshin/shigaichi
  都市の中心/市街地
post office
  yūbinkyoku　郵便局
restaurant
  resutoran/shokudo
  レストラン/食堂
tourist information office
  yūbinkyoku　　観光案内所

Food
food stall
  yatai　　　屋台
restaurant
  resutoran　　レストラン
I am vegetarian.
  watashi wa bejitarian desu
  私はベジタリアンです
How much is it?
  ikura desuka?　いくらですか？

Time & Dates
When?
  itsu　　　いつ
today
  kyō　　　今日
tomorrow
  ashita　　明日
in the morning
  asa　　　朝
in the afternoon
  gogo　　　午後

Emergencies
Help!
  tasukede kudasai　助けで下さい
Go away!
  itte shimae!/ike!
  行ってしまえ！/行け！
Call a doctor!
  isha o yonde kudasai.
  医者を呼んで下さい
Call the police!
  keisatsukan o yonde kudasai.
  警察官を呼んで下さい
I'm allergic to penicillin.
  penishirin ni arerugi ga arimasu.
  ペニシリンにアレルギがあります
I'm allergic to antibiotics.
  kōseibutsushitsu ni arerugīmasu.
  抗生物質
I'm diabetic.
  watashi wa tōnyōbyō kansha desu.
  私は糖尿病患者です

The counting system in Japan comprises two separate sets of numbers, one to be used with counters, one without. There are many different counters attached to numbers (ie: *-nin*, people; *-ji*, time; etc) – too many to list here.

To get by, use counterless numbers or write the number down – Japanese people will understand Arabic numerals.

counterless with counters

	counterless	with counters	
0	re;	maru	零
1	hitotsu	ichi	一, 一
2	futatsu	ni	二, 両
3	mitsu	san	三
4	yotsu	yon; shi	四
5	itsutsu	go	五
6	mutsu	roku	六
7	nanatsu	shichi; nana	七
8	yatsu	hachi	八
9	kokonotsu	kyu	九
10	to	ju	十

After 10 one set of numbers prevails:

11	ju-ichi
12	ju-ni
13	ji-san
20	ni-ju
30	san-ju
49	you-ju-kyu
100	hyaku
200	ni-hyaku

There are certain rules of linguistic politeness. Direct statements are avoided. Things are alluded to. Direct disagreement is avoided, being usually suggested by a pause in the conversation. Men and women use different forms of speech, with women using a more polite form to men.

Facts for the Visitor

VISAS & EMBASSIES

Many visitors who are not planning to work while in Japan are exempt from obtaining visas. Stays of up to six months are permitted for citizens of Austria, Germany, Ireland, Mexico, Switzerland and the UK; and stays of up to three months for citizens of Argentina, Belgium, Canada, Denmark, Finland, France, Iceland, Israel, Italy, Malaysia, Netherlands, New Zealand, Norway, Singapore, Spain, Sweden, the USA and a number of other countries.

Visitors from Australia and South Africa are amongst those nationals requiring a visa. This is usually issued free, but passport photographs are required and a return or onward ticket must be shown.

Anyone, and this includes tourists, who stays more than 90 days is required to obtain an Alien Registration Card. You can usually get a single 90-day extension on a tourist visa but further extensions require a letter of guarantee. Some foreigners get around this by leaving the country and then returning, but immigration officials can be very difficult.

Japanese Embassies

Australia
112 Empire Circuit, Yarralumla, Canberra, ACT 2600 (☎ 733244); there are also consulates in Brisbane (☎ 2215188), Melbourne (☎ 2673244), Perth (☎ 3213455) and Sydney (☎ 2313455)

Canada
255 Sussex Drive, Ottawa, Ontario K1N 9E6 2368541); there are also consulates in Edmonton (☎ 4223752), Montreal (☎ 8663429), Toronto (☎ 3637038), Vancouver (☎ 6845868) and Winnipeg (☎ 9435554)

Hong Kong
25th floor, Bank of America Tower, 12 Harcourt Rd, Central (☎ 5221184)

Ireland
22 Ailesbury Rd, Dublin 4 (☎ 69-40-33)

New Zealand
7th floor, Norwich Insurance House, 3-11 Hunter St, Wellington 1 (☎ 731-540); there is also a consulate in Auckland (☎ 34-106)

Singapore
16 Nassim Rd, Singapore 1025 (☎ 2358855)

Thailand
1674 New Petchburi Rd, Bangkok 10310 (☎ 2526151)

UK
43-46 Grosvenor St, London W1X OBA (☎ 4936030)

USA
2520 Massachusetts Ave, NW Washington DC 20008-2869 (☎ 9396700); there are also consulates in Anchorage (☎ 2798428), Atlanta (☎ 8922700), Boston (☎ 9739772), Chicago (☎ 2800400), Honolulu (☎ 5362226), Houston (☎ 6522977), Kansas City (☎ 4710111), Los Angeles (☎ 6248305), New Orleans (☎ 5292101), New York (3718222), Portland (☎ 2211811) and San Francisco (☎ 7773533)

Foreign Embassies in Japan

All of the following embassies and consulates are in Tokyo:

Australia
1-1-12 Shiba-kōen Park, Minato-ku (☎ 3435-0971)
Canada
7-3-38 Akasaka, Minato-ku (☎ 3408-2101)
China
3-4-33 Moto Azabu, Minato-ku (☎ 3403-3380)
Ireland
No 25 Kowa Building, 8-7 Sanban-cho, Chiyoda-ku (☎ 3263-0695)
New Zealand
20-40 Kamiyama-cho, Shibuya-ku (☎ 3467-2270/1)
Philippines
11-24 Nanpeidai-cho, Shibuya-ku (☎ 3496-2731)
South Korea
1-2-5 Minami Azabu, Minato-ku (☎ 3452-7611)
Taiwan (Visitors' Association)
A-9, 5th floor, Imperial Tower, Imperial Hotel, 1-1-1 Uchisaiwai-cho, Chiyoda-ku (☎ 3501-3591)
Thailand
3-14-6 Kami Osaki, Shinagawa-ku (☎ 3441-7342)
UK
1 Ichiban-cho, Chiyoda-ku (☎ 3265-5511)
USA
1-10-5 Akasaka, Minato-ku (☎ 3224-5000)
USSR
2-1-1 Azabudai, Minato-ku (☎ 3583-4224)

Korean visas can be obtained in the following cities: Tokyo (☎ (03) 452-7611), Sapporo (☎ (011) 621-0288), Nagoya (☎ (052) 935-9221), Osaka (☎ (06) 213-1401), Fukuoka (☎ (092) 771-0461), Shimonoseki (☎ (0832) 66-5341).

CUSTOMS

Customs allowances include the usual tobacco products, three 760 ml bottles of alcoholic beverages, 57 grams of perfume and gifts and souvenirs up to a value of Y200,000 or its equivalent. The penalties for importing drugs are very severe.

Customs officers also confiscate literature, such as men's magazines, which shows pubic hair. Depictions of just about every kind of sexual liaison and contortion is readily available at newsagents in Japan, but all pubic hair is carefully erased.

There are no limits on the importing of foreign or Japanese currency. The exporting of foreign currency is also unlimited, but a Y5 million limit exists for Japanese currency.

MONEY
Currency

The currency in Japan is the *yen* (Y) and banknotes and coins are easily identifiable. There are Y1, Y5, Y10, Y50, Y100 and Y500 coins, Y1000, Y5000 and Y10,000 banknotes.

You can change cash or travellers' cheques at an 'Authorised Foreign Exchange Bank' or at some of the large hotels and stores. These are easy to find in cities, but much less common elsewhere. Changing money at a regular bank is slow, often taking half an hour. Exchanging Korean or Taiwanese currency in Japan is a fruitless task, so avoid bringing any if you're arriving from those countries. The use of credit cards is becoming more widespread in Japan, but outside major cities, cash still reigns supreme. An interesting variation on all this is to have a post office savings account – there are branches almost everywhere the traveller is likely to go.

Exchange Rates

A$1	=	Y101
C$1	=	Y114
HK$1	=	Y17
NZ$1	=	Y73
UK£1	=	Y230
US$1	=	Y130

Costs

These are astronomical, but there are ways to minimise the expense. A skeleton daily budget, assuming you stay at the cheapest places (Y2000 per night in a hostel), eat modestly (Y1500) and spend Y1500 on short-distance travel, would be Y5000 (US$35). Add at least Y1000 for extras like

snacks, drinks, admission fees and entertainment.

Tipping
The total absence of tipping does reduce costs a little. Nobody expects a tip so it's best to keep it that way.

Bargaining
Prices in Japan are fixed, though in some of the bargain electronic shopping areas, such as Akihabara in Tokyo, a certain amount of bargaining is usually required to get the best possible price. Generally, shops will only come down 10% to 15% from the original price. Don't push too hard; asking politely for a discount is enough in Japan – the sales clerk will tell you if one is available. In the big department stores, as in the West, the marked price is as low as you're going to get.

Consumer Taxes
Shopping for tax-free goods in Japan may not necessarily give you the bargains you'd hoped for. Although tax-free shops enable foreigners to get an exemption from the 10% to 30% sales tax levied on most items, other bulk-buying shops are often a better deal. Shop around and compare prices before making a purchase.

WHEN TO GO
The best time to visit is from September to late November. If you are planning to tour all the main islands it would be best to start with Hokkaidō in the north and work your way south as the cool weather advances in the same direction. Early November is the peak time to visit Kyoto, with its beautiful autumn foliage, but the peak crowds arrive then as well.

The spring is the time to see Japan's famous cherry blossoms, but pinning down the exact time of this occurrence is problematic. It varies from year to year according to rainfall and temperature, and is also affected by latitude. It's best not to plan your trip around this elusive event. Furthermore, this is a peak time for Japanese travellers so accommodation and transport become tight.

Summer may be hot and humid, but fewer Japanese travel at this time than during spring or autumn. Winter can be miserably cold and many buildings are not well heated.

WHAT TO BRING
You'll have no trouble finding whatever you need in Japan, but since costs are high, it might be wise to make your expensive purchases before arrival. Even Japanese-made cameras cost more in Japan than in Hong Kong!

Medications of any kind are expensive in

Japan. Bring oral contraceptives if you need them, as the Japanese mainly rely on condoms.

Bring a stack of business cards and hand them out like confetti whenever you meet people.

TOURIST OFFICES
Local Tourist Offices

The Japan National Tourist Organisation (JNTO) is the best source of information. It publishes a number of maps, booklets and pamphlets in English and other foreign languages.

JNTO operates three Tourist Information Centres (TICs): one at Narita International Airport (☎ 0476-32-8711), another in the Ginza in central Tokyo (☎ 350-21461) and the third near the railway station in Kyoto (☎ 075-371-5649).

TIC offices do not make reservations or bookings, but will direct you to agencies which can, such as the Japan Travel Bureau (JTB) or the Nippon Travel Agency (NTA). The TIC offices in Tokyo (☎ 350-32911) and Kyoto (☎ 361-2911) operate 'Teletourist', a round-the-clock taped information service on current events in town. JNTO also operate Goodwill Guides, a volunteer programme with over 30,000 members who wear a blue and white badge with a dove and globe logo.

JNTO operate a nationwide toll-free phone service available from 9 am to 5 pm, seven days a week. The main aim is to provide assistance for visitors unable to get to the TIC offices in Tokyo or Kyoto. To contact an English-speaking travel expert, call 0120-2228000 for information on eastern Japan; 0120-4448000 for western Japan.

JNTO Offices Overseas

Australia
115 Pitt St, Sydney, NSW 2000 (☎ (02) 2324522)
Canada
165 University Ave, Toronto, Ontario M5H 3B8 (☎ (416) 3667140)
Hong Kong
Suite 3606, Two Exchange Square, 8 Connaught Place, Central (☎ 5227913)

South Korea
10 Da-dong, Chung-gu, Seoul (☎ (02) 7527968)
Thailand
Wall Street Tower Building, 33/61, Suriwong Rd, Bangkok 10500 (☎ (02) 2335108)
UK
167 Regent St, London W1 (☎ (071) 7349638)
USA
Chicago: 401 North Michigan Ave, IL 60611 (☎ (312) 2220874)
Dallas: 2121 San Jacinto St, Suite 980, LB53, TX 75201 (☎ (214) 7541820)
Los Angeles: 624 South Grand Ave, Suite 2640, CA 90017 (☎ (213) 6231952)
New York: Rockefeller Plaza, 630 Fifth Ave, NY 10111 (☎ (212) 7575640)
San Francisco: 360 Post St, Suite 401, CA 94108 (☎ (415) 9897140)

BUSINESS HOURS & HOLIDAYS

Shops are typically open seven days a week from around 10 am to 8 pm. Department stores close slightly earlier, usually 6.30 or 7 pm, and also close one weekday each week. If a city has five major department stores they will probably organise it so that Mitsukoshi closes on Monday, Daimaru closes on Tuesday, and so on. Large companies usually work a 9 am to 5 pm five-day week; some also operate on Saturday mornings. Banks are open from 9 am to 3 pm, Monday to Friday. They are closed on the second and third Saturday of the month and open on the others from 9 am to 12 noon.

Public holidays include: New Year's Day, 1 January; Adult's Day, 15 January; National Foundation Day, 11 February; Spring Equinox, 21 March (approximately); Green Day, 29 April; Constitution Day, 3 May; Children's Day, 5 May; Respect-for-the-Aged Day, 15 September; Autumn Equinox, 23 September (approximately); Sports Day, 10 October; Culture Day, 3 November; Labour Thanksgiving Day, 23 November; the Emperor's Birthday, 23 December.

POST & TELECOMMUNICATIONS
Postal Rates

The airmail rate for postcards is Y70 to any overseas destination; aerograms cost Y80. Letters weighing less than 10 grams are Y80 to other countries within Asia, Y100 to North

distance or overseas calls require a handful of coins which are used up as the call progresses, and any unused coins are returned.

Most pay phones accept prepaid phone cards in Y500, Y1000 and Y5000 denominations. The cards are sold from vending machines, telephone company card outlets and many shops. After each call, a small hole is punched to show how much value remains.

Japanese telephone numbers consist of an area code plus a local code and the number. You do not dial the area code when making a call within that area.

Only a few phones handle international calls. An overseas call (paid or operator-assisted) can only be made from a phone with a sign which says that it handles international calls. Look for these in big hotels, the main railway station, the main shopping arcade or Nippon Telegraph & Telephone (NTT) offices.

To place an international call through the operator, dial 0051 – international operators speak English. To dial direct, dial 001 then the international country code, the local code and the number. Another option is to dial 0039 plus a national code for home country direct, which takes you straight through to a local operator in the country dialled. You can then make a reverse-charge (collect) call or a credit card call. In some hotels or other tourist locations, you may find a home country direct phone where you simply press the button labelled USA, UK, Canada, Australia, NZ or wherever to be put through to your operator.

America or Oceania (including Australia and New Zealand) and Y120 to Europe, Africa and South America.

Sending Mail

District post offices (the main post office in a ward or *ku*), are normally open 8 am to 7 pm on weekdays, 8 am to 3 pm on Saturdays and 9 am to 12.30 pm on Sundays and public holidays. Local post offices are open 9 am to 5 pm on weekdays and 9 am to 1 pm on Saturdays. Central post offices in the larger cities may have some counters open 24 hours a day.

Receiving Mail

Although any post office will hold mail for collection, the poste restante idea is not well known and can cause confusion in smaller places. It is probably better to have mail addressed to you at a larger central post office. Letters are usually only held for 30 days before being returned to sender. When inquiring about mail for collection ask for *kyoku dome yūbin*.

Telephones

Local calls cost Y10 for three minutes; long-

International Dialling Codes		
country	*direct dial*	*home country direct*
Australia	001-61	0039-611
Canada	001-1	0039-161
Hong Kong	001-852	0039-852
Netherlands	001-31	0039-311
New Zealand	001-64	0039-641
Singapore	001-65	0039-651
Taiwan	001-886	0039-886
UK	001-44	0039-441

Fax, Telex & Telegraph

Japan may be an economic miracle but sending a fax from there can be a real hassle. Most post offices do not offer a fax service, and large hotels generally do not allow you to use their facilities unless you are a guest.

In Tokyo, the Kokusai Denshin Denwa (KDD) international telegraph office (☎ 3270-511), one block north of Otemachi Subway Station, has fax and telex facilities. Budget travellers, particularly those staying at the Kimi Ryokan, can use the Kimi Information Centre, around the corner from the ryokan. You have to pay a registration fee of Y2000, but after this you pay the fax charges individually. The centre will also receive faxes for you.

TIME

Despite Japan's east-west distance, the country is all on the same time, nine hours ahead of Greenwich Mean Time (GMT). Thus, when it is 12 noon in Japan, it is 3 am in London, 11 am in Hong Kong, 1 pm in Sydney, 3 pm in Auckland, 10 pm the previous day in New York, 7 pm the previous day in San Francisco and 5 pm the previous day in Honolulu. Daylight-saving time is not used in Japan. Times are all expressed on a 24-hour clock.

LAUNDRY

Laundromats are common enough in Japan, and a few odd hostels even have a washing machine.

WEIGHTS & MEASURES

Japan uses the international metric system. One odd local unit is the size of rooms, usually given in standard tatami mat measurements known as jō. There are several tatami sizes, but generally one tatami mat equals one jō which is 1.8 metres by 0.9 metres (1.62 sq metres).

ELECTRICITY

The Japanese electric current is 100 V AC, an odd current found almost nowhere else in the world. Furthermore, Tokyo and eastern Japan are on 50 cycles, while western Japan including Nagoya, Kyoto and Osaka is on 60 cycles. Most North American electrical items, designed to run on 117 V, will function reasonably well on Japanese current. The plugs are flat two pin.

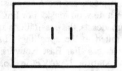

BOOKS & MAPS

Inside Japan (Penguin, 1987) by Peter Tasker, is probably the best wide-ranging introduction to modern Japanese culture, society and the economy.

Views on the growth of Japan as an economic superpower are found in *Trading Places: How America Allowed Japan to Take the Lead* by Clyde V Prestowitz Jr (Charles E Tuttle) and *The New Masters – Can the West Match Japan?* by Phillip Oppenheim (Hutchinson Business Books, 1990). Ezra Vogel saw it coming more than 10 years ago in *Japan as Number One: Lessons for America* (Harvard University Press, 1979).

The Japanese Today by Edwin O Reischauer (Belknap, 1988), is a recently revised standard textbook on Japanese society and a must for those planning to spend time in Japan.

For more detailed travel information, look for the Lonely Planet guidebook *Japan – a travel survival kit*.

MEDIA
Newspapers & Magazines

The *Japan Times* is undoubtedly the best of the English-language newspapers. The *Mainichi Daily News* and the *Yomiuri Daily* are a definite second to the *Japan Times*. The *Asahi Evening News* is available in the afternoon.

As for magazines, the Tokyo-based *Tokyo Journal* is the pick of the crowd with its comprehensive what's-on listings and informative, readable articles on local cultural and topical issues. Also based in Tokyo is the very similar *Tokyo Time Out*. Other magazines include *Kansai Time Out*, *Tokyo Journal*, *Discover Kinki* and *Eyes*.

Radio & TV

Japanese radio is pretty dismal, mainly because it places far more emphasis on DJ jive than it does on music. For English-language broadcasts, the possibilities are pretty much limited to the appallingly banal US armed services' Far East Network (FEN). The FM station J-WAVE in Tokyo has recently tried to increase the music content and cut the talk. Bring a good supply of tapes and a Walkman if music is essential to your sanity.

Like radio, most television is inaccessible to the non-Japanese speaker, and even if you do speak the language most programmes seem to be inane variety shows.

TVs can be fitted with an adapter so that certain English-language programmes and movies can be received in either Japanese or English. NHK broadcasts a nightly bilingual news report. Unfortunately, Japanese TV news is not highly informative, often running extended reports on the daring rescue of a cat from a tree.

Finally, many Japanese hotel rooms will have a pay cable TV with video channels. It is unlikely that English-language movies will be available but the porn channel needs no translation.

FILM & PHOTOGRAPHY

The Japanese are major producers of both photographic equipment and film, and you'll have no problem buying what you need. The very popular disposable cameras are even sold from vending machines! Slide film is harder to come by than print film, but you can still find it in large cities. Kodachrome film can be bought and processed in Japan.

HEALTH

Japan is a very healthy country, though there is always the chance of having a heart attack when you see the price tags. Food and water are perfectly safe everywhere.

Medical treatment is equally reliable. In the larger cities there are a number of Western doctors if you find it difficult to talk to a Japanese one. There are also several hospitals offering Western-style treatment – these have mostly been founded by Christian groups. Contact the TICs for details. Medical treatment is expensive so have your own insurance.

WOMEN TRAVELLERS

Japan is certainly a male-oriented society. This is evident in the career options available for women, which mainly consist of being receptionists whose purpose is to serve tea and brighten up the office with their looks. By the time she is aged 25, a woman is expected to be married and to have resigned from her job. A woman who remains unmarried and employed after this age is regarded as peculiar, and most Japanese men would suspect there must be a flaw in her character.

Perhaps most disturbing for Western women visiting Japan is the way in which women feature in the mass media. It's not just that they are often treated as giggling sex objects, but the fact that in comic strips, magazines and movies, women are so often shown as brutalised, passive victims in bizarre, sado-masochistic rites.

While these fantasies are disturbing, it is possible to take refuge in the thought that they *are* fantasies, and women are in fact a great deal safer in Japan than they are in other parts of the world. Harassment, when it does occur, is usually clandestine, occurring in crowded areas such as trains; however, with direct confrontation, almost all Japanese men will be shamed into withdrawing the groping hand.

DANGERS & ANNOYANCES

The crime rate is very low in Japan, but this should not lure you into carelessness. Pickpocketing does occasionally occur in crowded places like trains. With reasonable precautions you should have no problem.

WORK

Many foreigners come for a six to 12-month stint as English teachers, hostesses, technical rewriters, models or itinerant pedlars of paintings, jewellery and other odds and ends.

There is still plenty of work for foreigners but the competition is fiercer, pay and conditions are getting worse and the government is clamping down on foreign workers.

Finding casual work is certainly still possible, particularly if you look neat and tidy. Appearance is *very* important in Japan: suit and tie for the men please, businesslike dresses for the women. Once upon a time, blonde hair and blue eyes were all that was needed for an English teaching job, but nowadays real qualifications are becoming increasingly important. Be wary of anyone who is prepared to employ you without qualifications – there are some very exploitative deals, especially in Tokyo. Nevertheless, blond hair helps, and if you have charm and persuasiveness, it's still a seller's market in Japan.

Australians, Canadians and New Zealanders between the ages of 18 and 25 (the age limit can be pushed up to 30) can apply for a working holiday visa. This visa allows a six-month stay and two six-month extensions.

ACTIVITIES
Skiing
There are now more than 300 ski resorts, many with high-standard runs and snow-making equipment. The majority of resorts are concentrated on the island of Honshū, where the crowds are huge, the vertical drops rarely more than 400 metres and all runs start at altitudes of less than 2000 metres. Skiers on Hokkaidō, however, can look forward to powder skiing matching anything in the Alps. Niseko and Furano, two of Hokkaidō's best resorts, have excellent facilities. JNTO's *Skiing in Japan* pamphlet covers 20 resorts on Honshū and Hokkaidō. Skiing is normally possible from December to April.

Resort accommodation ranges from hostels to expensive hotels but is heavily booked during the ski season. Lift passes cost Y2600 to Y4200 per day. Daily hire of skis, stocks and boots can cost up to Y5000 but finding larger-size ski boots may be difficult. It's wise to bring your own equipment from abroad as it's expensive in Japan.

Cross-country skiing is a good way to escape the crowds. The best terrain for this is in the Hakodate region of Hokkaidō. The Japanese are very hospitable and foreigners are welcome to join in races and festivities organised by the local authorities – one of the most famous is the Sapporo Marathon Cross-country Ski Race.

Hiking
Japan is a good country for hiking, and this activity has the advantage of being free. Some hiking areas, like Mt Fuji, can be very crowded during the summer season. *Hiking in Japan* by Paul Hunt (Kodansha, Tokyo & London, 1988) is a useful guide.

Courses
Studying Japanese is expensive – out of reach unless you are also able to take on paid work. The TIC leaflet *Japanese & Japanese Studies* lists government-accredited schools that belong to the Association of International Education.

To find out more about courses for foreigners in ikebana (flower arranging) contact Ikebana International (☎ 03-293 8188), Ochanomizu Square Building, 1-6 Surugadai, Kanda, Chiyoda-ku, Tokyo. Some schools provide instruction in English; prices start around Y3000 per hour.

HIGHLIGHTS
Japan's temples, shrines, gardens and castles are major attractions.

Mt Fuji, the much-climbed symbol of Japan, can actually seem like Tokyo Station at rush hour when you get close up, but from a distance it's as beautiful as it has ever been. Mt Bandai and its lakes in the Tohoku region offer more superb scenery.

Hokkaidō, the second largest but least densely populated island, offers wonderful mountain scenery around Mashun-ko Lake in the east and around Toya-ko and Shikotsu-ko lakes in the west. The Shiretoko-hantō and Shakotan-hantō peninsulas have fine coastal scenery.

Kyūshū has some wonderful volcanic scenery, particularly in the immense caldera of Mt Aso, the bleak, volcano-studded Kirishima Plateau, and rumbling Sakurajima near Kagoshima. At the extreme western end of the country, Iriomote Island has dense jungle and good scuba diving.

The atomic bomb museums at Hiroshima and Nagasaki may not be pleasant, but they are something no visitor to Japan should avoid.

It's easy to arrange a factory visit at many centres in Japan, but the huge Mazda car factory in Hiroshima is certainly worth a visit.

ACCOMMODATION

Compared to the rest of Asia, Japanese budget places make a sizeable dent in the pocket, the lowest price per person per night being around Y1400. The average cost at a youth hostel is around Y1900.

Camping

Camping is one of the cheapest forms of accommodation but official campgrounds are often only open during the Japanese 'camping season' (July and August) when you can expect an avalanche of students. Facilities range from bare essentials to de luxe. JNTO publishes *Camping in Japan* (MG-084), a selection of campgrounds which includes details of prices and facilities.

Youth Hostels

Reservations are a good idea at youth hostels. Phoning ahead the day before arrival is usually sufficient, though the Tokyo hostels are often booked solid. Hostels definitely prefer you to phone first rather than just showing up, even if you phone from across the street. Advance reservations are essential for the New Year holiday weeks, March, the late April/early May Golden Week, and July and August. You should state the arrival date and time, number of nights, number and sex of the people for whom beds are to be reserved and the meals required.

When corresponding from abroad *always* include two International Reply Coupons.

JNTO publishes *Youth Hostels in Japan*, a concise English listing of youth hostels. By far the best source of information on hostels is the (Japan) *Youth Hostel Handbook* available for Y580 from the Japan Youth Hostel Association (JYHA) (☎ 3269-5831), Hoken Kaikan, 1-2 Sadohara-cho, Ichigaya, Shinjuku-ku, Tokyo 162.

Branch offices in Tokyo which stock the handbook and can supply information are in the second-level basement of Sogo Department Store, Yurakucho (two minutes on foot from TIC); the 4th floor of the Keio Department Store, Shinjuku-ku; and the 7th floor of the Seibu Department Store, Ikebukuro.

Hostellers are expected to check in between 3 and 8 pm. Checkout is usually required before 10 am and dormitories are closed between 10 am and 3 pm.

Gaijin Houses

This is the cheapest category of accommodation, especially for long-term stays. Prices for the cheapest houses start around Y1400 per night. Some places offer reductions for stays longer than a month.

Most of the gaijin houses are in Tokyo and Kyoto where listings are available from TIC. You can also find advertisements or listings in publications such as *Tokyo Journal*, *Kansai Time Out* or *Kyoto Visitor's Guide*.

Cycling Terminals

Cycling terminals provide low-priced accommodation of the bunk-bed or tatami-room variety and are usually found in scenic areas suited to cycling. If you don't have your own bike, you can rent one at the terminal.

At around Y2200 per person per night or Y3500 including two meals, terminal prices compare favourably with those of a youth hostel. For more information contact the Japan Bicycle Promotion Institute (☎ 3583-5444), Nihon Jitensha Kaikan Building, 9-3 Akasaka 1-chome, Minato-ku, Tokyo.

Minshuku

A *minshuku* is usually a family-run private home, rather like a B&B in Europe or the USA. Minshuku can be found throughout Japan and offer one way to peep into daily Japanese life. The average price per person per night with two meals is around Y5000. You are expected to lay out and put away your bedding and bring your own towel. JNTO publishes a booklet, *Minshukus in Japan*.

Ryokan

For a taste of traditional Japanese life, a stay at a *ryokan* – a Japanese-style inn – is mandatory. Prices start around Y3800 (per person, per night) for a 'no-frills' ryokan without meals. Classier ryokan start at Y8000. High-class ryokan can charge Y25,000 or more. The Japanese Inn Group (☎ 075-351-6748), c/o Hiraiwa Ryokan, 314, Hayao-cho, Kaminoguchi-agaru, Ninomiya-cho-dori, Shimogyo-ku, Kyoto 600, publishes an excellent listing of inexpensive ryokan.

Capsule Hotels

Forget these if you have claustrophobia. Your room (the 'capsule') measures two metres by one metre by one metre – about the size of a coffin. Inside is a bed, a TV, reading light, radio and alarm clock. Personal belongings are kept in a locker room.

This type of hotel is common in the major cities and often caters to male travellers who have partied too hard to make it home or have missed the last train. There are a few for women only, but the majority are only for men. Some capsule hotels have the added attraction of a sauna.

An average price is Y3800 per night or Y1400 for a three-hour stay. A lot of money to sleep in a box.

Business Hotels

Cheap single rooms average Y4000 to Y5000. Some business hotels also have twin rooms. Cheaper business hotels usually do not have a service charge, though places costing Y6000 or more often add a 10% charge.

The Japan Business Hotel Association at 43 Kanda-Higashi, Matsusita-cho, Chiyoda-ku, Tokyo, publishes the *Business Hotel Guide*.

Love Hotels

To find one on the street, just look for flamboyant facades with rococo architecture, turrets, battlements and imitation statuary. The design of the hotels emphasises discretion: entrances and exits are kept separate; keys are provided through a small opening without contact between desk clerk and guest; photos of the rooms are displayed to make the choice easy.

The rooms can fulfil most fantasies with themes ranging from harem extravaganza to sci-fi. Further choices can include vibrating beds, wall-to-wall mirrors, bondage equipment and video recorders to recall the experience – but don't forget to take the video cassette with you when you leave.

Charges on an hourly basis are at a peak during the day and early evening. Love hotels are of more interest to foreign visitors after 10 pm, when it's possible to stay the night for about Y5000 per room (rather than per person), but you should check out early enough in the morning to avoid a return to peak-hour rates. Outside love hotels there will usually be a sign in English announcing the rates for a 'rest' (usually two hours) or a 'stay' (overnight).

FOOD

Japanese food gets mixed reviews from travellers. Apparently, it also gets mixed reviews from younger Japanese, many of whom prefer Big Macs and pizza to rice, pickles, seaweed and other traditional cuisine.

Nevertheless, some Westerners really do get into Japanese cooking. Typical dishes include a bowl of *gohan* (rice), with a bowl of *miso shiru* (soup based on soybeans) and feature one or more kinds of vegetable plus a small portion of meat. More economical dishes are based on noodles, either *soba*

234 Japan – Facts for the Visitor

(buckwheat), *rāmen* (yellow), or *udon* (wheat).

Sashimi (raw fish) is not a myth, but needs to be fresh. Japanese cooking has few spices, and much of the flavour comes from pickles or seaweed. Appearance seems to be more important than taste. Whatever else you can say about Japanese food, it certainly looks nice.

Some restaurants have menus in English but most have plastic replicas of their meals that you can point to for ordering. You'd be wise to learn how to use chopsticks, though Western cutlery is sometimes available.

Some common Japanese dishes are sashimi, slices of raw fish served with horse-radish; *sushi*, raw fish, pickles and rice wrapped in seaweed; *tempura*, fried portions of fish, prawns and vegetables; *sukiyaki*, vegetables, meat, noodles and tofu (soybean curd), all cooked together at the table; *yakitori*, chicken pieces skewered on a stick and cooked over a charcoal fire; *okonomiyaki*, a pancake or omelette with anything that's lying around in the kitchen thrown in; rāmen, noodles in a chicken stock with vegetables and or meat; *unagi* – eel cooked over hot coals and brushed with soy sauce and *saké*.

In cities, look in the basements of department stores to find cheap restaurants, takeaway food, or supermarkets.

You may find yourself resorting to Western food more often than you expected. McDonald's and Kentucky Fried Chicken are everywhere, but not especially cheap. *Shakey's Pizza* has a fixed-price all-you-can-eat luncheon special between 11 am and 2 pm, giving you a rare chance to fill up cheaply. Chinese restaurants are often a good deal, with cheap noodle dishes providing you with an alternative to the ubiquitous pickles and seaweed.

DRINKS

Both sexes drink in public, but the men especially take it to excess. A recent survey estimated that around 12% of the male population gets drunk every day, whilst nearly 70% get drunk once a week. By 11 pm in Tokyo, it can seem that everyone on the streets is in various stages of inebriation.

Beer is dispensed everywhere, from vending machines to beer halls and even in temple lodgings. Major brewers are Asahi, Suntory, Sapporo and Kirin. A standard can of beer from a vending machine is about Y220; elsewhere the price of your beer starts around Y500.

Saké (rice wine) is strong stuff, and usually served warm. Bars favour the slim clay flask holding 180 ml, which usually costs around Y250. Custom dictates that you never eat rice at the same time as you drink saké.

ENTERTAINMENT

Cinemas

Foreign movies are screened with their original soundtracks and Japanese subtitles. Tickets average Y1600.

Karaoke

If you like amateur singing contests, visit a *karaoke* (empty music). The Japanese love singing and if you visit a karaoke you will certainly be asked to perform. No matter how badly you sing, you will undoubtedly receive polite applause.

Discos

These are popular and attract Japanese and foreigners alike. Typical costs are Y3000 to Y4000.

Nightclubs

It's possible to enjoy an evening out in a nightclub, but you have to be careful. Some are nice places with dinner and a show, and are suitable for both sexes. However, many of these are male-oriented, and when the customer has had a few drinks and light conversation with the hostesses, he's presented with a bill that would bankrupt some Third World countries. Touts often try to lure foreigners into these places. Proceed at your own risk.

THINGS TO BUY

Compare prices – Japanese goods are not

necessarily cheaper in Japan than back home.

Cameras can be a reasonably good buy, with prices comparable to Hong Kong and Singapore. One possibility that few visitors consider is buying second-hand camera equipment. Both Shinjuku and Ginza have a fair number of second-hand shops where prices are around half what you would pay for new equipment. Buying second-hand is a good option if you are only in the market for lenses, which are much more easily tested in the shop.

Electronic goods are sometimes a good deal, but those produced for Japan's virtually unique 100-V electricity may have to be adapted to work in other countries. Other problems include the incompatibility of Japanese TVs, video recorders and FM radios with foreign models. The safest bet is to go for export models.

From CDs to electric guitars, musical equipment can be a lot cheaper in Japan than elsewhere.

In well-heeled and fashionable districts, most of the clothes shops are exclusive boutiques with exclusive prices. In less fashionable areas, there are countless cheaper retail outlets. It is possible to pick up a suit for around Y12,000 – perfect if you're a newly arrived English-language teacher with a backpack full of travel-soiled jeans and T-shirts.

As well as all the hi-tech knick-knacks produced by the Japanese, it is also possible to go home loaded down with Japanese traditional arts and crafts. Anything from carp banners to kimono can make good souvenirs for the converted Japanophile.

Getting There & Away

AIR
Almost all international flights to Tokyo land at Narita Airport. China Airlines (of Taiwan) uses Haneda Airport, which also handles most of Tokyo's domestic flights.

The other way to avoid Narita is to use one of the other international airports at Niigata, Nagoya, Osaka, Fukuoka, Kumamoto, Kagoshima or Naha. Of these, Osaka is a good starting or departure point as it is close to Kyoto (one of Japan's must-see areas) and has flights to and from many Asian cities and Los Angeles. Fares change daily, but what follows are some recent quoted prices.

To/From the USA
Seven-day advance-purchase return fares from the USA are around US$1000 to US$1200 from the west coast (depending on the season) and US$1200 to US$1400 from the east. Regular economy fares are much higher – around US$900 to US$1000 (one way) from the west coast, US$1200 to US$1300 from the east coast.

Better deals are available if you shop around. From the east coast, return fares as low as US$800 and one-way fares of US$750 are possible. From the west coast fares can drop to US$600 and US$700 with Korean Airlines. There are also good deals available via Vancouver with Canadian Airlines International. From San Francisco or Los Angeles, fares to Tokyo range from US$650 to US$800 or to Nagoya from US$600 to US$800.

To/From Canada
Fares from Canada are similar to those from the USA. Canadian Airlines International, which operates out of Vancouver, often matches or beats the best fares available from the USA. Travel Cuts, the Canadian student travel organisation, offers one-way Vancouver-Tokyo flights from C$800 and returns from C$1000 or more depending on the season.

To/From Australia
Japan Airlines (JAL), All Nippon Airways (ANA) and Qantas all have direct flights between Australia and Japan. You can fly from most Australian state capitals to Tokyo, Osaka, Nagoya and Fukuoka. There's only a one-hour time change between Australia and Japan, and a direct Sydney-Tokyo flight takes about nine hours.

A return excursion Sydney-Tokyo fare is around A$1500. Discount deals will involve round about routes via other Asian capitals like Kuala Lumpur or Manila. If you shop around, you can find one-way flights from Sydney or Melbourne for around A$750, return flights for A$1100. The STA student travel offices or the numerous Flight Centres International are good places to look for discount ticket deals.

To/From New Zealand

From New Zealand, Auckland-Tokyo return excursion fares are around NZ$1900 in the low season rising to NZ$2500 in the high.

To/From the UK

The fastest nonstop London-Tokyo flights on the USSR route take just under 12 hours. Flights that stop in Moscow take an extra 2½ hours.

Return economy air fares between London and Tokyo start from around UK£1000 and are valid for 14 days to three months. A ticket valid for a year away costs from around £1300. Although a wide variety of cheaper deals are available, generally the lower the price, the less convenient the route. Expect to pay around £900 to £1000 for a one-year valid return ticket with a good airline via a fast route. For a less convenient trans-Asian route, count on £700 or lower and about half that for one-way tickets.

To/From Asia

South Korea is particularly popular because it's used by many travellers as a place to take a short holiday from Japan when their visas are close to expiring. The immigration authorities treat travellers returning to Japan after a short break in South Korea with great suspicion. Hong Kong is popular because it is such a bargain basement for airline ticketing.

South Korea Numerous flights link Seoul and Pusan with cities in Japan. A one-way/return Seoul-Tokyo flight costs around US$160/320. It is a lot cheaper to go by boat from Pusan.

Hong Kong There are direct flights between Hong Kong and a number of cities in Japan, though the biggest choice and best deals will to Tokyo. For a ticket bought in Hong Kong, a one-way/return to Tokyo starts at around US$250/400.

Taiwan There are direct flights from Taipei to Fukuoka, Naha, Osaka or Tokyo. Tokyo one-way/return costs around US$250/450.

China You can fly directly between Tokyo and Beijing, Shanghai or Dalian.

SEA

To/From South Korea

There are several ferries linking Japan to Korea – see the chapter on South Korea for details.

To/From North Korea

There is a monthly passenger ferry between Nagasaki and Wonsan on the east coast of North Korea – see the chapter on North Korea for details.

To/From China

There is a regular boat service between Shanghai and Osaka/Kōbe. The trip takes two days. The one-way fare is around US$120 for tickets bought in China, or US$175 for tickets bought in Japan. A 10% student discount is available for 2nd class only. The ship departs once weekly: one week to/from Osaka and the next week to/from Kōbe.

To/From Taiwan

A weekly ferry operates between Taiwan and Okinawa via Ishigaki and Miyako in Okinawa Prefecture. The Taiwan port alternates between Keelung (about US$113 economy class) and Kaohsiung (about US$130), and the trip takes one day.

For tickets bought in Japan, the one-way fare from Keelung/Kaohsiung is US$113/130. For tickets bought in Taiwan, it's US$106/145.

To/From the USSR

There's a weekly ferry service between Yokohama and the Soviet port of Nakhodka near Vladivostok. This is mainly for travellers taking the Trans-Siberian Railway. Your rail ticket will be timed to connect with a specific sailing.

LEAVING JAPAN

Airport tax at Narita is Y2000 for adults, and Y1000 for children aged two to 12 years.

Getting Around

You can get almost anywhere using Japan's immense variety of public transport. The problem lies in sorting out the maze of fares and timetables. Most transport runs efficiently and on time – the railways even go on strike almost on schedule, usually for a few days in the early spring.

AIR

Domestic carriers include Japan Air Lines (JAL), All Nippon Airways (ANA), Japan Air Systems (JAS), Air Nippon Koku (ANK) and South-West Airlines (SWAL). ANK links many smaller towns all over Japan while SWAL is particularly good for connections through Okinawa and the other South-West Islands.

There's a 10% discount on round-trip fares if the return flight is made within seven to 10 days. The airlines have some weird discounts if you know what to ask for. JAL has a women's group discount available for groups of three or more women. Or a husband and wife discount if their combined age totals 88 or more!

Some sample one-way fares (return fares are 10% less than two one-way fares) include:

From Tokyo

Chitose/Sapporo	Y25,500
Sendai	Y12,200
Nagoya	Y12,400
Osaka	Y15,600
Hiroshima	Y23,100
Fukuoka	Y27,100
Nagasaki	Y31,100
Kagoshima	Y31,500
Naha	Y37,300

From Nagoya

Nagasaki	Y23,000
Kagoshima	Y23,100
Naha	Y35,000

From Osaka

Nagasaki	Y19,000
Kagoshima	Y19,700

From Hiroshima

Kagoshima	Y18,500

BUS

In addition to its local city buses, Japan also has a comprehensive long-distance bus network. These 'highway buses' are nowhere near as fast as the *shinkansen* (super-express trains) and heavy traffic can delay them even further, but the fares are comparable with those of the local train without any reservation or express surcharges.

The main inter-city bus services run on the expressways and usually stop at expressway bus stops where local transport is available to adjacent centres. The main expressway bus route runs between Tokyo, Nagoya, Kyoto and Osaka and stops are made at each city's main railway station. There are also overnight bus services, and the comfortable reclining seats are better for a night's sleep than sitting up in an overnight train. Bookings can be made through Japan Travel Bureau (JTB) offices or at the green window in large Japan Railways (JR) stations. The Japan Rail Pass is valid on highway buses although, of course, the shinkansen would be far preferable!

TRAIN

Japanese rail travel is usually fast, frequent, clean, comfortable and often very expensive.

Japan Railways (JR) is actually a number of separate private railway systems which provide one linked service.

Tickets can be bought at any JR station to

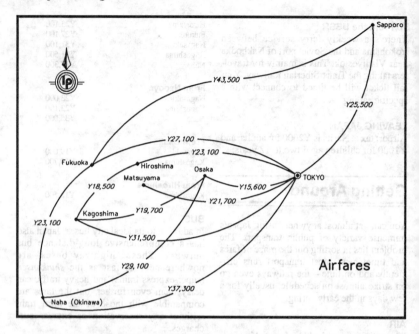

Y43,500

Y25,500

Y27,100

Y23,100

Fukuoka

Hiroshima

Matsuyama

Osaka

Y18,500

Y15,600

Y19,700

Y21,700

Kagoshima

Y23,100

Y31,500

Y29,100

Naha (Okinawa)

Y37,300

Sapporo

TOKYO

Airfares

any other JR station. Tickets for local services are usually dispensed from a vending machine but for longer distances you must go to a ticket window.

The slowest trains stopping at all stations are called *futsū*. A step up from this is the 'ordinary express' or *kyūkō* which stops at only a limited number of stations. A variation on the kyūkō trains is the *kaisoku* or 'rapid' services. The fastest regular trains are the *tokkyū* or 'limited express' services. Top of the line is the *shinkansen* super-expresses or 'bullet trains' which have become a symbol of modern Japan.

One of Japan's few travel bargains is the unlimited travel Japan Rail Pass. The pass lets you use any JR services for seven days for Y27,800, 14 days for Y44,200 or 21 days for Y56,600. Green Car (1st-class) passes are Y37,000, Y60,000 and Y78,000 respectively. Children aged six to 11 get a 50% discount. The only additional surcharge levied on the Japan Rail Pass is for overnight

sleepers. Since a reserved seat Tokyo-Kyoto shinkansen ticket costs Y12,970, you only have to travel Tokyo-Kyoto-Tokyo to make a seven-day pass come close to paying off.

The pass can only be bought overseas and

Distances & Fares from Tokyo

from Tokyo or Ueno	distance	futsū	shinkansen
Nagoya	366 km	Y5,970	Y10,380
Kyoto	514 km	Y7,830	Y12,970
Osaka	553 km	Y8,340	Y13,480
Okayama	733 km	Y9,990	Y16,050
Hiroshima	895 km	Y11,120	Y17,700
Shimonoseki	1089 km	Y12,570	Y20,690
Hakata	1177 km	Y13,180	Y21,300
Fukishima	273 km	Y4,530	Y8,330
Sendai	352 km	Y5,670	Y10,190
Morioka	535 km	Y8,030	Y15,370
Niigata	334 km	Y5,360	Y9,880

cannot be used by foreign residents in Japan. The clock starts to tick on the pass as soon as you validate it, which can be done at certain major railway stations or even at the JR counter at Narita Airport if you're intending to jump on a JR train immediately. Don't validate it if you're just going into Tokyo and intend to hang around the city for a few days. The pass is valid *only* on JR services, you will still have to pay for private railway services. The convenient Keisei Skyliner between Narita Airport and Tokyo Narita Station is a private line.

CAR & MOTORBIKE
Road Rules
Driving is on the left side of the road. To drive in Japan, you need your licence from your home country and an international driving permit. Be certain you're sober before getting behind the wheel – there are draconian penalties for drinking and driving.

Rental
Rental costs are generally a flat rate including unlimited km. Typical hire rates for a small car (a Toyota Starlet or Mazda 121 – one step up from the Japanese microcars) is Y7000 to Y8000 for the first day and Y4500 to Y6000 per day thereafter. Move up a bracket (a Mazda 323 or Toyota Corolla) and you're looking at Y9000 to Y12,000 for the first day and Y6000 to Y7000 thereafter. On top of the hire charge there's a Y800 per day insurance charge.

Purchase
Buying a car in Japan has pitfalls beside the usual ones encountered in Western countries. Once it's three years old, every car has to go through a *shaken* (inspection) every two years which is so severe that it quickly becomes cheaper to junk your car and buy another. The shaken costs about Y100,000 and once the car reaches nine years of age it has to be inspected every year. This is the major reason you see so few old cars on the road in Japan. A car approaching an unpassable shaken drops in value very rapidly and,

if you can find one, could make a good short-term purchase.

Motorcycles
As with car driving, your overseas licence and International Driving Permit are all you need to ride a motorcycle in Japan. Crash helmets are compulsory.

The 400 cc machines are the most popular large motorcycles in Japan, but for general touring a 250 cc machine is probably the best bet. Apart from being quite large enough for a compact country like Japan, machines up to 250 cc are also exempt from the expensive shaken. Also, motorcycles over 250 cc are not allowed on main city streets from 11 pm to 6 am! This curious law is to stop motorcycle gangs (*bososuku*) cruising late at night but it's another reason sub-250 cc bikes are so popular. Smaller machines are banned from expressways and are generally less suitable for long-distance touring but people have ridden from one end of Japan to another on little 50 cc 'step-thrus'. An advantage of these is that you can ride them with just a driving licence, and don't need to get a motorcycle licence.

BICYCLE
A bicycle can be a practical proposition for touring. It is possible to bring your own as part of your luggage on most airlines, or you can rent or buy one in Japan, although tall people may have trouble finding one big enough. Also, most Japanese bikes are one-speed clunkers. Bringing your own touring bike is best.

Many youth hostels have bicycles to rent – there's a symbol identifying them in the Japanese *Youth Hostel Handbook*. Cycling Inns are similar to youth hostels but are intended specifically for cyclists, and they all rent bikes. Rental rates vary from Y50 to Y250 per hour.

The Japan Bicycle Promotion Institute (Nihon Jitensha Kaikon Biru) (☎ 3583-5444) is also known as the Bicycle Cultural Centre and is across from the US Embassy at 9-3 Akasaka 1-chome, Minato-ku, Tokyo. The institute has a museum and is a useful source of information about the special inns for cyclists.

HITCHING

Japan can be an excellent country for hitch-hiking, though this may partly be because so few Japanese hitchhike and gaijin with their thumbs out are also a very rare sight. Nevertheless, there are many hitchhikers' tales of extraordinary kindness from motorists who have picked them up. There are equally numerous tales of motorists who think the hitchhiker has simply lost his or her way to the nearest railway station, and accordingly takes them there!

The rules for hitchhiking are similar to anywhere else in the world. Make it clear where you want to go – carry cardboard and a marker pen to write in kanji the name of your desired destination. Write it in romaji as well, as a car-driving gaijin may just be coming by. Look for a good place to hitch: it's no good starting from the middle of town, though unfortunately in Japan many towns only seem to end as they merge into the next one. Expressway entrance roads are probably your best bet. Women who hitch alone should of course be especially careful, even in Japan.

Truck drivers are particularly good bets for long-distance travel as they often head out on the expressways at night. If a driver is leaving before your intended destination, try and get dropped off at one of the expressway service centres. The Service Area Parking Area (SAPA) guide maps (☎ 3403-911 in Tokyo) are excellent for hitchhikers. They're available free from expressway service areas and show full details of each interchange (IC) and rest stop – important orientation points if you have a limited knowledge of Japanese.

In Japan, as anywhere else in the world, it's a hitchhiker's duty to entertain. Although the language gap can make that difficult, get out your phrasebook and try and use at least *some* Japanese. Finally, be prepared to reciprocate kindnesses. You may find your driver will insist on buying you food or drinks at a rest stop and it's nice if you can offer fruit, rice crackers or even cigarettes in return.

BOAT

Being a country of islands, Japan has a comprehensive ferry system. On longer routes, the ferries are ocean-going ships with bar and restaurant facilities. The lowest fare, 'tatami class', is usually cheaper than land transport. At that price you share the floor with your fellow passengers, and very probably share their saké too. Many ferries leave at night so you save a night's accommodation but may miss seeing the scenery, such as the Inland Sea.

The TICs have information sheets with details of many ferry services, including fares. Tickets may be bought from JTB offices or from the ferry office at the departure pier. Some sample fares:

Hokkaidō to Honshū

Otaru to Niigata	Y5150
Tomakomai to Nagoya	Y15,450
Tomakomai to Sendai	Y8850

Routes from Tokyo

to Kōchi (Shikoku)	Y13,910
to Kokura (Kyūshū)	Y12,000
to Kushiro (Hokkaidō)	Y14,420
to Naha (Okinawa)	Y19,670
to Tokushima (Shikoku)	Y8200
to Tomakomai (Hokkaidō)	Y11,840

Routes from Osaka

to Beppu (Kyūshū)	Y5870
to Kagoshima (Kyūshū)	Y10,300
to Kōchi (Shikoku)	Y4530
to Matsuyama (Shikoku)	Y4430
to Naha (Okinawa)	Y15,450
to Takamatsu (Shikoku)	Y2370

Other Routes from Honshū

Hiroshima to Beppu (Kyūshū)	Y3600
Kōbe to Kokura (Kyūshū)	Y4840
Kōbe to Matsuyama (Shikoku)	Y3500
Kōbe to Naha (Okinawa)	Y15,450
Nagoya to Sendai (Honshū)	Y9580

Other Routes from Kyūshū

Hakata to Naha (Okinawa)	Y12,970
Kagoshima to Naha (Okinawa)	Y11,840
Kokura to Matsuyama (Shikoku)	Y3500

LOCAL TRANSPORT
Train
There are subway systems in Tokyo, Osaka, Nagoya, Yokohama and Sapporo. They are a quick and convenient way of getting around. In each city the stations are well marked above ground and can usually be used by foreigners without difficulty because there is adequate information in English. City maps show the locations of stations.

Taxi
Taxis are convenient but expensive and are found in even quite small towns; the railway station is the best place to start looking. Drivers are often reluctant to stop and pick you up near a station taxi stand, so either wait at the correct spot for a taxi off the rank or walk a couple of streets away. Fares vary little throughout the country – flagfall is Y540 for the first two km, after which it's Y80 for each 395 metres. There's also a time charge if the speed drops below 10 km/h. A red light means the taxi is available, a green light means there's an additional night-time surcharge, a yellow light means the cab is on a call. Drivers open and close the door for you with a remote lever.

Taxi drivers have just as much trouble finding Japanese addresses as anyone else. Just because you've gone round the block five times does not necessarily mean your driver is a country boy fresh in from the sticks. Asking directions and stopping at police boxes for help is standard practice.

Tipping is not a standard practice unless you've got a lot of bags or your destination has been particularly difficult to find. A 20% surcharge is added after 11 pm at night or for taxis summoned by radio.

Tokyo 東京

Tokyo is one of the most populous cities on earth and is the centre of government and commerce in Japan. It's a good city for shopping and entertainment but has relatively little of historic or sightseeing interest.

Orientation
Tokyo sprawls endlessly, but nearly everything of interest for visitors lies either on or within the JR Yamanote line, the rail loop that circles central Tokyo.

Information
The Tourist Information Centres (TICs) are the best sources for information and maps. They also have lists of low-cost accommodation, but they do not make bookings.

There is a TIC at Narita Airport, at the junction of the central block and the south wing.

The Tokyo TIC (☎ 3502-1461) is at 1-6-6 Yūraku-cho, Tokyo 100, just beyond the expressway from the central Ginza area. To get there take the A2 exit of Hibiya Subway Station – the centre is directly opposite, on the other side of the road running towards Hibiya-kōen Park.

The Tokyo centre is open Monday to Friday from 9 am to 5 pm and on Saturdays from 9 am to noon. It is closed on Sundays and public holidays. The Narita TIC stays open until 8 pm.

Their *Tourist Map of Tokyo* is the best available, showing the parts of the city of most interest to visitors, plus detailed maps of popular areas such as Shinjuku.

Post & Telecommunications Look for the red and white T with a bar across the top. Post boxes have two slots: red-lettered for Tokyo mail and blue-lettered for all other mail. The Tokyo central post office (☎ 3284-9527) is next to Tokyo Station in the Tokyo Station plaza, Chiyoda-ku. Poste restante mail will be held there for 30 days: it should be addressed to Poste Restante, Central Post Office, Tokyo, Japan. International parcels and registered mail can be sent from the Tokyo international post office (☎ 3241-4891) next to Otemachi Subway Station.

All except the pink phones take telephone cards, and international phones are labelled in English. Tokyo also has an English-language directory assistance service (☎ 3201-1010) available Monday to Saturday from 10 am to 7 pm.

Foreign Embassies These are listed in the Facts for the Visitor section.

Cultural Centres Nō performances are held at the *Kanze Nō-gakudō Theatre* (☎ 3469-6241), which is a 10 to 15-minute walk from Shibuya Station. From the Hachikō exit, turn right at the 109 building and follow the road straight ahead past the Tōkyū Department Store. The theatre is on the right, a couple of minutes down the third street on the left after Tōkyū.

Nō is also performed at the *Ginza Nō-gakudō Theatre* (☎ 3571-0197), which is about a 10-minute walk from Ginza Subway Station. Turn right into Sotobori-dōri Ave at the Sukiyabashi Crossing and look for the theatre on the left.

Bunraku performances take place several times a year at the *Kokuritsu Gekijō Theatre* (☎ 3265-7411). Check with the TIC or the theatre for information.

Sumō wrestling tournaments at Tokyo's *Ryōgoku Kokugikan Stadium* (☎ 3866-8700) in Ryōgoku take place in January, May and September and last 15 days. The stadium is adjacent to Ryōgoku Station on the northern side of the railway tracks.

Travel Agencies Japan is not the place to look for cheap air tickets, but try looking for discount deals in the classified advertisements of the *Tokyo Journal*. Some agencies to try include:

Arch, 1st floor, New Shimbashi Building, 2-16-1 Shimbashi, Minato-ku (☎ 3595-1491)
Fuji Coin, 3-2-4 Kanda Kajimachi, Chiyoda-ku (☎ 3241-0005)
Just Travel, 1st floor, Koike Building, 2-13-7 Takadanobaba, Shinjuku-ku (☎ 3348-6303)
Kennedy Stamp, 1-9 Yotsuya, Shinjuku-ku (☎ 3353-5443)
Kinokuniya Gift, 3-31-5 Shinjuku, Shinjuku-ku (☎ 3352-7011)
Number One Travel, 3rd floor, Shoritsu Building, 7-8-12 Nishi Shinjuku, Shinjuku-ku (☎ 3366-2481)
Sakura Coin, 4-3 Nihombashi Muromachi, Chūō-ku (☎ 3241-4553)
Across Traveller's Bureau, Haneda Building, 2-5-1 Yoyogi, Shibuya-ku (☎ 3374-8721)

There is a Student Travel Association (STA) office (☎ 3221-1733) in Tokyo with Western, Chinese and Japanese staff. Ring the office and someone there will tell you how to find the place, which is in the Sanden Building, 3-5-5 Kojimachi, Chiyoda-ku. Council Travel (☎ 3581-7581) is also a student travel specialist and can be found at Room 102, Sanno Grand Building, 2-14-2 Nagata-cho, Chiyoda-ku.

Bookshops The big bookshop area in Tokyo is Jimbō-cho, and although most shops cater only to Japanese readers, there are a couple of foreign-language bookshops. The best is Kitazawa Shoten (☎ 3263-0011). If you leave Jimbō-cho Subway Station on Yasukuni-dōri Ave and set off westwards in the direction of Ichigaya, Kitazawa is about 50 metres away on the left.

Kinokuniya (☎ 3354-0131) in Shinjuku has a good selection of English-language fiction and general titles on the 6th floor. Kinokuniya is a good place to stock up on guidebooks. It's closed on the third Wednesday of every month.

Maruzen (☎ 3272-7211) in Nihombashi near Ginza. Take the Takashimaya Department Store exit at Nihombashi Subway Station and look for Maruzen on the other side of the road. It's closed on Sunday.

The 3rd floor of Jena (☎ 3571-2980) in Ginza doesn't have quite the range of some other foreign-language bookshops. Take the Sukiyabashi Crossing exit from Ginza Subway Station and walk along Harumi-dōri Ave towards the Kabuki-za Theatre. Jena is on the third block on your right. It's closed on public holidays.

Finally, the World Magazine Gallery (☎ 3545-7227) has a huge selection of magazines from all over the world and a coffee shop. It's in a big building behind the Kabuki-za Theatre in Ginza. It's open Monday to Saturday from 10 am to 7 pm.

Libraries The National Diet Library (☎ 3581-2331) is the largest in Japan, with over 1.3 million books in Western languages. The library is close to Nagata-cho Subway

Station on the Yūraku-cho and Hanzomon lines and is open from Monday to Saturday, 9.30 am to 5 pm.

The library at the American Center (☎ 3436-0901) has books and magazines concerning the USA. It's close to Shiba-kōen Subway Station on the TOEI Mita line, and is open Monday to Friday from 10.30 am to 6.30 pm.

The Australia-Japan Foundation (☎ 3498-4141) has books published in Australia and a large number of magazines. The foundation, close to Omote-sando Subway Station on the Ginza, Chiyoda and Hanzomon lines, is open from 11 am to 12.30 pm and from 1.30 to 6 pm.

The British Council (☎ 3235-8031) has a library and is close to Iidabashi Subway Station on the Yūraku-cho line. The library is open from Monday to Friday, 10 am to 8 pm.

Emergency There are emergency numbers for police (110) and fire or ambulance (119). For general hospital information, phone 3212-2323.

The Japan Helpline (☎ 0120-461-997) provides emergency information in the event of travel or life crises. It's available seven days a week, 24 hours a day.

Things to See
Close together are the **Imperial Palace** and **Ginza**, Tokyo's high-class shopping area. The palace can be reached by various subway lines and JR. The actual palace grounds may not be entered except on special occasions such as New Year, but you are allowed to walk through the Higashi-Gyoen (East Garden).

The cross-street at Ginza is Chūō-dōri (Centre Boulevard), which has many shops and passes Maruzen Department Store, leading to Akihabara (an hour on foot), which is a good area for buying electrical goods. You can also get there by subway (Akihabara Station). In the nearby Ueno area are the **Zoo**, popular for its giant pandas, and the **Tokyo Metropolitan Museum of Art**, the **Tokyo National Museum** and the **National Science Museum**.

Meiji-jingu Shrine, possibly the finest shrine in Japan, was built early this century to honour Emperor Meiji, and has extensive, heavily wooded grounds. It is close to Harajuku Station (Yamanote line) or Meiji-jingu-mae Station (Chiyoda line).

For a little peace and quiet, visit **Rikugi-en, Koshikawa Kōraku-en** and **Kiyosumi** gardens. The JNTO pamphlet on Tokyo has a good listing of museums.

Shinjuku is a major shopping and entertainment area. It appeals to a younger crowd than Ginza and Asakusa. West of Shinjuku Station is the 52-storey Sumitomo Building, for a free view of the city and beyond.

The Asakusa area is popular for theatres. The **Asakusa Kannon Temple** (now called Sensō-ji Temple) and its pagoda are postwar concrete constructions, and not really worth seeing except during the festival in March.

Activities
Tokyo has a large number of associations for foreigners with special interests:

Association of Foreign Teachers in Japan. Meets monthly (☎ 3238-3909)

Buddhist English Academy. Lectures every Friday at a location near Shinjuku (☎ 3342-6605)

Corn Popper Club. Very much an American affair, but if you're from the USA and into popcorn, coffee, tea, billiards and the occasional party, this could be the club for you (☎ 3715-4473)

Ikebana International. Monthly meetings (☎ 3295-0720)

Japan Association of Translators (☎ 3385-5709)

Japan Foundation. Library classes and free screenings of Japanese films with English subtitles – a real rarity in Japan (☎ 3263-4503)

Japan-IrelandSociety. Meets monthly (☎ 3561-1491, ask for Mr Nishi)

St Andrew's Society. A Scottish social and cultural association (☎ 3264-2171)

Tokyo British Club (☎ 3443-9083, after 5 pm)

Tokyo Canadian Club. Has a pub night on the first Thursday of every month at Zest in Nishi Azabu (☎ 3581-5765)

Places to Stay
As well as the places listed here remember that Yokohama and Kamakura have youth

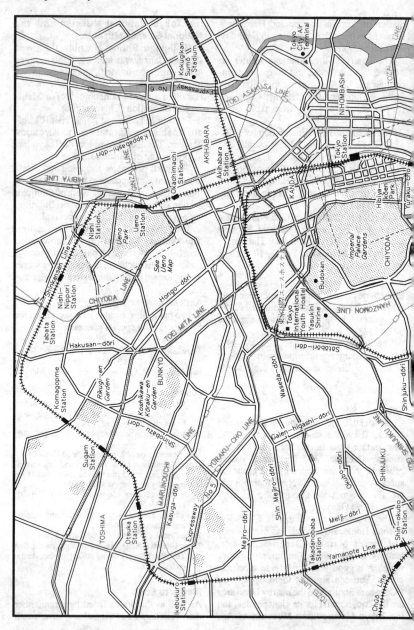

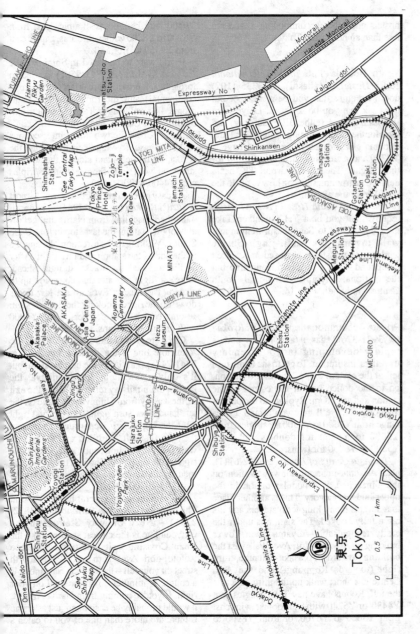

hostels and other accommodation, and are less than an hour from Tokyo.

Youth Hostels The *Tokyo International Youth Hostel* (Iidabashi) (☎ 3235-1107) doesn't require that you be a member but does ask that you book ahead. Leave from Iidabashi Station (either JR or subway) and look for the tallest building in sight (it's long, thin and glass-fronted). The basic charge is Y2250 and a sleeping sheet costs Y150 for three nights. The Narita Airport TIC has a detailed instruction sheet on how to get to the hostel from the airport.

The *Yoyogi Youth Hostel* (☎ 3467-9163) requires that you be a YHA member. Take the Odakyū line to Sangubashi Station and walk towards the Meiji-jingū Shrine gardens. The hostel is enclosed in a fenced compound – not a former prison camp but the National Olympics Memorial Youth Centre – in building No 14.

Private Accommodation The *Kimi Ryokan* (☎ 3971-3766) has tatami rooms and is rapidly developing into a legendary travellers' institution. To get to the Kimi, turn left at the eastern exit of Ikebukuro Station, go to the police box at the corner of the station and say 'Kimi Ryokan' to the policeman on duty. He'll give you a map. Prices range from Y2600 to Y3500 for singles, from Y5000 to Y5500 for doubles and from Y5500 to Y6000 for twins.

The *Asia Centre of Japan* (☎ 3402-6111), near Aoyama-Itchome Subway Station on the Ginza line, is a popular option in the upper-budget category. This is another place that attracts many long-term stayers and it's often fully booked. The station is under the easily recognisable Aoyama Twin Tower building on Aoyama-dōri Ave. Walk past the building towards Akasaka-Mitsuke, turn right (towards Roppongi) and the Asia Centre is a short walk up the third street on the left. Rooms have pay TVs. Singles cost Y4430, or Y5240 with bathrooms; twins cost from Y5600 to Y6700, or from Y8900 to

Y9400 with bathrooms; doubles cost from Y6900 to Y8200 with bathrooms; triples cost from Y9450 to Y11,550.

If you want to be based in Shinjuku, the *Inabaso Ryokan* (☎ 3341-9581) is used to foreigners. It provides breakfast (Japanese or continental) and the rooms include bathrooms, TVs and fridges. Take the eastern exit of Shinjuku Station and follow Yasukuni-dōri Ave. Cross the two major intersections – the Inabaso Ryokan is just around the corner, on the left-hand side of the seventh street on your left. Singles/doubles/triples cost Y4400/8000/10,500.

An easy place to get to from Narita Airport is *Suzuki Ryokan* (☎ 3821-4944) in Nippori. Take the Keisei line from Narita and get off at Nippori Station, the last stop before Ueno Station. Walking in the direction of Ueno, go to the end of the station and turn right. After you've crossed the tracks straight ahead, there's a flight of stairs that takes you up to a road. The Suzuki Ryokan is a few doors down on the right – look for the English sign. Rooms cost Y3500 per person, or Y4000 with private bathrooms.

Close to JR Gotanda Station on the Yamanote line is the *Ryokan Sansuisō* (☎ 3441-7475). This is not the best location, but it's only a few stops from Shibuya, the nearest main railway terminus. Take the exit furthest away from Shibuya and leave on the left-hand side. Turn right, take the first right after the big Tōkyū Department Store and then the first left. Turn left and then right, walk past the bowling centre and look for the sign on the right directing you down the side road to the ryokan. Singles/doubles/triples cost Y4000/7000/9600.

In Ueno there are several budget ryokan. The cheapest is *Ryokan Sawanoya* (☎ 3822-2251) – Nezu Subway Station on the Chiyoda line is the closest station. Take the Nezu Crossing exit and turn right into Kototoi-dōri Ave. Turn left at the fourth street on your left – the Ryokan Sawanoya is a couple of minutes down the road on your right. If you're coming from Narita Airport, it would probably be easier and just as cheap if there are more than one of you to catch a

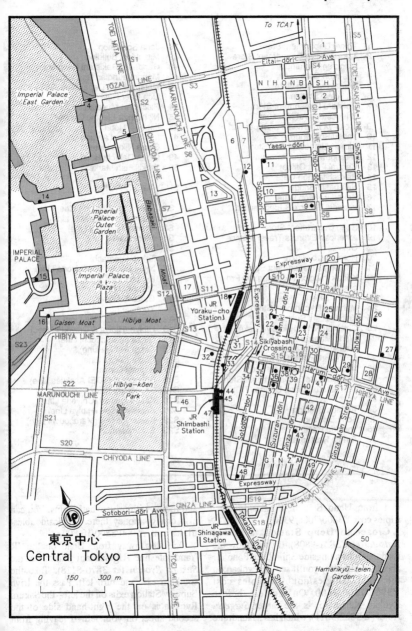

Central Tokyo / 東京中心

1	Tōkyū Department Store	38	Jena Bookshop
2	Takashimaya Department Store	39	Mitsubishi Building
3	Maruzen Bookshop	40	Gandhara Pakistani Restaurant
4	Ote-mon Gate	41	Maharaja Indian Restaurant
5	Wadakura-mon Gate	42	Matsuzakaya Department Store
6	JR Tokyo Station	43	Lion Beer Hall
7	Daimaru Department Store	44	Riccar Art Museum
8	Bridgestone Art Museum	45	Nishiginza Electric Centre
9	Meidi-ya International Supermarket	46	Imperial Hotel
10	Yaesu Bookshop	47	International Arcade
11	Airport Limousine Bus Stop	48	Ginza Nikkō Hotel
12	JR Highway Bus Terminal	49	Ginza Dai-Ichi Hotel
13	Central Post Office	50	Tsukiji Fish Market
14	Sakashita-mon Gate		
15	Nijū-bashi Bridge		**SUBWAY STATIONS**
16	Sakadura-mon Gate		
17	Imperial Theatre & Idemitsu Art Museum	S1	Otemachi (Chiyoda Line)
18	Sogo Department Store	S2	Otemachi (TOEI Mita Line)
19	American Express Travel Service Office	S3	Otemachi (Tōzai Line)
20	Hotel Seiyo Ginza	S4	Nihombashi
21	Printemps Department Store	S5	Edobashi
22	Kodak Imagica (Kodachrome Processing)	S6	Tokyo-Otemachi
23	Nikon Gallery	S7	Nijū-bashi-mae (Chiyoda Line)
24	Matsuya Department Store	S8	Kyobashi
25	Kaiten-zushi Sushi	S9	Takara-cho
26	Chichibu Nishiki Nomiya Saké Pub	S10	Ginza-Itchome
27	World Magazine Gallery	S11	Yūraku-cho
28	Kabuki-za Theatre	S12	Hibiya (TOEI Mita Line)
29	Nair's Indian Restaurant	S13	Hibiya (Hibiya & Chiyoda Lines)
30	Mitsukoshi Department Store	S14	Ginza (Marunouchi Line)
31	Hankyū & Seibu Department Stores	S15	Ginza (Hibiya Line)
32	Tourist Information Centre (TIC)	S16	Ginza (Ginza Line)
33	Yakitoris	S17	Higashi-Ginza
34	Toshiba Building	S18	Shimbashi (TOEI Asakusa Line)
35	Sony Building	S19	Shimbashi (Ginza Line)
36	Yoseido Gallery	S20	Kasumigaseki (Chiyoda Line)
37	Torigin Restaurant	S21	Kasumigaseki (Hibiya Line)
		S22	Kasumigaseki (Marunouchi Line)
		S23	Sakuradamon

taxi from Ueno Station. Singles/doubles/triples cost Y3800/7000/9300.

Closer to Ueno Station is *Ryokan Katsutaro* (☎ 3821-9808). If you follow the road that runs alongside Shinobazu Pond for about 10 minutes, you'll see the ryokan on the right. Singles/doubles/triples cost Y3900/7000/9600. On the left, before Ryokan Katsutaro, is the larger *Suigetsu Hotel* (☎ 3822-9611), which has a laundrette

and rooms with private bathrooms. You can also change money there. Singles/doubles/triples cost Y5000/8800/10,800.

One stop away from Ueno on the JR Yamanote line (Uguisudani Station) is the *Sakura Ryokan* (☎ 3876-8118). Take the southern exit and turn left. Pass the Iriya Subway Station exits on the left – the Sakura Ryokan is on the right-hand side of the second street on your left. If leaving from

1 東急百貨店	39 三菱ビル
2 高島屋百貨店	40 ガンダーラ
3 丸善書店	41 マハラジャ
4 大手門	42 松坂屋百貨店
5 和田倉門	43 ラィオンビルホール
6 東京駅	44 リッカー美術館
7 大丸百貨店	45 西銀座電力センター
8 ブリヂストン美術館	46 帝国ホテル
9 明治屋	47 イントナショナルアーケード
10 八重洲ブックセンター	48 銀座日光ホテル
11 空港リムジン、バスの停	49 銀座第一ホテル
12 ハイウェイバスタミナル	50 東京中央卸売市場
13 中央郵便局	
14 坂下門	**SUBWAY STATIONS**
15 二重橋	
16 桜田門	S1 大手町(千代田線)
17 帝国劇場/出光美術館	S2 大手町(都営地下鉄三田線)
18 そごう百貨店	S3 大手町(東西線)
19 アメリカンエクスプレス	S4 日本橋
20 ホテルセイヨ銀座	S5 江戸橋
21 プランタン	S6 東京大手町
22 コダック現像所	S7 二重橋前(千田線)
23 ニコンギャラリー	S8 京橋
24 松屋銀座	S9 宝町
25 かいてんずし	S10 銀座一丁目
26 ちちぶにしきのみやパーブ	S11 有楽町
27 ワールドマガジンギャラリー	S12 日比谷(都営地下鉄三田線)
28 歌舞伎座	S13 日比谷(日比谷線と千代田線)
29 ナイア	S14 銀座(丸内線)
30 三越百貨店	S15 銀座(日比谷線)
31 阪急と西武有楽町	S16 銀座(銀座線)
32 TIC	S17 東銀座
33 焼き鳥	S18 新橋(都営地下鉄浅草線)
34 東芝ビル	S19 新橋(銀座線)
35 ソニビル	S20 霞ケ関(千代田線)
36 よせいどビル	S21 霞ケ関(日比谷線)
37 鳥ぎんレストラン	S22 霞ケ関(丸内線)
38 イエナ書店	S23 桜田門

Iriya Subway Station on the Hibiya line, take the No 1 exit and turn left. Singles/doubles/triples cost Y4500/8400/12,000.

Three stops away from Ueno on the Ginza line is Asakusa, which also has a few reasonably priced ryokan. *Ryokan Mikawaya Bekkan* (☎ 3843-2345) is just around the corner from the Sensō-ji Temple in an interesting area. It's on a side street off the shop-lined street leading into the temple. From the Kaminari-mon Gate, the street is a few streets up on the left – there's a toy shop and a shoe shop on the corner. The ryokan is on the left-hand side of the road. Singles/doubles cost Y4800/9200.

Just outside the Sensō-ji Temple precinct is the *Sukeroku-no-yado Sadachiyo Bekkan* (☎ 3842-6431). Singles/doubles/triples with private bathrooms and air-con cost Y5500/9000/12,000.

In Nishi Asakusa (near Tawaramachi Subway Station, which is one stop away on the Ginza line from Asakusa Station) is the *Kikuya Ryokan* (☎ 3841-6404). It is just off Kappabashi-dōri Ave and has singles/doubles/triples for Y4000/7000/ 9000.

In Ikebukuro, *House Ikebukuro* (☎ 3984-3399) has singles/doubles/triples for Y3090/5150/6180. Near Kotake-Mukaihara Subway Station, a few stops out of Ikebukuro on the Yūraku-cho line, is the *Rikkō Kaikan Guest Room*, with singles/doubles from Y3605/7210. Near Shin-Nakano Subway Station on the Marunouchi line is the *Shin-Nakano Lodge* (☎ 3381-4886), which has singles from Y3500 to Y4000 and doubles from Y6500 to Y7000.

The *YMCA Asia Youth Centre* (☎ 3233-0631) takes both men and women but is pretty expensive. It's halfway between Suidobashi and Jimbō-cho subway stations. Singles/doubles/triples with attached bathrooms cost Y6180/10,300/13,905. The *Japan YWCA Hostel* (☎ 3264-0661) is cheaper but only accepts women. It's a few minutes from the Kudan exit of Ichigaya Subway Station and costs Y4738 per person. The *Tokyo YWCA Sadohara Hostel* (☎ 3268-4451), near the Ichigaya exit of Ichigaya Subway Station, accepts couples and is

cheaper. Singles/doubles with toilets cost from Y4635/9785.

Capsule Hotels Capsule hotels are a strictly male domain and you find them wherever there are large numbers of bars, hostess clubs and other drains for company expense accounts. Close to the western exit of Ikebukuro Station is the *Ikebukuro Puraza* (☎ 3590-7770), which costs Y3800 per night.

Places to Eat

The best cheap eats are either the Western-style fast-food barns or the Japanese and Chinese restaurants that are popular with office workers. You can usually get a large bowl of noodles for between Y350 and Y450. Other budget options are the curry rice shops and the sushi shops where three sushi pieces cost between Y100 and Y150.

Department stores often have branches of famous Tokyo restaurants offering special lunch-time prices. On the 8th floor of the Matsuya Department Store is *Restaurant City*, which has a wide variety of restaurants with prices that are not too outrageous. It's close to the centre of Ginza, on Ginza-dōri Ave, and is open until 9 pm except on Thursdays. The store itself closes at 6 pm, but the restaurant floor has its own elevator.

Another floor of restaurants can be found in the second basement level of the *Matsuzakaya* Department Store, also on Ginza-dōri Ave but just the other side of Harumi-dōri Ave.

Also try the top two floors of the *Shibuya NS* building on the western side of Shinjuku Station, and the *Tōbu Hope Centre* by the Tōbu Department Store on the western side of Ikebukuro Station. Ditto for the *Sunshine City* building, also in Ikebukuro.

During the day, the best eating areas are the big shopping districts like Shibuya, Shinjuku, Harajuku and Ginza. Shinjuku could well take the prize as Tokyo's best daytime gourmet experience, with restaurants in the big department stores, small restaurants at the street level and the best affordable Chinese food in Tokyo. Look

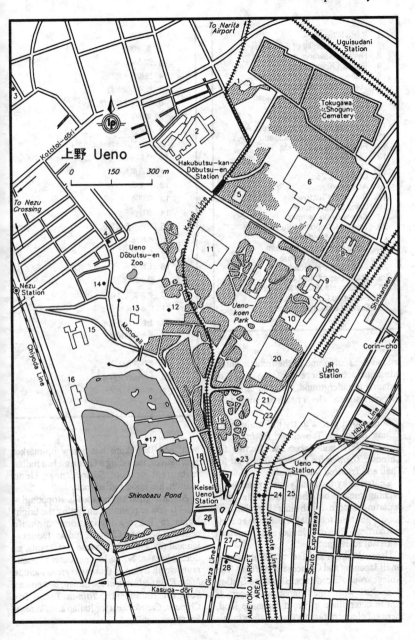

上野 Ueno

0   150   300 m

Kototoi-dōri

To Narita Airport

To Nezu Crossing

Uguisudani Station

Tokugawa Shogun Cemetery

Hakubutsu-kan Dōbutsu-en Station

Keisei Line

Ueno Dōbutsu-en Zoo

Nezu Station

Chiyoda Line

Monorail

Shinobazu Pond

Ueno-koen Park

Shinkansen

Corin-cho

JR Ueno Station

Hibiya Line

Ueno Station

Keisei Ueno Station

Yamanote Line

Shuto Expressway

Ginza Line

Kasuga-dōri

AMEYOKO MARKET AREA

1	Kane-ji Temple
2	Tokyo University of Fine Arts
3	Ryokan Sawanoya
4	Ryokan Katsutaro
5	Gallery of Hōryū-ji Treasures
6	Tokyo National Museum
7	Gallery of Eastern Antiquities
8	Rinno-ji Temple
9	National Science Museum
10	National Museum of Western Art
11	Tokyo Metropolitan Museum of Art
12	Five Storeyed Pagoda
13	Tōshō-gū Shrine
14	Suigetsu Hotel
15	Children's Zoo
16	Aquarium
17	Benzaiten Temple
18	Ueno Station Hotel
19	Kiyomizu-dō Temple
20	Tokyo Metropolitan Festival Hall
21	Japan Art Academy
22	Ueno no Mori Art Museum
23	Saigō Takamori Statue
24	Ameyoko-cho Arcade
25	Marui Department Store
26	Shitamachi History Museum
27	Ameyoko Centre Building
28	Samrat Indian Restaurant

1	寛永寺
2	東京芸術大学
3	澤の屋旅館
4	旅館勝太郎
5	法隆寺宝物殿
6	東京国立博物館
7	東洋館
8	りんの寺
9	国立科学博物館
10	東京国立西洋美術館
11	東京都美術館
12	五重塔
13	東照宮
14	水月ホテル
15	こどもの動物園
16	水族館
17	弁天堂
18	上野スティションホテル
19	清水堂
20	東京文化会館
21	日本美術協会
22	上野の森美術館
23	西郷隆盛銅像
24	アメ横
25	丸井百貨店
26	下町風俗資料館
27	アメ横センタビル
28	サムラート

around the station and in the frenetic entertainment area. There are also a lot of restaurants underground, along the 1.5 km of shopping streets which run from around the station.

Some good places to try in Shinjuku are *Tainan Taami* for Taiwanese; *Pekin, Tokyo Kaisen Ichiba* and *Tokyo Dai Hanten* for Chinese; *Tōkaien* for Korean; *Ban Thai* for Thai; and *Istanbul* for Turkish.

Central Tokyo is usually too expensive for evening meals, but there are some great department-store lunch-time bargains and good night-time food stalls. Ginza has excellent curries – try *Nair's* Indian and *Gandhara* Pakistani restaurants.

Ueno, Asakusa and Ikebukuro abound in small Japanese and Chinese noodle bars. The Ameyoko-cho arcade near the Ueno Station is packed with small Japanese places. If you're determined to avoid Japanese food, there are plenty of fast-food specialists in this area, and Ikebukuro has a few up-market alternatives, including a Greek and an Italian restaurant or two. *Samrat*, near Ueno Station, has good Indian food.

Another good eating spot is Roppongi – ideal if you're planning on hitting the bright lights in Tokyo's international nightlife centre. It has great Chinese, Indian, Indonesian and (expensive) Japanese restaurants, as does Akasaka. Some less expensive restaurants worth trying in these two areas include *Moti, Raja* and *Samrat* for Indian, *Bengawan Solo* for Indonesian, *Tainan Taami* for Chinese, *Capricciosa* for Italian and *Bodaiju* for vegetarian.

Shibuya and Harajuku – the crowded crossroads on the JR Yamanote line – have numerous fast-food restaurants and places serving a wide variety of international cuisines. Try *Maharaja* and *Samrat* for Indian, *Tainan Taami* for Chinese, *Capricciosa* for Italian, *Kiku* for Japanese and *Siam Thai* for Thai.

Rick Kennedy's *Good Tokyo Restaurants* is the gourmet's bible, but many restaurants which the book suggests are too expensive for budget travellers.

Shakey's Pizza, *Kentucky Fried Chicken* and *McDonald's* seem to have a branch next to every railway station in Tokyo. Others such as *El Polo Loco* and *Pizza Hut* also have a shop here and there. The *McDonald's* phenomenon has spawned some Japanese variations on the same theme: *Mos Burger*, *Lotteria* and *Love Burger*, to name a few.

Entertainment

Roppongi is an expensive nightlife centre. Areas like Shinjuku can be cheaper, but even there clubs often have a nominal entry fee, and a bottle of beer costs about Y800.

Live music in Tokyo has its drawbacks. Entry charges and drinks prices are very high, apart from in some of the more alternative 'live houses'. Also, the quality of the local music often leaves a lot to be desired.

A place that should be high on any list of live houses in Tokyo is *Club Z* (☎ 3336-5841). The club is next to Koenji Station on the Chūō line. Facing in the direction of Shinjuku, leave on the left side of the station and make a sharp right. Follow the road beside the railway tracks for about 50 metres and then cross the road. Club Z is opposite the railway tracks, next to Nippon Rent-a-Car, in the basement.

Not far from Club Z is a very special bar, *Inaoiza* (☎ 3336-4480), with a small stage for live music. The people who run the bar are musicians, and often if no-one is booked to perform there'll just be an impromptu jam session. Live music has to stop at 10.30 pm because of the neighbours, but the action continues with lots of foreigners and locals

who drop in after work. Inaoiza also has good food and a friendly atmosphere. The only problem is finding it. Your best bet is to ask someone at Club Z, as most of that crowd also frequent Inaoiza.

In Harajuku, *Crocodile* (☎ 3499-5205) has something happening nightly. To get there from the JR Harajuku Station, walk down Omote-sando and turn right at Meiji-dōri Ave. Cross the road and continue straight ahead, passing an overhead walk way. Crocodile is on your left, in the basement of the New Sekiguchi building.

Also in Harajuku is *Petite Rue* (☎ 3400-9890). To get there, walk down Omote-sando from the JR Harajuku Station, cross the intersection at Meiji-dōri Ave and take the next right. Petite Rue is on your left a few doors down.

Another good live house is *Rock Mother* (☎ 3460-1479) in Shimokitazawa. The whole area around there is popular with students. To get to Rock Mother, take the Odakyū line to Shimokitazawa Station and leave via the southern exit (Minami-guchi). After you leave the station, turn left, then right, then left again. Follow the road around to the right and look for the club on your left.

Look for information about what's happening in the mainstream music scene in *Pia*, or in the *Tokyo Journal*, the English-language magazine. Both have information on all the high-culture stuff (operas, philharmonics, etc) as well as details about jazz and rock. For information on alternative rock music, check *Infozine*.

In Shinjuku, a cheap place popular with students is *Yamagoya*. You enter by a narrow flight of stairs and end up in what seems like the hull of an old wooden ship. The bottom level is the gloomiest and most dungeon-like and the most fun. To get there, walk along Shinjuku-dōri Ave away from Shinjuku Station and turn left after the Isetan Department Store. Cross the road and turn right into the lane next to the cinema. You'll pass an advertisement for a Tokyo Playboy club; afterwards take the first left. Yamagoya is down the road a little, on your right – a wooden sign hangs outside with kanji

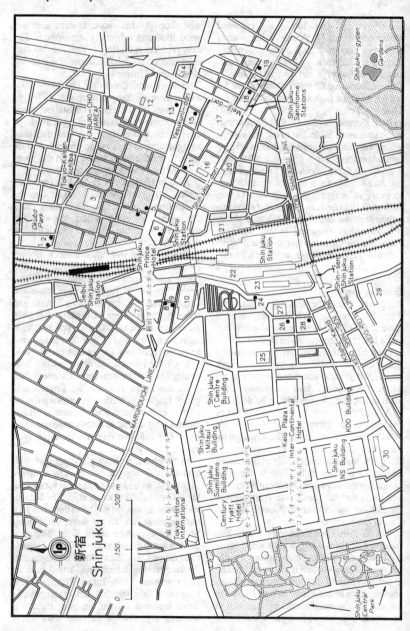

新宿
Shinjuku

Shinjuku-gyoen
Gardens

Shinjuku-
Sanchome
Stations

KABUKI-CHO
AREA

Tokyo-Kaisen
Iichiba

Okubo
Park

Shinjuku
Prince
新宿プリンスホテル Hotel

Shinjuku
Station

Shinjuku
Station

Seibu
Shinjuku
Station

Shin-Sen
Shinjuku
Station

Shinjuku
Centre
Building

Shinjuku
Mitsui
Building

Keio Plaza
Inter-Continental
Hotel

KDD Building

Shinjuku
Sumitomo
Building

Shinjuku
NS Building

Century
Hyatt Hotel

Tokyo Hilton
International

Shinjuku
Central
Park

MARUNOUCHI LINE

JR SHINJUKU LINE

KEIO NS-KOSEN LINE

Yasukuni-dori

Shinjuku-dori

Meiji-dori

300 m
150
0

1	Pekin Chinese Restaurant
2	Tainan Taami Taiwanese Restaurant
3	Koma Theatre
4	Ban Thai Restaurant
5	Tōkaien Korean Restaurant
6	Ibuki Restaurant
7	Star Hotel Tokyo
8	Volga Japanese Restaurant
9	Tori-jun Japanese Restaurant
10	Odakyū Department Store
11	El Borracho Mexican Restaurant
12	Hanazono Shrine
13	Tokyo Dai Hanten Chinese Restaurant
14	Marui
15	Shinjuku Pit Inn
16	Kinokuniya Bookshop
17	Isetan Department Store
18	Istanbul Turkish Restaurant
19	Rolling Stone
20	Mitsukoshi Department Store
21	My City Department Store
22	Odakyū Department Store & Station
23	Keio Department Store
24	Airport Limousine Bus Stop
25	Post Office
26	Yodobashi Camera
27	Highway Bus Terminal
28	Sakuraya Camera
29	Hotel Sun Route
30	Shinjuku Washington Hotel

1	北京レストラン
2	台南担仔麺
3	コマ劇場
4	バンタイレストラン
5	東海苑
6	いぶき
7	スターホテル
8	ボルガレストラン
9	とりじゅんレストラン
10	小田急百貨店
11	エルボラチョレストラン
12	花園神社
13	東京大飯店
14	丸井百貨店
15	Pit Inn 新宿
16	紀伊国屋書店
17	伊勢丹本店
18	イスタンブルレストラン
19	Rolling Stone
20	三越百貨店
21	My City 百貨店
22	小田急駅
23	京王百貨店
24	空港のリムジンバスの停
25	郵便局
26	ヨドバシカメラ
27	ハイウェイバスのタミナル
28	カメラのさくらや
29	ホテルサンルート
30	新宿ワシントンホテル

written on it. Look for the stairs going down into the building.

Just down the road from Yamagoya is the *Rolling Stone* (☎ 3354-7347) – not for the faint-hearted. The music is rock & roll from the '70s onwards and it's a hang-out for Tokyo's heavy metal kids. Avoid Friday or Saturday night when the place is packed out. There's a Y200 cover charge. To get there, walk along Shinjuku-dōri Ave past the Isetan Department Store, cross the main road and keep walking until you come to the next main road; turn left and take the next left. The Rolling Stone is a few doors down, next door to a soapland (a bathhouse/brothel).

Things to Buy

Department stores are mostly expensive, but there are a number of flea markets. The Tōgō Jinja Shrine has a flea market from 4 am to 4 pm on the first and second Sundays of each month. To get there from the JR Harajuku Station, turn left and take the next right after Takeshita-dōri.

A market operates at the Nogi Jinja Shrine from dawn to dusk on the second Sunday of each month. You get there from Nogi-zaka Subway Station on the Chiyoda line – the shrine is on the other side of Gaien-higashi-dōri.

Sunshine City also has a flea market, in the Alpa shopping arcade. It runs from 8 am to 10 pm on the third Saturday and Sunday of each month. It's five minutes from the western exit of Ikebukuro Station.

The Ramura building plaza has a market from 6 am to sunset on the first Saturday of each month. It's next to Iidabashi Subway Station.

Getting There & Away

Air Tokyo is the point of arrival for most travellers. Domestic flights are available between Tokyo and the major cities. See the Getting Around section in this chapter for details.

Most international flights land at Narita and most domestic flights at Haneda. Taiwan-based China Airlines is the exception – its international flights land at Haneda.

Bus Long-distance buses are little or no cheaper than the trains but are sometimes a good alternative for trips to areas serviced by expressways. The buses will often run direct, so that you can relax instead of watching for your stop.

Overnight buses leave at 10 pm from Tokyo Station and arrive at Kyoto and Osaka between 6 and 7 am the following morning. They cost from Y8000 to Y9000. The buses are a JR service and can be booked at one of the Green Windows in a JR station. Direct buses also run from Tokyo Station to Nara and Kōbe. And from Shinjuku Station there are buses running to the Fuji and Hakone regions, including, for Mt Fuji climbers, direct services to the 5th stations.

Train Most of the major train lines terminate at either Tokyo or Ueno stations, both of which are on the JR Yamanote line. As a general rule of thumb, trains for the north and north-east start at Ueno Station and southbound trains start at Tokyo Station. For day trips to areas such as Kamakura, Nikkō, Hakone and Yokohama, the most convenient means of transport is usually one of the private lines. With the exception of the Tōbu Nikkō line, which starts in Asakusa, all of them start from somewhere on the Yamanote line.

There are three shinkansen (bullet train) lines that connect Tokyo with the rest of Japan: the Tōkaidō line passes through Central Honshū, changing name along the way to the San-yō line before terminating at Hakata in Northern Kyūshū; the Tōhoku line runs north-east via Utsunomiya and Sendai as far as Morioka; and the Jōetsu line runs north to Niigata. Of these lines, the one most likely to be used by visitors to Japan is the Tōkaidō line, as it passes through Kyoto and Osaka in the Kansai region. The Tōkaidō line starts at Tokyo Station, while the Tōhoku and Jōetsu lines start at Ueno Station.

Boat From Tokyo, there are long-distance ferry services to Kushiro in Hokkaidō (Y14,420), to Kōchi (Y13,910) and Tokushima (Y8200) in Shikoku, to Kokura in Northern Kyūshū (Y12,000) and to Naha in Okinawa (Y19,670).

Departures may not always be frequent (usually once every two or three days for long-distance services) and ferries are sometimes fully booked so it pays to make inquiries early.

Getting Around

Tokyo has a fine but complex public transport system, including 11 private rail lines and 10 subway lines.

The JNTO's *Tourist Map of Tokyo* is invaluable for understanding the system. It includes small maps of the subway and railway systems with the names printed both in romaji (Roman script) and Japanese.

On timetables the symmetrical kanji (character) indicates weekdays (Monday to Saturday), the other is for Sundays and holidays. Private railways may use red numbers for expresses, black numbers for locals.

To/From the Airport Narita International Airport is used by almost all the international airlines but only by a small number of domestic operators. The airport is 66 km from central Tokyo, which means that getting into town is going to take at least

1½ hours. During holiday peak times it may be wise to book a seat on the Keisei Skyliner train service or on the limousine bus services.

A taxi to Tokyo will cost about Y20,000. The limousine buses are Y2500 or Y2700. Cheapest, and usually fastest, is a Keisei line train, at Y840 or Y1680.

Bus The trains are better. The bus system is complicated and at the mercy of Tokyo's sluggish traffic. Services also tend to finish about 9 pm, making buses a pretty poor alternative all round.

Train JR runs several lines in and around Tokyo. All services stop just after midnight. The Tokyo train system can be a bit daunting at first, but you soon get the hang of it. All the subway lines are colour coded, so even if you can't read a thing you soon learn that the Ginza line is orange. For all local journeys, tickets are sold by vending machines called *jidō kippu uriba*. Above the vending machines will be a rail map with fares indicated next to the station names. Unfortunately for visiting illiterates, the names are almost always in kanji only. Probably the best way around this problem is to put your money in the machine and push the lowest fare button (usually Y120). This will get you on the train and when you get to your destination you can correct the fare at the fare adjustment office. You can get your money back before you press the ticket button by pressing the button marked *torikeshi*.

If you get tired of fumbling for change every time you buy a ticket, the JR system offers the option of 'orange cards'. The cards are available in denominations of Y1000, Y3000 and Y5000. Fares are automatically deducted from the cards when you use them in the orange-card vending machines.

For long-term residents, passes called *teiki-ken* are available between two stops over a fixed period of time, but you have to use the ticket at least once a day for it to pay off. However, it beats queueing to buy tickets.

There are also the *furii kippu* tickets for a day's unlimited travel on either the subway system or the JR system, within the bounds of the Yamanote line. Given that you generally need to use both systems, it's difficult to get your money's worth from these tickets.

Taxi Taxis are so expensive that you should only use them when there is no alternative. Rates start at Y540 and rise by Y80 every 370 metres. You also click up Y80 approximately every two minutes while you relax in a typical Tokyo traffic jam.

If you have to get a taxi late on a Friday or Saturday night and are able to find one, be prepared for delays and higher prices. At these difficult times, gaijin may find themselves shunned like lepers because their ride is likely to be a short one, whereas the drunken salaryman holding up two fingers (to indicate his willingness to pay twice the meter fare) is probably bound for a distant suburb.

Tours Tours are expensive, but if interested, check with the TIC.

Around Tokyo
東京の附近

Some of the nation's main attractions, including Mt Fuji, Kamakura and the Chichibu-tama National Park, are quite close to Tokyo.

KAWASAKI 川崎

Kawasaki is a typical Japanese industrial city with very little to interest visitors except Jibeta Matsuri, an annual festival. Processions of costumed people carry wooden phalluses to celebrate the vanquishing of a sharp-toothed demon with an appetite for male sexual organs who had taken up residence in a fair maiden.

The festival takes place in the late afternoon of 15 April, commencing with a procession, followed by a re-enactment of the victory and rounded off with a banquet.

The action takes place close to Kawasaki Taishi Station.

Getting There & Away
Access from Tokyo is by Odakyu line from Shinjuku Station to Muko-ga-oka Yuen Station; the express from track No 5 takes about 30 minutes.

YOKOHAMA 横浜
Yokohama is the port city for Tokyo and has become the second largest city in Japan. It's close to Tokyo and has practically merged with it, making this whole area one huge megalopolis.

Things to See
The **Silk Centre Building** has a display of all aspects of the silk industry. Bus Nos 26, 8 and 58 from near the station will get you there. Nearby is the tall Marine Tower with good views, even of Mt Fuji on a clear day.

Sankei-en Park is one of the finest garden parks in Japan, with several historic buildings in its wooded grounds. Take bus No 8 to Sankei-en-mae stop.

Places to Stay
The *Kanagawa Youth Hostel* (☎ 045-241-6503) costs Y2000. From Sakuragi-cho Station, leave on the opposite side to the harbour, turn right and follow the road alongside the railway tracks. Cross the main road, turn left into the steep street with a bridge and a cobblestoned section and the youth hostel is up the road on the right.

Places to Eat
Chinatown is undoubtedly the place for a meal in Yokohama. It's about a five to ten-minute walk from the Marine Tower, away from the harbour.

Getting There & Away
There are numerous trains from Tokyo, the cheapest being the Tōkyū Toyoko line from Shibuya Station to Yokohama Station for Y160. The trip takes 40 minutes.

The Keihin Tōhoku line from Tokyo Station is a bit more convenient, going through to Kannai Station, but at Y610 it's considerably more expensive. If you only want to go as far as Yokohama Station, take the Tōkaidō line from Tokyo Station or Shinagawa Station; the 30-minute trip costs Y470.

It is convenient to continue on to Kamakura on the Yokosuka line from Yokohama Station. There is also a shinkansen connection for those continuing to the Kansai region.

Yokohama is a port of call for cruise ships and is served by regular sailings to and from Nakhodka (USSR) at the eastern extremity of the Trans-Siberian Railway. Passenger ships arrive at the modern international port terminal at Osambashi Pier.

Local buses terminate on both sides of the station; use the east exit for buses to the port, Sankei-en, etc.

KAMAKURA 鎌倉
Kamakura may not have as much to offer historically as Kyoto or Nara, but a wealth of notable Buddhist temples and Shinto shrines make this one of Tokyo's most interesting day trips.

Things to See
The most famous single sight in Kamakura is the **Great Buddha** (Daibutsu). Take bus No 7 from in front of Kamakura Station and get off at the Daibutsu-mae bus stop. The Great Buddha can be seen daily from 7 am to 5.30 pm, and admission is Y120.

Engaku-ji Temple is on the left as you leave Kita-Kamakura Station. **Tōkei-ji Temple**, across the railway tracks from Engaku-ji Temple, is notable for its grounds as much as for the temple itself. A couple of minutes further on from Tōkei-ji Temple is **Jōchi-ji Temple**.

Kenchō-ji Temple is about a 10-minute walk beyond Jōchi-ji Temple. It is on the left after you pass through a tunnel. This is Kamakura's most important Zen temple.

Across the road from Kenchō-ji Temple is **Ennō-ji Temple**, distinguished primarily by its collection of statues depicting the judges of hell.

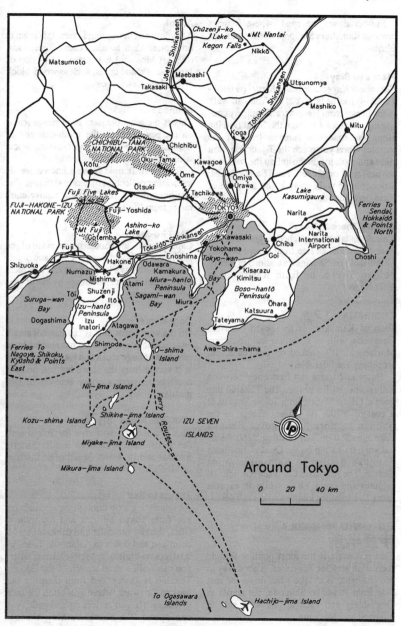

Around Tokyo

0   20   40 km

Further down the road, where it turns towards Kamakura Station, is **Hachiman-gū Shrine**.

Places to Stay
Kamakura Kagetsuen Youth Hostel (☎ 0467-25-1238) has beds at Y2100. You can walk to the hostel from Hase-dera Temple by continuing to walk away from the Great Buddha along the road that runs in front of the temple. When you reach the T-junction, turn right and look for the hostel on the corner of the next road on the left. Hase Station is also a five-minute walk away in the direction of Hase-dera Temple.

Getting There & Away
Kamakura is easily reached in just under an hour by Yokosuka line from Tokyo Station, Shimbashi and Shinagawa stations in metropolitan Tokyo, or from Kawasaki or Yokohama.

ENOSHIMA 江ノ島
West of Kamakura is the beach resort of Enoshima, with an aquarium and Enoshima Marineland. It's packed on weekends, but weekdays are tolerable.

Buses and trains run frequently between Kamakura and Enoshima. The Tōkaidō line goes to Ofuna Station from Tokyo Station, at a cost of Y780. At Ofuna, change to the Shonan monorail and go to Shonan Enoshima Station, a trip costing Y260. Alternatively, trains run on the Odakyū line from Shinjuku Station to Katase-Enoshima Station. The Romance Car takes one hour 10 minutes and costs Y870, while an express takes five minutes longer and costs Y460.

IZU-HANTO PENINSULA 伊豆半島
This peninsula is the most popular seaside recreation area for Tokyoites. A good way to see Izu-hanto is to take a bus down the east side from Atami to Shimoda, cut across to Dogashima and back up the west side to Numazu and Mishima.

Atami
A favourite of hot-spring lovers, this town is little more than hotels. Atami Bijutsu-kan (the Art Museum) has a good collection of Japanese arts and crafts, such as wood-block prints, lacquerware, etc.

Shimoda
This is the most pleasant hot springs resort on the peninsula. At the south-east end of Izu-hanto, Shimoda is a major summer resort with a few good beaches.

Ryosen-ji Temple is well known for its interesting collection of erotic statuary. The phallic symbols (and female equivalents) range from life-size upwards.

Cape Irō-zaki
Cape Irō-zaki, the southernmost point of the peninsula, is noted for its cliffs and lighthouse. It also has a jungle park and a tropical garden. You can get to the cape by bus or boat from Shimoda.

Dogashima
On the west coast, this is Izu-hanto's single most scenic place. Erosion has shaped large numbers of huge rocks that jut out of the sea. It is scenic from the shore but can be seen much better from a cruise boat out of Dogashima.

HAKONE AREA 箱根
This is a major resort area for Tokyo residents. Its main attractions are its historic remains and its views (weather permitting) of Mt Fuji.

Things to See
An interesting loop through the region takes you from Tokyo by train and toy train to Gōra, then by funicular and cable car up Mt Soun-zan and down to Ashino-ko Lake, by boat around the lake to Moto-Hakone, where you can walk a short stretch of the Edo era Tōkaidō Highway, and from there by bus back to Odawara, where you catch the train to Tokyo. (If you're feeling energetic, you can spend 3½ hours walking the old

highway back to Hakone-Yumoto, which is on the Tokyo line.)

Odawara's main attraction is a modern reconstruction of Odawara-jo Castle. Apart from that it is the start of the switchback Tozan railway to Gora. On the way you pass through Chokoku-no-mori, with sculptures in an open-air museum.

Places to Stay

Hakone Soun-zan Youth Hostel (☎ 0460-2-3827) costs the standard Y2100. The hostel is on the left-hand side of the road that goes off to the right of the cable car. Look for the wooden sign with Japanese writing and the YHA triangle outside the hotel.

The Japanese Inn Group has a comfortable, clean and reasonably priced guesthouse in the area. The *Fuji Hakone Guest House* (☎ 0460-4-6577) has singles from Y4500 to Y5000 and twins from Y8000 to Y9000. It is a 45-minute bus journey from stop No 4 at Odawara to the Senkyoro-mae bus stop. When you get off the bus, turn back and take the first right, then turn left into the road opposite the swimming pool.

Getting There & Away

There are basically three ways of getting to the Hakone region: by the Odakyu express bus service from the Shinjuku Bus Terminal on the western side of Shinjuku Station; by JR from Tokyo Station; and by the private Odakyu line from Shinjuku Station.

The Odakyu Express Bus Service has the advantage of running directly into the Hakone region, to Ashino-ko Lake and to Hakone-machi for Y1650. The disadvantage is that the bus trip is much less interesting than the combination of Romance Car, toy train (Hakone-Tozan line), funicular, cable car (ropeway) and ferry.

JR trains run on the Tōkaidō line between Tokyo Station and Odawara. Ordinary trains take 1½ hours, cost Y1420 and run every 15 minutes or so. Shinkansen do the journey in 42 minutes, cost Y3570 and leave Tokyo Station every 20 minutes.

Trains also service Odawara from Shinjuku Station on the Odakyu line. Quick-

est and most comfortable is the Romance Car, which takes one hour 25 minutes, costs Y1490 and leaves every half hour. There's also an express service, taking one hour 35 minutes, which at Y610 is by far the cheapest way of reaching Odawara.

At Odawara, it is possible to change to the Hakone-Tōzan line, which takes you to Gōra. Alternatively, if you are already on the Odakyū line, you can continue on to Hakone-Yumoto and change to the Hakone-Tōzan line there simply by walking across the platform.

For those coming from or continuing on to the Kansai region, kodama shinkansen run between Odawara and Shin-Osaka Station. The journey takes three hours 20 minutes, costs Y11,380 (you can use your Japan Rail Pass) and runs every 20 minutes.

Getting Around

Buses run between Moto-Hakone and Odawara. The trip takes one hour and costs Y1000. At Moto-Hakone, the buses depart from the stop next to the jetty.

The Odakyū line offers a Hakone *furii pasu* (Hakone free pass), which costs Y4520 and allows you to use any mode of transport within the Hakone region for four days. The fare between Shinjuku and Hakone-Yumoto is also included in the pass. This is a good deal for a Hakone circuit, as the pass will save you at least Y1000 even on a one-day visit to the region.

It's a pleasant journey to Gōra from Odawara or Hakone-Yumoto stations on the the Hakone-Tōzan line (literally the 'Hakone climb mountain line').

Ferry services crisscross Ashino-ko Lake, running between Togendai, Hakone-machi and Moto-Hakone for Y870 every 30 minutes or so. Ferries also go to Hakone-machi and Moto-Hakone from Kojiri for Y820. There are also frequent ferries between Togendai and Moto-Hakone.

MT FUJI AREA
富士山の附近

Japan's best-known feature is visited by thousands of foreigners and Japanese each year. Mt Fuji, or Fuji-san as the Japanese call it (never Fuji-yama!), is the universal symbol of Japan. It is one of the world's most beautiful mountains and is always a spectacular sight.

Be warned, however, that Fuji-san is very bashful in spring, summer and early autumn, and is usually totally obscured by clouds, even from close up.

Climbing Mt Fuji

Officially the climbing season on Fuji is July and August, and the Japanese, who love to do things 'right', pack in during those busy months. The climbing may be just as good either side of the official season but transport services to and from the mountain are less frequent then and many of the mountain huts are closed.

Don't climb Mt Fuji without adequate clothing for cold and wet weather: even on a good day at the height of summer, the temperature on top is likely to be close to freezing.

The mountain is divided into 10 'stations' from base to summit but these days most climbers start from one of the four 5th stations, which you can reach by road. From the end of the road, it takes about 4½ hours to climb the mountain and about 2½ hours to descend. Once you're on the top, it takes about an hour to make a circuit of the crater. The Mt Fuji Weather Station on the south-western edge of the crater is on the actual summit of the mountain.

Although nearly all climbers start from the 5th stations, it is possible to climb all the way up from a lower level. Gluttons for punishment could climb all the way on the Yoshida Route from Fuji-Yoshida or on the Shoji Route from near Shoji-ko Lake.

There are alternative sand trails on the Kawaguchi-ko/Yoshida, Subashiri and Gotemba routes which you can descend very rapidly by running and sliding.

There are four 5th stations around Fuji, and it's quite feasible to climb from one and descend to another. On the northern side of Fuji is the Kawaguchiko 5th station, at 2305 metres, which is reached from the town of Kawaguchiko. This station is particularly popular with climbers starting from Tokyo. The Yoshida route, which starts much lower down, close to the town of Fuji-Yoshida, is the same as the Kawaguchiko route for much of the way.

The Subashiri 5th station is at 1980 metres, and the route from there meets the Kawaguchiko one just after the 8th station. The Gotemba 5th station is reached from the town of Gotemba and is much lower than the other 5th stations, at 1440 metres. From the Gotemba station it takes seven to eight hours to reach the top, as opposed to the 4½ to five hours it takes on the other routes. The Fujinomiya or Mishima 5th station, at 2380 metres, is convenient for climbers coming from Nagoya, Kyoto, Osaka and western Japan. It meets the Gotemba route right at the top.

Things to See

The road around Mt Fuji passes Fuji Five Lakes. Of these, **Kawaguchi-ko Lake**, the second largest, is a popular resort. The area around the smaller **Sai-ko Lake** is less developed. Close to the road are the **Narusawa Ice Cave** and the **Fugaku Wind Cave**, both formed by lava flows from a prehistoric eruption of Mt Fuji. There's a bus stop at both caves, or you can walk from one to the other in about 20 minutes. The **Fuji-fūketsu Cave**, further to the south, is often floored with ice.

The views of Mt Fuji from further west are not so impressive, but tiny **Shoji-ko Lake** is said to be the prettiest of the Fuji Five Lakes. Continue to Mt Eboshi-san, a one to 1½-hour climb from the road to a lookout over the **Aokigahara** (the Sea of Trees) to Mt Fuji. Next is Motosu-ko Lake, the deepest of the lakes, while further to the south is the wide and attractive drop of the **Shiraito-no-taki Waterfall**.

Places to Stay

Marimo (Yamanaka-ko) (☎ 0555-62-4210), *Kawaguchi-ko* (☎ 0555-72-1431) and *Fuji Sai-ko* (☎ 0555-82-2616) youth hostels are by their namesakes. The first two cost Y2100 a night, while the Sai-ko is Y2250 or Y2450,

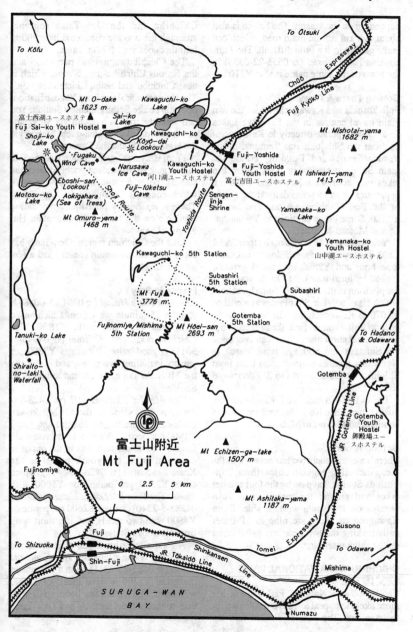

To Ōtsuki

Chūō Expressway

To Kōfu

Mt O-dake 1623 m

Kawaguchi-ko Lake

富士西湖ユースホステル
Fuji Sai-ko Youth Hostel ■

Sai-ko Lake

▲ Mt Misholai-yama 1682 m

Shoji-ko Lake

Kawaguchi-ko
河口湖ユースホステル

Kōyō-dai Lookout

Fuji Kyōko Line

Fugaku Wind Cave

Narusawa Ice Cave

Kawaguchi-ko Youth Hostel

Fuji-Yoshida ■

Fuji-Yoshida Youth Hostel
富士吉田ユースホステル

Mt Ishiwari-yama 1413 m ▲

Eboshi-san Lookout

Fuji-fūketsu Cave

Aokigahara (Sea of Trees)

Motosu-ko Lake

Sengen-jinja Shrine

▲ Mt Omuro-yama 1468 m

Shoji Route

Yoshida Route

Yamanaka-ko Lake

Yamanaka-ko Youth Hostel
山中湖ユースホステル ■

Kawaguchi-ko 5th Station

Subashiri 5th Station

Subashiri

Mt Fuji ▲ 3776 m

Fujinomiya/Mishima 5th Station

Mt Hōei-san 2693 m

Gotemba 5th Station

To Hadano & Odawara

Tanuki-ko Lake

Shiraito-no-taki Waterfall

Gotemba

LP

富士山附近
Mt Fuji Area

Gotemba Youth Hostel
御殿場ユースホステル

0   2.5   5 km

▲ Mt Echizen-ga-take 1507 m

Fujinomiya

JR Gotemba Line

▲ Mt Ashitaka-yama 1187 m

Fuji

Susono

To Shizuoka

Shin-Fuji

JR Tōkaidō Line

Shinkansen Line

Tomei Expressway

To Odawara

Mishima

SURUGA-WAN BAY

Numazu

depending on the season. The Sai-ko is also about two km off the main road, which can make getting to it a little difficult. The *Fuji-Yoshida Youth Hostel* (☎ 0555-22-0533) in the town of the same name is also Y2100.

Getting There & Away
Fuji-Yoshida and Kawaguchi-ko are the two main travel centres in the Fuji Five Lakes area. Buses operate directly to Kawaguchi-ko from the Shinjuku Bus Terminal in the Yasuda Seimei 2nd Building, beside the main Shinjuku station in Tokyo. The trip takes one hour 45 minutes and there are departures up to 16 times daily at the height of the Fuji climbing season. The fare is Y1520. Some buses continue to Yamanaka-ko and Motosu-ko lakes.

You can also get to the lakes by train. A JR Chūō line train goes from Shinjuku to Otsuki (one hour and Y2890 by limited express, Y1260 by local train). At Otsuki you cross the platform to the Fuji Kyūkō line local train which takes another 50 minutes at a cost of Y1070 to Kawaguchiko. The train actually goes to Fuji-Yoshida first, then reverses out for the final short distance to Kawaguchiko. On Sundays and holidays from March to November there is a direct local train from Shinjuku which takes two to 2½ hours and costs Y2200.

From Fuji-Yoshida and Kawaguchiko, buses run north to Kōfu, from where you can continue north-west to Matsumoto.

Getting Around
There's a comprehensive bus network in the area, including regular buses from Fuji-Yoshida Station that pass by the four smaller lakes and around the mountain to Fuji-nomiya on the south-western side. From Kawaguchiko, there are nine to 11 buses daily making the two-hour trip to Mishima on the shinkansen line.

CHICHIBU-TAMA NATIONAL PARK
秩父国立公園
Chichibu-Tama National Park's hikes are more likely to appeal to Tokyo residents than to travellers. The park is divided into the

Chichibu and the Oku-Tama regions, although the two are connected by a hiking trail that goes via Mt Mitsumine.

The Chichibu region has two walks and the famous Chichibu-jinja Shrine, which is near Chichibu and Seibu Chichibu stations. The shorter walk starts from Yokoze Station, one stop before Seibu Chichibu Station. You can walk the trail as a circuit via Mt Buko-san or turn off to Urayama-guchi Station via the Hashidate Stalactite Cavern.

From Urayama-guchi Station it is possible to continue to Mitsumine-guchi Station, the starting point for the longer 10-km walk which connects Chichibu with Oku-Tama. There is reasonably priced accommodation available on the trail at the Mountain Hut Kumitori Sanso.

Like the Chichibu region, Oku-Tama has some splendid mountain scenery and a few good hiking trails.

Places to Stay
Chichibu Youth Hostel (☎ 04945-5-0056) is about a 15-minute walk from Chichibu-ko Lake bus stop and costs Y1800. The *Chichibu Nagatoro SL Hotel* (☎ 04946-6-3011) is good value. It charges Y3800 per person, including two meals, and is close to the Mt Hodo-san cable car and to Nagatoro Station.

The *Mitake Youth Hostel* (☎ 0428-78-8501) is very close to the Mt Mitake-san cable-car terminus and charges the usual Y1900 per person. About a 15-minute walk from the cable-car terminus in the opposite direction from the youth hostel is the *Komadori Sanso* (☎ 0428-78-8472), which costs Y3500 per person or Y5000 with meals. The *People's Lodge Hatonosu-so* (☎ 04288-5-2340) charges Y2600 per person or Y4800 with two meals, and is a short walk from Hatonosu Station.

A good alternative if you're in the mood for hiking is the *Mountain Hut Kumotori Sanso* (☎ 0485-23-3311), with a per person charge of Y2300 without meals or Y4000 with them. The hut is a few hours up the trail that connects the Chichibu and Oku-Tama regions.

Getting There & Away

The cheapest and quickest way of getting to the Chichibu area is via the Seibu Ikebukuro line from Seibu Ikebukuro Station. The limited express Red Arrow service goes direct to Seibu Chichibu Station in 1½ hours for Y1170. If Ikebukuro is not a convenient spot to commence your trip, JR trains depart from Ueno Station to Kumagaya Station on the Takasaki line, where you will have to change to the Chichibu Tetsudō line to continue to Chichibu Station.

You can get to Oku-Tama by taking the JR Chūō line from Shinjuku Station to Tachikawa Station (Y430) and changing there to the JR Ome line, which will take you on to Oku-Tama Station (Y590). The first leg takes 40 minutes; the second, 70 minutes.

NIKKO 日光

Nikkō is not only one of the most popular day trips from Tokyo, it's also one of Japan's major tourist attractions due to the visual splendour of its shrines and temples. However, you can expect it to be crowded.

Information

First stop in Nikkō (after the cheesecake shop next to the Tōbu Nikkō line railway station, of course) should be the excellent Tourist Information Office on the road up to Tōshō-gū Shrine.

Things to See

Prominent sights include the Shin-kyō Bridge, Rinnō-ji Temple, Tōshō-gū Shrine, Futāra-san-jinja Shrine, Taiyūin-byō and Chūzenji-ko Lake.

Places to Stay

Nikkō Daiyagawa Youth Hostel (☎ 0288-54-1974) is the more popular of the town's two hostels. It costs Y1900 per night and is just behind the post office. A 10-minute walk away is the *Nikkō Youth Hostel* (☎ 0288-54-1013); it is slightly cheaper, at Y1800, but meals there are a little more expensive.

Far and away the most popular of Nikkō's pensions is the *Pension Turtle* (☎ 0288-53-3168), with rooms from Y3300 per person. It's by the river, beyond the shrine area. Also justifiably popular is the *Lodging House St*

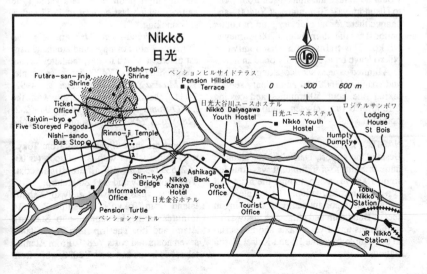

Bois (☎ 0288-53-0082). This place touts itself as a mountain lodge and has both Western and Japanese-style singles/doubles starting at Y4500/9200 for rooms without baths. It's across the river, north of the station.

Getting There & Away

The best way to visit Nikkō is via the Tōbu Nikkō line from Asakusa Station in Tokyo. The station, which is separate from Asakusa Subway Station, is in the basement of the Tōbu Department Store, but is well signposted and easy to find from the subway. Limited express trains cost Y2200 and take one hour 55 minutes. These trains require a reservation (on a quiet day you'll probably be able to organise this before boarding the train) and run every 30 minutes or so from 7.30 to 10 am; after 10 am they run hourly. Rapid trains require no reservation, take 15 minutes longer than the limited express and cost Y1100. They run once an hour from 6.20 am to 4.30 pm.

As usual, travelling by JR trains works out to be more time-consuming and more expensive and is only really of interest to those on a Japan Rail Pass. The quickest way to do it would be to take the shinkansen from Ueno to Utsunomiya – 50 minutes, at Y4400 – and change there for an ordinary train (no other options) for the 45-minute, Y700 journey to Nikkō. The trains from Utsunomiya to Nikkō leave on average only once an hour.

A limited express service taking 1½ hours and costing Y3600 and an ordinary service taking one hour 50 minutes and costing Y1800 also run between Ueno and Utsunomiya.

NARITA 成田

Besides the airport, Narita's other claim to fame is Shinshō-ji Temple. It was founded some 1000 years ago, though the main hall is a 1968 reconstruction. The temple itself remains an important centre of the Shingon sect of Buddhism and attracts as many as 10 million visitors a year. Taxis and buses run to the temple from the JR and Keisei Narita stations.

If you've got to kill time in the airport area, there's also the Museum of Aeronautical Sciences and the Chiba Prefectural Botanical Garden, both right beside the airport. There's a brochure *For Passengers Transiting at Narita* about the attractions in the vicinity of the airport, and tours are operated from the airport.

IZU SEVEN ISLANDS 伊豆諸島

The Izu Seven Islands are peaks of a submerged volcanic chain that projects out into the Pacific from the Izu-hantō Peninsula. There is still considerable volcanic activity.

Until recently the chain was considered more appropriate as a place of exile than of scenic beauty, but today it's a popular holiday destination for Tokyo residents. To escape the crowds, avoid holidays and head for the remoter islands.

The Izu Seven Islands Tourist Federation (☎ 03-436-6955) in Tokyo has information on minshuku, and there is also the O-shima Tourist Association (☎ 04992-2-2177), which offers help to depressed travellers.

O-shima 大島

This is the largest of the islands (91 sq km) and its high point is Mihara-yama (758 metres), which last erupted in 1957 and is still smoking.

The *O-shima-kōen Park* and *Umi no Furusatsu-mura* campground are the cheapest places at which to stay, the latter having pre-pitched tents at Y4000 for seven people. The *Mihara Sansō Youth Hostel* (☎ 04992-2-1111) charges Y2800 per person, while the *Izu O-shima People's Lodge* (☎ 04992-2-1285) costs Y4800 per person, including two meals.

There are three flights a day from Tokyo to O-shima Island with Air Nippon (☎ 03-552-6311). The 40-minute flight costs Y6550 one way and Y11,800 return.

Boat services run twice daily to O-shima Island from Tokyo's Takeshiba Pier (10 minutes from Hamamatsu-cho Station), Atami and Itō. The trip from Tokyo takes seven hours and costs Y2840. From Atami it takes two hours and costs Y2030, while from

Itō it takes 1½ hours and costs Y1770. High-speed services taking about one hour are available from Atami (Y4590) and Itō (Y4050).

To-shima 利島

To-shima Island, 27 km south-west of O-shima Island, is the smallest of the Izu Seven Islands, with a circumference of only eight km. The island is mountainous, although its volcano is now dormant, and there are no swimming beaches. Much of the island is used for the cultivation of camellias, which makes it a picturesque place to visit between December and February, when the flowers are in bloom.

The island has a few ryokan and min-shuku. Boats leave from Tokyo's Takeshiba Pier. The trip takes around nine hours and fares start at Y3160 in 2nd class.

Nii-jima 新島

Nii-jima Island has an area of 23 sq km, and its beaches have made it so popular that there are now over 200 minshuku on the island. Even with this abundance of accommodation, it's a good idea to ring the Nii-jima Tourist Association (☎ 04992-5-0422) if you're visiting during a holiday. The 10-hour boat trip from Tokyo's Takebashi Pier costs Y3810 in 2nd class.

Shikine-jima 式根島

Six km south of Nii-jima Island is tiny Shikine-jima Island, with an area of only 3.8 sq km. The island has swimming beaches, hot springs and plenty of accommodation. Contact the island's Tourist Information Office (☎ 04992-7-0170) for accommodation details. Boats to Shikine-jima Island depart from Takeshiba Pier daily, take 10 hours and cost Y3810 in 2nd class.

Kozu-shima 神津島

This 18 sq km island is dominated by an extinct volcano, Mt Tenjo. The island also has good beaches, Tokyo-ji Temple and a cemetery for former exiles, including 57 feudal warriors, from the days when the island served as a resort for Japanese unwanted by their compatriots on the mainland.

There are around 200 minshuku on the island and bookings can be made through the Kozu-shima Tourist Association (☎ 04992-8-0321). Boats leave from Takeshiba Pier and cost Y4040 2nd class.

Miyake-jima 三宅島

Known as Bird Island due to the 200 species of birds that live there, this island is 180 km south of Tokyo and is the third largest of the Izu Seven Islands, with a circumference of 36 km. It has a volcano, which last erupted in 1962, some good beaches, a couple of small lakes and an onsen. You can either explore the island in a hired car or on a rented bicycle or make use of the local bus services.

For reasonably priced minshuku, contact the Village Office (☎ 04994-6-1324). There are campgrounds at Sagiga-hama, Okubo-hama and Miike-hama beaches.

By boat from Tokyo costs Y4280 in 2nd class. There are also two flights a day with Air Nippon (☎ 03-552-6311) for Y8210 one way or Y14,780 return.

Hachijo-jima 八丈島

Hachijo-jima Island, 290 km south of Tokyo, is the southernmost and second largest of the Izu Seven Islands. It has a pleasant semi-tropical climate and is becoming very popular among young Japanese. Sights include the now dormant volcano, some good beaches, a botanical garden, Tame-tomo-jinja Shrine and Sofuku-ji Temple. Bicycles and cars can be rented.

There are some interesting local customs which are now maintained as tourist attractions, including a form of bull fighting found throughout Asia in which two bulls try to push each other out of a ring. Bull fights are held daily at Jiyugaoka and admission is Y800. The Runin Matsuri (Exile Festival) is held from 28 to 30 August, with a costumed procession, drum beating and folk dancing.

For accommodation information, ring the local tourist association (☎ 04996-2-1377). Boats from Tokyo, via Miyake-jima Island, taking around 10½ hours, cost Y5340 and depart six days a week. Alternatively, there is a more frequent air service (six flights a day) between Haneda Airport and the island. The flight takes one hour and costs Y11,110 one way, Y20,160 return.

OGASAWARA ISLANDS 小笠原諸島

Although they are also part of Tokyo-ko, these islands are far to the south of the Izu Seven Islands. They have a climate similar to that of the Okinawa islands.

The main group of islands include Chichi-jima, Haha-jima and Ani-jima islands, on which you will find a number of minshuku. Scuba diving is popular here. Further south are the Kazan, or Volcano, islands, which include Iwo-jima Island, one of the most famous battle sites of WW II. The island is still off limits to visitors because it contains live ammunition.

Northern Honshū 東北地方

Northern Honshū island, or Tōhoku (east-north), has a cold climate. As a result, this area is relatively unpopulated and therefore a great place to enjoy nature. Furthermore, local traditions still survive along with the fantastic scenery.

The few cities generally merit no more than a cursory stop before heading off into the back country to hike in volcanic and mountainous regions or along spectacular coastlines. Tōhoku has scores of hot springs tucked away in the mountains; and there are also cultural sights such as temples, festivals and folkcrafts. Several excellent skiing resorts benefit from the long and severe winters.

LAKE OZENUMA 尾瀬沼湖

This lake and its swampy surroundings, on a plateau about 70 km north of Nikkō, provide a popular destination for hikers to follow trails along boardwalks and admire the mountain flora. There are plenty of mountain huts providing basic accommodation – prices start around Y5500 per person and include two meals. *Oze Tokura Youth Hostel* (☎ 0278-58-7421) is opposite the bus stop in Oze Tokura.

Getting There & Away

There are buses running from Nikkō JR Station via Chūzenji to Yumoto Onsen. From Yumoto Onsen there are infrequent buses to Kamata (Y1250, 75 minutes) where you change to a bus for Oze Tokura. From Oze Tokura, there are infrequent and separate bus services – both take about 20 minutes – to the two major trailheads (Hatomachi Tōge Pass; and Oshimizu).

If you're heading down from Fukushima-ken, the lake can be reached by taking a bus from from Aizu-Kōgen Station (Aizu line) to Numayama Tōge Pass (Y1250, two hours) where trails lead into the swamp.

MT BANDAISAN & BANDAI KOGEN PLATEAU 磐梯山、磐梯高原

Mt Bandai-san erupted on 15 July 1888 and in the course of the eruption it destroyed dozens of villages and their inhabitants. At the same time it did a complete facelift on the landscape to create a plateau and dam local rivers which then formed numerous lakes and ponds. Now designated as a national park, the whole area offers spectacular scenery.

The most popular walk – sometimes jammed with hikers – takes about an hour and follows a trail between a series of lakes known as Goshikinuma (Five-Coloured Lakes). The trailheads for the Goshikinuma walk are at Goshikinuma Iriguchi; and at Bandai Kōgen Eki – the main transport hub – on the edge of Lake Hibara-ko. As can be expected of a main transport hub, Bandai Kōgen Eki is geared to a tourist circus – souvenir shops, restaurants, and a vast asphalt expanse to accommodate the tour buses. The pleasure boat rides can safely be skipped, but there are various walking trails along the eastern side of the lake. Nearby are several other lakes, including Lake Onagawa-ko and Lake Akimoto-ko, which also offer scope for walks along their shores.

Ura Bandai Youth Hostel is very close to Goshikinuma Iriguchi and makes a convenient base for extended hikes. The hostel has maps in Japanese which outline routes.

The most popular hiking destination is Mt Bandai-san which can be climbed in a day – start early and allow up to nine hours. A popular route for this hike starts from Kawakami Onsen (about 10 minutes by bus from the youth hostel) and climbs up to Mt Bandaisan, then loops around the rim of the crater before descending to Bandai Kōgen Eki.

Places to Stay

Ura Bandai Youth Hostel (☎ 0241-32-2811) seems a little the worse for wear, but it's in a quiet spot next to one of the trailheads for the Goshikinuma walk, and it's also a good base for longer mountain hikes. The hostel manager can provide maps and basic information for hikes in the area. Bicycle hire is available here – much cheaper than the hire at Lake Hibara-ko.

Take the bus bound for Bandai Kōgen from Inawashiro Station and get off 30 minutes later at Goshikinuma Iriguchi bus stop. The hostel is seven minutes on foot from the bus stop.

Getting There & Away

There are buses from Aizu Wakamatsu Station and Inawashiro Station to the trailheads for the Goshikinuma walk. From Aizu Wakamatsu and Inawashiro to Lake Hibara-ko, buses take 1½ hours (Y1450) and 25 minutes (Y750) respectively.

Between Bandai Kōgen Eki and Fukushima there is a bus service along two scenic toll roads – Bandai Azuma Lakeline; and Bandai Azuma Skyline. The trip provides great views of the mountains and is highly recommended if you are a fan of volcanic panoramas.

The bus makes a scheduled stop (30 minutes) at Jōdodaira, a superb viewpoint, where you can climb to the top of Mt

Azumakofuji (1705 metres) in 10 minutes; and, if you still feel energetic, scramble down to the bottom of the crater. Across the road is Mt Issaikyōyama which belches steam in dramatic contrast to its passive neighbour – a steepish climb of 45 minutes is needed to reach the top with its sweeping views.

The fare between Fukushima and Bandai Kōgen Eki is Y2560; the trip takes about three hours. This service only operates between late April and late October.

Between Bandai Kōgen Eki and Yonezawa there is another bus service along the scenic Sky Valley toll road. The trip takes two hours and the fare is Y1590. This service only operates between late April and late October.

SENDAI 仙台

The dominant figure in Sendai's history is Date Masamune (1567-1636) who earned the nickname, 'one-eyed dragon', after he caught smallpox as a child and went blind in his right eye. Date adopted Sendai as his base and used his military might and administrative skills to become one of the most powerful feudal lords in Japan.

Information

Sendai City Tourist Information Centre (☎ 022-222-4069) is on the second floor of Sendai Station and has English-speaking staff who can help with information not only for Sendai, but also for other parts of Tōhoku. It's open daily from 8.30 am to 8 pm. The Sendai English Hotline (☎ 022-224-1919) also offers travel information.

Things to See

Date Masamune built **Aoba-jō Castle** in 1602. Its ruins – a restored turret and that's about it – lie inside Aobayama-Kōen Park where you can pause for a look at **Gokoku Jinja Shrine** or walk south to Yagiyama Bashi Bridge which leads to a zoo. Admission costs Y400. It's open from 9 am to 4.15 pm. From Sendai Station, take bus No 9 for the 15-minute ride to Aoba-jōshi Uzumimon bus stop.

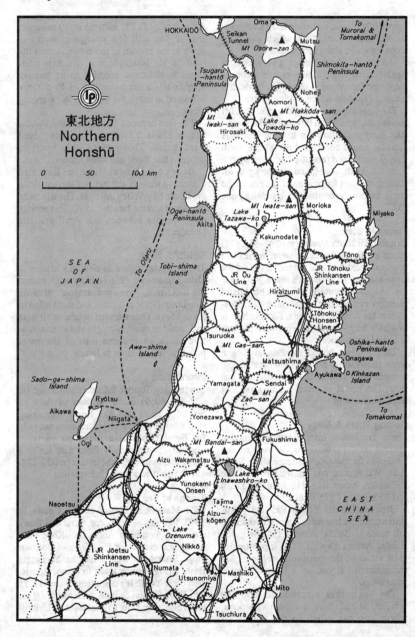

Zuihōden Hall is the mausoleum of Date Masamune. It was originally built in 1637, but it was destroyed by bombing in WW II. The present building is an exact replica. Admission costs Y500. It's open from 9 am to 4 pm. From Sendai Station, take bus Nos 11 or 12 for the 15-minute ride to Otamaya-bashi bus stop.

The original **Osaki Hachiman Jinja Shrine** dates from the 12th century and was moved from outside Sendai to its present site by Date Masamune in 1607. The main building is a luxurious, black-lacquered edifice with eye-catching carved designs. Admission costs Y300. It closes at sunset. From Sendai Station, take bus No 10 for the 15-minute ride to Hachiman-jinja-mae bus stop.

Places to Stay

Sendai Dōchu-an Youth Hostel (☎ 02-247-0511) is just south of Sendai in an old farmhouse and has a high reputation for hospitality to foreigners. From Sendai Station, take the subway to Tomizawa Station; then walk eight minutes to the hostel. Alternatively, you can walk to the hostel in 18 minutes from Nagamachi Station which is one stop south of Sendai Station. If you get lost, the hostel manager can give directions over the phone.

Sendai Onnai Youth Hostel (☎ 022-234-3922) is north of Sendai Station. Take bus No 24 (the stop is in front of Sendai Hotel, opposite the station) bound for Shihei-cho and get off after about 15 minutes at Tōhokukai Byō-in Shigakubu-mae stop. The hostel is two minutes away on foot. Bicycle hire is available at Y200 for the day.

Sendai Akamon Youth Hostel (☎ 022-264-1405) is north-west of Sendai Station – about 15 minutes by bus No 16 to Nakanose-bashi bus stop; then five minutes on foot. *Isuzu Ryokan* (☎ 022-222-6430), a member of the Japanese Inn Group, is five minutes on foot from Sendai Station. Prices for singles/doubles/triples start at Y3400/6000/8400.

Japanese Inn Aisaki (☎ 022-264-0700), also a member of the Japanese Inn Group, is right behind the Sendai post office which is a 12-minute walk from Sendai Station.

Prices for singles/doubles start at Y4000/7000.

Getting There & Away

From Sendai there are flights to Osaka; Sapporo (Chitose Kūko Airport); Nagoya; Fukuoka; Komatsu (Kanazawa); and Okinawa.

The Tōhoku Kyuko Express Night Bus runs between Tokyo and Sendai. The trip takes 7¾ hours and the one-way fare is Y5300 – reservations necessary.

The JR Tōhoku Shinkansen line provides a super-fast connection between Tokyo (Ueno) and Sendai – there are dozens of trains daily and the fastest ones do the run in a mere two hours. The same line connects Fukushima with Sendai in 26 minutes, and continues north to Morioka in 50 minutes.

The JR Senzan line connects Sendai with Yamagata in one hour. The JR Senseki line links Sendai with Matsushima in 40 minutes.

Sendai is a major port with daily ferries operating to Tomakomai (Hokkaidō). The trip takes just under 17 hours and the passenger fare is Y8850. There are also ferries operating every other day to Nagoya. The trip takes just over 21 hours and the passenger fare is Y9300.

The port is called Sendai-Ferry Futo. From Sendai Station, take the JR Senseki line to Tagajō Station; then take a 10-minute taxi ride to the port.

Getting Around

Most of the sights can be reached by bus direct from Sendai Station where the Tourist Information Centre provides a bilingual leaflet with relevant bus numbers. Short hops by taxi are inexpensive.

The present subway system runs from north to south. Apart from the subway station close to Sendai JR Station, it's not really useful for sightseeing. An extension of the subway is planned to run from east to west.

MATSUSHIMA 松島

Matsushima and the islands in Matsushima-wan Bay are meant to constitute one of the 'three great sights' of Japan – the other two are Miyajima and Amanohashidate. Besides the islands, there's also a lot of unprepossessing industrial scenery.

It's certainly a picturesque place which merits a half-day visit, but try to spend a day or so visiting the impressive and less-touristed seascapes further east.

Matsushima-kaigan Station and the main sights of Matsushima are within easy walking reach of the dock for the cruise boats.

Things to See

The present buildings of the **Zuigan-ji Temple** were constructed in 1606 by Date Masamune to serve as a family temple, but it dates back to 828. This is one of Tōhoku's finest Zen temples. Admission costs Y500 and includes an English leaflet. The temple is open from 7.30 am to 5 pm from April to mid-September; opening hours vary almost month by month at other times during the year, but the core opening hours are from 8 am to 3.30 pm. The temple is five minutes on foot from the dock and is approached along an avenue lined with tall cedars.

Godai-dō Hall is a small wooden temple reached by two bridges, just a couple of minutes on foot to your right as you get off the boat. The interior is opened only once every 33 years.

Kanran-tei Pavilion is about five minutes on foot from the dock; bear left after leaving the boat. Admission to the pavilion costs Y200 and includes entrance to the museum. It's open from 8.30 am to 5.30 pm (April to October), and closes an hour earlier during the rest of the year.

About five minutes on foot south of Kanran-tei, you'll see **Ojima Island** connected with the mainland by a red wooden bridge.

Places to Stay

Matsushima has dozens of ryokan, min-shuku and hotels catering to the tidal waves of visitors – Tourist Information Offices in Sendai or at the boat dock in Matsushima can help with booking accommodation.

One useful option, close at hand, but further removed from the madding crowds is *Matsushima Youth Hostel* (☎ 0225-88-2220) which is at Oku-Matsushima to the east of Matsushima Bay, near Nobiru Station.

OKU-MATSUSHIMA　奥松島

On the eastern curve of Matsushima-wan Bay, Oku-Matsushima is less touristed and offers scope for exploration by bicycle or on foot along several hiking trails.

To reach Oku-Matsushima, take the JR Senseki line east from Matsushima-kaigan to Nobiru Station (two stops). From Nobiru Station, it's a 10-minute bus ride to Otakamori village, where a 20-minute climb up the hill will give you a very fine panorama of the bay.

Matsushima Youth Hostel is about 20 minutes on foot from Nobiru Station. Bicycle hire is available and the manager can provide directions for the hiking trails.

OSHIKA-HANTO PENINSULA　牡鹿半島

The gateway to this beautiful, secluded peninsula is Ishinomaki which is on the JR Senseki line, about 30 minutes from Matsushima-kaigan by limited express.

From Ishinomaki Station there are buses (Y1430, 90 minutes) to Ayukawa at the base of the peninsula – you may be able to get a Y100 discount by asking for a *shūyū-ken* or block of tickets. There is also a boat connection between Ishinomaki and Ayukawa which leaves at 9.50 am. The trip takes two hours and the fare is Y1850.

The drive down the peninsula is particularly enjoyable, as the bus repeatedly climbs across forested hills before dropping down into bays and inlets where tiny fishing villages are surrounded by mounds of seashells and the ocean is full of rafts and poles for oyster and seaweed cultivation.

KINKAZAN ISLAND　金華山

This island consists of a pyramid-shaped mountain (well, 445 metres high to be precise); an impressive and drowsy shrine; a handful of houses around the boat dock; no cars; droves of deer and monkeys; and mostly untended trails.

The island is considered one of the three holiest places in Tōhoku – women were banned until late last century – and you should respect the ban on smoking.

From the boat dock, it's a steep 20-minute walk up the road to **Koganeyama Jinja Shrine**, which has several attractive buildings in its forested precincts.

A steep trail leads from the shrine up the thickly forested slopes via several wayside shrines to the summit in round about 50 minutes.

A map of the island on green paper is provided by the shrine or the Tourist Information Office in Ayukawa. It has neither contour lines nor scale and its only use is to demonstrate that there *are* trails and to provide the kanji for various places on the island – of moderate use when you come across one of the weatherbeaten trail markers.

There are very few people here. It's a wonderful place to enjoy some peace and fine scenery away from the crushing masses of Japan's cities and touristy spots. Before setting off for an extended hike, stock up on food and drink either at the dock or at the shrine shop. Apart from the route to the summit shrine, the trails are mostly untended and you should be cautious with some of the wooden walkways along the summit which are collapsing into rotten pulp. If you do get lost, head downhill towards the sea – there's a dirt road around all but the northern part of the island.

Places to Stay

Koganeyama Jinja Shrine (☎ 02254-5-2264), 15 minutes on foot up the steep hill from the dock, has spartan rooms set aside for hostellers; and basic meals are served. You can supplement the meals with food purchased from the shop outside the shrine – careful, the deer can mug the unwary! If you get up before 6 am you may be allowed to attend morning prayers. Most Japanese visitors seem to be day trippers – this means

the island is virtually deserted in the early morning and late afternoon.

The shrine also has a lodge for pilgrims which provides classier accommodation and food. Near the dock are a couple of unexciting minshuku.

Getting There & Away

Ferries to Ayukawa depart hourly between 9 am and 5 pm; the trip takes 25 minutes and the fare is Y1550/780 for a return/single.

A variation in routing is provided by the ferry – a high-speed catamaran – between Kinkazan Island and Onagawa which is the eastern gateway to the peninsula. There are four daily departures in both directions; the first ferry leaves between 9 and 10 am; the last leaves between 2 and 3 pm. The trip takes 30 minutes and the fare is Y3020/1600 for a return/single.

HIRAIZUMI 平泉

Of the few cultural sights in Tōhoku, Hiraizumi is one that should not be missed.

From 1089 to 1189, three generations of the Fujiwara family created a political and cultural centre in Hiraizumi which was claimed to approach the grandeur and sophistication of Kyoto. This short century of fame and prosperity was brought to an end when the last Fujiwara leader, Fujiwara Yasuhira, displayed such greed and treachery that he incurred the distrust of Minamoto Yoritomo who ordered the annihilation of the Fujiwara clan and the destruction of Hiraizumi.

Only a couple of the original temple buildings now remain; the rest have been restored or added over the centuries.

Things to See

Originally established in 850, **Chūson-ji Temple** was later expanded into a complex with over 40 temples and hundreds of residences for priests. A massive fire in 1337 destroyed most of the complex – even so, what you can see now is still most impressive.

Konjiki-dō (Golden Hall) was built in 1124. It's small but packed with gold ornamentation, black lacquerwork, and inlaid mother-of-pearl. Admission costs Y500 – the ticket is also valid for admission to Kyōzō Sutra Treasury and Sankōzō Treasury. It's open daily from 8.30 am to 5 pm but closes 30 minutes earlier from November to March.

Sankōzō Treasury houses temple treasures including the coffins and funeral finery of the Fujiwara clan.

Mōtsū-ji Temple once rivalled Chūson-ji in size and fame. All that remains now are foundation stones and the attractive Jōdo (paradise) garden. Admission to the gardens costs Y500. It's open from 8 am to 5 pm. Those staying at the youth hostel in the grounds do not have to pay for admission.

Takkoku-no-Iwaya Cave houses a temple. It's a few km south-west of Mōtsū-ji Temple. Admission costs Y200. It's open from 8 am to 5 pm but closes 30 minutes earlier from November to March. The cave can be reached in 10 minutes by bus or taxi; or cycle if you like.

Gembikei-kyō Gorge is a small canyon which is easily explored on foot. It's easily accessible by bus or taxi from Hiraizumi or Ichinoseki. This is not to be confused with **Geibikei-kyō Gorge**, which is much more impressive. The best way to reach the latter is either to take a taxi from Hiraizumi; or take a 45-minute bus ride (Y570) from Ichinoseki Station to Geibikei-kyō Iriguchi which is the entrance to the gorge. Between April and November, there are flat-bottomed boats with singing boatmen ferrying their passengers up and down the river between the sheer cliffs of the gorge. The trip takes 1½ hours and costs Y1030. Boats depart hourly between 8.30 am and 4 pm.

Places to Stay

Mōtsū-ji Youth Hostel (☎ 0191-46-2331) is part of Mōtsū-ji Temple and a pleasantly peaceful place to stay – guests at the hostel are not charged admission to the gardens. The temple is eight minutes on foot from Hiraizumi Station.

Getting There & Away

To reach Hiraizumi from Sendai, take the JR Tōhoku Shinkansen line to Ichinoseki (35 minutes); then take the bus which goes via Hiraizumi Station to Chuji Temple (Y320, 26 minutes). You can also take the JR Tōhoku Honsen line from Sendai to Hiraizumi Station, but a change of trains is usually necessary at Ichinoseki and the trip takes about two hours.

From Morioka to Ichinoseki on the JR Tōhoku Shinkansen line takes 43 minutes. Trains between Ichinoseki and Morioka on the JR Tōhoku Honsen line are less frequent and take about 1¾ hours.

Getting Around

Frequent buses run from Ichinoseki Station via Hiraizumi Station to Chūson-ji Temple. The walk from Hiraizumi Station to Chūson-ji Temple takes about 20 minutes and is not particularly appealing. To reach Mōtsū-ji Temple from the station requires an easy walk for about 10 minutes. Bicycles are available for hire outside the station.

MORIOKA 盛岡

From its origins as a castle town in the late 16th century, Morioka has developed into one of the largest cities in Tōhoku. Although there are very few sights in the city, it is a terminus for the JR Tōhoku Shinkansen line and this makes it a useful staging-point for visiting the northern part of Tōhoku.

Places to Stay

The Tourist Information Centre at the station has lists for moderate or inexpensive accommodation and can help with making reservations.

Morioka Youth Hostel (☎ 0196-62-2220) can be reached from Morioka Station. Take a bus from terminal No 11 – not all buses are suitable so check first – and get off after 15 minutes at Takamatsu-no-ike-guchi bus stop. It's a three-minute walk from there to the hostel.

Ryokan Kumagai (☎ 0196-51-3020), a member of the Japanese Inn Group, is eight minutes on foot from the station. Singles/doubles/triples start at Y3700/6800/9000.

Another Japanese Inn Group member,

Tamaya Ryokan (☎ 0196-22-8500), is 10 minutes by bus from Morioka Station and close to the Hachiman-gū Shrine. Singles/doubles/triples start at Y4000/7000/10,000.

Getting There & Away

From Morioka to Tokyo (Ueno) on the JR Tōhoku Shinkansen line the fastest trains take a mere 2¾ hours. If you are heading further north to Aomori by train, you should change to the JR Tōhoku line for the 2½-hour trip.

Lake Tazawa-ko, just west of Morioka, is reached via the JR Tazawako line. To visit the Hachimantai area, north-west of Morioka, take the JR Hanawa line to either Obuke Station or Hachimantai Station; then continue by bus. To reach Miyako, on the eastern coast of Tōhoku, take the JR Yamada line.

MT IWATE-SAN

The volcanic peak of Mt Iwate-san is a dominating landmark, north-west of Morioka, and a popular destination for hikers. From Morioka Station, you can take a bus north-west to Amihari Onsen (Y1240, 65 minutes) which is the start of one of the main trails to the summit. Another popular approach is to take the train north on the JR Tōhoku line to Takizawa Station; then change to a bus for Yanagisawa where you can join the steep trail to the summit.

MT OSORE-ZAN 恐山

This volcano has been held in awe as a mysterious, sacred place for many centuries. As you approach Osore-zan by road, the stench of sulphuric gas intensifies – it's definitely the mountain, not the passengers! Rhododendrons are the only plants that can hack it in this environment. After paying Y300 admission, you can walk through the temple grounds, past the bathhouses, and crunch your way along the trails of volcanic rock crisscrossed by rivulets of green and yellow sludge. It's an unworldly scene: hissing vents in the ground; flocks of ravens; shrines dotted across the barren slopes surrounded with garishly coloured toys and childrens' whirligigs spinning in the breeze. Paths lead down to the leaden waters of the lake that has formed in the caldera. The small statues of Jizō, the Buddhist deity in charge of the spirits of departed children, are covered with bibs and sweets.

Places to Stay

The staff at the information office inside Mutsu Bus Terminal don't speak English, but they will do their best to help you book accommodation. There are plenty of minshuku in the drab confines of Mutsu; and there are more expensive hotels and ryokan at Yagen Onsen, a scenic hot spring resort in the mountains, about 80 minutes by bus from Mutsu.

Of the two youth hostels on the peninsula – both in remote locations – you might find the most useful one is *Wakinosawa Youth Hostel* (☎ 0175-44-2341) which is handy for the excursion along Hotokegaura, the spectacular western coast of the peninsula, and for the ferry connection to Aomori.

Getting There & Away

From Mutsu Bus Terminal, it's a 35-minute bus ride (Y640) to Mt Osore-zan. The last bus to the mountain is at 3.20 pm; 4.45 pm during the festivals. The service closes down for the winter between November and April.

There are buses running between Aomori and Mutsu Bus Terminal via Noheji. From Mutsu Bus Terminal – the centre of transport action for the peninsula, but a real dump of a place otherwise – there are buses to Oma where you can catch the ferry to Hokkaidō.

From Oma, there are ferries to Hakodate and Muroran on Hokkaidō. There are three daytime departures (6.30 and 11.25 am, and 5.25 pm) to Hakodate. The trip takes just over 1½ hours and the cheapest passenger fare is Y1000. During August, there are also two sailings in the evening (8.35 and 10.20 pm).

There is one daily ferry to Muroran at 3 pm. The trip takes five hours and the cheapest passenger fare is Y1400. During June and July there is usually an extra sailing at 9.20 am.

There is also a ferry service which takes about an hour for the trip between Aomori and Wakinosawa. From Wakinosawa, there are boat excursions via Hotokegaura to Sai. The trip takes 1½ hours (Y2160). A bus service links Sai with Mutsu Bus Terminal in 2¼ hours (Y1960).

MT HAKKODA-SAN 八甲田山

Just south of Aomori is a scenic region around Mt Hakkōda-san which is popular with hikers, hot spring enthusiasts, and skiers.

A bus service from Aomori reaches the Hakkōda cable car in 70 minutes, then continues to Lake Towada-ko. The cable car whisks you up to the summit of Mt Tamoyachiyama in nine minutes (Y980 one way). From there you can follow a network of hiking trails. Some trails in this area are covered in *Hiking in Japan* by Paul Hunt.

HIROSAKI 弘前

With the exception of its dreary modern centre – which can be avoided – Hirosaki has retained much of its original architecture including a large portion of its castle area, temple districts, and even a few buildings from the Meiji era. There are just a few sights that can be covered in a day at an easy walking pace.

Things to See

There are festival floats and crafts on display at the **Neputa Mura (Neputa Museum)**, which is set up as a type of 'village' and allows visitors to follow a circuit through several sections devoted to different topics. Admission costs Y500. It's open from 9 am to 5 pm (April to mid-November) but closes an hour earlier during the rest of the year.

Hirosaki-jō Castle was completed in 1611, but the main keep burnt down in 1627 after being struck by lightning. It was rebuilt in 1810 and this attractive structure has survived. **Saishō-in Temple** is south of the castle, about 15 minutes on foot. From there, about 20 minutes to the north on foot, you come to an avenue – flanked by temples on

either side – which leads to **Chōshō-ji Temple**.

Places to Stay

Hirosaki Youth Hostel (☎ 0172-33-7066) is in a good location for the sights, but it's a bit drab.

From Hirosaki Station, take a bus from the No 3 bus stop and get off after about 15 minutes at Daigaku-byōin. Walk straight up the street for five minutes and the hostel is on your left down an alley.

Hotel Hokke Club Hirosaki (☎ 0172-34-3811) is in the centre, 10 minutes on foot from the station. Most of the rooms are Western-style and prices for singles start around Y6000.

Getting There & Away

Between mid-April and early November, there are up to six buses from Hirosaki Bus Centre to Lake Towada-ko.

The bus climbs through the mountains and passes remote hot spring hamlets. To reach Aoni Onsen (☎ 0172-52-3243), a rustic group of ryokan that prefer oil lamps to electricity and serve wholesome mountain food, you'll have to get off the bus at Aoni Onsen Iriguchi then walk about an hour up the track. Advance reservations are necessary and you should expect to pay around Y6000 per person including two meals.

The bus makes a short stop at Taki-nozawa, a scenic lookout across the lake, before descending to Nenokuchi beside the lake.

Morioka is linked with Hirosaki by a JR bus service which takes 2¼ hours (Y2880).

From mid-April to late October, there are buses from Hirosaki Bus Centre to Mt Iwaki-san.

If travelling by train, Hirosaki is connected with Aomori on the JR Ou line in 35 minutes by limited express. The same line runs south from Hirosaki to Akita in about 2½ hours by limited express.

MT IWAKI-SAN 岩木山

Soaring above Hirosaki is this sacred volcano which is a popular climb for both pilgrims and hikers.

From mid-April to late October, there are buses from Hirosaki Bus Terminal to Mt Iwaki-san. The trip takes 80 minutes to Hachigōme at the foot of the cable car below the summit. After a seven-minute ride (Y350) on the cable car, it then takes another 45 minutes to climb to the summit (1625 metres). This route is the shortest and easiest – the youth hostel in Hirosaki has maps showing other climbing routes and times.

An autumn festival known as *Oyamasankei* is celebrated on the mountain, usually in September. A colourful procession of local farmers climbs from Iwaki-san Jinja Shrine to the summit to complete ancient harvest thanksgiving rites.

LAKE TOWADA-KO

This is a large crater lake with impressive scenery. It is rated by Japanese as the top tourist spot in Tōhoku, which means you can expect lots of company! The main town on the lake is Yasumiya which is nothing special, just a staging post and centre for boat trips around the lake.

Nenoguchi, a small tourist outpost on the east shore of the lake, marks the entrance to the **Oirase Valley**. The 3½-hour hike up this valley to Ishigedo (refreshment centre and bus stop) is the most enjoyable thing to do around the lake.

There are frequent buses from mid-April to early November which link the valley with Aomori and Hirosaki. You can take a boat or a bus between Yasumiya and Nenoguchi.

Places to Stay

Hakubutsu-kan Youth Hostel (☎ 0176-75-2002) is tucked away *inside* the Grand Hotel, a few metres from the pier at Yasumiya. The Grand Hotel has a quota of rooms reserved for hostellers – you just front up at the reception desk and receive the keys to a comfortable room for the price of a bunk bed elsewhere.

The *Oirase Youth Hostel* (☎ 0176-74-2031) is at Yakeyama, just north of Ishigedo. It charges a very reasonable Y1500 per person between April and September; Y1900 during the rest of the year.

Getting There & Away

There are two bus centres in Yasumiya: one is for JR buses; the other is for the other services. Both are a couple of minutes on foot from the pier.

Between mid-April and early November, there are up to six buses from Hirosaki Bus Terminal to Lake Towada-ko – more details are provided in the Getting There & Away section for Hirosaki.

Between mid-April and mid-November, JR operates a frequent bus service from Aomori to Lake Towada-ko (three hours; Y2470) – more details are provided in the Getting There & Away section for Aomori.

There are also direct buses from Odate (two hours; Y1570) and Morioka (2¼ hours; Y2380).

If you want to visit the region around Mt Hachimantai, there are buses from Lake Towada-ko to Hachimantai Chōjō bus stop, the main point of access to the summit. This service only operates three times a day from May to late October; the trip takes about 2¾ hours and the ticket costs Y2260 – a reserved seat costs Y210 extra. From Hachimantai you can continue east to Morioka by bus; or take the bus south to Lake Tazawa-ko.

TSURUOKA 鶴岡

Tsuruoka was formerly a castle town and has now developed into a modern city with a couple of sights, but it is of primary interest to travellers as the main access point for the nearby trio of sacred mountains – Mt Haguro-san, Mt Yudono-san and Mt Gassan, known collectively as Dewa Sanzan.

Places to Stay

There are dozens of *shukubō* (temple lodgings) at Tōge, a convenient base at the foot of Mt Haguro-san. The Tourist Information Centre at the station has lists and can help with reservations. Expect prices to start around Y5500 per person including two meals – *sansai* (mountain greens) and vegetarian temple food are a speciality. The bus terminal at Tōge also has an information centre which can give help with accommodation.

Tsuruoka Youth Hostel (☎ 0235-73-3205) is not in a convenient location – a 15-minute walk from Sanze Station, three stops southwest of Tsuruoka Station.

Getting There & Away

Between April and November there is a bus service between Tsuruoka and Yamagata – the trip takes 1¾ hours. Three of the daily departures go via the Yudonosan Hotel, which provides access to Mt Yudono-san. There is also a bus service between Tsuruoka and Sendai which takes 3¾ hours.

Buses to Mt Haguro-san leave from Tsuruoka Station and take 35 minutes to reach Haguro Bus Terminal, in the village of Tōge; then continue for 15 minutes to the terminus at Haguro-sanchō. From July to October, there are a couple of buses which save pilgrim sweat by doing the climb from this terminus towards the peak of Mt Gas-san as far as Hachigōme (the Eighth Station) in 50 minutes (Y660).

Between June and late October there are infrequent buses direct to Sennin-Zawa on Mt Yudono-san. The trip takes 80 minutes (Y1390).

Tsuruoka is on the JR Uetsu train line with connections north to Akita in 1¾ hours by limited express; or connections south to Niigata in 2¼ hours by limited express.

DEWA SANZAN 出羽三山

Dewa Sanzan or 'the Three Mountains of Dewa', is the collective title for three sacred peaks (Mt Hagurosan, Mt Gassan and Mt Yudonosan) that have been worshipped for centuries by *yamabushi* (mountain priests) and followers of the Shugendō sect.

Mt Haguro-san

This mountain has several attractions with ease of access which ensures a busy flow of visitors. From Tsuruoka Station, there are buses to Tōge, a village consisting mainly of shukubō at the base of the mountain. The orthodox approach to the shrine on the summit of the mountain requires the pilgrim to climb hundreds of steps from here; the less tiring approach is to take the bus to the top.

The climb is well worth the trouble and can be done at a very leisurely pace in about 50 minutes – take your time and enjoy the woods.

From the bus terminal at Tōge, walk straight ahead through an entrance gate and continue across a bridge into beautiful cryptomeria woods with trees forming a canopy overhead. On the way you pass a marvellous, weatherbeaten, five-storeyed pagoda which dates from the 14th century. Then comes a long slog up hundreds of stone steps arranged in steep sections. Pause halfway at a teahouse for refreshment and a view across the hills to the sea.

As you continue up the steps, you come to a small water font on your right. You can make a pleasant excursion away from the main track by taking the path branching off to the right to visit a peaceful glade with a simple pavilion and a pond full of fat, crimson-bellied newts, water lilies and croaking frogs. To return to the main track, you'll need to retrace your steps.

Mt Gas-san

Mt Gas-san (1980 metres), the highest peak of the three, attracts pilgrims to Gassan Jinja Shrine on the peak itself. The peak is linked by a trail from Mt Haguro-san to Mt Yudono-san. The usual hiking route starts from Hachigōme (the Eighth Stage on Mt Hagurosan), passes through the alpine plateau of Midagahara to the Ninth Stage in 1¾ hours; and then requires an uphill grind for 70 minutes to the shrine. The trail between Hachigōme and Gassan Jinja Shrine is *only* open between 1 July and 10 October.

The descent on the other side to Yudonosan Jinja Shrine takes another 2½ hours. After about 40 minutes of this descent, you also have the choice of taking the trail to Ubazawa, the main ski resort on Mt Gassan, with its own cable car.

Mt Yudono-san

The mountain is approached via a three-km toll road from Yudonosan Hotel to Sennin-Zawa. From there, you can either walk uphill for another three km or pay Y150 to take the convenient bus (nice little earner for the shrine management) to the shrine approach. The shrine is then a 10-minute hike further up the mountain.

Yudonosan Jinja, the sacred shrine on this mountain, is not a building, but a large orange rock continuously lapped by water from a hot spring. Admission costs Y300 – another nice little earner! Take off your shoes and socks, pay the fee, receive your blessing with a type of feather duster, deposit your prayer slip into a nearby channel of water, then proceed into the inner sanctum where you perform a barefoot circuit of the rock, paddling through the cascading water. Respect the signs outside the shrine prohibiting photos.

NIIGATA 新潟

Niigata, the capital of the prefecture, is an important industrial centre and functions as a major transport hub. The city itself has few sights. Most foreign visitors use Niigata as a gateway for Sado-ga-shima Island or as a connection with Khabarovsk (USSR) as part of a trip on the Trans-Siberian Railway.

Information

The Tourist Information Centre (☎ 025-241-7914), on your left as you leave on the north side of Niigata Station, has to win top marks for friendly service.

Places to Stay

The Tourist Information Centre can help with accommodation suggestions to suit most budgets. There are plenty of business hotels around the station. *Ben Cougar Hotel – No 3* (☎ 025-243-3900) has singles/doubles from Y3800/5900. Similar hotels, with slightly higher prices, in the same area are *Green Hotel* (☎ 025-246-0341) and *Hotel Rich Niigata* (☎ 025-243-1881).

Ryokan Furukawa-tei Honten (☎ 0250-62-2013), a member of the Japanese Inn Group, is on the outskirts of Niigata in the town of Suibara. Prices for singles/doubles/triples start at Y4000/7000/9000. The ryokan is 15 minutes on foot from Suibara Station on the JR Uetsu line.

Getting There & Away

Niigata has flights to Khabarovsk (USSR) which connect with departures on the Trans-Siberian railway. The Aeroflot office (☎ 025-244-5935) is a couple of minutes on foot from the station. Flights link Niigata with Ryōtsu on Sado-ga-shima Island in 25 minutes (Y7,400). There are also flights to Tokyo, Osaka, Nagoya, Sendai and Sapporo.

There are long-distance buses to Tokyo (five hours, Y5150), and a night bus to Kyoto (8¼ hours, Y8750) and Osaka.

Niigata is connected with Tokyo by the JR Jōetsu Shinkansen line in 96 minutes (Asahi) or 2¼ hours (Toki).

Travelling north, Niigata is linked via the JR Uetsu line with Tsuruoka (two hours) and Akita (four hours). Travelling south-west on the JR Hokuriku line, it takes four hours to Kanazawa, and direct trains also continue to Kyoto and Osaka. To travel from Niigata to Matsumoto requires a routing via Nagano which takes 3¾ hours.

The Shin-Nihonkai Ferry from Niigata to Otaru (Hokkaidō) is excellent value at Y5150 for a passenger ticket. The trip takes 18 hours and there are six sailings per week. The appropriate port is Niigata kō which is 20 minutes by bus from Niigata Station.

The ferry to Ryōtsu on Sado-ga-shima Island takes 2½ hours and the cheapest passenger fare is Y1780; there are between five and seven departures daily. The hydrofoil (also known as the 'jet foil') zips across in a mere hour, but costs a hefty Y5460. There are at least five departures daily between April and early November; just two or three during the rest of the year.

The ferries leave from Sado Kisen Terminal which is 10 minutes (Y160) by bus from the station.

Central Honshū
中部地方

Central Japan, often referred to as Chūbu, extends across the area sandwiched between Tokyo and Kyoto.

Chūbu divides into three geographical areas with marked differences in topography, climate and scenery. To the north, the coastal area along the Sea of Japan features rugged seascapes, whilst the central area inland encompasses spectacular mountain ranges and highlands which are dominated by the Japan Alps. In the south, the Pacific coast area is heavily industrialised, urbanised and densely populated.

The attractions of Chūbu lie in the central and northern areas, each of which can be skimmed in five days, but preferably give yourself two weeks for both. In terms of variety and interest, these areas of Chūbu amongst the star attractions in Japan.

The central area highlights includes some well-preserved traditional architecture (Takayama and the Kiso Valley), superb mountain scenery and hiking (especially Kamikōchi), and remote rural communities such as those in the Shōkawa Valley.

The northern area highlights include the cultural and artistic centre of Kanazawa, the seascapes and rural relaxation of the Noto-hantō Peninsula, and Eihei-ji Temple in Fukui-ken.

TAKAYAMA 高山
Takayama lies in the ancient Hida District tucked away between the mountains of the Japan Alps.

The town – particularly the centre (San-machi Suji) with its traditional inns, shops, and saké breweries – has retained much of the traditional architecture and intimacy that is mostly lacking in other cities in Japan. It's also an ideal size for walking or cycling round sights without being swamped by asphalt and traffic.

Takayama makes a good base for trips into the mountains (Kamikōchi, Hirayu Onsen, Shin-Hotaka cable car or Norikura), or to the Shōkawa valley with its traditional farmhouses. For Takayama itself, you should reserve a couple of days.

Orientation
All the main sights, except Hida Folk Village, are in the centre of town, which is a short walk from the station. The streets are arranged in a grid pattern, similar to Kyoto or Nara, and this makes it easy to get around. Hida Folk Village is a 10-minute bus ride to the west of the station.

Information
The fount of all brochures, maps, reservations and knowledge on Takayama and the surrounding region is the Hida Tourist Information Office (☎ 0577-32-5328) which is in front of the station.

Things to See
You can get an idea of how the authorities used to govern at **Takayama Jinya** (Historical Government House) – brutally. **Hida Minzoku Kōko-kan** (Archaeology Museum) displays craft items and archaeological objects in a traditional house which was constructed with secret passages and windows in case the owners needed to make a quick exit. **Fujii Bijutsu Mingeikan** (Folk Craft Museum) is close to the Archaeology Museum and displays folk art from Japan, China, and Korea. **Hirata Kinen-kan** (Folk Art Museum) is a merchant's house dating from the turn of the century. **Kyōdo Gangu-kan** (Gallery of Traditional Japanese Toys) is the place to go if you are keen on dolls and folk toys from the 17th century to the present day. **Takayama Shi Kyōdo-kan** (Local History Museum) is devoted to the crafts and traditions of the region. Pride of place is allotted to rustic images carved by Enshū, a woodcarving priest who wandered around the region in the 17th century. **Oita Yacho-kan** (Wild Bird Museum) is devoted to wild birds of the Japan Alps and surrounding areas. **Kusakabe Mingei-kan** (Kusakabe Heritage House) is a fine example of a wealthy merchant's house.

The best way to link **Teramachi** (Temple District) with **Shiroyama Kōen Park** is to follow the walking trail from the station, which takes a couple of hours. The Tourist Information Office in front of the station has a small, green booklet entitled *Temples & Shrines in Higashiyama Preserved Area* which gives details for many of the temples. Teramachi has over a dozen temples – the youth hostel is in Tenshō-ji Temple – and several shrines which you can wander round at your leisure before continuing to the lush greenery of the park. Various trails lead through the park and up the mountain to the ruins of Takayama-jō Castle. As you go down, you can take a look at **Shōren-ji Temple**.

Hida Minzoku Mura (Hida Folk Village) is a large open-air museum with dozens of traditional houses which once belonged to craftsmen and farmers in the Takayama region. The houses were dismantled at their original sites and rebuilt here. You should definitely include this museum in your visit to Takayama. Admission costs Y500 and your ticket is good for entry to both western and eastern sections of the Hida Folk Village. A glossy brochure gives more detail on the individual houses. It's open from 8.30 am to 5 pm. Although Hida Folk Village is itself an enjoyable place to walk around, the approach to the village from the station offers only an urban stroll – the bus ride zips you through the ugliness in 10 minutes.

Drop in on the **Sukyo Mahikari Suza** (Main World Shrine). This colossal, Orwellian structure with a golden roof topped by a glacé cherry, is visible from several km away. Sukyo Mahikari is the name given to a movement started in 1959 by Kotama Okada who emphasised a spiritual life centred around the basic principles of the universe. The founder's daughter, Oshienushihisama, arranged completion of the Main World Shrine in 1984. The activities of this spiritual movement, which has over half a million followers all over the world, concentrate on purification and include healing through the laying on of hands. The shrine is a 20-minute walk north-west of Hida Folk Village, or you can take a bus from Takayama Bus Station.

Festivals

Takayama is famed all over Japan for two major festivals which attract over half a million visitors. Book your accommodation well in advance.

Sannō Matsuri Festival takes place on 14 and 15 April. The starting point for the festival parade is Hie Jinja Shrine. *Hachiman Matsuri* Festival, which takes place on 9 and 10 October, is a slightly smaller version of Sannō Matsuri.

Places to Stay

If you are going to stay in Takayama for the big festivals in April or October, you must book months in advance and expect to pay up to 20% more than the rates during the rest of the year. Alternatively, you could stay elsewhere in the region and commute to Takayama for the festival.

Hida Takayama Tenshō-ji Youth Hostel (☎ 0577-32-6345) is a temple in the pleasant surroundings of Teramachi (temple district), but hostellers should be prepared to stick to a rigid routine. From the station, it takes about 20 minutes to walk across town to the hostel. A bed for the night costs Y1900.

Hachibei (☎ 0577-33-0573) is a minshuku place close to Hida No Sato Village. Take a bus to the Hida No Sato bus stop; from there it's an eight-minute walk to the north. Prices start at Y5500 per person including two meals.

Ryokan Seiryu (☎ 0577-32-0448) is modern in architecture, but centrally located. Prices start at Y7000 per person including two meals.

The *New Alps Hotel* (☎ 0577-32-2888) is just a minute's walk from the station. Singles/doubles start at Y4200/8000.

Places to Eat

There are numerous restaurants and teahouses in the San-machi Suji area, close to the breweries.

Suzuya (☎ 0577-32-2484) is a well-known restaurant with rustic décor, in the

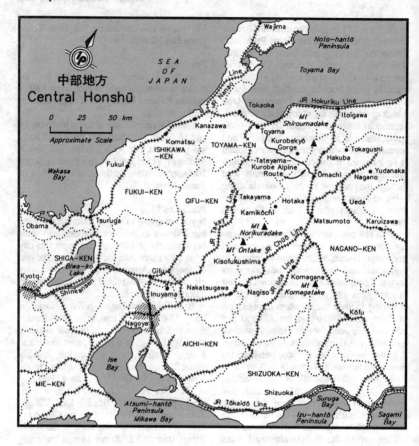

centre of town but on the other side of the river from San-machi Suji. It serves all the local specialities, and its lunchtime teishoku are good value at prices starting around Y1000. Opening hours are from 11 am to 8 pm, but it's closed on Tuesdays. If you turn left when leaving Kokubun-ji Temple, cross the intersection and continue towards the river; Suzuya is down the first street on your right.

For a complete change, you could try *Tom's Bellgins Bell* (☎ 0577-33-6507) at 24 Asahi-machi which is a couple of blocks west of Yayoibashi Bridge. The best way to find it is to phone for directions from the amiable Swiss owner, Tom Steinmann. Pizzas are a speciality and prices start around Y1200.

Getting There & Away

Winter snows disrupt or cancel bus schedules. A bus service connects Takayama with Hirayu Onsen (one hour) and takes another hour to reach Kamikōchi. Direct buses run from Takayama via Hirayu Onsen to Shin Hotaka Onsen and the nearby cable car.

Another bus route runs on the spectacular

Norikura Skyline highway connecting Norikura with Takayama in 1¾ hours.

The bus service between Kanazawa and Nagoya runs via Takayama and Shirakawa-gō, but only operates during the middle of the summer.

Takayama is connected with Nagoya on the JR Takayama line. The fastest limited express takes two hours and 50 minutes.

Express trains run from Osaka and Kyoto to Gifu or Nagoya and continue on the JR Takayama line to Takayama. The trip takes about five hours from Osaka and half an hour less from Kyoto.

Toyama is connected with Takayama on the JR Takayama line. The fastest express from Toyama takes around 1½ hours; the local train rambles to Takayama in just under three hours.

Providing you are equipped for mountain conditions, hitching is quite feasible in the Japan Alps between May and late September.

Getting Around

With the exception of Hida Folk Village, the sights in Takayama can easily and enjoyably be covered on foot.

The bus station is on your left as you leave the station. There is a circular bus route round the town and bus passes are available for one day (Y890) or two days (Y1350).

There are several bicycle hire shops near the station, in town and at the youth hostel.

SHOKAWA VALLEY 荘川

This unique region to the west of Takayama makes an interesting side trip. Although much of what you see here has been specially preserved for and supported by tourism, it still presents a view of rural Japan far removed from the usual images of the country as a giant urban factory or a genteel collection of temples. If you want to avoid large contingents of tourists, bear in mind that the peak seasons for this region are May, August and October.

The Shirakawa-gō District and Ogimachi consist of several clusters of houses in villages stretching for several km in the middle of the valley. Ogimachi, the central cluster,

is the most convenient place for bus connections, tourist information and orientation. When arriving by bus, ask to get off at the Gasshō-shuraku bus stop.

Things to See

To get your bearings on the village, you can climb up to **Tenbōdai** (Lookout Point), which has the view you will see on most tourist brochures. From Gasshō-shuraku bus stop, walk north down the main road for about 10 minutes. On your right you will see a wooded hill beside the road with a side road leading round the foot of the hill.

You can either follow the side road to the top of the hill, or, after walking about 10 metres down the side road, take the steep path on your right which gets you to the top in about 15 minutes.

The **Shirakawa-gō Gasshō No Sato Village** is a well presented collection of over a dozen *gasshō-zukuri* buildings (built in the 'hands in prayer' architectural style) mostly collected from the surrounding region and reconstructed in this open-air museum.

In the centre of Ogimachi, **Myōzen-ji Temple** is combined with a museum displaying the traditional paraphernalia of daily life.

Places to Stay

If you want to stay in a typical gasshō-zukuri house, the office has lists of these places which operate as ryokan or minshuku, and will make reservations. Ryokan prices start at Y7000 per person including two meals; minshuku prices for the same deal start at Y5500. *Juemon* (☎ 05769-6-1053) is one minshuku which has received consistently favourable comments from foreign visitors.

If you want the cheapest option in the area, you'll have to travel to *Etchū Gokayama Youth Hostel* which is a gasshō-zukuri house in a more remote location (about two km on foot from the bus stop on the main road) close to Gokayama.

Getting There & Away

There are direct JR buses, running twice daily, between Nagoya and Ogimachi during the following peak seasons: from 28 April to

10 May, from 20 July to 31 August, from 10 October to 3 November, and from 28 December to 15 January. The price for a one-way ticket is about Y4500 and the trip takes 5½ hours. Advance bookings are recommended. Slight alterations are made to these dates every year so you should check exact details before travelling.

Another bus service is operated once a day by Nagoya Tetsudo and runs between Nagoya and Kanazawa via Ogimachi between 1 July and 12 November. The price for a one-way ticket on this service from Ogimachi to Kanazawa costs about Y2200 and the trip takes about three hours.

Bus connections between Takayama and Ogimachi run four times daily and are made in two stages. The first stage is a bus service operated by Nohi bus company between Takayama and Makido. The trip takes just over an hour and a one-way ticket costs Y1800.

The second stage is a connecting bus service operated by JR between Makido and Ogimachi. The trip takes about an hour and a one-way ticket costs Y1200 – unless, of course, you have a JR Railpass.

KISO VALLEY (KISOJI) 木曽川

A visit to this region is highly recommended if you want to see several small towns with architecture carefully preserved from the Edo period. As a bonus, there's the opportunity to combine your visit to Magome and Tsumago with an easy walk. The thickly forested Kiso Valley lies in the south-west of Nagano-ken and is surrounded by the Japan Alps.

Things to See

A favourite pastime is hiking the old post road between Magome and Tsumago. **Magome** is a small post town with rows of traditional houses and post inns (and souvenir shops!) lining a steep street. The Tourist Information Office (☎ 0264-59-2336) is a short way up, on the right-hand side of the street. The office is open from 8.30 am to 5 pm and dispenses tourist literature as well as

making reservations for accommodation. Close by is a museum devoted to the life and times of Shimazaki Tōson (1872-1943) – a famous literary figure. His novel *Ie* (published in English under the title *The Family*) draws on his experiences here.

To walk from Magome to Tsumago, continue toiling up the street until the houses eventually give way to a forest path which winds down to the road leading up a steep hill to Magome kōge (pass). This initial walk from Magome to the pass takes about 45 minutes and is not particularly appealing because you spend most of your time on the road. You can cut out this first section by taking the bus between Magome and Tsumago and getting off after about 12 minutes at the pass.

There's a small shop-cum-teahouse at the top of the pass where the trail leaves the road and takes you down to the right along a pleasant route through the forest. From the teahouse to Tsumago takes just under two hours – allow time to stop at waterfalls or ponder the Latin names thoughtfully labelled on plants beside the trail.

Tsumago is geared to tourism, and so well preserved it feels like an open-air museum. Designated by the government as a protected area for the preservation of traditional buildings, no modern developments such as TV aerials or telephone poles are allowed to mar the picture. The Tourist Information Office (☎ 0264-57-3123), open from 8.30 am to 5 pm, is halfway down the main street. Tourist literature on Tsumago and maps are available, and the staff are happy to make reservations for accommodation.

As a special service for walkers on the trail between Magome and Tsumago, both the tourist offices offer a baggage forwarding service. For a nominal fee of Y300 per piece of luggage, you can have your gear forwarded; the deadline for the morning delivery is 9 am, and the deadline for the afternoon delivery is 1 pm. The service operates daily from 20 July to 31 August; but is restricted to Saturdays, Sundays and national holidays between 1 April and 19 July and throughout September and November.

Places to Stay & Eat

Both the Tourist Information Offices special-ise in helping reserve accommodation for visitors – telephone enquiries can only be dealt with in Japanese. There are many ryokan and minshuku. Prices for a room and two meals at a ryokan start around Y8000; minshuku prices for a similar deal start around Y5500. *Minshuku Daikichi* (☎ 0264-57-2595) is a friendly place just four minutes on foot from the bus terminal.

Magome and Tsumago have several res-taurants on the main streets. The local specialities include *gohei-mochi* (rice dump-ling coated with nut sauce, on a stick), and sansai (mountain greens) which can be ordered as a set meal (sansai teishoku) for about Y800.

Getting There & Away

The main railway stations on the JR Chūō line for access to Magome and Tsumago are Nakatsugawa Station and Nagiso Station respectively. Some services do not stop at these stations, which are about 12 minutes apart by limited express – check the time-table. The trip between Nagoya and Nakatsugawa takes 55 minutes by limited express; the limited express between Naka-tsugawa and Matsumoto takes 85 minutes. Direct buses also operate between Nagoya and Magome; the trip takes just under two hours.

Buses leave hourly from in front of Nakatsugawa Station for Magome (30 minutes) where you can do the walk to Tsumago. There's also an infrequent bus service between Magome and Tsumago (30 minutes). If you decide to start your walk from the kōge (pass), take this bus and get off at the bus stop at the top of the pass.

From Tsumago, either walk (1½ hours) to Nagiso Station or take the bus (nine minutes).

KISO-FUKUSHIMA & MT ONTAKE
木曽福島、御岳

Kiso-Fukushima was an important barrier gate and checkpoint on the old post road. From the station, it takes about 20 minutes on foot to reach several old residences, museums and temples.

Mt Ontake (3063 metres) is an active volcano – entry to the crater area is prohib-ited. For centuries the mountain has been considered sacred and an important destina-tion for pilgrims.

There are several trails to the summit. One popular trailhead is at Nakanoyu, 80 minutes by bus from Kiso-Fukushima Station. From the trailhead, it takes about 3½ hours to hike to the summit. Another railhead is at Tan-ohara, which is 1¾ hours by bus from Kiso-Fukushima Station; the hike to the summit takes about three hours.

An inexpensive place to stay is *Kiso Ryōjōan Youth Hostel* (☎ 0264-23-7716) which is a short bus ride from Kiso-Fukushima Station. Take the 25-minute bus ride to Ohara Bus Terminal – the hostel is three minutes on foot from there and pro-vides a useful base for hiking or sightseeing in the area.

Kiso-Fukushima is on the Chūō line, and limited expresses run to Nagoya in 1½ hours, or to Matsumoto in 40 minutes.

TENRYUKYO GORGE & MT KOMAGATAKE
天竜峡、駒ケ岳

Both Tenryūkyō Gorge and Mt Komagatake lie east of the Kiso Valley and are easily reached via the JR Iida line which runs roughly parallel to the Chūō line.

The main sightseeing approach for Tenryūkyō Gorge is a 1½-hour boat trip down the Tenryū River and through the gorge. Boats leave from the dock close to Ichida Station.

Mt Komagatake (2956 metres) is a popular hiking destination. From Komagane Station, a 55-minute bus ride takes you up to the base station of the cable car at Shirabi-taira. The eight-minute cable-car ride whisks you up to Senjōjiki. From there, the hike to the peak takes about 2½ hours.

There are numerous pensions, minshuku and ryokan around the town, and several mountain huts along the trails. If you stay at *Komagane Youth Hostel* (☎ 0265-83-3856), you need to take a 15-minute bus ride from the station, then walk for 12 minutes.

KARUIZAWA 軽井沢

This place lies at the foot of Mt Asamayama and lays claim to being Japan's trendiest summer resort. The Japanese will all tell you it's a great place and urge you to go there. Unfortunately, it's become a booming centre for outdoor pursuits such as golf, tennis and horse-riding. Naturally, the pursuit of shopping has received due attention in the shape of a 'Ginza' street duplicating all the fashionable boutiques. In other words, unless your idea of nature includes vending machines and crushed velvet carpeting, this is a place to avoid. The one thing worth doing here is to climb **Mt Asamayama**, but this is currently prohibited because it is known to have erupted at least 50 times and has recently become active again.

BESSHO ONSEN 別所温泉

This town was established around the hot springs during the Heian period. It flourished as an administrative centre during the Kamakura period and this cultural influence encouraged the construction of several temples, notably **Anraku-ji Temple** which is renowned for its octagonal pagoda, **Chūzen-ji Temple**, and **Zenzan-ji Temple**. Anraku-ji Temple is 10 minutes on foot from Bessho Onsen Station. If you have a couple of hours to spare for a five-km rural hike, you can continue east to visit the temples of Chūzen-ji and Zenzan-ji.

If you want an inexpensive place to stay in Bessho Onsen, the *Ueda Mahoroba Youth Hostel* (☎ 0268-38-5229) is eight minutes on foot from the station.

To reach Bessho Onsen, first travel on the JR Shin-etsu Honsen line to Ueda, then change to the Ueda Railway for the 30-minute ride to Bessho Onsen.

NAGANO 長野

Nagano is a thriving industrial centre and transport hub. The star attractions are **Zenkō-ji Temple**, which attracts millions of pilgrims every year, and the superb recreational facilities in the surrounding region.

Kyōju-in Youth Hostel (☎ 0262-32-2768) is a temple in a side street a couple of minutes on foot east of Zenkō-ji Temple. As you might expect, shukubō (temple lodgings) are available around Zenkō-ji Temple (☎ 0262-34-3591).

TOGAKUSHI 戸隠

Togakushi is a popular destination for hikers, particularly in late spring and during autumn. In the winter, skiers favour the slopes around **Mt Menōyama** and **Mt Kurohimeyama**. The one-hour hike to **Togakushi-Okusha Sanctuary** includes a pleasant section along a tree-lined approach.

For an inexpensive place to stay, there's *Togakushi Kōgen Yokokura Youth Hostel* (☎ 0262-54-2030) which is a couple of minutes from the bus stop.

Togakushi is north of the highway between Hakuba and Nagano.

YUDANAKA 湯田中

This town is famous for its hot springs, particularly those known as Jigokudani Onsen (Hell Valley Hot Springs), which attract monkeys keen to escape the winter chill with a leisurely immersion.

Uotoshi Ryokan (☎ 0269-33-1215), a member of the Japanese Inn Group, charges Y4000 per person per night. You can either arrange to be picked up at the station or walk from there to the ryokan in seven minutes.

From Nagano, take the Nagano Dentetsu Railway for the 40-minute ride to Yudanaka.

HAKUBA 白馬

The town of Hakuba is a staging point providing access for outdoor activities in the nearby mountains. Skiing in the winter and hiking or mountaineering in the summer attract large numbers of visitors. The ascent of Mt Shirouma-dake is very popular, but you should be properly prepared. There are several mountain huts which provide meals and basic accommodation along the trails.

Things to See

For alpine flora, visit **Tsugaike Shizen-en** (Tsugaike Natural Park), which lies below Mt Norikura-dake in an alpine marshland. A three-hour hiking trail takes in most of the park.

Happō-one is a busy ski resort in the winter, and hiking area in the summer. From Hakuba Station, a five-minute bus ride takes you to Happō, then walk for eight minutes to the gondola base station. From the top station of the gondola you can use two more lifts, and then hike along a trail for an hour or so to Happō Ike Pond on a ridge below Mt Karamatsu-dake. From this pond you can follow a trail leading to Mt Maruyama (one hour), continue for 1½ hours to the Karamatsudake Sansō (mountain hut), and then climb to the peak of Mt Karamatsu-dake (2696 metres) in about 30 minutes.

OMACHI 大町

The city of Omachi has several stations, but the one to use is called Shinano-Omachi which has facilities for tourist information. The main reason for visiting Omachi is to start or finish the Tateyama-Kurobe Alpine Route, which is an expensive but impressive jaunt by various means of transport across the peaks between Nagano-ken and Toyama-ken.

An inexpensive place to stay is the *Kizaki-ko* Youth Hostel (☎ 0261-2-1820) which is 15 minutes on foot from Inao Station next to Lake Kizaki-ko – three stops north of Shinano-Omachi Station.

HOTAKA 穂高

This is a small town with a couple of sights, but it's especially popular with hikers and mountaineers who use it as a base to head into the mountains. The station office or the bicycle hire shop – to your right as you leave on the east side of the station – have basic maps for the town. You can either walk around the area or rent a bicycle – Y200 per hour. If you're staying at the youth hostel, you can also hire a bicycle there.

From Toyoshina Station, two stops south of Hotaka, it takes 10 minutes by taxi to reach Kitakaido, which is the start of a trail for experienced hikers to climb **Mt Jonen-dake** (2857 metres) – the ascent takes about eight hours.

MATSUMOTO 松本

Matsumoto is worth a visit for its superb castle and as a convenient base for exploration of the Japan Alps.

Information

Matsumoto Tourist Information Office (☎ 0263-32-2814) is on your right at the bottom of the steps at the east exit of Matsumoto Station.

Places to Stay & Eat

Asama Onsen Youth Hostel (☎ 0263-46-1335) is a bit distant, regimented and drab, but it's cheap. It closes at 9 pm and lights go out punctually at 10 pm. Just round the corner from the hostel is a student eatery, the *Tambien Coffee Shop*, which does inexpensive teishoku (set meals).

Utsukushigahara Sanjiro Youth Hostel (☎ 0263-31-2021) is on an alpine plateau, nearly an hour's bus ride from Matsumoto. It's closed from December to April. Take the bus for Utsukushigahara Bijutsukan and get off after 50 minutes at Sanjiro bus stop. The hostel is two minutes on foot from there.

Enjoh Bekkan (☎ 0263-33-7233) is a member of the Japanese Inn Group. The charges in this ryokan start at Y4800/Y9000 for a single/double – excluding meals. The total bill will include an additional 3% consumption tax, 3% local consumption tax, and Y150 spa tax per person. The hot spring facilities are available day and night. Western breakfast is available for Y800.

KAMIKOCHI 上高地

Kamikōchi lies in the centre of the northern Japan Alps and has some of the most spectacular scenery in Japan.

If you want to avoid immense crowds, don't plan to visit between late July and late August, or during the first three weeks in October. Between June and mid-July, there's a rainy season which makes outdoor pursuits depressingly soggy.

Despite the thousands of visitors, Kamikōchi has so far resisted the commercial temptation of development that might – as has happened elsewhere in Japan – destroy the original attractions. Let's hope it stays that way.

Information

Hiking in Japan by Paul Hunt covers some trails in the area.

At the bus terminal, an information office (☎ 0263-95-2405, late April to mid-November only), geared mostly for booking accommodation, also has leaflets and maps, but it's preferable to make prior use of the Tourist Information Offices in Takayama or Matsumoto, which have English-speaking staff.

Things to See

It's perfectly feasible to visit Kamikōchi from Matsumoto or Takayama in a day, but you'll miss out on the pleasures of staying in the mountains and the opportunity to take early morning or late evening walks before the crowds appear.

If you want to do level walking for short distances, without any climbing, then you should stick to the river valley. A sample three-hour walk (round trip) of this kind would proceed east from **Kappa Bashi Bridge** along the right-hand side of the river to **Myōjin Bashi Bridge** (45 minutes) and then continue to **Tokusawa** (45 minutes) before returning. For variety you could cross to the other side of the river at Myōjin Bashi Bridge.

West of Kappa Bashi Bridge, you can amble along the right-hand side of the river to **Wilson Monument** (15 minutes), or keep to the left-hand side of the river and walk to **Taishō Ike Pond** (20 minutes). A bridge across the river between Wilson Monument and Taishō Ike Pond provides variation for the walk.

There are dozens of long-distance options for hikers and climbers, varying in duration from a couple of days to a week. The large Japanese maps of the area show routes and average hiking times between huts, major peaks and landmarks – but you've got to be able to read Japanese or get someone to help with reliable decipherment. Favourite trails and climbs (which can mean human traffic jams on trails during peak seasons!) include **Mt Yarigatake** (3180 metres) and **Mt Hotaka-dake** (3190 metres), also known as Mt Okuhotaka-dake, and more distant destinations, such as **Nakabusa Onsen** and **Murodō** which is on the Tateyama-Kurobe Alpine Route.

If you want to hike between Kamikōchi and **Shin-Hotaka Onsen**, there's a steep trail which crosses the ridge below Mt Nishi Hotaka-dake (2909 metres) at Nishi Hotaka Sansō (Nishi Hotaka Mountain Cottage) and continues to Nishi Hotaka Guchi, the top station of the cable car for Shin-Hotaka Onsen. The hike takes nearly four hours (because of a steep ascent) – softies might prefer to to do the hike in the opposite direction!

Places to Stay

Accommodation is relatively expensive, advance reservations are essential during the peak seasons, and the whole place shuts down from November to May. You'd be well advised to make reservations before arriving in Kamikōchi – the Tourist Information Offices at Takayama and Matsumoto are convenient since they have English-speaking staff.

There is a handful of hotels mostly ranged around Kappa Bashi Bridge, a short walk from the bus terminal. *Gosenjaku Lodge* (☎ 0263-95-2221) and *Kamikōchi Nishiitoya Sansō* (☎ 0263-95-2206) provide a bed and two meals at prices starting from Y9000; for a bed only, you may get a reduction to around Y6000.

Dotted along the trails and around the mountains are dozens of mountain cottages or mountain huts (*san-sō* or *yama-goya*) which provide two meals and a bed at an average price of around Y6000. Given the usually lower standards of their food and lodging these are expensive, but they have to contend with a short season and difficult access, and most hikers are prepared to pay the premium for somewhere out of the cold.

There are campgrounds at Konashidaira (about 10 minutes beyond Kappa Bashi Bridge) and Tokusawa (about two hours from Kamikōchi).

The closest youth hostels are at Shirahone Onsen and on Norikura Kōgen Plateau – both within easy reach of Kamikōchi.

Getting There & Away

Bus services for Kamikōchi don't run between mid-November and late April; the exact dates can vary. If you plan to travel at the beginning or end of this period, check first with a tourist office or call Japan Travel-Phone toll free on 0120-222800.

The connection between Kamikōchi and Matsumoto involves rail and bus travel. For more details, refer to Matsumoto – Getting There & Away.

Between Takayama and Kamikōchi there are frequent bus connections but *only* from April to October. The bus runs via Nakanoyu and you have to change to another bus at Hirayu Onsen. The whole trip takes just over two hours (Y1480).

Between Norikura and Kamikōchi there are buses running via Hirayu Onsen approximately three times a day. The whole trip takes about two hours. The Norikura Skyline Highway is *only* open from 15 May to 31 October.

There is an infrequent bus service between Kamikōchi and Shirahone Onsen.

NORIKURA KOGEN PLATEAU & NORIKURA ONSEN
乗鞍高原、乗鞍温泉

This alpine plateau below Mt Norikura-dake (3026 metres) is popular with hikers and famous for the Norikura Skyline Highway (closed from November to May) – a scenic bus route which leads to Tatami-daira bus stop at the foot of the mountain. From there, a trail leads to the peak in about 1½ hours. Norikura Onsen is a hot spring resort on the plateau and a base for skiing and hiking which is open all year round.

Places to Stay

There is a choice of accommodation including ryokan, pensions and mountain huts. An inexpensive place to stay near the ski lifts is *Norikura Kōgen Youth Hostel* (☎ 0263-93-2748).

Getting There & Away

The bus between Norikura and Takayama operates along the Norikura Skyline Highway between May and October and usually runs via Hirayu Onsen. The ride takes about 1½ hours.

From July to mid-October, there's a bus between Norikura and Shin-Shimashima Station. The trip takes about an hour.

There are infrequent buses between Norikura and Shirahone Onsen and Kamikōchi.

Western Honshū
中国地方

Western Honshū has two main areas of interest. One is the southern region which, while heavily industrialised and densely populated, contains a number of interesting cities including Kurashiki and Hiroshima. Here you also find the island-dotted waters of the Inland Sea, sandwiched between Honshū and Shikoku.

The other major area of interest is the north coast. By Japanese standards, this region is comparatively uncrowded and rural. The north coast route takes you to the historically interesting towns of Hagi, Matsue, Tsuwano and Izumo.

KURASHIKI 倉敷

Kurashiki's claim to fame is a small quarter of picturesque buildings around a stretch of moat. There are a number of old black-tiled warehouses which have been converted into an eclectic collection of museums. Bridges arch over and willows dip into the river, and the whole effect is quite delightful; it's

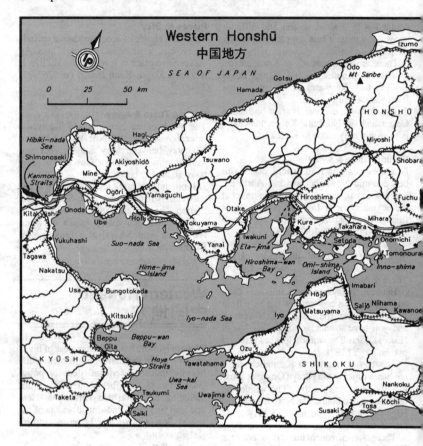

hardly surprising that the town is a favourite with tourists.

Things to See

The museums and galleries which are the town's major attraction are concentrated along the banks of the canal. The **Ohara Museum of Art** is undoubtedly Kurashiki's No 1 museum. Entry is Y600, opening hours are from 9 am to 5 pm and the museum is closed Mondays.

Between the Ohara Museum and the tourist office is the interesting **Kurashiki Ninagawa Museum** which houses a collec-

tion of Greek, Etruscan and Roman antiquities. Entry is Y600 and it's open from 8.30 am to 5 pm daily.

The **Japan Rural Toy Museum** displays folkcraft toys from Japan and around the world. Japanese rural toys are also on sale. Entry is Y310 and it's open from 8 am to 5 pm daily.

Places to Stay

Kurashiki Youth Hostel (☎ 0864-22-7355) is south of the canal area and costs Y2100 per night. It's a long climb to its hilltop location.

There are several good value minshuku

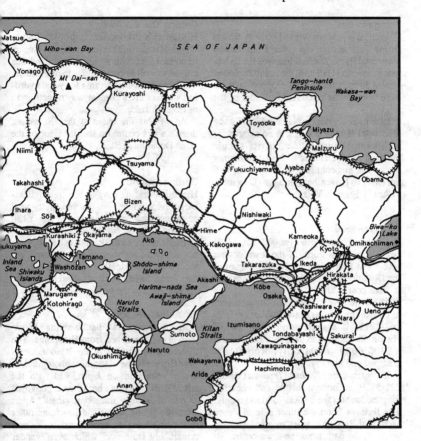

conveniently close to the canal. The *Tokusan Kan* (☎ 0864-25-3056) is near Ivy Square and offers a room-only price as well as a room and two meals at Y5500 per person. Right by the canal near the toy museum the small *Kawakami Minshuku* (☎ 0864-24-1221) is slightly cheaper.

Getting There & Away

Kurashiki, only 16 km from Okayama, is not on the shinkansen line. Travelling westwards, it's usually faster to disembark at Okayama and take a San-yō line local train to Kurashiki. These operate several times an hour; the trip takes just over 15 minutes and costs Y470. If you're going east, get off at the Shin-Kurashiki Station, two stops on the San-yō line from Kurashiki.

HIROSHIMA 広島

Although it's a busy, prosperous, not unattractive industrial city, visitors would have no real reason to leave the shinkansen in Hiroshima (population 1,070,000) were it not for that terrible instant on 6 August 1945 when the city became the world's first atomic bomb target.

Things to See

Hiroshima's modern symbol is the **A-Bomb Dome** just across the river from **Peace Memorial Park**. The building was the Industrial Promotion Hall until the bomb exploded almost directly above it. Its propped-up ruins have been left as an eternal reminder of the tragedy.

Like its equivalent in Nagasaki, the **Peace Memorial Museum** will win no awards for architectural inspiration but its simple message is driven home with sledgehammer force. The museum is open from 9 am to 6 pm (May to November), or 5 pm (December to April). Entry is Y50.

Places to Stay

Hiroshima Youth Hostel (☎ 082-221-5343) is about two km north of the town centre; take a bus from platform No 22 in front of the JR station or from platform No 29 behind it. Beds cost Y2090.

There are two Japanese Inn Group places in Hiroshima. The *Mikawa Ryokan* (☎ 082-261-2719) is a short stroll from the JR Hiroshima Station and has singles/doubles at Y3300/6000, room only. Rooms are cramped and gloomy.

In contrast, the *Minshuku Ikedaya* (☎ 082-231-3329) is modern, bright and cheerful. Singles/doubles are Y4000/7000 room only. The Ikedaya is on the other side of Peace Memorial Park in a quiet area but an easy walk via the park from the town centre. To get there, take tram No 6 or a Miyajima tram from the station and get off at the Dobashi stop.

Places to Eat

The familiar assortment of fast-food outlets including Shakey's Pizza, McDonalds and Mister Donut can be found in the Hon-dōri shopping arcade. *Andersen's* on Hon-dōri is a popular restaurant complex with an excellent bakery section, a good place for an economical breakfast. There are a variety of other restaurant sections in the Andersen's complex.

Getting There & Away

Hiroshima is an important stop on the Tokyo-Osaka-Hakata shinkansen route, and also an important port with a variety of Inland Sea cruises as well as connections to other cities. The Hiroshima-Matsuyama ferry and hydrofoil services are a popular way of getting to or from Shikoku.

As well as the buses at the JR station, there's a bus centre on the 3rd floor of the Sogo Department Store.

Getting Around

Hiroshima has an easy-to-use tram (streetcar) service which will get you pretty well anywhere you want to go for a flat Y130 (Y90 on the short No 9 route).

Buses are more difficult to use as they are not numbered and the names are in kanji, but the stands outside the station are clearly numbered. Take a bus from stand No 1 to the airport, No 2 to the port.

MIYA-JIMA ISLAND 宮島

Correctly known as Itsuku-shima, Miyajima is easily reached from Hiroshima. The famous floating torii of the **Itsukushima-jinja Shrine** is one of the most photographed tourist attractions in Japan, and with the island's Mt Misen as a backdrop is classified as one of Japan's 'three best views'. Apart from the shrine, the island has some other interesting temples, some good walks and remarkably tame deer which even wander the streets of the small town.

The ascent of 530-metre **Mt Misen** is the island's finest walk; the uphill part of the round trip can be avoided by taking the two-stage cable car for Y800 one way, Y1400 return. It leaves you about a 15-minute walk from the top. There are superb views from the summit and a variety of routes leading back down. The descent takes a good hour and walking paths also lead to other high points on the island, or you can just follow the gentle stroll through Maple Valley (Momiji-dani) which leads to the cable-car station.

There's also an aquarium, a popular

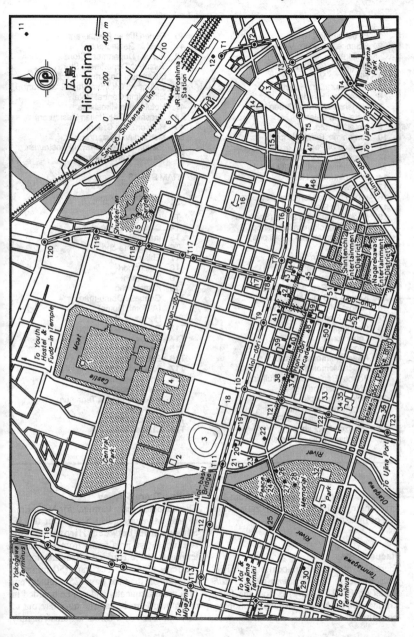

広島
Hiroshima

1	Hiroshima-jō Castle	40	Denen Italian Restaurant
2	Science & Culture Museum for Children	41	Suishin Restaurant
		42	Fukuya Department Store
3	Hiroshima Carp's Baseball Stadium	43	Tenmaya Department Store
4	Hiroshima Museum of Art	44	Mitsukoshi Department Store
5	Prefectural Art Museum	45	Tokugawa Okonomayaki Restaurant
6	Hotel New Hiroden	46	Hiroshima Central Hotel
7	Hiroshima Ekimae Green Hotel	47	Hotel Union Hiroshima
8	Hotel Sun Palace	48	Hiroshima T&K Italian Restaurant
9	Hotel Yamato	49	Hobson's Ice Cream
10	Hiroshima Terminal Hotel	50	Moti Indian Restaurant
11	Pagoda of Peace	51	Tokugawa Okonomayaki Restaurant
12	Hiroshima Station Hotel	52	Sera Bekkan Ryokan
13	Hiroshima Century City Hotel		
14	Hiroshima City Hotel		TRAM STOPS
15	Mikawa Ryokan		
16	World Peace Memorial Cathedral	T1	Hiroshima ekimae
17	Hotel Silk Plaza	T2	Enkobashi
18	Sogo Department Store (Sogo Bus Centre, Kinokuniya Bookshop)	T3	Matoba-cho
		T4	Danbara Ohata-cho
19	KDD (International Telephone)	T5	Inarimachi
20	ANA	T6	Kanayama-cho
21	A-Bomb Dome	T7	Ebisu-cho
22	Hiroshima Green Hotel	T8	Hatchobori
23	Atomic Bomb Epicentre	T9	Tatemachi
24	Children's Peace Memorial	T10	Kamiya-cho
25	Korean A-Bomb Memorial	T11	Genbaku Domu-mae (A-Bomb Dome)
26	Tourist Information Office		
27	Peace Flame	T12	Honkawa-cho
28	Cenotaph	T13	Tokaichimachi
29	Laundromat	T14	Dobashi
30	Minshuku Ikedaya	T15	Teramachi
31	Peace Memorial Museum	T16	Betsuin-mae
32	Peace Memorial Hall	T17	Jogakuin-mae
33	Former Bank of Japan Building	T18	Shukkeien-mae
34	ANA Hiroshima Hotel	T19	Katei Saibansho-mae
35	Hokke Club Hotel	T20	Hakushima Line Terminus
36	Hiroshima Tōkyū Inn	T21	Hon-dōri
37	Andersen's Bakery & Restaurant	T22	Fukuromachi
38	Maruzen Bookshop	T23	Chuden-mae
39	Hiroshima Kokusai Hotel		

beach, a seaside park and, across from the ferry landing, a display of local crafts in the Hall of Industrial Traditions.

Places to Stay

There is no cheap accommodation on Miyajima although the *Miyajima-guchi Youth Hostel* (☎ 0829-56-1444) is near the ferry terminal and JR Miyajima-guchi Station on the mainland.

Getting There & Away

The mainland ferry terminal for Miya-jima is near Miyajima-guchi Station on the JR San-yō line between Hiroshima and Iwakuni. Miya-jima trams from Hiroshima terminate at the Hiroden-Miyajima stop by the ferry terminal. The tram (50 minutes) takes longer than the train (25 minutes) but runs more frequently and can be boarded in downtown Hiroshima. The tram fare out to Miya-jima is Y250. On some trams you may

1 広島城
2 こども文化科学館
3 広島市民球場
4 広島市美術館
5 広島県立美術館
6 ホテルニューヒロデン
7 広島駅前グリーンホテル
8 ホテルサンパラス
9 ホテルやまと
10 広島ターミナルホテル
11 平和塔
12 広島ステイションホテル
13 広島センチュリーシティホテル
14 広島シティホテル
15 三河旅館
16 世界平和記念聖堂
17 ホテルシルクプルザ
18 そごう百貨店
19 KDD（国際電話）
20 ANA
21 原爆ドーム
22 広島グリーンホテル
23 広島市道路元標
24 原爆の子の像
25 韓国人原爆犠牲者慰霊碑
26 観光案内所
27 平和灯
28 原爆慰霊碑
29 洗衣店
30 民宿池田屋
31 平和記念資料館
32 平和記念館
33 以前の日本銀行ビル
34 広島全日空ホテル
35 法華クラブ
36 広島東急イン
37 アンデルセン
38 丸善本店
39 広島国際ホテル

40 テネンイタリャン料理
41 酔心レストラン
42 福屋百貨店
43 天満屋百貨店
44 三越
45 徳川おこのみやきレストラン
46 広島セントラルホテル
47 ホテルユニオン広島
48 広島TK イタリレストラン
49 ホブソン
50 モテイ
51 徳川おこのみやきレストラン
52 セラ別館旅館

TRAM STOPS

T1 広島駅前
T2 猿猴橋
T3 的場町
T4 段原大畑町
T5 稲荷町
T6 銀山町
T7 胡町
T8 八丁堀
T9 立町
T10 紙屋町
T11 原爆ドーム前
T12 本川町
T13 十日市町
T14 土橋
T15 寺町
T16 別院前
T17 女学院前
T18 縮景園前
T19 家庭裁判所前
T20 白島
T21 本通
T22 袋町
T23 中電前

have to transfer at the Hiroden-Hiroshima stop.

From the terminal, ferries shuttle across to Miya-jima in just 10 minutes for Y170. One of the ferries is operated by JR so Japan Rail Pass holders should make sure they use this one. Ferry services also operate to Miya-jima direct from Hiroshima. High-speed ferries (Y1120) take just over 20 minutes from Hiroshima's Ujina Port. The SKK Inland Sea cruise on the *Akinada* starts and finishes at Miya-jima; the Miyajima-Hiroshima leg costs Y1480.

Getting Around

Bicycles can be rented from the ferry building or you can walk. A free bus operates from in front of the Iwasō Ryokan to the Mt Misen cable-car station, although that isn't a long walk either.

HAGI 萩

If there were a single reason for travelling along the northern coast of Western Honshū it would have to be Hagi, with its interesting combination of temples and shrines, a fascinating old samurai quarter, some picturesque castle ruins and fine coastal views.

Places to Stay

Hagi Youth Hostel (☎ 0838-22-3558) is south of the castle at the western end of the town, has beds at Y2100 and hire shop bicycles are available. Tamae is the nearest JR station.

Pension Hagi (☎ 0838-28-0071) is a pleasant, modern pension 10 km east of town in the fishing port of Nagato-Ohi (pronounced *oy*). The pension is just back from the main road and costs Y4000 per person including breakfast. JR Nagato-Ohi Station is two stops from Higashi-Hagi and the pension's owner, Eukio Yamazaki, who learnt his excellent English in Papua New Guinea, will meet you at the station. Hagi also has a number of ryokan and minshuku and a people's lodge (kokuminshukusha).

Getting There & Away

The JR San-in line runs along the north coast through Tottori, Matsue, Masuda and Hagi to Shimonoseki. The faster expresses take four hours to or from Matsue.

JR buses to Hagi take 1½ hours from Ogōri, south of Hagi on the Tokyo-Osaka-Hakata shinkansen line. The buses go via Akiyoshi-dai and there are also buses from Yamaguchi. Buses also operate between Tsuwano and Hagi, taking a little under two hours.

Getting Around

There are plenty of bicycle hire shops including one at the youth hostel and several around the castle and JR Higashi-Hagi Station. Bocho Bus Company tour buses operate from Bocho Bus Station.

MATSUE 松江

Matsue straddles the Ohashi River which connects Shinji-ko Lake to the Nakanoumi-ko Lake and then the sea. A compact area in the north of the town includes almost all of Matsue's important sites: an original castle, a fine example of a samurai residence, the former home of British writer Lafcadio Hearn (whose book *Glimpses of Unfamiliar Japan*, written a century ago, is a classic) and a delightful teahouse and garden.

Places to Stay

Matsue Youth Hostel (☎ 0852-36-8620) is about five km from the centre of town in Kososhi-machi, on the north side of the lake at the first station you come to along the Ichibata line from Matsue-onsen Station. Beds cost Y2100.

The *Pension Tobita* (☎ 0852-36-6933) in Hamasada-machi is in the same direction as the youth hostel and has Japanese and Western-style rooms at Y4000 per person with breakfast only.

Getting There & Away

Matsue is on the JR San-in line which runs along the north coast. It takes a little over 2½ hours to travel via Yonago to Kurashiki on the south coast. See the Izumo section which follows for information on the two railway lines running west from Matsue.

Matsue is also a jumping-off point for the Oki Islands (see the Oki Islands section of this chapter for details).

Getting Around
Matsue is a good place to explore by bicycle: these can be hired at the Matsue and Matsue-onsen stations for Y500 for two hours or Y1000 per day.

TSUWANO 津和野
Inland from Masuda is Tsuwano, a pleasant and relaxing mountain town with a fine castle, some interesting old buildings and a wonderful collection of carp swimming in the roadside water channels. The town is noted as a place to get to by the superb old steam train service from Ogōri and as a place to get around by bicycle, of which there is a phenomenal number for hire.

Places to Stay
Tsuwano Youth Hostel (☎ 08567-2-0373) has beds at Y2100 and is a couple of km south of the station.

Wakasagi no Yado Minshuku (☎ 08567-2-1146) is not in the town centre but it's a pleasant place at Y5500 per person with two meals. Other similarly priced minshuku and ryokan include the *Hoshi Ryokan, Hiroshimaya Minshuku* and *Minshuku Mitsuwa*. All are near the centre.

Getting There & Away
The JR Yamaguchi line runs from Ogōri on the south coast through Yamaguchi to Tsuwano and on to Masuda on the north coast. It takes about one hour 15 minutes by limited express from Ogōri to Tsuwano and about 30 minutes from Masuda to Tsuwano. A bus to Tsuwano from Hagi takes nearly two hours.

IZUMO 出雲
Only 33 km west of Matsue the small town of Izumo Taisha, just north of Izumo itself, has one major attraction, the great **Izumo Taisha Shrine**.

Places to Stay
There's no imperative reason to stay overnight in Izumo Taisha since it's easy to take a day trip there from Matsue or simply pause there while travelling along the coast. If you do want to stop, there is a host of places along the main street of Izumo Taisha, which runs down from the shrine to the two stations.

The *Ebisuya Youth Hostel* (☎ 0853-53-2157) is just off the main street and costs Y2100. On the street nearby is *Hotel Katō* (☎ 0853-3-2214) with Japanese-style rooms at Y7000 per person including excellent meals.

Getting There & Away
Izumo has an airport with JAS flights to and from Tokyo.

Izumo Taisha has two railway stations, the JR one at the end of the street leading down from the shrine and the private Ichihata line station about halfway up the street. The Ichihata line starts from Matsue-onsen Station in Matsue and runs on the northern side of Shinji-ko Lake to Izumo Taisha Station. The JR line runs from JR Matsue Station to JR Izumo Station, where you transfer to an Izumo Taisha train. The private-line service also requires a change of train, at Kawato, but is more frequent (20-plus services a day) and also takes you closer to the shrine; the trip takes less than an hour and passes by rows of trees grown as windbreaks.

Kinki District 近畿地方

The term Kansai (west of the barrier) is loosely used to describe the core area around Kōbe, Osaka, Kyoto, and Nara. This section concentrates on the Kinki District, a geographical division in the heart of Kansai, which covers the prefectures of Shiga, Mie, Nara, Kyoto, Wakayama, Osaka and Hyōgo. Much of Japan's history and tradition has its roots here: a prime reason to visit.

Kyoto, with its hundreds of temples and gardens, was the imperial capital between

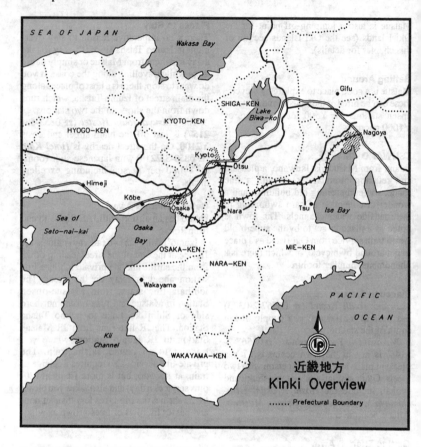

近畿地方
Kinki Overview
.... Prefectural Boundary

794 and 1868 and is now a magnet for domestic and international tourism. It continues to function as the major cultural centre of Japan, but business and industry are closing in on the traditional architecture. Nara predates Kyoto as an imperial capital and has an impressive array of temples and burial mounds and other relics from early times.

Osaka and Kōbe are part of a large industrial belt and of limited interest to travellers. Himeji, just east of Kōbe, is famed for its magnificent castle, which survives in its original (non-concrete) form.

KYOTO 京都

A visit to Japan simply *has* to include Kyoto, a city embodying the key qualities of Japanese culture and tradition yet undeniably marked by its growing industrial role.

From 794 to 1868, Kyoto was the capital of Japan, but at times its power was usurped and it remained capital in name only. During WW II, Kyoto was one of the few cities in Japan to be spared from bombing raids. Since the '50s, it has become a major industrial centre.

Despite modern urban intrusions, Kyoto has over 2000 temples and shrines, a trio of palaces, dozens of gardens, plenty of museums and the finest cultural and artistic choices in Japan. Some of these places are only accessible on guided tours.

The tour can evolve into an interesting cultural experience with Japanese sticking close to the guide whilst the foreigners hang back. Both groups eagerly jostle for camera positions: the Japanese want everyone *in* the picture, the foreigners want everyone *out*.

Information

Before you do anything else, drop into the Tourist Information Centre (☎ 371-5649). It is four minutes on foot north of Kyoto Station. Opening hours are 9 am to 5 pm on weekdays, 9 am to noon on Saturday, closed on Sunday and holidays.

Things to See

Central Kyoto Start your explorations with a visit to the **Nijō-jō Castle**, built in 1603 as the official Kyoto residence of the first Tokugawa shogun, Ieyasu. Admission to the inner palace and garden is Y500. The place is so inundated with visitors that you have to choose your exit according to the numbered location of your shoes! Bus Nos 9, 12, 50, 52, 61 and 67 go past the castle – the stop is called Nijō-jō-mae. Alternatively you can take the subway to Oike and then walk for 12 minutes.

Higashi Hongan-ji Temple is one of those rare places in Japan where admission is free. The temple is open from 9 am to 4 pm. It's a five-minute walk north of Kyoto Station.

Kikokutei Shōsei-en Garden is just east of Higashi Hongan-ji Temple and dates back to 1657. The landscaped garden arranged around a lake is gently falling into disrepair – a pleasant spot for a quiet stroll. Ask at the temple office for permission to enter.

Tō-ji Temple was established in 794 by imperial decree to protect the city. Admission costs Y400; there's an extra charge for entry to special exhibitions. An explanatory leaflet in English is provided. It's open 9 am to 4 pm. The temple is a 15-minute walk south-west of Kyoto Station.

Kanchi-in Temple is just outside the north gate of Tō-ji Temple. It's an excellent temple because of its striking combination of garden, interior design, statues, and tearoom on a small, intimate scale. Admission is Y400 and it's open 9 am to 5 pm.

Eastern Kyoto The eastern part of Kyoto, which includes the core district of Higashiyama (Eastern Mountains), is a top priority for a visit to its fine temples, peaceful walks and traditional night entertainment in Gion.

Sanjūsangen-dō Temple derives its name from the 33 ('sanjūsan') spaces between the columns in this long, narrow building which houses 1001 statues of Kannon (Deity of Mercy). Admission is Y400. The temple is a 15-minute walk east of Kyoto Station, or take bus No 206 or 208 and get off at Sanjūsangen-dō-mae stop.

Kyoto National Museum is housed in two buildings opposite Sanjūsangen-dō Temple. There are excellent displays of fine arts, historical artefacts and handicrafts. Admission costs Y300. It's open from 9 am to 4 pm, closed on Monday.

Kiyomizu-dera Temple has a main hall with a huge verandah, supported on hundreds of pillars, jutting out over the hillside. Just below this hall is the Otawa waterfall; visitors drink or bathe in the sacred waters which are believed to have therapeutic properties. The steep approach to the temple, known as 'teapot lane', is lined with shops selling Kyoto handicrafts, local snacks, and souvenirs. Shopkeepers hand out samples of *yatsuhashi*, a type of dumpling filled with a sweet bean paste. Admission costs Y300, and it's open from 6 am to 6 pm. From Kyoto Station take bus No 207, 206, or 202 and get off at Kiyomizu-michi or Gojō-zaka stops. Plod up the hill for 10 minutes to reach the temple.

Gion is the famous entertainment and geisha district on the east bank of the Kamogawa River. Modern architecture, congested traffic and contemporary night-life establishments have cut a swathe through the

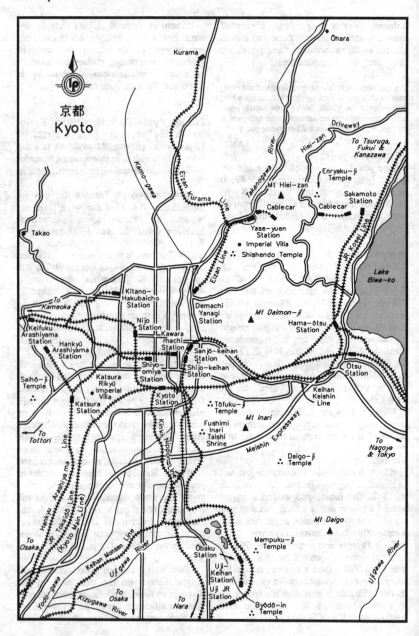

historical beauty, but there are still enough places left for an enjoyable walk.

North-East Kyoto There is a collection of contemporary Japanese ceramics and paintings at the **National Museum of Modern Art**. Admission costs Y500. It's open 10 am to 5 pm, closed on Monday.

Nanzen-ji Temple started as a retirement villa for Emperor Kameyama, but was dedicated as a Zen temple on his death in 1291. It operates now as headquarters for the Rinzai school of Zen. Admission costs Y350. It's open from 8.20 am to 5 pm. It's a ten-minute walk south-east from Heian-jingū Shrine; from Kyoto Station take bus No 5 and get off at Eikan-dō-mae stop.

Eikan-dō Temple is also known as Zenrin-ji Temple. The variety of architecture, gardens and works of art make this one of Kyoto's best temples. The best approach is to follow the arrows and wander slowly along the covered walkways connecting the halls and gardens. Admission costs Y350. It's open from 9 am to 4 pm.

Ginkaku-ji Temple is definitely worth seeing, but be warned that it is often swamped with busloads of visitors jamming the narrow pathways. Admission costs Y400. It's open from 9 am to 5 pm. From Kyoto Station, take bus No 5 and get off at Ginkaku-ji-mae stop.

North-West Kyoto The north-western part of Kyoto is predominantly residential, but there is a number of superb temples with tranquil gardens in secluded precincts. For Zen fans, a visit to **Daitoku-ji Temple** and **Ryōan-ji Temple** is recommended. **Kinkaku-ji Temple** is another major attraction. The JNTO leaflet on walks also covers this area, but most of the walk is along unremarkable city streets.

Takao is a secluded district tucked far away in the north-west of Kyoto. It is famed for autumn foliage and for the temples of **Jingo-ji**, **Saimyō-ji**, and **Kōzan-ji**. To reach Jingo-ji Temple, take bus No 8 from Shijō Omiya Station – allow one hour for the ride.

The other two temples are within easy walking distance.

Western Kyoto Arashiyama and Sagano are two districts worth a visit in this area if you feel like strolling in pleasant natural surroundings and visiting temples tucked into bamboo groves. The JNTO leaflet *Walking Tour Courses in Kyoto* has a rudimentary walking map for the Arashiyama area.

Bus Nos 71, 72 and 73 link Arashiyama with Kyoto Station. Bus No 11 connects Sanjō Keihan Station with Arashiyama. The most convenient rail connection is the 20-minute ride from Shijō-Omiya Station on the Keifuku-Arashiyama line to Arashiyama Station. There are several bicycle hire shops (three hours for Y600, Y1000 for the day) near the station, but it's more enjoyable to cover the relatively short distances between sights on foot.

Places to Stay

Kyoto has plenty of places to stay to suit all budgets. You have a choice ranging from the finest and most expensive ryokan in Japan to youth hostels or gaijin houses. Bear in mind that most of the cheaper places are further out of town.

TIC offers advice, accommodation lists and help with reservations. Two useful TIC leaflets are *Reasonable Ryokan and Minshuku in Kyoto* and *Inexpensive Accommodations in Kyoto* (dorm style).

Seven minutes walk from TIC is the *Kyoto Minshuku Reservation Centre*, On Building, 7th floor, Shimogyo-ku (☎ 351-4547) which provides computer reservations for minshuku not only in Kyoto, but also all over Japan. Some English is spoken.

In the central area of Kyoto is *Tani House Annex* (☎ 211-5637), which has doubles with bath and air-con for Y5500 per night. Take bus No 5 from Kyoto Station (bus terminal No A1) and get off at Kawaramachi-sanjō-mae stop. The trip takes about 20 minutes.

Also in the central area is *Uno House* (☎ 231-7763), another of the celebrated gaijin houses. Rates start at Y1400 for a dorm bed for the night; private rooms cost Y1600 per person. Take bus No 205 or 'special' No 17 – make sure the kanji character for *toku* ('special') is in front of the number – from Kyoto Station (bus terminal A3) to Kawaramachi-marutamachi-mae stop. The trip takes about 20 minutes.

Moving over to the eastern district, there's *Higashiyama Youth Hostel* (☎ 761-8135). It's a spiffy hostel which makes an excellent base very close to the sights of Higashiyama. For a dorm bed and two meals, the charge is Y3200. Private single/twin rooms are available for Y4600 per person (including two meals). Take bus No 5 from Kyoto Station (bus terminal No A1) to Higashiyama-sanjō-mae stop. The trip takes about 20 minutes.

Also on the east side of town is *I. S. E. Dorm* (☎ 771-0566), which provides basic accommodation at rates between Y1350 and Y2600 per day. Take bus No 206 from Kyoto Station (bus terminal No A2) to Kumano Jinja-mae stop. Allow 30 minutes for the ride.

On the western side of Kyoto is *Utano Youth Hostel* (☎ 462-2288), which offers dorm beds and two meals for Y2250. Take bus No 26 from Kyoto Station (bus terminal C1) to Yūsu hosuteru-mae stop. The ride takes about 50 minutes.

In northern Kyoto, there's *Aoi-So Inn* (☎ 431-0788), a quiet place where dorm beds cost Y1000 and a private room for two costs Y3000. It's near the Old Imperial Palace, five minutes' walk from subway Kuramaguchi Shin-mei (exit No 2), west between Kuramaguchi Hospital buildings.

Tani House (☎ 492-5489) is in northern Kyoto and charges Y1400 per person per night for a space on the floor in a tatami room. No curfew, free tea and coffee, can become crowded, so book ahead. This is an old favourite for short-term and long-term visitors on a tight budget. Take bus No 206 from Kyoto Station (bus terminal No B4) and get off at Kenkun-jinja-mae stop. The ride takes about 45 minutes.

Also in the north is *Kitayama Youth Hostel* (☎ 492-5345). It offers a dorm bed without meals for Y2200, Y3200 with two meals. Take bus No 6 from Kyoto Station (bus terminal B4) to Genkoan-mae stop (allow 35 minutes for the trip). Walk west past a school, turn right and continue up the hill to the hostel (five minutes on foot).

Guest House Kyoto (☎ 491-0880) has single rooms at Y2500 a day. Take bus No 205 from Kyoto Station (bus terminal B3) to Senbon-kitaoji-mae stop. The ride takes about 50 minutes and it's in the north part of town.

Takaya (☎ 431-5213) provides private rooms at Y2500 a day or Y45,000 a month. Take the subway from Kyoto Station to Imadegawa Station (15 minutes). It's in the northern area.

Kyoto Ohara Youth Hostel (☎ 744-2528) is a long way north out of town, but the rural surroundings are a bonus. A dorm bed costs Y2100. From Kyoto Station, you can take the subway to Kitaoji Station and then take bus No 'north' 6 (make sure the kanji for 'north' precedes the number or ask for 'kita rokku') to Ohara. Get off at 'To-dera' (Todera Temple).

Mid-range accommodation is provided at *Ryokan Hiraiwa/Annex Hiraiwa* (☎ 351-6748). They are well used to foreigners and offer basic tatami rooms conveniently close to central and eastern Kyoto. Singles/twins cost Y3500/7000. Take bus No 205, 42 or 'special' 17 – make sure the kanji for *toku* ('special') precedes the number – from Kyoto Station (bus terminal A3). Get off at the third stop, 'kawaramachi shomen'. Then it's a five-minute walk; alternatively you can walk there in 15 minutes from the station.

Ryokan Kyōka (☎ 371-2709) is a member of the Japanese Inn Group and has 10 spacious, Japanese-style rooms. Singles/twins cost Y3600/7200. If you give advance notice, a traditional formal *kaiseki* dinner is available for Y3500. It's about eight minutes on foot from Kyoto Station, close to Higashi Hongan-ji Temple.

Matsubaya Ryokan (☎ 351-4268) is a member of the Japanese Inn Group. Prices for singles/twins/triples are Y3800/7000/10,000. It's close to Higashi Hongan-ji Temple.

Ryokan Murakamiya (☎ 371-1260) is a

member of the Japanese Inn Group Prices for singles/twins/triples are Y3500/7000/9000. It's seven minutes on foot from Kyoto Station, close to Higashi Hongan-ji temple.

Riverside Takase (Annex Kyōka) (☎ 351-7920) is a member of the Japanese Inn Group with five Japanese-style rooms. Prices for singles/twins/triples start at Y3100/5150/7750. Take bus No 205 from Kyoto Station (bus terminal No A3) and get off at Kawaramachi Shomen – the third stop.

Pension Station Kyoto (☎ 882-6200) is a member of the Japanese Inn Group. It's a quiet place, built only recently. Prices for singles/twins/triples are Y3600/7200/10,000. From the station it's an eight-minute walk.

Yuhara Ryokan (☎ 371-9583) has a family atmosphere and riverside location popular with foreigners. Prices for a single/twin are Y3500/7000. It's a 15-minute walk from Kyoto Station.

Ryokan Hinomoto (☎ 352-4563) is a member of the Japanese Inn Group with a position right in the centre of the city's action. Prices for singles/twins/triples are Y3500/7000/9000. Take bus No 17 or 205 from Kyoto Station (bus terminal A3) and get off at Kawaramachi-matsubara-mae stop.

Places to Eat

At the lower end of the food budget, there are plenty of fast-food eateries (Shakey's Pizza, McDonalds, Kentucky Fried Chicken, Mr Donut, etc) all over town.

Coffee shops and noodle restaurants are good for inexpensive meals or snacks. Good value is offered by the chain of *Doutor* coffee shops (big yellow and brown signs) which sell coffee for Y150 and inexpensive snacks.

Most of the major department stores have restaurants usually offering teishoku (set meals) which are good value at lunchtime. Locals favour *Seven-Eight*, the 7th and 8th floors of Hankyu Department Store, which together form a large complex of inexpensive restaurants and are open until 10 pm. In the Porta shopping centre below Kyoto

Station there are also rows of restaurants with reasonable prices.

For Italian food, the *Ristorante Chiaro* (☎ 231-5547) does reasonable lunches from Y850 (closed on Wednesday). It's opposite the Kyoto Royal Hotel on Kawaramachi-dōri St (just north of the intersection with Sanjō-dōri St). Also opposite the Kyoto Royal Hotel is *Kerala* (☎ 251-0141), a restaurant serving regional Indian dishes; lunch prices start at Y1500.

In the Gion area, you can enjoy Chinese food at *Gasshotei Gion* (☎ 531-2100). Prices start at Y800 and it stays open until 3 am (closed on Sunday). It's on Tominagacho-dōri, one block north of Shijō-dōri.

In eastern Kyoto, a couple of minutes' walk north of Heian-Jingū Shrine, you can find *Time Paradox* (☎ 751-7531), a quirky eatery-cum-bar popular with university students and as a foreigners' den. The Western-style menu includes pizzas, omelettes, salads, soups, etc – prices start around Y800. It's open from 5 pm to 1 am, closed Thursday.

Things to Buy

Kyoto offers probably the best shopping opportunities for traditional arts and handicrafts in Japan.

Getting There & Away

Kyoto is served by Osaka Itami Airport which is a one-hour bus ride away.

There is a JR bus running frequently during the day between Osaka and Tokyo via Kyoto and Nagoya. Passengers change buses at Nagoya. Travel time for the express buses between Kyoto and Nagoya is about 2½ hours (Y2200). The journey between Nagoya and Tokyo takes about 6¼ hours (Y5000).

The overnight bus (JR Dream Bus) runs between Tokyo and Kyoto (departures in both directions). The trip takes about eight hours and there are usually two departures at 10 pm and 11 pm. Tickets are Y8050 plus a reservation fee. You should be able to grab some sleep in the reclining seats. If you find sleep a bit of a struggle, you can console

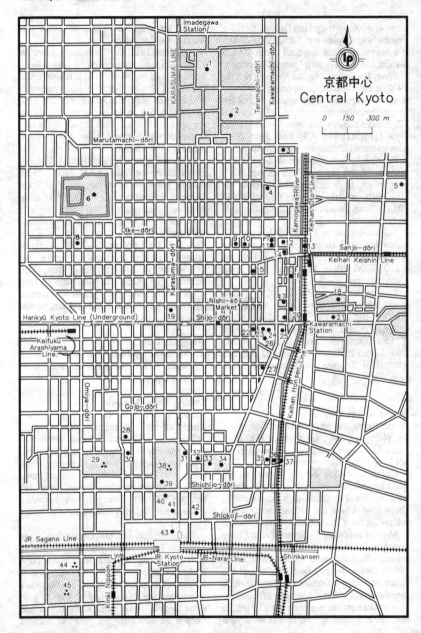

京都中心
Central Kyoto

1	Imperial Palace	24	Takashimaya Department Store
2	Sentō Gosho Palace	25	Fujii Daimaru Department Store
3	Uno House	26	Ninomiya
4	Ippō-dō Teashop	27	Ryokan Hinomoto
5	Kanze Kaikan Nō Theatre	28	Costume Museum
6	Nijō-jō Castle	29	Nishi Hongan-ji Temple
7	Kerala	30	Kungyoku-dō
8	Nijō-jinya	31	Matsubaya Ryokan
9	Hiiragiya Ryokan	32	Ryokan Kyōka
10	Tawaraya Ryokan	33	Ryokan Murakamiya
11	Ristorante Chiaro	34	Kikokutei Shōsei-en Garden
12	Kyoto Royal Hotel	35	Yuhara Ryokan
13	Taka Jyo Noodle Restaurant	36	Ryokan Hiraiwa
14	Ukiya Noodle Restaurant	37	Riverside Takase & Annex Kyōka
15	Tani House Annex	38	Higashi Hongan-ji Temple
16	Pontochō	39	Pension Station Kyoto
17	Far East Bar & Restaurant	40	Kintetsu Department Store
18	Gion	41	TIC
19	Kongō Nō Theatre	42	Kyoto Minshuku Reservation Centre
20	Yamatomi	43	Porta Shopping Centre
21	Gonbei	44	Kanchi-in Temple
22	Kinmata Ryokan	45	Tō-ji Temple
23	Hankyū Department Store		

1	京都御所	24	高島屋
2	仙洞御所	25	大丸
3	うのハウス	26	にのみや
4	一保堂	27	旅館ひのもと
5	カンゼ会館能座	28	服装博物館
6	二条城	29	西本願寺
7	ケララ	30	くんこょくどう
8	二条陣屋	31	松葉屋旅館
9	柊屋旅館	32	旅館京花
10	俵屋旅館	33	旅館むらかみや
11	リストランテチャロ	34	渉成園
12	京都ロイヤルホテル	35	ゆはら旅館
13	高城麺店	36	平岩旅館
14	うきや麺店	37	リバサイドたかせアネクス
15	谷ハウスアネクス	38	東本願寺
16	先斗町	39	ペンションステーション京都
17	ファーイーストバー	40	金鉄デパート
18	祇園	41	TIC
19	こんごう能座	42	民宿予定センター
20	やまとみ	43	ボータショッピングセンター
21	ごんべい	44	観智院
22	近又旅館	45	東寺
23	阪急デパート		

yourself with the thought that you are saving on accommodation and will be arriving at the crack of dawn to make good use of the day.

There is a JR shinkansen line between Kyoto and Shin-Osaka – the trip takes only 16 minutes. To connect between Shin-Osaka and Osaka proper, you can either take the JR Tōkaidō-Sanyo line to Osaka Station, or switch to the Midosuji subway line for Osaka's Namba District.

The railpass is also valid on the JR Tōkaidō-Sanyo line which runs via Osaka. The trip between Kyoto and Osaka Station takes 45 minutes; it costs Y530 for a one-way ticket.

The Hankyū Kyoto line runs between Kyoto (Kawaramachi) and Osaka (Umeda Station – close to JR Osaka Station). The fastest trip takes 47 minutes; it costs Y330 for a one-way ticket.

The Keihan line runs between Kyoto (Keihan-sanjō Station) and Osaka (Yodobashi Station). The fastest trip takes 40 minutes; it costs Y330 for a one-way ticket.

Unless you have a JR Railpass, the best option between Kyoto and Nara is the Kintetsu line (Kintetsu Nara Station) which costs Y900 one way on limited express. If you take a local or express train on this line, the ticket price drops to Y500 for the 45-minute ride, but you will need to change at Yamato-Saidaiji which is a five-minute ride from Kintetsu Nara Station.

The JR Nara line connects Kyoto with Nara JR Station. The ticket costs Y740 one way.

For getting to Tokyo, the JR shinkansen line is the fastest and most frequent rail link. The Super Express takes two hours and 40 minutes from Tokyo Station.

TIC has a leaflet which gives examples of a cheap route using local trains for eight hours on the JR Tōkaidō line between Tokyo and Kyoto. A one-way ticket should cost about Y8000.

Getting Around

There's a limousine bus service every 20 minutes from early morning until early evening between Kyoto and Osaka Airport which takes about one hour. The buses serve Kyoto Station as well as the major hotels in Kyoto.

Most buses run between 7 am and 9 pm. The main bus terminals are Kyoto Station, Sanjō-keihan Station, and Shijō-karasuma. On the north side of Kyoto Station is a major bus terminus. Inner city buses charge a flat fare (Y180) which you drop into a machine next to the driver.

To save time and money, you can buy a *kaisū-ken* (book of six tickets) for Y1000 at bus centres or from the driver. There is also a deal offering 11 tickets for the price of 10.

There's a one-day pass, *ichinichi jōshaken*, valid for unlimited travel on city buses, private Kyoto buses and the subway. It costs Y1050 and is available at bus centres and subway stations.

Bus No 59 is useful for travel between the sights of north-west Kyoto and Keihan-Sanjō Station. Bus No 5 connects Kyoto Station with the sights of Eastern Kyoto.

Three-digit numbers denote loop lines. Bus No 204 runs round the northern part of the city, bus Nos 205 and 206 circle the city via Kyoto Station.

The quickest way to travel between the north and the south of the city is to take the subway which operates from 5.30 am to 11.30 pm. There are eight stops: the most useful ones are those in the centre of town. Minimum fare is Y160.

Both the youth hostels at Higashiyama and Utano provide bicycle hire. In Higashiyama you could try *Taki Rent-a-Bicycle* on Kaminokuchi St, east of Kawaramachi; Arashiyama Station has several places for bicycle hire; *Nippon Rent-a-Cycle* is in front of Kyoto Station, close to the Hachijo exit.

OSAKA 大阪

Osaka is Japan's second city in economic importance, and third largest in population (after Tokyo and Yokohama). As you might imagine, it's a city of commerce and industry rather than temples and gardens. It has a few sights, but for most travellers, it's basically a gateway to Kyoto and other attractions in central Japan.

Orientation

Kita-ku, the northern ward, and Minami-ku, the southern ward, each have distinct features. Kita-ku is the business part of town with a scattering of high-rises and trendy department stores, while Minami-ku, with its bustling entertainment quarters, great restaurants and discount shopping, is a living area. Osaka Station is in Kita-ku, but if you're coming from Tokyo by shinkansen you arrive at Shin-Osaka Station. Osaka Station is two stops or about 10 minutes from Shin-Osaka by subway on the Midosuji line. The same line continues to Minami-ku, where most of the cheaper accommodation is located.

Things to See

The city's foremost attraction is **Osaka-jō Castle**. It's a 1931 re-creation of the original. The castle is open 9 am to 5 pm daily; admission is Y400. The Ote-mon Gate is about a 10-minute walk north-east of Tanimachi-yonchome Station on the Chūō and Tanimachi subway lines. From the JR Kanjo line that circles the city, get off at Morinomiya Station and look for the castle grounds a couple of minutes to the north-west. You enter through the back of the castle.

Shitennō-ji Temple has the distinction of being one of the oldest Buddhist temples in Japan. It's open from 9 am to 5 pm daily, and admission is Y500. It's most easily reached from Shitennō-ji-mae Station on the Tanimachi line. Take the south exit, cross to the left side of the road and take the small road that goes off at an angle away from the subway station. The entrance to the temple is on the left.

The 32-storey **Hankyū Grand Building** next to Osaka Station is renowned for its restaurants which occupy the 27th to the 31st floors. There is a free observatory on the 32nd floor.

Umeda Chika Centre is a labyrinthine underground shopping complex. The complex links Osaka Station with Umeda Station and can be entered from either.

The **Museum of Oriental Ceramics** has more than 1000 exhibits and is claimed to have one of the finest collections of Chinese and Korean ceramics in the world. Opening hours are 9.30 am to 5 pm, closed on Mondays; admission is Y400. Go to Yodoyobashi Station on either the Midosuji line or the Keihan line (different stations). Walk north to the river and cross to Nakanoshima Island. Turn right, pass the City Hall on your left, bear left with the road and the museum is on the left.

Billed as a 'Futuristic Electro-Fun Zone' **Panasonic Square** is a display forum for high-tech gadgetry, and it's open from 10 am to 6 pm, closed Wednesdays; admission is Y200. The easiest way to get there is to take the Keihan line to Kyobashi Station, take the south exit, cross the river and turn right. Panasonic Square is on the 2nd floor of the Twin 21 Tower Building.

Minami-ku is the part of town south of Shinsaibashi Station, and comes into its own after night falls. North of Dōtomburi, between Midosuji-dōri Ave and Sakaisu-ji Dōri, the narrow streets are crowded with hostess bars, discos and pubs.

Expo Memorial Park is the legacy of Expo '70. To get there take the Midosuji line to Senri Chūō Station and change to bus No 114 or 115 to the park, if the monorail from the station to the park is not already in operation.

Places to Stay

The best place to stay when visiting Osaka is Kyoto, less than 20 minutes away by shinkansen.

Osaka Shiritsu Nagai Youth Hostel (☎ 06-699-5631) near Nagai Station on the Midosuji line is only about 10 minutes from Minami-ku and costs Y1600 or Y1850 depending on the season. Further out, about 15 minutes from Kita-ku or 30 minutes from Minami-ku, is the *Osaka-fu Hattori Ryokuchi Youth Hostel* (☎ 06-862-0600), where beds are Y1600. Take the Midosuji line to Ryokuchi-kōen Station and leave through the west exit. Enter the park and follow the path straight ahead past a fountain and around to the right alongside the pond; the youth hostel is a little further on the right.

Rinkai Hotel Dejimaten (☎ 0722-41-3045) and *Rinkai Hotel Kitamise* (☎ 0722-47-1111) are close together and good for short or long-term stays. They're much cheaper by the month. Singles start from Y2500, from Y3000 with attached bathroom. For long-term stays rooms are Y1800/3200 for singles/doubles. There are cooking facilities and dining areas. Take an express from platform Nos 5 or 6 at Namba Station, change to a Nankai line local train at Sakai and get off at Minato Station, the next stop. Take the east exit, turn right, then left at the first intersection to the Dejimaten. Walk back along the road that the Dejimaten is on until you reach a T-junction. The Kitamise is on the opposite side of the road, to the left.

The *Ebisu-so Ryokan* (☎ 06-643-4861) is a bit more expensive but more convenient and has rooms from Y3800/7000. The rooms are small, but have TV, heater and fan. The ryokan is a 10-minute walk from exit No 4 of Namba Station or from exit No 1 of Ebisu-chō Station.

Without a doubt, the best mid-range hotel in town is the wonderfully kitsch *Hotel California* (☎ 06-243-0333). The rooms, slightly larger than those of the average business hotel, start at Y7000/10,000 with private bath. Take exit No 8 of Shinsaibashi Station, turn right into the small street that runs off the main road next to the big Hotel Nikko Osaka and the hotel is about 50 metres down on the left.

Places to Eat

The eating options in Kita-ku are more expensive and not as exciting as in Minami-ku. One place to try is the *Food Park* in the Umeda Chika Centre, which has about 20 small restaurants. On the 27th to 31st floors of the Hankyū Grand Building there are plenty of restaurants, although they're a bit pricey.

The place to eat in Minami-ku is the restaurant-packed street of Dōtomburi. You can't miss *Kuidaore* (☎ 06-211-5300); it has

a mechanical clown posted outside its doors, attracting the attention of potential customers by beating a drum. The restaurant has eight floors with meals starting from Y1000.

Indian food can be had at the popular Tokyo restaurant *Moti* (☎ 06-211-6878), which has a branch in Osaka. It's on the 3rd floor a few doors down Dōtomburi from its intersection with Midosuji-dōri Ave – great curries from around Y1000.

Entertainment

Osaka has a very active nightlife, not all of it aimed at businessmen with fat expense accounts. Forget Kita-ku and head for Minami-ku's Dōtomburi. The very popular *Kirin City Bar* on the 2nd floor of the Kirin Plaza Building next to the river is a good place to meet young locals.

Cross the bridge next to the Kirin Plaza Building, turn right, take the next left, and walk a couple of streets down where, in the midst of all the hostess bars and exclusive clubs, on the right-hand side is *Shanghai*. The name is displayed only in kanji; look for a darkened doorway into a tiny bar whose walls are decorated with rock posters and the complete Keith Richard guitar collection. Shanghai gets *very* crowded from about midnight.

Most of the local gaijin and a lot of the more 'international' Japanese hang out at the *Pig & Whistle* (☎ 06-213-6911), an English pub.

In the vicinity of the Pig & Whistle and Shanghai there are a number of discos, among which *Maharaja* and *Dynasty* are the most popular. They charge the usual Y4000 to Y4500 admission, which includes a few drink tickets.

Getting There & Away

Osaka is a major international air centre.

Kōbe is a mere 30 minutes away, even quicker by shinkansen, while Kyoto and Nara are each about 50 minutes from Osaka.

Shinkansen services operate between Tokyo Station and Shin-Osaka Station (just under three hours) via Kyoto, and from Shin-

Osaka Station on to Hakata in northern Kyūshū (around three hours 30 minutes).

To get to Kyoto from Osaka, the quickest route (other than the shinkansen, which takes only 17 minutes) is with the private Hankyū line, departing from Umeda Station.

To get to Nara your best bet is to take the JR Kansai line from Tennō-ji Station and get off at Horyuji Station. The private Kintetsu line also operates between Namba Station and Nara Station, taking about 30 minutes.

It is also possible to travel between Osaka and Koyasan from Shiomibashi Station via the private Nankai-Koya line.

Osaka has international ferry services to and from Pusan (South Korea) and Shanghai (China). The ferries leave from the Nanko International Ferry Terminal, which can be reached by taking the 'New Tram' service from Suminoekoen Station to Nankoguchi Station. Call for information about Shanghai-bound ferries (☎ 06-261-9924) or for Pusan ferries (☎ 06-263-0200).

Ferries also depart from Nanko, Kanome-futo and Benten-futo piers for various destinations around Honshū, Kyūshū and Shikoku.

Getting Around

There are frequent limousine buses running between the airport and various parts of Osaka. To Shin-Osaka Station buses run every 15 minutes from 6.50 am to 8.15 pm and cost Y320. The trip takes around 25 minutes. To Umeda and Namba stations buses run at about the same frequency and the 30-minute trip costs Y410.

Osaka has a bus system though it is nowhere near as easy to use as the rail network.

Osaka has a good subway network and like Tokyo a JR loop line that circles the city area. If you're going to be using the rail system a lot on any day, it might be worth considering getting a One-Day Free Ticket. For Y800 you get unlimited travel on any subway, the so-called New Tram and the buses, but unfortunately you cannot use the JR line. You'd really need to be moving around all day to save any money but it might save the headaches of working out fares and where to buy tickets.

KOBE 神戸

Kōbe (population 1,450,000) is popular among young Japanese for its cosmopolitan atmosphere. Among Japanese Kōbe is renowned for Kōbe beef and for its foreign houses, the former being too pricey for the average traveller and the latter probably not too exciting to anyone who grew up in the West.

All things considered, Kōbe shouldn't be a high priority on your itinerary.

Things to See

Best known for its collection of *namban* art, influenced by Spanish and Portuguese painting, **Kōbe City Museum** is open from 10 am to 5 pm, closed Mondays; admission is Y200.

Chinatown (*nankin-machi*) is nothing to write home about if you've seen Chinatowns elsewhere. Eating is the main reason to come here. Chinatown is easy to find: a five-minute walk south of Motomachi Station.

Port Island is an artificial island touted as one of Kōbe's premier tourist destinations. A monorail does a circuit from Sannomiya Station, and sights along the way which you may or may not want to stop and have a look at include a container terminal, a science museum and an international trade show hall.

Featured prominently in all the tourist literature is 931-metre **Mt Rokko-san**. It's not a bad trip by cable car to the top – 'nice' would be the word to sum up the experience. To get there take bus No 16 from Rokko Station on the Hankyū line. Get off the bus at the Rokko cable-car station.

Fifteen minutes north of Motomachi Station is the Japanese-style **Soraku-en Garden** with a pond and some old buildings. The garden is a pleasant enough place for a stroll and is open from 9 am to 5 pm, closed Thursdays; admission is Y150.

Places to Stay

Kōbe Tarumi Youth Hostel (☎ 078-707-

2133) has beds for Y1900, breakfast for Y450 and dinner for Y700, but it's a bit far out of town. From Tarumi Station, six stops from Kōbe Station on the Tōkaidō line, it's an eight-minute walk to the east along the road that runs parallel to the south side of the railway tracks.

Kōbe Mudō-ji Youth Hostel (☎ 078-581-0250) is a 10-minute bus journey north of Shin-Kōbe Station, followed by a further 10 minutes on foot. A bed here is Y1500, breakfast Y450, dinner Y650.

Tor Ryokan (☎ 078-331-3590) has rooms from Y4300 per person. Book ahead, its small size and reasonable rates mean that this place is frequently booked out.

Middle-price places are almost all in the familiar business hotel category, where from Y5500 you get a tiny room with attached bathroom, pay TV and fridge.

Places to Eat

Kōbe is famous among Japanese for its restaurants, but foreigners don't usually find it that special. The Japanese make a big deal out of Kōbe beef, which to most foreigners may seem both too expensive and too fatty.

Most of the numerous Chinese restaurants are in Nankin-machi, Kōbe's Chinatown, but they're all pretty similar with plastic offerings in the window displays. Kōbe is well known for its Indian restaurants, best known of which is *Gaylord* (☎ 078-251-4359). It's not exactly cheap but the food is good and lunch time sets range from Y1200. The restaurant is south of Sannomiya Station on the left side of Flower Road and has an English sign.

Getting There & Away

By shinkansen it's about 15 minutes from Shin-Osaka Station to Shin-Kōbe Station, which in turn is about five minutes from Sannomiya Station in the centre of town.

Ferries from Kōbe operate to destinations as diverse as Okinawa, Shikoku, Kyūshū and Awaji-shima Island. The departure point for the ferries is Naka Pier, next to the Port Tower.

Getting Around

It is possible to take a bus directly from Osaka International Airport to Kōbe.

The JR, Kankyū and Hanshin lines run east to west across Kōbe, providing fairly easy access to most of Kōbe's sights. A subway line also connects Shin-Kōbe Station with Sannomiya Station.

HIMEJI 姫路

If you see no other castles in Japan you should at least make an effort to visit Himeji Castle, unanimously acclaimed as the most splendid Japanese castle still standing.

Himeji can be easily visited as a day trip from Kyoto. A couple of hours at the castle, plus the 10 to 15-minute walk from the station, is all the time you need here. The only other attraction worth lingering for is Himeji's historical museum, which has some interesting exhibits on Japanese castles. Walk to the castle down one side of the main street and back on the other to see the statuary dotted along both sides.

Places to Stay

There *are* some places to stay in Himeji, but in general they are overpriced and have little to recommend them. Basing yourself elsewhere and visiting Himeji as a day trip would be a far better option.

The *Tegarayama Youth Hostel* (☎ 0792-93-2716) gets consistently bad reports from travellers even though beds are only Y1300 and the place does not require a Youth Hostel Card. The hostel is a 10-minute walk south of Tegara Station.

Getting There & Away

From Shin-Osaka Station the trip takes around 40 minutes, from Okayama it takes 30 to 40 minutes on the shinkansen. JR trains also run between Osaka, Kyoto, Kōbe and Himeji, and the private Hankyū line runs between Kōbe and Himeji.

NARA 奈良

Prior to the 8th century, it had been the custom amongst the rulers of Japan to change the capital with each successive emperor. In 710 Nara was made the permanent capital under Empress Gemmyō. The permanent status lasted a mere 75 years. Several decades later, after a few more moves, the capital was shifted to Kyoto where it remained until 1868.

Although brief, the Nara period was extraordinarily vigorous in absorbing influences from China, which set the foundations for Japanese culture and civilisation. Once Nara had lost its role as a capital it was spared the subsequent destruction that occurred in Kyoto, and a number of magnificent buildings have survived.

Nara tends to be skipped in favour of Kyoto's huge choice of sights, but Nara's smaller scale does make it easier for a visitor to concentrate on a smaller selection of attractions – some of the finest in Japan.

Information

If you are heading for Nara from Kyoto, the TIC in Kyoto has extensive material. In Nara, the best source of information is the *Nara City Tourist Centre* (☎ 22-3900), open from 9 am to 9 pm. The area code if you're phoning from outside Nara is 0742. It's a short walk from JR Nara and Kintetsu Nara Stations.

Things to See

JNTO publishes a leaflet called *Walking Tour Courses in Nara* which includes a map of **Nara-kōen Park**. Although walking time is estimated at two hours, you'll need at least half a day to see a selection of the sights and a full day to see the lot.

The park was created in 1880. It is famous for its deer which provide a cutesy backdrop for photos and are fed by tourists who buy special packets of biscuits for Y100 from vendors. These creatures, numbering over a thousand, have been spoilt rotten and can be a nuisance.

Kōfuku-ji Temple was transferred here from Kyoto in 710 as the main temple for the Fujiwara family. The **National Treasure Hall** (Kokuhōkan) contains a variety of statues and art objects salvaged from previ-

ous structures. A descriptive leaflet is provided in English.

Nara National Museum is devoted to Buddhist art and is divided into two wings which are linked by an underground passage.

Tōdai-ji Temple is the star attraction in Nara. It is the largest wooden building in the world and houses the Great Buddha – one of the largest bronze images in the world.

Daibutsu-den (Hall of the Great Buddha) is the largest wooden building in the world, but the actual structure is not remarkably ancient because it is a reconstruction dating from 1709. A short walk west of the entrance gate to the Daibutsu-den is **Kaidan-in Hall**.

Shōsō-in (Treasure Repository) is a short walk north of Daibutsu-den. If you discount the slight curve to the roof, the structure is reminiscent of a log blockhouse from North America.

If you walk east from the entrance to the Daibutsu-den, climb up a flight of stone steps, and continue to your left, you reach **Nigatsu-dō Hall** and **Sangatsu-dō Hall**.

Kasuga Taisha Shrine was founded in the 8th century by the Fujiwara family and completely rebuilt every 20 years according to Shinto tradition until the end of the 19th century. It lies at the foot of the hill in a pleasant wooded setting with herds of sacred deer waiting for handouts.

The **Hōmotsu-den** (Treasure Hall) is just north of the entrance torii for the shrine. The hall displays Shinto ceremonial regalia and equipment used in *Bugaku* (court dance music), Nō, and *Gagaku* (court music) performances.

Places to Stay

Although Nara is favoured as a day trip from Kyoto, accommodation can still be packed out for festivals, holidays and at weekends so try and make reservations in advance. The City Tourist Centre can help with reservations and has extensive lists of hotels, minshuku, pension, ryokan, and shukubō.

Seishōnen Kaikan Youth Hostel (☎ 0742-22-5540) is of nondescript, concrete character, but cheap at Y1900 per person per

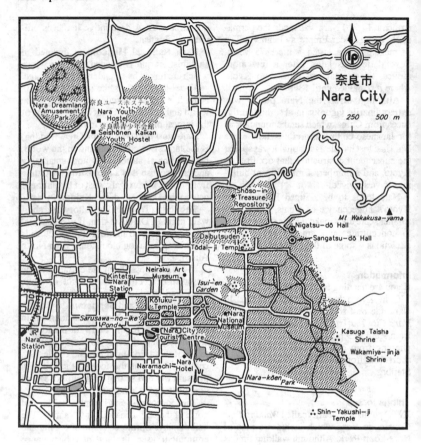

Isui-en
Garden

Kōfuku-ji
Temple

Sarusawa-no-ike
Pond

JR
Nara
Station

Nara City
Tourist Centre

Naramachi

Nara
Hotel

Kintetsu
Nara
Station

Neiraku Art
Museum

Shōsō-in
Treasure
Repository

Daibutsuden
Tōdai-ji Temple

Nara
National
Museum

Nara-kōen Park

Nara Dreamland
Amusement
Park

奈良ユースホステル
Nara Youth
Hostel
奈良県青少年会館
Seishōnen Kaikan
Youth Hostel

奈良市
Nara City

0   250   500 m

Mt Wakakusa-yama

Nigatsu-dō Hall

Sangatsu-dō Hall

Kasuga Taisha
Shrine

Wakamiya–jinja
Shrine

Shin–Yakushi–ji
Temple

night. It's a 30-minute uphill walk from the centre of town to the hostel. From JR Nara Station you can take bus No 21 (in direction of Dreamland south entrance) and get off at Sahoyama-mae stop which is opposite the hostel. Buses run about twice an hour between 7 am and 9 pm.

Nara Youth Hostel (☎ 0742-22-1334) is close to Kōnoike Pond which is a short walk from the other youth hostel, and charges Y2100. It tends to be booked out and is often swarming with schoolkids on excursion. From Kintetsu Nara Station, take a bus in the direction of Dreamland or Kamo or

Takanohara and get off at Yakyujo-mae stop which is in front of a baseball stadium beside the hostel.

Ryokan Seikan-so (☎ 0742-22-2670) is a 15-minute walk from Kintetsu Nara Station, close to Sarusawa-no-ike Pond. Prices for a Japanese-style room without bath start at Y3500/7000 for singles/doubles.

The quaintly named *Cotton 100% (Cotton Hyakupasento)* (☎ 0742-22-7117) is a 10-minute walk from the city centre. Most of the rooms are Western-style, but the place has a bright atmosphere. Per person charges start at Y5000 without meals.

Places to Eat

There are plenty of inexpensive restaurants and fast-food places around both the stations. Opposite Kintetsu Station are *Lotteria* and *Mister Donut* outfits which do cheap set breakfasts for about Y350. On the streets leading south from Kintetsu Station are restaurants offering teishoku (set lunches) for around Y1200.

Getting There & Away

Bus There is an overnight bus service between Tokyo and Nara which costs Y8,240 one way or Y14,830 return. The bus leaves Nara at 10.30 pm and reaches Tokyo next day at 6.20 am. The bus from Tokyo leaves at 11 pm and arrives in Nara next day at 6.50 am.

Train Unless you have a JR Railpass, the best option is the Kintetsu line linking Kyoto and Nara (Kintetsu Nara Station) in 33 minutes by limited express (Y900 one way) which runs direct. If you take a local or express train on this line, the ticket price drops to Y500 for the 45-minute ride, but you will need to change at Yamato-Saidaiji which is a five-minute ride from Kintetsu Nara Station.

The JR Nara line connects Kyoto with Nara JR Station. The ticket costs Y740 one way, and the ride takes just over an hour.

The Kintetsu Nara line connects Osaka (Kintetsu-Namba Station) with Nara (Nara-Kintetsu Station). The limited express takes about half an hour and costs Y880; express and local trains take about 40 minutes and cost Y460.

The JR Kansai line links Osaka (Tennō-ji Station) and Nara (JR-Nara Station) via Hōryu-ji; the express trip takes about 40 minutes and costs around Y750.

Getting Around

Nara has an excellent bus system geared to tourists, and most of the buses have taped announcements in English. Outside Kintetsu Station there's even a machine which gives advice in English for your destination. Just push the right destination button to find out your boarding terminal, bus number, ticket cost, and time of the next bus.

Most of the area around Nara Kōen Park is covered by two circular bus routes. Bus No 1 runs counter-clockwise, bus No 2 runs clockwise. There's a Y130 flat fare. You can easily see the main sights in the park on foot.

The most useful buses for western and south-western Nara (Tōshōdai-ji Temple, Yakushi-ji Temple, and Hōryū-ji Temple) are Nos 52 and 97 which have taped announcements in English and link all three destinations with Kintetsu Station and the JR Station. Buses run about every 30 minutes between 8 am and 5 pm, but are much less frequent outside these times.

From Kintetsu Station, allow about 20 minutes and a fare of Y200 for the trip to Tōshōdai-ji Temple and Yakushi-ji Temple; add another 30 minutes and an extra Y400 if you continue to Hōryū-ji Temple.

Nara is a convenient size for bicycling. The *Kintetsu Rent-a-Cycle Center* (☎ 0742-24-3528) is close to the City Tourist Centre. From the tourist centre, walk east down the main street to the first intersection, turn left into Konishi-dōri street and walk about 70 metres until you see Supermarket Isokawa on your right. Opposite the supermarket is a small side street on your left – the bicycle hire centre is at the bottom of this street.

Hokkaidō 北海道

Hokkaidō is the northernmost of Japan's islands, and although it accounts for over one-fifth of Japan's land area, only 5% of the Japanese population lives there. The real beauty of the place lies in the unpopulated, wilderness regions where – in contrast to Honshū – there are no cultural monuments, but superb opportunities for outdoor activities such as hiking, camping, skiing, sampling of hot springs, and observing wildlife.

Without hesitation we'd rate Hokkaidō as the best destination in Japan for outdoor pursuits. Sapporo and Hakodate are the only cities worth a brief stop before visiting the rest of the island, especially the five major national parks: Daisetsuzan National Park, Rishiri-Rebun-Sarobetsu National Park, Shiretoko National Park, Akan National Park, and Shikotsu-Tōya National Park – given in order of preference.

HAKODATE 函館

Hakodate is a convenient gateway for Hokkaidō and the most interesting city on the island. In contrast to Sapporo which emphasises sleek modernity, Hakodate has retained architectural influences from the last century when it was chosen as an international trading port and attracted foreign communities.

Information

The Hakodate Tourist Information Office (☎ 0138-23-5440) is to your right as you leave the station. It's open from 9 am to 7 pm, and closes at 5 pm in the winter. The office has plenty of detailed maps and brochures in English.

Things to See

The star attraction of Hakodate is the view from the summit of **Mt Hakodate-yama**, preferably enjoyed on a clear night. A cable car whisks you up to the top in a few minutes and relieves you of Y1130 for the return trip. Operating hours extend into the evening: 10 am to 8 pm during winter, and 9 am to 10 pm in summer. To reach the base station of the cable car from Hakodate Station, take tram Nos 2, 3 or 5 and get off after about six minutes at Jūjigai tram stop. The base station is then a seven-minute walk uphill. There is also a trail winding up the mountain – closed from late November to late April. From Hakodate Station, you can also take a 20-minute bus ride (Y280) direct to the summit, but this service is suspended from late October until late April.

If you're an early bird, the **Asaichi** (morning market) is open from 5 am to noon, closed on Sundays. It's a two-minute walk from the west exit of Hakodate Station.

Goryōkaku was Japan's first Western-style fort, built in 1864 in the shape of a five-pointed star. All that's left now is the outer walls, and the grounds have been made into a park with the obligatory squads of cherry trees. Inside the grounds, keen historians or militarists can pay Y100 admission to visit the **Hakodate Hakubutsukan Museum**. Close to the entrance to the park is **Goryōkaku Tower** which provides a bird's-eye view of the ruins. To reach the fort, take tram Nos 2, 3, or 5 for a 15-minute ride to Goryōkaku-kōen-mae tram stop. From there, it's a 10-minute walk to the fort.

Places to Stay

The Tourist Information Office outside the station can provide details of ryokan, minshuku and hotels. There are plenty of business hotels in the centre of town.

In the station area is the *Hotel Ocean* (☎ 0138-23-2200), an efficient business hotel with helpful staff. Singles start at Y4800. There are two hotels of this name in the station area. To reach this one, walk out of the station exit to the main road, then turn right and continue for about 100 metres until you see the neon sign – the walk takes about three minutes.

Minshuku Ryorō (☎ 0138-26-7652) is a member of the Toho network. Prices start at Y3000 without any meals. To reach the minshuku – close to the morning market – take the west exit (*nishi guchi*) from the station then walk six minutes down the street, keeping to the left until you come to the seventh side street. Go left down the side street and the minshuku is about 30 metres on your right.

Akai Boshi (☎ 0138-26-4035) is a popular minshuku, 13 minutes on foot from the station. Prices start at Y2500 per person without meals. English is spoken.

In the western district beneath Mt Hakodateyama is *Free Station* (☎ 0138-26-6817) is a member of the Toho network. Prices start at Y2000 and use of the nearby hot spring is included in the price. From Hakodate Station, take tram No 2 for the 15-minute ride west to the terminus at

Yachigashira, then walk for about 15 minutes.

Ikusanda Onuma Youth Hostel (☎ 0138-67-3419) is a 10-minute walk from Onuma Station, which itself is to the north of Hakodate. Bicycle hire is available at the hostel and there are hot springs nearby.

Places to Eat

For a meal with a view, there's the restaurant on Mt Hakodateyama. At the foot of the mountain, in the Motomachi District, there are plenty of trendy eateries in converted Western-style buildings.

Getting There & Away

An overnight bus service links Hakodate with Sapporo in 6½ hours (Y4600).

Hakodate is connected with Aomori by the JR Tsugaru Kaikyō railway line which runs via the Seikan Tunnel beneath the Tsugaru Kaikyō Straits to Hakodate in 2½ hours. Sapporo is linked with Hakodate in 3¾ hours by limited express via Chitose Kūkō Airport and Tomakomai.

Ferries link Hakodate with ports on Honshū such as Oma (Y1000, 1¾ hours), Noheji (Y1400, 4¾ hours), and Aomori (Y1400, 3¾ hours). Hakodate-kō Port does not have convenient access for the centre of the city. The taxi ride to the station costs Y1140. The closest bus stop, Hokkudai-mae, is a seven-minute walk from the ferry terminal; from there you can catch bus No 1 or 19 to the station.

Getting Around

One-day (Y900) and two-day (Y1500) open tickets, which entitle you to unlimited bus and tram travel, are available from the Tourist Information Centre or on buses or trams.

SAPPORO 札幌

Sapporo is the capital of Hokkaidō and the island's focal point for administration, culture and transport. The Sapporo Snow Festival, held in Odōri Kōen Park in early February, is a major drawcard, but accommodation is very tight at this time and must be booked in advance.

For the foreign visitor, the ordered streets provide easier orientation at the expense of architectural variety. The city has few sights and is best used briefly as a staging post. However, the residents of Sapporo are as good a reason as any to visit the city. They appear to be more open towards outsiders than in many other parts of Japan, and they certainly know how to have a good time, whether in the bright lights of Susukino – the largest nightlife district north of Tokyo – or during the Snow Festival held in February.

Information

There are several tourist offices in Sapporo, including the *Tourist Section, Sapporo City Government* (☎ 011-211-2376) and the *Sapporo Tourist Association* (☎ 011-211-3341) which have English speakers on the staff.

An office with English-speaking staff has been opened in the western concourse of Sapporo Station – it's next to the tourist information counter.

Things to See

If you want to take a look at Hokkaido's flora, **Shokubutsu-en** (Botanical Garden) has over 5000 varieties of plant spread around 14 hectares. From 4 November to 28 April, only the greenhouse is open (Y50 admission) from 10 am to 3 pm; it's closed on Sunday.

Beer enthusiasts may like to visit the **Sapporo Brewery** which was the first one in Japan and dates from 1878. Tours are free, but you should phone (☎ 011-731-4368) before you go, to reserve a place and increase your chances of being allotted an English-speaking guide. Tours lasting about 80 minutes are given throughout the year from 9 am to 5 pm; the hours are extended between June and August from 8.40 am to 6 pm. From the north exit of the station, the brewery is a 15-minute walk east – or take the Higashi No 63 bus and get off at Kita-hachi Higashi-nana bus stop.

If you like bars, cabarets, nightclubs, res-

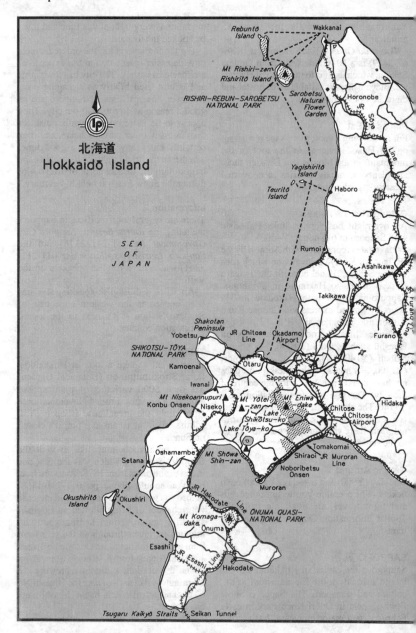

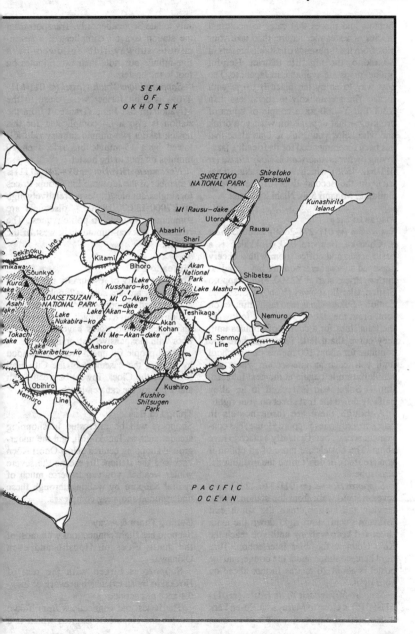

taurants and places that cater to nocturnal fancies of a steamier nature, then take your pick from the thousands of establishments in **Susukino**, the nightlife district. Helpful 'guide' maps are available in Japanese. The best way to enjoy the place is to go with locals. You are unlikely to spend less than Y3000 to Y4000 for a couple of hours of drinking – that depends on what you drink and who helps you drink it. One place that has been recommended for its friendly, jazz-loving owner is *American Melody House* (☎ 011-512-4388) which is in Susukino District, on the second floor of the Liberty Building, Minami 5 jō, Nishi 5 chome.

Places to Stay

Sukarakan (☎ 011-271-2668), South 3 West 8, Chūō-ku, Sapporo 060, Hokkaidō is a basic hostel and coffee room with a cheery crashpad atmosphere: nothing fancy, and no curfew. Prices start at Y2500. From Sapporo Station, take the subway (Y160) to Susukino Station – Sukarakan is then eight minutes on foot. From the station, walk west following the tram lines for a couple of minutes until they curve sharp left. Turn right here and continue for about 100 metres past a school until you reach an intersection where you turn left; turn left again at the next intersection – Sukarakan is tucked in an alley halfway down the first street on your right.

Although there are three hostels in Sapporo, only one (Sapporo House) has convenient access, but it's hardly a place to rave about. The hostels are more of an option if you are stuck or don't mind the institutional atmosphere.

Sapporo House (☎ 011-726-4235) is a seven-minute walk from the station. When leaving the station, take the south exit (Minami guchi), turn right down the main street and keep walking until you reach the Keio Hotel at the third intersection. Turn right here, continue under the bridge, and the hostel is about 20 metres further ahead on your right.

Sapporo Miyagaoka Youth Hostel (☎ 011-611-9016) is close to Maruyama Kō-en Park in the west of Sapporo, but it's open from July to late September only. Transport from the station is a bit complicated: a seven-minute subway ride followed by a five-minute bus ride, then two minutes on foot to the hostel.

Sapporo Lions Youth Hostel (☎ 011-611-4709) is a bit further west, close to the Miyanomori Ski Jump. Transport from the station is also a bit complicated for this hostel: take a two-minute subway ride followed by a 15-minute bus ride, then 10 minutes on foot to the hostel.

Nakamuraya Ryokan (☎ 011-241-2111) is a member of the Japanese Inn Group. Prices for singles/doubles/triples are relatively high at Y7000/13,000/18,000 – discounts are sometimes available on polite request. The ryokan is a seven-minute walk west of the station.

Places to Eat

There are plenty of restaurants and eateries in shopping arcades such as Tanuki-kōji, the underground shopping centres beneath the station and Odōri Kōen Park, and most of the major department stores have at least one floor with inexpensive restaurants.

Local people fill up on inexpensive food by visiting the basement of the City Hall (opposite the Clock Tower) between 1 pm and 2 pm for the canteen lunch.

Things to Buy

Shoppers will be interested in shopping arcades such as Tanuki-kōji, and the underground shopping centres below Odōri Kōen Park and the station. To escape the severe winter weather, you can traverse much of central Sapporo by walking through these underground shopping complexes.

Getting There & Away

Sapporo has flight connections with most of the major cities on Honshū and even Okinawa.

Sapporo is linked with the rest of Hokkaidō by an extensive network of long-distance bus services

The fastest rail connections from Tokyo include the Hokutōsei Express which is a direct sleeper to Sapporo in 16 hours, and a combination of the shinkansen to Morioka followed by a limited express via Aomori and Hakodate to Sapporo in 11 hours. If you are using a JR Railpass, you will have to pay the sleeper supplement.

Sapporo is linked with Hakodate in 3¾ hours by limited express via Chitose Kūkō Airport and Tomakomai.

The trip from Sapporo to Otaru on the JR Hakodate line takes 36 minutes. There are frequent trains running north-east on the JR Hakodate line to Asahikawa in 90 minutes (limited express). If you're going from Sapporo to Wakkanai, there's a sleeper service that leaves Sapporo round 10 pm and arrives in Wakkanai around 6 am, nicely timed to take the early ferry across to Rishiritō or Rebuntō islands. If you're travelling on a JR Railpass, you'll need to pay about Y7400 in supplementary charges.

Getting Around

There are several bus terminals in Sapporo, but the main one is next to the railway station.

The subway is the most efficient way to get around Sapporo. There are three lines, the two most useful being the Nanboku line, which runs on a south-north axis, and the Tozai line which runs on an east-west axis. Special one-day passes for sightseeing are available for Y700 and are valid for buses and trams as well.

DAISETSUZAN NATIONAL PARK
大雪山国立公園

This is Japan's largest national park, consisting of several mountain groups, volcanoes, lakes and forests. It is spectacular hiking and skiing territory. The main centres of interest are Sōunkyo, Asahidake Onsen, Tenninkyō Onsen, Furano and Tokachidake Onsen. Pick up maps and information about the park in English in Sapporo or try the Tourist Information Offices locally.

The main gateways to the park are Asahikawa and Kamikawa in the north, Kitami in the east, and Obihiro in the south. Bus services through the park are restricted to routes between Kitami and Kamikawa (continuing to Asahikawa) via Sōunkyo, and a service between Asahikawa and Tenninkyō Onsen via Asahidake Onsen.

Things to See

At the foot of Mt Asahi-dake (2290 metres), the highest mountain on Hokkaidō, is **Asahidake Onsen**, an unspoilt hot spring resort consisting of several houses surrounded by forests. The Mt Asahi-dake cable car runs in two stages (Y1300, 12 minutes) from the resort to a point within easy hiking distance of the peak.

The base station at the cable car has a restaurant and shop where you can buy *Daisetsuzan Attack*, a very detailed map (Y1500) in Japanese. There are *rotemburo* (open air, natural hot springs) at Yudoku Onsen and Nakadake Onsen along the trails over the peaks. During the peak hiking seasons, cable cars and lifts operate from as early as 6 am until as late as 7.30 pm.

There are dozens of hiking options in this region; the most popular one follows trails from the Mt Asahi-dake cable car via several peaks to Sōunkyo – allow about 6½ hours. From the top station of the Mt Asahi-dake cable car, it takes 1¾ hours to climb along a ridge overlooking steaming, volcanic vents to reach the peak of Mt Asahi-dake.

From there, you can continue via Mt Hokkai-dake (1½ hours) to Mt Kuro-dake Ishimuro (1½ hours) for a pause at the mountain hut, and then continue via the peak of Mt Kuro-dake (30 minutes) to the top station of Sōunkyo ski lift (40 minutes). The lift takes 15 minutes to connect with a cable car which whisks you down to Sōunkyo in seven minutes.

From Asahidake Onsen there's a trail through the forest to Tenninkyō Onsen, a small hot spring resort with a scenic gorge and waterfall, which can be used as a base for extended hiking into the park.

Sōunkyo is the touristic hub of the park and consists of Sōunkyo Onsen, the hot spring resort with an array of brutally ugly hotels, and Sōunkyo Gorge itself – 'kyo' means gorge in Japanese.

The gorge stretches for about eight km beyond Sōunkyō Onsen and is renowned for its waterfalls – Ryūsei-no-taki and Ginga-no-taki are the main ones – and two sections of perpendicular columns of rock which give an enclosed feeling, hence their two names which are Obako (big box) and Kobako (little box).

Since the view from the road is restricted by tunnels, a separate cycling path has been constructed and local entrepreneurs derive a sizable income from bicycle hire at Y1200 per day – the local youth hostels probably offer the best deals for bicycle hire. You could also speed things up by taking a taxi to Obako (20-minute ride) and walking back in a couple of hours.

Hiking Routes The combination of a cable car (Y750, seven minutes) and a ski lift (Y220, 15 minutes) provides fast access to Mt Kuro-dake for skiers and hikers. Discounts are given to youth hostellers, and for return tickets.

The most popular hike is the one across to Mt Asahi-dake. You can arrange to leave your baggage at either end and pick it up later after making the tedious loop back through Asahikawa by bus, or simply restrict your baggage to the minimum required for an overnight stay and return on foot on a different trail.

If you want to do simple day hikes out of Sōunkyō Onsen and return there at the end of the day, you could climb from the top station of the ski lift to the peak of Mt Kuro-dake in an hour and then descend in about 20 minutes to the mountain hut called Mt Kuro-dake Ishimuro which provides basic accommodation and food during the peak hiking season. The return trip to this hut from Sōunkyō Onsen takes about four hours at a leisurely pace.

Places to Stay

Yuwanto-Mura (☎ 01658-2-2772) is a member of the Toho network, about four km from Kamikawa Station. From the station, take the bus bound for Sōunkyō and get off after six minutes at Rubeshibe Bashi bus

stop; from there, it's about 20 minutes on foot. It might be easier either to take a taxi, or to phone from the station and enquire if you could be fetched. Prices start at Y3600 per person including two meals. It's closed during November.

Daisetsu-zan Shirakaba-sō (☎ 0166-97-2246) is an outstanding youth hostel at Asahidake Onsen.

Ginsenkaku Youth Hostel (☎ 01658-5-3003) is a five-minute walk from the bus terminal at Sōunkyō. As you leave the terminal, cross over the bridge to the right-hand side of the river and continue up the steep hill to another bridge below the cable car – the hostel is down the road on your right. Hot spring baths are available for an additional fee of Y150.

There is another youth hostel in Sōunkyō, but judging from personal experience, the attitude of the manager towards foreigners doesn't make for a pleasant stay.

Getting There & Away

Kamikawa is a useful gateway to Sōunkyō. Local trains from Asahikawa take about 1¼ hours to Kamikawa on the JR Sekihoku line. Buses run from Kamikawa to Sōunkyō in 32 minutes (Y600).

Buses run from Sōunkyō to Kamikawa in 32 minutes (Y600). The bus service from Sōunkyō to Kitami takes about two hours. The price is a hefty Y2400, but you get to ride in a deluxe sightseeing bus with plush seats and chandeliers!

If you want to head south towards Obihiro, you'll have to use Route 273 which follows a scenic route via Lake Nukabira-ko, but has *no* bus services – hitch or hire a car. From Obihiro, there's a bus (1¾ hours, Y1600) to Lake Shikaribetsu-ko which is about 15 km from Lake Nukabira-ko.

A bus service runs twice daily (three times daily from mid-June to mid-October) from Asahikawa to Tenninkyō Onsen via Asahidake Onsen. The last bus to Asahidake Onsen is at 3 pm, the last bus from Asahidake Onsen is at 5 pm. The trip takes 1½ hours and the ticket costs Y1180.

RISHIRITO ISLAND 利尻島

This is part of the Rishiri-Rebun-Sarobetsu National Park. Rishiritō Island is dominated by the volcanic peak of Mt Rishiri-zan which soars majestically out of the sea. A road circles the island and a bus service links the small fishing communities. The main activity for visitors is hiking around the various trails and lakes below the summit of the mountain. Providing you have warm clothes and proper footwear, the hike to the summit can be comfortably completed in a full day. Oshidomari and Kutsugata are the main ports for the island.

Information

Information booths at the ferry terminals of these two ports provide maps and information on transport, sights and hiking, and make reservations for accommodation. The booths are opened for the arrival or departure of ferries.

Things to See

There are three trails to the summit of **Mt Rishirizan** (1718 metres), but the most reliable ones lead from Oshidomari and Kutsugata. It doesn't make much difference which of these trails you take up, and which one you take down. Prepare properly for a mountain hike, aim for an early start, and allow a total of 10 hours for the ascent and descent. Advice and maps in Japanese (excellent hiking details with contours) are available from the information booths at the ports, and from the youth hostels.

Just below the summit is **Rishiridake-Sangoya**, an unstaffed mountain hut, which perches on the edge of a precipice and provides the bare minimum for a roof over your head. Take your own food (purchase from shops in the ports) and water. If you stay here, be warned that it's bloody cold at night and the wind contributes generously to the drop in temperatures. If you can't sleep, the night views are absolutely amazing, and providing the clarity holds, the views during the day extend as far as Sakhalin Island (USSR).

If you don't feel like hiking to the summit, there are several enjoyable light hikes. One of these follows the trail from Oshidomari for an hour towards the summit, but branches left in thick forest, about 10 minutes after reaching a group of A-frame chalets at the end of a paved road. This trail leads to **Himenuma Pond** in 1¾ hours with the option of a 30-minute side trip to **Mt Ponyama**.

Places to Stay

The information booth at Oshidomari-kō Port is opened when ferries arrive or depart and can help with booking accommodation both on this island and on Rebuntō Island. There are plenty of minshuku and a couple of youth hostels.

Rishiri Youth Hostel (☎ 01638-4-2523) is a 15-minute walk from Kutsugata-kō Port. If you arrive on the other side of the island, at Oshidomari-kō Port, take the 20-minute bus ride to Kutsugata. Bicycle hire available.

Rishiri Green Hill Youth Hostel (☎ 01638-2-2507) is a five-minute bus ride or 25-minute walk from Oshidomari-kō Port. Bicycle and scooter hire is available.

Herasano-ya (☎ 01638-2-2361) is a member of the Toho network, three minutes on foot from Oshidomari-kō Port. Prices start at Y4500 per person including two meals. It's closed from November until the end of April.

Getting There & Away

It's a 20-minute flight with ANK (Air Nippon) from Wakkanai and the round-trip ticket costs Y10,580 – there are two flights daily during the peak summer season.

A daily ferry service connects Kutsugata with Otaru in about 11 hours and the cheapest ticket costs Y7210 – the same service also extends to Kafuka on Rebuntō Island.

Getting Around

There are six buses daily which complete a 1¾-hour (Y1880) circuit of the island.

Taxis are available in Kutsugata and Oshidomari. Hitching is feasible.

Bicycles are a great way to get around the island and are available for hire at the youth hostels. You can complete a leisurely circuit (53 km) of the island in about five hours.

REBUNTO ISLAND 礼文島

This island is also part of Rishiri-Rebun-Sarobetsu National Park. In contrast to the conical heights of neighbouring Rishiritō Island, Rebuntō is a low, sausage-shaped island with one major road down the east coast. The main attractions are the hiking trails which follow routes along the west coast past remote fishing communities. Between June and August, the island's alpine flowers – over 300 species – pull out all the stops for a floral extravaganza. I'd rate my hikes on this island among the most memorable days I spent in Japan.

Kafuka and Funadomari are the main communities and ports, at the southern and northern ends of the island, respectively.

Things to See

The classic hike down the entire length of the western coast of the island is known as the **Hachi-jikan-haiking-kursu** (Eight-Hour Hiking Course). It's a marvellous walk across varied terrain: grassy clifftops, fields of dwarf bamboo, forests of conifers, deserted, rocky beaches, and remote harbours with clusters of fishing shacks and racks of seaweed. There doesn't seem to be much sense in following the example of many Japanese hikers who turn it into an endurance race – complete with certificate of survival! If you have the extra day, or simply want to pack less into the day, it may be more enjoyable to break the hike into two four-hour sections, known as **Yonjikan Haiking-kursu** (Four-Hour Hiking Course) starting or finishing at Nishi-uedomari.

All the youth hostels and other places to stay on the island provide information on hiking, transport to trailheads, and assign hikers to groups.

Although the Eight-Hour Hike is not a death-defying feat, it has some tricky stretches, including steep slopes of loose scree and several km of boulder-hopping along beaches, which can become very nasty in the unpredictable weather of these north-

ern regions. Much of the trail is several hours away from human habitation, and for the most part, access to pick up those who slip off a cliff or twist an ankle will require a rescue operation by boat. There's no need to be paranoid, but this is the reason why group hiking is encouraged. Beware of being marshalled into large groups because things can then become too regimented. The best size is a group of four.

You'll need proper footwear, warm clothes, and some form of rainwear. The hostels often provide packed lunches which hikers affectionately refer to as 'the Japanese Flag' – an aluminium container of rice with an *umeboshi* (sour salted plum) stuck in the centre! Take water or soft drinks with you. Do *not* drink the water from the streams. During the '30s, foxes were introduced from the Kurile Islands (USSR) and their faeces now contaminate the streams – it may be tapeworm gunk or something else.

Rebun Youth Hostel in Kafuka has an excellent guide book in English entitled *Hiking Maps of Rebun*. The author details seven hikes and grades them according to difficulty, and a really useful point is the inclusion of place names in kanji and romaji. The book is not for sale, but you can look through it and make notes, sketch maps and lists of place names.

The Eight-Hour Hike runs from Cape Sukotonmisaki on the northern tip, down to Moto-chi on the southern tip. The Four-Hour Hike starts or finishes at Nishi-uedomari, a small fishing village midway down the trail. You can follow the trails in either direction – most people seem to hike from north to south – but make sure you have got transport arranged and keep your timetable flexible to avoid spoiling things with the rush of a forced march.

Another popular hike is the one from Nairo, halfway down the east coast, to the top of Mt Rebun-dake. The peak is a tiddler at 490 metres, but it's a pleasant 3½-hour return hike.

Places to Stay

The information booth at the port can help

find accommodation. There are many minshuku, a couple of hotels and a trio of youth hostels on the island.

Rebun Youth Hostel (☎ 01638-6-1608) in Kafuka is a very friendly place, 13 minutes on foot from Kafuka-kō Port. If you phone ahead, they'll pick you up at the port, and when you leave you may be given a lift back to the port by two staff members who insist on playing guitar and harmonica to serenade your departure!

Momoiwa-sō Youth Hostel (☎ 01638-6-1421) is a 15-minute bus ride from Kafuka-kō Port. Take the bus bound for Moto-chi and get off at Momoiwa iriguchi, then walk for seven minutes. The hostel is in a convenient spot, close to one of the trailheads for the Eight-Hour Hike. It's open from June to late September only.

Rebuntō Funadomari Youth Hostel (☎ 01638-7-2717) is a 20-minute walk from Funadomari-kō Port. It's open from 10 May to the end of October only.

Seikan-sō (☎ 01638-7-2078) is a member of the Toho network, just a couple of minutes on foot from Funadomari-kō Port. Prices start at Y4120 per person including two meals. It's closed from October until the beginning of May.

Getting There & Away

It's a 20-minute flight with ANK (Air Nippon) from Wakkanai and the round-trip ticket costs Y12,080 – two flights daily during the peak summer season. The information office (☎ 01638-7-2175) at Rebun Kūkō Airfield is open from 9 am to 5 pm.

There is a ferry service from Kafuka providing connections to Oshidomari (Rishiritō Island) and to Wakkanai. There is one daily ferry between Funadomari and Wakkanai.

A daily ferry service connects Kafuka via Kutsugata (Rishiritō Island) with Otaru in about 11 hours and the cheapest ticket costs Y7720.

Getting Around

Most of the time you'll be getting around the island on foot. The youth hostels and other places to stay will usually help with your transport arrangements on arrival or departure. A couple of the minshuku also have bicycles to rent.

The main bus service follows the island's one major road from Kafuka in the south, to Cape Sukotonmisaki in the north. En route it passes Funadomari, the Kūkō-shita or Airport bus stop, and Nishi-uedomari. Buses run on this route up to six times daily, but only four go to Cape Sukotonmisaki. Top marks go to the solitary splendour of the hi-tech toilet on this cape where you can follow the needs of nature whilst listening to the recorded sounds of the waves outside! Another useful bus service runs five times daily from Kafuka to Moto-chi, a trailhead for the hiking trail along the western coastline of the island. Pick up a copy of the island's bus timetable at the information office in Kafuka Port.

Since there is only one major road, hitching is relatively simple, but most rides will be short.

SHIRETOKO NATIONAL PARK
知床国立公園

This remote park features a peninsula with a range of volcanic peaks leading out to the rugged cliffs around Cape Shiretokomisaki. The main season for visitors is from mid-June to mid-September – most of the hikes are not recommended outside this season.

Orientation

Shari is the gateway to the peninsula. Utoro is the largest resort on the peninsula, but the boat excursions are about the only things it has to offer. Iwaobetsu is a hamlet, further up the coast from Utoro.

Information

There's a Tourist Information Office just behind the bus centre in Utoro.

Things to See

About 10 minutes by bus from Iwaobetsu Youth Hostel are the **Shireto-ko Goko** (Shireto-ko Five Lakes) where wooden walkways have been laid out for visitors to stroll around the lakes in an hour or so.

Another 45 minutes by bus down the rough road towards the tip of the peninsula, you come to Ohashi Bridge just below the spectacular rotemburo (natural, open-air hot springs) which form part of **Kamuiwakka-no-taki Falls**. It takes about 20 minutes to climb up the rocky bed of the stream until you come to cascades of hot water emptying into a succession of pools. Bathers simply strip off and soak in the pools which command a superb panorama across the ocean. Between mid-June and mid-September, a special sightseeing bus service operates once daily to the lakes and the open-air hot springs – passengers are given time to take a dip in the pools.

There are several hikes on the peninsula; Iwaobetsu Youth Hostel can provide more detailed advice on routes, trail conditions, and organisation of transport. Proper footwear and warm clothes are essential.

The hike to the top of **Mt Rausu-dake** starts from the hotel at Iwaobetsu Onsen. There's only one bus a day out to the hotel, so you'll probably have to walk for an hour up the side road from Iwaobetsu Youth Hostel to reach the start of the trail – allow 4½ hours from there to reach the top (1660 metres) at a comfortable pace.

The hike to the summit of **Mt Iō-zan** (1562 metres) starts about 500 metres beyond Ohashi Bridge and requires about eight hours for the return trip.

The youth hostel owner also recommends another short hike from Shiretoko Pass – midway between Utoro and Rausu – to Lake Rausu-ko.

Places to Stay

Kaze-no-Ko (☎ 01522-3-1121) near Shari is a member of the Toho network. From Shari Station, take the bus bound for Utoro and get off after 10 minutes. Prices start at Y3800 per person including two meals.

Shiretoko Youth Hostel (☎ 01522-4-2764) in Utoro is a massive place ready to cater for large numbers. Bicycle hire is available.

Iwaobetsu Youth Hostel (☎ 01522-4-2311) in Iwaobetsu is a convenient base. Bicycle hire is available at Y300 per day. The hostel is closed from late October to the beginning of June. To get there, take a direct bus from Shari via Utoro to Iwaobetsu (70 minutes, Y1600). Alternatively, change at Utoro for the bus bound for Shireto-ko Goko (Shireto-ko Five Lakes) and get off after about 20 minutes – just ask the bus driver to drop you off at the hostel. If you've missed the bus from Utoro, either hitch (it's only nine km) or phone the hostel manager. A side road almost opposite the youth hostel leads four km uphill to Iwaobetsu Onsen, a hot spring hotel, at the start of the trail up Mt Rausu-dake.

Getting There & Away

From Shari, which is the gateway to the peninsula, there is an efficient bus service to the large and rather bland resort of Utoro, but Iwaobetsu Youth Hostel is a more convenient base for hiking.

There are up to eight buses daily from Shari to Utoro, but only three or four continue to Iwaobetsu – the full trip from Shari to Iwaobetsu takes 70 minutes (Y1600). Buses to Rausu operate twice daily from July to mid-October.

Getting Around

Roads run along each side of the peninsula, but they peter out well before its tip, which can be viewed as part of a long boat excursion from Utoro. Another road crosses the peninsula from Rausu to Utoru. Transport is restricted to infrequent buses, bicycle hire and hitching.

Between May and early September, two boat excursions are operated from Utoro: one runs once daily out to the soaring cliffs of Cape Shiretokomisaki (Y4910, 3¾ hours); the other runs up to five times daily for a short cruise along the coastline as far as Kamuiwakka-no-taki Falls (Y1900, 90 minutes).

BIHORO 美幌

Bihoro lies east of Asahikawa, and north of Akan National Park. If you're not going to Shiretoko National Park, you can head south from here into Akan National Park.

From Bihoro, sightseeing buses follow a scenic route to the park, pausing after 50 minutes at Bihoro Pass which provides a superb view across Lake Kussharo-ko, and then continuing round all the sights of the park for another 2¾ hours before reaching the terminus at Akan Kohan. It's best to use this expensive service in small doses – the incessant commentary and packaged feel can be oppressive. The trip from Bihoro to Kawayu Onsen on the shore of Lake Kussharo-ko takes 65 minutes (Y2590).

Places to Stay

Bihoro Youth Hostel (☎ 01527-3-2560) is close to the town centre. From Bihoro Station it's a six-minute bus ride followed by a 10-minute walk. Bicycle hire is available, and there are hot springs nearby.

KUSHIRO 釧路

Kushiro is the industrial and economic centre of eastern Hokkaidō and one of the main gateways to Akan National Park.

Places to Stay

Charanke-sō (☎ 0154-41-2386) is 12 minutes by bus from Kushiro Station. Prices at this minshuku start at Y5500 per person including two meals.

Kushiro Makiba Youth Hostel (☎ 0154-23-0852) is a 15-minute walk from the station. Bicycle and scooter hire available.

Kushiro Youth Hostel (☎ 0154-41-1676) is a 15-minute bus ride from the station – take bus Nos 8 or 15, then walk for two minutes.

Getting There & Away

Flights connect Kushiro with Sapporo (40 minutes) and Tokyo (105 minutes).

There are bus services from Kushiro to Akan Kohan (2¼ hours, Y2440), and to Rausu (3½ hours, Y2730) on the Shiretoko Peninsula. There's also a night bus to Sapporo (seven hours, Y5700).

The JR Senmō rail line runs north through Akan National Park to Shari. The JR Nemuro line runs west to Sapporo (4¾ hours by limited express).

A regular ferry service connects Kushiro

with Tokyo in 32 hours – the cheapest passenger fare is Y14,000. Kushiro Nishi Kō Port is a 15-minute bus ride from Kushiro Station.

AKAN NATIONAL PARK
阿寒国立公園

This large park in eastern Hokkaidō contains several volcanic peaks, some large caldera lakes, and extensive forests.

The main gateways on the fringe of the park are Bihoro in the north and Kushiro in the south. The major centres inside the park are the towns of Teshikaga, Kawayu Onsen and Akan Kohan.

Things to See

You can use **Kawayu Onsen** as a convenient base for visiting the nearby sights of Lake Kussharo-ko, Mt Iō-zan, and Lake Mashū-ko. Unfortunately, Kawayu Onsen, a hot spring resort, is notable for hordes of tourists disgorged from tour buses and greeted by loudspeakers playing a 'welcome cassette' which is endlessly repeated to entice customers into the souvenir shops.

About three km from Kawayu Onsen is **Lake Kussharo-ko**, the largest inland lake in Hokkaidō and a popular spot for swimming and camping. At Sunayu Onsen on the eastern shore, the hot springs warm the sand on the beach, and at Wakoto Onsen on the southern shore there are hot springs bubbling into open-air pools.

Mt Iō-zan, just outside Kawayu Onsen, is unmistakable for its steam and distinctive smell. A pleasant nature trail leads from the bus centre through dwarf pines to the mountain in 35 minutes. The scene is certainly impressive with hissing vents, billowing clouds of steam and bright yellow sulphur deposits.

Lake Mashūko is about 15 km south-east of Kawayu Onsen. If you are fortunate enough to visit when the lake is not wreathed in mist, the clarity of the water and its intense blue colour are quite startling.

Akan Kohan is a hot spring resort on the edge of Lake Akan-ko. You can safely skip the boat trips on the lake and the atrocious tourist facilities, but it's good to use this resort as a base for doing some interesting mountain hikes in the area.

You can start your hiking activities with **Mt O-Akan-dake** (1371 metres), about six km south of Akan Kohan. The hiking trail starts at Takiguchi and the ascent takes about three hours; the descent takes two hours. From the peak there are fine views of Lake Penketō and Lake Panketō. Hiking maps are available from the visitors' centre and the owner of Akan Angel Youth Hostel can provide more details.

Also accessible from Akan Kohan is **Mt Me-Akan-dake** (1499 metres), an active volcano and the highest mountain in the park. Keep a close watch on the weather which can change very quickly. When hiking round the crater, watch out for the noxious effects of the sulphur fumes from the vents. There is a clear trail up the mountain which requires about 4½ hours for the ascent and 3½ hours for the descent if you return by the same trail. It's also possible to descend a different trail on the west side of the mountain which joins the road leading to Nonaka Onsen Youth Hostel. Hiking maps are available from the visitors' centre and the owner of Akan Angel Youth Hostel can provide more details.

Places to Stay

Kussharo-ko Youth Hostel (☎ 01548-3-3539), four km from Kawayu Onsen, is part of a large ryokan on the shore of the lake. Hostellers are given comfortable rooms in the ryokan. For an additional fee of Y150 you can use the hot spring bath – lined with smooth rocks and offering a view across the lake – on the premises. There is a shuttle service operated by the ryokan to transport guests to the bus terminal in Kawayu Onsen. The hostel is open from May to late October.

Sanzoku-no-ie (☎ 01548-3-2725), a member of the Toho network, is a small minshuku about six minutes on foot from Kawayu Onsen Station. Prices start at Y3800 per person including two meals. It's open from May to late October.

Mashumaro (☎ 01548-2-2027), a member

of the Toho network, is a five-minute walk from Biruwa Station – the stop between Kawayu Onsen and Teshikaga. Prices start at Y3800 per person including two meals. It's closed during November and April.

Akan Angel Youth Hostel (☎ 0154-67-2309) is a 12-minute walk from the bus terminal at Akan Kohan. Bicycle hire and hot spring baths (Y150 additional fee) are also available.

Akan-Kohan Youth Hostel (☎ 0154-67-2241) is a four-minute walk from the bus terminal at Akan Kohan. Bicycle hire and hot spring baths are available. It's open from June to late October.

Nonaka Onsen Youth Hostel (☎ 01562-9-7454), about 20 km west of Lake Akan-ko, also provides a base for climbing Mt Me-Akan-dake. It's reached by a very infrequent direct bus service, or you can use the more frequent bus service between Akan Kohan and Ashoro Station – get off at Noboriyama guchi (about 55 minutes from Akan Kohan) then take the side road south for the 45-minute walk to the hostel.

Getting There & Away

Sightseeing buses run north-east from Akan Kohan to the main sights in the rest of the park as far as Kawayu Onsen. Other services connect with Ashoro and Obihiro (Y3500, 2¾ hours) to the south-west, Bihoro (Y1950, 1¼ hours) and Kitami to the north, and Kushiro (Y2440, 2¼ hours) to the east.

The JR Senmō line links Kawayu Station with Shari in 55 minutes, and Kushiro in 1½ hours. Kawayu Onsen Bus Centre is a 10-minute bus ride from Kawayu Station.

Getting Around

The only efficient and speedy transport in the park is provided by sightseeing buses which get you to the sights but also have the disadvantages of 'packaged' travel. Bus services are most frequent between June and October. Kushiro would be a convenient choice to rent a car – ask at the Tourist Information Centre at Kushiro Station. The JR Senmō line runs from Shari to Kushiro – trains are slow and infrequent. Hitching is also a possibility.

SHIKOTSU-TOYA NATIONAL PARK
支笏洞爺国立公園

This park in southern Hokkaidō is centred around Lake Shikotsu-ko, Lake Tōya-ko, and Noboribetsu Onsen. The lakes have the added attractions of mountain hikes or close-up encounters with volcanoes, whilst Noboribetsu Onsen will appeal to hot spring enthusiasts. Fast and easy access to the park from Sapporo or Chitose Kūkō Airport makes it a favourite with visitors who have only a short time to spend in Hokkaidō.

JNTO publishes a leaflet entitled *Southern Hokkaidō (MG-12)* which provides a map of the park with information on sights, transport and accommodation.

Things to See

For mountain hiking, try **Lake Shikotsu-ko**, a caldera lake surrounded by several volcanoes. The main centre for transport and information is Shikotsu Kohan which consists of a bus terminal, a visitor centre, a pier for boat excursions, and assorted souvenir shops, restaurants, and places to stay.

The visitor centre (☎ 01232-5-2453), close to the bus terminal, is open from 9.30 am to 4.30 pm and has maps and information. From the boat pier, there are rather tame sightseeing cruises which stop off at a couple of places round the lake before returning to the pier (1½ hours, Y1580). If you cross the bridge on your far left as you walk down to the lake shore, you can follow a nature trail around the forested slopes for an hour or so. The youth hostel provides bicycle hire (Y250 per hour or Y800 per day) and this is a good way to follow the road round the edge of the lake, which is not served by a bus service.

The mountain hikes are the most interesting things to do around the lake. The youth hostel or the visitor centre can give more advice on access, routes and timings.

Mt Eniwa-dake (1320 metres) lies on the western side of the lake. The start of the trail is about 10 minutes on foot from Poropinai – the appropriate bus stop is called Eniwa-dake Yamaguchi. It takes about 3½ hours to hike to the summit where there is a fine panorama of the surrounding lakes and peaks. Don't hike in the rain as the steeper sections of the trail become dangerously slippery.

Mt Tarumae-dake (1038 metres) lies on the southern side of the lake and offers the rugged delights of wandering round the crater of an active volcano. The crater is an easy 40-minute hike from the 7th station which can be reached from Shikotsu Kohan in three hours on foot – or in 20 minutes if you use the bus service that seems to run only on Sunday. From the crater, you can either return to the 7th station, or follow the trail north-west down the mountain for 2½ hours to **Koke-no-Dōmon**, a mossy gorge, which is 10 minutes from the car park at Shishamonai on the lake shore. From Shishamonai you'll have to walk or hitch the 15 km to Shikotsu Kohan.

Places to Stay

There are over a dozen minshuku, ryokan and hotels on the edge of the lake; campgrounds are also available at Morappu, Poropinai and Bifue. The visitor centre can help with booking accommodation.

Shikotsu-ko Youth Hostel (☎ 0123-25-2311) is at Shikotsuko Kohan, and just a couple of minutes from the bus terminal there. This is a well-organised and friendly hostel which has family rooms as well as the usual dorm accommodation. Bicycle hire and hot spring baths (additional fee of Y150) are also available. Overseas hostellers are eligible for a Y500 discount.

Getting There & Away

The bus service from Sapporo to the lake takes 80 minutes (Y990), other bus services run from Chitose Kūkō Airport (47 minutes, Y660) and Tomakomai (45 minutes, Y540).

Shikoku 四国

Although Shikoku is Japan's fourth largest island, it's predominantly rural and very much off the tourist track. The Ritsurin-kōen

Garden in Takamatsu and the castles in Matsuyama and Uwajima are the main cultural attractions. The island has some impressive coastline and a few interesting mountains.

Japan's best known pilgrimage is the 88 Temple Circuit of Shikoku - set aside six weeks and be prepared to walk over 1000 km if you want to join those hardy souls who make the journey on foot. Most pilgrims these days travel by tour bus.

TAKAMATSU 高松

The completion of the Seto-ōhashi Bridge has reinforced Takamatsu's importance as a major arrival point on Shikoku. The town has an important garden, the nearby Shikoku Mura Village Museum and the very popular Kotohira-gū Shrine is an easy day trip.

Things to See

Although not one of Japan's 'big three' gardens, the **Ritsurin-kōen Garden** could easily be a contender for that list. The garden, which was first constructed in the mid-1600s, winds around a series of ponds with lookouts, tearooms, bridges and islands.

The 292-metre-high table-top plateau of **Yashima** stands five km from the centre of Takamatsu. Today it's the site for the Yashima-ji Temple and offers fine views over the surrounding countryside and the Inland Sea.

From the left of the shrine at the bottom of the hill a funicular railway runs up to the top of Yashima Hill. The cost is Y510 one way or Y1010 return. At the top you can rent a bicycle (Y300 plus Y1000 deposit) to pedal around the attractions, it's a long walk otherwise.

You can get to Yashima by private Kotoden train or by JR train which also drops you a bit further from the base of the hill. It takes about 20 minutes and costs Y190 by JR, slighty less by Kotoden. Buses also run directly to the top of the hill.

At the bottom of Yashima Hill is **Shikoku Mura Village**, an excellent village museum with old buildings brought from all over Shikoku and neighbouring islands.

Places to Stay

Takamatsu-shi Youth Hostel (☎ 0878-85-2024) is some distance south of Takamatsu, and can be reached via the Kotoden line to Kotohira. The hostel charges Y1740 per night. *Yashima-Sansō Youth Hostel* (☎ 0878-22-3656), near the Shikoku Mura Village at Yashima, costs Y1900 per night.

A few minutes' walk away from the station is the *New Getukōen Hotel* (☎ 0878-22-0953) which is definitely at the grotty end of the business hotel spectrum. Singles with sink and toilet but no bath (these rooms are upstairs and more or less on the roof) are Y3200. The beds are clean but otherwise well worn.

Places to Eat

Every larger railway station in Shikoku seems to have an *Andersen's Bakery*, often rejoicing in the name *Willie Winkie*. The one at JR Takamatsu Station is good for an economical breakfast. Across the road is a *Mister Donut* and there are a number of other restaurants nearby. Kotoden Kawaramachi Station is also a centre for a variety of cheap eats.

Getting There & Away

JAS have flights to and from Fukuoka and Tokyo; ANA to and from Osaka and Tokyo.

Direct buses operate between Tokyo and Takamatsu; the 'Hello Bridge' service costs Y10,300 one way.

The Seto-ōhashi Bridge has brought Takamatsu much closer to the main island of Honshū. From Tokyo, you can take the shinkansen to Okayama, change trains there and be in Takamatsu in five hours. The Okayama-Takamatsu section takes about an hour.

From Takamatsu, the JR Kotoku railway line runs south-east to Tokushima and the JR Yosan line west to Matsuyama. The Yosan line branches off at Tadotsu and becomes the Dosan line, turning south-west to Kotohira and Kōchi. The private Kotoden line also runs direct to Kotohira.

Takamatsu is also an important ferry terminus with services to ports in the Inland Sea

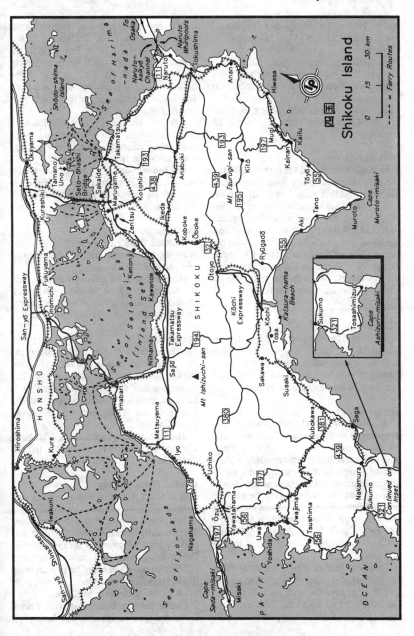

Shikoku Island

四国

0   15   30 km

---- = Ferry Routes

and on Honshū including Kōbe (4½ hours) and Osaka (5½ hours). Uno, to the south of Okayama, is a quick way to make the Honshū-Shikoku connection, since Uno-Okayama trains connect with the ferry departures. Takamatsu is also the easiest jumping-off point for visiting attractive Shōdo-shima Island. Takamatsu's ferry terminal buildings are right beside the JR station.

Getting Around

Takamatsu Airport is 16 km from the city and the bus, which departs from outside JR Takamatsu Station, takes about half an hour.

Takamatsu has a local bus service, but for most visitors the major attractions, principally the Ritsurin-kōen Garden and Yashima, can easily be reached on the JR Kotoku line or the more frequent Kotoden line service. The main Kotoden junction is Kawaramachi although the line ends at Chikko Station, just across from JR Takamatsu Station.

TOKUSHIMA 徳島

Tokushima (population 225,000), on Shikoku's east coast, is a pleasant enough modern city, but offers few attractions in its own right. However, some of Shikoku's best sights are in the nearby countryside.

Things to See

The **Naruto Whirlpools** are near Tokushima. At the change of tide, the water whisks through the narrow Naruto Strait with such speed that ferocious whirlpools are created. Boats venture out into the strait, which separates Shikoku from nearby Awaji-shima Island, and travel under the modern Naruto-ōhashi Bridge to inspect the whirlpools close up. A brochure on the boat trips (Y1300) is available at the JR Tokushima Station information counter and it details tide times.

There's a fine view over the strait from Naruto Park at the Shikoku end of the bridge, and you can save the walk up to the top of the lookout by taking a long Y200 escalator ride. Getting to the bridge by public transport

can be very time-consuming although it's not a great distance. From Tokushima, take a train to JR Naruto Station (Y310, 40 minutes) and an infrequent bus from there to the bridge (Y300, 20 minutes). It might be better to take a bus directly from Tokushima Bus Station. Ferries also run to the park from Awaji-shima Island.

About 35 km directly west of Tokushima is **Dochū**, where erosion has formed curious sand pillars standing about 15 metres high. It's reached via JR Anabuki Station.

Mt Tsurugi-san (1955 metres) is the second highest mountain in Shikoku. A chairlift takes you to a point which is a 40-minute walk from the summit.

Places to Stay

Tokushima Youth Hostel (☎ 0886-63-1505) is by the beach some distance out of town and costs Y2100.

Hotels close to the railway station include the *Station Hotel* (☎ 0886-52-8181) with singles/doubles at Y4900/9300, the *Astoria Hotel* (☎ 0886-53-6151) and *Aivis Hotel*.

Places to Eat

Fast-food places can be found around the station and include an *Andersen's/Willie Winkie* bakery and a nearby *Lotteria*. The arcade south of the river has a selection of fast-food outlets including a *McDonald's, Mister Donut, Andersen's* and *Kentucky Fried Chicken*.

The hotel area just north of the river bank has a good selection of restaurants and red lantern bars.

Getting There & Away

JAS connect Tokushima with Osaka and Tokyo.

Tokushima is less than 1½ hours from Takamatsu by limited express. There are also railway lines westward to Ikeda on the JR Dosan line (which runs between Kotohira and Kōchi) and south along the coastal Mugi line as far as Kaifu from where you will have to take a bus to continue to Kōchi.

Ferries connect Tokushima with Tokyo, Osaka and Kōbe on Honshū, with Kokura on

Kyūshū and with various smaller ports. It only takes two hours to Kōbe by hydrofoil.

Getting Around

It's easy to get around Tokushima on foot: from the railway station to the Mt Bizan cable-car station is only 700 metres. Bicycles can be rented from the underground bicycle park in front of the station.

CAPE MUROTO-MISAKI 室戸岬

Cape Muroto-misaki, east of Kōchi, has a lighthouse topping its wild cliffscape. The **Higashi-dera Temple** here is No 24 on the Shikoku temple circuit and also houses the *Higashi-dera Youth Hostel* (☎ 0887-22-0366). Just north of Muroto is a chain of black sand beaches known by local surfers as 'Little Hawaii'.

You can reach the cape by bus from Kōchi and you can continue right round to Tokushima on the east coast. The JR Mugi line runs around the east coast from Tokushima as far as Kaifu.

CAPE ASHIZURI-MISAKI 足摺岬

West of Kōchi, Cape Ashizuri-misaki, like Cape Muroto-misaki, is a wild and scenic promontory ending with a lighthouse. As well as the coastal road, there's also a central skyline drive. Cape Ashizuri-misaki also has a temple (the **Kongōfuku-ji**, No 38 on the temple circuit) which, like the temple at Cape Muroto-misaki, also has its own youth hostel (☎ 0880-88-0038).

From Tosashimizu, at the top of the cape, ferries operate to Kōbe on Honshū. From Kōchi there is a railway as far as Nakamura; travel from Nakamura around the cape and on to Uwajima is by bus.

MATSUYAMA 松山

Shikoku's largest city, Matsuyama, is a busy north coast town (population 400,000) and an important transport hub with frequent ferry links to Hiroshima.

Things to See

Picturesquely sited on top of a hill in the middle of town, **Matsuyama-jō Castle** is one of the finest original surviving castles from the feudal era.

Dōgo Onsen is a popular spa centre a couple of km east of town but easily reached by the regular tram service which terminates at the start of the spa's shopping arcade. The arcade leads to the front of Dōgo Onsen Honkan. A high priority for any visitor to Matsuyama should be a bath at this rambling old public bathhouse which dates from 1894.

Places to Stay

Matsuyama has three accommodation areas – around the JR station (business hotels), around the centre (business hotels and more expensive hotels) and at Dōgo Onsen (ryokan and Japanese-style hotels).

Matsuyama Youth Hostel (☎ 0899-33-6366) is near the Isaniwa Shrine in Dōgo Onsen and costs Y2100 a night.

Around JR Matsuyama Station is the *Central Hotel* (☎ 0899-41-4358/59), a cheaper business hotel with singles/doubles from Y3800/7000.

In central Matsuyama is the *Tokyo Dai Ichi Hotel* (☎ 0899-47-4411) on the station side of the town centre. Singles are from Y5500, doubles or twins from Y9500. Rooms at the *Chateau-tel Matsuyama* (☎ 0899-46-2111) are almost identical in price.

For Japanese tourists, Dōgo Onsen is the big attraction. Hotel are usually expensive, but *Minshuku Miyoshi* (☎ 0899-77-2581), behind the petrol station near the Ishite Temple, is an exception with per person costs at around Y4000 to Y4500.

Places to Eat

The long Gintengai and Okaidō shopping arcade in central Matsuyama has the usual fast food: *McDonald's, Kentucky Fried* and *Mister Donut.* There's another *Mister Donut* near Matsuyama City Station. The arcade leading from the Dōgo Onsen tram stop to the Dōgo Onsen Honkan bathhouse also has a number of restaurants with plastic meal replicas.

Next to the post office in the town centre, *Restaurant Goshiki* offers sōmen (fine wheat) noodles and other dishes.

Close to the Okaidō arcade is the small *Tandoor* Indian restaurant offering various curries at Y750 to Y1000, thali dinners at Y2000 and tandoori dinners at Y2500.

Getting There & Away

ANA has flights between Matsuyama and Osaka, Nagoya and Tokyo. JAS has connections to Fukuoka, Miyazaki and Kagoshima, all in Kyūshū. JAL also fly to Tokyo while SWAL have direct flights between Matsuyama and Naha in Okinawa.

The north coast JR Yosan line connects Matsuyama with Takamatsu and there are also services across the Seto-ōhashi Bridge to Honshū. Another line runs south from Matsuyama to Uwajima and then east to Kōchi, though this is a rather circuitous route: it's much faster to take a bus directly to Kōchi.

There are frequent ferry and hydrofoil connections with Hiroshima. Take the Iyo-tetsudo private railway line from Matsuyama City (Shi-eki) or Otemachi Station right to the end of the line at Takahama (Y440 from Otemachi). From Takahama, a connecting bus whisks you the remaining distance to Matsuyama Kanko Port. The hydrofoils zip across to Hiroshima in one hour for Y4950. The ferry takes 2¾ to three hours depending on the port in Matsuyama and costs Y3710 1st class, Y1850 2nd class to Hiroshima from Matsuyama Kanko.

Other ferries operate to and from Beppu, Kokura and Oita on Kyūshū as well as Iwakuni, Kure, Mihara, Onomichi and Yanai in Honshū.

Getting Around

Matsuyama has the private Iyo-tetsudo railway line and a tram (streetcar) service. The railway line is mainly useful for getting to and from the port for Hiroshima ferries.

The tram services cost a flat Y150 anywhere in town. There's a loop line and major terminuses at Dōgo Onsen and outside Matsuyama City Station. The Ichiban-chō stop outside the Mitsukoshi Department Store and ANA Hotel is a good central stopping point.

MT ISHIZUCHI-SAN

Ishizuchi-san (1982 metres) is the highest mountain in Shikoku (indeed in all western Japan) and easily reached from Matsuyama. It's also a holy mountain and many pilgrim climbers make the hike.

From Matsuyama, you can take a bus to Tsuchi Goya, south-east of the mountain. Alternatively, take a bus from Iyo Saijō Station on the Matsuyama-Takamatsu line to the Nishi-no-kawa cable-car station on the north side. This route passes through the scenic **Omogo-kei Gorge**, an attraction in its own right. Out of season, bus services to the mountain are infrequent. You can climb up one way and down the other or even make a complete circuit from Nishi-no-kawa to the summit, down to Tsuchi Goya and then back to Nishi-no-kawa. Allow all day from an early start for the circuit.

The cable car takes about eight minutes straight up and down and costs Y800 one way or Y1500 return. The ride is followed by an optional chair lift (Y200, Y350) which slightly shortens the walk to Jōju where there is a good view of the mountain from the **Ishizuchi-jinja Shrine**. From Jōju, it's 3.6 km to the top, first gently downhill through forest, then uphill through forest, across a more open area and finally a steep and rocky ascent. Although there's a path, and often steps, all the way to the top, the fun way to make the final ascent is up a series of *kusari*, heavy chains draped down the very steep rock faces. Clambering up these chains is the approved pilgrimage method. The actual summit is a little beyond the mountain hut on the top, reached by climbing along a sharp ridge.

UWAJIMA 宇和島

Uwajima is a relatively quiet and peaceful place with a small but original castle, the shabby remnants of a fine garden, some pleasant temples and a notorious sex shrine.

Things to See

Dating from 1665, **Uwajima-jō Castle** was never a great castle but it is original, not a reconstruction. It once stood by the sea, and although land reclamation has moved the sea well back, there are still good views over the town. Entry is free and it opens at 9 am.

Once upon a time, many Shinto shrines had a connection to fertility rites but this aspect was comprehensively purged when puritanism was imported from the West following the Meiji Restoration. A handful of holdouts survived and Uwajima's **Taga-jinja Shrine** is certainly one of them: it's totally dedicated to sex. There's a tree trunk phallus and various other bits and pieces around the temple grounds but the three-storey sex museum is the temple's major attraction. Entry is Y600.

The **Tenshaen Gardens** (entry Y200) are definitely not among Japan's classic gardens, they look distinctly worn and thin compared to the well-tended lushness of most Japanese gardens. Nearby is the Municipal Date Museum (entry Y200, closed Mondays).

Places to Stay

The *Uwajima Youth Hostel* (☎ 0895-22-7177) is a long walk from the town centre: when you get to the temples overlooking the town, its another 650-metre walk, uphill. From the shrine, the hostel is a 1.25 km walk. Beds cost Y2100.

The *Kiya Ryokan* (☎ 0895-22-0101) is a relaxed and friendly place with single rooms at Y4120. It's just south of the shopping arcade.

Places to Eat

Remarkably, Uwajima is free of the usual US-dominated fast-food chains, having only a *Willie Winkie/Andersen's* bakery in the station and a burger place in the arcade. The arcade is principally inhabited by coffee bars, the entertainment district, with many places to eat, sprawls on both sides.

Getting There & Away

You can approach Uwajima by train from Matsuyama (via Uchiko and Uno); the trip by limited express takes one hour 40 minutes. From Kōchi it takes 3¾ to 4½ hours by limited express via Kubokawa where you change trains. If you want to head further south and on to Cape Ashizuri-misaki, you'll have to resort to buses as the railway line from Kōchi terminates at Nakamura.

Direct bus services operate to Honshū from Uwajima and there is also a ferry connection to Beppu in Kyūshū via Yawatahama.

Getting Around

Uwajima is a good place to explore by bicycle since it's quiet and the traffic is not too bad. The tourist office across from the station rents bicycles for Y100 an hour.

Kyūshū 九州

Kyūshū is the furthest south of the four major islands of Japan. Some of the earliest evidence of Japanese civilisation can be seen at the archaeological excavations around Miyazaki and at the many ancient stone carvings in the Usuki area.

For visitors, prime attractions in Kyūshū include Nagasaki with its European-influenced history and its atomic tragedy. In the north, Fukuoka/Hakata is a major international arrival point and the terminus for the shinkansen line from Tokyo. In the centre of the island there is the massive volcanic caldera of the Aso National Park, while more volcanic activity can be witnessed in the south at Mt Sakura-jima. Larger towns like Kagoshima and Kumamoto offer fine gardens and magnificent castles. There are some good walking opportunities, particularly along the Kirishima volcano chain.

FUKUOKA/HAKATA 福岡、博多

Fukuoka/Hakata (population 1.2 million) is a somewhat confusing city as the airport is always referred to as Fukuoka, and the shinkansen terminus as Hakata. Today it is the biggest city in Kyūshū.

Although there are no compelling tourist attractions in Fukuoka it's a pleasant city and easy to get around.

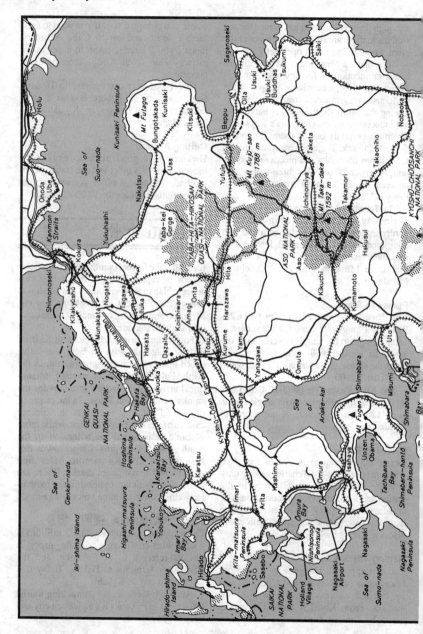

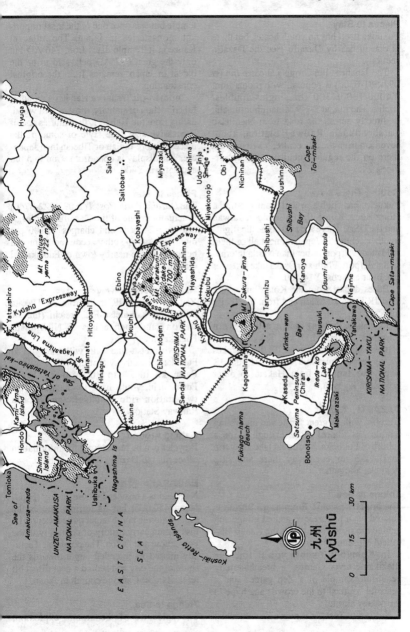

Places to Stay

Fukuoka itself has no youth hostel, but there is one in nearby Dazaifu (see the Dazaifu section).

The Japanese Inn Group's *Suehiro Inn* (☎ 092-581-0306) is popular, with rooms from Y4000/7300/9300 for singles/doubles/triples. The inn, at 2-1-9 Minamihon-machi, is directly across the road from Nishitetsu Zasshonokuma Railway Station, about seven km from the city centre; it's easy to get there on the regular suburban railway services.

Getting There & Away

Fukuoka has flights to and from Australia, Hong Kong, Korea, the Philippines, Taiwan and the USA. There are also domestic flights to other centres in Japan, almost all of them to Haneda Airport rather than Narita International Airport. Flights to Osaka take just over one hour and cost Y14,400.

Buses depart from the Kōtsū bus centre near JR Hakata Station and from the Tenjin bus centre.

JR Hakata Railway Station is the western terminus of the 1177 km Tokyo-Osaka-Hakata shinkansen service. To Tokyo takes six to seven hours and costs Y21,300. JR lines also fan out from Hakata to other centres in Kyūshū.

DAZAIFU 太宰府

Dazaifu, with its great shrine and interesting temples, is almost close enough to be a suburb of Fukuoka. You could take a day trip to Dazaifu or even stay there and skip Fukuoka altogether.

Things to See

The brightly painted **Tenman-gū Shrine** is entered via a picturesque arched bridge and behind the shrine building is the Kankō Historical Museum (entry Y200).

In **Kōmyō-ji Temple** you'll find the Ittekikaino-niwa Garden, a breathtakingly beautiful example of a Zen garden and a peaceful contrast to the crowds and hype in the nearby shrine.

Kaidan-in Temple is now a Zen Buddhist

temple but was once one of the most important monasteries in Japan. The adjacent Kanzeon-ji Temple dates from 746 AD but only the great 697 AD bell, said to be the oldest in Japan, remains from the original construction.

Tenman-gū Treasure Hall has a wonderful collection of statuary, most of it of wood, dating from the 10th to 12th centuries and of impressive size. The style of some of the pieces is more Indian or Tibetan than Japanese. The display is open from 9 am to 5 pm and entry is Y400.

Places to Stay

The *Dazaifu Youth Hostel* (☎ 092-922-8740) is actually in one of the Dazaifu temples; it has only 24 beds and charges Y2100 per night. Ryokan and other accommodation can be found in the nearby town of Futsukaichi Onsen.

Getting There & Away

You can take a JR train from JR Hakata Station to Kokutetsu-Futsukaichi (the JR station) and then a bus to Nishitetsu-Futsukaichi.

A Nishitetsu line train will take you to Futsukaichi Railway Station from Tenjin in Fukuoka in 20 to 30 minutes. From Futsukaichi, you'll have to change for the two-station ride to Nishitetsu-Dazaifu Railway Station.

Getting Around

Bicycles can be rented from the information office next to Dazaifu Railway Station.

NAGASAKI 長崎

Nagasaki is a busy and colourful city (population 450,000) but its terrible fate as the second atomic bomb target quite obscures its fascinating early history of contact with the Portuguese and Dutch. The bomb itself actually missed its intended target towards the south of the city and scored a near direct hit on the largest Catholic church in Japan.

Things to See

The epicentre of the atomic explosion,

Urakami is today a prosperous, peaceful suburb with modern shops, restaurants and even a couple of love hotels just a few steps from the epicentre. Hypocentre Park has a black stone column marking the exact point above which the bomb exploded. Nearby are bomb-blasted relics including a section of the wall of the Urakami Cathedral and a buckled water tower. The Matsuyama tram stop, the eighth stop north of the JR Urakami Station on tram route Nos 1 or 3, is near the site.

The **A-Bomb Museum**, or International Cultural Hall as the museum is curiously named, is an ugly and badly designed building overlooking the Hypocentre Park. The four floors of photographs, reports, equipment and displays telling the story of the blast are enough to leave most visitors decidedly shaken. Entry to the museum is Y50 and it is open from 9 am to 6 pm (April to October) and 9 am to 5 pm (November to March). Behind the museum is the Nagasaki Municipal Museum; entry is Y100.

Places to Stay

Nagasaki Youth Hostel (☎ 0958-23-5032) has 132 beds at Y2100 and is within walking distance of JR Nagasaki Station; it's well signposted in English.

The *Oranda-zaka Youth Hostel* (☎ 0958-22-2730) is south of the centre on the hilly Dutch Slopes street and can be reached on tram No 5; get off at the Shimin-Byoin-mae stop. Beds are Y2100.

The other two youth hostels are inconveniently located about 20 minutes by bus from JR Nagasaki Station. They are the *Nanpoen Youth Hostel* (☎ 0958-23-5526) in Hamahira-cho and the *Uragami-ga-Oka Youth Hostel* (☎ 0958-47-8473) in Miyoshi-machi.

Minshuku Tanpopo (☎ 0958-61-6230) is at 21-7 Hoeicho, north of JR Nagasaki Station and near the A-bomb site. Get off at the Matsuyama tram stop or JR Urakami Station, cross the river, and walk to the street with a petrol (gas) station. Follow that street, turn left at the first junction and take the right side of the fork. Rooms are Y3300 for singles or Y3000 per person in double or triple rooms.

Places to Eat

The railway station area has a selection of restaurants with plastic meal displays and fast-food places but Nagasaki's restaurant centre is around the Hamano-machi arcade and Maruyama entertainment area. For a cheap, quick breakfast in the railway station try the *Train D'Or* bakery.

Getting There & Away

There are flights between Nagasaki and Kagoshima, Tokyo (Haneda Airport), Osaka and Okinawa as well as flights to and from a variety of lesser locations.

Buses operate between Nagasaki and Kumamoto. The four-hour trip costs about Y2750, but note the following section about the interesting route via the Shimabara Peninsula. From the Ken-ei Bus Terminal opposite JR Nagasaki Station, buses go to Unzen from stand No 3 (express buses from stand No 2), Shimabara from stand No 5, Sasebo from stand No 6 (bus S) or stand No 9 (bus E), Fukuoka from stand No 8, Kumamoto from stand No 11 and sightseeing buses from stand No 12.

By local train, it takes about 2½ to three hours from Hakata to Nagasaki on the JR Nagasaki line for Y2470 (add Y2060 if you want to travel by limited express). Kyoto to Nagasaki by shinkansen takes about six hours. To get to Kumamoto from Nagasaki, take a JR Nagasaki main line train north to JR Tosu Station (two hours) and a Kagoshima main line train from there (one hour).

Getting Around

The best way of getting around Nagasaki is on the excellent and easy-to-use tram service. There are four colour-coded routes numbered 1, 3, 4 and 5 (there's no No 2 for some reason). It costs Y100 to travel anywhere in town or you can get a Y500 all-day pass. The passes are available from the shop beside the station information centre, from

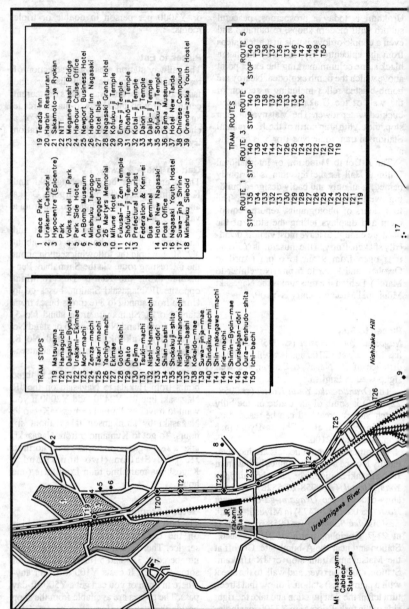

1 Peace Park
2 Urakami Cathedral
3 Hypocentre (Epicentre)
4 Volks Hotel In Park
5 Park Side Hotel
6 A-Bomb Museum
7 Minshuku Tanpopo
8 One Legged Torii
9 26 Martyrs Memorial
10 Mifune Hotel
11 Fukusai-ji Zen Temple
12 Shōfuku-ji Temple
13 Prefectural Tourist
   Federation & Ken-ei
   Bus Terminal
14 Hotel New Nagasaki
15 Post Office
16 Nagasaki Youth Hostel
17 Suwa-jinja Shrine
18 Minshuku Siebold

19 Terada Inn
20 Harbin Restaurant
21 Sakamoto-ya Ryokan
22 NTT
23 Megane-bashi Bridge
24 Harbour Cruise Office
25 Newport Business Hotel
26 Harbour Inn Nagasaki
27 Hotel Ibis
28 Nagasaki Grand Hotel
29 Kōfuku-ji Temple
30 Ema-ji Temple
31 Chosho-ji Temple
32 Kotai-ji Temple
33 Daion-ji Temple
34 Daijo-ji Temple
35 Sofuku-ji Temple
36 Dejima Museum
37 Hotel New Tanda
38 Chinese Compound
39 Oranda-zaka Youth Hostel

TRAM STOPS

T19 Matsuyama
T20 Hamaguchi
T21 Daigaku-Byoin-mae
T22 Urakami-Ekimae
T23 Mori-machi
T24 Zenza-machi
T25 Takari-machi
T26 Yachiyo-machi
T27 Ekimae
T28 Gotō-machi
T29 Ohato
T30 Dejima
T31 Tsuki-machi
T32 Nishi-Hamanomachi
T33 Kanko-dōri
T34 Shian-bashi
T35 Shokakuji-shita
T36 Nishi-Hamanomachi
T37 Nigiwai-bashi
T38 Kokaido-mae
T39 Suwa-jinja-mae
T40 Shindaiku-machi
T41 Shin-nakagawa-machi
T46 Irie-machi
T47 Shimin-Byoin-mae
T48 Ourakaigan-dōri
T49 Oura-Tenshudo-shita
T50 Ichi-bachi

TRAM ROUTES

ROUTE 1 STOP	ROUTE 3 STOP	ROUTE 4 STOP	ROUTE 5 STOP
T35	T40	T40	T40
T34	T39	T39	T39
T33	T45	T38	T38
T32	T44	T37	T37
T31	T27	T36	T36
T30	T26	T33	T31
T29	T25	T34	T46
T28	T24	T35	T47
T27	T23		T48
T26	T22		T49
T24	T21		T50
T22	T20		
T19	T19		

Nishizaka Hill

Urakami Station

Urakamigawa River

JR Urakami Station

Mt Inasa-yama Cablecar Station

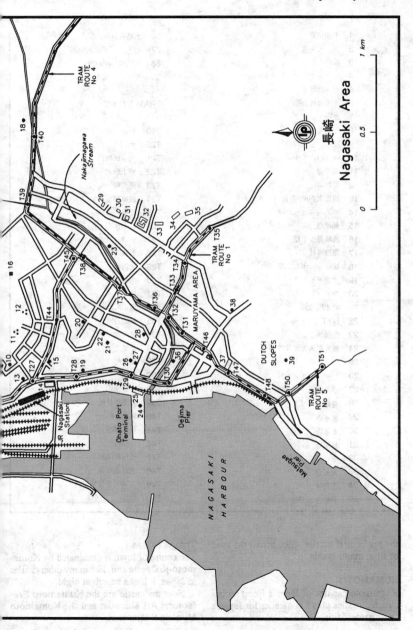

TRAM ROUTE No 4

Nakaōmagawa Stream

TRAM ROUTE No 1

TRAM ROUTE No 5

MARUYAMA AREA

DUTCH SLOPES

JR Nagasaki Station

Ohato Port Terminal

Dejima Pier

Matsugae Pier

NAGASAKI HARBOUR

長崎 Nagasaki Area

0   0.5   1 km

1	平和公園	36	出島資料館
2	浦上天主堂	37	ホテルニュータンダ
3	原爆中心公園	38	新地町(中華街)
4	フォルクスホテルインパーク	39	オランダザカユースホステル
5	パークサイドホテル		
6	原爆福祉会館	**TRAM STOPS**	
7	民宿タンポポ		
8	片足鳥居	T19	松山
9	二十六聖人殉教地	T20	浜口
10	みふめホテル	T21	大学病院前
11	福済寺	T22	浦上駅前
12	聖福寺	T23	茂里町
13	観光案内所/県営バスタミナル	T24	銭座町
14	ホテルニュー長崎	T25	宝町
15	郵便局	T26	八千代町
16	長崎青少年館	T27	駅前
17	諏訪神社	T28	五島町
18	民宿シーボルト邸	T29	大波止
19	テラダイン	T30	出島
20	ハビンレストラン	T31	築町
21	坂本屋旅館	T32	西浜町
22	NTT	T33	観光通
23	眼鏡橋	T34	思案橋
24	観光船大波止発着所	T35	正覚寺下
25	ニューポートビジネスホテル	T36	西浜町
26	ハーバーイン長崎	T37	賑橋
27	ホテルアイビス	T38	公会堂前
28	長崎グランドホテル	T39	諏訪神社前
29	興福寺	T40	新大工町
30	えま寺	T41	新中川町
31	長照寺	T46	入江町
32	皓台寺	T47	市民病院前
33	大音寺	T48	大浦海岸通
34	大光寺	T49	大浦天主堂下
35	崇福寺	T50	石橋

the prefectural tourist office across the road or from major hotels.

KUMAMOTO

Kumamoto has one of Japan's finest reconstructed castles plus a contender for Japan's 'best garden' title.

Things to See

The centre of town is dominated by **Kumamoto-jō Castle** and, like many other castles in Japan, it looks superb at night.

Near the castle are the **Kumamoto Prefectural Art Museum** and the **Kumamoto Municipal Museum**.

Suizen-ji-kōen Garden is open from 7.30 am to 6 pm in summer and from 8.30 am to 5 pm in winter; entry is Y200. The garden actually remains open after hours and entry is then free but only the north gate is open. A tram No 2 will take you there from JR Kumamoto Station or Nos 2 or 3 from the downtown area. Get off at the Suizenji-kōen-mae stop.

Honmyō-ji Temple is to the west of the centre, on the hills sloping up from the river. The temple complex contains the mausoleum of Kato Kiyomasa, the architect of Kumamoto's great castle.

Continue up the hill beyond the cheap ryokan and minshuku near the JR Kumamoto Station, past the large collection of love hotels and you eventually reach the **pagoda** topping the hill. The effort of the climb is rewarded with superb views over the town.

Places to Stay

Suizen-ji Youth Hostel (☎ 096-371-9193) is about halfway between the town centre and Suizen-ji Garden and costs Y2100 per night. The Misotenjin-mae stop on tram route Nos 2 or 3 is close by. The *Kumamoto-Shiritsu Youth Hostel* (☎ 096-352-2441) is west of town, across the Iserigawa River, and costs Y1600 or Y1800 depending on the time of year. A bus from platform No 36 at the Kumamoto Kōtsū bus centre will take you there.

The *Tsukasa Besso Minshuku* (☎ 096-354-3700) at 1-12-20 Kasuga has rooms at Y3500 or from Y6000 with meals. To get there from JR Kumamoto Station, turn left onto the road by the railway tracks, not the main road at the front of the railway station car park.

Getting There & Away

There are flights to Kumamoto from Tokyo, Osaka, Nagoya and Naha (Okinawa). The JR Kagoshima line between Hakata and Nishi-Kagoshima runs through Kumamoto and there is also a JR line to Miyazaki on the south-eastern coast. Buses depart from the Kōtsū bus centre for Hakata, taking just over 1½ hours. The cost is Y1850 for the basic futsū fare, add Y1750 for limited express service.

MT ASO 熊本

In the centre of Kyūshū, halfway from Kumamoto to Beppu, is the gigantic Mt Aso volcano caldera. There has been a series of eruptions over the past 30 million years but the explosion which formed the outer crater about 100,000 years ago must have been a big one. It's 20 to 30 km across the original crater from north to south, 15 to 20 km east to west and 80 to 130 km in circumference. Inside this huge outer crater there are towns, roads, railways, farms, 100,000 people and a number of smaller volcanoes.

Things to See

The 'five mountains of Aso' are the five smaller mountains within the outer rim. They are Mt Eboshi-dake (1337 metres), Mt Kishima-dake (1238 metres), Mt Naka-dake (1216 metres), Mt Neko-dake (1408 metres) and Mt Taka-dake (1592 metres). Mt Naka-dake is currently the active volcano in this group.

Recently **Mt Naka-dake** has been very active indeed. The cable car to the summit of Naka-dake was closed from August '89 to March '90 due to eruptions and had only been opened for a few weeks when the mountain erupted again in April '90, spewing dust and ash over a large area to its north. When Mt Naka-dake is not misbehaving, the cable car whisks you up to the summit in just four minutes (Y410 one way or Y820 return). There are departures every eight minutes. The walk to the top takes less than half an hour.

There are plenty of interesting walks around Mt Aso. You can walk all the way to the Aso-nishi cable-car station from the Aso Youth Hostel in about three hours. From the top of the cable-car run you can walk around the crater rim to the peak of Naka-dake and on to the top of Taka-dake. From there you can descend either to Sensui-kyō, the bottom station of the old cable-car run on the north-eastern side of Naka-dake, or to the road which runs between Taka-dake and Neko-dake. Either road will then take you to Miyaji, the next railway station east from Aso. The direct descent to Sensui-kyō is very steep, however, so it's easier to continue back from Taka-dake to the Naka-dake rim and then follow the old cable-car route down to Sensui-kyō.

Despite the usual shortage of non-Japanese labelling, the **Aso Volcanic Museum** will undoubtedly fill a few gaps in the average person's knowledge of volcanoes.

Places to Stay

The *Aso Youth Hostel* (☎ 0967-34-0804) is a 15 to 20-minute walk or a three-minute bus ride from JR Aso Station and costs Y1800 or Y1950 depending on the time of year. There's a campground further along the road from the hostel. *Aso No Fumoto* (☎ 0967-32-0264) is a good minshuku, conveniently close to JR Aso Station, and costs Y5000 per person. There's also a good little restaurant with an English menu in the station.

The *Murataya Ryokan Youth Hostel* (☎ 0967-62-0066) costs Y2100 and is right in Takamori. The *Minami Aso Kokumin Kyūkamura* (☎ 0967-62-2111), a people's vacation village, costs from Y4500, and is crowded in July-August.

The *YMCA/Youth Hostel Aso Camp* (☎ 0967-35-0124) is near JR Akamizu Station, the third stop west of JR Aso Station. Cost per night is Y1900. The *Minami Aso Kokuminshukusha* (☎ 096-67-0078) is a people's lodge near the Aso-shimoda Private Railway Station, the third stop west of Takamori. Rooms cost from Y3000 without meals.

Getting There & Away

The JR Hōhi rail line operates between Kumamoto and Beppu via Aso. From JR Aso Station there are buses to the Aso-nishi cable-car station. From Kumamoto to Aso takes one to 1½ hours and costs from Y1000 for the basic (futsū) fare. The Beppu-Aso limited express service costs Y2800 and takes 2½ hours. To get to Takamori on the southern side of the crater, transfer from the JR Hōhi line to the Minamiaso private railway line at Tateno.

Bus No 266 starts from the Sanko Bus Terminal at JR Kumamoto Station, stops at the Kumamoto Kōtsū bus centre then continues right across Kyūshū with an excursion to the Aso volcanic peaks and then along the Yamanami Highway to Beppu. The trip takes seven hours, including a short photo stop at the Kusasenri meadow in front of the Aso Volcanic Museum, and costs from Y7500. Buses from Beppu to Aso take 2½ to three hours and cost Y3000, plus another Y1100 for the services that continue to the Aso-nishi cable-car station.

From Takamori, buses continue south to the mountain resort of Takachiho, a 1½-hour trip along a very scenic route.

Getting Around

Buses operate approximately hourly from the JR Aso Station via the Aso Youth Hostel to the Aso-nishi cable-car station on the slopes of Mt Naka-dake. The trip takes 40 minutes up, 30 minutes down and costs Y600. There are less frequent services between Miyaji and Sensui-kyō on the northern side of Mt Naka-dake.

Buses also operate between Aso and Takamori. Cars can be rented at Aso and at Uchinomaki Onsen, one stop west from the JR Station.

KIRISHIMA NATIONAL PARK
霧島国立公園

The day walk from the village on the Ebino-kōgen Plateau to the summits of a string of volcanoes is one of the finest volcanic hikes in Japan. It's about 15 km from the summit of Mt Karakuni-dake to the summit of Mt Takachiho-no-mine and there's superb scenery all the way. If your time or energy are limited there are shorter alternatives such as a pleasant lake stroll on the plateau or a walk up and down Mt Karakuni-dake or Mt Takachiho. The area is also noted for its spring wildflowers and has fine hot springs and the impressive 75-metre Senriga-taki Waterfall.

Information

There are Tourist Information Centres with maps and some information in English at Ebino-kōgen Village and at Takachiho-gawara, the two ends of the volcano walk. There are restaurant facilities at both ends of the walk as well but Ebino-kōgen has most of the hotels, camping facilities and the like. Kobayashi to the north and Hayashida, just to the south, are the main towns near Ebino-kōgen.

Things to See

The Ebino-kōgen lake circuit is a pleasantly relaxed stroll around a series of volcanic lakes – Rokkannon Miike Lake has the most intense colour, a deep blue-green. Across the road from Fudou Lake, at the base of Mt Karakuni-dake, is a steaming hot springs. From there you can make the stiff climb to the 1700-metre summit of Mt Karakuni-dake, skirting round the edge of the volcano's deep crater before arriving at the high point on the eastern side.

The view across the almost lunar landscape from any of the volcano summits is other-worldly. If you have time you can continue from Mt Karakuni-dake to Mt Shishiko, Mt Shinmoe-dake, Mt Naka-dake and Takachiho-gawara, from where you can make the ascent of Mt Takachiho-no-mine.

Places to Stay

Ebino-kōgen Village has a good choice of accommodation including the *Ebino-kōgen Hotel* (☎ 0984-33-1155) and a kokumin-shukusha (☎ 09843-3-0161) with rooms from Y5250 including two meals. Just to the north-east of the centre is the *Ebino-kōgen Rotemburo* with basic but cheap huts around a popular series of open-air hot-spring baths. There's also a campground. More accommodation can be found at Hayashida Onsen, between Ebino-kōgen and the Kirishima-jinja Shrine.

Getting There & Away

JR Kobayashi Station to the north of Ebino-kōgen and Kirishima-jinja Station to the south are the main railway junctions. From Miyazaki or Kumamoto take a JR Ebino-go limited express train to Kobayashi on the JR Kitto line, from where buses operate to Ebino. From Kagoshima (around one hour) or Miyazaki (1½ hours) you can take a JR Nippō limited express to Kirishima-jinja Railway Station. From there buses operate to Takachiho-gawara (about 45 minutes) and Ebino-kōgen.

Buses arrive and depart from Ebino-kōgen (the village on the Ebino Plateau, not to be confused with the town of Ebino down on the plains). You can arrive there from Kobayashi to the north, Miyazaki to the east or Kagoshima to the south and continue on another service. From Nishi-Kagoshima Railway Station in Kagoshima buses depart for Kirishima Shrine and Hayashida Onsen at least hourly and some continue on to Ebino-kōgen. It takes about 2½ hours to Hayashida Onsen.

KAGOSHIMA 鹿児島

Kagoshima is the southernmost major city in Kyūshū and a warm, sunny and relaxed place, except when Sakura-jima's huge cone, across Kinkō-wan Bay, spits out clouds of dust and ash.

Things to See

The Shimazu family dominated Kagoshima's history, and also left the city its principal attraction, the beautiful bayside **Iso-teien Garden**. Adjacent to the garden is **Shōko Shuseikan Museum**. The garden is north of the centre (10 minutes by Hayashida line bus No 11 from the stop outside JR Kagoshima Station) and open from 8.30 am to 5.30 pm, except in winter, when it closes half an hour earlier. Entry is Y720.

Places to Stay

Fujin-Kaikan Youth Hostel (☎ 0992-51-1087) is at 890 Shimoarata 27-12, 2-chome, towards the waterfront east of Nishi-Kagoshima Station. It costs Y1700 or Y1900, depending on the time of year. The hostel is a short walk from the Kōtsū-kyoku stop on tram route No 1.

There's a good selection of business hotels

in the Nishi-Kagoshima Station area. The *Business Hotel Gasthof* (☎ 0992-52-1401) at 7-3 Chūō-cho, has good, low-priced rooms at Y3800/6600 for singles/doubles; ones without bathrooms are even cheaper. Across the road from the Gasthof, right on the corner, is the small *Tkuba* hotel, which is also very low priced: rooms without bathroom cost from Y2500.

Places to Eat
The main restaurant area is in the town centre but there's also a good selection around the Nishi-Kagoshima station area including an old railway carriage converted into a restaurant called the *Vesuvio*.

Getting There & Away
Kagoshima's airport has overseas connections as well as domestic flights to Tokyo, Osaka, Nagoya and a variety of other places in Honshū and Kyūshū.

Hayashida buses to Kirishima and Ebinokōgen go from the Takashimaya Department Store in the centre.

Both the Nishi-Kagoshima and Kagoshima stations are arrival and departure points for other areas of Japan. It takes about five hours by train from Fukuoka/Hakata via Kumamoto to Kagoshima on the JR Kagoshima line.

There are car ferry services from Kagoshima to Tokyo and Osaka on Honshū and to a number of the South-West Islands, including Okinawa.

Getting Around
As in Nagasaki and Kumamoto, the tram service in Kagoshima is easy to understand, operates frequently and is the best way of getting around town. You can pay by the trip (Y150) or get a one-day unlimited travel pass for Y500. The pass gets you a 20% discount on the Iso-teien Garden entry fee. There are two tram lines. Line No 1 starts from Kagoshima Station, goes through the centre and on past the suburb of Korimoto to Taniyama. Line No 2 follows the same route through the centre, then diverges at Takamibaba to Nishi-Kagoshima Station and terminates at Korimoto.

SAKURA-JIMA 桜島
Dominating the skyline from Kagoshima is the brooding cone of this decidedly overactive volcano.

Sakura-jima actually has three peaks – Kita-dake (1117 metres), Naka-dake (1060 metres) and Minami-dake (1040 metres) – but at present only Minami is active.

Things to See
The visitors' centre near the ferry terminal has a variety of exhibits about the volcano. The centre is open from 9 am to 5 pm daily but is closed Mondays. Entry is free. There are also several good lookout points, although visitors are not allowed to climb to the top of the volcano.

Places to Stay
Sakura-jima Youth Hostel (☎ 0992-93-2150) is near the ferry terminal and visitors' centre and has beds at Y1800 or Y2000, depending on the season. The ferry service is so short that it's possible to stay here and commute to Kagoshima.

Getting There & Away
The passenger and car ferry service shuttles back and forth between Kagoshima and Sakura-jima. The trip takes 15 minutes and costs Y150 per person, payable at the Sakura-jima end. From Kagoshima Station or the Sakura-jima Sanbashi-dōri tram stop, the ferry terminal is a short walk through the Nameriwaka market area.

Getting Around
Getting around Sakura-jima without your own transport can be difficult. You can rent bicycles from near the ferry terminal but a complete circuit of the volcano would be quite a push, even without the climbs to the various lookouts. Three-hour bus sightseeing tours operate several times daily from the ferry terminal and cost Y1500.

South-West Islands
南西諸島

Nansei means south-west, and the South-West or Nansei-shoto Islands extend for over 1000 km in that direction from Kagoshima on Kyūshū to Yonaguni-jima Island, just over 100 km from the east coast of Taiwan.

A warm climate, fine beaches, excellent scuba diving and traces of the old Okinawan culture are the prime attractions. But don't think of these islands as forgotten backwaters with a mere handful of visitors – 747s regularly regurgitate platoons of camera-clicking tourists and their megaphone-toting guides.

OKINAWA 沖縄

Okinawa gives its name to the prefecture and is also the largest and most important island in the Nansei-shoto chain. Okinawa had developed distinct cultural differences to mainland Japan, particularly in architecture, but WW II obliterated almost every trace of the old buildings. The USA retained control of Okinawa after the war, handing it back in 1972.

The 26 years of US management did a pretty effective job of wiping out any remaining traces of the old Okinawan ways but for good measure the Japanese have turned the island into a major tourist resort. Okinawa is still the biggest US military base in Japan, with 50,000 military and non-military personnel and dependents.

The US military bases are principally in the southern part of central Okinawa, the resorts in the northern part. Dotted around this stretch of Okinawa is an amazing number of artificial tourist attractions where many thousands of yen could be squandered on entry fees.

Orientation
Naha (population 300,000) is the capital of Okinawa; it was flattened in WW II and little trace remains of the old Ryūkūan culture.

Today Naha is chiefly a gateway to other places.

Okinawa City is the US military centre on Okinawa, centred around the Kadena Air Force Base which was the initial target of the US invasion. The prewar village has mushroomed to a population of over 100,000. The city has all the hallmarks of American influence, from pizzerias to army surplus stores.

The Tuttle Bookstore at the Plaza House shopping mall is the best English-language bookshop on Okinawa.

Places to Stay
Naha has three youth hostels. The *Naha Youth Hostel* (☎ 0988-57-0073) is the largest, with room for 100 people at Y2100 a night. It's south of the Meiji Bridge, near the road to the airport in Onoyama.

The other two are both north of the city centre. The *Tamazono-sō Youth Hostel* (☎ 0988-67-5377) in Asato has room for 30 people and costs Y1500. It's near the end of Kokusai-dōri Ave, before the Sōgen-ji gates. A little further north-west from the Tamazono-sō, towards Route 58, is the *Harumi Youth Hostel* (☎ 0988-67-3218/4422), which accommodates 38 people at Y2100.

Just off Kokusai-dōri Ave in Naha is *Hotel Sankyo* (☎ 0988-67-5041), a basic but comfortable enough business hotel with rooms from Y3600. There are other similar places in the alley directly behind the Sankyo.

Places to Eat
Perhaps due to the US military presence, Naha has just about every variety of fast-food restaurant available in Japan. Along Kokusai-dōri Ave alone you'll find *McDonald's, Kentucky Fried Chicken, Mos Burger, Lotteria, Mister Donut, Shakey's Pizza, A&W Burgers* and probably a few others. Shakey's offers unlimited quantities of pizza from 10 am to 3 pm for Y520.

Among the restaurants with plastic-meal models along Kokusai-dōri it's hard to pass by *Rawhide* when the sign outside announces that it specialises in 'Stake & Robster' but the food's just average (and the plastic replicas look awful). Okinawa is said

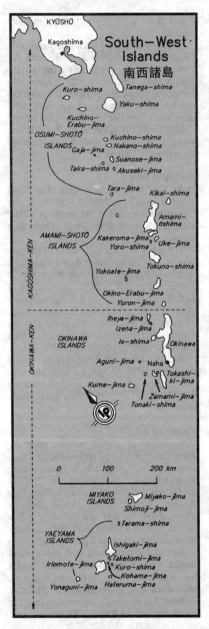

to have the best priced steaks in Japan, and there are plenty of steakhouses along Kokusai-dōri although the best of them are in the Tsuji red-light district near the Naminoue-gū Temple. Within a couple of blocks there you've got a choice of *Restaurant George, Jackie's Steak House, Restaurant Stateside, Restaurant Texas, Restaurant 88* and others. The restaurants offer steaks from around Y1000 to Y2500 plus other exotic dishes including pizzas and tacos.

Getting There & Away

There are direct flights from the USA, Guam, Hong Kong and Taipei. There are domestic flights from Naha to Fukuoka, Kagoshima, Osaka and Tokyo. SWAL have the most connections to the other South-West Islands. There are plenty of travel agencies in central Naha which can handle bookings.

Various operators have shipping services from Tokyo, Osaka, Kagoshima and other ports to Naha. The schedules are complex and there is a wide variety of fares.

From Naha Port boats head south to Ishigaki-jima and Miyako-jima islands, north to Yoron-jima Island and Kagoshima. From Naha New Port there are boats to Fukuoka/Hakata, Kagoshima, Kōbe, Osaka and Tokyo and also to Miyako-jima and Ishigaki-jima islands. From the Tomai Port, boats operate to a number of the smaller islands including Kume-jima, Aguni-jima and the Daito Islands far to the east.

The Arimura Sangyo shipping company (☎ 0988-68-2191 in Naha, 03-562-2091 in Tokyo), operates a weekly boat service between Okinawa and Taiwan. Boats depart from Naha Port on Fridays and from Keelung (or sometimes Kaohsiung) in Taiwan on Sundays. From Naha, boats travel via Ishigaki and sometimes Miyako.

Getting Around

The busy Naha Airport is only three km from the town centre – 12 minutes by bus Nos 24 or 102 for Y160.

The bus system is relatively easy to use.

You collect a ticket showing your starting point as you board and pay the appropriate fare as you disembark; a board at the front shows the various starting numbers and the equivalent fares. Buses run from Naha to destinations all over the island.

There are many bus tours around the island, particularly to the war sites in the south.

Okinawa is a good place to get around in a rented vehicle since the traffic is not too heavy and the northern end of the island has poor public transport. There are numerous hire companies in Nara with cars from around Y5000 per day plus Y1500 insurance. Try Japaren (☎ 0988-61-3900), Nippon Rent-a-Car (☎ 0988-68-4554) or Toyoto Rent-a-Car (☎ 0988-57-0100), among others.

A number of places rent scooters and motorcycles. A 50 cc scooter costs from Y1500 for three hours to Y3000 for a day; a 250 cc motorcycle Y4000 to Y8000. Try Sea Rental Bikes (☎ 0988-64-5116) or Trade (☎ 0988-63-0908).

ISLANDS AROUND OKINAWA

Apart from the islands just a stone's throw from the Okinawan coast, there are three other island groups a little further away.

Iheya-jima & Izena-jima Islands

North of Okinawa, these two islands have good beaches and snorkelling and a number of hotels and minshuku. A daily ferry runs from Motobu's port to Izena (1½ hours) and to Iheya (another 20 minutes).

Kerama Islands

There are about 20 islands in this group west of Okinawa, only four of them inhabited. The largest one is Tokashiki-jima Island. The islands have fine beaches, some good walks, great lookouts and some of the best scuba

diving in Japan. Ferries from Naha take one to 1½ hours; flights are also available.

Kume Island

Further west from the Kerama Islands is beautiful Kume Island, with its superb scenery, excellent beaches and the long curving sweep of sandbank at Sky Holiday Reef, just east of the island. The Uezu House is a samurai-style home dating from 1726. There are ryokan and minshuku on the island, particularly near Eef Beach where there is also a small resort hotel. Day trips can be made from Eef Beach to Sky Holiday Reef.

From Naha, ferries to the island take about 3½ hours, and SWAL have regular daily flights, taking 35 minutes at a cost of Y5360. You can get around the island by rented car, scooter or bicycle.

OTHER ISLANDS

Miya-ko Islands

About 300 km south-west of Okinawa, directly en route to the Yaeyama Islands, is the small Miya-ko group, comprising Miyako-jima Island itself and, a few km to the west, Irabu-jima and Shimoji-jima islands, plus a scattering of smaller islands.

Yaeyama Islands

At the far south-western end of the Nansei-shoto chain are the islands of the Yaeyama group, consisting of two main islands (Ishigaki-jima and Iriomote-jima) and a scattering of smaller islands between and beyond the two main ones. There are some fine diving sites around the islands, particularly on Yonaguni-jima Island, the westernmost point in Japan, and Hateruma-jima Island, the southernmost point. Although there are many Japanese visitors to the islands, most of them, in true Japanese fashion, are day-trippers. Come nightfall on Iriomote or Taketomi most of the tourists will have scuttled back to the comfort of their hotels on Ishigaki.

South Korea

Despite the nonstop efforts of the national tourist organisation, South Korea still remains very much off the beaten track. Many travellers get to the capital, Seoul, and a handful of intrepid individuals make it to Cheju-do and Kyongju, but very few take the time to explore South Korea's numerous other attractions.

Yet Korea is an enigma of the Far East, with the fascinating yet turbulent history of a small nation's struggle for survival against seemingly impossible odds. Sandwiched between vastly more powerful neighbours – China and Japan – Korea has always managed to preserve its unique character and cultural identity.

South Korea offers numerous opportunities for adventurous travellers; 20 national parks where you can hike amongst waterfalls, brilliant autumn leaves, and craggy granite formations; beautifully crafted temples; tombs from Korea's ancient dynasties; the world's longest lava tube; one of the world's rare waterfalls that plunges directly into the sea; numerous rugged islands off the south and east coasts barely touched by foreign visitors; ski resorts and other modern sports facilities; Seoul with its bustling markets and nightlife; exotic (and fiery hot) cuisine.

Most people are friendly, and despite language difficulties they will try hard to establish a rapport with a foreigner. You'll constantly be approached by people who want to strike up a conversation – soldiers, students, businesspeople or whatever.

Transport is well organised on both buses and trains and all but the most remote roads are paved. South Korea is prosperous and clean, yet relatively cheap compared to Japan. If you manage to get out of Seoul you will encounter a culture that has maintained strong links with the past, striking a fine balance with the environment, thus preserving the best of South Korea for motivated travellers to discover.

Facts about the Country

HISTORY
Origins
Folk legend fixes the date of the nation's birth at 2333 BC, but scientific research places it at around 30,000 BC, when migrating tribes from central and northern Asia first arrived in the peninsula.

The nomads brought with them a distinct language and culture, and an animistic religion. During the Han dynasty in China, a Chinese outpost was established at Pyongyang. Constant wars with the Chinese made it necessary for an early alliance between the tribes of the north which eventually led to the formation of the first Korean kingdom, Koguryo, around the 1st century AD, and the uniting of the northern half of the peninsula approximately four centuries later.

Three Kingdoms
By the 3rd century AD two powerful kingdoms – Silla and Paekje – had emerged to dominate the southern half of the peninsula. This was the beginning of the Three Kingdoms period, which was to last for the next four centuries.

China continued to influence Korean arts and religion. Probably the single most formative influence was Buddhism which, in time, became the state religion. At the same time Korea began to have a powerful impact on Japan. Architects and builders from Paekje, for instance, were primarily responsible for the great increase in temple construction in Japan in the 6th century.

The Three Kingdoms – Silla, Paekje and Koguryo – were often at war during this time, but it wasn't until 668 AD, with the rise of the Tang dynasty in China, that Silla formed an alliance with the two others. This unity was to last through various changes of regime, right up until the partition of the country after WW II.

Silla, Koryo & Yi Dynasties

Unified Silla presided over one of Korea's greatest eras of cultural development, and this is apparent in the countless tombs, temples, pagodas, palaces, pleasure gardens and other relics that dot the countryside in and around Kyongju, the Silla capital. Buddhism flourished during this period. Monks were sent to China and as far away as India to study. By the beginning of the 9th century discontent, fostered by rival warlords, threatened to break the kingdom apart, and the last Silla king offered his kingdom to the ruler of Later Koguryo to avoid further destruction.

The capital was moved to Kaesong, north of Seoul, and the new dynasty was called Koryo. Stability was restored. The ruling oligarchy and its sons reigned over a Confucian bureaucracy, and Buddhism reached new heights through royal patronage.

Throughout the later years of the Koryo dynasty marauding Khitan tribes on the northern borders began to threaten the kingdom. A treaty was made with the Mongols to keep this threat in check, but when the treaty was rescinded the Mongols invaded and laid waste to the peninsula for the next 25 years. In 1259 the Koryo monarchy was restored, but the heirs to the throne were held prisoner in Beijing until such time as they might marry Mongolian princesses, and Koryo resumed paying tribute to the Mongols. The extortionate demands made and obligations placed on the Koreans eventually led to the downfall of the Koryo monarchy.

A new dynasty was formed by Yi Songgye, one of the king's former generals. The ideals and practices of neo-Confucianism replaced Buddhism, which was regarded as an enemy and a rival and was suppressed. Neo-Confucianism, which combined the sage's original ethical and political ideas with a quasi-religious practice of ancestor worship and the idea of the eldest male as spiritual head of the family, remains the moral foundation of the nation today.

Sejong (1418-50) was the most enlightened of the kings who reigned during the next 150 years. He presided over the invention of a phonetic script *(hangul)* for the Korean language, which led to a vast increase in literacy.

Foreign Invasions

In 1592 the country was invaded by the Japanese, who, with the aid of superior weaponry (muskets supplied by the Portuguese), overran the peninsula in just one month. At sea, however, they were defeated by Yi Sun-sin, the inventor of the *geobugseon* (iron-clad ship), the 'turtle' ship – immortalised on every packet of cigarettes bearing that brand name.

The Japanese invasion was an unprecedented disaster for Korea. Craftsmen and intellectuals were taken hostage while temples and pagodas were burnt to the ground. The war dragged on for four years until Korean guerrilla resistance and Chinese intervention forced it to a conclusion.

The next years saw further fighting against the Chinese, which the depleted kingdom could ill afford. Throwing in their lot with the Ming dynasty, the Koreans were eventually invaded by the powerful Manchus. The Korean forces were disastrously defeated and severe restrictions were placed on their sovereignty.

Hermit Kingdom

Korea withdrew for almost a century after this series of events, becoming known as the 'Hermit Kingdom'. Meanwhile the surrounding countries were increasingly being influenced by Western ideas, culture and religion. The Korean policy of excluding foreigners was abandoned by the late 19th century, following the Tonghak uprising and the Sino-Japanese war. When Japan won this war it found itself pitted against the Russians, with Korea the meat in the sandwich. The Japanese began their occupation of Korea in 1905 and formally annexed the country in 1910. For the next 35 years, Korea was harshly ruled and exploited by Japan, and Korean resentment of the Japanese

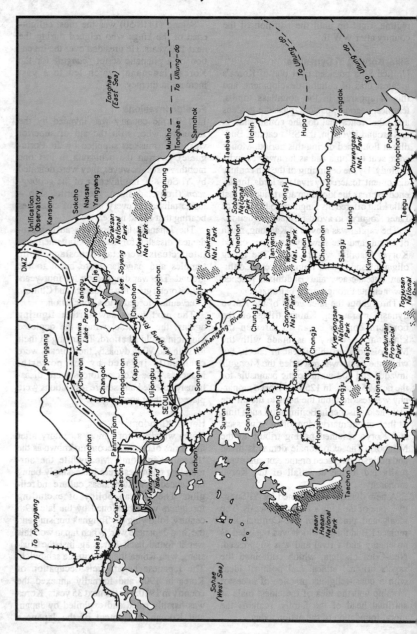

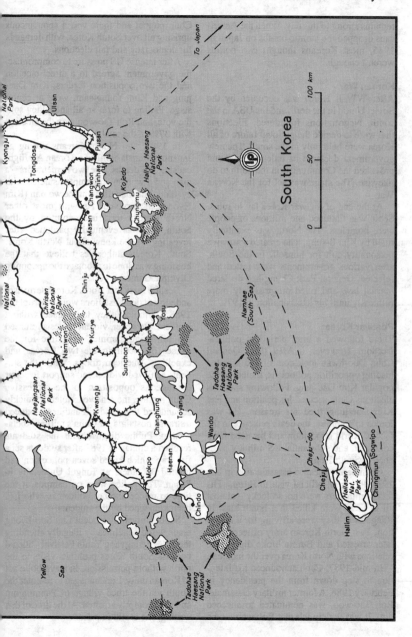

remains strong to this day. When the Americans dropped the atomic bombs on Japan in 1945, most Koreans thought two bombs weren't enough.

Korean War

After WW II Korea was occupied by the Soviet Union in the north and the USA in the south. Negotiations foundered. Elections that were to decide the political future of all Korea were held only in the south. The new government declared its independence and provoked the Communists in the north to do likewise. The stage was set for the Korean War.

At the end of the war Korea lay in ruins. Seoul was flattened and millions of people were homeless. The North was eventually ruled by Kim Il-sung, who created a massive personality cult for himself. In the South, after various governments were tested and rejected, General Park Chung-hee declared martial law, and ruled progressively more ruthlessly until his assassination in 1979.

Postwar Korea

There followed a brief period of political freedom. However, in May 1980, General Chun Doo-hwan took control and arrested leading opposition politicians, including the popular Kim Dae-jung. Following spurious elections Chun secured his position and had Kim Dae-jung tried for treason. He was forced to commute the death sentence in the face of world opposition and his need for a continued and substantial US military presence in South Korea.

Chun barely escaped assassination in late 1983 during an official visit to Burma. His fellow ministers were not so lucky – almost all of them were killed in a bomb blast in Rangoon as they were arriving for a reception. Two North Korean army officers were later arrested and Burma broke diplomatic relations with North Korea over the incident.

In mid-1987, Chun announced his intention to step down from the presidency in February 1988. A former military classmate, Roh Tae-woo, was nominated to succeed him. It was widely felt that Roh would be a Chun puppet and there was a spontaneous uprising all over South Korea, with demands for democracy and fair elections.

After intense US pressure to compromise, the government agreed to a direct election and the two opposition leaders, Kim Dae-jung and Kim Young-sam, were at centre stage. Failing to form an alliance, they split the vote, and Roh Tae-woo won the election with 37% of the total.

In 1987, two North Koreans posing as Japanese tourists bombed a Korean Air flight causing 115 deaths. The two perpetrators – a man and a woman – attempted suicide with cyanide. The man died but the woman (Kim Hyon-hee) survived. As with most other North Korean terrorists captured by the South, she was eventually pardoned after revealing all she knew about North Korea. South Korean authorities believe that the bombing was done to sabotage the upcoming Olympic Games.

Despite fears that North Korean terrorism and violent demonstations would disrupt the 1988 Olympics, they took place without incident. However, violent protests returned the following summer, this time for the causes of reuniting the two Koreas and expelling American troops. While the students achieved widespread support for their courageous opposition to the repressive Chun regime, the renewed violence quickly squandered this goodwill and has produced a strange nostalgia for Chun's military dictatorship. Public disgust with the students reached a climax in 1989 after students set a fire trap which killed seven policemen and injured 30 others at Tongui University in Pusan. The police were on campus at the time to rescue another policeman who had been kidnapped by the students.

Seoul University student Lim Soo-kyong made world headlines by illegally attending the 1989 Pyongyang Youth Festival – illegal because South Korea prohibits visits to the north without permission. In a symbolic act of Korean unity, Lim managed to re-enter the South via the truce village of Panmunjom and was promptly arrested. At the time of this writing, she is still in prison.

Under pressure from the Soviet Union and China, North Korea has opened a grudging dialogue with the South. Actual reunification of the two Koreas – which both sides claim to want – will almost certainly have to wait until after Kim Il-sung passes from the scene.

GEOGRAPHY

The peninsula is divided roughly at the 38th parallel, with North Korea holding 55% of the land and the remainder going to South Korea. The dividing line is the ludicrously misnamed Demilitarised Zone (DMZ) – probably the most militarised border in the world. A favourite pastime of North Korean infiltrators is digging tunnels under the DMZ or trying to paddle around it in rubber rafts.

The Korean Peninsula borders on Manchuria and the Soviet Union in the north, and faces China across the Yellow Sea, and Japan across the East Sea (Sea of Japan) to the east and south-east. Its length from north to south is about 1000 km while at its narrowest point it is 216 km. Taken together, the land area of North and South Korea is about the same as that of Britain.

The great bulk of the peninsula is mountainous, although none of the peaks are very high by world standards. The tallest peak in South Korea is 1950-metre Hallasan on Cheju-do (Cheju Island).

South Korea's early efforts at industrialisation resulted in much air and water pollution, but efforts to clean it up have paid off and today the country is mostly clean. Unfortunately, prosperity has brought a rapid explosion in the automobile population, resulting in serious air pollution in Seoul and Pusan.

CLIMATE

Korea has four distinct seasons. Autumn is the best time to visit – the forests are riotously colourful – and at its best in late October and early November. April, May and June are generally good months, before the summer monsoon rains. Winter, from November to March, sees temperatures hovering around both sides of 0°C, but it can be bitter in the mountains with temperatures down to minus 15°C. The snow, however, is picturesque.

Cheju-do off the south coast is the warmest place in South Korea and also the wettest. Winter is particularly dreary and will leave you wondering why the whole island doesn't wash away.

GOVERNMENT

Power emanates from the Blue House (the president's residence and office), which is behind Kyongbok Palace in Seoul. In theory, the president shares power with the legislative and judicial branches, but in practice the president is far stronger than the entire 299-member National Assembly. The president is democratically elected. There has been no vice-president since the 1960s. The president and members of the National Assembly serve five-year terms.

Until recently, there was no local autonomy – provincial governors, top county officials and mayors of cities were appointed by the Blue House. However, the first local elections were about to be held at the time of writing.

The prime minister – the head of the cabinet – in theory wields considerable power, but in practice is mostly a figurehead. In the National Assembly, there is one

	Jan	Feb	Mar	Apr	May	Jun	Jul	Aug	Sep	Oct	Nov	Dec
Seoul Temperatures & Rainfall												
Temp (°C)	-5.9	-0.3	4.3	11.6	18.1	20.1	25.8	26.3	20.2	14.7	5.6	-3.3
Rain (mm)	21	28	49	105	88	151	383	263	160	48	42	24

elected member from each constituency and up to 10 non-elected members 'at large' for each party. All the parties have been known to sell the 'at large' seats to the highest bidder as a means of raising money.

Federal judges are appointed by the executive branch and confirmed by the National Assembly, but it would be stretching things to say that South Korea has an independent judiciary.

In early 1990, several parties merged to form the ruling Democratic Liberal Party, which has since been riven by factionalism. Current opposition parties include the Party for Peace and Democracy (PPD), the Democratic Party and the Minjung (People's) Party.

ECONOMY

South Korea is one of Asia's 'little dragons' whose manufacturing industries live and die on foreign trade, though the domestic market is taking on increasing importance. South Korea now enjoys a standard of living approaching that of Hong Kong and Taiwan, but there are significant differences. Unlike the other dragons, South Korea's economy is dominated by just four huge, corporate conglomerates (chaebol) whose charitable contributions to the government have raised more than a few eyebrows. The 'Big Four' are Daewoo, Goldstar, Hyundai and Samsung. These companies are concentrated around Seoul, but there are some manufacturing plants in Taegu and Pusan.

South Korea does not have the true freewheeling sort of capitalism found in Hong Kong. Rather, the government is heavily involved in all sectors of the economy. The bureaucratic controls extend through the chaebol and the banking system right down to small enterprises – by government decree, a pastry shop cannot sell coffee and a coffee shop cannot sell pastry. Many South Korean economists have theorised that these heavy-handed controls do more harm than good, and attempts at reform are starting to get off the ground. Under constant threats of trade retaliation, the USA and EC countries are dragging South Korea (kicking and scream-

ing) into a more open economic system. South Korea runs a large trade surplus with the West, but a big deficit with Japan.

POPULATION & PEOPLE

Korea is one of the most ethnically homogeneous countries in the world. The population of South Korea is 42 million, 25% of whom live in Seoul.

Over 20% of the population uses the surname 'Kim' and 15% are named 'Lee', though there are some variations in the romanised spellings. In traditional Confucian culture, it is considered incest to marry someone with the same surname, which certainly limits marriage prospects among Koreans! Only recently was the law changed to permit couples with the same surname to marry, to great protest from the Confucianists.

ARTS

Traditional Korean folk dances, drum dances (sungmu) and operas are well worth watching. There are performances at the Korean Folk Village near Suwon.

CULTURE

Koreans don't have the Japanese obsession with bowing, but a short nod or bow is considered respectful when greeting somebody or departing.

Politeness is the key word to remember when dealing with Koreans. Koreans are a proud people – which basically means they have a short fuse. Avoid criticism – some polite bowing and smiling will smooth things over when you must complain about something or disagree on a topic of discussion.

If you're ever invited out for a meal or even just a drinking and dancing session with Korean friends, you'll find it difficult to pay for the bill yourself or even contribute to it. The same applies even if it's you that's doing the inviting. All manner of ruses will be used to beat you to the cashier even if it means that the person who pays is going to have to live on bread and water for the next week. The bill for a group is always paid by one person and one only. If you want to contribute then make these arrangements before you go out and square up after you leave. Never attempt to do it in front of the cashier. You will seriously embarrass your host. Indeed, by doing anything like this, you may embarrass them to such a degree that they'll never be able to return to that particular restaurant or club. If you're a man taking a woman out for the night, you pay. She won't even offer.

Never wear short trousers inside a temple, and be careful about taking liberties photographing monks.

RELIGION

Buddhists comprise about half of the total population, yet the majority also adhere to Confucianism. It is said that Korea is probably the most Confucian nation on earth today, and this doctrine permeates every aspect of society. Shamanism is said to be largely a religion of the past, yet it still flourishes throughout the peninsula in many different guises ranging from 'spirit posts' at the entrance to villages to strings of chillis, charcoal and pine needles over the front door of houses where a son has recently been born. Nevertheless, don't expect all Korean Buddhists to be vegetarians and ascetic – in Seoul, you may even get to see a monk eating a Big Mac at McDonald's.

Christianity also has a high profile in South Korea as the number of churches – even in rural areas – bears witness.

LANGUAGE

The Korean language is a member of the Ural-Altaic group, which includes Mongolian, Turkish and Finnish. The spoken language has been around for 5000 years but it was only in the 15th century that the alphabet, known as hangul, was invented. Hangul is one of the most phonetic alphabets in the world and can be learned in one day, though it normally takes a few weeks to get proficient with it. However, maps, books and timetables published in South Korea are often partially or wholly in Chinese. This can be a source of frustration but it doesn't compare with the confusion you're likely to experience initially with the two accepted systems of romanising the Korean language.

These are the Ministry of Education system and the McCune-Reischauer, the latter being an internationally recognised scheme. To illustrate the differences, a few examples: Pusan = Busan; Cheju-do = Jeju-do; Chongno = Jongro; Kyongju = Gyeongju; Halla = Hanra; Kangnung = Gangneung; Poshingak = Bosingag; Soraksan = Seolagsan.

Three cities in South Korea sound very similar to the uninitiated – Kyongju (Gyeongju), Kongju (Gongju) and Kwangju (Gwangju). More than a few travellers have got on the wrong bus. The obvious thing to do in situations like this is to know the Korean characters of the places you're heading for. Fortunately, the Ministry of Education system is gradually falling into disuse, but you may still come across it on some maps, street signs and in bus terminals. In this guide the McCune-Reischauer system is used to render Korean into English because it is simpler and more common.

Vowels

ㅏ	a	like the 'a' in 'car'
ㅑ	ya	like the 'ya' in 'yard'
ㅓ	ŏ	like the 'o' in 'or'
ㅕ	yŏ	like the 'yo' in 'York'
ㅗ	o	like the 'o' in 'home'
ㅛ	yo	like the 'yo' in 'yoke'
ㅜ	u	like the 'u' in 'flute'
ㅠ	yu	like the word 'you'
ㅡ	ŭ	like the 'oo' in 'look'
ㅣ	i	like the 'ee' in 'beet'

Vowel Combinations

ㅐ	ae	like the 'a' in 'hat'
ㅒ	yae	like the 'ya' in 'yam'
ㅔ	e	like the 'e' in 'ten'
ㅖ	ye	like the 'ye' in 'yes'
ㅚ	oe	like the 'wa' in 'way'
ㅟ	wi	like the 'wi' in 'wield'
ㅢ	ŭi	like u + i
ㅘ	wa	like the 'wa' in 'waffle'
ㅝ	wŏ	like the 'wa' in 'warp'
ㅙ	wae	like the 'wa' in 'wax'
ㅞ	we	like the 'we' in 'wet'

Consonants

The pronunciation of several consonants changes according to the position they occupy in a word. Thus, the Korean *k* is pronounced like a *g* when it appears between vowels. Aspirated consonants are articulated with a stronger puff of air, and are indicated in romanised form with an apostrophe, such as *k'* or *ch'*.

Korean Letters	Initial Position	Medial Position	Final Position
ㄱ	k	g	k
ㄴ	n	n	n
ㄷ	t	d	t
ㄹ	r	r	l
ㅁ	m	m	m
ㅂ	b	b	p
ㅅ	s	s	t
ㅈ	ch	j	t
ㅊ	ch'	ch'	t
ㅋ	k'	k'	k
ㅌ	t'	t'	t
ㅍ	p'	p'	p
ㅎ	h	h	ng

Hyphens

Many Korean words appear with hyphens when written in romanised form, but there is no compelling reason to do this other than to show where to break syllables. For example, we can hyphenate *tong-il* so it doesn't mistakenly get pronounced as *ton-gil*.

Greeting & Civilities

Hello.
 an-nyŏng ha-sim-ni-ka (formal)
 an-nyŏng ha-se-yo (less formal)
 안녕하십니까?
 안녕하세요?
Goodbye (when someone is leaving your place).
 an-nyŏng-hi ka-ship-shi-o
 안녕히 가십시오
Goodbye (when you are leaving someone's place).
 an-nyŏng-hi kye-ship-shi-o
 안녕히 계십시오
Please.
 pu-t'ak ham-ni-da 부탁합니다

Thank you.
 kam-sa ham-ni-da 감사합니다
Yes.
 ye / he 예
No.
 anio 아니오
Excuse me.
 sil-lye-ham-ni-da 실례합니다

Getting Around

I want to go to...
 ...e ka-go ship-sŭm-ni-da
 ……에 가고 싶습니다
What time does...leave?
 myŏt-shi-e ch'ul-tal ham-ni-kka?
 몇시에 출발합니까?
What time does...arrive?
 myŏt-shi-e to-ch'ak ham-ni-kka?
 몇시에 도착합니까?
bus/tram
 pŏ-sŭ / chŏn-ch'a 버스/전차
train
 ki-ch'a 기차
boat/ferry
 pae / yŏl-lak-sŏn 비/연락선
one-way (ticket)
 p'yŏn-do 편도
return (ticket)
 wang-bok 왕복
station
 yŏk / chŏn-gŏ-chang 역/정거장
ticket
 ch'a-p'yo 차표
ticket office
 mae-p'yo-so 매표소
entrance
 ep-gu 입구
exit
 ch'ul-gu 출구
information
 an-nae-so 안내소
open/closed
 yŏng-ŏp-chung / chung-ŏp
 영업중/종업
prohibited
 kŭm-chi 금지

Necessities

toilets
 hwa-chang-shil 화장실

toilet paper
hwa-chang-ji 화장지
tampons
tem-po
sanitary pads
saeng-ni-dae
How much does it cost?
ol-ma-ye-yo
Too expensive
nŏ-mu pis-sam-ni-da

Accommodation
hotel
ho-t'el 호텔
inn
yŏgwan 여관
What is the address?
chu-so-ga ŏ-di-im-ni-ka?
주소가 어디 입니까?
Please write it down.
chŏk-ŏ chu-ship-shi-o
적어 주십시오
Do you have a...available?
...ga (i) i-ssŭm-ni-ka?
......가(이) 있습니까?
bed
ch'im-dae 침 대
cheap room
ssan-bang 싼 방
How much is it per night?
ha-sut-pam-e-ŏl-ma im-ni-ka?
하룻밤에 얼마입니까?
How much is it per person?
han-sa-ram-e-ŏl-ma im-ni-ka?
한사람에 얼마입니까?

Around Town
Where is the/a...?
o-di-e i-ssŭm-ni-kka?
어디에 있습니까?
bank/exchange office
ŭn-haeng / oe-hwan-ŭn-haeng
은행/외환은행
city centre
to-shim-chi 도심지
post office
u-ch'e-guk 우체국
tourist information office
kwan-gwang an-nae-so
관광 안내소

Food
food stall
no-chŏm shiktang 노점 식당
restaurant
shiktang 식당
I am vegetarian.
ch'ae-shik chu-i-cha im-ni-da
채식주의자 입니다
I can't eat spicy food.
mei-wun um-shig-un muk-ji mo-tam-ni-da
How much is it?
ŏl-ma-im-ni-kka? 얼마 입니까?

Time & Dates
When?
ŏn-che-im-ni-ka? 언제 입니까?
today
o-nŭl 오늘
tomorrow
nae-il 내일
in the morning
o-chŏn-e 오전에
in the afternoon
o-hu-e 오후에

Numbers
1
il 일
ha-na 하나
2
i 이
tul 둘
3
sam 삼
set 셋
4
sa 사
net 넷
5
o 오
ta-sŏt 다섯
6·
yuk 육
yŏ-sŏt 여섯
7
chil 칠
il-gop 일곱
8
p'al 팔
yŏ-dŏl 여덟

9
ku 구
a-hop 아홉
10
ship 십
yŏl 열
11
ship-il
20
i-ship
30
sam-ip
40
sa-ip
48
sa-ship-pal
50
o-ship
100
paek
200
i-paek
300
sam-paek
846
p'al-paek-sa-ship-yuk
1000
chon
2000
i-chon
5729
o-chon-chil-paek-i-ship-ku
10,000
man

Emergencies

Help!
sa-ram sal-lyŏ! 사람 살려 !
Thief!
tod-duk-nom! 도둑놈 !
Fire
pul i-ya 불이야 !
Go away!
chŏ-ri-ga-yo 저리 가요 !
Call a doctor!
ŭi-sa-rul pu-rŭ-se-yo! 의사를 부르세요
Call the police!
kyŏng-ch'al-ŭl pu-rŭ-se-yo!
경찰을 부르세요

I'm allergic to penicillin.
pe-ni-shil-lin al-le-ru-gi-ga-i-ssŏ-yo.
페니실린 알레르기가 있어요
I'm allergic to antibiotics
hang-saeng mul-chil al-le-ru-gi-ga-i-ssŏ-yo.
항생물질 알레르기가 있어요
I'm diabetic.
tang-nyo-pyŏng-i i-ssŏ-yo.
당뇨병이 있어요

Facts for the Visitor

VISAS & EMBASSIES

Visitors with confirmed onward tickets can stay up to 15 days without a visa and this is not extendable after arrival. In addition, South Korea grants visa exemptions to nationals of any west European nation except the Irish Republic – if you fall into this category you'll be given a 30-day, 60-day or 90-day permit, depending on where you come from. Nationals of all other countries – including Australia, Canada, and New Zealand – require visas for stays over 15 days – visas are difficult to obtain after you arrive in South Korea, so get one beforehand. Tourist visas are usually issued for a stay of 90 days. Onward tickets and/or proof of 'adequate funds' are not normally required.

Extensions of visas are now difficult to get – you can apply at the Seoul Immigration Office (☎ (02) 6798321/2) which is very inconveniently located out near the airport. Don't take the airport bus. The most direct way to get there is by bus Nos 67 or 631-1 from the Sejong Cultural Centre area in central Seoul. The closest subway station is Yongdungpo-gu, and from there you'd have to take a taxi to the Moktong apartment area. The immigration office is open from 9 am to 6 pm Monday to Friday, and on Saturdays until 1 pm. Extensions cost W500; no photographs are necessary. The fine for overstaying your visa varies between W50,000 and W200,000.

If you have a work, study or resident visa, and you stay for over 90 days, you must apply for an Alien Resident Card – don't forget!

Many South Korean embassies are notoriously slow when it comes to processing visa applications. Figure on three working days no matter what they tell you over the telephone.

Passports should be carried as identification, as you may be asked to produce them when buying ferry or air tickets.

South Korean Embassies

Australia
    113 Empire Circuit, Yarralumla, ACT 2600 (☎ 2733044)
    Sydney Consulate, 12th floor, 115 Pitt St (☎ (02) 2212751)
Canada
    151 Slater St, 5th floor, Ottawa, Ontario K1P 5H3 (☎ (613) 2321715)
    Toronto Consulate (☎ (416) 5984608)
    Vancouver Consulate (☎ (604) 6819581)
Hong Kong
    5th floor, Far East Finance Centre, 16 Harcourt Rd, Central (☎ 5294141)
Japan
    205 Minami-Azabu, 1-Chome, Minato-Ku, Tokyo (☎ (03) 4527611)
    Fukuoka Consulate (☎ (092) 7710461)
    Kobe Consulate (☎ (078) 2214853)
    Nagoya Consulate (☎ (052) 9354221)
    Niigata Consulate (☎ (025) 2434771)
    Osaka Consulate (☎ (06) 2131401)
    Sapporo Consulate (☎ (011) 6210288)
    Sendai Consulate (☎ (022) 2212751)
    Shimonoseki Consulate (☎ (0832) 665341)
New Zealand
    86 Victoria St, 6th Elders, Wellington (☎ (04) 739073)
Philippines
    Alpap 1 Building, 140 Alfaro St, Salcedo Village, Makati, Manila (☎ 8175827)
Taiwan
    345 Chunghsiao East Rd, Section 4, Taipei (☎ (02) 7619360)
Thailand
    Salthorn Thani Building, 12th floor, 90 North Sathorn Rd, Bangkok (☎ 2340723)
UK
    4 Palace Gate, London W8 5NF (☎ (071) 5810247)
USA
    2370 Massachusetts Ave, Washington DC (☎ (202) 9395600)
    Anchorage Consulate (☎ (907) 5615488)
    Atlanta Consulate (☎ (404) 5221611)
    Boston Consulate (☎ (617) 3483660)
    Chicago Consulate (☎ (312) 8229485)
    Honolulu Consulate (☎ (808) 5956109)
    Houston Consulate (☎ (713) 9610186)
    Los Angeles Consulate (☎ 213) 3859300)
    Miami Consulate (☎ (305) 3721555)
    New York Consulate (☎ (212) 7521700)
    San Francisco Consulate (☎ (415) 9212251)
    Seattle Consulate (☎ (206) 4411011)

There is no South Korean embassy in China and you cannot get a South Korean visa there.

Foreign Embassies in South Korea

Foreign embassies which are represented in Seoul include:

Australia
    11th floor, Kyobo Building, 1-1 Chongno 1-ga, Chongno-gu (☎ (02) 7306491)
Canada
    10th floor, Kolon Building, 45 Mugyo-dong, Chung-gu (☎ (02) 7532605)
Japan
    18-11 Chunghak-dong, Chongno-gu (☎ (02) 7335626/8)
New Zealand
    18th floor, Kyobo Building, Chongno 1-ga, Chongno-gu (☎ (02) 7307794)
Philippines
    559-510 Yoksam-dong, Kangnam-gu (☎ (02) 5689131)
Thailand
    653-7 Hannam-dong, Yongsan-gu (☎ (02) 7953098)
Taiwan (Republic of China)
    83, Myong-dong 2-ga, Chung-gu (☎ (02) 7762721)
UK
    4 Chong-dong, Chung-gu (☎ (02) 7357341)
USA
    82 Sejong-ro, Chongno-gu (☎ (02) 7322601)

There are also consulates of Japan, New Zealand, Taiwan and the USA in Pusan (see the Pusan section).

CUSTOMS

Although the government likes to deny it, South Korea's economy is heavily protected against imports. Things are getting more liberal, but many consumer goods are still much more expensive in South Korea than in Singapore, Hong Kong or Japan. For this reason, Customs are pretty thorough, but they're much stricter with returning South Koreans than with foreigners. If you're carrying items with a value below W300,000 (US$450), you shouldn't have any trouble.

There is a duty-free allowance of 400 cigarettes, two ounces of perfume, and two bottles of spirits (not exceeding a total of 1½ litres). It's prohibited to bring in two-way radios (walkie-talkies). You can leave any prohibited items in bonded baggage for about US$2 per day.

MONEY
Currency
The US dollar is the most acceptable currency, but you won't have trouble exchanging other major currencies. The South Korean unit of currency is the won (W) with coins of W1, W5, W10, W50, W100 and W500. The W1 coins are rarely seen outside of banks. Notes come in denominations of W1000, W5000 and W10,000.

Up to US$100 can be reconverted into hard currency on departure without exchange receipts, but if you save your receipts you can reconvert the amount you originally converted within 90 days.

South Korea is gradually lifting its exchange controls and it's becoming easier to send money out of the country.

Exchange Rates
A$1	=	W586
C$1	=	W663
HK$1	=	W97
NZ$1	=	W422
UK£1	=	W1331
US$1	=	W750
Y100	=	W578

Costs
It's possible to live on as little as W15,000 a day exclusive of airfares if you stay in cheap yogwan and don't go on a shopping spree.

To save money on haircuts, men should go to a women's beauty shop – barbershops do manicures and massage, and some are fronts for prostitution. A haircut costs around

W3000 in a beauty shop while a barbershop charges about W10,000.

Tipping
South Korea is one of those marvellous countries where tipping isn't necessary or expected. A 10% service charge is added to the bill at tourist hotels so tipping isn't required there either.

Bargaining
There is some latitude for bargaining in cheaper hotels, in street markets and with taxi drivers. Remember that Koreans are very proud people – they get hot under the collar really fast if they think you're looking down at them. Bargaining should be polite and done with a smile.

Consumer Taxes
Most items purchased in South Korea are subject to a 10% value added tax (VAT), a defence tax and special excise tax, all of which are included in the purchase price. Under some circumstances, you can get these taxes refunded to you. Unfortunately, this is only possible if you buy from one of the following department stores in Seoul, all of which are expensive: Dongbang Plaza, Hotel Shilla Arcade, Livart Furniture Store, Hyundai Department Store, Lotte, Midopa, New Core, Samick Musical, Shinsegae or Youngdong. Also at Minsokkwan in Kyongju.

There are two other restrictions: the goods must be taken out of South Korea within three months from the date of purchase, and the purchase must exceed W50,000 (including tax).

If you meet these stringent qualifications, do the following: complete the tax refund form provided by the store (you must show your passport); take two copies of the Certificate of Selling Goods plus self-addressed, postage-paid envelope; indicate currency desired for refund; give two copies of Certificate to Customs officer on departure. Your refund (minus a service charge) will be mailed to you within 20 days. If you don't receive it, you can complain to the South

Korean Embassy in your country which will probably ignore you.

Better yet, buy your goods from cheap places like the street markets and forget about the tax refund.

WHEN TO GO

The best times to visit Korea are April, May and June before the monsoon and September, October and early November after the rains. You should not be put off by the monsoon, however, as the country is incredibly green at that time of year.

WHAT TO BRING

Dental floss, mosquito repellent and sunblock (UV) lotion are hard to come by. Shaving cream, vitamins and medicines are very expensive in South Korea. Deodorant is only available from big tourist hotels – try the Lotte Hotel Pharmacy in Seoul. Tampons *(tempo)* are available from some pharmacies and supermarkets. It's totally impossible to buy an electric immersion heater for making hot water in a teacup.

TOURIST OFFICES
Local Tourist Offices

The Korean National Tourism Corporation (KNTC) produces an extensive range of well-illustrated booklets and maps. You can pick them up at the three international airports – Kimpo Airport (☎ (02) 6650088) near Seoul; Kimhae Airport (☎ (051) 981100) at Pusan; and Cheju Airport (☎ (064) 420032).

KNTC has an information centre (☎ (02) 7570086) in Seoul, but even more useful is the municipal Seoul City Tourist Information Centre (☎ (02) 7316337) at the rear of Seoul City Hall. Both KNTC and the Seoul City TIC are open daily from 9 am to 6 pm, except from November through the end of February when they close at 5 pm.

Pusan also has a municipal information centre (☎ (051) 227289, 231465), at the Tourist Section in the City Hall; and there's one in Kyongju (☎ (0561) 23843), at the Tourist Information Kiosk in the express bus terminal.

KNTC Overseas Tourist Offices

Australia
    Suite 14/15, Level 17, Tower Building, Australia Square, George St, Sydney 2000 (☎ (02) 2524147)
Canada
    Suite 406, 480 University Ave, Toronto (☎ (416) 3489056)
Hong Kong
    Room 506, Bank of America Tower, 12 Harcourt Rd, Hong Kong (☎ 5238065)
Japan
    Room 124 Sanshin Building, 4-1 1-chome, Yuraku-cho, Chiyoda-ku, Tokyo (☎ (03) 5803941, 5082384). There are branch offices in Fukuoda (☎ (092) 4717174) and Osaka (☎ (06) 2660847)
Singapore
    24 Raffles Place, 20-03 Clifford Centre, Singapore 0104 (☎ 5330441)
Taiwan
    Room 1813, 18th floor, 333 Keelung Rd, Section 1, Taipei 10548 (☎ 7208049)
Thailand
    11th floor, CCT Building, 109 Surawongse Rd, Bangkok 10500 (☎ 2362880, 2331399)
UK
    2nd floor, Vogue House, 1 Hanover Square, London W1R 9RD (☎ (071) 4092100)
USA
    3435 Wilshire Blvd, Suite 350, Los Angeles, Ca 90010 (☎ (213) 3823435)
    205 North Michigan Ave, Suite 2212, Chicago, IL 60601 (☎ (312) 8192560)
    2 Executive Drive, 7th floor, Fort Lee, NJ 07024 (☎ (201) 5850909)

USEFUL ORGANISATIONS

If you have trouble or need help or advice, there is a Tourist Complaint Centre (☎ (02) 7350101), CPO Box 903, Seoul. Outside of Seoul, the provincial governments have offices to assist travellers experiencing difficulties: Taegu (☎ (053) 4225611); Chongju (☎ (0431) 520202; in all other cities, dial the area code followed by 0101.

BUSINESS HOURS & HOLIDAYS

For most government offices, business hours are from 9 am to 6 pm Monday to Friday, and from 9 am to 1 pm on Saturdays. From November to February, government offices close at 5 pm.

Private businesses normally operate from 8.30 am until 7 pm on weekdays, and from

8.30 am to 2 pm on Saturdays. Department stores are open from 10.30 am to 7.30 pm daily, while small shops may stay open from dawn until late at night.

Banking hours are from 9.30 am to 4.30 pm weekdays, and 9.30 am until 1.30 pm on Saturdays.

There are two types of public holidays – those that go according to the solar calendar and those that follow the lunar calendar. Solar holidays include: New Year's Day, 1 & 2 January; Independence Movement Day, 1 March; Arbour Day, 5 April; Children's Day, 5 May; Memorial Day, 6 June; Constitution Day, 17 July; Liberation Day, 15 August; Armed Forces Day, 1 October; National Foundation Day, 3 October; Hangul Nal, 9 October; Christmas, 25 December.

Lunar holidays will of course fall on different solar calendar dates every year. The Lunar New Year – 1st day of the 1st moon – falls somewhere between mid-January and late February; see the introductory chapter Facts for the Visitor for dates. Buddha's Birthday (Feast of the Lanterns) is the 8th day of the 4th moon. Chusok is the 15th day of the 8th moon.

CULTURAL EVENTS

A fascinating ceremony is held twice a year according to the lunar calendar (1st day of the 2nd moon, and 1st day of the 8th moon). The ceremony is held in the courtyard of the Confucius Shrine at Sungkyunkwan University in the north of Seoul. The nearest subway stop is Hyehwa.

If you're in Seoul on Buddha's birthday, there is an evening lantern parade from Youido Plaza to Chogye-sa Temple, starting around 6.30 pm. On the same evening, there is a similar lantern parade at Popchu-sa Temple in Songnisan National Park in the central part of the country.

There is a week-long cherry blossom festival held in the southern city of Chinhae, usually occuring in the first half of April.

POST & TELECOMMUNICATIONS
Postal Rates

Domestic rates are W100 for up to 50 g and postcards cost W70. International rates vary according to region, but for Europe and North America it's as follows: aerograms, W350; airmail letters (10 g), W440; postcards, W300; printed matter (20 g), W250; registered mail, W1240.

Sending Mail

Post offices are open all day on Monday to Friday and a half day on Saturday. Public mail boxes are always coloured red. Domestic mail can be delivered in about two days if it bears an address in Korean characters – if written in English, figure on a week.

Receiving Mail

Poste restante is available at all main city post offices but only in Seoul and Pusan will you find a counter dealing exclusively with poste restante. Elsewhere such letters may go astray because few postal workers speak English.

Telephones

There is a 30% discount on calls made from 9 pm to 8 am daily, and all day on Sunday and public holidays.

Public pay telephones come in different flavours – orange, blue and grey. The orange phones can only be used for local calls and will cut off automatically after three minutes no matter how much money you put in. Blue or grey pay phones can be used for local and long distance calls, and there is no time limit as long as you keep feeding money into it. The cost for local calls is W20 for three minutes.

There are also card telephones, and these can be used for local, long-distance and international calls. The magnetic telephone cards come in denominations of W3000, W5000 and W10,000, but you get a discount and only have to pay W2900, W4800 and W9500 respectively. The cards can be bought from banks and shops near the card telephones. It's wise to buy the cheapest denomination (W3000) because the phones have a tendency to eat the cards, though you get a larger discount on the big denominations.

To dial an international call direct, first dial 001, then the country code, area code (minus the initial zero if it has one) and then the number you want to reach. You can place an international reverse charge call through the operator by dialing 007.

The country code for dialling to South Korea is 82.

Fax, Telex & Telegraph

Every major city has a main telephone office usually near the GPO. From these offices you can make international calls and send fax messages, telexes and telegrams. Telegrams are of two types – ordinary (ORD) which take 12 hours, and letters and telegrams (LT) which take 24 hours.

TIME

The time in South Korea is Greenwich Mean Time plus nine hours. When it is noon in South Korea it is 2 pm in Sydney, 3 am in London, 10 pm the previous day in New York and 7 pm the previous day in Los Angeles or San Francisco.

LAUNDRY

Most hotels including cheap yogwan can do laundry if you prefer not to do it yourself. Charges for this service are usually reasonable.

WEIGHTS & MEASURES

South Korea uses the international metric system.

ELECTRICITY

Both 110 V and 220 V are in common use. The way to tell the difference is from the design of the electrical outlets – two flat pins is 110 V and two round pins is 220 V. There is no third wire for ground (earth).

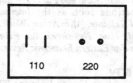

BOOKS & MAPS

Discovering Seoul by Donald Clark & James Grayson is available from the Royal Asiatic Society in Seoul and covers everything you ever wanted to know about this city. *Living in Korea* by the American Chamber of Commerce is – like the title implies – geared for those who plan to live here. *Korea Guide* by Edward Adams (Seoul International Publishing House) is an excellent, scholarly work with good photos and provides a glimpse of Korea's cultural legacy.

Those interested in South Korea's economy should pick up a copy of *The Chaebol* by Steers, Shin & Ungson (Harper & Row, New York, 1989).

Lonely Planet publishes a comprehensive guide, *Korea – a travel survival kit*, and the pocket-sized *Korean Phrasebook*.

For maps, the best place by far is the Chung-ang Atlas Map Service (☎ (02) 7209191-3), 125-1 Gongpyeong Dong, Chongno-gu. Maps of specific cities are also available from the city halls throughout the country.

MEDIA
Newspapers & Magazines
There are three English-language newspapers published in South Korea, the *Korea Times*, *Korea Herald* and *Korea Daily*. These papers are printed daily except Monday.

You'd probably enjoy the newspapers more if you could read Korean – it's here where you'll find xenophobic diatribes against foreigners committing heinous crimes against the Korean people – like trying to force open South Korea's closed markets.

Some local monthly magazines include the *Korea Post* and *Business Korea*. Large bookstores in Seoul and Pusan sell imported publications such as the *International Herald Tribune*, the *Asian Wall Street Journal*, *Time*, *Newsweek*, the *Economist* and the *Far Eastern Economic Review*.

Radio & TV
There are three Korean-language TV networks: KBS, MBC and EBS. A few programmes are bilingual. AFKN is an English-language station run by the US military and features typical US shows. AFKN is popular among foreign residents and South Koreans learning English, but this will soon end. A coalition of left and right-wing nationalists stopped fighting with each other long enough to launch a campaign against foreign 'cultural pollution' – as a result, the government has asked the US military to stop broadcasting and put AFKN on cable TV only. The guardians of cultural purity also forced Japan to turn down the power on their satellite broadcasts so that South Koreans wouldn't be able to pick up Japanese stations, even though most South Koreans who own satellite dish antennas bought them specifically to watch Japanese TV.

AFKN radio broadcasts in English on AM (549 kHz) and FM (102.7 mHz), and so far the xenophobes haven't been able to shut it

down even though it culturally pollutes the airwaves. Whether or not the nation can survive this invasion of foreign cultural pollution remains to be seen.

A complete schedule of TV and radio programmes is listed in the daily English-language newspapers.

FILM & PHOTOGRAPHY
Major brands of colour print film (Agfa, Fuji and Kodak) are readily available. Slide film is harder to find – generally only in big cities. Kodachrome is not available nor can it be processed in South Korea. Photoprocessing facilities are of a high standard and the cost is moderate.

The traditional Korean form of underfloor heating can cook your film if you leave your camera or bags on the floor.

Cameras and camera accessories are mostly imported and ridiculously expensive in South Korea. Korean-made cameras are not particularly cheap unless you buy them outside of South Korea.

Photography is prohibited around military installations, certain high buildings and from the windows of aircraft.

HEALTH
South Korea is a very healthy country to travel in and you are unlikely to encounter any of the things that might have you running for the nearest pharmacy in Thailand, the Philippines or Indonesia. The people are very hygiene-conscious and the government fosters and funds many public health schemes. Malaria has been eliminated and cholera and typhoid are things of their past. If you need medical advice or treatment for any reason, help is always close at hand and the standards are excellent.

Most South Koreans drink the water straight from the tap without boiling it. If you have some trouble with travellers' diarrhoea, you might consider boiling the water until your body adjusts to the local microbes, but there is little chance of contracting dysentery or other serious intestinal infections.

Korea has two systems of medicine – Western and traditional. The traditional system, known as *hanyak*, is based on Chinese herbal remedies and acupuncture.

Emergency medical care in hospitals is excellent and reasonably cheap, but normal outpatient care leaves much to be desired. Westerners are liable to become very frustrated with Korean doctors because most will not answer questions from patients regarding illness, laboratory tests or the treatment being given. Questions are regarded as insults to the doctor's competence, thus causing a loss of face. Doctors who have studied and worked abroad may be more used to Western ways.

WOMEN TRAVELLERS

Confucius is the world's most celebrated male chauvinist, and South Korea is still a Confucian society, though things are now changing. By watching South Korean-made movies, it's easy to get the impression that rape and wife-beating are national sports. As for foreign women, the chance of being physically attacked is small, but sexual harassment can be a problem. There are more than a few drunken men wandering around Seoul at night and they can be obnoxious. Groping on crowded buses and trains is not uncommon – South Korean women sometimes carry sharp pins to fend off unwelcome probing hands. Wearing miniskirts or shorts will invite stares and rude comments.

DANGERS & ANNOYANCES

South Korea is one of the safest countries in Asia, but there are problems. South Korea has very strict gun control laws, and almost no drug addicts – both of these factors undoubtedly keep crime rates down. Unfortunately, South Korea is no longer the crime-free country it once was. In Seoul, burglaries have become common while muggings and rapes are on the rise. It's still much safer than cities like Manila or New York, but you should keep your valuables secure. The back alleys of Itaewon late at night should be avoided, but you can walk major streets after dark without fear. However, pickpockets work in all crowded areas.

Student rioting is a seasonal sport most common in late spring or early summer. Although fatalities are rare, injuries are common. It's best to avoid riots unless your idea of a good time is getting clubbed or tear-gassed (by police) or firebombed (by students) or stoned (with rocks). Riots seemed until recently to be tapering off, partly because the government had made some major political concessions, but also because legal prosecution against firebomb-throwers was stepped up. However, 1991 was a record-setting year for rioting.

In winter, Koreans use a form of heating known as *ondol* in which the floor is heated, turning into a giant radiator. In traditionally constructed houses, coal is burned in an oven right under the floor and there is a danger of carbon monoxide poisoning if the floor develops any cracks. Concrete floors are usually safe, but older buildings usually have a floor made of stone or clay with a wood surface – these are prone to leaking carbon monoxide. Modern houses use a safer system – hot water is pumped through pipes in the floor. In the older buildings, it would be prudent to leave a window partially open at night.

Air raid drills are held once a month at unannounced times – when you hear the sirens you must get off the streets and keep away from doors and windows. If you're on a bus during an air raid, the bus will stop and you'll have to get off and seek shelter. After the all-clear signal is given, you are permitted to get back on the bus again without paying an additional fare – some people take advantage of this to get a free ride.

Because of the threat of North Korean infiltrators, there is a dusk to dawn curfew applying to most beaches.

WORK

Employment is not permitted on a transit or tourist visa and the immigration authorities have become very strict. There are now stiff fines and deportations of travellers working illegally – those who can't pay the fine are usually imprisoned. It is still possible to get a job teaching English and other European languages, but to do it legally you must first line up the job, then leave South Korea and apply for the work visa while outside the country. Most travellers do this from Japan or Taiwan. If a work visa is issued, it is only valid for one job only – if you want to change jobs, you must first get another work visa. You are not permitted to work a second job on the same visa without government approval. When your employment contract ends, or if you quit or get fired, you must leave the country within three days. Check with the immigration authorities in Seoul for the latest requirements. Documentation is needed, usually in the form of a formal letter of invitation for employment. Don't sign any contracts until *after* you receive the work visa.

Some travellers have complained of 'misunderstandings' (cheating) on wages – be sure to get everything written down airtight. More and more schools are requiring academic credentials. Many private schools now want a bachelor's degree and university teaching positions usually require a master's degree.

One unusual method of fund-raising is to turn in a North Korean spy – the government pays from W1,000,000 to W5,000,000 for each one you report. The telephone number for the spy hotline is 113.

ACTIVITIES
Skiing

Although Korea's mountains don't compare with the Swiss Alps, there are some good places where you can practise the art of sliding downhill. The ski season is from about early December through mid-March. Facilities include hotels, artificial snow and equipment hire. These places can be crowded at weekends – get there early if you need to hire equipment. Since ski resorts are on remote mountaintops, some of them don't have a regular bus service, but numerous travel agencies run tour buses up to these places as part of a package tour. Otherwise, hire a taxi for the last leg of the journey, or hitchhike.

For half a day of skiing at the Alps resort,

prices for equipment hire are W11,800 and lift tickets are W9900. For a full day, equipment hire costs W16,000 and lift tickets are W16,700.

The United Service Organisation (USO) runs inexpensive weekend ski trips to Bear's Town, Alps and Yongpyeong resorts. They also sell tickets for the daily shuttle bus to Bear's Town and Yongpyeong. Korea Travel Bureau (☎ (02) 7780150) organises full-day trips to the Bear's Town resort for W27,000 which includes transport from Seoul, equipment, lift tickets and lunch – KTB is on the 3rd floor of the Lotte Hotel.

All ski resorts have a representative office in Seoul that you can call for information. The seven resorts are as follows:

Yongpyeong (Dragon Valley) (☎ (02) 5482251), 16 slopes, just south of Odaesan National Park on the east coast about 3½ hours from Seoul. This is South Korea's premier resort – the slopes are equipped with lighting for night skiing. There is a youth hostel here charging W5500 for a dormitory bed, while double rooms cost W66,000.

Alps Ski Resort (☎ (02) 7565481), eight slopes, about 45 minutes north-west of Sokcho and just north of Soraksan National Park. This area gets the most snow and has the longest season.

Bear's Town (☎ (02) 5467210), seven slopes, about 40 minutes north-east of Seoul.

Chonmasan (☎ (02) 7446019), six slopes, about 50 minutes north-east of Seoul.

Yangji (☎ (02) 5113033), seven slopes, near the Korean Folk Village in Suwon, about one hour from Seoul.

Suanbo Aurora Valley (☎ (02) 5465171), seven slopes, by Suanbo Hot Springs about three hours south-east of Seoul near Soraksan National Park.

Muju (☎ (02) 5155500), three slopes (more planned), 3½ hours from Seoul near Togyusan National Park (south-east of Taejon).

Skating

Both roller skating and ice skating are popular pastimes. A few large cities have good indoor ice-skating rinks, but in most other areas it's outdoors and therefore strictly a winter sport.

Taekwondo

An effective form of self-defence, *taekwondo* was developed in Korea. If you're interested in either observing or studying, call the Korea Taekwondo Association (☎ (02) 4204271).

Courses

It is very important that you obtain a student visa *before* enrolling in any kind of course – the schools will not tell you this! Even if you already have a work visa, you cannot legally enrol in a school without first getting a student visa. The fine for breaking this rule is at least W100,000.

Gambling

If you're a compulsive gambler and can't wait to get to Macau, then you can lose your fortune in South Korea at one of the special casinos which are designed to milk foreign tourists only (no Koreans allowed). Japanese and Arabs are the most favoured customers, but all non-Koreans with excess cash can participate. The casinos are in the Sheraton Walker Hill Hotel, Seoul; Olympos Hotel, Inchon; KAL Hotel, Cheju; Hyatt Regency Hotel, Cheju; Sorak Park Hotel, Soraksan; Riviera Yusung Hotel, Taejon; Paradise Beach Hotel, Pusan; Kolon Hotel, Kyongju; and the Songnisan Hotel, Songnisan.

HIGHLIGHTS

In terms of culture and history, South Korea's top attractions include Kyongbok Palace and the adjacent National Museum in Seoul. Kyongju in south-east Korea has an overwhelming collection of cultural sights.

The most outstanding natural beauty spot is Soraksan National Park on the east coast. Cheju-do island off the south coast is worthwhile for the chance to climb South Korea's highest peak, Hallasan. Both of these areas are best visited in summer or fall.

ACCOMMODATION
Hostels

There are youth hostels scattered around the country. Unlike their counterparts in Europe, America and Australia, South Korean hostels are generally huge, modern places with incredible facilities and some private rooms – real luxury at a reasonable price. Dorm beds vary between W6000 and W9000 but the private rooms cost as much as W30,000. All the hostels have their own restaurants with meals at very reasonable prices.

For more information and reservations contact the Korean Youth Hostel Association (☎ (02) 2662896, fax (02) 2798002), Room 604, 27 Supyo-dong, Chung-gu, Seoul 100-230. Some of the hostels have separate offices where you can make bookings.

Cheap Hotels

Western-style accommodation in the major centres is generally very expensive so budget travellers usually head for the traditional Korean inns known as *yogwan* or *yoinsuk* (sometimes spelled *yoinsook*). These can be found everywhere and are classified by the government according to the standard of accommodation offered. Yogwan usually, but not always, have at least some rooms with private bath, while yoinsuk almost never do. There is often a price list in each room indicating its cost as a single and additional charges for extra people. The proprietors are highly unlikely to speak English but they'll expect you to want to see the room and bathroom facilities before you decide to stay.

Never wear your shoes into the room – take them off and leave them outside or place them on a sheet of paper so they don't touch the floor.

Basic yoinsuk rooms, with communal washing facilities, generally cost around W6000 to W8000, while yogwan with private bath cost around W8000 all the up to W16,000. Prices in Seoul are higher than elsewhere.

The washing facilities are often rather primitive in yoinsuk. If you want a good hot wash and possibly a sauna, then visit a public bathhouse known as a *mok yok tang* easily identified by the symbol ♨. At bathhouses you can rent towels and soap and bathe for as long as you like for around W1500. Most bathhouses close for the summer. Men and women have separate facilities. Many bathhouses also double as yogwan.

Minbak

Another form of traditional accommodation is *minbak* – a room in a private house. Bathing and cooking facilities are shared with the family, although occasionally you may find separate facilities for guests. Some of these places will be signposted but many are not. Souvenir shops, teashops and small restaurants can usually point you in the right direction and may actually be minbak themselves. In many rural areas, minbak may be the only form of accommodation available. Prices are always on a 'per room' basis and should cost W8000 except in Seoul where they charge around W12,000. Meals can generally be provided on request. Minbak offer considerable discounts if you plan to stay for a month or more.

FOOD

Traditional Korean food is heavily based on vegetables, often pickled and preserved with hot spices to last through the cold winters.

The basic Korean meal is known as *pekpan* and consists of rice, soup and vegetable dishes that vary in type and number from restaurant to restaurant. They can number a dozen or more but will always include *kimchi* – a fiery hot fermented cabbage which makes a reasonable substitute for tear gas. A basic pekpan meal will cost W1500 to W2500, but if you want something more substantial, with meat or fish, the main possibility is the national dish, *pulgogi*. In descending order of cost this will be thinly sliced marinated beef, marinated ribs, unmarinated sliced beef or unmarinated sliced pork. Pulgogi is cooked at your table so if that's what you plan to have make sure you sit down at a properly equipped table. For pulgogi or *kalbi*, marinated beef or pork short ribs, grilled over charcoal, you can expect to pay around W6000.

An inexpensive dish is *om rice*, consisting of rice with a fried egg and sauce on top – about W1500. The Koreans also love sushi *(kimbap)*, which as far as they're concerned isn't Japanese food. A typical sushi meal costs around W1300 which often includes a bowl of soup and pickled radishes. A good meal can be made from steamed dumplings *(mandu)* which are on sale everywhere.

With such an extensive coastline it is not surprising that Koreans also love their seafood. Many restaurants, especially in coastal towns and cities, serve nothing else. Dishes run the whole gamut from cockles, mussels and oysters to sea cucumbers, octopus, squid, crab, prawns and fish.

Chinese restaurants are identified by two black swinging signs in Chinese characters above the entrance which are flanked by red streamers on either side. The cheapest dishes are usually noodles with sauce *(jajang myon)* which will cost W1000 to W1500 but meat dishes (sweet and sour pork, etc) will be in the W4000 to W5000 range. They're primarily designed for quick meals and include a variety of traditional Cantonese dishes.

Japanese restaurants are nowhere near as common as Korean and Chinese ones and tend to be expensive. Here you'll find tempura and other Japanese dishes. Sushi is very cheap if you buy it from a Korean restaurant, but the price doubles as soon as it's officially labelled 'Japanese'.

Western-style fast food restaurants are catching on, especially in Seoul. Fried chicken is available in many Korean restaurants as well. High-class Western restaurants are found in either expensive hotels or the top floors of big department stores.

DRINKS

Koreans love their booze and there is no shortage of drinking establishments. The traditional drink is *makkoli*, a kind of white-coloured rice brew which is cheap but, like kimchi, an acquired taste. It's sold in raucous beverage halls known as *makkoli jip*.

Soju is the local firewater – potent stuff similar to bad vodka. Makkoli and soju are often drunk with various snacks known as *anju*. They include fresh oysters, dried squid, salted peanuts and *kim* (seaweed).

Korea's best wine is *Kyongju Beobjoo*. Beer *(maekju)* comes in two brands – OB and Crown. If you drink in a beerhall, the management expects you to buy some snacks (peanuts, etc) along with it.

Tea/coffee rooms *(tabang)* are great social centres. No food is served (by government edict), but it is possible to take sandwiches in. A tabang is a good place to inquire about the quality of local yogwan. Most tabangs employ a girl to take coffee to yogwan and shops in the area, so they know the local situation well.

Korea produces some fine herb teas. Ginseng tea is most famous, but also check out *ssanghwang* tea, made from three different roots and often served with an egg yolk or pine nuts floating in it. Ginger tea *(saengkang cha)* is also excellent. There are lots of instant herb teas available from supermarkets.

THINGS TO BUY

Traditional craftwork and the arts are alive and well in Korea, and even the impecunious traveller will have a wide range of things to choose from. Many visitors take a liking to the lacquerware boxes inlaid with mother-of-pearl. Ceramics and carved wooden masks are other traditional items. As in Japan, Koreans produce their own versions of Chinese-style brush pens (for calligraphy) and name seals. If you get a name seal carved, have a friend help you choose a Korean name.

Korea is not famous for jewellery, but you can get good deals on amethyst, smoky topaz (quartz) and pale green jadeite.

If you're not an art or jewellery collector, South Korea does produce a wide range of practical consumer goods – home appliances, Reebok shoes (both real and fake), unreliable fake Rolex watches, luggage, handbags, cookware and camping equipment. Clothing is a good buy – one of the great mysteries is who buys all those bikinis on display in the stores, because the Korean women certainly don't wear them (at least not in public). Those who take their caffeine straight will find numerous blends of Korean tea.

Ginseng is one of Korea's major exports; its sale is controlled by a government monopoly and you won't find it cheaper or better anywhere in the world.

Getting There & Away

AIR

Most travellers arrive in South Korea by air. There are three international airports – Seoul (Kimpo), Pusan (Kimhae) and Cheju-do. All manner of ticket deals are available and the ticketing jargon can be confusing, so to get the best deal you need to do some research and planning before you buy. The cheapest places to buy airline tickets in Asia are Penang and Hong Kong, the latter being the best as a rule. Japan and Taiwan are expensive for air tickets.

You can get pretty good deals on air tickets purchased in South Korea. Quoted prices on economy tickets bought in Seoul one way/return are as follows: Bangkok, US$400/504; Hong Kong, US$220/385; London, US$1000/1200; Los Angeles, US$462/741; Manila, US$215/425; Sydney, US$1000/1200; Taipei, US$133/265; Tokyo, US$156/310.

SEA
To/From Japan

There are several ferries linking Japan to South Korea. Most popular is the Pukwan (Pusan-Shimonoseki) Ferry which takes 15½ hours. Daily departures from either Pusan (South Korea) or Shimonoseki (Japan) are at 5 pm and arrival is at 8.30 am. Fares in 1st class cost US$80 to $90; 2nd class costs US$55 to $65. Students can receive a 20% discount. Tickets are available in Shimonoseki (☎ (0832) 243000) and Pusan (☎ (051) 4633161) or Seoul (☎ (02) 7380055). In addition, there are combination ferry-train tickets allowing you to make the Tokyo-Seoul run without taking to the air. Many travel agents can sell these – try contacting Nippon Travel Agency (☎ (06) 3120451), Osaka; or Aju Travel Service (☎ (02) 7535051), Seoul.

The Kuk Jae Ferry connects both Kobe and Osaka with Pusan. The trip takes 22 hours and tickets cost from US$90 to US$200. A 20% student discount is available in 2nd class. Departures from Osaka (☎ (06) 2661111) are on Wednesday and Saturday at noon; from Pusan (☎ (051) 4637000) to Osaka on Monday and Thursday at 5 pm. Departures from Kobe are on Monday and Friday; and from Pusan to Kobe on Wednesday and Saturday. Tickets can be purchased in Seoul (☎ (02) 7547786), 8th floor, Centre Building, 118 Namdaemunno 2-ga, Chung-gu.

The Fukuoka International Ferry links Fukuoka (Hakata), Japan with Yosu. Actually, the ferry begins its journey in Okinawa and makes a stop in Fukuoka before ending up in Yosu. Since there is a ferry from Taiwan to Okinawa, this offers one way to get from Taiwan to South Korea by ship. Departures are twice weekly in winter and three times weekly in summer. The Fukuoka-Yosu journey takes 14½ hours and costs from US$55 to US$124 (student discounts available). In Japan, call the ferry office in Fukuoka (☎ (092) 2725151); in South Korea, there's an office in Seoul (☎ (02) 7764927) and Yosu (☎ (0662) 629689).

Perhaps the most interesting sea route is the jetfoil connecting Nagasaki with Cheju-do. The jetfoil takes 4½ hours. It makes one round trip daily, departing Nagasaki at 8 am and arriving in Cheju at 12.30 pm. It departs Cheju at 1.15 pm and arrives in Nagasaki at 5.45 pm. Seats in 1st class cost US$170; 2nd class costs US$130.

To/From China

The Weidong Ferry links the South Korean port of Inchon to Weihai in China's Shandong Province (twice weekly, 17 hours). The cost is US$90 in economy class, US$110 (2nd class), US$130 (1st class) and US$150 (luxury class). Students can receive a 20% discount. In China, tickets are available from the Weihai branch of China International Travel Service (CITS). In South Korea, tickets are sold by Universal Travel Service (UTS) just behind City Hall in Seoul (near the Tourist Information Centre). If you're going from South Korea to China, getting the Chinese visa is tricky because there is no Chinese embassy in South Korea. UTS can get the visa for you, but charges US$100 for the service. If you get it before coming to South Korea, you'll save considerably but note that Chinese visas are only valid for three months from date of issue, though they can easily be extended in China.

LEAVING KOREA

Airport departure tax on international flights is W6000. If departing by ship it's W1000. There are no places to change money after you pass immigration so take care of this beforehand.

Getting Around

Koreans are very helpful to lost-looking foreigners, so if you stand around looking bewildered with a map in your hands, someone will probably offer to assist you.

AIR

Given the small distances, you won't have to take to the air often, although you may prefer to fly rather than take a ferry to Cheju-do island. The two domestic carriers, Korean Air and Asiana Airlines, have a good network connecting all the main cities and both charge the same fares which are pretty reasonable. You must have your passport handy when boarding domestic flights. You can carry a camera on board domestic flights but don't take photographs of the airports or out the windows of a flying aircraft.

From Seoul there are flights to Cheju-do, Chinju, Kangnung, Kwangju, Pusan, Pohang, Sokcho, Taegu, Ulsan and Yosu.

From Cheju-do there are flights to Chinju, Kwangju, Pusan, Seoul, Taegu and Yosu.

BUS

South Korean bus travel is a dream come true – fast, frequent and on time. It's even safe – quite a luxury after China. Major cities are served by air-con express *kosok* buses. These buses usually operate from their own separate terminal and, except at peak seasons, it's

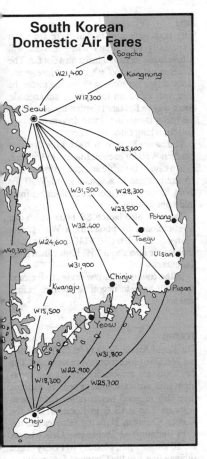

South Korean Domestic Air Fares

Sogcho

W21,400

Kangnung

W17,300

Seoul

W25,600

W31,500   W28,300

W23,500

Pohang

W32,400

W24,600   Taegu

Ulsan

W40,300   W31,900

Kwangju   Chinju

Pusan

W15,500

Yeosu

W31,800

W22,900

W18,300   W25,700

Cheju

---

not necessary to book more than a few hours ahead. Fares are very reasonable.

Next down are the *chikheng* buses, which operate along local roads and expressways. These are limited express buses which make scheduled stops at various towns and rest areas along the expressways. The terminal is generally separate from the kosok buses and often shared with the local or wanheng buses.

Wanheng buses operate on set routes and will pick up and drop off anywhere. There are no reserved seats, often as many standing as sitting passengers, and all but the bulkiest of freight may also be squeezed on. There may often be chikheng and wanheng buses on the same routes.

TRAIN

South Korea has an excellent railway network connecting all major cities and the ticketing system is computerised. There are four classes of trains. The fastest are called *saemaul-ho*. Then come the limited stop *mugunghwa-ho*. Similar, but not air-con, are the *tongil-ho* trains – the best deal (reserve a seat). Finally there are the incredibly slow 4th-class (local) trains known as *bidulgi-ho* – avoid these! Seats on the 4th-class trains cannot be booked; on the two middle-range trains there are 1st and economy-class seats and standing tickets.

Some of the larger stations have English signs indicating special ticket windows for foreigners, but these seem to be out of operation. They were installed for the 1988 Olympics and have since gone to pot. However, you can buy train tickets from the Korean National Tourism Corporation (KNTC) office in the basement of the KNTC building, 10 Ta-dong, Chung-gu, Seoul.

Few ticket clerks speak any English. There's a monthly timetable available from bookstores for W1400 – this contains schedules for all forms of transport throughout the country, but only the rail portion is in English.

TAXI

Share taxis are available at some major tourist sites – they often meet incoming ferries (such as the boat on Lake Soyang near Chunchon). Meters are not used – negotiate the fare in advance. Try to find a group of Koreans and let them do the bargaining.

CAR & MOTORBIKE

It makes no sense to rent a car in South Korea – the cost is outrageous and public transport is excellent. Motorcycles are seldom available for hire, but if you're obsessed with driving yourself, you could purchase one and sell it when you leave. Driving is on the right side of the road. Police love to issue traffic summonses, although motorcycles are at least partially immune to the law and often drive on the pedestrian footpaths. Driving in the larger cities can be hair-raising, but rural areas are bliss – very little traffic, and the roads are usually excellent. It is wise not to expect any consideration at all from other road users.

If you're determined to hire a car, you must be at least 21 years old and have your passport and an international driver's license. Costs begin at W30,000 for a 12-hour hire. Cars can be rented from the following agencies in Seoul:

88 Rent-Car (☎ (02) 7330888); Hertz Korean Rent-a-Car (☎ (02) 5850801); Korea Express Rent-a-Car (☎ (02) 7197295); Sae Han Rent-a-Car (☎ (02) 6760031); Seoul Arirang Rent-a-Car (☎ (02) 7804200); Seoul Rent-a-Car (☎ (02) 4740011); Sungsan Rent-a-Car (☎ (02) 7973601).

LOCAL TRANSPORT
Bus
Inside cities and their outlying suburbs, buses are classified as ordinary (*ipsok*) and seat (*chwasok*). The former generally cost W180 regardless of distance (or W170 if you buy tokens from a booth beforehand) but they get incredibly crowded at rush hours. A chwasok bus over the same route will cost W470. All city buses carry a route number and a destination on the front and the sides. Bus stops, likewise, carry panels on the post indicating the route served. None of these will be in English so you need to be able to recognise the name of your destination in Korean.

Underground
Seoul and Pusan have underground railways, which are a very convenient and cheap way of getting around. All signs for both the trains and the stations are in Korean and English. Tickets are bought at vending machines or at ticket windows.

Taxi
City taxis have meters, but there are times (especially rush hour) when drivers will refuse to use them and insist on a flat fee. The Koreans get this too, it's not just foreigners. If the driver isn't going to use the meter, be sure you agree on the fare in advance. In some ways a flat fare is better, because when the meter is running, some drivers may take you for a long ride.

The basic charge is W700 for the first two km then W50 for each additional 353 metres. When caught in traffic and going slower than 15 km/h, there is a surcharge of W50 for every 85 seconds. Fares are 20% higher from midnight to 4 am.

There are also larger '88' taxis which can be summoned by phone for a W1000 surcharge (in Seoul, ☎ (02) 4140150). The basic charges are also about 15% higher than standard taxis.

In the countryside, few taxis are metered so you'll have to negotiate the fare before you set off.

TOURS
The Royal Asiatic Society (☎ (02) 7639483, fax 7663796) does tours every weekend. The day tours are reasonably priced, but overnight trips are somewhat expensive because they stay in good hotels rather than cheap yogwan. The RAS is in Room 611 of the Korean Christian Building (also called the CBS Building) on Taehangno. Office hours are 10 am to 5 pm, Monday to Friday. Take subway line 1 to the Chongno 5-ga station.

The Korean Travel Bureau (☎ (02) 5851191) runs commercial tours of Seoul, Panmunjom, Korean Folk Village, Kyongju, Pusan, Cheju-do island and Soraksan. You can also contact their office on the 3rd floor of the Hotel Lotte (☎ (02) 7780150) for more information.

The USO (☎ (02) 7953063, 7953028) runs tours at bargain prices and you don't have to be a member of the US military to join. The office is opposite Gate 21 of the Yongsan military compound. There is also a USO in Pusan (☎ (051) 4623732).

Seoul 서울

Seoul is a city of incredible contrasts. It was flattened during the Korean War but has risen from the ashes to become a modern metropolis with a population of more than 10 million. Although the city now boasts highrise buildings, 12-lane boulevards and urban problems to match, the centuries-old royal palaces, temples, pagodas and imposing stone gateways set in huge traditional gardens remain timeless and elegant.

Seoul dates from the establishment in 1392 of the Yi dynasty, which ruled Korea until 1910. During this time, when Korea was largely closed to the outside world, the shrines, palaces and fortresses that still stand today were built. Government funding for the repair and restoration of historic sites is outstanding in South Korea and is the reason the very new and the ancient continue to exist side by side.

Seoul is the cultural hub of the country, catering for every taste. It's a magnet for foreigners. It has excellent public transport and cheap accommodation, even right in the centre. It's certainly worth spending a week in Seoul, but do make the effort to get down to the Kangnam express bus terminal – the gateway to the rest of South Korea – and board an outbound bus. Many travellers never do.

Orientation

Locating addresses in Seoul is much like in Tokyo – chaos reigns supreme! Few roads are signposted, and most smaller streets and alleys have no name at all. But there is a system of sorts, and it helps if you learn it.

A *gu* is an urban district only found in large cities like Seoul and Pusan. A *dong* is a neighbourhood smaller than a gu. Seoul presently has 22 gu and 494 dong. Thus, an address like 104 Itaewon-dong, Yongsan-gu, means building No 104 in the Itaewon neighbourhood of the Yongsan district. Buildings have names, and the name is crucial to finding the correct address.

The word for a large street or boulevard is *no* or *ro*. So Chongno means Chong St, Ulchiro is Ulchi St, etc. Also worth knowing is that large boulevards are divided into sections called *ga*. Thus, you'll see on the Seoul subway map that there is a station for Ulchiro 3-ga, Ulchiro 4-ga – these are just different sections of a street named Ulchi St. A *gil* is a smaller street than a no/ro – Sambonggil is one such example.

Chung-gu is the central district around the city hall area south to Namsan Park. Chongno-gu is from Chongno (Chong St) northwards to the Kyongbok Palace area. This district has most of the budget hotels and the city's best sights. Itaewon-dong is a neighbourhood on the south side of Namsan Park famous for its shopping, bars and nightlife.

Kangnam-gu is the district on the south side of the Han River and includes two of Seoul's most high-class neighbourhoods – Yong-dong and Chamshil-dong.

If you can't find a certain address, try the police boxes which are in every neighbourhood. A surprisingly large number of police speak English, though it still helps considerably if you have your destination written in Korean script.

Information

The best source of information is the Seoul City Tourist Information Centre (☎ (02) 7316337, 7358688) at the back of City Hall. It's open every day from 9 am to 6 pm, but closed from noon to 1 pm.

Another place offering similar services is the KNTC Tourist Information Centre (☎ (02) 7570086), in the basement of the KNTC Building, 10 Ta-dong, Chung-gu. There are also tourist information kiosks at various points in the city.

The Royal Asiatic Society (☎ (02) 7639483, fax 7663796) is in Room 611 of the Korean Christian Building on Taehangno. The RAS is a gold mine of information for people who want to dig deep into Korea's culture, history, economy and geography. The society sells books, sponsors free lectures and runs weekend trips. Take subway

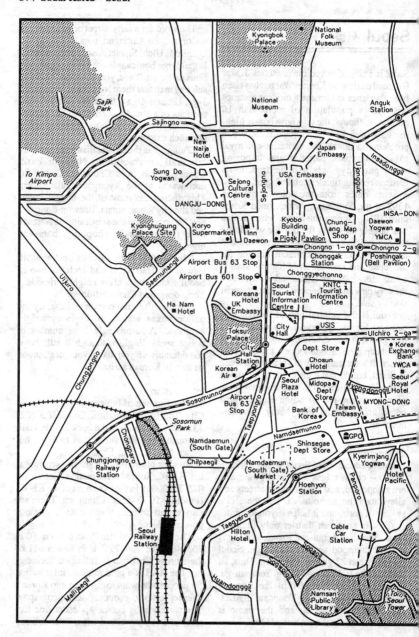

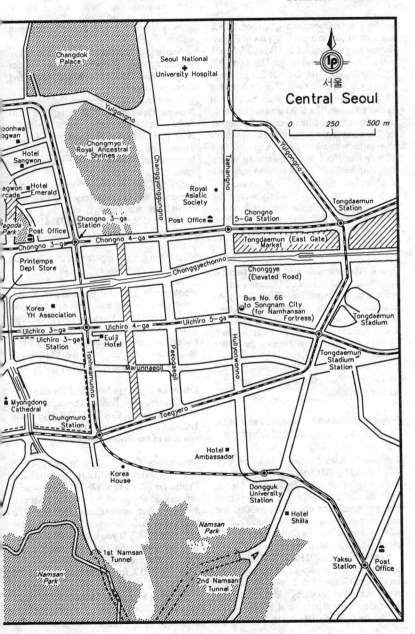

Central Seoul
서울

0 250 500 m

line No 1 to the Chongno 5-ga station. Office hours are 10 am to 5 pm, Monday to Friday. The mailing address is CPO Box 255, Seoul.

It's also worth trying the USO (☎ (02) 7923028/3063), 104 Galwol-dong, Yongsan-gu, just opposite Gate 21 of the Yongsan US army base down the road past Seoul Railway Station. The USO is an information, entertainment and cultural centre that serves the US army base here, though you don't have to be with the military to get in. Take subway line No 1 to the Namyong station (one stop south of Seoul station) and walk south for five minutes. Office hours are daily from 8 am to 8 pm. Possibly within the lifespan of this book, the Yongsan base and the USO with it will be moved out of Seoul which will free up this valuable real estate to alleviate Seoul's severe housing shortage.

Post & Telecommunications Poste Restante is on the third floor of the GPO, usually known in Seoul as the Central Post Office (CPO). All incoming letters are entered into a logbook which you have to sign when you pick up a letter or package – look over this logbook carefully for your name because they often misfile letters.

The telecommunications building is just behind the GPO – fax, telephone and telex service is available.

Foreign Embassies These are listed in the Facts for the Visitor section of this chapter.

Cultural Centres The Seoul Arts Centre (☎ (02) 5853151), 700 Socho-dong, Socho-gu, is the best place to go to see folk dances, court dances and other traditional performances. Admission costs only W3000 and there are performances every Saturday. Take subway line No 3 to the Cargo Truck Terminal at the south end of town.

Korea House (☎ (02) 2678752, 2669101) has similar performances to those of the Seoul Arts Centre, but they are performed every weekday evening. Unfortunately, these shows are expensive at W12,000. It's on the north side of Namsan Park – take

subway line No 3 or 4 to the Chungmuro station.

Nanjang is a privately run music house near Shinchon station which features various programmes of traditional Korean music and dance performances.

The National Theatre on the slopes of Namsan Park (just behind Dong-Guk University and right across from the Shilla Hotel) has various performances (opera, dance, etc). Check with one of the Tourist Information Centres for the current programme.

Sejong Cultural Centre does modern performances and exhibits – classical music, art exhibitions, piano recitals, etc.

The Seoul Nori Madang (☎ (02) 4141985) is an open-air theatre for traditional dance performances. It's just behind the Lotte World Shopping Complex near the Chamshil subway station (subway line No 2).

Bookshops The best place is the Kyobo Book Centre in the basement of the Kyobo Building on the north-east corner of Sejongro and Chongno – you can enter through the pedestrian subway. Chongno Book Centre – just across the street from the YMCA – is Seoul's second largest bookshop.

Libraries There are two good libraries with English-language books. The largest is at USIS, just east of City Hall. The other is the British Council, just north of Toksu Palace and east of the British Embassy.

Emergency During office hours, you can call the Seoul City Tourist Information Centre (☎ (02) 7316337, 7358688) – they can arrange an ambulance or relay your call to the proper authorities. Outside office hours, call Asia Emergency Assistance (☎ (02) 3536475/6). If you want to try your luck with someone who probably won't speak English, the emergency telephone number for police is 112; for an ambulance or fire it's 119.

Seoul has a number of good hospitals with English-speaking doctors, but most are horribly overcrowded. For emergencies, the biggest, best and jam-packed is Seoul National University Hospital (☎ (02) 7625171). For normal outpatient treatment, the best place to go is the Foreigners' Clinic at Severance Hospital (☎ (02) 3920161) which is attached to the Yonsei University Medical School – several American doctors work here. Other hospitals with English-speaking doctors include Cheil (☎ (02) 2692151), Ewha (☎ (02) 7625061), Soonchunhyang (☎ (02) 7947191) and Saint Mary's (☎ (02) 7891114).

The Foreign Community Service (FOCUS) (☎ (02) 7987529, 7978212) provides referrals to hospitals, doctors, lawyers, schools and other services in South Korea. The office is open Monday to Friday, 9 am to 5 pm, and there's a 24-hour answer phone for emergencies. The address is 5th floor, B Building, Namsan Village Apartments, San 1-139, Itaewon-dong, Yongsan-gu.

Lost & Found If you leave something in a taxi or on public transport, there is a chance of recovering it from the lost & found at the Korean Broadcasting System (KBS) Building (☎ (02) 7811325) on Youido Island. However, first try calling the Citizen's Room of the Seoul Police Bureau (☎ (02) 7554400), 201-11 Naeja-dong, Chongno-gu.

Things to See

The **Kyongbok Palace**, at the back of the former Capitol Building at the end of Sejongro, was first built in 1392 by the founder of the Yi dynasty, King Taejo. It was burnt down during the Japanese invasion of 1592 and left in ruins until it was rebuilt in 1867, when it became the residence of the 26th ruler. The walled grounds contain some exceptionally beautiful buildings and a collection of old stone pagodas from other parts of the country, many of them moved there by the Japanese during their occupation of Korea.

The palace is open daily from 9.15 am to 6.30 pm from April to October, and from 9.30 am to 5.30 pm from November to March. Entry costs W550.

Also in the grounds are the **National Folk Museum** and the **National Museum**. The National Folk Museum (closed Tuesdays) has life-like recreations of traditional houses, festivals and clothing styles and a display of movable metal type that was invented and used in Korea around 1234 – 200 years before Gutenberg's invention of movable type printing in Europe. Entry costs W110.

The National Museum (closed Mondays) has displays of ancient pottery and a collection of stone and brass buddhas and bodhisattvas. Entry costs W500.

Chongmyo Royal Ancestral Shrines is a forested park east of the Kyongbok Palace. It contains a collection of beautiful traditional Korean temples that house the ancestral tablets of the 27 Yi dynasty kings and queens. The two main shrines are only open to the public on certain ceremonial days. One of these is the first Sunday of May each year when the descendants of the royal family come to honour the spirits of their ancestors in a very colourful Confucian ceremony. Don't miss it if you happen to be in Seoul at the time. Entry costs W1000 and the park is open daily between 9 am and 6 pm.

The best preserved of Seoul's five palaces is **Changdok Palace**, once the residence of Korea's royal family. It was originally built in 1405 and rebuilt in 1611. It is also the site of the enchanting **Secret Garden (Piwon)**, a landscaped wooded retreat covering 32 hectares and incorporating over 40 pleasure pavilions as well as many ponds and stone bridges. This is Korean landscape gardening at its best. The garden was originally reserved for members of the royal family and the king's concubines. The palace and the Secret Garden are open daily but to see them you must join a tour group. Each tour lasts about 1½ hours and costs W1800 which includes the admission price. The tour guides speak English.

Toksu Palace is opposite the Seoul Plaza Hotel. The grounds contain the **Museum of Modern Art**. It's open from 9.15 am to 6.30 pm from April to October, and from 9.30 am to 5.30 pm from November to March. Entry costs W550.

In the centre of the city you will find **Pagoda Park**, famous for its 10-storey Koryo pagoda. **Poshingak** – near the Chonggak subway station – houses Seoul's city bell.

For superb views over the city (smog permitting), go to **Seoul Tower**, which is on top of Namsan (South Mountain), between Seoul and Itaewon. Admission to the tower is W1200. It's an additional W1400 round trip if you want to take the optional cable car up the mountain – otherwise, it's a 20-minute walk up from the Namsan Public Library at the base of the mountain. For a different perspective, go up here at night – operating hours are from 10 am to 9.30 pm (10.30 pm in summer).

One sight often overlooked by visitors is the **Subterranean City** – the underground shopping arcades and interconnecting passages. There is a maze of these arcades twisting and winding under the city – the tourist bureau maps show only part. Longest is the Ulchiro Underground Arcade running from City Hall to the Ulchiro 7-ga subway station – about 2.8 km. More interesting is the Sogong Arcade (near the Seoul Plaza Hotel) which connects to the Myong-dong Arcade (near the GPO) and connects to the basement of the Lotte Department Store – a good walk with plenty to see.

Lotte World is an interesting though bizarre place to visit – it's a huge mass of stores, restaurants and movie theatres, with a monorail, indoor swimming pool, ice-skating rink and laser light-show thrown in for good measure. Just behind Lotte World is **Magic Island**, South Korea's answer to Disneyland. Take subway line No 2 to the Chamshil station.

The enormous **Olympic Stadium** on the south bank of the Han River accommodates around 100,000 spectators and the surrounding sports complex covers almost three sq km. The stadium and sports complex are open to the public.

Youido (*do* means island) is in the Han River and is Seoul's answer to Manhattan. Actually, it doesn't look much like Manhattan, but it's certainly got Seoul's densest collection of high-rises and is very different from the rest of the city. Youido is home to the ugly National Assembly Building, the stock exchange and South Korea's tallest structure, the DLI 63 Building. You can visit the observation platform in DLI 63, though the view is nowhere near as good as from Seoul Tower or Pukansan. There is an outdoor collection of warplanes and tanks at the **Korean War Museum**. Overall, Youido isn't much of a tourist attraction – the best sight in Youido is the park along the Han River.

Activities

River Cruise During the summer there are six different cruises on the Han River. Most last about one hour and cost W3000, except the Ttuksom to Chamshil cruise which takes only 10 minutes and costs W600. Cruises are offered by two companies, Won Kwang and Semo. Won Kwang has an office in Youido (☎ (02) 7855522) and Chamshil (☎ (02) 4166811). Semo also has an office in Youido (☎ (02) 7854411) and Chamshil (☎ (02) 4168611). Cruises depart from either Youido or Chamshil.

Swimming Thanks to the 1988 Olympics, there are several indoor Olympic-size swimming pools. One is in the Seoul Sports Complex and another is in Olympic Park.

Language Courses There are several large government-run language schools such as the Yonsei University Foreign Language Institute (FLI) and Ehwa Women's University in Seoul. The Language Research Teaching Centre (LRTC) in Seoul is a well-known private language school. Other language schools advertise in the *Korea Times* and *Korea Herald*. Remember that you *must* obtain a student visa *before* enrolling.

Places to Stay

Hostels Hotels are generally a better deal – the hostels operated by the Korea Youth Hostels Associaton (KYHA) are not particularly cheap and tend to be inconveniently located. However, they are very clean and comfortable. At the KYHA hostels, an International Youth Hostel Association card is required and the buildings are closed from 10 am to 3 pm. Seoul's oldest hostel is the *Bando Youth Hostel* (☎ (02) 5672141). It's a long way out south of the Han River, but reachable by subway line No 2 – exit at the Yoksam station. Airport bus No 600 can drop you 15 minutes by foot from the hostel. A bed in a beautiful, modern dormitory costs W8800.

The KYHA also operates the *Seoul Olympic Youth Hostel* (☎ (02) 4101521) where dorm beds cost W9900. Take subway line No 2 and exit at the Songnae station.

Hotels Urban renewal has swept through central Seoul, taking with it most of the old buildings along with the cheap yogwan once common in this area. The cheapest remaining is *Inn Daewon* (☎ (02) 7357891), 26 Tangju-dong, Chongno-gu. A dormitory bed costs W4500 and double rooms cost W8000. All share one grotty washroom with barely functional plumbing. This hostel is scheduled for demolition and may be gone by the time you read this – progress marches on.

The second most popular place with budget travellers is the *Sung Do Yogwan* (☎ (02) 7388226), 120 Naesu-dong, Chongno-gu. Singles/doubles with shared bath cost W7000/8000, and a double with private bath costs W12,000. This yogwan has a sign in English, but there are several other similarly priced yogwan on the same street with signs in Korean.

Highly recommended is the *Moonhwa Yogwan* (☎ (02) 7654659), 69 Unni-dong, Chongno-gu, where beautiful double rooms with shared bath cost W8000. With private bath it's W12,000. This place is very close to Duksung Women's University, a few blocks north of Pagoda Park. The English sign is yellow with blue letters and only says 'Hotel'.

As you face the YMCA, on the right side of the building you'll find an alley. If you head up this alley, you'll find a sign in English saying 'Hotel' – this is the *Daewon*

Yogwan (☎ (02) 7351588) where doubles with shared bath cost W8000. In this same alley is *Yongil Yogwan* (☎ (02) 7340525) where singles/doubles are W8000/10,000, but they have no English sign.

The *Kyerimjang Yogwan* (☎ (02) 7784294) has comfortable singles/doubles with private bath for W12,000/13,000. There is no English sign, but it's easy to find – as you face the huge Hotel Pacific, immediately to your left is an alley with a sign saying 'yogwan' in Korean and an arrow pointing the way.

An outstanding place to stay is *Ha Nam Hotel* (☎ (02) 7777181-5, 7529926/8), 16-1 Chong-dong, Chung-gu, on Toksugunggil just to the west of Toksu Palace. A comfortable double room costs W17,500. The only problem with this place is that it's often full.

If you're willing to spend significantly more for your comforts, there is the *YMCA* (☎ (02) 7328261) on Chongno 2-ga on the north side of the street just west of Pagoda Park. Singles/doubles cost W26,400/34,100.

In an alley just to the north of Pagoda Park by the Nagwan elevated arcade is the *Hotel Emerald* (☎ (02) 7432001), 75 Nagwon-dong, Chongno-gu. A comfortable double with private bath goes for W20,000. In another alley just slightly to the north is the relatively luxurious *Hotel Sangwon* (☎ (02) 7650441-9) 33 Nagwon-dong, Chongno-gu, where doubles are W32,000.

In an alley right by the south-east corner of Ulchiro and Tonhwamunno is the *Eulji Hotel* (☎ (02) 2785000-9), 291-45 Ulchiro 3-ga, Chung-gu. Korean-style doubles are W22,000 and Western-style rooms are W25,000.

Places to Eat

The only problem finding food is deciding where to start – the supply is limitless. If you're on a tight budget, the best bargains are found in the basements of large department stores, where you can often find supermarkets and lunch counters. Best of the bunch is the basement of *Lotte Department Store* where you'll find an excellent bakery and numerous, cheap restaurants. The 10th floor has a wide selection of more expensive Korean food. The 11th floor has a Japanese restaurant complete with a waterfall and babbling brook, though the prices on the menu might also leave you babbling. The *Sky Cafe* on the 12th floor is quite cheap.

The nearby Shinsegae Department Store also has some cheap lunch counters in the basement, but selection is limited. The Printemps Department Store has excellent restaurants in the basement and on the 7th floor.

If you're in the area of the Inn Daewon or the Kyobo Bookstore, a place you should definitely check out is *Koryo Supermarket* (no English sign). The lunch counters are hidden in the back and to your right – you can eat well for around W1500. The supermarket itself is one of the cheapest and has sustained many a budget traveller in Seoul.

Yet another place to look is in the large subway stations and underground shopping malls – sushi with soup and pickled vegetables should go for around W1200.

Western chain restaurants like *McDonald's*, *Wendy's* and *Kentucky Fried Chicken* have made their debut in Seoul. *Lotteria* is a South Korean clone of McDonald's and Kentucky Fried combined but with lower prices – the fried chicken dinners (W2000) aren't bad at all.

Entertainment

Itaewon-dong (just call it Itaewon) is on the south side of Namsan Park. It's an area of bars, music and dancing clubs, restaurants, brothels and more. The area used to cater solely to US soldiers, but it's becoming more and more Koreanised. One place which has become a legend in Itaewon is the *King Club*, which features disco music, a dance floor and no cover charge, though you're expected to buy drinks. Just across the street is another lively place, *Heavy Metal*. Also in the neighbourhood is *All That Jazz*. From directly in front of the YMCA, you can catch bus No 23 which goes to Itaewon – you can also catch this bus from in front of the Samsung Building.

Besides Itaewon, the other part of Seoul

that has numerous discos is in Myong-dong, east of the GPO.

The Hyehwa district is the place to go for plays, teashops, cafes and to hang out with Seoul's trendy set. There are often street plays, but only Korean is spoken. You can get there on subway line No 4 – exit at the Hyehwa or Hansung University station.

Seeing a movie is as much fun in South Korea as anywhere else. Imported films will usually be in English (or German, French, etc) with Korean subtitles. Movies are sometimes advertised in the English newspapers, but you'll need to get a Korean paper to find out show times. Tickets cost around W2500 to W4000.

Things to Buy

The best deals are to be found in the open-air markets such as Namdaemun (South Gate Market) and Tongdaemun (East Gate Market). Insa-dong is a shopping street north of the YMCA which is a popular area for buying antiques, arts and crafts. Itaewon is a neighbourhood well known for its nightlife, but it's also a good shopping district for all clothing and all manner of goods.

The Yongsan Electronics Market is to the west of Itaewon and is a good place to look for all manner of appliances – Walkmans, computers, Nintendo games, etc. You can reach the market by taking the Suwon train on subway line No 1 and getting off at Yongsan station – from there follow the elevated walkway over the tracks to the 'Tour Bus Terminal'. Part of the electronics market is in this bus terminal and also in the many shops outside.

Although not the cheapest place to buy things, the large department stores near the GPO are worth exploring, at least to see what's available. Popular stores in this area include Lotte (closed on Tuesdays), Midopa (closed Wednesdays) and Shinsegae (closed 1st & 3rd Mondays). Just east of the GPO is a shopping district called Myong-dong. It's expensive, but you can try bargaining. Lotte World at the Chamshil subway station (line No 2) is a long way out from the city centre but is one of the largest shopping malls in the world.

Getting There & Away

Air Seoul is the main international arrival point in South Korea with flight connections to cities all over the world. See the Getting There & Away section in this chapter.

Bus The main bus terminal in Seoul is the Kangnam express bus terminal on the south side of the Han River – take subway line No 3 and leave at the Express Bus Terminal station. The terminal is very well organised, with signs in English and Korean over all the ticket offices and bus bays so you can't go wrong as long as you don't confuse places like Kongju, Kwangju and Kyongju.

In addition to this terminal there are a further six local bus terminals. The one that most travellers come in contact with is the Sangbong local bus terminal in the eastern suburbs. This is the terminal for buses to and from Chunchon and other destinations on the east coast. It is connected by bus with Chongnyangni railway station, which is also the terminus of subway line No 1. There are buses to Chunchon from Sangbong terminal every 10 minutes daily from 5.15 am to 9.30 pm. The fare is W1340 and the journey takes two hours and 20 minutes.

From the Kangnam express bus terminal there are the following buses:

To Chinju Every 30 minutes from 6.30 am to 6 pm. The fare is W5820 and the journey takes 5½ hours.
To Chongju Every 10 minutes from 5.50 am to 10 pm. The fare is W1870 and the journey takes one hour and 40 minutes.
To Kangnung Every 10 minutes from 6 am to 7.40 pm. The fare is W3530 and the journey takes about 3¾ hours.
To Kongju Every 40 minutes from 7 am to 7 pm. The fare is W2240 and the journey takes 2½ hours.
To Kwangju Every five minutes from 5.30 am to 8 pm. The fare is W4530 and the journey takes about four hours.
To Kyongju Every 35 minutes from 7 am to 6.10 pm. The fare is W5090 and the journey takes 4¼ hours.

To Mokpo Every 30 minutes from 6 am to 6.30 pm. The fare is W5520 and the journey takes about 5½ hours.
To Nonsan About every hour from 6.30 am to 7.50 pm. The fare is W2990 and the journey takes 2¾ hours.
To Pohang Every 20 minutes from 6.30 am to 6.30 pm. The fare is W5570 and the journey takes five hours.
To Pusan Every five or 10 minutes from 6 am to 6.40 pm. The fare is W5970 and the journey takes 5¼ hours.
To Sokcho Every 50 minutes from 6.30 am to 6.40 pm. The fare is W4460 and the journey takes 5¼ hours.
To Taegu Every 10 minutes from 6 am to 8 pm. The fare is W4220 and the journey takes 3½ hours.
To Taejon Every 10 minutes from 6 am to 9.40 pm. The fare is W2240 and the journey takes two hours.
To Yosu Every hour from 6.40 am to 5.40 pm. The fare is W6120 and the journey takes 5½ hours.

Train Most trains departing from Seoul leave from Seoul Station. The one important exception is the train heading east towards Chunchon. For this, go to Chongnyangni Railway Station, which you reach by taking subway line No 1 to its terminus.

Getting Around

To/From the Airport Kimpo International Airport is the usual arrival point, a considerable distance west of the city. Airport shuttle buses connect Kimpo with the city centre every 10 minutes from 7.40 am to 9.30 pm (6 am to 8.10 pm from the city). The 40-minute journey costs W500 on bus No 601. Most travellers get off at the Koreana Hotel, though another useful stop is Chongno 3-ga further along the route.

Bus No 63 costs W470 and stops just north of the Koreana Hotel and also just to the south of Toksu Palace. It has several advantages over bus No 601: it runs more frequently; it starts service earlier and ends later; if all seats on bus No 601 are full, it will not stop whereas No 63 will allow additional passengers to stand.

Airport bus No 600 travels along the area south of the Han River and is only useful if you're heading directly to the Express Bus Terminal or Bando Youth Hostel (get off at

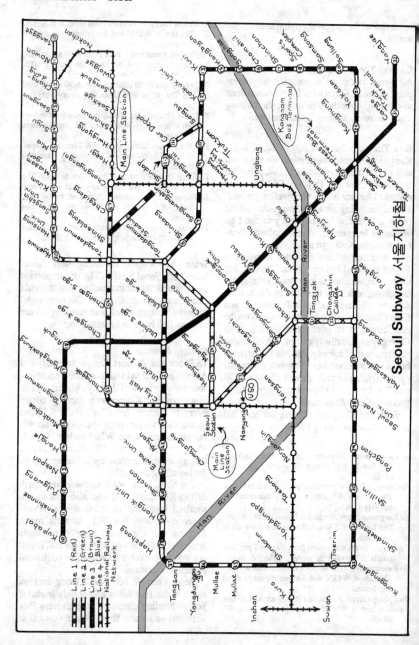

Seoul Subway 서울지하철

Line 1 (Red)
Line 2 (Green)
Line 3 (Brown)
Line 4 (Blue)
National Railway Network

Samjung Hotel). It terminates at Lotte World near the Olympic Park.

Bus City buses run from approximately 5.30 am until midnight. The ordinary buses are colour-coded purple & white or blue & white, and cost W180 (exact change please) or W170 with a token (same word in Korean) bought from one of the bus token booths found at most major bus stops. The green & white chwasok buses (the ones with seats) cost W470 and no tokens are available. The token booths sell a *Bus Line Guide (Bus Nosunannae)* for W500, but it's written entirely in Korean despite the English title on the cover.

Minibuses are privately owned and operate illegally, but are tolerated by the government because they provide services to isolated areas not reached by public transport. The fare depends on the distance travelled.

Underground The Seoul subway system is modern, fast and cheap, but can be so crowded that if you drop dead, you'll never hit the ground. The basic charge is W250 for Zone 1 which includes most of the city. The fare rises to W350 if you cross into Zone 2 – the machines where you buy tickets have a self-explanatory fare map, but you'll rarely need to go outside Zone 1. There are additional charges for suburban lines like the one to Suwon – buy these tickets from the ticket windows. Trains run at least every six minutes from 5 am until midnight. There are four lines in total, all of them colour-coded. You can get to all of the bus terminals using the subway except for Sangbong local bus terminal out in the north-eastern suburbs.

The subway system is still expanding. By 1997, the city hopes to have completed four new lines, thus doubling capacity. Most useful will be line No 5 which will extend all the way out to Kimpo International Airport via Youido.

Taxi Seoul taxi drivers have a sordid reputation – even the Koreans are fed up with them. Demand is so much greater than supply that you practically have to throw yourself in front of a cab to get the driver's attention. Sometimes they use the meter, but often ask for a set fee. More disconcerting is that they may stop and pick up other passengers along the way, thereby doubling or tripling their profit. While this might not be so terrible, single women travelling late at night should be especially wary about this practice – rapes have occured when the driver and other 'passengers' turn on the unsuspecting victim.

Around Seoul

PUKANSAN 북한산
Just to the north of Seoul is Pukansan National Park, a popular area for hiking, rock climbing and photography. The summit of Pukansan is 836 metres high and offers the best views of Seoul if the smog doesn't get in the way. The rugged landscape of granite peaks and cliffs offers stunning scenery. Within the park is Pukhansansong (North Mountain Fortress).

Getting There & Away
Take bus No 156 from the Sejong Cultural Centre to the Pukansan entrance *(Pukansan ipku)*.

PANMUNJOM 판문점
This is a good place to visit for a sobering dose of reality. Situated 56 km north of Seoul, Panmunjom is the truce village on the ceasefire line established at the end of the Korean War in 1953. It's in a building here that the interminable 'peace' discussions continue.

Tours are run by Korea Travel Bureau (☎ (02) 7780150), which has an office on the 3rd floor of the Hotel Lotte. Tours cost W26,000 – if it helps any, lunch is thrown in free. The tour includes a visit to the third invasion tunnel which North Korea dug under the DMZ and which was discovered in 1978. The trip takes seven hours and runs daily except weekends.

The USO (☎ (03) 7953063, 7953028) also

arranges tours at the bargain price of US$18 or equivalent in Korean won, but without lunch or a tour of the invasion tunnel. You *do not* have to be a US citizen or military personnel to attend, but USO tours are extremely popular so book in advance.

While you are permitted to take photos and use binoculars, there are a number of restrictions that visitors must adhere to. You must bring your passport; children under 10 years of age are not allowed; Korean nationals are not allowed; there is strict dress code which civilians must follow – many travellers run afoul of this rule! The military lists the following as examples of inappropriate clothing for this formal occasion:

1) Shirts (top) without sleeves, T-shirts, tank tops and shirts of similar design.
2) Dungarees or blue jeans of any kind, including 'designer jeans'.
3) Shorts of any style, including hiking, bermuda, cut-offs, or 'short-shorts'.
4) Miniskirts, halter tops, backless dresses and other abbreviated items of similar design.
5) Any item of outer clothing of the sheer variety.
6) Shower shoes, thongs or 'flip-flops'.
7) Items of military clothing not worn as an integral part of a prescribed uniform.
8) Any form-fitting clothing including tight-knit tops, tight-knit pants and stretch pants.

NAMHANSAN 남한산

To the south-east of Seoul high up on the mountains is Namhansan Provincial Park. Namhansansong (South Mountain Fortress) is probably the nearest thing you'll find in Korea to the Great Wall of China. The stone walls – up to seven metres high – and massive gates of this fortress snake for some eight km around the mountains above Songnam City east of Seoul. The views from the top are stupendous.

Getting There & Away

Take Seoul city bus No 36 from Kangnam express bus terminal or bus No 66 from Ulchiro 5-ga (others that go there include Nos 239 and 570) to Songnam City – the trip takes about one hour and costs W210. If you take the No 66 bus, which is the preferred one, watch out for a large sign saying 'City

Hall' when you get to Songnam City. Get off the bus just after that. From there you will find minibuses going to Namhansansong – the fare is W350 one way and it takes about 15 minutes.

TONGGURUNG 동구능

Outside central Seoul are five Yi dynasty royal tomb sites. The best preserved of these is Tonggurung (East Nine Tombs) in the far north-east part of the city. All of these tombs consist of the traditional earthen burial mound (similar to those of the Silla kings in Kyongju) but most of them are guarded by beautifully carved granite sentries and real or mythical animals. All the Yi kings have been buried at one or other of these sites from the first, King Taejo in 1408, to the last crown prince, Yongchinwang, in 1970.

Getting There & Away

The national tourist organisation, USO and other private touring companies offer organised trips to one or other of the burial sites, but you can also get there individually by local buses. To get to Tonggurung, take subway line No 1 to Chongnyangni station, then bus No 55-1 to the tomb site.

SUWON 수원

Suwon is an ancient fortress city 48 km south of Seoul. The walls were constructed in the later part of the 18th century by King Kongjo in an unsuccessful attempt to make Suwon the nation's capital. The walls, gates, a number of pavilions and an unusual watergate have all been reconstructed along original lines.

To get there take subway line No 1 heading south all the way to the last stop, making sure the train is marked Suwon. The journey takes about 45 minutes and costs W600 one way.

KOREAN FOLK VILLAGE 민속촌

This major attraction (*min sok chon*) is as near to being authentic as throngs of tourists will allow. The village has examples of the traditional peasants', farmers', and civil officials' housing styles from all over the country as well as craft workshops, a brewery, Confucian school, Buddhist temple and a market place.

To get there, go to Suwon by subway and cross the road to find the office of the Folk Village. You can catch a free bus from there. Admission to the Folk Village costs W3100 and opening hours are from 9 am to 5 pm.

YOJU 여주

About two km to the east of Yoju is **Shiluk-sa**, a magnificent temple built around 580 AD. The temple is open from 8 am to 4 pm.

A short bus ride to the west of Yoju is Yongnung, where you can find the **Tomb of King Sejong**. Sejong, whose face adorns the W10,000 bill, invented the modern Korean script (hangul) and is considered the greatest of Korea's kings. The tomb site is open from 8.30 am to 6 pm, and there is a small museum on the grounds.

Yoju is to the south-east of Seoul. You can get there by bus from Seoul's Sangbong bus terminal.

North-East Korea

CHUNCHON 춘천

This is the provincial capital of Kangwon-do (Kangwon Province) and the urban centre of South Korea's northern lake district, which includes lakes Soyang and Paro. The main attraction is a boat trip on the lakes. Set in a beautiful mountainous area, Chunchon makes a good stopover en route to such places as the Soraksan and Odaesan national parks.

Places to Stay & Eat

The two main places for cheap yogwan are around the bus terminal and just beyond the main roundabout in the centre of town on the right-hand side. One good place near the bus terminal is *Kumhwajang Yogwan* (☎ 546850) where a double with shared/private bath is W8000/12,000.

There are plenty of restaurants in the market area (off to the right-hand side just before the main roundabout).

Getting There & Away

Bus Buses to Chunchon depart from Seoul's Sangbong bus terminal, but the train is certainly more convenient. The same bus continues on from Chunchon to Sokcho on the east coast.

Train Trains to Chunchon depart from Seoul's Chongnyangni Railway Station at the terminus of subway line No 1. The one-way trip takes a little over 1½ hours.

Boat Trips

There are two excellent boat trips on Lake Soyang. A popular short trip is the one from Chunchon to Chongpyong-sa, a Buddhist temple up in the hills north of the lake. The boats run daily every half hour or so depending on sufficient numbers. The trip takes about 10 minutes.

Much more interesting is to travel by a combination of boat and bus or taxi to Soraksan National Park via the town of Inje. The boat follows Lake Soyang from Chunchon to just outside of Inje where you catch a bus or share-taxi into town. Many of these share-taxis will take you all the way to Paektam-sa at Inner Sorak, the best part of Soraksan National Park. Negotiate the fare before heading out.

SORAKSAN NATIONAL PARK 설악산

This is the most scenically beautiful area in South Korea, with high craggy peaks, forests, tremendous waterfalls, crystal clear water, old temples and hermitages. Though most of the trails are well marked you'll need a map if you intend to go out into the real wilderness. Soraksan is an excellent place to go walking for a few days or even longer if you have camping equipment with you. Entry to the national park costs W900 (W500 for students).

Unfortunately, during the summer peak season, Soraksan gets so crowded it's a wonder the whole mountain doesn't collapse. Your best chance of avoiding the

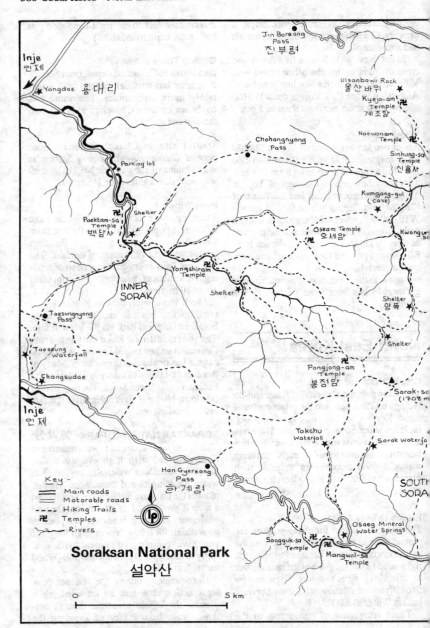

Soraksan National Park
설악산

Inje 인제

Yongdae 용대리

Jin Boreong Pass 진부령

Ulsanbawi Rock 울산 바위

Kyejo-am Temple 계조암

Naewonam Temple

Chohangnyong Pass

Sinhung Temple 신흥사

Parking lot

Kumgang-gul (cave)

Kwongur

Paektam-sa Temple 백담사

Shelter

Oseam Temple 오세암

Yongshiram Temple

INNER SORAK

Shelter

Shelter 양폭

Taesungnyong Pass

Taesung Waterfall

Pongjong-am Temple 봉정암

Changsudae

Shelter

Sorak-sa (1708 m)

Inje 인제

Tokchu Waterfall

Sorak Waterfa

Hon Gyereong Pass 한계령

SOUTH SORA

Key:-
Main roads
Motorable roads
Hiking Trails
卍 Temples
Rivers

Osaeg Mineral Water Springs

Songguk-sa Temple

Mangwol-sa Temple

0   5 km

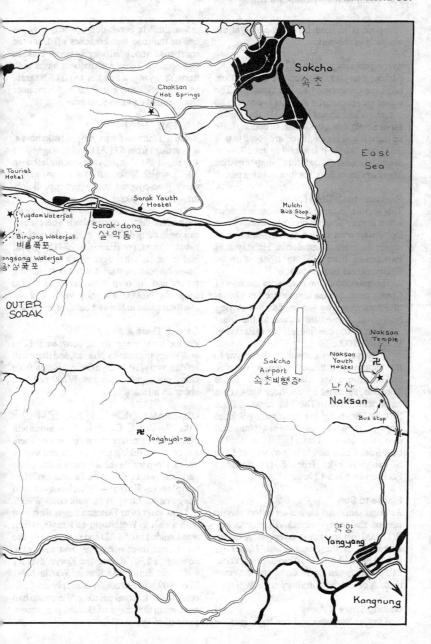

stampede is to head for Inner Sorak at the west end of the park.

Kwongumsong 권금성

Almost everyone who comes to Soraksan takes the cable car to Kwongkumsong. The views are spectacular and this is one way to get immediate access to the trails that lead to Inner Sorak, though you can, of course, walk up there if you prefer. If you are going to trek into Inner Sorak, it is useful to get a *Tourist Map of the East Coast* from Chung-ang Atlas Map Service in Seoul before heading out.

Paektam-sa 백담사

This temple in Inner Sorak became famous when former South Korean President Chun Doo-hwan went to live here in seclusion to repent for various misdeeds. He stayed at Paektam-sa from 1988 to 1990, when he finally moved back to Seoul.

The main attraction here is not the saga of Chun's exile, but the temple itself in a beautiful natural setting and the fact that staying here gives immediate access to the Inner Sorak area. You can find minbak at Paektam-sa for W10,000.

There is no public transport all the way to the temple. The nearest town is Yongdae (where there are also minbak). From Yongdae it's about a three-hour walk south on a sealed road. The bus running from Seoul's Sangbong bus terminal to Sokcho stops at Yongdae. Alternatively, you could also get a share-taxi from Inje if you take the boat from Chunchon to Inje by way of Lake Soyang. A hike from Sorak-dong to Paektam-sa takes 12 hours.

Places to Stay

At Soraksan, most budget travellers stay in one of the many minbak. Expect to pay W12,000 per room on average. A cheap alternative is the *Sorak Youth Hostel* (☎ (0392) 347540-50), 155 Tomun-dong, about halfway between Sorak-dong and the coast road. A bed in the dormitory costs W6000.

Getting There & Away

You get to Soraksan and the trails into the mountains via Sorak-dong, which is at the end of the road that branches off from the coast road about halfway between Naksan and Sokcho. There are frequent buses both from Yangyang, a few km south of Naksan, and from Sokcho every 10 to 15 minutes from around dawn to 9.30 pm.

NAKSAN 낙산

Naksan is famous for its temple, **Naksan-sa**, which dates from 671 AD, and its huge white statue of Avalokitesvara (completed in 1977), which looks out to sea from atop a small pine-covered rocky outcrop. Below the temple is Naksan beach.

There are several yogwan and yoinsuk on the beach side of the coast road, where meals can be arranged. There is also the *Naksan Youth Hostel* (☎ (0396) 6723416/7) near Nakan-sa. It's a huge, plush place with English-speaking staff, hot and cold running water, and its own restaurant and coffee shop. At W6000 it's good value and the cheapest place to use as a base for Soraksan.

Getting There & Away

All the local buses plying between Sokcho and Yangyang pass by Naksan, and there will be one every 10 to 15 minutes. Buses from either place to Naksan cost W200 and take about 25 minutes.

ODAESAN NATIONAL PARK 오대산

Like Soraksan, Odaesan is a mountain massif where nature reigns supreme. There are excellent hiking possibilities and superb views. Deep inside the western section of the park are two of the most famous Buddhist temples in Korea – Wolchong-sa and Sangwon-sa. Entry to the park costs W900.

Most visitors to Odaesan begin their tour with a visit to **Wolchong-sa** temple, which was founded in 654 AD and destroyed by fire on at least three occasions over the years, notably in 1307 during the Koryo dynasty and again during the Korean War in 1950. The 1969 reconstruction is simply magnificent and the internal painting of the main hall containing the image of Buddha is a masterpiece of religious art.

Much deeper into Odaesan, some nine km beyond Wolchong-sa at the end of a forested pass, is **Sangwon-sa** temple, whose most famous possession is its bronze bell, one of the oldest and largest in Korea. It was cast in 663, one year after construction of the temple began.

Getting There & Away

A trip to Odaesan National Park starts in Kangnung, and there's a choice of direct bus or local buses that involve a change at Jinbu, just off the expressway.

There are four direct buses per day from Kangnung to Wochang-sa temple, the first at 9.10 am and the last at 4.05 pm. The fare is W900 and the journey takes about 1½ hours. These buses will have Wolchong-sa on their destination indicator.

UNIFICATION OBSERVATORY
통일 전망대

A visit to the Unification Observatory *(tongil chunmangtae)* on the DMZ north of Sokcho has become almost as popular these days as a trip to Panmunjom north of Seoul. From the observatory there are fine views over into North Korea and the Diamond Mountains.

A number of commercial tour companies in Sokcho and Sorak-dong run trips to the Observatory. The round trip costs W5000 and takes about five hours.

West-Central Korea

TAEJON 대전

Taejon is the capital of Chung Cheong Nam Province and a major industrial centre. It's also an excellent base from which to explore the nearby temples and national parks. Transport facilities are very good. You'll also come here if you're heading south to Mokpo by rail and from there to Cheju-do.

If you find yourself in Taejon with an evening to while away, try the tents by the river opposite the Taejon Department Store, where you'll meet half the locals having a party.

Places to Stay

The *Yongsong Yogwan* (☎ (042) 2829060) is excellent value at W8000 a single and W9000 a double. More luxurious is the nearby *Sunji Hotel* (☎ (042) 2566388) where doubles cost W12,000.

Getting There & Away

There are three bus terminals in Taejon: west chikheng, east chikheng, and the express (kosok). The latter two are side by side on the eastern outskirts of town. The east chikheng is most useful for getting to the Sogrisan and Togyusan national parks. Buses from here go to the temples in these parks.

There are also two railway stations. Taejon station serves the main line between Seoul and Pusan. Seodaejon station, on the west of town, serves the line to Mokpo via Nonsan, Iri and Kwangju, though if you're heading for Kwangju you must change at Yeong San Po.

Getting Around

The most important local bus for travellers is the No 841, which connects the east chikheng and express bus terminal with the west chikheng bus terminal via Taejon Railway Station and the city centre. The fare is the same on all city buses – W160 or W150 if you buy the ticket from a booth.

KWANCHOK-SA TEMPLE 관촉사

Just outside Nonsan, this temple is famous throughout Korea for possessing the largest stone buddha in the country, built in 968 AD. The temple complex and the 18-metre-high statue made from three pieces of granite are well worth seeing. Admission costs W600 (W500 for children and students). If you'd like to stay at the temple overnight, there's a small yogwan just below the temple entrance.

To get to the temple, take a bus from Taejon to Nonsan (W650, 45 minutes). From the local bus terminal there you can get a bus every few minutes directly to the temple. The fare is W150 and the journey takes about eight minutes.

TAEDUNSAN PROVINCIAL PARK
대둔산

This park offers some of the most spectacular views in Korea, but the climbing is steep. It's no place for acrophobes – the ascent involves crossing a hair-raising steel rope bridge stretched precariously between two rock pinnacles, then climbing an extremely steep and long steel stairway.

To get to Taedunsan, take a bus from either the east chikheng bus terminal or the express (kosok) bus terminal in Taejon. There are buses every hour from 7.30 am to 6.20 pm. The fare is W530 and the journey takes about one hour.

POPJU-SA TEMPLE 법주사

Popju-sa is one of the largest temple sites in Korea – an absolute must for all travellers. Until recently the temple area was most famous for the largest statue of Buddha in Korea – possibly in the whole of North-East Asia – a 27-metre-high figure above the temple compound. It took 30 years to build and was completed in 1968. In the 1980s the statue began to crack and it was demolished in late 1986. A new statue was erected in its place at a cost of US$4 million – 33 metres in height, made out of 160 tonnes of brass.

Popju-sa is surrounded by the luxuriously forested mountains of the Songnisan National Park. There are many well-marked hiking trails in the mountains above the temple and several hermitages where you may be able to stay the night.

Places to Stay & Eat

Songnidong, the village before the temple where the buses terminate, is quite large and there's a good selection of yogwan, yoinsuk and minbak. Expect to pay W5000 to W6000 for a room in a minbak.

There is a very good restaurant called the *Myongshin Shiktang* on the left-hand side of the main street as you walk up from the bus station towards the temple entrance.

Getting There & Away

Direct buses to Popju-sa from Taejon depart from the east chikheng bus terminal about

every 20 minutes. The fare is W1100 and the journey, over an exceptionally scenic route, takes 1¾ hours.

KONGJU 공주

This second capital of the Paekje kingdom was established in 475 AD, and the tombs of many of the Paekje kings are here. Over the centuries most of the tombs were looted of their treasures but in 1971 archaeologists came across the undisturbed tomb of King Muryeong (501-23 AD). The find was one of 20th-century Korea's greatest discoveries and the hundreds of priceless artefacts uncovered now form the basis of the Kongju National Museum.

Things to See

The **Kongju National Museum**, opened in 1972, was built to resemble the inside of King Muryeong's tomb. It houses the finest collection of Paekje artefacts in Korea, including two golden crowns, part of a coffin, gold, jade and silver ornaments, bronze mirrors and utensils. The museum is open daily, except Mondays, from 9 am to 6 pm during the summer and 9 am to 5 pm in the winter. Admission is W110.

The **Royal Paekje Tombs** are clustered together on Songsan-ri Hill, a 20-minute walk from the centre of town. Three of the chambers of King Muryeong's tomb are open for viewing from 9 am to 6 pm. Entry costs W330.

Places to Stay & Eat

The *Samwon Yoinsuk* is clean and friendly – it costs W5000 a single.

For good, basic Korean food try the *Hwanggum Shiktang*, which has a range of dishes starting from W2000. The *Taewu Shiktang*, about 100 metres from the express bus terminal down the main street of town, is similar.

Getting There & Away

The express bus terminal in Kongju has express and chikheng buses. It is well organised and you shouldn't have any difficulty finding the bus you want.

PUYO 부여

This is the site of the last capital of the Paekje kingdom, before its fall in 660 AD. Very little remains except a few foundation stones. It is a quiet provincial town surrounded by wooded hills and paddy fields with a friendly and very traditionally minded people.

At the **Puyo National Museum** you will find artefacts from the Paekje kingdom, as well as pottery and musical instruments from the 5th to 4th centuries BC. It is open daily except Mondays from 9 am to 4 pm in summer and 9 am to 5 pm in winter. Entry costs W110.

The museum stands at the foot of **Pusosan**, a pine-forested hill that was once part of the royal palace grounds. The hill is associated with the legend of the 3000 court ladies who threw themselves off a high cliff above the Paek Ma River rather than be captured by invading Chinese and Silla warriors at the end of the Paekje empire.

Also dating from the Paekje era is a five-storey pagoda on the site of the Chongnim-sa temple and a weather-beaten seated stone buddha which bears an uncanny resemblance to the Easter Island statues. Up the road is the **Gungnam Ji Pond & Pavilion**, once the pleasure garden for Paekje court ladies. Until a few years ago this place had been sadly neglected but there has been recent restoration work and the bridge to the pavilion is in good repair.

Places to Stay & Eat

Kyongbuk Yoinsuk is one of the cheapest places at just W5000/7000 for singles/doubles. There's also plenty of minbak. The *Puyo Youth Hostel* (☎ (0463) 23102), 105-1 Kugyo-ri, where beds go for W6000. Meals are available.

Most of the restaurants are pretty expensive. There are a few cafes around the express bus station where you can eat well for around W2000.

Getting There & Away

There are frequent local buses from Kongju to Puyo.

KYERYONGSAN NATIONAL PARK 계룡산

The area around Kongju is replete with fascinating old temples set amidst forested mountains and crystal clear streams. The most accessible of these are found in Kyeryongsan National Park between Kongju and Taejon.

The real jewel of the Kongju area is **Kapsa** temple, one of the oldest Buddhist temples in Korea. It is still in use, and the head monk speaks English. Several trails lead from here to Tong Hak-sa temple on the other side of the mountain. The walk from Kap-sa to Tong Hak-sa will take about four hours at a comfortable pace. Entry to the national park, in which both temples are situated, costs W800.

If you want to stay overnight near Kap-sa temple ask around for a minbak in the village below the temple.

Getting There & Away

Getting to Kap-sa temple is probably easiest from Kongju. There are direct buses from the express and chikheng bus terminal in Kongju. The fare is W390 and the journey takes 45 minutes.

East-Central Korea

KYONGJU 경주

For almost a thousand years Kyongju was the capital of the Silla dynasty and for nearly 300 years of that period it was the capital of the whole peninsula. Its origins date back to 57 BC and it survived right through to the 10th century AD, when it fell victim to division from within and invasion from without. After its conquest by the Koryo dynasty the capital of Korea was moved far to the north and Kyongju fell into decline.

Despite being ransacked by Mongols in the early 13th century and by the Japanese in the late 16th it survived to experience a revival early this century that still continues. There has been a great deal of restoration work and archaeological excavations are still

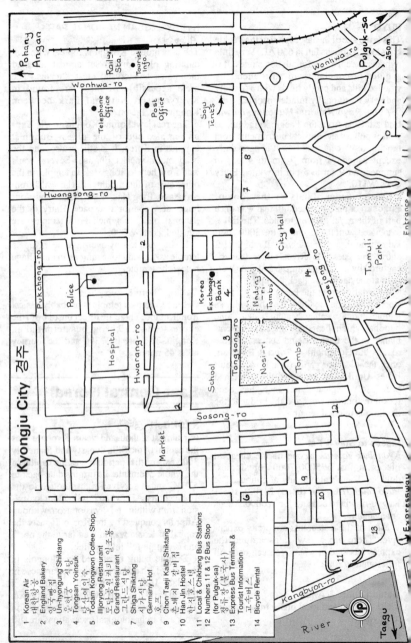

Kyongju City 경주

1 Korean Air
   대한항공
2 England Bakery
   영국 베커리
3 Un-hyongung Shiktang
   운혀궁 식당
4 Tongsan Yoinsuk
   당산여인숙
5 Todam Kongwon Coffee Shop.
   도담공원 커피 임즈숍
   Illjoryong Restaurant
   도담보원식당
6 Grand Restaurant
   그린드식당
7 Shiga Shiktang
   시가식당
8 Germany Hof
   홍프
9 Chon Taeji Kalbi Shiktang
   천태지 갈비집
10 Han Jin Hostel
   한진호스텔
11 Local & Chikheng Bus Stations
12 Numbers 11 & 12 Bus Stop
   (for Pulguk-sa)
   (불국사)
13 Express Bus Terminal &
   Tourist Information
   고속버스
14 Bicycle Rental

uncovering treasure troves of precious relics that throw more light on what life was like during this magnificent period of Korean history.

A small, provincial town with easy-going people, Kyongju is an open-air museum. Temples, tombs, shrines, the remains of palaces, pleasure gardens, castles and even an observatory survive as fine examples of Silla artistry. In the forested mountains that surround the city, magnificent views still do not overshadow the beauty of thousands of Buddhist temples, rock carvings and statues. Just how much time you want to devote to Kyongju depends on your level of interest in ancient culture and history, but most of the main sites can be seen in about four days.

Although Kyoto in Japan is famous as the place to see cherry blossoms, a similiar experience can be had in Kyongju, especially in the area around Pulguk-sa.

Things to See

Right in the centre of Kyongju city is **Tumuli Park**, a huge walled area with 20 royal tombs. One huge tomb, the Chonmachong (Heavenly Horse Tomb), is open in cross-section to show the method of construction. Facsimiles of the golden crown, bracelets, jade ornaments, weapons and pottery found here are displayed in glass cases.

Tumuli Park is open daily from 8.30 am to 6.30 pm from 1 April to 31 October, and from 8.30 am to 5 pm from 1 November to 31 March. A multiple-entry ticket for W2200 gives you access to the park and nine other sites.

A few hundred metres away is the stone observatory of **Chomsongdae**. A little further on is the **Castle of the Crescent Moon** or Panwolsong. This was once the royal castle and the site of a fabled palace, which dominated the whole area. Little is left of this fortress but thousands of relics were dredged up from the pond when it was drained in 1975. Outside this beautiful building is the legendary Emille Bell, one of the largest and most resonant bells ever made in Asia. Across the road is **Anapji Pond**, constructed by King Munmu in 674 AD as a pleasure garden to commemorate the unification of Silla.

Also on this circuit is the **Punhwang-sa Pagoda**, the oldest datable pagoda in Korea. Only three of the original nine storeys are left. The magnificently carved Buddhist guardians and stone lions are a major feature.

Just a little to the south on the road to Pulguk-sa is the superb **Kyongju National Museum**, the second best museum in the country (Seoul's National Museum still reigns supreme). This museum is very worthwhile, but it's often jammed with bored, screaming school kids who are being force-fed Korean culture. The museum is closed on Monday.

Crossing the river bridge south from the city brings you to the **Onung Tombs**, five of the most ancient tomb mounds in the area. A long walk further on is the beautiful Posokjong Bower, elegant gardens from the Silla dynasty. Less than a km down the road are the mysterious **Triple Buddhas**, which were only discovered in 1923. They are not in the Silla style but display the massive boldness characteristic of the Koguryo style. Last on this circuit are the four **Samnung Tombs**, nearly 1000 years younger than the tombs in the Onung compound.

Local bus No 23 will get you to any of these sites.

In the western area are the **Muyol Tombs**. Note the tortoise monument as you enter the compound. The main tomb is that of King Muyol who, in the mid-7th century, paved the way for the unification of Korea by conquering the rival Paekje kingdom. Back towards town is the tomb of General Kim Yu-shin, one of Korea's greatest military heroes. He led the armies of both Muyol and his successor, Munmu, in the 7th-century campaigns that resulted in the unification of the country. The tomb stands on a wooded bluff overlooking the city.

To the south-east is the crowning glory of Silla temple architecture, **Pulguk-sa**, built on a series of stone terraces about 16 km from Kyongju. It's Korea's most famous temple and is simply magnificent. From the top level, the view down over the rolling sea

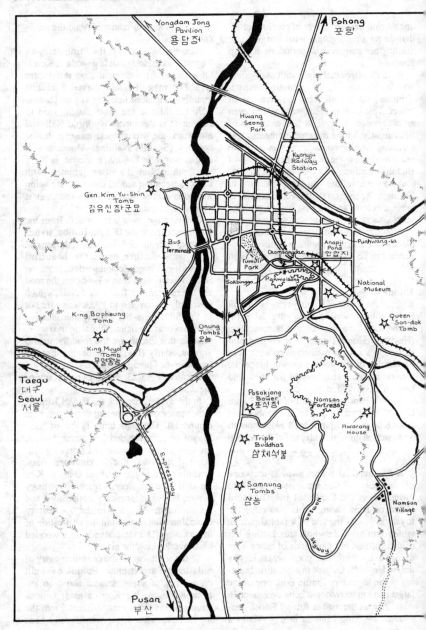

Yongdam Jong
Pavilion
용담정

Pohang
포항

Hwang
Seong
Park

Kyongju
Railway
Station

Gen. Kim Yu-Shin
Tomb
김유신장군묘

Bus
Terminals

Tumuli
Park

Chomsongdae

Anapji
Pond
안압지

Punhwang-sa

Sokbinggo

Panwolsong

National
Museum

King Bopheung
Tomb

Onung
Tombs
오릉

Queen
Son-dok
Tomb

King Muyol
Tomb
무열왕릉

Taegu
대구
Seoul
서울

Posokjong
Bower
포석정

Namsan
Fortress

Hwarang
House

Triple
Buddhas
삼체석불

Samnung
Tombs
삼릉

Namsan
Skyway

Namsan
Village

Expressway

Pusan
부산

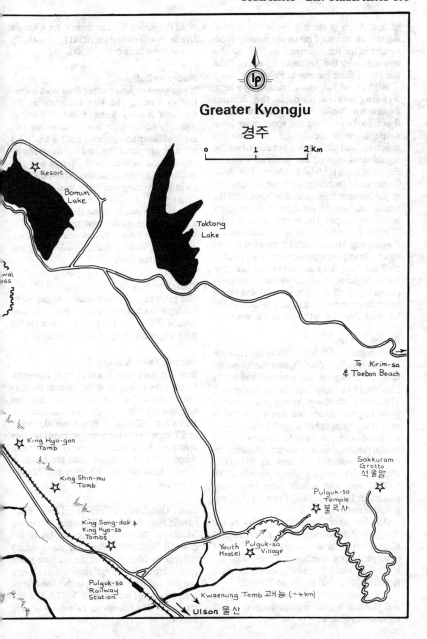

Greater Kyongju
경주

0   1   2 km

Resort

Bomun Lake

Toktong Lake

To Kirim-sa & Taebon Beach

King Hyo-gon Tomb

King Shin-mu Tomb

King Song-dok & King Hyo-so Tombs

Pulguk-sa Railway Station

Youth Hostel

Pulguk-sa Village

Pulguk-sa Temple 불국사

Sokkuram Grotto 석굴암

Kwaenung Tomb 괘능 (~4 km)

Ulsan 울산

of tiled roofs is superb, while the internal woodwork and roof eaves are equally spectacular. In the first courtyard are two pagodas that survived the Japanese invasion. Take bus No 11 from the city to Pulguk-sa.

High above Pulguk-sa, reached by a long, winding sealed road, is the famous **Sokkuram Grotto**, where a seated buddha figure looks out over the spectacular landscape towards the distant East Sea. Its simplicity and perfection have caused it to be regarded as one of the greatest works of Buddhist art in the whole of North-East Asia. To get to the grotto from Pulguk-sa, take one of the frequent minibuses that leave from the tourist information pavilion in the car park below the temple. The return fare is W840.

Further south-east along the main road is **Kwaenung Tomb**, with its unusual carved figures lining the approach – military guards, civil officials, lions and monkeys. Take bus No 11 to get to this little-visited tomb compound – get off at the main road and take a bus running down this road. It's then a one-km walk from the billboard on the road.

Places to Stay

Most popular with travellers is the *Han Jin Hostel* (☎ (0561) 24097), two blocks north-east of the express bus terminal and easily identified by a large English sign on the roof. The owner, Mr Kwon Young-joung, speaks good English, hands out free maps and is very knowledgeable about local sights. Unfortunately, you have to bargain to get a decent price. He usually starts the bidding for a double without/with bath at W14,000/16,000. This quickly drops to W12,000/14,000, and with a little more bargaining reaches W10,000/12,000. For a third person it's 30% more.

Another excellent place to stay is the *Tongsan Yoinsuk* which is a traditional Korean-style house surrounding a quiet courtyard. It's spotlessly clean, has hot water, and laundry can be dried on the roof. Rooms with shared bath cost W8000.

There are other numerous cheap yogwan and yoinsuk behind the bus station, but all signs are in Korean.

At Pulguk-sa Village there's the *Kyongju Kyelim Youth Hostel* (☎ (0561) 7460601/7), where dorm beds cost W6600.

Places to Eat

If you want to put together your own breakfast or snacks, the two branches of the *England Bakery* bake a mean pastry. Kyongju has its soju tent street where you can find cheap snacks, soup and the like. This street is almost at the end of Tongsong-ro close to the junction with Wanhwa-ro just south of the railway station. The tents open up in the evening and begin closing around 11.30 pm.

One block south of the Han Jin Hostel is a Chinese restaurant with noodles for W1000. The *Grand Restaurant* does decent pulgogi for W6000. The *Shiga Shiktang* has good Western food.

Things to Buy

The price tags in many shops are geared to the Japanese tourist market – you can often get a 30% discount simply by pointing to the price tag and saying, 'I'm not Japanese'.

Getting There & Away

Bus There are three bus stations in Kyongju. Nearest the link road is the express (kosok) bus terminal. Next to that is the chikheng terminal and after that the local bus terminal. Buses run to Kwangju, Pusan, Seoul, Taejon and Taegu. There are also five buses per day direct to Kim Hae (Pusan) International Airport, but they depart from the hotels at Bomun Lake between Kyongju and Pulguk-sa temple.

Train There are only two direct trains daily connecting Seoul to Kyongju (three on Sunday). These are saemaul-ho trains costing W12,900. You can do it much cheaper by taking one of the cheaper trains from Seoul to Tongdaegu (east Taegu station) and then changing to the Tongdaegu – Kyongju bus which costs W970. The bus station at Tongdaegu is called Dongyang Kosok.

AROUND KYONGJU

Many other Silla kingdom relics can be found in the mountains from Kyongju to Pohang on the east coast, Taegu in the west and Pusan in the south. A rewarding area to explore within easy reach of Kyongju is **Namsan mountains**, south of the city. The hiking trails take you through areas of natural scenic beauty. The mountains are strewn with royal tombs, pagodas, rock-cut figures, pavilions and the remains of fortresses, temples and palaces.

Taewang-am, a small rocky island just off the coast south of Taebon Beach and east of Kyongju, is the site of the famous underwater tomb of the Silla king Munmu (661 to 681 AD). It's perhaps the only underwater tomb in the world and at low tide it can be seen through the clear water of the pool in the centre of the island.

A little way up the coast from Taewang-am is **Taebon Beach**, well known and fairly popular among Koreans but hardly ever visited by foreigners. About half way between Kyongju and Pohang is the village of Yang-dong, a traditional Yi dynasty village which the 20th century has passed by.

TAEGU 대구

This is South Korea's third largest city and although of little interest to travellers it is the most convenient place from which to visit one of the country's most famous and largest monasteries – **Haein-sa** temple.

High up on the steep, forested slopes of Kayasan National Park, outside Taegu, this temple is the repository of the 80,000 carved wooden blocks that make up the *Tripitaka Koreana*. If you don't manage to get into the library to see these Buddhist scriptures (ask a monk), there's plenty of interest in other buildings. The original set, completed in 1251, was destroyed during a 14th-century Mongol invasion. The current replacement set dates from that time.

Entry to the temple costs W600 plus another W400 to the park. It's a 20-minute walk from the bus stop. You can day-trip from Taegu or stay near the temple, if you're thinking of exploring the hiking trails in the area.

Places to Stay & Eat

There are plenty of cheap and mid-range yogwan around the bus terminals and the Tongdaegu Railway Station. The *Sujong Yogwan* (☎ (053) 2386) by the west chikheng bus terminal is recommended – W10,000 with attached bathroom. It's clean and friendly although there are cheaper places around.

Getting There & Away

Taegu Station in the town centre is for local trains only, and unless you're staying in Taegu, don't get off the train here! The Tongdaegu Station on the east side of the city is where express trains stop, and this is where you should get off if you're carrying on to Kyongju by bus. Taegu has five bus terminals – one express plus north, south, east and west chikheng.

Bus Nos 33 or 120 connect the west and east chikheng. Bus No 76 connects Tongdaegu with the west chikheng. Bus Nos 1, 12, 31, 32, 35, 71, 75, 88, 89 and 101 also go to the west chikheng. From there buses go to the Haein-sa temple three or four times hourly from 6.45 am to 7 pm. The trip takes almost two hours and costs a little over W880. There are also up to seven buses an hour to Kyongju from this terminal.

The east chikheng terminal handles buses to Kyongju and Pohang. The trip takes about an hour and buses depart frequently throughout the day.

POHANG 포항

Pohang is a fairly small city on the east coast. You can stay here before taking the ferry to Ullung-do, over 260 km to the north-east, about half way between Korea and Japan.

ULLUNG-DO 울릉도

If you have a yen for remote, mysterious islands where foreign tourists haven't overrun the place, then this is the place to go. Isolated out in the storm-ravaged East Sea between Korea and Japan, this beautiful island is difficult to get to if the weather doesn't cooperate (the ferries are frequently cancelled due to gales) but well worth the effort.

Most of the people live in small villages along the coast, making their living from the sea. There are virtually no roads and only two buses; people get around on foot or in fishing boats. Dodong is the largest town, almost hidden away like a pirate outpost in a valley between two craggy, forested mountains with a very narrow harbour front. It was only settled in the late 19th century – few tile-roofed houses here – but what it lacks aesthetically it makes up for in friendliness.

Places to Stay & Eat
The cheapest places to stay are in rooms with families – minbak. The usual price is W10,000 per room. For campers with their own tents, there's a landscaped site just below the mineral springs that costs W3000 per tent.

For a cheap place to eat, try the *Kum Kang Shiktang*, which has Chinese food. More expensive, but one of the best restaurants on the island is the *Ullung-do Hae-gwan*, about 100 metres up the hill from the harbour front.

Getting There & Away
From Pohang, there are daily boats at 1 pm from 20 April until 15 August, and every other day from at 12 pm or 1 pm from 16 August until 19 April. The trip takes 7½ hours and costs W29,500 in 1st-class berth; W19,670 in 2nd-class berth; W19,670 in 1st class (no berth); and W13,110 in 2nd class.

From Hupo there are daily boats at 10 am and 9 pm between 26 July and 14 August; daily at 2 pm from 1 May to 25 July; every other day at 2 pm from 1 March to 30 April, and from 15 August to 31 October; every three days at 2 pm from 1 November to 28 February. The trip takes four hours and costs W15,630.

The fastest boats (2½ hours) are from Mukho, but these only run from here during summer and the fare is W18,650.

South-East Korea

PUSAN 부산
Pusan is the second largest city and principal port of South Korea. It was also the only major city to have escaped capture by the Communists during the Korean War, though at the time its population was swelled by an incredible four million refugees. It is superbly located between several mountain peaks, though the city itself has that gone-to-seed appearance common in major seaports. Many people regard Pusan as a concrete jungle to be avoided, so they come here only to take the ferries to Yosu, Cheju-do or Japan.

Information
Tourist Office The Tourist Information Office (☎ (051) 4629734) is in the Pusan Chamber of Commerce and Industry close to City Hall.

The USO (☎ (051) 4623732) is in the Dae Yang Building, Room 1195, 19-Tong, 2-Ban, Choryang 3-dong, Tong-gu.

Foreign Consulates Pusan is the only city outside Seoul to have foreign consulates, as follows:

Japan
    1147-11 Choryang-dong, Tong-gu (☎ (051) 4655101/5)
New Zealand
    Room 202, Dong-il Building, 84-10 Chungang-dong 4-ga, Chung-gu (☎ (051) 4645055)
Taiwan
    6th floor, Tong Yang Building, No 4 (☎ (051) 2463617, 2424557)
USA
    American Consulate Building 24, Taechong-dong, Chung-gu (☎ (051) 2467791/2)

Things to See
Take the lift to the top of **Pusan Tower** for incredible views over the city, but note that photography is not allowed from the observation decks. At night head to **'Texas St'** opposite the railway station, a colourful area with music clubs, bars and pick-up joints. At **Chagalchi fish market** you can watch

catches being unloaded from the boats and buyers haggling with fishermen.

Places to Stay

There are very few cheap yogwan and yoinsuk around the bus terminals (but quite a lot of expensive Western-style hotels). The best area for yogwan is around the Bando, Ferry and Cosmos hotels up against the hill close to the International Ferry Terminal and the GPO. There are plenty to choose from; an average place without own bathroom will cost around W8000.

In the city centre, two cheap places to stay are the *Hyundae Yoinsuk* or *Munha Yoinsuk* where doubles with shared bath cost W7000. More luxurious is the *Junghwajang Yogwan* (☎ (051) 4637268) where doubles with private bath are W12,000 but can be bargained to W10,000.

There are many cheaper mid-range hotels in the central area. Room prices are government-controlled and range from W12,700 to W15,000, depending on the facilities offered.

Places to Eat

There are plenty of restaurants on streets off Chungangno between the central post office, ferry piers and the Bando Hotel. If you're looking for seafood, then make sure you know the price of a meal before you order. Seafood – particularly if it's raw – can be very expensive.

One restaurant which stands out as exceptional value as far as fried fish goes is the *Songpo Haechip* behind the Posonjang Yogwan. Here they'll serve you with a variety of fried fish complete with all the usual accompanying dishes for just W4000.

Getting There & Away

Air There are flights to Seoul (W31,500) and Cheju (W25,700). Bus No 201 connects the city centre to Kim Hae International Airport. The trip costs W470 and takes 45 minutes.

Bus The express (kosok) bus terminal and the Tongbu local bus terminal are a long way from the city centre out in Tongnae suburb near the hot springs of the same name.

To get to or from the city centre, take local bus No 35 (W180) or chaesok bus Nos 301 or 306 (W470), or go by subway. The nearest station to the bus terminals is Tongnae – one of the exits is marked 'Express Bus Terminal'. Going into the city, buy a ticket to Chung-ang-dong Station, which is near the ferry terminals.

The following buses are available from the express bus terminal:

To Kwangju Every 20 minutes from 6 am to 6.20 pm. The fare is W3860 and the journey takes 4¼ hours.

To Kyongju Every 30 minutes from 7 am to 7.30 pm. The fare is W1150 and the journey takes one hour.

To Seoul Every 10 minutes from 6 am to 6.40 pm. The fare is W5970 and the journey takes 5½ hours.

To Taegu Every 15 minutes from 6 am to 7.50 pm. The fare is W1980 and the journey takes nearly two hours.

To Taejon Every 50 minutes from 6 am to 6.30 pm. The fare is W4030 and the journey takes 3½ hours.

To Yosu Every 50 minutes from 6 am to 6.10 pm. The fare is W3280 and the journey takes about four hours.

Train Pusan is the southern terminus of the Seoul-Pusan railway. There are frequent departures throughout the day. Depending on class, trains to/from Seoul take around five hourse.

Pusan's main railway station is located right in the city centre.

Getting Around

Bus Buses which run down Chungangno as far as City Hall include Nos 26, 34, 42, 55, 127 and 139.

Train Pusan has a subway system connecting such vital places as the express bus terminal with the city centre and the ferry piers.

AROUND PUSAN

The **Tongdo-sa** temple, one of the largest and most famous in Korea, sits amidst beau-

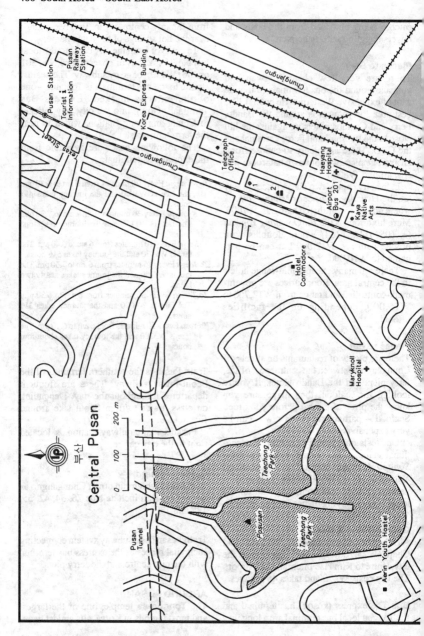

Central Pusan

부산

Pusan Station
Tourist Information
Pusan Railway Station
Korea Express Building
Texas Street
Chungangno
Telegraph Office
Chungjangno
Haeyang Hospital
Airport Bus 201
Kaya Native Arts
Hotel Commodore
Maryknoll Hospital
Taechong Park
Pusan
Taechong Park
Pusan Tunnel
Aerin Youth Hostel

0 100 200 m

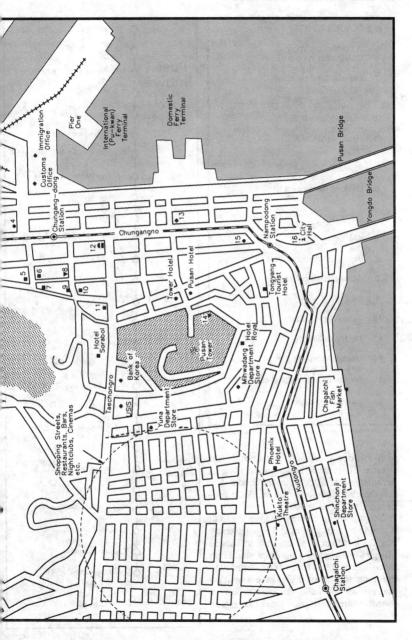

■ **PLACES TO STAY**

5   Junghwajang Yogwan
6   Cheun Cho Yogwan
    천조장, 보서장여관
7   Ferry & Bando Hotels
    훼라 반도 호텔
9   Poson Jang Yogwan
    보성장여관
10 Munha Yoinsuk
    문호여인숙
11 Hyundae Yoinsuk
    현대여인숙

▼ **PLACES TO EAT**

8   Umijong Restaurant
    우미정식당

    OTHER

1   KAL Office
    대한항공
2   Pusan International Post Office
    우체국
3   Korea Exchange Bank
    외환은행
4   Asiana Airlines
    아시아나 항공
12 Central Post Office
    우체국
13 Japanese Airlines
    (JAL)
14 Taiwan Consulate
    대만 영사관
15 Korean Tourist Association
    관광안내소
16 Tourist Information
    관광안내소

Pusan Subway
부산 지하철

Nopodong 노포동
Pomosa 보모사
Namsandong 남산동
Tushil 두실
Kusodong 구서동
Changjondong 장전동
Pusan Univ. 부산대
Onchonjang 온천장 ← Kumgang Park
Myongnyundong 명륜동 ← Express Bus Terminal
Tongnae 동래역
Teachers' College 교육대입구
Yonsandong 연산동
Yonje 연제
Yangjong 양정
Pujondong 부전역
Somyon 서면
Pomnaegol 봄내골
Pomildong 범일동
Chwachondong 좌천동
Pusanjin Sta. 부산진역
Choryangdong 초량동
Pusan Station 부산역
Chungangdong 중앙동 ← Ferryboat Terminals & Central Yogwan
Nampodong 남포동
Chagalchi 충무동 ← Fish Market
Tosongdong 토성동
Tongdaeshindong 부민동
Sodaeshindong 서대신동

N.B. Chagalchi = Chungmudong
      Tongdaeshindong = Pumindong

tiful forested mountains and crystal-clear streams. There are 65 buildings including 13 hermitages behind the main temple complex, and there are still about 200 monks in residence. Entry costs W300.

You can visit it on the way from Pusan to Kyongju by taking a Pusan-Taegu chikheng bus. It's less than a one-km walk to Tongdo village from where the bus drops you. From the village you can take a taxi the final 1½ km to the temple, or if you have time it's a really beautiful walk; the road follows a mountain stream with many rock carvings on the way.

South-West Korea

YOSU 여수

Yosu lies half way along the mountainous and deeply indented southern coast of Korea. A spectacular area of islands and peninsulas, a large section now makes up the Hallyo Waterway National Park. The hydrofoil trip from Yosu to Pusan via Namhae, Samchonpo, Saryangdo, Chungmu and Songpo is extremely popular and costs W6110. Contact the ferry office in Pusan (☎ (051) 443851) or Yosu (☎ (0662) 631824).

Yosu's historical claim to fame is in connection with Admiral Yi, who routed the Japanese navy on several occasions during the 16th century. On display here is a full-size recreation of one of the admiral's famous iron-clad war vessels or turtle ships.

Things to See

The **Jinnamgwan Pavilion**, one of the longest and most beautiful in Korea, stands in the centre of town. Inside you can see two full-scale replicas of the turtle ships that Admiral Yi used to defeat the Japanese naval forces during the 1592 invasion. Up on a hill, offering a spectacular view, is **Chungmin-sa shrine**, but it's a steep climb.

Odong-do island is linked to the mainland by a 730-metre causeway. In spring the island is covered with camellia blossoms.

Hansan-sa temple, high up on the wooded mountain, was built in 1194 AD. It is reached by a substantial trek and the views are superb.

Places to Stay

Most yogwan and yoinsuk are between the railway station and city hall. The *Sam Song Yogwan* near the docks has been recommended.

Getting There & Away

Air The airport is about seven km out of town and served by local buses. Simply walk from the terminal building to the road and wait. The fare is W290 and the journey takes about 40 minutes finishing up at the chikheng bus terminal.

Bus The express and chikheng bus terminals are near each other on the western side of town on the road out to Suncheon and the airport. City bus Nos 3, 5, 6, 7, 8, 9, 10, 11, 13 and 17 go past the two bus terminals but probably the most useful is bus No 11, which connects the bus terminals with the railway station via the centre of town. The local ferry terminal is nearby.

Boat The Yosu to Pusan hydrofoil, *Angel*, used to operate out of the new port near the railway station but now it docks at the local ferries quay, which is a much more convenient entry point into Yosu. It is only necessary to book in advance during the holiday season, July and August. The ferry is operated by the Hanryeo Development Co Ltd in Pusan (☎ (051) 443851/3) – the office in Yosu is at (☎ (0662) 631824).

KWANGJU 광주

Though Kwangju has been the capital of Chollanam-do Province for centuries, there is precious little left of its traditional heritage. This is an all-modern concrete and glass city with few redeeming features, so it's not surprising that most travellers give it a miss or, at the most, spend a night en route to somewhere else. Its one saving grace is that Kwangju has the cheapest flights to Cheju (W15,500).

MOKPO 목포

The fishing port of Mokpo is at the end of the railway line near the south-western tip of mainland Korea. Mokpo is the departure point for the cheapest ferries to the island of Cheju-do; the town itself is not very interesting.

Offshore Islands

There are scores of local ferries from Mokpo to the small islands west and south of the town. One beauty spot well known to Koreans but rarely visited by foreigners is **Hong-do** island, one of the most westerly islands and part of the Tadohae National Park.

Places to Stay & Eat

The best yogwan are on the side streets directly opposite the railway station immediately to the left of the footbridge across the main road. They include the *Seoul Yogwan, Kwyangyong Yoinsuk*, and *Kukdo Yoinsuk*.

There are many restaurants around the railway station. Recommended for value and the quality of the food is the *Yonghwa Um Shiktang*.

Getting There & Away

The bus terminal is a considerable distance from the town centre, but is served by local bus No 1.

The boat terminal at Mokpo handles all ferry departures and arrivals. Advance booking isn't necessary – just get to the boat terminal about two hours before departure time. There are two ferries daily to Cheju-do, at 10 am and 4 pm, which take seven hours and 5½ hours respectively.

WANDO 완도

The island of Wando, off the south-western tip of the mainland, is noted for the quality of its seaweed (kim), which at certain times of year can be seen drying in racks around the island in much the same way as squid are dried on Ullung-do and along the north-east coast. The island has sandy and pebble beaches. It's connected to the mainland by bridge and there is a ferry service to Cheju-do that takes about four hours.

Cheju-do 제주도

Cheju-do (Cheju Island) lies 85 km off the southern tip of the peninsula. Centuries of isolation resulted in the island acquiring its own history, cultural traditions, dress, architecture and even language.

The island landscape is dominated by the volcano of Hallasan, the highest mountain in

South Korea, and at Sogwipo on the south coast the impressive Chongbang Falls cascade directly into the sea. There is also the enigma of the *harubang*, or grandfather stones, carved from lava rock. Their purpose is still debated by anthropologists, but they may have represented legendary guardians of the gates of Cheju's ancient towns.

The island is part of the Korean cultural tradition but its differences are sufficiently evocative to draw people here from all over the world in search of a legend.

Since the government realised the island's tourist potential, things have changed. The island's supposed matriarchal society, exemplified by the skin-diving women who are the subject of folk songs, trinkets and photographs in tourist literature, is on the wane. Commercialisation has arrived – activities include power boating, scuba diving, golfing, and helicopter and submarine rides. Nevertheless, Cheju retains much of its charm and is one of the most interesting places to visit in Korea, especially if you can get up the energy to climb Hallasan.

Summer is the peak season. Avoid the place in winter unless you like rain.

CHEJU CITY 제주시

The island's capital has the most easy-going and festive atmosphere of any city you're likely to encounter in Korea. It's compact, and despite the modern construction going on you'll still run into many gems of the traditional local thatched-roof houses made from lava stone.

Right in the centre of town is Cheju's oldest building, the 15th-century **Kwandok-chong Pavilion** complete with grandfather stone. Also worth seeing are the **Samsong-hyol Shrine** and the **Yongdu-am** or Dragon's Head Rock on the shore between the city centre and the airport. About six km outside of Cheju city on the cross-island highway is **Moksukwon**, a natural sculpture garden of stone and wood. Along with the natural objects, there are many old grinding stones and even harubang.

Places to Stay

Only a short distance away from the boat terminal on Sanji-ro are three yoinsuk which have been popular for years – the *Namyang Yoinsuk* (☎ (064) 229617); *Hanil Yoinsuk* (☎ (064) 231598); and *Yangsando Yoinsuk* (☎ (064) 229989). All three cost W7000 but can be bargained to W6000, at least in the off season (winter).

Places to Eat

Not surprisingly, seafood is a speciality here but check prices as certain kinds of fish are amazingly expensive.

Getting There & Away

Air There are flights to Seoul (W31,900), Kwangju (W15,500), Pusan (W25,700) and Yosu (W18,300). Bus No 100 connects the airport and the budget hotel area on Sanji-ro, costs W200 and takes 35 minutes.

Boat There are boats from Pusan, Mokpo and Wando. The *Ansungho* departing from Mokpo is your cheapest alternative, though the ship has seen better days. The fastest boats are from Wando.

From **Pusan** *Car Ferry Queen* departs Tuesday, Thursday and Sunday at 7 pm. The trip takes 12½ hours. *Tong Yang Car Ferry No 1* departs Monday, Wednesday and Friday at 7.30 pm and takes 11½ hours. *Tong Yang Car Ferry No 5* departs Tuesday, Thursday, and Saturday at 7.30 pm and takes 11½ hours. For all three ferries, fares for a deluxe berth are W84,550; 1st-class berth, W34,170; 2nd-class berth, W23,290; 2nd class, W15,400; 3rd class, W11,820.

From **Mokpo** *Tong Yang Car Ferry No 2* departs daily except Sunday at 4 pm and takes 5½ hours. *Tong Yang Car Ferry No 3* departs every other day at 10 am and takes 6½ hours. For both of these ferries a 1st-class berth costs W22,020; a 2nd-class berth is W17,130; 2nd class is W10,240; 3rd class costs W7790. The cheapest ferry is the *Ansungho* which departs every other day at 10 am and takes seven hours with fares ranging from W11,660 (1st-class berth) to W5250 for 3rd class.

From **Wando** *Hanil Car Ferry* departs at 4 pm daily except the 1st and 3rd Wednesday of every month. The trip takes just over three hours and costs W16,590 for a 1st-class berth, and W7740 for 2nd class. *Hanil No 2* departs at 3 pm but does not run in winter – the crossing takes less than 2½ hours and costs W9240 in 1st class and W7710 in 2nd class.

Getting Around

Cheju city has a bus service which you probably won't use, except to get to the airport or to the chikheng bus terminal. There are plenty of buses from the terminal to most places of interest around the island.

There are only four main roads out of Cheju city, all leading to Sogwipo on the southern coast. There are four or five buses an hour along these roads. Going west you will reach the best selection of beaches. Going east you will get to Gim Nyeung and the Man Jang Caves, around to Pyosun, and then to Sogwipo. The two cross-island highways skirt Hallasan and are the ones you will need if you are going to climb the mountain.

AROUND THE ISLAND

At Sogwipo the main attraction is the 23-metre-high waterfall of **Chongbang**, 10 to 15 minutes' walk from the centre of town. The falls are an impressive sight, and among the few in Asia where the water plunges directly into the sea. **Chonjiyon** is another waterfall on the other side of town, about 20 minutes' walk from the centre. Entry to both waterfalls is W700, or W350 for students.

Chungmun Beach is near the small village of Chungmun, west of Sogwipo at the junction of the coast road and the second cross-island highway. This is probably the best and longest beach on the island but it has developed into a tourist resort and it can get very crowded in the holiday season.

A short bus ride north of Pyoson is **Song-up**, Cheju's ancient capital, which dates from the early 15th century and is now designated as a Folk Village. The whole village has been preserved in the traditional style and there are plenty of well-illustrated billboards in Korean and English pointing out the history and the main features of the most

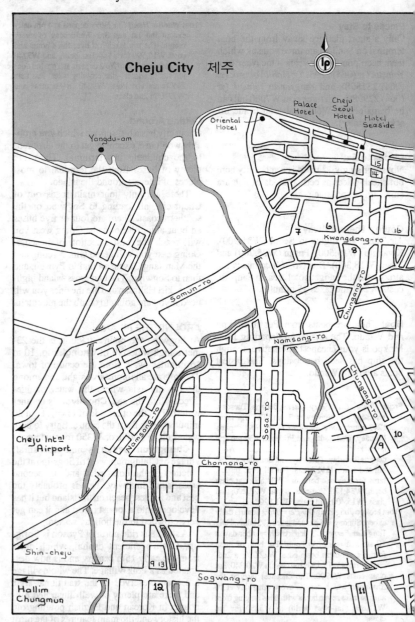

Cheju City 제주

Yongdu-am

Oriental Hotel

Palace Hotel

Cheju Seoul Hotel

Hotel Seaside

15
14
16

7   6

Kwangdong-ro

8

Chungang-ro

Somun-ro

Namsong-ro

Chungang-ro

Namsong-ro

Sosa-ro

Cheju Intʼl Airport

10

9

Chonnong-ro

Shin-cheju

9 13

Hallim Chungmun

12

Sogwang-ro

11

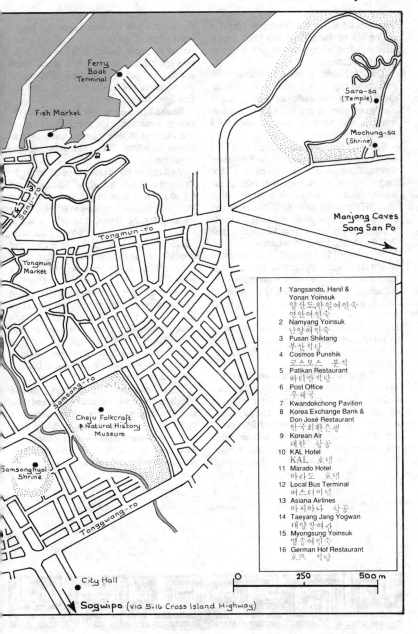

Ferry Boat Terminal

Fish Market

Sara-sa (Temple)

Mochung-sa (Shrine)

Sanji-ro

Tongmun-ro

Manjang Caves
Song San Po

Tongmun Market

Samsong-ro

Cheju Folkcraft & Natural History Museum

Samsonghyol Shrine

Tonggwang-ro

City Hall

Sogwipo (via 5.16 Cross Island Highway)

1 Yangsando, Hanil & Yonan Yoinsuk
   양산도,한일여인숙
   연안여인숙
2 Namyang Yoinsuk
   남양여인숙
3 Pusan Shiktang
   부산식당
4 Cosmos Punshik
   코스모스 분식
5 Patikan Restaurant
   바티칸식당
6 Post Office
   우체국
7 Kwandokchong Pavilion
8 Korea Exchange Bank & Don José Restaurant
   한국외환은행
9 Korean Air
   대한 항공
10 KAL Hotel
   KAL 호텔
11 Marado Hotel
   마라도 호텔
12 Local Bus Terminal
   버스터미널
13 Asiana Airlines
   아시아나 항공
14 Taeyang Jang Yogwan
   태양장여관
15 Myongsung Yoinsuk
   명승여인숙
16 German Hof Restaurant
   호프 식당

0   250   500 m

important sites. The old Confucian school in the centre of the village has been reconstructed and many of the harubang or grandfather stones are here.

The main street of Song-up is lined with restaurants and *makkoli* (rice beer) halls and many of them play traditional Korean music over their sound systems. If you want somewhere to stay, then try asking around for a minbak.

East of Cheju and about 2½ km off the coast road from Kimnyong are the **Man Jang Caves**. The main section of the caves is 7 km long – the longest known lava tube in the world with a height and width varying from three to 20 metres. It is well lit but damp and cool so take appropriate clothing. Entry is W1000. Direct buses from Cheju city cost W410 and take about 45 minutes.

Just south of Hallim on the north-western side of the island is **Hyopchae**, another lava-tube cave complete with stalagmites and stalactites. This one is actually a system of two interconnected caves, the larger of which is the spectacular Sochon-gul with a length of 2500 metres. Due to an abundance of subtropical vegetation its two entrances resemble huge subterranean botanical gardens.

At **Songsan Po** you can watch women diving for seaweed, shellfish and sea urchins. This is the town at the extreme eastern tip of Cheju-do, nestled at the foot of the spectacular volcanic cone of **Songsan-ilchubong** (Sunrise Peak), whose sides plunge straight down into the surf. Unlike Hallasan, there's no longer any crater lake on

the summit and the area below the jagged outer edges of the peak is continuously harvested for cattle fodder. It is one of Cheju-do's most scenically beautiful areas. There are ferries from here heading north-east to the island of U-do, which is very rural and free from motor cars.

Sanbanggul-sa temple is carved into the side of a volcanic cone overlooking the sea and the Andok valley in the south-western part of the island. Take a bus from Sogwipo to get there.

Walking up **Hallasan** is one of the highlights of a visit to the island. Be sure to get off to an early start as the summit is often shrouded in cloud by late afternoon. Wear jogging/hiking shoes, and take a warm sweater – it gets cold. Entry to the area, which is a national park, is W200, and detailed trail maps are available free at the ticket offices at the beginning of the five trails.

The climb up the shortest trails takes about 2½ hours on average, the descent about two hours. From the eastern side the ascent is about four to five hours. There are several campsites.

There's quite a large and active Buddhist monastery – **Kwanum-sa** – close to the trail of the same name.

To get there from Cheju city simply decide which trail you want to start off on and then take the appropriate bus along either the '5.16' or the second cross-island highway. Tell the driver or his assistant which trail you want to go on and they'll make sure you're put down on the right spot.

North Korea

Workers' paradise or totalitarian dictatorship – your image of North Korea may depend on your ideology. While Eastern Europe and China are opening up to Western-style capitalism, North Korea remains devoutly Marxist. No other country maintains such a rigid Stalinist system.

This may not sound like a travellers' paradise. Indeed, few people outside of the Communist bloc have been allowed to visit North Korea since the Korean War. However, it is now possible to tour the country. Unfortunately, you are restricted to seeing certain places, you must be accompanied by a guide all the time and your visit will be very expensive. Also, you will be subjected to nonstop propaganda – the 'US imperialist aggressors' and 'South Korean puppet stooges' are the favourite themes.

So why go?

Simply put, North Korea is fascinating. Western tourists are drawn to this country out of pure curiosity. Furthermore, it's an education, one you aren't likely to forget. Lastly, it is a beautiful country, and you won't have to worry about it being overrun by tourists.

Some travellers come away from North Korea impressed by the cleanliness and orderliness of the society. Many come away horrified. So why has the country opened its doors (slightly) to the bourgeoisie of the world? The main reason is economic. Despite showcase cities like Pyongyang, the country's economy is on the skids and hard currency is desperately needed to buy food, oil and other basic necessities. Another motive is to propagandise – much of your tour will be devoted to proving the North Korean version of history, but this in itself is fascinating and says much about the mentality of the regime.

Perhaps another reason why foreigners are permitted to visit is that with the disintegration of the Communist bloc North Korea is worried that it will find itself totally isolated. North Korea is especially concerned about its neighbours and former sources of aid – China and the USSR. In September, 1990, the USSR established diplomatic relations with South Korea. In 1991, South Korea and China opened up trade offices in each other's capitals which serve as unofficial embassies. Increasingly isolated, armed to the teeth and led by a regime that is intractably hostile, North Korea is being forced to react to a new world order.

Facts about the Country

HISTORY

See the South Korean chapter of this book for Korean history prior to 1945.

North Korea's history as a separate political entity began from the end of WW II. The USA, the UK and the USSR had made a deal at the Yalta Conference in the closing days of the war – the USSR was temporarily to occupy Korea north of the 38th parallel to accept the Japanese surrender, while the USA would occupy the south. This 'temporary' partitioning was also done to Germany, with the same tragic result. In 1948, the uncompromising Kim Il-sung became head of North Korea, and the temporary division became permanent as neither side was willing to yield. Negotiations failed to resolve the problem, but the USA and USSR pulled most of their troops out of Korea by 1949. However, the Soviets gave Kim Il-sung massive military assistance, and on 25 June 1950, with US aid to the South on its way, North Korea invaded the South.

The Korean War

The North Koreans swiftly pushed the South Korean and US troops into a tiny enclave around Pusan. Under US prompting, the United Nations passed a resolution calling for other countries to send in troops to halt the aggression. The war effort took a dra-

CHINA

Onsong

USSR

Hoeryong Tumangang

To Vladivostok

Paekdusan

Chunggang

Chongjin

Hyesan

Kilju

Manpo

Kanggye

To Beijing

Pukchong

Dandong

Sinuiju

Hyangsan

Mt Myohyang

Hamhung

North Korea

GULF OF
WEST
KOREA

Wonsan

0   50   100 km

PYONGYANG

Sinpyong

Mt Kumgang

Nampo

Pyonggang

DMZ

SEA
OF
JAPAN

Sariwon

Kumgang

Kansong

Haeju

Kaesong

Yangyang

Yonan

Panmunjom

Kumchon

DMZ

To Seoul

matic turn when UN forces landed behind
enemy lines at Inchon on 15 September.
Within a month, UN forces defeated the
North Koreans, pushing them back to the
Chinese border. Fortunes changed again
when China's Mao Zedong decided to
support the North Korean effort and sent in
180,000 Chinese 'volunteers'. UN forces
were pushed back again to the 38th parallel.
The war reached a stalemate while negotiations for a truce dragged on for two years. In
1953 the war ended with the Korean peninsula split at the ironically named Demilitarised
Zone (DMZ). The Korean War resulted in four

million deaths and devastated the country's
economy and infrastructure.

North Korea, which refers to this conflict
as the 'Fatherland Liberation War', gives a
different account of how the Korean War
started. One propaganda pamphlet, *An
Earthly Paradise for the People*, has this to
say about the war:

The US imperialists, who had boasted of being the
strongest in the world, frantically pounced upon the
Korean people in league with the south Korean
puppet army plus the troops of 15 satellite countries.

However, the American imperialists who were
assured of a glorious victory in this grim war were

covered all over with wounds and surrendered to the heroic Korean people. As a result, the Korean people and their young People's Army held a military parade in honour of their victory in the presence of President Kim Il-sung, the ever-victorious and iron-willed brilliant commander.

This was a great victory and natural outcome attained under the wise leadership of the great President Kim Il-sung.

Postwar Standoff

Constant provocations by the North have kept relations between the two Koreas at the subzero level for more than 40 years. In the 1970s, it was discovered that the North was drilling invasion tunnels under the DMZ. In 1983, North Korean terrorists tried to murder South Korean President Chun while he was making an official visit to Burma – Chun survived the bomb blast but several of his fellow ministers were killed. North Korea denied involvement, and suggested the whole thing was a stunt by South Korean agents trying to discredit the North. Burma's leaders needed no convincing that Pyongyang was behind the bombing, and promptly broke off diplomatic relations with North Korea.

In 1987, two North Koreans posing as Japanese tourists boarded a South Korean civilian airliner and planted a bomb, causing 115 deaths. Both terrorists tried to commit suicide with cyanide, but one – Kim Hyun-hui – survived. She later revealed to South Korean authorities that she learned Japanese from a former bar hostess who was abducted from Japan in 1978 by North Korean kidnappers – which of course did nothing to improve Japan's already bad relations with North Korea. As in previous terrorist attacks, North Korea claimed the whole thing was a trick by the South Korean 'puppet clique' trying to discredit the North.

North Korea's position regarding the USA and the present South Korean government is well summed up in the following quote from *Women of Korea* (1991, volume 2), a magazine published in Pyongyang:

The US imperialists have stationed more than 40,000 troops and more than 1000 nuclear weapons in south Korea, and they, with the nearly one million puppet troops, are preparing an invasion against north Korea...Their aim is to create 'two Koreas', to divide Korea permanently and to continuously occupy south Korea as their colony and, using south Korea as a bridgehead, to make an invasion of north Korea and the other countries of Asia.

Japan – Enemy No 2

If the USA is North Korea's No 1 enemy, then Japan is certainly No 2. The North Korean book entitled *Kim Il-sung on the Five-Point Policy for National Reunification* has this to say:

The Japanese militarists, dancing to the tune of the US imperialists, have also hampered the north-south dialogue and taken many actions against the reunification of our country. The US imperialists and the Japanese militarists aim, in the final analysis, at keeping our country divided indefinitely, and making south Korea their permanent colony and commodity market.

In November 1990, Kim Il-sung surprised everyone by telling a visiting Japanese politician that his country was ready to establish diplomatic relations with Japan. However, the first round of talks with Japan did not go well – North Korea demanded billions of US dollars as war reparations from Japan, and billions more for the 45 years of 'cold war' following WW II.

An issue which continues to anger Japan is that of the 'Japanese spouses'. In the 1950s, about 100,000 Koreans who had been living in Japan were repatriated to North Korea (by their own will, not forcibly). They took with them nearly 3000 Japanese wives. Then the door was slammed shut and no-one was allowed to leave. So for the past 35 years or so, these women have been unable to visit their families. Pleas on their behalf from Japan have been ignored. However, Pyongyang has turned them into a convenient source of revenue, having made it clear to their families in Japan that the way these women are treated depends on how much cash the family contributes to North Korea. Recent talks with Japan on this issue produced this official statement from the North Koreans:

That the Japanese in the DPRK have failed to visit their native towns freely is due to the abnormal relations between the two countries; the Japanese spouses are leading a stable life in our country; and when the relations between the two countries have been normalised, their free travel will be possible.

Translated, this means that Japan must pay billions of US dollars so that relations with North Korea can be 'normalised', and only then will the women be free to leave.

In spite of electric fences and heavy patrols, some North Koreans have successfully escaped to Japan on makeshift boats. North Korea responded in 1983 by kidnapping two Japanese sailors on the high seas; this was known as the 'Fujisanmaru' incident. The Koreans said they would only return the sailors if Japan handed over all the North Korean escapees. Japan refused and the sailors were held until 1991, when North Korea finally released them in an attempt to woo the Japanese into establishing diplomatic relations.

Cold War Continues
Apparently, this was not enough. Normalisation talks between Japan and North Korea ground to a halt when US military experts rolled out satellite photos showing that North Korea appears to be developing nuclear weapons at its reprocessing centre near Yongbyon, north of Pyongyang. Japan now says it will not establish diplomatic relations with North Korea unless international inspections of the Yongbyon site are permitted. Pyongyang turned the argument around and said it would only open Yongbyon to international inspection if the USA also opened its military bases in the South to inspection for nuclear materials. The North claims that the USA has over 1000 nuclear warheads based in the South.

In 1991, the USA surprised North Korea by offering to withdraw all nuclear weapons from the Korean Peninsula. Western military sources also say North Korea posesses huge quantities of chemical and biological weapons which could kill millions if launched against the South. Many assume

that the USA would respond to a nerve gas attack on Seoul with an equally devastating nuclear attack against Pyongyang. But all this is speculation unless it actually happens, which no sane person wants to see.

In spite of this ultra-tense atmosphere, 1991 saw tother signs of a thaw in the icy relations between the two Koreas. Officials from Pyongyang visited Seoul for talks and, to the great surprise of the rest of the world, emerged with a non-aggression accord at the end of the year. The agreement sidestepped the difficult issue of nuclear weapons, but the South Korean prime minister offered to open his country's facilities to inspection by officials from the North – indicating that the USA had probably removed its weapons already.

It seems likely, however, that further steps towards unity will proceed at a snail's pace, at least until the death of Kim Il-sung.

GEOGRAPHY
North Korea occupies 55% of the land area on the Korean peninsula. The northern and eastern regions are mostly rugged mountains and not well suited for agriculture. The official name is the Democratic People's Republic of Korea (DPRK).

A trip to North Korea makes an interesting comparison to the South. While South Korea suffers from some serious environmental problems, there is almost no pollution in the North, whether it be industrial waste or just pure trash. The one thing which strikes most visitors to North Korea is its squeaky-clean appearance. This is a function not just of the lack of consumer goods and their packaging but of determined policies which keep it that way. The streets of Pyongyang are washed down twice a week, and before dawn each day street cleaners are out sweeping up any litter or leaves which they can find. You'd be hard pressed to find a single piece of paper on the streets despite the absence of litter bins. Even in the countryside, women are assigned a particular stretch of the main road to sweep and keep clean – each and every day. It's a far cry from the situation in South Korea where litter has become a major eyesore – especially plastic rubbish which clogs many a major river and fouls up popular beauty and picnic spots.

The apparent lack of people is also one of the most striking features of the countryside (or, at least, of that part which you're allowed to see) and you may get to wondering where all those 21 million people actually live and work. Even in Pyongyang, only on Sunday do you see substantial numbers of people out on the streets.

The other major contrast is the lack of traffic on the highways. Most of what you'll see will be army vehicles. There are very few passenger cars. North Korea has no automobile manufacturing plants and must import them from abroad. As a result, there's nothing remotely like the traffic congestion and vehicle exhaust pollution which characterises many South Korean cities.

CLIMATE

The weather is similar to South Korea, but colder and drier in winter. There are four distinct seasons. Autumn is the preferred time for a visit, with crisp, dry weather and a chance to see the leaves changing colour. Over 60% of the annual rainfall falls from June to September. Average monthly temperatures for Pyongyang are as follows:

GOVERNMENT

The government consists of Kim Il-sung and Kim Jong-il, with window-dressing provided by the Korean Workers' Party.

This country has been so closed for so long, and maintains the world's fifth largest army, principally because of Kim Il-sung (the 'Great Leader'), who has totally domi-nated the politics of North Korea ever since 1948. If there's anyone who has outdone Stalin or Mao Zedong in the cult of person-ality then it has to be Kim Il-sung. Not only is his word God's will, but huge statues and portraits of him litter the North Korean coun-tryside and the cities. Furthermore, the Great Leader has been grooming his son, Kim Jong-il (the 'Dear Leader'), to take over after his death – highly ironic given that classic Marxist theory absolutely opposes dynastic succession. Both leaders are periodically referred to as 'His Excellency'. You'll see political slogans (in Korean) mounted on every hillside, and you need never be in doubt as to whether someone is a North Korean or not. Everybody, young or old, at home or abroad, wears a small metal badge with the face of the 'Great Leader' on it.

This sort of cult following and passionate belief in every gem of wisdom which falls from the 'Great Leader's' lips is a corner-stone of the education system and no-one escapes it. It even has its attraction for some university students in South Korea, who display the utmost naivety by uncritically espousing his totalitarian strictures on the evils of South Korea's political, economic and social policies and his passionate anti-Western rhetoric. Of course, many things are far from perfect in the South, but it's true to say that few would prefer Kim's brand of utopia, given the choice. Within North Korea, opposition to Kim's regime is bru-tally suppressed. You may take with a pinch of salt claims by North Koreans that prisons don't exist, though they do admit to main-taining 're-education centres'. Photos taken by Western spy satellites confirm the exis-tence of these, and Amnesty International

Pyongyang Temperatures & Rainfall											
	Jan	Feb	Mar	Apr	May	Jun	Jul	Aug	Sep	Oct	Nov	Dec
Temp (°C)	-8.1	-4.8	1.7	9.5	15.5	20.6	24.2	24.4	18.9	11.9	3.4	-4.8
Rain (mm)	15	11	26	46	67	76	237	228	112	45	41	21

estimates that there are over 100,000 political prisoners in North Korea.

It may seem incredible to a Western liberal accustomed to multiparty democracy that such totalitarianism could exist in the late 20th century, but it does. If any society comes close to the nightmare depicted in George Orwell's book *1984*, North Korea is it. The system is likely to remain in place until Kim Il-sung dies, but after that anything could happen. Little is actually known about heir-apparent Dear Leader Kim Jong-il, but all accounts indicate that he lacks the charisma of his father – he is never seen publicly, not even for official functions held in his honour. Western intelligence reports indicate that he is heavily introverted and devotes much of his time to watching foreign videos. Whether or not he can control his own military is the all-important question.

ECONOMY

Capitalism does not exist here, not even street vendors. The Marxist economy has been augmented with Kim Il-sung's ideology of *juche* (self-reliance) which has resulted in the country spurning overseas aid and trade, especially with the West. The country has poured its resources into the military, heavy industries, monuments and statues of the Great Leader, all at the expense of agriculture and consumer goods. The country is believed to have suffered from severe food and energy shortages since the USSR ended subsidies in 1990. However, outsiders can only make educated guesses about the North Korean economy since the government's statistics are pure fantasy.

North Korea owes more than US$800 million in defaulted loans to Western banks – the country borrowed the money, then simply refused to repay. As a result, North Korea has a zero credit rating and cannot borrow additional funds for development projects, nor will most countries sell anything to North Korea on other than a cash or barter basis. As for exports, North Korea has little to sell, except weapons and ammunition which have found a ready market in Africa and the Middle East.

POPULATION & PEOPLE

The population is approximately 21 million – less than half the population of the South. The government has encouraged population growth which is estimated at 2.1% annually.

You won't be seeing any minority groups; Korea is ethnically almost totally homogeneous.

ARTS

One thing you must say for Kim Il-sung – he has indeed promoted traditional Korean arts and culture. His motives for doing so are a subject of debate. Kim is a fierce nationalist, relentlessly emphasising the superiority of Korean culture. North Koreans are told they are culturally superior, their country is the best in the world, and Kim Il-sung is the greatest man in the world. The focus on Korea's cultural superiority reinforces Kim's position as the greatest leader in the world and also helps divert attention from North Korea's genuinely serious problems.

Whatever his motives, tourists with an interest in traditional arts can benefit – visits to Korean song-and-dance performances can easily be arranged. Some even argue that in terms of traditional culture, the North is the 'real Korea'.

RELIGION

As far as Buddhist temples go, they do exist, and in some cases have been renovated, but they no longer function, as the religion is regarded as an expression of a so-called bourgeois mentality and is therefore proscribed. Confucianism has been similarly suppressed. The traditional arts associated with such temples and shrines, on the other hand, have been harnessed to serve the greater glory of Kim Il-sung's 'vision'. Christians and Christian churches do exist here though they're few in number and any belief in the holy trinity is likely to be expressed in the form of the Great Leader (Kim Il-sung), the Dear Leader (Kim Jong-il), and the holy spirit of Juche – the national ideology of self-reliance.

LANGUAGE

This is essentially the same as that of South

Korea, but the North has developed a somewhat different accent and vocabulary. Very few people speak English or any other foreign language.

Facts for the Visitor

VISAS & EMBASSIES

North Korea was opened up to Western group tourism in 1986 and to individual Western travellers in 1989, so getting a visa is now possible but certainly not guaranteed.

Your best bet is to first approach the North Korean Visa Office in Macau. They are in the business of selling tours, and will normally respond much more favourably to travellers than the North Korean Embassy in Beijing. They offer several standard tours of varying lengths, or you may put together a specialised itinerary of your own. You fill out a visa application which they fax off to Pyongyang straight away. They can usually give you an approval or rejection within 10 minutes. The first question you will be asked is 'Are you a journalist?' If you really want to go to North Korea, you'd better say 'No'. They normally issue your visa as soon as you pay the full charge. Three photographs are required and there is a US$15 visa fee. If you're with a group of over 16 people, the 16th person visits free of charge.

The fee you pay only covers your tour within North Korea. You still must book your transport to and from Pyongyang. The normal starting point is Beijing, and you book at China International Travel Service (CITS) in the Beijing International Hotel. You must then inform the North Korean Visa Office in Macau. They will call ahead to make sure that your guide is there to meet you and that your hotels are booked and transport within Korea is arranged. You'd better also call or fax the Visa Office in Macau – the North Korean Embassy in Beijing has often proved to be unreliable.

Trying to book your tour directly with the North Korean Embassy in Beijing is much less certain. Some travellers have received a warm welcome at the embassy, while others have been told 'the person you need to see won't be back for two months'. Assuming they respond favourably, you may be issued the visa in anything between 10 minutes and three weeks. As in Macau, you must pay for the entire trip in advance in hard currency before your visa is issued, and then arrange your own transport for getting to/from North Korea.

There are no little tricks like entering on a transit visa and then extending after arrival. Don't even think about sneaking in to North Korea. This is one country where you dare not thumb your nose at the authorities.

Getting your visa extended is easy as long as you pay. Just how much your extended stay will cost is subject to negotiation, but include in your calculations your hotel bill, meals and a service charge for your guide. If you want a visa extension and can come up with the cash, your guide will make all the arrangements.

Even citizens of the USA have been allowed to visit, despite North Korea's vehemently anti-US stand. The same goes for Japanese nationals (enemy No 2). Only Israelis are officially prohibited entry. However, policies in North Korea change.

The visa is not stamped into your passport (which might prejudice future visits to the USA or South Korea) but onto a separate sheet of paper which will be retained by the immigration authorities on leaving North Korea.

If your time is limited and you want to arrange everything before arriving in Macau or China, there are a few travel agents (very few!) who deal with tours to North Korea. See the Tours section for details.

Most likely, you'll be entering and returning through China. This means you should get a dual or multiple-entry visa for China. Otherwise, you can arrange a return visa at the Chinese embassy in Pyongyang, but this will consume some of your scarce time and North Korea is an expensive place to hang around.

Booking a tour through a travel agent usually requires a minimum wait of six weeks, two weeks of which are needed to process your visa application – you must part with your passport for these two weeks. In the UK, try Regent Holidays Ltd (☎ (0272) 211711), 13 Small St, Bristol BS1 1DE. In Australia, try Orbitours (☎ (02) 2217322), 7th floor, Dymocks Building, 428 George St, Sydney 2000. In Hong Kong, the agent specialising in these trips is Wallem Travel (☎ 5286514), 46th floor, Hopewell Centre, 183 Queen's Rd East, Wanchai.

The China International Travel Service (CITS) office in Shenyang, Liaoning Province, has been known to book tours to North Korea. The Beijing CITS does not book these tours or help you obtain a visa, but they do arrange transport.

If you feel burdened by all the red tape and restrictions, then spare a thought for the North Korean people. Even within the country, special permission is required for a change of location. Those who are allowed to go overseas for study invariably have to choose a Communist country as their destination. Most go to Chinese universities, though for a few Tanzania is a possible alternative. At all these universities where there's a Korean contingent they form an exclusive bloc and never, at any time, socialise with non-Koreans, even at a departmental level. In addition, there's always a political cadre to keep watch over them and report any misdemeanours. Likewise, all North Korean businesspeople are required to attend special political education classes once a week to keep them doctrinally pure.

North Korean Visa Offices

China
> Embassy of the Democratic People's Republic of Korea, Ritan Beilu, Jianguomenwai, Chaoyang District, Beijing (☎ 5321186)

Macau
> DPR Korea-Macau International Tourism Company, 23rd floor, Nam Van Commercial Centre, 57-9 Rua da Praia Grande (☎ 333355, fax 333939)

USSR
> Embassy of the Democratic People's Republic of Korea, PO Box ulitsa Mosfilmovskaya 72 (☎ 5787580) (telex 413272 ZINGG SU)

Foreign Embassies in North Korea

There are about 25 embassies, but the only ones of significant size are the Chinese and Soviet embassies. The rest are small offices staffed by one or two persons representing mostly Third World countries in Africa and the Middle East. The only Western country with a full-time representative is Sweden.

CUSTOMS

North Korean Customs are surprisingly easy – we were not hassled at all. Besides the usual prohibitions against guns and narcotics, the government lists several other things which you may not bring in:

1) Telescopes and magnifiers with over six magnification
2) Wireless apparatus and their parts
3) Publications, video tapes, recording tapes, films, photos and other materials which are hostile to our socialist system or harmful to our political, economic and cultural development and disturb the maintenance of social order
4) Seeds of tobacco, leaf tobacco and other seeds

MONEY
Currency

The unit of currency is the won = 100 jon. There are bank notes for W1, W5, W10, W50 and W100, and coins for W1 and jon 1, 5, 10 and 50.

In addition, there are three types of North Korean currency. The first is coloured green (for won) or blue (for jon) if you're converting hard currency. The second is coloured red if you're exchanging 'non-convertible' currency (basically Communist bloc and Third World currency). The last is local currency for use by Koreans only. Local currency comes in both banknotes and coins whereas green/blue and red currency comes only in banknotes. As a foreigner, you must pay for hotels, restaurants and goods bought in stores in either green/blue or red banknotes and change will only be given in matching notes.

Red currency is North Korea's way of saying it doesn't particularly want roubles or the like. There are certain limits on consumer goods that can be bought with red currency. The object of this is to prevent East Europeans and particularly people from the Soviet Union from stripping stores bare – something which wouldn't be too hard to do!

There are also two sets of prices for certain goods – a green price and a red price. The red price is often up to 10 times greater than the green price.

The only time you're likely to need local currency is if you use the Metro in Pyongyang since the escalator takes only coins. You'll also need coins if you want to make a call from a public pay phone.

Foreigners must exchange money at hotels. You are much better off changing cash rather than travellers' cheques since the hotels have a W3 service charge for cashing cheques. There's no black market but you can, with some people, swap green for red or local currency. Most Koreans would love to have the green currency since it can be used to buy rare imported goods.

Currency declaration forms are usually issued when you get your visa or at the border/airport on entry and you must fill in an exit currency form when you leave. It's probably best to make sure you get a currency form to avoid hassles on leaving, but if you don't it seems that the guides assigned to you can generally sort things out without too much trouble.

Exchange Rates

The only convertible currencies you are able to exchange easily are the Deutschmark, French franc, British pounds, US dollars and Japanese yen. Exchange rates are as follows:

DM1 = W1.24
FFr1 = W0.37
UK£1 = W3.64
US$1 = W2.22
Y100 = W1.59

There is also a highly punitive 'external exchange rate' of US$1=W0.97. Usually, you will not have to worry about this, but some travellers have run into it when trying to buy air tickets from outside North Korea (see the Getting There & Away section in this chapter).

Costs

All in all, it's going to be an expensive trip, even more so than Japan. You're looking at between US$70 and US$190 per day all-inclusive (not including transport to and from North Korea). You can save up to US$25 per day by choosing 'standard'

accommodation rather than 'deluxe'. There are also four price levels depending on the number of persons in your group: one person, two to five persons, six to nine persons or 10 to 15 persons. A 16th person can go for free.

Prices quoted by the DPR Korea travel office in Macau for a single traveller are as follows: four days all-inclusive tour in deluxe/ standard accommodation, US$646/544; five days, US$840/717; eight days, US$1487/1272; and 11 days, US$2130/1821.

Transport to/from Pyongyang costs extra. See the Getting There & Away section for details.

If it's any consolation, they do give very good service for the money.

WHAT TO BRING
There is a shortage of basic consumer items, so bring everything you think you'll need. Korean men smoke like chimneys and foreign cigarettes make good gifts – you can buy a carton of Dunhills at the hard currency shops for US$14, but if you have a cheaper source, bring them. Marlboro reds are especially valued since they are not available in North Korea. Postage stamps seem to be glueless, so a gluestick will prove valuable.

TOURIST OFFICES
Local Tourist Offices
Ryohaengsa (☎ 850-2-817201), the government tourist agency, is also known as the Korea International Tourist Bureau. You can reach them by telex (5998 RHS KP) or fax (850-2-817607). The mailing address is: Ryohaengsa, Central District, Pyongyang, Democratic People's Republic of Korea.

Overseas Reps
DPR Korea-Macau International Tourism Company (☎ 333355, fax 333939) is on the 23rd floor, Nam Van Commercial Centre, 57-9 Rua da Praia Grande, Macau. This is currently the easiest place to arrange a visa.

BUSINESS HOURS & HOLIDAYS
Official working hours are Monday to Satur-

day from 9 am to 6 pm. Public holidays include: New Year's Day, 1 January; Kim Jong-il's birthday, 16 February; Kim Il-sung's birthday, 15 April; Armed Forces Day, 25 April; May Day, 1 May; National Foundation Day, 9 September; Korean Workers' Party Foundation Day, 10 October.

CULTURAL EVENTS
By all means try to be in Pyongyang during Kim Jong-il's birthday (16 February) or Kim Il-sung's birthday (15 April). Both events are huge extravaganzas with military-style parades and portraits of the Great and Dear Leaders being carried through the streets.

An interesting thing about the Dear Leader's birthday is that it's been changed: he was born in 1942 but this was recently changed to 1941 and all previous North Korean history books had to be altered to reflect the new 'reality'. Just why Kim Jong-il was made one year older is subject to speculation, but the currently accepted theory is that the Great Leader likes even numbers and wants his son to be exactly 30 years younger than him.

POST & TELECOMMUNICATIONS
Postal Rates
A postcard to Australia costs W1.30. To the USA it's W1.50.

Sending Mail
You needn't bother trying to track down the post office, since most major hotels offer postal service.

You're best off sending postcards since these give the authorities a chance to read what you've said without having to tear open your letters. Saying a few nice things about how clean and beautiful North Korea is will increase the chances of your mail getting through.

Receiving Mail
You can forget about the GPO and poste restante. Given the short time you're likely to be spending in North Korea, it's hardly worth bothering trying to receive any letters. However, if you want to try, the most likely

Fax, Telex & Telegraph

Fax and telex services are readily available from major hotels like the Koryo in Pyongyang. Telegraph (cable) service does not seem to be avaiable.

TIME

The time in Korea is Greenwich Mean Time plus nine hours. When it is noon in Korea it is 2 pm in Sydney or Melbourne, 3 am in London, 10 pm the previous day in New York and 7 pm the previous day in Los Angeles or San Francisco.

ELECTRICITY

Electric power is 220 V, 60 Hz, though luxury hotels often have an outlet for 110 V. If so, this will be clearly labelled. All outlets are of the US type with two flat prongs, but no ground (earth) wire.

place to receive your mail is at the Pyongyang Koryo Hotel, Tonghung-dong, Central District, Pyongyang; or care of the Korea International Tourist Bureau (Ryohaengsa), Central District, Pyongyang. There is a better than average chance that your letters will be opened and read.

Telephone

It's easy to book an overseas call from major hotels, and some even offer international direct dialling (IDD) right from your room. Phone calls usually go through without much trouble.

Public pay phones require 10 jon coins, which means you'll need some local money if you want to use them. Coin-operated phones are not very common even in Pyongyang, but you probably won't find too many people to call anyway.

If you are dialling direct to North Korea from abroad, the country code is 850. A number of Western countries do not have phone connections with North Korea, but making an IDD call from Beijing to Pyongyang is very easy.

BOOKS & MAPS

Literature about North Korea is rare, and tourist literature is even rarer. The easiest place to get travel brochures is from the DPR Korea-Macau International Tourism Company in Macau. These are printed in several languages – English, German, French, Japanese, Chinese etc, and give all the major sites open to foreign tourists, the hotels, an airline schedule, and a breakdown of suggested itineraries ranging from three days to 16 days. The North Korean Embassy in Beijing has these brochures but does not give them to Westerners, though ethnic Koreans seem to be able to obtain them without difficulty. If you get into the North Korean embassy, immediately to your right is a waiting room. If you manage to get in there, they have free copies of various glossy-colour magazines such as *Women of Korea* and *Democratic People's Republic of Korea*. You may take these with you.

Another source of information is the book *Korean Review* by Pang Hwan Ju (Foreign Languages Publishing House, Pyongyang, 1987), which gives information on North Korea's flora, fauna, minerals, history, economy, politics and sightseeing.

Within North Korea, there are numerous propaganda books and pamphlets. Though these have scant useful information, they are rare gems for collectors.

Maps of Pyongyang and Korea can be purchased at major tourist hotels.

As for getting a general feel for the place, what could be more relevant than George Orwell's *1984* or *Animal Farm*? Read these before or after you arrive, as it would not be wise to carry them through North Korean Customs.

Perhaps more to the point is a report on human rights in North Korea published jointly by Asia Watch (Washington DC, USA) and the Minnesota Lawyers International Human Rights Committee. A brief summary of this report appeared in the Far Eastern Economic Review, 19 January 1989, which should be available from libraries in Hong Kong. North Korea has harshly denounced this report.

MEDIA

Information about the rest of the world is hard to come by in North Korea. The press is rigidly controlled and prints only what the government tells it to print, which is mostly stories about happy workers, loyal soldiers, US imperialist aggressors, South Korean puppets, and the superhuman feats of Kim Il-sung. Likewise, TV programmes are all designed to reinforce the reigning ideology. North Koreans cannot receive foreign news broadcasts because all radio and TVs are designed to only pick up the government broadcasting frequencies.

One thing about the North Korean media is fairly consistent: the propensity for exaggeration. If a riot occurs in South Korea and a dozen people are injured, the North Korean media reports 'hundreds of injuries'. When production statistics are released for the

North Korean economy, you can just about divide by 50 to get the real figure.

Newspapers & Magazines

There are no foreign publications available, so if you want to read *Time* or *Newsweek*, you'll have to bring your own copies.

As for local publications in English, the selection is severely limited. There are free magazines everywhere in a variety of languages, especially the colourful *Democratic People's Republic of Korea* magazine. This is filled with the usual tirade against US imperialists and South Korean puppets, plus articles about the Great Leader and Dear Leader. You'll also learn that the Juche idea is a shining beacon of hope which has swept the world by storm. At the tourist hotels you can pick up a free weekly English-language newspaper, the *Pyongyang Times*, but every issue is virtually the same.

Radio & TV

There are two AM radio stations and two regular TV stations. It is said that there is a third TV station which broadcasts cultural events on holidays only, but we haven't seen it. The two TV stations broadcast approximately from 6 pm to 11 pm.

FILM & PHOTOGRAPHY

You can buy colour print film at reasonable prices from the hard currency gift shops, but everything else is expensive so bring what you need. There are photoprocessing facilities on the second floor at the Koryo Hotel, but you'd probably be better off waiting until you return to China, Hong Kong or elsewhere. This same place can do visa photos in case you need some.

If you visit the International Friendship Exhibition (IFE) centre at Mt Myohyang, you'd be wise to bring a tripod and cable release for time exposures because an electronic flash is not permitted. Since many of the exhibits are behind glass, a polarising filter would also come in handy.

You are surprisingly free to photograph what you like, but ask first before taking pictures of soldiers. In many cases, permission *will* be given. The only time we had a problem was when we tried to photograph a long queue of people trying to buy ice-cream cones. A man jumped out of the crowd and put his hand over the lens.

HEALTH

There seems to be no problem with food and most Koreans drink their water unboiled. You won't have to worry about eating from dirty street stalls either, because there aren't any.

That having been said, North Korea does not seem like a good place to get sick since there are shortages of basic Western medicines. On the other hand, you can try traditional Korean medicine which is similar to the Chinese variety.

WOMEN TRAVELLERS

We saw a few foreign women travelling in North Korea, but they were always part of a group that included men. This isn't to say that a single woman or group of women couldn't travel without male companions in North Korea, but it seems to be a very rare occurrence. Also, we never saw a female guide leading any of these tour groups, though Ryohaengsa claims that female guides are available. It's the opposite situation in South Korea, where most tour guides are women.

One thing we can say for sure – Korea is a very male-dominated society. In spite of the regime's constant attempts to show complete equality between the sexes, there are no women holding any positions of importance. This is not mere speculation on our part – we talked to numerous embassy people who had spent years in North Korea, and all assured us that of the hundreds of high government officials they met, not a single one was female. While no North Korean woman holds any position of power, there are two who are revered: the Great Leader's mother, Kang Ban-sok, sometimes referred to as the 'Mother of Korea', and Kim Jong-suk, mother of the Dear Leader.

DANGERS & ANNOYANCES

As far as we can tell, crime is not a problem. The North Korean penal system is an enigma, but we'd be willing to guess that thieves are dealt with harshly – possibly with the death penalty. This doesn't mean you should be careless with your valuables, but the chance of theft is probably lower than in most countries.

The one thing which will get you into serious trouble fast is to insult the Great Leader or the Dear Leader. We know of one Austrian visitor who put out his cigarette butt on a newspaper, right on the face of a photo of Kim Il-sung. The maid found it in his hotel room and informed the police. This resulted in a frightening confrontation, with threats, shouting, pushing and shoving before he was finally booted out of the country.

Male travellers should not even think about touching a North Korean woman regardless of how friendly, charming and receptive she might seem to be. Even something fairly innocent like shaking hands could be construed as an 'immoral act' and could result in serious punishment for both parties to this 'crime'. As for relations between North Korean men and foreign women, it's a big unknown. Most North Korean men would probably not dare touch a foreign woman, but given the fact that Korea is a bastion of male chauvinism, it would probably be viewed less seriously than contact between a foreign man and a Korean woman.

Besides thinking about dangers to yourself, give some thought to the Koreans you meet. Giving them gifts like foreign coins or photos of yourself could have unpredictable consequences for them. What might seem like an innocent act for you might result in them spending time in a concentration camp.

The US Treasury Department has a list of regulations (available from US embassies) governing the economic conduct of US citizens abroad. One little-known rule is that US citizens may not use a credit card in North Korea – not for the purchase of goods or even to pay living expenses! Breaking this rule is a crime and the violator may be prosecuted.

ACCOMMODATION

You will have to stay at certain designated hotels everywhere you go. These are modern, multi-star hotels which have been built specifically for foreign tourists and, as you might expect, they're expensive, though there are several grades of them. Local *yogwan* undoubtedly exist, though not anywhere near in the same numbers as in South Korea, but you're not allowed to stay at them. And since you must stay in the large tourist hotels, this also limits where you can go.

FOOD

Despite reports of food shortages, foreigners at least eat very well. Your guide orders your food, so if you have any special requests, make your wishes known early. The food is heavily based on meat, fish and poultry – vegetarians are liable to have a difficult time. There is a tendency to order Western food for Westerners, so if you want Korean food, ask for it.

DRINKS

Korean beer is not bad, but most hard liquor is imported. As for nonalcoholic beverages, North Korea produces mineral water and some pleasant-tasting carbonated fruit drinks. There are plenty of imported drinks available in the hotels and hard currency shops, including Coca-Cola.

Getting There & Away

AIR

There are flights between Beijing and Pyongyang by either the Chinese national airline CAAC, once weekly, or the North Korean airline, Korean Airways (also known as Chosonminhang), twice weekly. The flight takes less than two hours.

The airfares are insane. The one-way Beijing-Pyongyang ticket costs US$120, but a one-way Pyongyang-Beijing flight is US$274 if the ticket is bought in China! If bought in Pyongyang, it's only US$120!

This is because CAAC calculates the fare using the absurd 'external exchange rate' of US$1 = W0.97. To make it more absurd, a round-trip Beijing-Pyongyang-Beijing air ticket bought in China costs US$220, or US$54 less than a one-way ticket.

There are flights between Khabarovsk and Pyongyang in either direction by either Aeroflot or Korean Airways and between Moscow and Pyongyang. There are also flights between Berlin and Pyongyang via Moscow.

You're advised to book as far in advance as possible, though most aircraft fly nearly empty. Occasionally, delegations of diplomats descend on Pyongyang for some special event and seats suddenly become scarce.

Sunan International Airport is 30 km west of Pyongyang, about 20 minutes by car.

TRAIN

There are four trains per week in either direction between Beijing and Pyongyang via Tianjin, Tangshan, Jinxi, Dandong and Sinuiju. The Chinese trains leave on Monday and Thursday and the North Korean trains leave on Wednesday and Saturday. All these trains leave Beijing at 4.48 pm and arrive at Pyongyang the next day at 3.55 pm (about 23 hours). Going the other way, trains depart Pyongyang at noon on Monday, Wednesday, Thursday and Saturday. The cost is US$77 one way.

Chinese trains are more comfortable than the North Korean ones. North Korean trains don't have air-conditioning even in the soft sleeper section, and the windows are locked so ventilation is nonexistent.

The North Korean train is actually just two carriages attached to the main Beijing-Dandong train, which are detached at Dandong (Chinese side) and then taken across the Yalu River bridge to Sinuiju (Korean side), where more carriages are added for local people. Non-Koreans remain in their original carriages.

Customs and Immigration on both sides of the border are relatively casual and your passport will be taken away for stamping.

The trains spend about four hours at the border for Customs and Immigration – two hours at Dandong and two hours at Sinuiju. You are permitted to wander around the stations but you should not attempt to go beyond the entrance gate.

Sinuiju Station will be your first introduction to North Korea and the contrasts with China will be quite marked. Everything is squeaky-clean and there are no vendors plying their goods. A portrait of the Great Leader looks down from the top of this station, and at all other railway stations in North Korea. You may wander around the station and take photos. One of the buildings is a rest area for foreign passengers, and here you will encounter the first of many billboards with photos and captions in English: 'The US Aggression Troops Transferring Missiles'; 'South Korean Puppet Police'; 'US Imperialists and South Korean Stooges' etc.

Soon after departing Sinuiju, you will be presented with a menu (complete with colour photographs) of what's for dinner. The food is excellent and the service is fine. It's all very civilised. Make sure you have some small denomination US dollar bills to pay for the meal, as this is not included as part of the package deal you paid for in advance. There are no facilities for changing money at Sinuiju or on the train. The dining car is for the use of non-Koreans only.

Your guide will meet you on arrival at Pyongyang Railway Station and accompany you to your hotel. Likewise, when you leave North Korea, your guide will bid you farewell at Pyongyang Railway Station or the airport and you travel to China unaccompanied.

When leaving North Korea, you can link up with the Trans-Siberian train at Sinuiju/Dandong in China. To make this connection you need to take the noon train from Pyongyang on Saturday which arrives in Moscow the following Friday. There's also the possibility of crossing directly from North Korea into the USSR in the north-east via Hasan and Tumangang and then taking the Trans-Siberian to Moscow. This connec-

tion leaves Pyongyang on Monday and Wednesday at 5.30 pm. These trains arrive in Moscow on Monday and Wednesday respectively.

BOAT

A passenger ship, the *Sam Jiyon*, plies between Wonsan on the east coast of North Korea and Nagasaki (Japan) once a month. It's a North Korean ship and is primarily intended to enable Koreans living in Japan to visit their homeland – most of the Koreans living in Japan originally came from North Korea. It's popular with youth groups from Japan, who get VIP treatment on arrival in the North, and is a possible port of entry if you already have a visa for North Korea.

If you have limited time at your disposal, you'll need to know the departure dates of this ship. North Korean embassies *may* know the details but don't be surprised if they don't or won't tell you. In Japan, contact the General Association of Korean Residents in Japan (Soren). Soren is Pyongyang's mouthpiece in Japan, with branches all over the country, and heavily-guarded headquarters in Tokyo. Don't just think you can hop on this ship even if you have a North Korean visa – you'd better clear it with the North Korean Embassy first, and in any event, a guide must be informed that you're coming so you will be met on arrival.

LEAVING NORTH KOREA

You should make your reservations for departure before you arrive in North Korea. The government tourist agency, Ryohaengsa, can easily do this for you as long as you inform them in advance.

If departing by air, your guide will accompany you to the airline office so you can buy your ticket, or to reconfirm your outbound flight if you've already bought one. You must pay an airport departure tax of W13 at the time you reconfirm, rather than at the airport.

Money-changing facilities are available at the airport but not at the railway station.

Getting Around

Public transport isn't anywhere near as well developed in North Korea as in the South. However, you will have a few opportunities to use it, usually only when accompanied by your guide.

One thing you'll notice is the distinct lack of traffic in the countryside. Most of the vehicles you'll see will be military transports.

AIR

There are no regularly scheduled domestic flights. There are occasional charters to Paekdusan for W2000 return, but these only fly if there are sufficient passengers, which is seldom the case.

BUS

There are hardly any public buses in the countryside or between major cities, a reflection of the fact that North Koreans are not allowed to move freely around their own country without permission. Most of the time, you'll be travelling by car accompanied by your driver and guide. If you're with a larger group, you'll ride in a specially arranged tourist bus. Naturally, this will limit your chances of meeting local people. On the other hand, if you can't speak Korean then this is probably an advantage of sorts, though it does mean you'll stand out a mile as a foreigner.

Being conspicuous is no great disadvantage in itself since Confucianism still rules, though under a different guise. Children will wave at you as you pass by, while adults will smile and maybe even chat (in Korean) if you happen to stop and get out on the streets. They've been encouraged to give visiting foreigners a warm welcome.

TRAIN

You'll probably take the railway to visit some of the major tourist sites such as Kaesong and Mt Myohyang. You'll be accompanied by your guide during these trips, and you'll ride in sleeper cars rather than the hard-seat carriages used by the masses.

BICYCLE

A major contrast with China is the distinct lack of bicycles. There are almost none in Pyongyang and very few elsewhere. Outside of Pyongyang, most people walk. Presumably, the absence of bicycles in Pyongyang indicates a ban on their use. Occasionally, you'll come across a few in a department store in Pyongyang, usually with no price tags on them. Certainly you cannot rent bikes anywhere.

Finally, even if you did have your own bike, you'd be hard-pressed to find your way around either in the cities or in the countryside because there are no street signs in the cities or direction signs in the countryside and road maps are almost impossible to find. The only street map you'll find available is for Pyongyang.

TOURS

You must be accompanied at all times by a guide whose fees you will already have paid. In a few places you are allowed to walk around alone – basically Pyongyang and a few of the beauty spots – though this is only reluctantly conceded. Guides are available who can speak English, French, German, Chinese, Japanese and Russian as well as a number of other languages.

Tours booked through a private travel agent are more expensive than booking directly with Ryohaengsa, but only slightly. Presumably, the travel agents are shielding you from all the hassles of dealing with the North Korean bureaucracy and China International Travel Service (CITS) in Beijing. For a five-day trip, Wallem Travel in Hong Kong charges US$880 for one person; US$683 each for two to five persons; US$502 each for six to nine persons; US$485 for 10 to 15 persons; a 16th person can go for free. If booked in conjunction with a Trans-Siberian tour, these charges are reduced by US$153 per person.

There are a number of special interest

tours. One is the 'Tour for Traditional Korean Medical Treatment'. This involves acupuncture, moxibustion, suction using vacuum flasks, manipulative (chiropractic) treatment and physical therapy. Cure rates of 90% are claimed for most illnesses. The costs for these treatments vary, but don't expect it to be cheap.

One of the more unusual manifestations of North Korea's cultural policy is the invention of 'alphabetical dance notation'. This is a method of writing down dance movements much the way music is recorded on paper using special notation. Tourists are invited to study this system by taking a dance tour. The cost per person runs from US$435 to US$750 for an eight-day course, depending on the number of persons in the class. The cost for a fifteen-day course is US$860 to US$1500. The price includes accommodation, meals, transport and some sightseeing as well as the course. Ryohaengsa can supply you with more details.

Pyongyang

Being the capital, Pyongyang is a superb example of the regime's determination to project its own image of progress, discipline and the wellbeing of its citizens. You won't find here the hustle and bustle, the noise and smells of other cities in Asia. Kim Il-sung's version of the model Communist city excludes people with disabilities (except the Great Leader, who has a large visible bulge on the back of his head from a benign brain tumour). Also excluded are the very old, bicycles, animals and street vendors. Even pregnant women were banned for a while. All this has attracted the critical attention of the foreign press, and possibly because of such criticism, there is now one token disabled man who is often seen riding a modified bicycle near the Koryo Hotel (even though bikes are banned in the city). A few elderly persons have also recently appeared around the Koryo Hotel (where most for-

eigners stay), but their numbers are exceedingly low.

It's said that only those with proven records of unswerving loyalty to the country's leaders are allowed to live in Pyongyang.

Pyongyang is the showpiece of North Korea and is peppered with distinctive landmarks and monuments, many of them in honour of the Great Leader. A notable one is the 170-metre high Tower of the Juche Idea, crowned with a beacon which flickers at night. There's also the extraordinary 13-lane boulevard which connects the city centre with the outer suburb of Kwangbok over three km away – a ridiculous extravagance given the scarcity of traffic, though no more of a profligate waste than many of the other grandiose monuments. Not surprisingly, a few things are named after the Great Leader: Kim Il-sung Square, Kim Il-sung Stadium, Kim Il-sung University and Kim Il-sung Higher Party School.

Fascinating indicators of the mentality of the regime are the stores with big glass display windows, well stocked with goods for all to see. The problem is that the doors are always locked and no-one is inside.

Orientation

Like Seoul, the city is built on the banks of a major river, in this case the Taedong, but unlike the Han River the Taedong appears to be refreshingly clean. Like the Han, it often freezes over in winter. One of the major sights here are the two mid-river fountains which rise to a height of 150 metres. Your guide will proudly tell you they're the highest in the world, and this is probably true (Canberra's single jet reaches only 140 metres and the one in Geneva only 122 metres).

If walking around the city, beware of jaywalking even if there's not a car in sight! There are underground walkways or pedestrian crossings at all major intersections and *everyone*, without exception, uses them. There are also traffic police at all such points standing on wooden plinths. If you attempt to jay-walk the nearest one will give a sharp blast of her whistle (they're mostly women) and a smart remonstration will quickly bring you back in line.

Things to See

Since Pyongyang is one of the few places where you'll be allowed to walk around unaccompanied (with a little gentle but persistent persuasion), it's a good idea to take this opportunity either before or after you've been chauffeured around the main sights. If you request it, you can, for instance, be dropped on the far side of the city at Liberation Tower and walk back from here to the centre calling in at department stores along the way if you want.

Your first day out in Pyongyang will undoubtedly be a guided tour of the monuments by car. How many of them you will see depends on the time available and what preferences you express. It's a good idea to make your preferences known as early as possible after arrival in North Korea or even beforehand if you want to be sure of being taken to the ones of your choice.

One of the principal monuments is the **Tower of the Juche Idea**, a 170-metre phallic symbol which you can get to the top of by express lift for an unencumbered view of the city. The ride costs W5. In an alcove at the bottom are commemorative messages from various parts of the world hewn in stone and brick extolling the concept of Juche. As the plaques indicate, the Juche idea is also referred to as *Kim Il-sungism*.

Other monuments include the **Arch of Triumph**, which marks the spot where Kim Il-sung made his rallying speech following the departure of the Japanese, and which is a full three metres higher than its counterpart in Paris, and the **Chollima Statue**, a bronze Pegasus representing the high-speed progress of the socialist reconstruction of North Korea. On Munsu Hill, overlooking the Taedong River, is the **Grand Monument** itself. As you might expect, this is where an enormous and highly polished bronze statue of the Great Leader stands, flanked by carvings of oppressed but ultimately victorious workers.

Of a more traditional nature are the **Chilsong** and **Taedong Gates**, two of the old city's gates, the latter with a two-tiered roof similar to its counterpart in Seoul.

For an exposition of North Korea's version of the country's history there is the **Korean Central History Museum**. The counterpart to the South's Independence Hall outside Chonan, the museum houses exhibits, artefacts and drawings tracing Korean history from prehistoric times right up to the revolution. Your guide will provide a running commentary.

If time permits, you may be taken to the **Pyongyang Maternity Hospital**. The most intriguing thing about this showcase hospital is that when the first foreign tour groups were herded through the maternity wards, all the 'patients' were beautiful, smiling young women who weren't pregnant.

Other institutes which may well be worth a visit include the **Students' & Children's Palace**, established in 1963 as a centre for after-school activities and where you can see students doing everything from pingpong to dance, gymnastics and playing music, and the **Pyongyang Embroidery Institute**, where you can see an exhibition of very impressive embroidery as well as prototype designs which are then copied by manufacturers around the country.

Although **Kim Il-sung University** is not on every tour, you might want to pay it a visit. It is here that Dear Leader Kim Jong-il graduated. The book *Kim Jong-il In His Young Days* makes it clear that the Dear Leader was the university's foremost scholar and was soon teaching his teachers. When the Dear Leader read his thesis about socialism, it was described thus:

> The professors and scholars, who were so strict about scientific matters, could not suppress their surging emotions, and approached the author who made immortal theoretical achievements, shaking his hands and congratulating him heartily and warmly.
>
> His thesis was highly assessed as an immortal document.

The major site of interest is the outer district of **Mangyongdae** – the so-called 'Cradle of the Revolution'. This where Kim Il-sung was born and spent his childhood. His old thatched house here, set in carefully tended gardens, has been turned into a shrine, and houses photographs of his family as well as a few everyday household utensils to indicate the humble background from which he came. The surrounding pine woods hold the burial mounds of his relatives. There's also a marble observation platform overlooking the Taedong River at the top of Mangyong Hill.

Near to Mangyongdae are two funfairs and pleasure grounds which you'll be told receive over 100,000 visitors a day, but you can take that with a pinch of salt.

On the way back from Mangyongdae, it's worth making a detour to see **Kwangbok Street**, a Kowloonesque suburb visible from high points in central Pyongyang. It's essentially a linearly laid-out suburb of high-rise apartment blocks, which stretch for over three km on either side of the virtually empty 13-lane highway.

Another worthwhile excursion is a visit to the **Movie Studio**. This is not part of the standard tours, so you must request it if you want to go there. It is not difficult to arrange, but give your guide as much advance notice as possible. Like everything else in North Korea, the movie studio is very politicised. Most of the films are anti-US and anti-South Korean. There are also a lot of anti-Japanese films. Kim Il-sung is credited with almost single-handedly defeating Japan in WW II (the Allied war effort is never acknowledged). His mother and father are also depicted as great revolutionaries. As part of the tour, they usually give you a sneak preview of films currently in production. Although the sound tracks are all in Korean, your guide will interpret for you. Fascinating stuff.

Places to Stay

Wherever you choose to stay in Pyongyang it's going to cost you heavily (unless you have contacts and/or are a member of your local Communist organisation). On the other hand, there is a choice between Deluxe, Class A, Class B and Class C accommodation. You'll probably be pressured to stay at the deluxe *Pyongyang Koryo Hotel* (☎ 38106), a 45-storey tower with a revolving restaurant on top. It's a five-minute walk from the railway station and it's where most foreigners stay. The hotel has 500 rooms, and given the small number of tourists, it's unlikely you'll have to worry about getting a reservation.

There are some other deluxe hotels, but most are inconveniently located. There's the *Tourist Hotel*, about seven km from the city centre; the *Angol Hotel*, at a similar distance from the centre; and the *Yanggakdo Hotel*, about four km from the centre.

The skyline of Pyongyang is dominated by the incredible *Ryugyong Hotel*, a 105-storey pyramid with 3000 rooms about four km from the centre. Originally conceived as the world's largest luxury hotel, the pyramid was erected in 1989 but the North Koreans apparently ran out of money before they could complete it. The building now sits as an empty shell and it's unlikely further work will be done unless there is a dramatic increase in tourism. Tourist pamphlets produced in North Korea often show the building photographed at night with lights on inside. The photos are a sham: the building is not even wired for elecricity.

Further down the scale in the B class are the *Potonggang Hotel* (☎ 48301), a fairly modest hotel about four km from the centre with 161 rooms; the *Sosan Hotel* about four km from the railway station; the *Ryanggang Hotel* with 330 rooms, also four km from the centre; and the *Youth Hotel*, about 10 km from the centre with 465 rooms.

The most popular C class hotel is the *Changgwangsan Hotel* (☎ 48366), with 326 rooms, less than two km from the railway station. In the heart of the city is the *Pyongyang Hotel* (☎ 38161) with 170 rooms. The *Taedonggang Hotel* (☎ 38346) with 60 rooms is also in the centre of the city.

Places to Eat

You'll usually eat at your hotel, but eating elsewhere can be arranged. Many foreigners

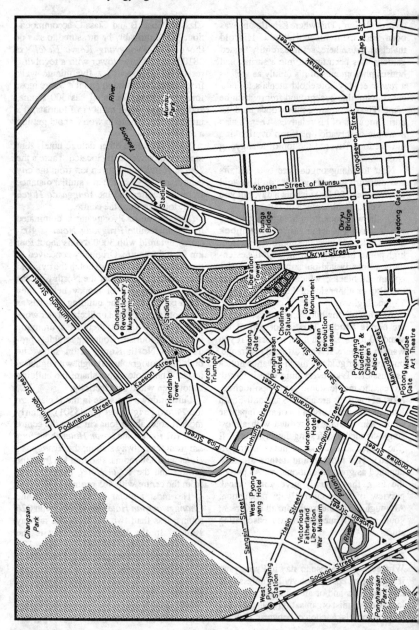

Pyongyang

0   250   500 m

hang out in the coffee shop of the *Changgwangsan Hotel*, but prices are high. As for the 'local restaurants', these in fact cater to foreigners or privileged Koreans with access to hard currency. Don't think you'll be able to eat along with the working class. Just where the locals eat is a mystery – either they bring food from home or they're fed at the workplace, but there are certainly no pavement restaurants or food stalls like you find all over South Korea. If you want to eat outside your hotel, you should make this clear to your guide.

Entertainment
The streets are deserted at night. For North Koreans, the evening is presumably spent sitting by the radio or TV listening to testimonials by happy workers and profound speeches by the Great Leader.

There are a few discos for decadent foreigners (no Koreans allowed). Don't get your hopes up though – the largest disco managed to attract 20 customers (19 males and one female) when we visited on a Saturday night during the peak summer season. The most popular disco is on the top floor of building No 2 in the Changgwangsan Hotel (☎ 48366). It's open from 9.30 pm until midnight and costs W2.

The Koryo Hotel has a dance hall, but the cover charge is W25 so it's usually empty except for a few Japanese karaoke enthusiasts. The second floor of the same hotel has a billiards room which is a good place to socialise with embassy staff, journalists and whoever else happens to be in town.

Things to Buy
While there are scarcely any consumer goods on the shelves, North Korea offers plenty of unique souvenirs which make fantastic conversation pieces.

Just to the south of the Pyongyang Koryo Hotel on Changgwang St is a place selling postage stamps (sign in English), and it's well worth your time to stop in here. One postage stamp shows a crowd of angry Koreans beating a US soldier to death while someone sticks a knife through his throat. Another shows two soldiers, one Korean and one Chinese, standing shoulder to shoulder while brandishing AK-47s. You might enjoy the stamps depicting North Korea's version of the space shuttle, but even more bizarre are the stamps proudly displaying the British royal family. Just why Charles and Diana are so popular in North Korea is one of those great mysteries. And finally, one guess whose picture is displayed on the largest stamps.

Many tourists have expressed an interest in purchasing the metal badge which every North Korean wears, with the Great Leader's picture printed on it. However, these are not for sale.

Ginseng is for sale in hotels, but prices are ridiculously high. You can buy it much more cheaply in the South. However, if you're an aspiring acupuncturist, you can find acupuncture needles in the medicine shops at rock-bottom prices.

Getting Around
All public transport in Pyongyang costs 10 jon. They want it in coins, so you'll need local money. As a general rule, foreigners are discouraged from using the public transport system except for the Metro (underground) which is something of a showcase.

Bus It's unlikely you'll ever use the urban bus network as the queues are phenomenally long and the buses crammed to bursting point, but if you do they run until 10 pm each day. Women with children form separate queues and have priority in boarding buses.

Tram Pyongyang's tram began service in 1991. It's not a bad way of getting around, but it's often extremely crowded.

Taxi You won't find taxis plying the streets like in most major capital cities, but you can book a taxi from a tourist hotel. The word 'taxi' is not written on the car, nor will you see a meter, but the fare is based on distance. The fare is approximately W2 per km, depending on the type of vehicle (Mercedes are most expensive). The price also rises slightly late at night. In the rare event that you don't find a taxi waiting outside your hotel, you can call one (☎ 10507).

Underground You should definitely visit a Metro station if only to see the extravagance with which the stations have been constructed. Each station is differently designed, with varying bronze sculptures, murals, mosaics and chandeliers, and all the pillars, steps, corridors and platforms are fashioned in marble. The trains themselves are nowhere near as impressive, being dim and dingy, but each car contains a picture of His Excellency. There are 17 stations in all served by two lines covering a total length of 24 km and the present system was completed in 1978. There are grand plans to extend it to Mangyongdae (Pyongyang's western district) and eventually to Nampo (Pyongyang's seaport). Each station has a map of the system indicating where you are. The cost of a ride on this system is a standard 10 jon and it's a very convenient way of quickly visiting different parts of the city.

Around the Country

What you get to see outside of Pyongyang depends on what sort of itinerary you request and how much time you have. It will also be limited to the places where tourist hotels are located. The following is a selection of places but isn't meant to be exhaustive. If you wish to go elsewhere then it's worth attempting to get permission. Few such requests, it seems, are refused, though they may initially cause raised eyebrows. On the other hand, if you do succeed in getting permission to visit places which aren't on the suggested tourist circuits, you must be prepared to accept last-minute cancellations. This even happens to group tours occasionally.

MT MYOHYANG
A visit here from Pyongyang can be adequately covered in a day trip using the train as your means of transport. It's 160 km from the capital.

The train leaves Pyongyang daily at 6 am and arrives at Hyangsan at 9 am. On the return journey, the train leaves Hyangsan at 7 pm and arrives Pyongyang at 10.20 pm. Breakfast is taken on the train in the foreigners-only dining car.

The main centre of interest in Hyangsan is the International Friendship Exhibition (IFE) centre, about three to four km from the railway station. It's another of those monuments to the greater glory of the Great Leader and, to a lesser extent, of the Dear Leader. It's a six-storey building in traditional Korean style which houses gifts given to Kim Il-sung and Kim Jong-il from all over the world and is magnificently set amongst densely wooded hills. You need to be on your best behaviour here, as the building is maintained as a hallowed shrine. You must take off your hat if you have one, and shoe covers must be worn when walking around. You may be permitted to open the golden doors to the shrine, but you must first put on a pair of gloves before touching the sacred handle. During your tour, you'll be escorted the whole time by a woman in traditional Korean costume. The building has been lavishly endowed with marble stairways, huge bronze doors and thick carpets. There are no windows and each room is thermostatically temperature-controlled. It's quite cold inside, so bring a jacket even in summer.

The gifts are quite interesting: a bullet-proof car from Stalin, a luxurious train carriage from Mao Zedong, a stuffed alligator from the Sandinistas, carvings, pottery and paintings, many of which are exquisitely executed. The gifts are arranged by country with a note, in English, of who sent them and when. There are 120 rooms in total and it's not possible to see them all in one day.

When you've seen the exhibition, it's possible to go for a three-km hike up the Sangwon Valley, via a clearly defined pathway, stone steps and a suspension footbridge to three sets of waterfalls (Kumgang, Taeha and Sanju). Nearby, there's an observation platform from which you can view the surrounding countryside. A short hike above the falls is a Buddhist temple – Sangwon-sa – which is in good order though no longer used.

There's also the Buddhist temple Pohyon-sa, just a short walk from the IFE at the start of the hike up Sangwon Valley, which consists of several small pagodas and a large hall housing images of the Buddha, as well as a museum which sports a collection of wood-block Buddhist scriptures. You'll be told that these wooden buildings are 950 years old and have never been rebuilt – if so, they must be made of petrified wood.

The village of Hyangsan itself consists of just one main street lined by traditional Korean houses. The main tourist hotel in this vicinity is the *Hyangsan Hotel*, about halfway between the station and the IFE, rated as class A. There is also the class C *Chongbyong Hotel* and the class D *Chongchon Hotel* about one km from the railway station.

KAESONG

Kaesong (population 200,000) is one of the few North Korean towns where burial sites of the former kings and queens of Korea can be seen. You can see here the burial mounds along with associated statuary of King Kongmin (the 31st Koryo king who reigned between 1330 and 1374) and his queen, about 13 km from the centre of the city. It's a very secluded site and there are splendid views over the surrounding tree-covered hills from a number of vantage points. You'll need a car to get there.

In the city itself are a number of obligatory tourist sights. Included among them are the **Sonjuk Bridge**, a tiny clapper bridge built in 1216 and, opposite, the **Pyochung Stele**, similar to those at the shrines outside of Kyongju and elsewhere in South Korea. A short drive from town is the **Songgyungwan Confucian College** which was originally built in 992 and rebuilt after fire in the 17th century. Today it's a museum of vases and other relics. The buildings surround a wide courtyard dotted with ancient trees.

Kaesong itself is a modern city with wide streets and of scant interest, though it does have an interesting old part consisting of traditional tile-roofed houses sandwiched between the river and the main street. There's also the Nam (South) Gate at the beginning of the main street which dates from the 14th century. From the main street, a wide driveway sweeps up Mt Chanam on top of which there's a massive bronze statue of – guess who?

If you stay in Kaesong, you'll be based at either the *Channamsan Hotel* or *Kaesong Minsok Hotel*. If you have a choice, definitely choose the latter, which is built in the traditional Korean yogwan style. Both hotels are rated class 'C'.

To get to Kaesong you can either take the train or a car, though a car is preferable if you want to see the towns en route. Driving time between Pyongyang and Kaesong is about 3¼ hours with a tea stop at a tourist halt built on a rocky outcrop overlooking the Sohung River along the way.

PANMUNJOM

This is one of the most morbidly fascinating sights in Korea. Even if you've visited this 'Truce Village' from the South, the trip from the northern side is well worth the effort.

To get there, you drive out of Kaesong on the 'Reunification Highway', a four-lane freeway devoid of traffic. The freeway is supposed to connect Pyongyang to Seoul, and the last exit before the DMZ has a large sign saying 'Seoul 70 km'. You drive up to a sentry box at the entrance to the DMZ where a military officer gives you a brief rundown of the history of Panmunjom aided by a large model of the 'Truce Village'. After that you'll be escorted to the Joint Security Zone by military officers in a car. From the car park, you enter a large building that faces the row of huts which straddle the demarcation line and then exchange glances with burly US marines, South Korean soldiers and the tourists on the other side in their pagoda viewing tower. Unless meetings are in progress, you'll permitted to visit the very room where the endless peace negotiations go on. After that, it's back to the main building for an exposition of the North Korean view of things.

The whole setting looks very serene, with well-tended gardens, trees, rice fields and chirping birds. Hard to imagine that all around the countryside is bristling with camouflaged tanks, nuclear warheads, nerve gas canisters, biological weapons and land mines. If war were to break out during your visit, you'd be incinerated in a minute. Imagine that.

On the way out of the DMZ, you are given a chance to visit the gift shop. There are some real collectors' items here, including a classic hate-mongering book called *Panmunjom* published in a variety of languages:

The US imperialist aggressors drew the Military Demarcation Line to divide Korea and her people by artificial means. Panmunjom is a place through which the line runs and a court which exposes and vehemently denounces the US imperialist criminal aggression in Korea to the whole world. The US imperialists started a war of aggression (1950-53) in order to swallow up the whole of Korea. But here at Panmunjom they went down on their knees before the Korean people and signed the Armistice Agreement.

The next stop on the agenda is the 'Wall'. According to the North, the Americans and South Koreans have built a concrete wall all the way across the peninsula (240 km) along the southern side of the DMZ. As the *Panmunjom* propaganda book puts it:

The south Korean puppets have hindered north-south dialogues against the burning desire of the Korean people for national reunification and their great expectations for the talks. They committed another ineffaceable crime against the nation. They built a reinforced concrete wall along the Military Demarcation Line to divide the country and cut the national ties forever at the dictates of the US imperialists.

The wall is in fact an anti-tank barrier which has been there for many years and attracted no attention whatsoever from the North until around 1990 when the Berlin Wall was torn down. Suddenly, the North realised the propaganda potential, and the 'Korean Wall' was added as one of the compulsory stops for

foreign tour groups. You'll be able to view the wall through telescopes from four km away. You'll then be taken into a room and be shown a video and given a lecture on the burning desire of the Korean people for reunification. All very gripping stuff.

KUMGANGSAN

South of Wonsan on the east coast, Kumgangsan (the Diamond Mountains) are the North Korean equivalent of the South's Soraksan and Odaesan mountains – an area of outstanding natural beauty. It's also the place where Kim Il-sung is believed to maintain large concentration camps for political prisoners, but don't expect to be shown these as part of your tour.

The usual route to Kumgangsan is by car from Pyongyang to Onjong-ri via Wonsan along the new highway (around 315 km or four hours in all). The first part of the journey to Wonsan can also be done by train, though it's not so interesting doing it this way.

Going by car, you stop off at a teahouse at Sinpyong Lake – a very attractive area and a centre of honey production. The new road is quite spectacular and involves passing through 18 tunnels between Sinpyong and Wonsan, the longest of which is some 4½ km long. The port city of Wonsan itself was shelled to rubble in the Korean War, so it's an entirely modern town with a seven-lane boulevard leading down to the waterfront. Tourists are taken to the class C *Songdowon Hotel* and the adjoining Kumgang Restaurant.

From Wonsan, the road more or less follows the coastline, and you'll get glimpses of the double electric fence which runs the entire length of the east coast – like its counterpart in South Korea. They'll be an obligatory stop for tea at Sijung Lake. Your final destination is the village of Onjong-ri and the *Kumgangsan Hotel*, rated class 'B'. The hotel is quite a rambling affair consisting of a main building and several outer buildings which include chalets, a shop, dance hall and bath-house (fed by a hot spring). The village itself, 15 minutes' walk from the hotel, is worthy of a guide-less visit and consists of a cluster of traditional Korean houses and small front plots crammed with vegetables.

Much like Soraksan in the South, Kumgangsan is divided into Inner, Outer and Sea Kumgang, and the main activities here are hiking, mountaineering, boating and sightseeing. The area is peppered with former Buddhist temples and hermitages, waterfalls, mineral springs, a lake (Samil Lake) and museum. It's up to you how long you spend here and what you do, but maps of the area are provided to help you decide where you want to go.

Two of the most popular excursions are to **Kuryong Falls** and **Samil Lake**. The Falls are a 15-minute drive from the hotel via Onjong-ri along an unsurfaced road through conifer forest to the Mongran Restaurant. The restaurant is hemmed in by steep rock faces and its balcony overlooks the waters of the river which flows down from the Falls. It's a pleasant place to eat lunch. From the restaurant it's a 4½ km walk along footpaths, over rocks and across suspension bridges to the Falls. Your guide will regale you with legends about the area and stories behind the rocks which supposedly resemble animals such as elephants, frogs, turtles, fried dumplings, etc. At the Falls, which are some 70 metres high, there's a viewing platform. It's a very attractive area and popular with artists (many of the paintings you see in Korea were inspired by the views in the area).

Samil Lake is located in an area of conifer forests and was once connected to the sea, and although you can see the ocean from here you're not permitted to go to the seashore at this point. Boats are available for hire at the lake, and for meals there's the Danpung Restaurant on the lakeside.

PAEKDUSAN

The highest mountain in the whole of Korea at 2750 metres, Paekdusan (Mt Paekdu) sits astride the Korean/Chinese border in the far north. It's a sacred spot to both South and North Koreans – according to Korean mythology, this is where the Korean race

began. The story goes that Hwanung (son of the lord of heaven) descended from heaven and met a bear and a tiger. He offered them a chance to become human, but first they had to pass a test – they had to stay in a cave all winter and eat only garlic. The tiger failed the test, but the bear succeeded and emerged from the cave as a beautiful woman. She mated with Hwanung and produced Tangun, the progenitor and first king of the Korean race.

It should be no mystery then why Kim Il-sung claims that his son was born here, even though all sources outside North Korea maintain that Kim Jong-il was born in the Soviet city of Khabarovsk.

North Korea's current history books also claim that Kim Il-sung established his headquarters at Mt Paekdu from where he defeated the Japanese. To prove this, you'll be shown revolutionary slogans which the Great Leader himself carved on the trees. You'll be told that more and more of these carvings are being discovered every year, and some are so well-preserved you'd almost think they were carved yesterday if you didn't know better. A North Korean pamphlet explains:

Slogan-bearing trees, relics and remains in the period of the anti-Japanese revolutionary struggle organised and led by the great leader Comrade Kim Il-sung are recently being discovered in various parts of the country...During the anti-Japanese revolutionary struggle the great leader Comrade Kim Il-sung set up more than ten districts of secret camps in the primitive forests of Mt Paekdu and led to victory the Korean revolution as a whole centered on the anti-Japanese armed struggle.

Kim Jong-il never got anywhere near WW II nor was Korea's highest mountain ever a battlefield. Nevertheless, the North Korean book *Kim Jong-il In His Young Days* describes the Dear Leader's difficult childhood during the nonexistent battles at Mt Paekdu:

His childhood was replete with ordeals.

The secret camp of the Korean People's Revolutionary Army in the primeval forest was his home, and ammunition belts and magazines were his playthings.

The raging blizzards and ceaseless gunshots were the first sounds to which he became accustomed.

Day in and day out fierce battles went on and, during the breaks, there were military and political trainings. On the battlefield, there was no quilt to warmly wrap the new-born child. So women guerrillas gallantly tore cotton out of their own uniforms and each contributed pieces of cloth to make a patchwork quilt for the infant.

On top of the now-extinct volcano is a crater lake (Lake Chon) which is some 14 km in circumference and reaches a maximum depth of 380 metres. This whole area is only accessible from around late June to mid-September. Access to Paekdusan is by air or train followed by car.

Hotels to stay at in this area include the *Hyesan Hotel*, in the town of the same name, the *Samjiyon Sin Hotel*, some 67 km from Hyesan, and the *Onsupyong Hotel*. The first two are 'B' class hotels whilst the latter is a 'C' class hotel.

You can also visit the mountain and crater lake from the Chinese side – a trip that's popular with South Korean tourists. Paekdusan is called Changbaishan in Chinese and the crater lake is named Tianchi (Lake of Heaven).

Macau

Sixty km west of Hong Kong, on the other side of the Pearl River's mouth, is the oldest European settlement in the East – the tiny Portuguese territory of Macau. The lure of Macau's casino gaming tables has been so actively promoted that its other attractions are almost forgotten. It's actually one of the most fascinating places in Asia – steeped in history and, with a little effort, reasonably cheap and comfortable. If you're in Hong Kong, don't miss Macau.

Facts about the Country

HISTORY

Macau has a far longer history than its younger and brasher sister Hong Kong – and it certainly shows. Portuguese galleons were dropping by here in the early 1500s, and in 1557, as a reward for clearing out a few pirates, China ceded the tiny enclave to the Portuguese. For centuries it was the principal meeting point for trade with China – a look around the intriguing old Protestant Cemetery will show just how international this trade was. In the 19th century European and American traders could operate in Canton, up the Pearl River, only during the trading season and would then retreat to Macau during the off season.

When the Opium Wars erupted between the Chinese and the aggressive (and somewhat unprincipled) British, the Portuguese stood diplomatically to one side and Macau soon found itself the poor relation of the more dynamic city of Hong Kong. More recently Macau's existence has depended on the Chinese gambling urge that every weekend sends hordes of Hong Kong's more affluent citizens shuttling off to the casinos. Today, however, Macau does very well as an overflow valve for booming Hong Kong with many thriving industries and an important role as a doorway to the People's Republic.

During the Cultural Revolution Macau suffered more than Hong Kong, virtually capitulating to Chinese management. Later, while the heavy negotiations went on over Hong Kong, the Macau situation was very much on the back burner. With Hong Kong sorted out the Chinese soon turned their attention to Macau, which will be handed back in 1999, two years after Hong Kong. It's said the Portuguese wanted to last out 500 years, which would have taken them well into the next century. They finally settled for any date which put them one up on Hong Kong!

GEOGRAPHY

Macau's 16 sq km consists of the city itself, which is part of the Chinese mainland, and the islands of Taipa and Coloane, which are joined together by a causeway and linked to Macau city by a bridge.

CLIMATE

The weather is almost identical to that of Hong Kong, with short, occasionally chilly

Macau Temperatures & Rainfall											
	Jan	Feb	Mar	Apr	May	Jun	Jul	Aug	Sep	Oct	Nov	Dec
Temp (°C)	14.5	14.9	18	21.9	25.8	27.5	28.5	28.2	27.2	24.5	20.5	16.3
Rain (mm)	30	57	73	174	335	362	240	326	235	107	36	24

winters, and long, hot and humid summers. November is usually the best month, with mild temperatures and dry weather. Typhoons are most common from June to October.

GOVERNMENT

Officially, Macau is not considered a colony. Instead, the Portuguese government regards Macau as a piece of Chinese territory under Portuguese administration. The colony/Chinese territory has a governor who is appointed by the president of Portugal, but in theory the main governing body is the 23-member Legislative Assembly of which eight members are elected by direct vote, while the remainder are appointed by the Governor and 'economic interest groups'.

ECONOMY

The spin of the wheel and the toss of the dice still play an important part in Macau's economy, but there's also a variety of local industries including textiles and toys. Macau is currently building an airport and deepwater port which are expected to give the economy a major boost.

POPULATION & PEOPLE

Macau has about half a million people. About 95% are Chinese, 3% are Portuguese and there is a sprinkling of other Western nationalities. Nearly 1% of the population is from Thailand, mostly female and employed in what is loosely called the 'entertainment industry'.

ARTS

Chinese art is covered in the Hong Kong and China sections of this book. As for the Portuguese, their art is most apparent in the old churches and cathedrals which grace Macau's skyline. It's here that you'll see some fine examples of painting, stained-glass windows and sculpture.

CULTURE

The Chinese population – 95% of the total – is culturally indistinguishable from that of Hong Kong. See the Hong Kong chapter of this book for details.

Of course, the Portuguese minority has a vastly different culture, which they have kept largely intact. Although mixed marriages are not uncommon in Macau, there has been surprisingly little cultural assimilation between the two ethnic groups – most Portuguese cannot speak Chinese and vice versa.

RELIGION

For the Chinese majority, Taoism and Buddhism are the dominant religions. However, nearly 500 years of Portuguese influence have definitely left an imprint, and the Catholic church is very strong in Macau. Many Chinese have been converted and you are likely to see Chinese nuns.

LANGUAGE

Portuguese is the official language and Cantonese the real one, but you will have little trouble communicating with English, in hotels at least. Mandarin Chinese (putonghua) is also very common. See the Hong Kong chapter for a few Cantonese phrases. Here are a few in Portuguese.

How much does this cost?
  Quanto custa isso?
Too expensive.
  Caro demais.
The bill, please.
  A conta por favor.
Leave me alone!
  Me deixa em paz!

Facts for the Visitor

VISAS & EMBASSIES

For most visitors, all that's needed to enter Macau is a passport. Everyone gets a 20-day stay on arrival. Visas are not required for nationals of the following countries: Australia, Austria, Belgium, Brazil, Canada, Denmark, France, Germany, Greece, Hong Kong, Ireland, Italy, Japan, Luxemburg, Malaysia, Netherlands, New Zealand,

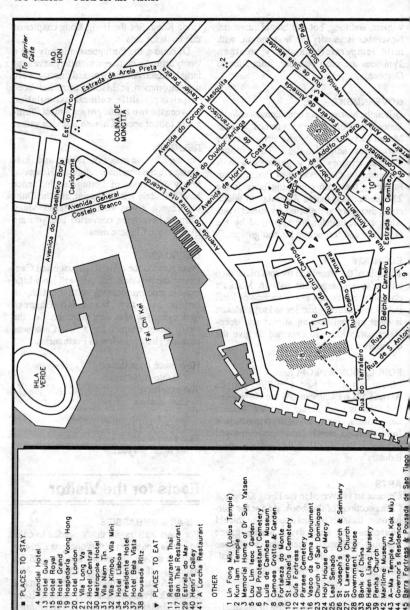

PLACES TO STAY

- 4 Mondial Hotel
- 13 Hotel Guia
- 15 Hotel Royal
- 18 Hotel Grand
- 19 Hospedaria Vong Hong
- 20 Hotel London
- 21 Vila Long Va
- 22 Hotel Central
- 30 Metropole Hotel
- 31 Vila Nam Tin
- 32 Vila Kimbo, Vila Mini
- 34 Hotel Lisboa
- 35 Presidente Hotel
- 37 Hotel Bela Vista
- 38 Pousada Ritz

▼ PLACES TO EAT

- 11 Restaurante Thai
- 17 Ban Thai Restaurant
- 29 Estrela do Mar
- 40 Henri's Galley
- 41 A Lorcha Restaurant

OTHER

- 1 Lin Fong Miu (Lotus Temple)
- 2 Kun Iam Temple
- 3 Memorial Home of Dr Sun Yatsen
- 5 Lou Lim Ieoc Garden
- 6 Old Protestant Cemetery
- 7 Luis de Camões Museum
- 8 Camoes Grotto & Garden
- 9 Fortaleza do Monte
- 10 St Michael's Cemetery
- 12 Guía Fortress
- 14 Parsee Cemetery
- 16 Vasco da Gama Monument
- 23 Church of San Domingos
- 24 Holy House of Mercy
- 25 Leal Senado
- 26 St Joseph's Church & Seminary
- 27 St Lawrence Church
- 28 Government House
- 33 Bank of China
- 36 Helen Liang Nursery
- 39 Penha Church
- 42 Maritime Museum
- 43 A-Ma Temple (Ma Kok Miu)
- 44 Governor's Residence
- 45 Barra Fortress & Pousada de Sao Tiago

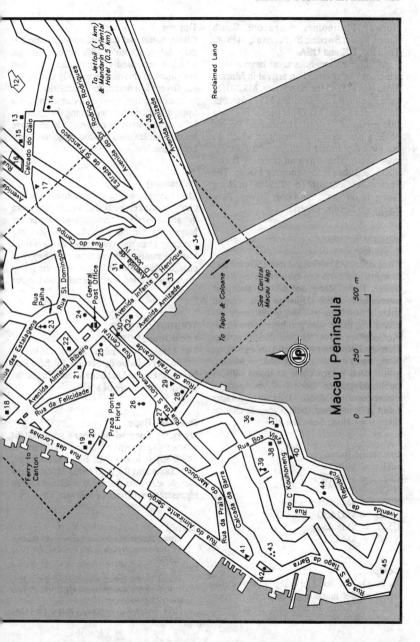

Macau Peninsula

To Jetfoil (1 km)
& Mandarin Oriental
Hotel (0.5 km)

Reclaimed Land

See Central
Macau Map

To Taipa & Coloane

0   250   500 m

Ferry to
Canton

Rua do Almirante Sérgio
Rua do Manduco
Calçada da Barra
Rua da Praia da Barra
Rua das Lorchas
Rua da Felicidade
Avenida Almeida Ribeiro
Rua das Estalagens
Rua Palha
Rua St Domingos
Rua Central
Rua da Praia Grande
Rua S Lourenço
Rua Boa Vista
Rua do C Kouhoheng
Avenida da Republica
Rua de S Tiago da Barra
Calçado do Gaio
Estrada de St Francisco
Avenida Rodrigo Rodrigues
Avenida Amizade
Avenida Infante D Henrique
Avenida do Campo
Praça Ponte E Horta
General Post Office

Norway, Philippines, Singapore, South Korea, Spain, Sweden, Switzerland, Taiwan, Thailand, UK and USA.

All other nationalities must have a visa, which can be obtained on arrival in Macau. Visas cost M$145 for individuals, M$290 for married couples and families, M$72 for children under 12 and M$72 per person in a bona fide group of at least 10 persons. People holding passports from countries which do not have diplomatic relations with Portugal must obtain visas from an overseas Portuguese consulate before entering Macau. The Portuguese Consulate (☎ 5225488) in Hong Kong is on the 10th floor, Tower Two, Exchange Square, Central.

MONEY
Currency
The pataca (M$) is divided into 100 avos and is worth about 3% less than the Hong Kong dollar. Hong Kong dollars are accepted everywhere, which is just as well because there's nowhere to change currency on arrival. So make sure you have some Hong Kong dollars or you'll have difficulty getting from the Jetfoil Pier to town! Although Hong Kong coins are quite acceptable in Macau, you'll need pataca coins to make calls at public telephones. Get rid of your patacas before departing Macau – they are hard to get rid of in Hong Kong, though you can change them at the Hang Seng Bank.

Exchange Rates
A$1   = $M6.35
C$1   = $M7.10
HK$1   = $M1.05
NZ$1   = $M4.50
UK£1   = $M14.30
US$1   = $M8.05
Y100   = $M6.21

Costs
As long as you don't go crazy at the roulette wheel or slot machines, Macau is cheaper than Hong Kong. To help keep costs down, avoid weekends.

Tipping
Classy hotels and restaurants will automatically hit you with a 10% service charge, which is supposedly a mandatory tip. Just how much of this money actually goes to the employees is a matter for speculation.

You can follow your own conscience, but tipping is not customary among the Chinese. Of course, porters at expensive hotels have become accustomed to hand-outs from well-heeled tourists.

Bargaining
Most stores have fixed prices, but if you buy clothing, trinkets and other tourist junk from the street markets, there is some scope for bargaining. On the other hand, if you buy anything from the pawnshops, bargain ruthlessly. Pawnbrokers are more than happy to charge Western tourists five times the going price for second-hand cameras and other goods.

TOURIST OFFICES
Local Tourist Offices
The Macau Government Tourist Office (☎ 315566) is at Largo do Senado, Edificio Ritz No 9, next to the Leal Senado building in the square in the centre of Macau.

Overseas Reps
On Hong Kong Island there's an excellent Macau Government Tourist Office (☎ 5408180) at Room 305, Shun Tak Centre, 200 Connaught Rd, next to the Macau Ferry Pier. Macau also maintains overseas tourist representative offices as follows:

Australia
    Macau Tourist Information Bureau, 449 Darling St, Balmain, Sydney, NSW 2041 (☎ (02) 5557548)
Canada
    Macau Tourist Information Bureau, Suite 305, 1530 West 8th Ave, Vancouver, BC V6J 1T5 (☎ (604) 7361095
    5059 Yonge St, Toronto, Ontario (☎ (416) 7338768)

Japan
> Macau Tourist Information Bureau, 4th floor, Toho Twin Tower Building, 5-2 Yurakucho 1-chome, Chiyoda-ku, Tokyo 100 (☎ (03) 35015022)

Singapore
> Macau Tourist Information Bureau, 11-01A PIL Building, 140 Cecil St, Singapore 0106 (☎ 2250022)

Thailand
> Macau Tourist Information Bureau, 150/5 Sukhumvit 20, Bangkok 10110, or GPO Box 1534, Bangkok 10501 (☎ 2581975)

UK
> Macau Tourist Information Bureau, 6 Sherlock Mews, Paddington St, London W1M 3RH (☎ (071) 2243390)

USA
> Macau Tourist Information Bureau, 3133 Lake Hollywood Drive, Los Angeles, CA, or PO Box 1860, Los Angeles, CA 90078 (☎ (213) 8513684, (800) 3317150)
>
> Suite 316, 70A Greenwich Ave, New York, NY 10011 (☎ (212) 2066828)
>
> 630 Green Bay Rd, PO Box 350, Kenilworth, IL 60043-0350 (☎ (708) 2516421)
>
> PO Box 22188, Honolulu, HI 96922 (☎ (808) 5887613)

BUSINESS HOURS & HOLIDAYS

The operating hours for most government offices in Macau are weekdays from 8.40 am to 1 pm and 3 to 5 pm, and Saturday from 8.40 am to 1 pm. Private businesses keep longer hours and some casinos are open 24 hours a day.

Banks are normally open on weekdays from 9 am to 4 pm, and on Saturdays from 9 am until noon.

Macau's main festival time is November when the Grand Prix is held – not a good time to go unless you're a racing fan, as the place is packed and prices skyrocket. As in Monte Carlo and Adelaide, the actual streets of the town make up the raceway. There are in fact two races, one for cars and one for motorcycles, plus various support races, and the six km circuit attracts contestants from all over the world.

CULTURAL EVENTS

Find out about cultural events, concerts, art exhibitions and other such activities from the tourist newspaper *Macau Travel Talk*. Free copies are available from the tourist office.

The Chinese in Macau celebrate the same religious festivals as their counterparts in Hong Kong but there are also a number of Catholic festivals and some Portuguese national holidays. Most important is the *Feast of Our Lady of Fatima* when the Fatima image is removed from São Domingos (St Dominic's) Church and taken in procession around the city.

The Dragon Boat Festival is a Chinese holiday well known for its exciting dragon boat races. Similar races are held in Hong Kong and Taiwan. The Dragon Boat Festival is scheduled according to the lunar calendar, but usually falls sometime during June.

The Miss Macau Contest is held every August. Whether this a cultural or an anti-cultural event depends on one's point of view.

The International Music Festival is held during the third week of October.

POST & TELECOMMUNICATIONS
Postal Rates

Domestic letters cost M$0.80 for up to 20 grams. As for international mail, Macau divides the world into zones. Zone 1 is east Asia, including Korea, Taiwan, etc. Zone 2 is everything else. There are special rates for China and Portugal.

Grams	Postal Rates from Macau			
	China	Portugal	Zone 1	Zone 2
10	1.70	3.00	3.50	4.20
20	2.70	4.70	4.80	6.10
30	3.70	6.40	6.10	8.00
40	4.70	8.10	7.40	9.90
50	5.70	9.80	8.70	11.80
Aero-grams	1.30	1.90	2.50	3.20

Sending & Receiving Mail

The GPO on Leal Senado is open from 9 am to 8 pm, Monday to Saturday. It has an efficient poste restante service and English-speaking postal clerks. Large hotels like the Lisboa also sell stamps.

Telephone

Companhia de Telecomunicacões (CTM) runs the Macau telephone system, and for the most part service is good. However, public pay phones can be hard to find, being mostly concentrated around the Leal Senado. Most large hotels have one in the lobby, but this is often insufficient and you may have to stand in line to use one. However, once you find a phone it generally works OK.

Local calls are free from a private or hotel telephone. At a public pay phone, local calls cost M$1 for five minutes. All pay phones permit international direct dialling (IDD). The procedure for dialling to Hong Kong is totally different to all other countries. You first dial 01 and then the number you want to call – you must *not* dial the country code.

The international access code for every country *except* Hong Kong is 00. To call into Macau from abroad, the country code is 853.

Telephone cards from CTM are sold in denominations of M$50, M$100 and M$200. Phones which accept these cards are numerous around Leal Senado, the Jetfoil Pier and at a few large hotels. You can also make a call from the telephone office at Leal Senado, next to the GPO. Leave a deposit with a clerk and they will dial the number for you. When your call is completed the clerk deducts the cost from the deposit and refunds the balance. The clerks speak English and the office is open 24 hours.

Fax, Telex & Telegraph

Unless you're staying at a hotel that has its own fax, the easiest way to send and receive faxes is at the GPO (not the telephone office) on Leal Senado.

Telex messages are sent from the telephone office next to the GPO. The telephone office also handles cables (telegrams).

TIME

Like Hong Kong, Macau is eight hours ahead of Greenwich Mean Time and does not observe daylight-saving time.

When it is noon in Macau it is also noon in Singapore, Hong Kong and Perth; 2 pm in Sydney; 8 pm the previous day in Los Angeles; 11 pm the previous day in New York; and 4 am in London.

WEIGHTS & MEASURES

Macau subscribes to the international metric system. As in Hong Kong, street markets and medicine shops sell things by the *leung* (37.5 grams) and the *catty* (600 grams).

ELECTRICITY

Macau's electricity system is the same as in Hong Kong and China – 220 V AC, 50 Hz. The electric outlets are the same as Hong Kong's and accept three round pins. There are still one or two old buildings wired for 110 V, but as long as you see three round holes on the outlets you can be assured it's 220 V.

BOOKS & MAPS

Hong Kong, Macau & Canton from Lonely Planet has a section on Macau with much more information. There are various books on Macau you can find in Hong Kong (try Wanderlust Books, 30 Hollywood Rd, Central) or the Macau Government Tourist Office on Leal Senado in Macau. The Tourist Office also publishes the useful little *Macau Guide Book*.

Books About Portugal has a good selection of books in English as well as Portuguese. It's on Rua Nolasco da Silva near the Cathedral.

MEDIA

Newspapers & Magazines

There is a monthly tourist newspaper, *Macau Travel Talk*, but otherwise there is no English-language newspaper published in Macau. However, both the *South China Morning Post* and *Hong Kong Standard* are readily available from big hotels and some bookshops. It's also easy to buy foreign news magazines.

Radio & TV

Macau has three radio stations, two of which

broadcast in Cantonese and one in Portuguese. There are no local English-language radio stations, but you should be able to pick up Hong Kong stations.

Teledifusão de Macau (TdM) is a government-run station which broadcasts on two channels. Shows are mainly in English and Portuguese, but with some Cantonese programmes. It's easy to pick up Hong Kong stations in Macau (but not vice versa) and you can also receive stations from China. Hong Kong newspapers list Macau TV programmes.

FILM & PHOTOGRAPHY

You can find most types of film, cameras and accessories in Macau, and photoprocessing is of a high standard. The best store in town for all photographic services is *Foto Princesa* (☎ 555959), 55-59 Avenida Infante D Henrique, one block east of Rua da Praia Grande. This is also the best place to get quickie visa photos.

HEALTH

The water is purified and chlorinated and is probably OK to drink. Nevertheless, the Chinese always boil it (more out of custom than necessity). Hotel rooms are always supplied with a thermos filled with hot water.

The emergency telephone number for ambulance (and for fire and police) is 999.

Treatment is available at the government-run Centro Hospital (☎ 514499, 313731), on Estrada São Francisco.

WOMEN TRAVELLERS

Wearing a skimpy bikini at the beach will elicit some stares, but travel in Macau is as safe for women as in any Western country.

DANGERS & ANNOYANCES

In terms of violent crime, Macau is pretty safe, but residential burglaries and pick-pocketing are problems. Most hotels are well guarded, and reasonable care with your valuables should be sufficient to avoid trouble.

Traffic is heavy and quite a few tourists have been hit while jaywalking. Macau police have been cracking down on this, and

though they go light with foreigners, you can still get fined. Be especially careful at rush hour when the traffic (and the police) come out in force.

Cheating at gambling is a serious criminal offence, so don't even think about it.

WORK

Unless you hold a Portuguese passport, you can pretty much forget it. Most Portuguese speak excellent English, so there is little need to import foreign English teachers. Most of the foreigners employed in Macau are Thai prostitutes and Filipino musicians. Unskilled labour is supplied by Chinese workers who are paid a pittance.

ACTIVITIES

Windsurfing is possible at Hac Sa Beach on Coloane Island, and equipment is readily available for rent. There are two good swimming beaches on Coloane, Hac Sa and Cheoc Van. Cheoc Van Beach also has a yacht club.

Bicycles are available for hire on the two islands of Taipa and Coloane.

HIGHLIGHTS

Although gambling is what draws most people to Macau, the fine colonial architecture is what makes this place unique. Highlights include the ruins of São Paulo, Fortaleza do Monte, Guía Fortress, Leal Senado and the Penha Church. St Michael's Cemetery is a fascinating place to walk through, and many visitors are impressed by A-Ma Temple (Ma Kok Miu). Taipa Village on Taipa Island is unique, and there is no better way to round off a trip to Macau than a fine meal at a Portuguese restaurant.

ACCOMMODATION

Weekends are a bad time to come to Macau; try to make your trip on a weekday. During the quieter midweek time it's worth bargaining a little.

The cheapest hotels in Macau are mostly clustered near the Floating Casino. There are also several cheap and cheapish hotels between the Hotel Lisboa and Rua da Praia Grande, a somewhat nicer part of town.

Finding them is easy as all the hotels have signs. Cheap hotels usually call themselves *vila*, but sometimes they are called *hospedaria* or *pensão*.

The key to finding a good, cheap room is patience. If one place waves you off or charges too much, then try another. As long as you haven't arrived on a weekend, you should find something acceptable in half an hour or so.

FOOD

A long, lazy Portuguese meal with a carafe of red to keep it company is one of the most pleasant parts of a Macau visit. The menus are often in Portuguese so a few useful words are *cozido* – stew, *cabrito* – kid, *cordeiro* – lamb, *carreiro* – mutton, *galinha* – chicken, *caraguejos* – crabs, *carne de vaca* – beef, *peixe* – fish. Apart from carafe wine you can also get Mateus Rosé, the best known of Portuguese wines. Another Macau pleasure is to sit back in one of the many little cake shops *(pastelarias)* with a glass of *cha de limão* (lemon tea) and a plate of cakes – very genteel! These places are good for a cheap breakfast too. People eat early in Macau; you can find the chairs being put away and the chef gone home at 9 pm.

DRINKS

For economy-minded wine lovers Macau is the best bargain in this book. At one of the cheaper Portuguese restaurants like the Estrela do Mar you can get a bottle of wine for M$30 to M$40 (Mateus Rosé is M$36). The more expensive Solmar has bottles for around M$55. You can bring a litre of wine or spirits back to Hong Kong, where it's more expensive. Beer in Macau is typically M$10 in restaurants.

THINGS TO BUY

Pawnshops are ubiquitous in Macau, and it is possible to get good deals on cameras, but you must be prepared to bargain without mercy.

The Macau Government Tourist Office has T-shirts for sale at the bargain price of M$25. They also sell a set of poster-size 'antique maps of Macau' (M$150), a set of postcards (M$5), umbrella (M$30) and raincoat (M$35).

The São Domingo Market is in the alley just behind the Hotel Central and next to the Macau Government Tourist Office. It's a good place to pick up cheap clothing.

Getting There & Away

LAND

Macau is an important gateway into China. You simply take a bus to the border and walk across. Bus No 3 runs between the Jetfoil Pier and the Barrier Gate at the Macau-China border. You can also catch a bus directly from Macau to Canton. Tickets are sold at Kee Kwan Motors, across the street from the Floating Casino.

SEA

To/From Hong Kong

Although Macau is separated from Hong Kong by 65 km of water, the journey can be made in as little as one hour. There is a variety of sea vessels plying this route, the fastest, smoothest and most popular being the jetfoils and jumbocats. There are frequent departures throughout the day from 7 am to 9.30 pm.

You have a wide selection of boats to choose from. There are jetfoils, hoverferries, jetcats (jet-powered catamaran), jumbocats (large jetcat) and high-speed ferries. There are still two old hydrofoils plying this route, but they are to be retired soon and will probably be out of service by the time you read this.

Most of the boats depart from the huge Macau Ferry Terminal next to Shun Tak Centre at 200 Connaught Rd, Sheung Wan, Hong Kong Island. This is easily reached by MTR to the Sheung Wan Station.

Hoverferries depart from the China Hong Kong City ferry pier in Tsimshatsui. However, these are far less numerous than jetfoils, so if you can't get a seat, go to Shun Tak Centre on Hong Kong Island.

If you have to return to Hong Kong the same day as departure, you'd be wise to book your return ticket in advance because the boats are sometimes full, especially on weekends and holidays. Even Monday mornings can be difficult for getting seats back to Hong Kong. If you can't get on the jetfoil, you might have a chance with the high-speed ferries which have a lot more room.

Jetfoil tickets can be purchased up to 28 days in advance in Hong Kong at the pier and at Ticketmate offices in some MTR stations, or booked by phone (☎ 8595696) if you have a credit card. Jumbocat bookings (☎ 5232136) can be made 35 days in advance by telephone if you pay with plastic. If you buy a ticket at any other place than the pier, be certain you understand which pier the boat departs from. You need to arrive at the pier at least 15 minutes before departure, but from our experience you'd be wise to allow 30 minutes because of occasional long queues at the immigration checkpoint.

There are different classes on the jetfoils and high-speed ferries. All other boats have only one class. The Hong Kong Government charges HK$20 departure tax which is included in the price of your ticket. There is no such tax when leaving Macau. The prices in the table do not include the tax.

In Hong Kong, tickets can be bought at the pier and at Ticketmate kiosks in the Tsimshatsui and Jordan Rd MTR Stations.

In Macau, you can book tickets on all boats at the Jetfoil Pier. You can also book tickets on the jetfoil and high-speed ferry right in the lobby of the Hotel Lisboa. A couple of blocks west of the Hotel Central is a window for booking tickets on the jumbocats. Tickets for the hoverferry can only be booked at the Jetfoil Pier.

To/From China

The daily Macau-Canton ferry leaves Canton from Zhoutouzui Pier south of the White Swan Hotel. From Macau, it departs from the terminus next to the Floating Casino at 8 pm and arrives in Canton at 7.15 am the next day.

Fares range from M$69 in 2nd class, for rooms with six to 22 beds, to M$100 in 1st class for a bed in a room with four beds, a shower and TV. Finally there's also special class, which costs M$147 for a cabin with just two beds, as well as a TV and shower.

To/From Taiwan

A ferry runs between Macau and the port of Kaohsiung in Taiwan. The name of the ship is the *Macmosa*.

From Taiwan, one-way 1st-class tickets cost NT$3700, and 2nd class is NT$3000. From Macau, a one-way 1st-class fare is M$1060; 2nd class is M$860. Round-trip fares are exactly double. There is one boat weekly during the winter, but at least twice weekly during the summer months. The journey takes 24 hours. In winter, the ship leaves Kaohsiung at 4 pm on Wednesday. Departures from Macau are at 2 am on Tuesday. Check departure times – they can change.

In Taiwan, you can buy tickets at the pier

Ferries between Macau & Hong Kong				
Vessel	*Travel Time*	*Weekday*	*Weekend*	*Night*
High-Speed Ferry	90 minutes	HK$48/62	HK$60/74	
Hoverferry	80 minutes	HK$60	HK$73	HK$86
Hydrofoil	75 minutes	HK$68	HK$75	
Jetcat	75 minutes	HK$68	HK$75	
Jetfoil	60 minutes	HK$72/82	HK$78/88	HK$95/108
Jumbocat	60 minutes	HK$78	HK$85	

in Kaohsiung or from Kwanghwa Tour & Travel Service in both Taipei and Kaohsiung. The Taipei office (☎ (02) 5310000) is on the 7th floor, 72 Sungchiang Rd. The Kaohsiung ticket office (☎ (07) 2821166) is on the 6th floor, 79 Chunghua 3rd Rd. In Kaohsiung, the boat departs from Pier 1 (*dìyī mǎtoú*) on Penglai Rd – take bus No 1 or a taxi to get there. In Macau tickets are most easily purchased at the Jetfoil Pier. In Hong Kong, you can buy tickets at Kwanghwa Tour & Travel Service (☎ 5457071), Room 803, Kai Tak Commercial Building, 317-321 Des Voeux Rd, Central, Hong Kong Island. Taiwan charges a departure tax of NT$200. Macau has no departure tax.

Getting Around

Macau is fairly compact and it's relatively easy to walk almost everywhere, but you'll definitely need motorised transport to visit the islands of Taipa and Coloane. The pedicabs are essentially for touristy sightseeing. They have to be bargained for and it's hardly worth the effort – if there are two of you make sure the fare covers both.

BUS

There are minibuses and large buses, and both offer air-conditioning and frequent service. They operate from 7 am until midnight.

You'll find it easier to deal with the bus system if you buy a good map of Macau showing all the routes. For most tourists, bus No 3A is the most important since it connects the Jetfoil Pier to the central area (Leal Senado), Floating Casino, then turns south and terminates at Ponte Praca e Horta. The fare is M$1.50.

Another very useful bus is No 3 which starts at the Jetfoil Pier, goes into the city centre past Leal Senado, then turns north at the Floating Casino and heads north, terminating at the China border. If you're going to or coming from China, this is the bus to take. The fare is M$1.50.

The buses to the islands are as follows:

No 11 Praça Ponte E Horta, Floating Casino, Avenida Almeida Ribeiro, GPO, Hotel Lisboa, Hotel Hyatt Regency (Taipa), Taipa Village, Macau Jockey Club. Fare: M$1.60

No 21 Praça Ponte E Horta, Floating Casino, Avenida Almeida Ribeiro, GPO, Hotel Lisboa, Hotel Hyatt Regency (Taipa), Restaurante 1999 (Coloane), Coloane Village. Fare: M$2.30

No 21A Praça Ponte E Horta, Floating Casino, Avenida Almeida Ribeiro, GPO, Hotel Lisboa, Hotel Hyatt Regency (Taipa), Taipa Village, Restaurante 1999 (Coloane), Coloane Village, Cheoc Van Beach, Hac Sa Beach. Fare: M$3

No 28A Jetfoil Pier, Hotel Lisboa, Hotel Hyatt Regency (Taipa), Macau University, Taipa Village, Macau Jockey Club. Fare: M$2

No 33 Fai Chi Kei, Lin Fong Miu (Lotus Temple), Avenida Almeida Ribeiro, Hotel Lisboa, Hotel Hyatt Regency (Taipa), Macau University, Taipa Village, Macau Jockey Club. Fare: M$2

No 38 Special bus running from the city centre to the Macau Jockey Club one hour before the races. Fare: M$3

TAXI

Macau taxis are black with cream roofs. They all have meters and drivers are required to use them. Flagfall is M$5.50 for the first 1.5 km, thereafter it's 70 avos every 250 metres. There is a M$5 surcharge to go to Taipa, and M$10 to go to Coloane, but there is no surcharge if you're heading the other way back to Macau. There is also an additional M$1 service charge for each piece of luggage carried in the boot (trunk). Not many taxi drivers speak English, so it would be helpful to have a map with both Chinese and English or Portuguese.

CAR

The mere thought of renting a car in Hong Kong is ridiculous but between a group it might make sense for exploring on Taipa and Coloane. On the Macau peninsula, the horrendous traffic and the lack of parking space make driving more of a burden than a pleasure.

As in Hong Kong, driving is on the left side of the road. Another local driving rule is that motor vehicles must always stop for pedestrians at a crosswalk if there is no traffic light. It's illegal to beep the horn.

Macau Mokes (☎ 378851) is Macau's rent-a-car pioneer. They are on Avenida Marciano Baptist, just across from the Jetfoil Terminal in Macau. There is also a Hong Kong office (☎ 5434190) at 806 Kai Tak Commercial Building, 317-321 Des Voeux Rd, Sheung Wan, near the Macau Ferry Terminal on Hong Kong Island. A moke costs M$280 on weekdays and M$320 on weekends and holidays.

BICYCLE

You can hire bicycles out on the islands of Taipa and Coloane. On the peninsula, there are no places to hire bikes, and it wouldn't be pleasant riding anyway with the insane traffic.

TOURS

A typical city tour (booked in Macau) of the peninsula takes three to four hours and costs about M$70 per person, often including lunch. Bus tours out to the islands run from about M$20 per person. You can also book a one-day bus tour across the border into Zhuhai in China, which usually includes a trip to the former home of Dr Sun Yatsen in Zhongshan County. There are large numbers of tour operators.

Around the Country

MAINLAND MACAU

There's far more of historical interest to be seen in Macau than Hong Kong. Simply wandering around is a delight – the streets are winding and always full of interest. Old hands say it's now getting speedy like Hong Kong – it has a way to go.

The **Ruins of São Paulo** (St Paul's) are the symbol of Macau – the facade and majestic stairway are all that remain of this old church, considered by many to be the greatest monument to Christianity in the East. It was designed by an Italian Jesuit and built in 1602 by Japanese refugees who had fled

anti-Christian persecution in Nagasaki. In 1853 the church was totally burned down during a catastrophic typhoon – the light from the burning church on its hilltop site lit the way for people escaping from the typhoon floods. *Macau Guide Book* has an description of the stone carvings on the facade.

The **Fortaleza do Monte** overlooks São Paulo and almost all of Macau from its high and central position. It was built by the Jesuits at about the same time as São Paulo, but the governor of Macau took it over by the neat trick of coming to dinner and at the close of the meal announcing he was going to stay and his hosts could depart. In 1622 a cannonball fired from the fort conveniently landed in a Dutch gunpowder carrier during an attempted Dutch invasion, demolishing most of their fleet.

The most historic and interesting temple in the city, the **Temple of Kun Iam**, has a whole host of interesting things to search out. In the temple study are 18 wise men in a glass case – the one with the big nose is said to be Marco Polo. It was here in 1844 that China and the US signed a treaty of 'undying friendship'. The 400-year-old temple complex is dedicated to Kun Iam, the queen of heaven and goddess of mercy.

The **Old Protestant Cemetery** is a fascinating place to wander around (if the door is closed, just knock on it). Lord Churchill (one of Winston's ancestors) and the English artist George Chinnery are buried here, but far more interesting are the varied graves of traders, seamen, missionaries and their families and the often detailed accounts of their lives and deaths. One US ship seems to have had half its crew 'fall from aloft' while in port.

On the Praça Luis de Camões, the fine little **Luis de Camões Museum** has items from China and a particularly fine collection of paintings, prints and engravings showing Macau in the last two centuries. It's right next door to the cemetery.

The **Portas do Cerco** (Barrier Gate) used to be of interest because you could stand 100 metres from it and claim that you'd seen into

China. You might even have seen a bus arriving from China or leaving Macau. Now you can be on the bus yourself so the Barrier Gate is of little interest.

The **Leal Senado** (Loyal Senate) looks out over the main town square and is the main administrative body for municipal affairs. At one time it was offered (and turned down) a total monopoly on all Chinese trade! The building also houses the National Library.

The highest point in Macau is the **Guía Fortress** overlooking the Jetfoil Pier, with a 17th-century chapel and lighthouse built on it. The lighthouse is the oldest on the China coast, first lit up in 1865.

One of the most beautiful churches in Macau is the **São Domingos Church**, a 17th-century building which has an impressive tiered altar. There is a small museum at the back, full of church regalia, images and paintings.

The beautiful and peaceful **Lou Lim Ieoc Gardens** and the ornate mansion with its columns and arches (now the Pui Ching School) once belonged to the wealthy Lou family. The gardens are a mixture of Chinese and European influences with huge shady trees, lotus ponds, pavilions, bamboo groves, grottoes and strangely shaped doorways.

Macau means the 'City of God' and takes its name from A-Ma-Gau, the Bay of A-Ma. The **A-Ma Temple** (Ma Kok Miu), which dates from the Ming dynasty, stands at the base of Penha Hill on Barra Point. According to legend, A-Ma, goddess of seafarers, was supposed to have been a beautiful young woman whose presence on a Canton-bound ship saved it from disaster. All the other ships of the fleet, whose rich owners had refused to give her passage, were destroyed in a storm. The boat people of Macau come here on a pilgrimage each year in April or May.

Beside the A-Ma Temple, a restored colonial-style building houses the **Macau Maritime Museum**. These are only temporary quarters; it should have its own building by the time you read this. Across the road at the waterfront there are a number of boats

including a tug, a dragon boat and a *lorcha*, a type of sailing cargo-vessel used on the Pearl River.

THE ISLANDS

Directly south of the mainland peninsula are the islands of Taipa and Coloane. In the past these islands were most notable for their pirates, the last raid being as recent as 1910. A bridge connects Taipa Island to the mainland, and a causeway connects Taipa and Coloane.

Taipa

Taipa seems to have become one big construction site with the Hyatt Hotel and Macau University just the first of numerous projects. Taipa village is a pleasantly relaxed place with some fine little restaurants to sample. You can rent a bicycle to explore the village and further afield. There's an interesting old church, a couple of Chinese temples and the interesting Taipa House Museum.

Coloane

This island also has a pretty little village where you can see junks under construction. Again bicycles can be rented there. Situated in a muddy river mouth, Macau is hardly likely to be blessed with wonderful beaches but Coloane has a couple that are really not bad. Hac Sa Beach is a long but not particularly inspiring stretch of sand but tiny Cheoc Van Beach is really quite pretty.

PLACES TO STAY - BOTTOM END

Rua das Lorchas is a hunting ground for cheap hotels. There are two numbering systems on this street, which causes some confusion. The *Hospedaria Vong Hong* on Rua das Lorchas is cheap. Depending on which numbering scheme you believe, it's either No 45 or No 253, but it's on the north side of Praça Ponte e Horta (the square) and south of the Floating Casino. Tiny single rooms cost M$25 and larger rooms are M$50.

Nearby at 175 Rua das Lorchas is *Hospedaria Namkio* where singles cost

M$37. It's a rather run-down sort of place, but it has character. Next to it is the *Hotel San Hou* at No 159 Rua das Lorchas, where singles/doubles are M$64/88. All rooms have shared bath, but the double rooms are huge with twin beds. Rooms with a balcony are the same price, so ask for one.

Just around the back is an alley called Rua do Bocage. At No 17 you'll find *Hotel Ung Ieong*, though a sign on the door says 'Restaurante Ung Ieong'. The rooms are so huge you could fit an army in there! Auditorium-sized doubles go for M$67 with attached bath, but look the place over before you pay because it's quite run-down.

Just opposite the Floating Casino and a few doors to the north is *Hoi Keng Hotel* (☎ 572033) where doubles are M$130 with shared bath and M$138 with private bath. The address is 153 Rua do Guimarães but you enter just around the corner on Rua Caldeira.

Two blocks to the south of the Floating Casino, on Rua das Lorchas, is a large square called Praça Ponte e Horta. It might once have been a park, but now it's just a car park (most of Macau's open space is buried under cars these days), and there are several vilas around it. On the east end of the square *Vila Kuan Heng* (☎ 573629) has clean rooms which cost M$150 with private bath. On the west side of the square, on the corner with Rua das Lorchas, is the tattered-looking *Vila Hoi Von* where singles are M$100, but not really worth it.

Moving a few blocks to the east of the Floating Casino, the very clean and very friendly *Vila Universal* (☎ 573247) is at 73 Rua Felicidade. The manager can speak good English and singles/doubles cost M$184/276. The price is amazingly cheap for the high standard of the rooms, but it's often full because it's known to offer such good value.

The *Vila Veng Va* is at the corner of Travessa das Virtudes and Travessa Auto Novo (which is a few doors to the south of the Floating Casino). It has rooms for M$150. They are attractive and the manager is friendly.

Moving to the east side of the peninsula, the area between the Hotel Lisboa and Rua da Praia Grande is fertile ground for finding budget accommodation, though prices are somewhat higher than by the Floating Casino. One good place to try is the *Va Lai Vila* at 44 Rua da Praia Grande. Singles cost M$180, the rooms look clean and the management is friendly. On the opposite side of the street at 93 Rua da Praia Grande is *Vila Nam Kok* where singles are M$188.

Intersecting with Rua da Praia Grande is a small street called Rua Dr Pedro Jose Lobo where there's a good line of accommodation houses, including *Vila Nam Loon* which has singles for M$150. Around the corner on Avenida Infante D Henrique, near Rua da Praia Grande, is *Vila Kimbo* where singles go for M$130.

On Rua Dr Pedro Jose Lobo, the *Vila Loc Tin* has comfortable doubles for M$180. In the same building the *Vila San Sui* costs M$150 for a double.

Running off Avenida D João IV is an alley called Travessa da Praia Grande which has several good places. Among the best is the bright, airy and friendly *Vila Nam Tin* (☎ 81513) where singles/doubles with private bath cost M$150/175. On the same alley is *Pensão Nam In* (☎ 81002), where singles with shared bath are M$110, or M$230 for a pleasant double with private bath.

Behind the Hotel Lisboa on Avenida de Lopo Sarmento de Carvalho is a row of vilas. The *Vila San Vu* is friendly and has nice rooms for M$160.

PLACES TO STAY – MIDDLE

The *Hotel London* (☎ 83388) on Praça Ponte e Horta has singles/doubles for M$200/240.

True to its name, the *Hotel Central* (☎ 373888) is in the centre of town at 28-26 Avenida Almeida Ribeiro, west of the GPO. Rather dumpy-looking double rooms with private bath cost from M$220.

Just on the north side of the Floating Casino on Rua das Lorchas is the *Peninsula Hotel* (☎ 318899). Singles/twins are M$250/300. This is a new hotel, clean and well air-conditioned.

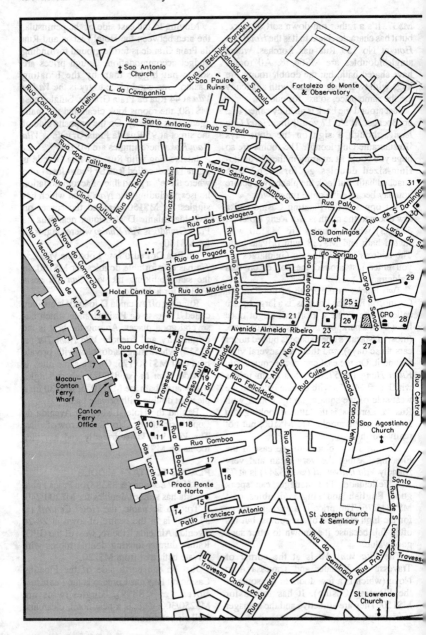

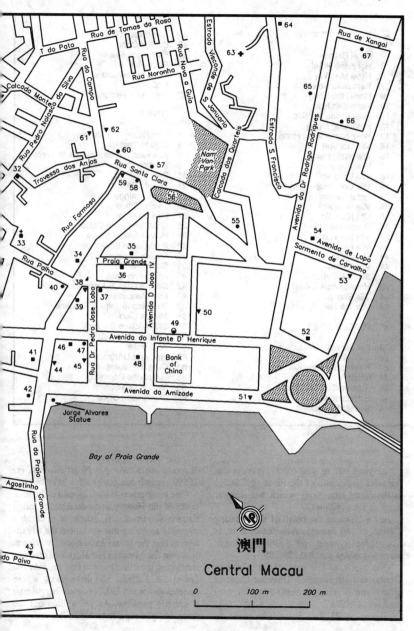

Rua de Tomas da Rosa
Rua de Xangai
Estrada Visconde de S Januario
64
63 †
67
T do Pato
Rua do Campo
Calçada Monteiro da Silva
65
Rua Pedro Nolasco da Silva
Rua Noronha
Rua Nova a Guia
66
62
Estrada S Francisco
61
Avenida do Dr Rodrigo Rodrigues
32
Travessa dos Anjos
60
57
Nam Van Park
Rua Santa Clara
Calçada dos Quarteis
59 58
56
33
Rua Formosa
55
Rua Palha
54
Avenida de Lopo
Sarmento de Carvalho
34
35
T Praia Grande
53
40
38
36
Avenida D João IV
39
37
50
Rua Dr Pedro José Lobo
49
Avenida do Infante D' Henrique
52
41
46
47
48
Bank of China
44
45
42
Avenida da Amizade
51
Jorge Alvares Statue
Bay of Praia Grande
Rua da Praia Grande
Agostinho Grande
澳門
Central Macau
43
do Poiva
0   100 m   200 m

■ PLACES TO STAY

2	Hotel Grand
3	Hoi Keng Hotel
5	Hotel Man Va
7	Peninsula Hotel
9	Hotel Hou Kong
10	Hotel San Hou
11	Hospedaria Namkio
12	Hotel Ung Ieong
13	Hospedaria Vong Hong
14	Vila Hoi Von
16	Vila Kuan Heng
17	Hotel London
18	Vila Veng Va
19	Vila Universal
23	Hotel Central
34	Vila Nam Kok
35	Vila Nam Tin
36	Pensao Nam In
37	Vila Nam Loon
39	Vila Loc Tin
41	Metropole Hotel
46	Vila Kimbo
48	Sintra Hotel
52	Hotel Lisboa & Casino
54	Vila San Vu
64	Vila Tak Lei

▼ PLACES TO EAT

20	Fat Siu Lau Restaurant
22	Café Safari
26	Restaurant Long Kei
31	Maxim's
38	Algarve Sol Restaurant
43	Estrela do Mar
44	Solmar Restaurant
45	Restaurant Ocean
50	Dai Pai Dong
51	Esplanade Macau
53	Pizza Hut
59	Pizzeria Toscana
61	McDonald's
62	Portugues Restaurant

OTHER

1	Hong Kung Miu Temple
4	Casino Kam Pek
6	Kee Kwan Motors (Buses to Canton)
8	Floating Casino
15	Park 'n Shop
21	Taifung Bank
24	Sao Domingo Market
25	Tourist Office
27	Leal Senado
28	CTM Telephone Office
29	Holy House of Mercy
30	Portuguese Bookshop
32	Capitol Theatre
33	Cathedral
40	Hongkong Bank
42	Days & Days Supermarket
47	Foto Princesa
49	Bus Stop to Taipa & Coloane
55	Military Club
56	St Francisco Gardens
57	Cineteatro Macau
58	Bookstore
60	Watson's Drugstore
63	Centro Hospital
65	Telephone Company
66	Main Police Station
67	Immigration Office

On your left as you enter Travessa das Virtudes (just south of the Floating Casino) is the *Hotel Hou Kong* which has singles/doubles for M$230/322.

Just a block to the north of the Floating Casino, at 146 Avenida Almeida Ribeiro, is the *Hotel Grand* (☎ 579922) where singles/doubles cost M$228/288.

One block to the east of the Floating Casino is a street called Travessa Caldeira where you'll find the *Hotel Man Va* with doubles at M$287.

Nearby at 71 Rua Felicidade, close to Travessa Auto Novo, is *Hotel Ko Wah* (☎ 75599), which has doubles for M$195.

One more place to look around is the area north of the Hotel Lisboa on a street called Estrada São Francisco. You have to climb a steep hill to get up this street, but the advantage is that the hotels have good sea views. Just past the Matsuya Hotel (out of reach of shoestring travellers) you'll find the *Vila Tak Lei* at 2A Estrada São Francisco, where doubles go for M$350. However, bargaining is entirely possible. As we walked out the price dropped rapidly to M$200!

PLACES TO EAT

Henri's Galley (☎ 556251) is right on the waterfront at 4 Avenida da Republica, the south end of the Macau Peninsula. Also known as *Maxims* (not the Hong Kong fast-food chain), Henri's Galley is known for its African chicken, spicy prawns and prawn fondue. They also serve Chinese food.

Right next door is *Cafe Marisol* where food is both cheap and excellent. They set up outdoor tables so you can take in the view across to the islands.

Also adjacent to Henri's Galley is *Ali Curry House*, which also has outdoor tables and a wide menu of curry dishes (M$25 to M$35) and steaks (M$30 to M$40) with a Portuguese flavour.

For good, cheap Portuguese and Macanese food, the *Estrela do Mar* (☎ 81270), at 11 Travessa do Paiva off the Rua da Praia Grande, is the place to go, as is the *Solmar* (☎ 74391) at 11 Rua da Praia Grande. Both places are famous for their African chicken and seafood.

Fat Siu Lau (☎ 73580) – or 'House of the Smiling Buddha' – serves Portuguese and Chinese food. It's at 64 Rua Felicidade, once the old red-light Street of Happiness. Turn left opposite the Central Hotel in Avenida Almeida Ribeiro. It's supposed to be the oldest restaurant in Macau or at least the oldest Macanese restaurant in the colony, dating back to 1903. The speciality is roast pigeon.

Another place known for good Portuguese food is *Português* (☎ 75445) at 16 Rua do Campo, and one place known for its good food and fine Spanish decor is *Algarve Sol* (☎ 89007), at 41-43 Rua Comandante Mata e Oliveira, two blocks west of the Hotel Lisboa between Rua da Praia Grande and Avenida D João IV.

An excellent place to eat is *Café Safari* (☎ 574313) at 14 Pateo do Cotovelo, a tiny square off Avenida de Almeida Ribeiro across from the Hotel Central. It has good coffee shop dishes as well as spicy chicken, steak and fried noodles. This is a good place to eat breakfast.

Lots of people hop over to Taipa village for the excellent restaurants found there. *Pinocchio's* is a very popular little Portuguese place where they serve up superb prawns and you can often sit outside. Most dishes are M$20 to M$30, wine is around M$30 a bottle. It gets frantically crowded for Sunday lunch.

Other popular Taipa village restaurants include the very Portuguese *Restaurante Panda*, the Italian (despite the name) *Restaurante Leong Un*, the cheaper *Casa de Pasto Tai Tung*, the *Kung Kai, Cozinha Ricardo's Kitchen* and the pleasant sidewalk-café-like *Cafe Tai Lei Lai Kei* opposite the Tin Hau Temple. Most of them are along, or in the case of Pinocchio just off, the Rua do Cunha.

At Hac Sa Beach on Coloane Island, *Fernando's* deserves honourable mention for some of the best food in Macau. The atmosphere is also pleasant, and it can get crowded in the evening. There are two main problems with this place. The first is that there is no sign above the door and it's possible to wander around for quite a while looking for it. The restaurant is at the far end of the car park, close to the bus stop. The other problem is that the menu is in Portuguese and Chinese only. Fernando himself (the manager) will gladly translate for you, and he recommends the clams.

Budget travellers should head to *Esplanade Macau* which sits on the traffic island on Avenida Amizade in front of the Hotel Lisboa and adjacent to the Bank of China. It's in an outdoor pavilion and opens only in the evening. They serve good Cantonese dishes like fried noodles for M$7 and drinks are also very cheap. Not much English is spoken, but they have an English menu.

One of the most conveniently located street markets is Rua da Escola Commercial, a tiny lane one block west of the Hotel Lisboa, just next to a sports field.

ENTERTAINMENT
Gambling

Even if gambling has no interest for you it's fun to wander the casinos at night. There are three main arenas for losing money. Largest is the Hotel Lisboa with all the usual games, a special private room for the really high rollers and row upon row of 'hungry tigers' – slot machines. It's gambling Chinese-style though, none of the dinner jacket swank of Monte Carlo or the neon gloss of Vegas – at Macau you put your money down, take your chances and to hell with the surroundings.

At the other end of the main street is the Macau Palace, usually known as the 'Floating Casino', and midway between is the Chinese casino where they play games like *Dai-Siu* (big and small). You can also bet on the games at the Jai-Alai Palace on the waterfront near the ferry terminal.

Discos

The most popular with the locals is the

Mondial Disco at the Hotel Mondial, Rua da Antonio Basto. There is no cover charge, but you are obligated to buy two drinks for M$70.

The Hotel Presidente is home to the Skylight Disco. There is no cover charge here, but you must buy one drink for M$80.

Other

For M$120 you can watch 10 graduates of the Crazy Horse in Paris cavort around the stage of Hotel Lisboa attired in outfits ranging from very little to nothing at all. It's called the Crazy Paris Show.

There's also horse racing on Taipa Island and dog racing at the 'canidrome' (yes, they really call it that).

Mongolia

The name 'Mongolia' has always stirred up visions of the exotic – Genghis Khan, the Gobi Desert, wild horses galloping across the Siberian steppes. Even today, Mongolia seems like the end of the earth – outside of the few major cities, you begin to wonder if you haven't stepped into another century rather than another country.

Paradoxically, many Western travellers visit Mongolia yet never set foot on it. The Trans-Siberian Railway runs right through the centre of the country, but most foreigners are only issued transit visas. As a result, few Westerners get to see more than the view from the train's window. There are numerous bureaucratic hurdles to clear before getting a tourist visa, and few want to waste the time and money just to see a tiny slice of Mongolia.

This is a pity, because this country has much to offer. A land of vast deserts, rolling grasslands, high mountains, forests and crystal clear lakes: Mongolia's environment is the most pristine in Asia. This is largely due to the harsh climate, which has always made human existence a precarious proposition in this part of the planet. Not surprisingly, the Mongols are a tough people – indeed, in the 13th century they conquered half the world.

The unique culture of the Mongols has fascinated Western travellers since the time of Marco Polo, but the door slammed shut in 1921 with a Marxist revolution. Now that the Cold War has been banished, Mongolia is cautiously opening up. With neighbouring China rapidly modernising, Mongolia is sure to follow. The country is desperate for foreign exchange, and the most likely way to earn it is to open up to Western tourism. Perhaps in another decade we'll be seeing Genghis Khan Burger chain restaurants in the Gobi Desert, but for now Mongolia remains a barely explored traveller's destination. If you hurry up, you may be among the first.

Facts about the Country

HISTORY

Early Chinese manuscripts refer to 'Turkic-speaking peoples' living in what we now call Mongolia as early as the 4th or 5th century BC. The name 'Mongol' was first recorded during China's Tang dynasty (618-907 AD). The Mongols at this time were scattered nomadic tribes, barely noticed by the outside world.

All this was to change dramatically in the 13th century. A Mongol by the name of Temüjin was born in 1162. He united the Mongols after 20 years of internal warfare, and in 1206 he was he was given the honorary name Genghis Khan (universal ruler). His swift troops on horseback launched themselves against Russia and China. By the time of his death in 1248, the empire already extended from Beijing to the Caspian Sea.

It was Genghis Khan's grandson, Kublai Khan, who completed the subjugation of China. He set himself up in Beijing as the emperor of the Yuan dynasty. This was the height of glory for the Mongol empire, which stretched from Sumatra to Hungary – the largest nation the world has ever known. The Mongols improved the road system linking China with Russia and promoted trade throughout the empire and with Europe. They instituted a famine relief scheme and expanded the canal system which brought food from the countryside to the cities. They were the first society to make paper money the sole form of currency. It was the China of the Mongols that Marco Polo and other Westerners visited, and their books described the empire to an amazed Europe.

The splendour of the Mongol empire didn't last for long. Kublai Khan died in 1294 and the Mongols became increasingly corrupted by the empire they ruled. They were deeply resented as an elite, privileged

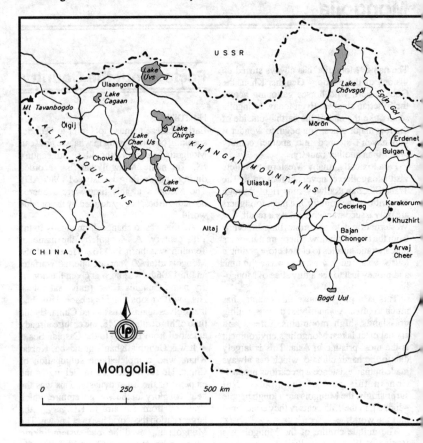

Mongolia

0   250   500 km

class exempt from taxation, and the empire became ridden with factions vying for power. By the 1350s, the empire was coming apart. The Mongols were driven out of Beijing as China came under the control of the Ming dynasty.

The Mongols then underwent a long period of stagnation and decline. Later, China's ruling Manchus (the Qing dynasty) took over Mongolia. As the Manchus extended their control, both Chinese and Mongolian peasants suffered ruthless exploitation, crushing debts and brutal pun-

ishment for the slightest offence. The country was ripe for rebellion.

The opportunity came in 1911 when the Qing dynasty was overthrown. The Mongol princes declared independence. China sought to re-establish control, and forced Mongolia to accept a 'request' to be taken over by China. A new opportunity was created by the Russian revolution of 1917. Mongolian revolutionaries asked the Communists for help. In July 1921, Mongol and Russian fighters captured Ulaan Baatar. On 26 November 1924, the Mongolian People's

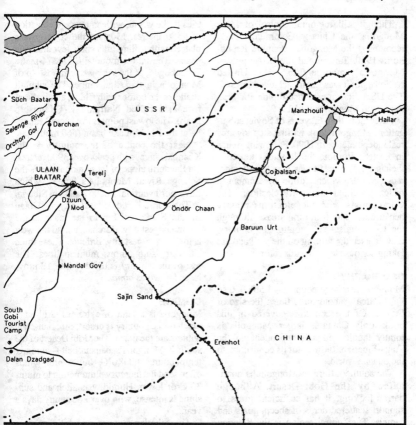

Republic (MPR) was declared and Mongolia became the world's second Communist country. This only applied to 'Outer Mongolia' – the southern part of the country, Inner Mongolia, remained part of China. Finally free of their Chinese masters, the 'independent' Mongolian nation quickly fell under Soviet domination.

In 1939, the Japanese occupied part of Inner Mongolia, but they were resoundingly defeated when they invaded Outer Mongolia. The Japanese military changed tactics and concentrated their efforts on eastern China, South-East Asia and the Pacific islands.

In 1945, Stalin extracted full recognition of the independence of Outer Mongolia from Chiang Kaishek when the two signed an anti-Japanese Sino-Soviet alliance. In 1949, the Chinese Communists defeated Chiang's Kuomintang (Nationalist Party) troops, which then fled to Taiwan. The Kuomintang subsequently withdrew recognition of Outer Mongolia's independence, and maps produced in Taiwan today still show Mongolia as a province of China.

Though still retaining control of Inner Mongolia, the Chinese Communist Party recognised the Mongolian People's Republic in 1950. Taiwan and the USA opposed Mongolia's membership in the United Nations, but it was finally achieved in 1961. The USA did not establish diplomatic relations with Mongolia until 1989.

After more than 60 years of Soviet subjugation, Mongolia took its first step towards real independence in 1990. Following trends in Eastern Europe, the Russians loosened their grip. The result was large pro-democracy protests, which led the government to resign and hold multiparty elections. The Communists won the elections mainly because of support in rural areas. Although the Communists still control the country, they can see the writing on the wall and are taking serious steps towards reform.

GEOGRAPHY

Mongolia is a large country – 1,566,000 sq km in area – about three times the size of France. Of the countries covered in this book, only China is larger. Mongolia is totally landlocked and dependent on the Trans-Siberian Railway for its connection to the outside world.

The southern third of Mongolia is dominated by the Gobi Desert. Although barren-looking, it has sufficient grass to support scattered herds of sheep, goats and camels. The central region is the Siberian steppes. This region is largely covered by grassland, home to Mongolia's famed horses which Genghis Khan used so successfully in his wars of conquest. About 10% of the land is forested, mostly in the north.

Mongolia is also one of the highest countries in the world, with an average elevation of 1580 metres. Most of the country is a plateau with rolling hills and a few dramatic peaks. The tallest mountain is 4374-metre Tavanbogdo, at the very westernmost tip of Mongolia in the Altai range. The summit straddles the border with China, and is therefore also called Nairamdal (Friendship Peak). The lowest point is in eastern Mongolia at the Khokh Lake basin (560 metres).

Near the centre of the country is the Khangai range, with peaks over 3900 metres. On the north slope of these mountains is the Selenge River, Mongolia's largest, which flows northward into Lake Baikal in Siberia.

The capital and largest city is Ulaan Baatar. Some 200 km to the north is the second largest city, Darchan, and to the west is the third largest city, Erdenet. These three cities are autonomous municipalities. The rest of the country is divided into 18 provinces known as *aimaks*.

CLIMATE

Mongolia is a land of extremes. Although much of the country is desert, Siberian-style winters are the norm. The Gobi Desert of the south is Mongolia's banana belt – summer temperatures hit 40°C, but winter winds often send the mercury plummeting to minus 30°C or lower. Humidity is zilch and sunshine is intense, with over 260 sunny days a year.

The Siberian steppes are chilly even in summer – the July average is only 10°C. Winter is no joke – minus 50°C is not unknown.

Even spring and autumn are frosty – July is ideal. There is a brief rainy season from mid-July to September, but the showers tend

| **Ulaan Baatar Temperatures & Rainfall** | | | | | | | | | | | |
Jan	Feb	Mar	Apr	May	Jun	Jul	Aug	Sep	Oct	Nov	Dec
Temp (°C) -25	-21	-13	-1	6	13	17	14	8	-1	-13	-22
Rain (mm) 0	0	3	5	10	28	76	51	23	5	5	3

to be brief. Because of the high altitude, evenings are cool even in summer. Mongolia is a windy place, especially in spring.

GOVERNMENT

The political landscape is changing rapidly. For years, the country stagnated under the fossilised rule of the Mongolian People's Revolutionary Party (MPRP) – all other political parties were banned. A political earthquake came in March 1990, when the government resigned after massive street protests. Multiparty elections were held in July, still leaving the MPRP in control, but hanging on by just a thread.

The major new political parties include the Mongolian Democratic Party (MDP), Social Democratic Party (SDP), National Progress Party (NPP), the Greens and Free Labour Party. The MDP is strongly anti-Communist and seems to be the most popular with young people.

The military does not seem to have any significant political role. In any event, the Mongolian army is very tiny, barely capable of repelling an invasion by budget travellers who arrive on the Trans-Siberian without a visa. By contrast, the USSR has stationed large numbers of troops in the country, but these are gradually being withdrawn.

ECONOMY

Mongolia is a Marxist state experiencing all the problems of a country which is trying to dump socialism in stages rather than all at once. In 1991, prices doubled overnight, but are still ridiculously cheap, which means state enterprises continue to lose money. Between 1989 and 1991, the official currency lost over 90% of its value relative to the US dollar. You can expect more devaluations and more inflation, which means the prices quoted in this book may not reflect reality by the time you read this.

Private businesses have only been permitted since 1989, and private ownership of land is still not allowed. The economy is still dominated by inefficient state-run companies. In the past Mongolia relied heavily on subsidies from the USSR, but these have ended and the result has been serious shortages of fuel and most consumer goods. An attempt by the Mongolian government to make up the subsidies has created a huge budget deficit. The government has tried to compel farmers to sell their goods to the state at low fixed prices – the farmers have refused, and this has worsened the food shortage, resulting in rationing of dairy products and other basic staples. Both the ruling and opposition parties agree on the need for an end to subsidies and price controls, privatisation of state enterprises and more foreign investment, but there is much debate on how to go about it. It will take Mongolia a while to work all this out.

Mongolia's economy rides the backs of sheep, goats, cattle, horses and camels. Sheep are most important, constituting two-thirds of all animals raised. Livestock raising is possible because of the extensive grasslands – the harsh, dry climate makes most forms of agriculture impossible. Less than 1% of the land is under cultivation, mostly wheat and potatoes.

The main manufacturing industries are the production of leather and wool plus a few finished products like boots and clothing. The country has a few important mineral resources, especially coal, copper, tin, tungsten, iron ore and zinc. There is also timber production along the USSR border. Overall, Mongolia is a poor country but there are hopeful signs for the future.

POPULATION & PEOPLE

The population stands at 2.2 million, with more than 25% living in the capital, Ulaan Baatar. With an average population density of about 1.3 persons per sq km, Mongolia is one of the most sparsely inhabited nations on earth. In the past, the government actively promoted population growth, which now stands at 2.8% annually, the highest in North-East Asia. Despite the fact that Mongolia is mostly empty space, the pastoral economy probably cannot sustain a large increase. In the past, the government also encouraged migration to urban areas in the belief that this would increase industrialisation – the result has been a labour shortage in agriculture and an excess of unemployed youths in the cities. These policies have now been reversed: the government encourages family planning and is trying to persuade people to move back to rural areas.

The Mongols are not a single ethnic group. Khalkhs make up 80% of the population. Another 5% of the population are Kazakhs. There are 18 other minorities, including Buryats, Derbets and Bayads.

ARTS

Mongolia has a mixture of local traditional arts and imports from the Soviet Union and the West. The government promotes operas, plays, folk music, folk dancing, ballet and circuses.

More recent artistic expression comes from the West. Rock music is the rage. You can draw your own conclusions, but two of the most popular songs are Bruce Springsteen's 'Born in the USA' and 'Money for Nothing' by Dire Straits. Roll over Marx and Lenin.

Disco has caught on. Scantily clad dancers perform the lambada on stage. It's enough to make Genghis fall off his horse.

CULTURE

The *Soyombo* is the national symbol of Mongolia which dates back at least to the 17th century. You'll most likely first see it on the covers of Mongolian passports and also on the Mongolian flag. It signifies freedom and independence.

Some aspects of Chinese culture have deeply influenced the Mongolians. You will often see Mongolian cashiers use a Chinese abacus to count up the bill. The Mongolians also use the Chinese zodiac with its 12 animal signs.

RELIGION

Under the Communists, religion was suppressed and nearly disappeared. Since the liberalisation of 1990, there has been a phenomenal religious revival. Monasteries have reopened.

There is a significant minority of Muslims, but the main religion is Lamaism (Tibetan or Tantric Buddhism). Lamaism originated in Tibet around the 7th century. It was heavily influenced by Tibet's pre-Buddhist Bon religion, which relied on priests or shamans to placate spirits, gods and demons. Lamaism is distinguished from classical Buddhism by several important features: the belief in mantras (sacred speech); the creation of sacred art; the performance of mudras (ritual postures); the system of Lamas who are reincarnations of highly evolved beings; and the supremacy of the Dalai Lama. It's worth noting that Buddhist monks are normally vegetarians, but Lamaist monks can eat meat.

Lamaism attracted Kublai Khan and other prominent members of the ruling class, but it was introduced to the masses under Altan Khan (1543-1583). There seem to have been several motives for promoting Tibetan Buddhism rather than Chinese Buddhism. One is that the Mongols feared the Chinese would eventually seduce and assimilate the Mongols – compared to China, Tibet was weak and not seen as a threat. Another reason may have been that the Tibetan writing system was much easier to learn and use, though eventually the Tibetan scriptures were translated into Mongol.

LANGUAGE

The national language is Mongolian, a member of the Ural-Altaic family of languages which includes Finnish, Korean and Turkish. Since 1944, a modified version of the Russian Cyrillic alphabet has been used to write Mongolian. The traditional Mongolian script was borrowed from China's Uigurs, who brought it from the Middle East. Since the collapse of authoritarian rule in 1990, the traditional script is back in fashion, though mostly for scholarly and artistic purposes rather than mass communication. Mongolian script is composed of 26 letters, written in a fashion that forms beautiful characters. The script is written downwards, starting from the top-left corner of the page. Since 1990, secondary schools have once again been teaching traditional Mongolian script.

As for romanisation, there was a spelling reform in 1987 so that the capital city, previously written as Ulan Bator, is now Ulaan Baatar.

The most common foreign language is Russian, but English is rapidly gaining popularity. A few Mongolians speak German.

Greetings & Civilities

Hello
sain bainuu   Сайн байна уу
Goodbye
baiyartai   Баяртай
Thank you
baiyarlalaa   Баярлалаа
You're welcome
zugeer   Зугээр

Necessities

toilet
jorlon   жорлон
toilet paper
jorlon giin tsaas
жорлонгийн цаас
sanitary pads (Kotex)
ariun tsevriin hereglel
ариун цэврийн хэрэглэл
How much does it cost?
ene yamar unetei ve
Энэ ямар унэтэй вэ
too expensive
heterhii untei yum
Хэтэрхий унэтэй юм

Drinks

hot water
haluun us   халуун ус
coffee
kofe   кофе
beer
piiv   пиво
tea
tsai   цай

Numbers

1	*neg*	10	*arav*
2	*hoyor*	11	*arvan neg*
3	*gurav*	12	*arvan hoyor*
4	*doruv*	13	*arvan gurav*
5	*tav*	20	*hori*
6	*zurgaa*	31	*guchin neg*
7	*doloo*	100	*zuu*
8	*naim*	101	*zuun neg*
9	*yus*	1000	*neg mianga*

Emergency

I'm sick.
bi ovchtei   Би овчтэй
Help!
toslaarai   Туслаарай
Thief!
holgaich   Хулгайч
Fire!
gal   Гал

Facts for the Visitor

VISAS & EMBASSIES

There are two kinds of visas: 'transit' and 'tourist'. Most travellers taking the Trans-Siberian get a transit visa, which means they cannot go beyond the train platform in the Ulaan Baatar station. In other words, they only get to watch Mongolia roll by from the train window. Some travellers have reckoned that they could arrive on a transit visa, get off and 'miss' their train. Until recently, this was a dangerous stunt that could easily get you arrested. Suddenly, the authorities have become more tolerant and many travellers are getting away with it. There are no longer immigration and Customs officials at Ulaan Baatar station, so it's easy to leave the train. The main problem with this method of getting into Mongolia is that getting out may prove difficult. Rail and train tickets are hard to get and delays of several weeks are not uncommon, and in the meantime your transit visa may expire. Getting a transit visa extended seems to be impossible, so if you choose this method of entering Mongolia, it's entirely at your own risk.

A tourist visa will allow you to visit almost anywhere in the country, but there is a catch. For most Western nationalities, you can only be issued a tourist visa if you're invited. To be invited, you must make all bookings for hotels and transport and pay for everything in advance. After this, your host will send a wire to the Mongolian embassy inviting you to visit the country. Only then will the visa watchdog let you pass.

The tail that wags this dog is Zhuulchin, Mongolia's national tourist organisation. Zhuulchin can book your hotel rooms, arrange transport within Mongolia, provide guides and extend the invitation that you need to get a tourist visa. Unfortunately, Zhuulchin charges high prices and will always try to book you into expensive hotels.

Fortunately, there is now a way to bypass Zhuulchin. The free market has just arrived, and fledgling private tour operators are appearing in Mongolia. There are very few of these, but their numbers will no doubt increase if the government leaves them alone. To do the research for this book, we booked a one-week tour for US$140 through Monkey Business (see 'Tours' section in this chapter), then stayed on after the tour was completed. Currently, this is the cheapest way to legally obtain a tourist visa. Of course, the situation may change by the time you read this. Hopefully, Mongolia will start issuing tourist visas to individual travellers, or perhaps they will permit short visa-free stays. At present, only citizens of the formerly Eastern Bloc countries can get tourist visas without being booked into tours.

The Mongolian embassy in Beijing, China, is open all day, but the visa section keeps short hours – only on Monday, Tuesday, Thursday and Friday from 8.30 am to 11.30 am. They close for all Mongolian holidays, and they shut down completely for the entire week of National Day (Naadam), which officially falls on 11-13 July. Visas cost US$20 (US$28 for UK citizens) if picked up the next day, or US$24 (US$36 for UK citizens) for same-day delivery. Some nationalities can get visas for free (India, Finland etc).

Mongolian Embassies

China
 2 Xiushui Beilu, Jianguomenwai, Beijing (☎ 5321203)
Czechoslovakia
 Koriska 5, Prague 6 (☎ 328992, 329067)
Hungary
 X 11 Istenhedyi UT-59-61, Budapest (☎ 15-14-12, 15-50-87)
Japan
 Shoto Pinecrest Mansion 21-4 Kamyamacho Chibuya KU, Tokyo 150 (☎ (03) 4692088, 4692092)
Poland
 al Ulazdowskie 12, Warsaw (☎ 289765, 281651)
Romania
 str Fagaras 6, Bucharest (☎ 496340, 560040)
UK
 7 Kensington Court, London W85 DL (☎ (01) 937-0150, 937-5235)
USSR
 ulitsa Stanislavskaya Dom 20, Moscow (☎ 229-67-65
 Irkutsk Consulate, ulitsa Lapina 11, Irkutsk (☎ 42370, 42266)

Foreign Embassies in Mongolia

No exact addresses can be given because there aren't any. See the map of Ulaan Baatar in this book for exact locations.

China
 north side of Sambuu St between Small Ring and Eldev-Ochir St, Ulaan Baatar (☎ 20955, 23940)
Germany
 north-west corner of United Nations St and University St, Ulaan Baatar (☎ 23325)
Poland
 Sambuu St and Eldev-Ochir St, Ulaan Baatar (☎ 23365, 22294)
UK
 eastern end of Peace Ave near Big Ring, Ulaan Baatar (☎ 51033)
USA
 inner north side of the Big Ring just west of the Selbe River, Ulaan Baatar (☎ 29095, 29639)
USSR
 south side of Peace Ave, one block west of the Central Post Office, Ulaan Baatar (☎ 25207, 27071)

CUSTOMS

Baggage searches tend to be light to non-existent for foreigners, but it's a different story for the Mongolians, who have become skilled smugglers. Chinese and Mongolian people on the train carry tremendous amounts of luggage and may ask you to carry it for them – in most cases this is not a good idea. Mongolian Customs have been strict about bringing pornography into the country. Their definition of pornography includes some pretty tame stuff like lingerie ads in women's magazines.

Other than that, there are few problems. For electronic goods (Walkmans, etc), you can usually bring one of each item duty-free, but you must pay 100% import duty on each additional one.

MONEY

Even if you don't want to play the black market game, it would be wise to bring lots of cash US dollars, preferably in small denominations. Imported items and certain other goods are only available if you pay in hard foreign currency. US coins would definitely prove helpful as the shops frequently run out and therefore cannot give any change smaller than US$1.

At the time of this writing, Mongolia's State Bank announced that it would soon allow Visa credit cards to be used in the country. There is no word yet on the introduction of other international credit cards.

Currency

The unit of currency is the *Tughrig* (Togrog), with 100 mongo to the Tughrig. Bills are issued in denominations of 1, 3, 5, 10, 20, 50 and 100 Tughrigs. There is a 1 Tughrig coin – other coins are in mongo in units of 1, 2, 5, 10, 15, 20 and 50. There are special gold collector coins which you won't see on the street, but many Mongolians are willing to sell these to you. All foreign currency and travellers' cheques must be declared on arrival and may be inspected on departure. Foreign currency can only be exchanged at the Mongolian State Bank, or designated branches which are found in Zhuulchin-approved tourist hotels, but the bank is best. Keep your exchange receipts for changing money back on departure.

The tight foreign exchange controls are an attempt (spectacularly unsuccessful) to keep a lid on the burgeoning black market in US dollars. Chinese renminbi have some black market value because Mongolians like to go shopping in China, but they're not nearly as useful as US dollars. At the time of this writing, the police were taking a very nonchalant attitude towards the black market, but that could change.

Exchange Rates

There is a raging black market, where US$1 will get you T100 or more depending on your bargaining ability. The currency will probably continue to be devalued, but at the time of this writing, official rates were as follows:

A$1	=	T31.15
C$1	=	T34.76
HK$1	=	T5.13
NZ$1	=	T23.54
UK£1	=	T66
US$1	=	T40
Y100	=	T28.9

In spite of what the official rates are, you may get considerably less at hotels, train ticket offices and foreign currency shops.

Costs

Mongolia is either dirt cheap or very expensive, depending on your willingness to obey the law. Costs can be less than US$5 per day if you enter illegally on a transit visa, travel independently and use black market currency. To obtain your visa legally, you need to sign up for a tour. These can cost from US$20 to US$200 per day. See the 'Tours' section in this chapter for more information.

Tipping

In restaurants, tipping is expected. However, it is not a custom to tip taxi drivers, so don't make it one.

Bargaining

Nobody bargains in government shops. In the budding private sector, bargaining is definitely catching on.

WHAT TO BRING

Shortages of basic consumer goods are the norm, so bring everything you need. There is an acute shortage of toilet paper, but if you run out you can always use Tughrigs. It's also recommended that you bring toothpaste, shampoo, soap, razor blades, tampons, condoms, tea or coffee and a cup. Hot water for making tea is seldom available, so an electrical immersion coil is worth its weight in gold, assuming you have the correct plug adaptor (see Electricity section). A gluestick will ensure that your postage stamps remain stuck to the envelope or postcard. Food supplies can be sketchy, so a few jars of peanut butter could prove useful. Warm clothes will be needed for any time of year – even summer evenings can be chilly. UV (sunblock) lotion and sunglasses are essential survival gear. Plastic bags and twist ties are hard to come by, but will prove valuable for storing bread, which the Mongolians live on. Also bring some candy and foreign cigarettes if you want to give gifts to the Mongolians.

BUSINESS HOURS & HOLIDAYS

There are few private businesses. Government offices are open from 8 am to 5 pm on weekdays, and from 8 am to 12 pm on Saturday. Banks stay open from 10 am to 3 pm weekdays, and from 8 am to 12 pm on Saturday. Most offices are closed on Sunday.

Many things are changing rapidly in Mongolia, including the holidays. In 1990, Labour Day was cancelled and the traditional Lunar New Year festival was restored. More changes can be expected, but as of now, the following are public holidays: 1 January, New Year's Day; Lunar New Year; 8 March, Women's Day; 11-13 July, National Day (anniversary of the 1921 Mongolian revolution); 26 November, Mongolian Republic Day. The Lunar New Year is celebrated some time in late January or early February.

CULTURAL EVENTS

The biggest event of the year that attracts foreigners and locals alike is Naadam, held on National Day (11-13 July) in Ulaan Baatar. Naadam is a Mongolian sports fair featuring horse riding, wrestling and archery, with prizes for the winners. The fair has its origins in the ancient Obo-worshipping Festival (an *obo* is a pile of stones with a hollow space for offerings – a kind of shaman shrine).

The fairs are held in other locations besides Ulaan Baatar, though these are less accessible. The Mongolian clans make a beeline for the fairs on any form of transport they can muster, and create an impromptu yurt city. There are signs that the fair may be staged more often with the addition of shooting, motorcycling, storytelling and dancing.

Come back in five years and they'll have added bungy-jumping.

POST & TELECOMMUNICATIONS
Postal Rates
Mongolia has some of the lowest international postal rates in the world. International postcards cost T2.60. International letters up to 20 grams cost T3, but if you want them registered the postage is T7. Domestic letters cost T1.2 to send if unregistered, or T2 if registered.

You can send parcels from the post office at low cost, but if you need airfreight service and are willing to pay a minimum of US$35, the privately run carrier DHL (☎ 23722) can be contacted at the Ministry of Communications, Sukhbaatar Square-9, Ulaan Baatar 210611.

Sending Mail
There is a mailbox just outside the front door of the Ulaan Baatar Hotel. Otherwise, take it to the Central Post Office on Peace Ave, on the west side of Sukhbaatar Square. The mail service appears to be reliable.

Receiving Mail
Poste restante at the Central Post Office in Ulaan Baatar seems to work OK.

Telephone
Public pay phones are a rare item, but if you find one, it costs 15 mongo. You can make free local calls from the reception desks of most hotels. The phone system is in decrepit condition and you'll often have to dial many times before you finally get connected.

If you need a connection to the outside world, you can try calling from the Central Post Office or a tourist hotel, but making an international call either to or from Mongolia is extremely difficult.

Fax, Telex & Telegraph
International fax can be sent from the post office, but is expensive and unreliable. Telex is most reliable, assuming the person you need to reach has one. Foreigners must pay hard currency for international telex and fax.

TIME
The standard time in Mongolia is Greenwich Mean Time plus eight hours. When it is noon in Mongolia it is also noon in Beijing, Hong Kong, Singapore and Perth; 2 pm in Sydney; 8 pm the previous day in Los Angeles; 11 pm the previous day in New York; and 4 am in London. Mongolia observes daylight saving time.

WEIGHTS & MEASURES
Mongolia follows the international metric system.

ELECTRICITY
Electric power is 220 V, 50 Hz. The sockets are designed to accommodate two round

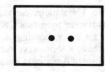

prongs in the European style. Unfortunately, the holes are very narrow in diameter, so a Hong Kong standard plug will not fit.

BOOKS & MAPS

Men, Beasts and Gods by Ferdinand Ossendowski is a sensationalised account of events in the late 1920s – well worth reading.

Within Mongolia, you can buy an excellent paperback book called *This is Mongolia* by Yunden, Zorig and Erdene. It's available at the post office in the Ulaan Baatar Hotel for US$4.

If you're in China, you can buy the large, bilingual *Map of the People's Republic of China* which also contains an excellent map of Mongolia. The map is available from Xinhua Bookstore which has branches all over China, or you can get it from most large bookstores in Hong Kong. Within Mongolia, any maps you find will be written in Cyrillic script.

MEDIA

Newspapers & Magazines

All media used to be state-controlled, but liberalisation has certainly changed the atmosphere. The major daily paper is the government-run *Unen* ('The Truth'), which is published in Mongolian. The new political parties have their own new publications, including *Ug* ('The Word') and *Ardchilal* ('Democracy').

There is one English-language newspaper, the weekly *Mongol Messenger*, available from the post office and major hotels. There are several magazines available in English. *Mongolia* magazine is published monthly. *Moscow News* is a Soviet weekly newspaper in English. *New Time* is an English-language weekly. Also available is *Soviet Union* magazine.

Radio & TV

There are two TV stations carrying both Mongolian and Soviet programs. CNN news in English is on every morning at various times. If you have a short-wave radio, you can pick up Voice of America in Russian and English. You can also get the BBC world service, mornings and evenings.

FILM & PHOTOGRAPHY

Kodak and Fuji colour print film is available from duty-free shops, but you must pay with hard foreign currency. You can get film processed at the Bayangol Hotel. Slide film is a rare item indeed, so bring what you need. Mongolia is definitely *not* the place to buy camera accessories, though you never know what sort of ancient relic you might find in the department stores.

Mongolians are not especially enthusiastic about having their photos taken. This is best accomplished surreptitiously, with a powerful telephoto lens.

HEALTH

Except for getting frostbite in winter, Mongolia is generally a healthy country to travel in. Mongolians insist that the tap water is safe to drink in Ulaan Baatar, and in any event you'll have a hard time finding boiled water unless you boil it yourself. Care should be taken drinking water in areas where it may be contaminated by livestock. In the countryside, there have been reports of rabies.

From all appearances, Mongolia seems like a bad place to get ill. If you need medical treatment, China would be better. However, herbal medicine and acupuncture are available in Mongolia, based on Tibetan medicine rather than the Chinese variety.

DANGERS & ANNOYANCES

Theft is becoming increasingly common in Ulaan Baatar. The locals say that walking around at night in Ulaan Baatar is not safe, especially in poorly lit areas. The 'yurt suburbs' are more dangerous than the centre. The problem is not severe, but caution with your valuables is still advised. There are few police on the streets and you'll have a hard time communicating with them unless you speak Mongolian.

Perhaps the biggest annoyance is the presence of drunken men who wander the streets and occasionally become very aggressive. Your chances of getting into a fight are greatly increased if you're mistaken for a Russian – apparently the locals don't like them at all. The Russians recognise that they aren't popular, and many of them have taken to wearing 'I Love Hong Kong' T-shirts so the Mongolians will think they're tourists.

WORK

Mongolia's new opening to the outside world has raised some speculation about English-teaching possibilities. You might approach the Mongolian embassy with the idea, but don't expect the pay to be anything more than dismal. Still, it's one way to experience the country.

ACCOMMODATION

If you book through Zhuulchin, you'll have little choice – you must stay at a Zhuulchin-approved (expensive) hotel. If you arrive on your own, there are several dirt-cheap hotels. Some of these are reasonably comfortable, though you may have to get used to no hot water in the showers. Budget hotels start at T150 per night.

You may have the opportunity to stay in a yurt, otherwise known as a *gher*. Gher is a Mongolian word, while yurt is what everyone else calls it. These can also be quite comfortable, but usually toilets and showers will be outside.

FOOD

There are some serious shortages of food in Mongolia, though hopefully this problem will be alleviated by the time you get there. Residents of Ulaan Baatar are issued ration coupons for scarce basic staples. Foreigners are less affected because they can afford the prices in the tourist hotels, which are actually absurdly cheap by Western standards. Bread is a basic staple and the quality is often good.

The most common dish is mutton, served in numerous styles. It's at its best in the form of *shorlog* (Mongolian barbecue, or shish kebab). Steamed buns *(buuz)* with mutton filling vaguely resemble the Chinese variety. There is also a pancake made with flour and mutton *(khoshor)*, and boiled dumplings *(bansh)*.

The problem is that most Mongolians prefer their mutton boiled, a cooking method which puts out a nauseating odour that sends most foreigners scurrying for the toilet. If you don't believe this, just walk into the Ulaan Baatar railway station restaurant and take a whiff of the air! The odour permeates everything – even Mongolian biscuits and butter smell like boiled mutton, and when you try to wash off the odour, you may find the soap smells like mutton too. Even the paper money soon develops that mutton smell.

There is no fresh fruit available and only a few vegetables mostly grown in green-houses. If you're a vegetarian, about the only way you'll survive is to get your protein from dairy products. Yoghurt and milk are available. There is a very sharp fermented cheese called *aarts*. For variety, try Russian food – primarily borscht with sour cream and potatoes.

DRINKS

Mongolians can drink you under the table if you challenge them. They brew their own unique firewater, *koumiss*, which is fermented horse's milk – definitely an acquired taste. The Russians have popularised vodka, which the Mongolians now make and even export to the USSR – a popular brand is Arkhi. The Mongolians also produce several brands of beer – quality varies but Borgio isn't bad. Mongolians take their tea with milk and salt. Coffee is a rare item.

THINGS TO BUY

Mongolian department stores specialise in empty shelves. Occasionally, you'll spot some interesting souvenirs such as traditional robes and ceremonial hats. You'll sometimes find nice-looking boots in the department stores, but on closer inspection the quality often leaves much to be desired. We found one with a large nail sticking right up through the bottom of the sole!

Mongolia produces some amazing postage stamps. The Mickey Mouse stamp is a favourite with travellers, but it's only available at the Ulaan Baatar Hotel, not in the post office.

You can buy imported goods at reasonable prices in the duty-free shops in the Ulaan Baatar and Bayangol hotels, but you must pay with hard foreign currency. There are a few other hard currency shops scattered around town. Acceptable currencies include US dollars, British pounds, German marks, French francs, Japanese yen and Swiss francs.

Getting There & Away

AIR

Only three airlines fly into Mongolia: the Mongolian state airline MIAT, the Chinese airline CAAC and the Soviet airline Aeroflot.

MIAT runs two flights weekly from Beijing to Ulaan Baatar for US$150 one way. CAAC also flies twice weekly. From Moscow to Ulaan Baatar, MIAT has two flights weekly and Aeroflot once weekly – these cost an outrageous US$700 one way. Ironically, Aeroflot is cheaper if you fly from Berlin to Ulaan Baatar via Moscow. There are also flights from Irkutsk, USSR, to Ulaan Baatar.

In China, MIAT (☎ 5002255) has a Beijing booking office on the 19th floor, CITIC Building, Jianguomenwai, just next to the Friendship Store. The office is open from Tuesday to Friday, 8 am to noon and 1 to 5 pm, and on Saturday from 9 am to 2 pm. International tickets with CAAC can be bookd through China International Travel Service (CITS) in the Beijing International Hotel. Aeroflot (☎ 5002412) has an office in the Hotel Beijing Toronto on Jianguomenwai.

Getting to Mongolia is only half the battle. Getting away can be a real problem, at least during the summer peak season. Buy your onward or return ticket in advance. If you can't get a ticket, try flying standby – there are often seats available on MIAT even when they claim to be 'all full'.

TRAIN

The Trans-Siberian from Beijing takes 1½ days to reach Ulaan Baatar. Moscow to Ulaan Baatar is four days. There are major delays at the China-Mongolia border, in part because of bureaucracy gone berserk. Also, about two hours are spent changing the bogies (undercarriage wheels) due to the different railway track gauges between the two countries. The ride through Mongolia is impressive: rolling grasslands with plenty of animals, including camels, wild horses and (if you look closely) marmots.

It's very important to realise that as soon as you cross into Mongolia, the food in the dining car is priced in Tughrigs. Many foreigners have the mistaken impression that they must pay in US dollars. The railway staff will gladly accept your dollars instead of Tughrigs, but you'll be paying anywhere from three to 10 times the real price. There are black market moneychangers at the Chinese border railway station in Erlian (Erenhot). Many Mongolians on the train are also willing to change money, but usually at a poorer rate. Still, it's a lot cheaper than paying with US dollars.

It's a good idea to bring food with you, because the food in the Mongolian dining cars is usually not enough, which is just as well since it generally tastes like stale camel fat.

If you enter Mongolia on the Trans-Siberian, arrange your onward ticket to Beijing or Moscow in advance. Otherwise, you'll be scrambling for tickets in Ulaan Baatar, and these can be very difficult to get. If you must buy tickets in Ulaan Baatar, it's often easier to do it yourself than to have a Mongolian 'help' you – they seem to be more easily intimidated by the system than foreigners are.

A few Mongolians do however have connections with the railway staff through the 'back door', and if you know someone like this, they could probably prove extremely useful.

LEAVING MONGOLIA

If you're on tour with Zhuulchin, they will

take you to the railway station or airport – you're paying for it anyway. If you're on your own, try to make arrangements in advance for a taxi to take you to the airport or railway station, especially if you have an early morning departure.

Air passengers can rejoice – Mongolia is one of those rare and wonderul countries where there is absolutely no airport departure tax.

Getting Around

AIR

Mongolia is a vast, sparsely inhabited country, and flying is about the only way to get around if you're going far afield from Ulaan Baatar. Air tickets are subsidised by the government and are insanely cheap, about US$3 on the average. Chances are these bargains won't last long since the price doesn't even cover the cost of fuel.

MIAT flies daily except Sundays to the following provincial capitals: Ölgij, Ulaangom, Chovd, Uliastaj, Altaj, Mörön, Cecerleg, Bajan Chongor, Arvaj Cheer, Dalan Dzadgad, Mandal Gov', Cojbalsan, Baruun Urt, Öndör Chaan. MIAT also flies on Tuesdays and Thursdays to Erdenet via the provincial capital of Bulgan.

There are three provincial capitals which MIAT does not fly to: Süch Baatar, Sajin Sand and Dzuun Mod. The first two are served by the railway, and Dzuun Mod is a short drive from Ulaan Baatar.

BUS

There are buses connecting Ulaan Baatar and Darchan. Other than that, there are no long-distance buses. The Ulaan Baatar-Darchan road is paved, but most other highways are dirt tracks.

TRAIN

There is only one train, the Trans-Mongolian line which is part of the international Trans-Siberian system. For domestic travel, the most useful line is the one between Ulaan Baatar and Darchan.

TAXI

There are very few taxis anywhere, even in Ulaan Baatar, but they will no doubt increase in the future. At present, there are two kinds of taxis, government and private. Government taxis have a meter while private ones don't. It's essential to agree on the fare before starting out, and bargaining is permissible.

BICYCLE

Until 1991, bicycles were scarcer than rainfall in the Gobi Desert. Evidently, the fierce climate and wide open spaces discourage this activity, not to mention the fact that no one could afford bikes. Now that Mongolia is opening to the outside world, 10-speed bicycles have suddenly appeared on the streets of Ulaan Baatar, but bike rentals are nowhere to be found. Bikes are in demand, so if you have one, keep it securely locked.

TOURS

Mongolia's official state-run tour agency is Zhuulchin. They can make all travel arrangements, but they always try to book you into expensive accommodation (US$45 to US$75 per night) with meals included. Furthermore, communicating with Zhuulchin is anything but easy. They don't have any offices outside Mongolia, so you must call them and make all arrangements before you arrive. They have two telephone numbers (☎ 20163, 20246), but these might as well be on the moon for all the good they will do you – getting a call through to Mongolia is virtually impossible. Your best hope of communicating is via telex (232 ZHULN MH). Zhuulchin needs to know: your nationality, purpose of tour, itinerary, and means of transport (air or train) for arrival and departure. You have to make these international transport arrangements yourself, though once you are in the country, a Zhuulchin guide will meet you at the railway station or airport and arrange transport around the country. Not everyone has been satisfied with the service they received from Zhuulchin. As one traveller wrote:

The Mongolian countryside was as beautiful as the tourist guide was horrible. The restaurant car had been disconnected at the border before we had our evening meal the night before, and we were starving! But the guide (who spoke German but hardly any English) took us all around town on the bus to make reservations for accommodation and onward travel before taking us to a touristy fake 'nomad camp' about an hour's drive out of town. By now we had not eaten for almost 24 hours, and when we arrived at the camp there was another long wait for the ghastly food to be prepared...The next day the abominable guide took us back into town and dropped us off at the museum, no English-speaking guide was available, and we were left on our own while the guide and the bus driver got drunk in the bus.

Mats Reimer

Hopefully, their service will improve now that they are starting to get some free market competition.

Zhuulchin claim they can organise special interest tours such as trekking, hunting, bird-watching, etc. Don't expect these ex peditions to be cheap, but if you get a decent guide, they could be interesting.

At the time of this writing, the cheapest tour we could find was offered through Monkey Business. For US$140, you get to spend a week in Mongolia. Accommodation is in a traditional yurt. Part of the time is spent in Terelj, 80 km from Ulaan Baatar. Meals and transport are included. After the tour is completed, you can still spend additional time on your own. The chief advantage of this tour is that they arrange a legal tourist visa. Monkey Business (also known as Moonsky Star) has two offices, one in Hong Kong and one in Beijing. The Hong Kong office (☎ 7231376, fax 7236653) is on the 4th floor, E-Block, Flat 6, Chungking Mansions, 40 Nathan Rd, Tsimshatsui, Kowloon. The Beijing office (☎ 3012244 ext 716) is in room 716 of the Qiaoyuan Hotel.

If you don't want to deal with Zhuulchin directly, some Western tour agencies can make the bookings for you, although they go through Zhuulchin too. Most of these agencies require that you make your bookings

months in advance, and they are even more expensive than trips that you book yourself. In the UK, try Regent Holidays Ltd (☎ (0272) 211711), 13 Small St, Bristol BS1 1DE. In Australia, try Access Travel (☎ (02) 2411128), 5th floor, 58 Pitt St, Sydney. In Hong Kong, the agent specialising in tours to Mongolia (and other former Eastern Bloc countries) is Wallem Travel (☎ 5286514), 46th floor, Hopewell Centre, 183 Queen's Rd East, Wanchai. The following prices are quoted by Wallem Travel. For a single traveller, a five-day tour costs US$1194. The price drops to US$727 each for two to four persons; US$569 each for five to nine persons; US$519 each for 10 to 15 persons; a 16th person can go for free. If booked in conjunction with a trip on the Trans-Siberian Railway, the price is reduced by US$153 per person. Wallem Travel needs six weeks to arrange this tour, plus you need to allow at least a day (preferably more) to pick up your Mongolian visa in Beijing.

Ulaan Baatar

Ulaan Baatar is the sprawling capital city of the MPR with a population of over half a million. There's plenty of open space – wide boulevards, squares, parks, monuments and very little traffic. There are a few high-rise apartments in the centre, but much of the population lives in yurts on the outskirts of town. These are enclosed by fences which protect from the fierce winds. Except for the central area, cows wander around town grazing on whatever greenery they can find. Ulaan Baatar has the look and feel of the 1950s, from the columned buildings to the vintage Soviet-built cars and old German motorcycles with sidecars attached. The city has changed names many times. The present name, Ulaan Baatar, was given in 1924 and means 'Red Hero'.

Orientation

We can't give exact addresses because there aren't any. It must be a real nightmare for

Mongolian postal workers, which probably explains why post office boxes are so popular in Ulaan Baatar.

The city is divided into districts, the centre being called Sukhbaatar District. The prominent landmark in the centre is Sukhbaatar Square, containing a monument of Sukh himself riding a horse. To the east is the Nairamdal District; to the west is the October District; to the south-west is the Workers or Azhilchin District. Within all these districts are numbered 'micro-districts'.

Information

Tourist Office Zhuulchin (☎ 20163, 20246) is next to worthless. They hide their office on the 11th floor of the Chamber of Commerce, Ministry for Foreign Economic Relations and Supply Building on Sambuu St. If he's awake, the security guard in the lobby won't let foreigners go up there, and it's really not worth the trouble.

There is a Zhuulchin office in Room 4 of the Ulaan Baatar Hotel. They had no information, maps or brochures. We asked them what they had, and they replied, 'An office'.

Money The Central Bank is on the north side of the MIAT office at the south-east corner of Small Ring and October St. You can change travellers' cheques to US dollars cash, but the operating hours are brief: Monday to Friday from 9 am to 12.30 pm, and on Saturdays from 9 to 11.30 am.

Post & Telecommunications The Central Post Office is on Peace Ave, just on the west side of Sukhbaatar Square. The east section of the building is devoted to international telephone service.

There is a mailbox just outside the front door of the Ulaan Baatar Hotel. As you enter the lobby, to your right is a small shop selling postcards and stamps, but you have to pay in US dollars at the rip-off exchange rate of US$1 = T5.20. However, it's well worth visiting because they sell the famed Mickey Mouse stamps, which are not available from the post office.

Cultural Centres Venues for cultural events include the State Academic Theatre of Opera and Ballet at Sukhbaatar Square, State Academic Theatre of Drama on Lenin Ave, the Puppet Theatre on Lenin Ave, State Circus on Kucherenko Ave and the State Philharmonic Society on Peace Ave.

Sadly, most cultural centres are closed during the summer. The Mongolian performers like to take their holidays at this time, which also happens to be the time when most foreign travellers arrive.

Bookshops There are two bookshops, neither of which is very good, but you can at least pick up a decent map of Ulaan Baatar. These are available in English, German or Mongolian. You can buy them from the bookshop on the north-west side of Sukhbaatar Square. This same bookshop also sells good maps of Mongolia, but only in the Cyrillic script.

The reception desk of the Ulaan Baatar Hotel sometimes has maps of Ulaan Baatar for sale.

There is another bookshop next to the State Department Store on the corner of Peace Ave and Natsagdorj St. They have a few nice picture books but their maps aren't too good.

Emergency There are emergency numbers for fire (01), police (02) and ambulance (03), but don't expect anyone to speak English.

Things to See

The **State Central Museum** on Sambuu St near the centre is well worth a visit. The natural history section is very interesting – the most astonishing sight is the two complete dinosaur skeletons which were found in the south Gobi Desert. The shorter skeleton was found in 1948 and belongs to a trabosaur. The tall skeleton is a duck-billed dinosaur, found in 1987. The museum has numerous other sections devoted to Mongolian history and culture. This museum and most others are closed on Tuesday.

The **Gandan Monastery** (Gandantegchinlen) was nearly deserted during the

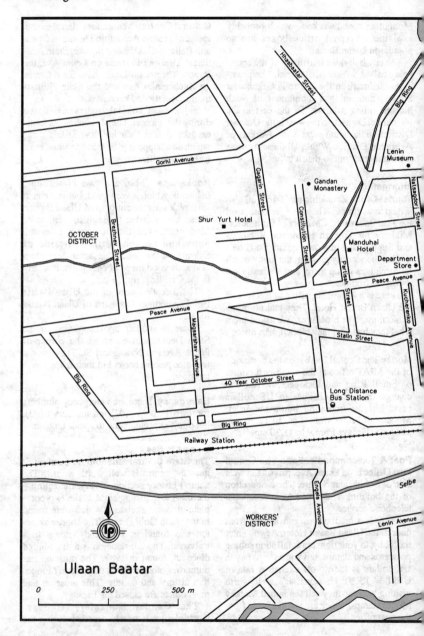

Ulaan Baatar

0   250   500 m

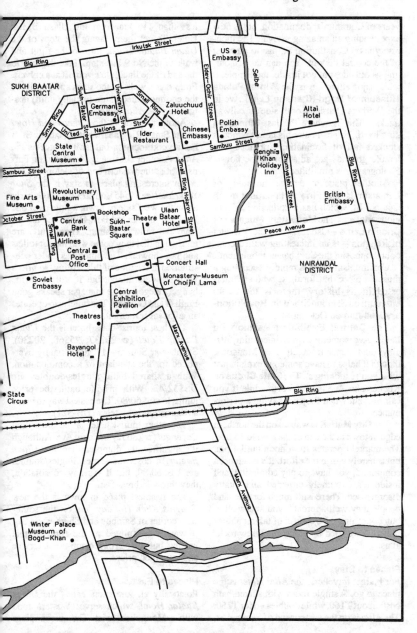

years of Communist domination, but is now experiencing an amazing revival. The monastery is on Constitution St, just to the west of the central district. You can take photographs outside, but not inside, the temple.

A major attraction is the **Winter Palace Museum of Bogd-Khan**, on Lenin Ave in the Workers District (south side of railway tracks). This is where the last Mongolian king lived. You can enter his house which is stocked full of fascinating artefacts. The temple grounds are adjacent to the house. Photography is prohibited.

Another place to pursue the study of Lamaism is the **Fine Arts Museum** on October St, which has a collection of religious artefacts. The **Monastery-Museum of Choijin Lama** – also known as the Museum of Religion – is an interesting walled compound opposite the Sukhbaatar monument.

Communism itself is rapidly becoming a museum piece, but for those who are interested in its history, there is the **Lenin Museum** on Sambuu St and the **Revolutionary Museum** on October St.

The **Central Exhibition Pavilion** on Lenin Ave sometimes has interesting displays and items from all over Mongolia, though it helps to have someone explain just what you're looking at. The **State Circus** on Kucherenko Ave is well worth while if you can find out when they are having a performance.

The **City Market** is way up on the northern edge of town at the end of the bus No 15 line. The market operates from noon until 4 pm, but is hardly worth the effort. It's in a fenced compound, you have to pay admission, and inside it's extremely crowded and totally disorganised. There isn't much for sale, and people may well approach you and want to buy your things. Be careful of taking photos in here – we tried it and people threw rocks at us.

Places to Stay

For budget travellers, the *Altai Hotel* is the place to go. A single room with shared bath costs about T160, while doubles go for T250. The *Altai* is on the eastern end of Sambuu St,

less than 1½ km from the Ulaan Baatar Hotel. To get there: facing the steps of the *Ulaan Baatar Hotel*, turn to the right and walk to the No 9 bus stop. Take this bus to the end of the line. It lets you off at a culvert. From there, walk up the steps and you'll see the enormous neon sign (usually unlit) designating the *Altai Hotel*.

Another option is the *Zaluuchuud Hotel* on the Small Ring near United Nations St. It has a good location but isn't as nice as the *Altai*. Another cheapie is *Manduhai* on Partisan St at the western end of October St.

An interesting place to stay is the *Shur Yurt Hotel* (☎ 54545), on an alley off Gagarin St on the west side of town, a little over one km from the Central Post Office and not far from the railway station. These yurts are unusual in that they come with indoor toilets and hot showers. The hotel was under construction at the time of this writing, so prices were not determined, but it will be in the budget category. The manager speaks good English and German. The hotel also operates an adjacent restaurant.

The best tourist-class hotel is the *Ulaan Baatar Hotel* (☎ 20237, 25368, 20230), Sukhbaatar Square – 17. It's certainly overpriced for the standard of accommodation. With a shared bath, singles/doubles are US$32/42. With private bath, the price jumps to US$60/80. The easiest way to make a reservation is by telex (UB-321).

The other tourist hotel is the crumbling *Bayangol* (☎ 28632) on Lenin Ave. Although it's significantly dumpier than the *Ulaan Baatar*, it costs the same. Singles/doubles are US$60/80, but if it's any consolation, they throw in breakfast.

The flashiest place in town is the new *Genghis Khan Holiday Inn*, on the southwest corner of Sambuu and Shumyatshi Sts. It wasn't completed at the time of this writing, but you can expect top-notch service and top-notch prices.

Places to Eat

Practically all foreigners eat at the *Ulaan Baatar Hotel*, which serves Western food with a Mongolian twist. The surroundings are fairly plush and a typical meal costs around T30. You don't have to be staying at this hotel to eat there. The service is not great – the waitresses scowl when you ask for a menu – but once you finally get served, the food is excellent. The cheap restaurant is on the ground floor and they accept Tughrigs. Upstairs is a more expensive restaurant which demands US dollars. Breakfast is served from 7.30 to 10 am; lunch from noon to 2 pm; dinner from 5 to 9 pm.

The other tourist hotel, the *Bayangol*, also provides excellent Western meals but isn't as popular because of its location. The *Altai Hotel* has very irregular supplies of food – one day they might only have rice pudding and eggs, the next day stale bread with boiled mutton. They often run out of food and close early.

Other restaurants in the centre include *Tuul* on October St, and *Ider* on the Small Ring next to the Zaluuchuud Hotel.

Entertainment
Ulaan Baatar is not Bangkok – nightlife is definitely tame. Locals either get plastered on Arkhi or visit the cinemas.

For foreigners, nightlife consists of the bars in the big hotels. You have to pay in hard currency. One can of beer costs US$1.50, Coca-cola is US$1.25 and a double whisky costs US$2. Mongolians with access to dollars also hang out in these bars.

Getting There & Away
Air The MIAT office is on the inner west side of Small Ring, just south of October St. It gets extremely crowded and there are no queues. However, if you ask at the information desk, they will assist you so that you don't have to engage in hand-to-hand combat in order to get your ticket.

The Aeroflot office is on Stalin St near the intersection with Partisan St.

Bus There are buses to Darchan and the suburbs surrounding Ulaan Baatar. The long-distance bus station is on the southern end of Constitution St.

Train Domestic tickets are sold at the railway station, but for international train tickets you must go to the Ulaan Baatar Hotel. The 'Booking Office for International Trains' is at rear of the hotel (north-east corner) which you enter from a separate door. Hours of operation are from Monday to Saturday, 9 am to 2 pm. On Tuesdays, there are additional afternoon hours from 3 to 5 pm.

Getting Around
To/From the Airport Airport buses meet incoming flights and charge T1 to go to the centre. If you're on a Zhuulchin tour, they will come to the airport to meet you. A taxi (if you can find one) from the airport to the centre costs around T55.

Bus There is a good network of electric trolley buses and regular buses, but they can get extremely crowded. All buses charge T1 to anyplace in the city. The Ulaan Baatar city map shows the routes. Beware of pickpockets.

Around the Country

TERELJ
The **Terelj Tourist Camp**, 80 km north-east of Ulaan Baatar, is usually included on most tours. At 1600 metres altitude, the area is cool, forested and alpine. The scenery is magnificent, and there are opportunities for hiking, swimming (in icy water!), Mongolian barbecue and horseback riding. On the way going up there, you pass grazing sheep, cattle, horses and yaks. The place has some nightlife too – a disco operates from 8.30 pm until midnight during the summer months.

That's the good news. The bad news is that this tourist camp is just that – it's being 'developed' for tourists. Zhuulchin's ideal tourist camp itinerary includes a picnic, demonstrations of 'genuine Mongolian sports', a disco party and a photo session with tourists dressed up in Mongolian garb. Dressing up the tourists is one thing, but Zhuulchin wants to dress up the scenery too – they've rigged up a few dinosaurs made out of concrete. This could be a sign of abominations to come. Most of the tourist horrors are being inflicted in the area around Tortoise Rock, a geological formation which – if you drink a litre of Arkhi – resembles a turtle. Fortunately, the area near the hotel has been spared the concrete reptiles, at least for now.

In spite of all this, Terelj is really worth visiting, at least if you don't go with Zhuulchin. Unfortunately, getting to Terelj is a real logistical problem. There is no public transport, and access is mostly by tour bus. Hitchhiking is one possibility, though the only vehicles going up there are usually trucks and tour buses. A mountain bike would be fine if you don't mind 80 km of uphill riding. Long-distance taxi is another possibility, but it will cost you. Once you do get to Terelj, hitching a ride back to Ulaan Baatar is relatively easy. Almost all tour groups, even the budget ones, usually include a trip to Terelj.

KARAKORUM

About 400 km to the south-west of Ulaan Baatar, Karakorum was the capital of the Mongolian empire before Kublai Khan moved it to Beijing. Modern-day Karakorum is just a small but pleasant town in the grasslands, while the ruins of the ancient capital are about two km away. There isn't much left of the ruins because many of the stones were hauled away to build the nearby **Erdenezuu Monastery**, which was constructed in 1586, the first Buddhist centre in Mongolia. This impressive monastery is enclosed in an immense walled compound, and inside are the Lavran Temple and 108 stupas.

About 50 km south of Karakorum by road is **Khuzhirt**, a Zhuulchin-promoted tourist camp noted for its hot springs. Soaking your body in these is claimed to cure everything from arthritis to nappy rash. After you've been properly soaked, you can also arrange an excursion to **Orkhon Waterfall**, 82 km west of Khuzhirt.

Places to Stay & Eat

Right in the hotel on the city square is an unnamed hotel (no sign), but just say the world 'hotel' to anyone and they'll point it out to you. Beds cost T60 per person in a four-bed room, and doubles are T70 per person. The hotel serves set meals for T10 which includes rice and mutton. They serve horrible salty tea, but most travellers drink unboiled water, apparently without ill effect. You can buy bread in the town.

The other place to stay is the *Orkhon Hotel* about two km from town right by the river. It's a lovely place, built in log cabin style, and they also have fancy yurts. All beds cost T110 per person. In the back of the log cabin, there is a room with ping-pong and billiards tables. Most amazing of all is the beach adjacent to the hotel, complete with beach chairs and tables. Meals in the plush dining room cost T15.

Getting There & Away

Getting to Karakorum is half the fun. Because there is no airport, the MIAT flight is in an old Soviet helicopter! Departures from Ulaan Baatar are on Monday, Wednesday and Friday at 7.10 am. The flight takes almost two hours and shortly after arrival in Karakorum, the helicopter loads up more passengers and returns to Ulaan Baatar. The landing field is three km from Karakorum, so you can either walk or hire a jeep for T50.

SOUTH GOBI

Zhuulchin plugs other trips, most of which are a lot more fun and certainly cheaper if you go by yourself. Part of the thrill is the chance to spend a night in a yurt.

The **South Gobi Tourist Camp** is 600 km south of Ulaan Baatar. You get there by taking a MIAT flight to Dalan Dzadgad (1½ hours) and then a short bus ride. The tour includes: a walk or camel ride on the sand dunes; a visit to Bayanzag where dinosaur eggs and skeletons have been found; a trip to a cattle breeding farm; and a movie about the Gobi Desert. The camp is open from 1 May to 1 October.

LAKE CHÖVSGÖL

Near the USSR border is Lake Chövsgöl,

Mongolia's deepest and largest lake, in an area noted for its numerous caves. To get there, first fly from Ulaan Baatar to the provincial capital of Mörön. From there, you must take either a chartered bus or taxi. There are quite a few foreign and local Mongolian groups going to Lake Chövsgöl, so finding a chartered bus is not as hard as it sounds.

ÖLGIJ & CHOVD

The north-west part of Mongolia has the best scenery in the country. The region is Mongolia's lake district – there are over 300 lakes in the vicinity. Along the Mongolia-China border is the splendour of the Altai mountains. This is Mongolia's highest range, and many of the mountains are covered by glaciers.

The two main cities of this region are the provincial capitals of Ölgij and Chovd, both of which can be reached by air from Ulaan Baatar. Of the two, Ölgij is higher in the mountains. Transport to the mountains is mainly on foot, and it's a real expedition for experienced mountaineers only.

Taiwan

A subtropical island – and officially a province of China – Taiwan is still the focus of a political tug of war between the mainland Chinese Communist Party and Taiwan's ruling Kuomintang, both of which claim to represent all of China. Like Hong Kong, Taiwan has been an embarrassment to the Communists; although the mainland has over 50 times the population and 265 times the area, Taiwan's per capita income is more than 20 times higher. Both sides continue to exchange verbal abuse (they used to exchange artillery shells), but these days Taiwanese tourists flock to the mainland in droves. Mainlanders also flock to Taiwan – illegally, on fishing boats and even rubber rafts.

Politics aside, Taiwan has much to offer the foreign traveller. There are unsurpassed mountains, gorges, beaches, forests, Taoist and Buddhist temples, and small offshore islands harbouring a fascinating aboriginal culture. Taiwan also preserves the finest of Chinese art, much of which was destroyed on the mainland during the Cultural Revolution. Taipei's National Palace Museum holds the world's richest collection of ancient Chinese art and is rated as one of the top four museums in the world.

Taiwan is one of the world's most densely populated regions – 395 km long, with a population of 20 million – yet over half of the island is extremely mountainous and almost uninhabited, offering numerous opportunities for mountaineering and exploring remote villages. Taiwan's tallest peak – Yushan – is the highest in North-East Asia outside of remote western China. The cities – crowded and noisy though they may be – provide excellent nightlife, outstanding food and very friendly people, who will go out of their way to make sure you are not lonely. For those who take the time to explore, Taiwan offers a unique and diverse environment – a fast-changing society that defies generalisation.

Facts about the Country

HISTORY

Little is known of Taiwan's earliest history, but it is thought that people have inhabited the island for at least 10,000 years. The first known inhabitants were not Chinese at all, but probably migrants from the Pacific islands.

Taiwan may have had contact with mainland China as early as the Sui dynasty (581 to 618 AD) but there was no significant migration until the 15th century. The Hakka (the name means 'guests') started trickling into Taiwan to escape persecution on the mainland. Starting in the 1400s, large numbers of Chinese from Fujian Province started migrating to Taiwan. Their language – Fujianese – is virtually the same as modern-day Taiwanese.

In 1517 the first Europeans – Portuguese sailors – landed on Taiwan's shores and were so impressed by the beautiful scenery that they named it Ihla Formosa, which literally means 'Island Beautiful'. The name Formosa has been used right up to the present. The Dutch invaded Taiwan in 1624 and established the island's first capital at Tainan. In 1626, the Spanish grabbed control of north Taiwan, but were expelled by the Dutch in 1641.

Soon thereafter, Cheng Chengkung (also known as Koxinga) arrived with 30,000 troops, fleeing the invading Manchus. In 1661, Koxinga expelled the Dutch, but by 1682 the Manchus had captured Taiwan. For the next 200 years, there was steady migration from the mainland. Taiwan remained a county of Fujian Province until 1887.

In 1895 the Japanese occupied the island and held it for the next 50 years. Although the Japanese were often cruel overlords, they provided education, built roads, railways and factories, and raised the standard of living to a level much higher than on the Chinese mainland.

Under the Yalta Agreement, China regained sovereignty over Taiwan with Japan's defeat in WW II. In 1949 the Communists took control of the mainland, and the Kuomintang (Nationalist Party) led by Chiang Kaishek fled to Taiwan. The Kuomintang has vowed ever since to retake the mainland – it hasn't happened yet.

In October 1971, the Kuomintang lost the Chinese United Nations seat. A further blow came in January 1979 when the USA withdrew recognition of the Republic of China (ROC) and established diplomatic relations with the Communists on the mainland. Recognition of two Chinas was impossible – the Kuomintang and the Communists agree on little else, but both sides insist that Taiwan is a province of China.

In 1975, Chiang Kaishek died, and in 1978 his son, Chiang Chingkuo, became president. Criticism mounted over the Kuomintang's one-party rule and the establishment of a 'Chiang dynasty'. Opposition candidates formed the Democratic Progressive Party (DPP) in 1986 and were permitted seats in the legislature. In 1987, 38 years of martial law ended. In 1988, Chiang Chingkuo died and was succeeded by his vice-president, Lee Tenghui, the first native-born Taiwanese to assume the presidency. The first really free election was in 1989, when the DPP took 30% of the vote.

One of the thornier political dilemmas for the Kuomintang has been what to do with the aging 'deputies' – legislators who were elected on the mainland before the Communist takeover. Unable to stand for re-election, they were frozen in office for over 40 years, still claiming to represent their constituents on the mainland. In 1991, those still living were finally forced to retire.

GEOGRAPHY

Shaped roughly like a tobacco leaf, Taiwan is an island just a mere 160 km from the Chinese mainland. The island's maximum length is 395 km and its maximum width is 144 km. A narrow plain on the west coast is where 90% of the population lives – it's overcrowded, industrialised and badly polluted. Fortunately, the rest of the island is extremely mountainous and mostly unspoilt. Taiwan's highest peak is Yushan (Jade Mountain) – at 3952 metres, it's higher than Japan's Mt Fuji.

In addition to Taiwan itself, there are a number of smaller offshore islands including the Penghu group, Lanyu, Green Island and Hsiao Liuchiu. The ROC also controls Kinmen and Matsu, two islands within sight of mainland China – these serve as military bases and are not open to visitors.

Taipei is the largest city and seat of government. Other large cities include Kao hsiung, Taichung and Tainan – all on the west side of the island.

CLIMATE

The island is subtropical, but the mountains can be cold even in summer. The north-east coast gets heavy rain in winter, while the south-west is noticeably warmer and drier. However, summer is uniformly hot and sticky at low elevations, and mountain areas get the heaviest rains. The typhoon season can run from June to the end of October, but is unpredictable. The best time for a visit is during October and November.

GOVERNMENT

The Kuomintang (KMT) has held power continuously since 1945. The Democratic Progressive Party (DPP) is by far the largest opposition party. They have won widespread recognition for getting into fist fights with Kuomintang legislators, though they also take time out for fighting amongst themselves.

Power is distributed among five major branches of government which are called Yuan – the Legislative, Executive, Judicial, Examination and Control Yuan. The first three are self-explanatory. The Examination Yuan oversees Taiwan's formidable system of exams, which determines one's access to education, jobs, business licences, etc. The Control Yuan is a watchdog agency that tries to keep things honest.

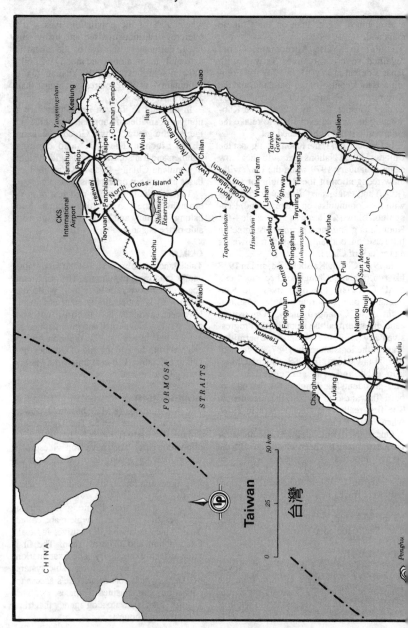

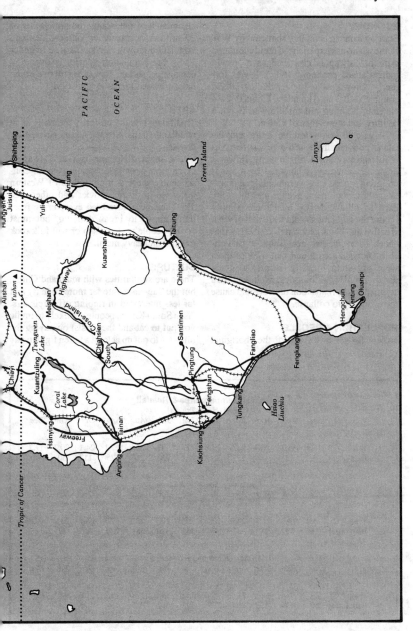

ECONOMY

Starting from an economy shattered by WW II, the island has experienced rapid economic growth. Taiwan is classified as a 'newly industrialised economy' (NIE). It was formerly known as a 'newly industrialised country' (NIC) until mainland China threw a tantrum, pointing out that Taiwan is not a country, but a province of China.

Taiwan lives on foreign trade and the island now has the world's largest reserves of foreign currency. Unfortunately, Taiwan's domestic economy is hindered by a mind-boggling morass of governmental red tape – everything requires a licence and these are hard to obtain. Many businesses simply ignore the regulations – they are part of what is called the 'black economy'. In 1991, a spot check of businesses near Taipei's fashionable Dinghao area found that 67% of them were operating illegally. Efforts to crack down on illegal businesses have been stymied by the realisation that it would cause the economy to collapse.

POPULATION & PEOPLE

Except for some 300,000 of the aboriginal inhabitants of the island, the population of 20 million is mostly of Chinese descent. Population growth rate has slowed to under 1.5%, but population density is over 550 persons per sq km. Taiwan is still one of the most crowded places in the world.

ARTS

Traditional arts are basically the same as in mainland China. See the China chapter for details.

The main difference is that Taiwan is much more open to the modern world. Consequently, there is a good deal of Western influence in music, movies and other arts. The Taiwanese have tried every craze from punk music to break dancing, but most young people go for disco or soft folk rock rather than heavy metal.

CULTURE

There are similarities with mainland China, but the Taiwanese are far more friendly and far less interested in ripping off foreigners. As in South Korea, people are likely to invite you out to eat and they insist on paying the bill – try to put up at least a token fight to pay

Taiwan Temperatures & Rainfall
Taipei (North Taiwan)

	Jan	Feb	Mar	Apr	May	Jun	Jul	Aug	Sep	Oct	Nov	Dec
Temp (°C)	15.3	15.7	17.7	21.6	24.8	27	29	28.8	27.1	24.1	20.7	17.2
Rain (mm)	92	13	184	153	233	282	233	268	325	117	80	74

Kaohsiung (South-west Taiwan)

	Jan	Feb	Mar	Apr	May	Jun	Jul	Aug	Sep	Oct	Nov	Dec
Temp (°C)	18.4	19.3	21.7	24.9	27.2	28.1	28.7	28.2	27.7	26.1	23.1	19.8
Rain (mm)	16	17	34	52	184	365	320	381	180	40	17	9

Alishan (elevation 2190 metres)

	Jan	Feb	Mar	Apr	May	Jun	Jul	Aug	Sep	Oct	Nov	Dec
Temp (°C)	5.3	6.4	8.6	11	12.6	13.8	14.2	13.9	13.3	11.6	9.5	6.6
Rain (mm)	89	114	159	209	537	743	592	820	464	126	54	54

your share, or reciprocate with some sort of gift (a cake or a bag of fruit).

Death is a totally taboo topic of conversation. The number four sounds just like the Chinese word for death – hospitals never put patients on the 4th floor and you never give anyone a gift of NT$400 or NT$4000. If you give someone flowers, you always give red flowers, not white. In Chinese symbolism white – not black – is the colour associated with death. The most popular brand of cigarettes in Taiwan is named 'Long Life'. There are lots of parks with names like 'Longevity Mountain' and 'Eternal Happiness Forest'. There is one national park in America the Taiwanese never visit – Death Valley. Sellers of life insurance have a hard time in Taiwan.

RELIGION

Depending on who's counting, about 2% to 5% of the population are Christian. The vast majority of the people in Taiwan today consider themselves Buddhist or Taoist with Confucian influence. Taiwan's original inhabitants have mostly adopted Christianity.

Taiwan has the most complete collection of Taoist temples in the world, and they are in far better condition than those on the Chinese mainland. These temples become extremely lively during worship festivals.

LANGUAGE

Mandarin Chinese is the official language – it's used on television, radio, in schools and for all formal purposes. Taiwanese – almost identical to the Fujian dialect on the mainland – is popular for informal occasions but has no written script.

Unfortunately there are three competing Romanisation systems for Chinese in common use. In mainland China, pinyin is used; on Taiwan you'll find Wade-Giles – the oldest system – in use for street signs, maps, books, newspapers and name cards. Romanisation is unfortunately not taught in Taiwan's schools, so the locals are usually unfamiliar with it and mistakes are common.

Most Taiwanese cannot even romanise their own names. The use of apostrophes is also a problem; they are usually omitted and it becomes impossible to distinguish between d and t, k and g, and so on.

See the chapter on mainland China for a vocabulary list and an explanation of pronunciation. Some of the vocabulary is unique to Taiwan, as follows:

Necessities

tampons
　wèishēng mián tiáo
pharmacy
　yàojú
Panadol
　pǔnátén
telephone card
　diànhùa kǎ

Places

Bank of Taiwan
　táiwān yínháng
Intl Commercial Bank of China
　gúojì shāngyè yínháng
immigration office (Taipei)
　wàijiāo bù
foreign affairs police
　wàishì jǐngchá
GPO
　zǒng yóujú
poste restante
　cún jú hòu lǐng

Accommodation

youth hostel
　húodòng zhōngxīn
hotel
　lǚgǔan
small cheap hotel
　lǚshè
dormitory
　tuántǐfáng
cheap room (shared bath)
　pǔtōngfáng
room with private bath
　tàofáng

Transport

1st-class train
zìqiáng hào
2nd-class train
jǔgūang hào
3rd-class train
fúxīng hào
slow local train
pǔtōng chē
bus station
gōng chē zhàn
left-luggage room
xínglǐ shì
taxi
jìchéngchē

Facts for the Visitor

VISAS & EMBASSIES

Visas are required for all nationalities, and these can generally be obtained on the same day if you apply early enough in the morning.

There are two types of visitor visas: single-entry and multiple-entry. Single-entry visas are easily obtained, but a multiple-entry visitor visa is usually only issued in your home country. Both of these permit a stay for 60 days. It is possible to extend a visitor visa twice for a total stay of 180 days, but you need some valid reason like study in a government-approved language school. Visa extensions can be obtained from the Foreign Affairs Police, who speak English and have a regional office in each of Taiwan's county seats (☎ (02) 3817475 in Taipei).

The Republic of China (ROC – the official name for Taiwan's government) is recognised by very few countries. This means you won't find many ROC embassies in the world. An exception is South Korea. Nevertheless, you can easily obtain a visa from Taiwan's various 'trade offices', 'travel services', 'friendship associations' etc, which are basically pseudo-embassies travelling under flags of convenience.

Taiwan Visa Offices

Australia
    Far East Trading Co Pty Ltd, D401, International House, World Trade Centre, Melbourne (☎ (03) 6112988)
    Suite 1902, MLC Centre, King St, Sydney (☎ (02) 2233207)
Canada
    Far East Trade Service Inc, Suite 3315, 2 Bloor St East, Toronto, Ontario M4W 1A8 (☎ (416) 9222412)
Hong Kong
    Chung Hwa Travel Service, 4th floor, East Tower, Bond Centre No 89, Queensway, Hong Kong Island (☎ 5258315)
Japan
    Association of East Asian Relations, 8-7, Higashi-Azabu 1-Chome, Minato-Ku, Tokyo 106 (☎ 5832171)
    Association of East Asian Relations, 3rd floor, Sun Life Building III, 5-19, 2-Chome, Hakataeki, Higashi Hakata-Ku, Fukuoka (☎ (092) 4736655)
Malaysia
    Taipei Economic & Cultural Centre, Lot 202, Wisma Equity, 150 Jalan Ampang, 50450 Kuala Lumpur (☎ 2435337, 2425549)
New Zealand
    East Asia Trade Centre, Level 21, Marac House,105-109 The Terrace, Wellington (☎ (04) 736474)
    3rd floor, Norwich Union Building, corner Queen and Durham streets, Auckland (☎ (09) 33903)
Philippines
    Pacific Economic & Cultural Center, 8th floor, BF Homes Condominium Building, Aduana St, Intramuros, Manila (☎ 472261)
Singapore
    Trade Mission of the Republic of China, 460 Alexandra Rd, 23-00 PSA Building, Singapore 0511 (☎ 2786511)
South Korea
    Embassy of the Republic of China, 83, 2-ga, Myong-dong, Chung-gu, Seoul (☎ 7762721, 7764309)
Thailand
    The Far East Trade Office, 10th floor, Kian Gwan Building, 140 Wit Thayu Rd, Bangkok (☎ 2519274, 2519393)
UK
    Free Chinese Centre, 4th floor, Dorland House, 14-16 Regent St, London, SW1Y 4PH (☎ (071) 9305767, 9305770)
USA
    Head Office, Coordination Council for North America Affairs (CCNAA), 4201 Wisconsin Ave NW, Washington, DC 20016-2137 (☎ (202) 8951800)
    CCNAA Atlanta (☎ (404) 8720123); Boston (☎

(617) 7372050); Chicago (☎ (312) 3721213); Honolulu (☎ (808) 5956347); Houston (☎ (713) 6267445); Kansas City (☎ (816) 5311298); Los Angeles (☎ (213) 3891215); New York (☎ (212) 6971250); San Francisco (☎ (415) 3627680); Seattle (☎ (206) 4414586)

Foreign Embassies & 'Trade Offices' in Taiwan

South Korea has an embassy in Taipei. Most other countries have 'trade offices' which can also issue visas and replace lost passports. Some of these are slow because they must process the paperwork through Hong Kong or some other location where they have a 'real embassy'. The Japanese pseudo-embassy in Taipei is pretty fast – visas are issued in three days.

American Institute in Taiwan (AIT)
    7 Lane 134, Hsinyi Rd, Section 3 (☎ (02) 7092000)
Anglo-Taiwan Trade Committee
    9th floor, 99 Jenai Rd, Section 2 (☎ (02) 3223235)
Australian Commerce & Industry Office
    Room 2605, International Trade Building, 333 Keelung Rd, Section 1 (☎ (02) 7202833)
Canadian Trade Office
    13th floor, 365 Fuhsing N Rd (☎ (02) 7137268)
Indonesian Chamber of Commerce
    3rd floor, 46-1 Chungcheng Rd, Section 2 (☎ (02) 8310451)
Japan Interchange Association
    43 Chinan Rd, Section 2 (☎ (02) 3517250)
Korean Embassy
    345 Chunghsiao E Rd, Section 4 (☎ (02) 7619361)

Malaysian Friendship & Trade Center
    8th floor, 102 Tunhua N Rd (☎ (02) 7132626)
New Zealand Commerce & Industry Office
    8th floor, Room 0812, CETRA Tower, 333 Keelung Rd, Section 1 (☎ (02) 7577060)
Manila (Philippines) Economic & Cultural Office
    8th floor, 47 Chungshan N Rd, Section 3 (☎ (02) 5851120)
Thai Airways International Ltd
    6th floor, 150 Fuhsing N Rd (☎ (02) 7121882)

DOCUMENTS
Mountain Permits

Permits are required to climb some of Taiwan's most spectacular peaks such as Yushan and Tapachienshan.

There are two basic types of mountain permit, one which is easy to obtain and another which is difficult. The difficult one is called a class A pass, and the easy one is a class B pass.

Class B permits can usually be obtained right at the roadside entrance or trail head in a few minutes, after you've filled out a simple form. You can also get them in Taipei from the Foreign Affairs Office, Taiwan Provincial Police Administration, 7 Chunghsiao E Rd, Section 1, Taipei – directly across the street from the Lai Lai Sheraton Hotel.

A class A pass is big trouble – usually you have to be accompanied by a group and licensed guide. If you go with a mountain club, they will need photocopies of your passport and alien resident certificate (if you have one) at least a week in advance. The club will apply for the permit and make all

the arrangements. The best club for arranging this is the ROC Alpine Association (☎ (02) 5911498), 10th floor, 185 Chungshan N Rd, Section 2, Taipei.

CUSTOMS

Unless you're carrying guns and drugs, you aren't likely to have much trouble with Taiwan's Customs. The rules were being liberalised at the time of this writing, so what follows might be out of date by the time you arrive.

Travellers arriving from Hong Kong, Australia or Japan are allowed a duty-free limit of US$1500 in goods. Those arriving from elsewhere are permitted a duty-free allowance of US$3000. The limit for children is half that of adults. These limits are not applicable to gold, liquor or cigarettes.

Any amount of foreign currency can be brought in but must be declared on arrival. Otherwise, only US$5000 in cash or the equivalent amount in another foreign currency can be taken out on departure. No more than NT$40,000 can be brought in or taken out. Travellers' cheques and personal cheques do not have to be declared.

MONEY
Currency

The official unit of currency is the New Taiwan dollar (NT$), which totals 100 cents. Coins in circulation come in denominations of 50 cents, NT$1, NT$5 and NT$10; notes come in denominations of NT$50, NT$100, NT$500 and NT$1000. An NT$50 coin will be introduced in January 1992, and it is likely that the NT$50 bills will eventually be phased out.

The easiest places to change money are at the airport, Bank of Taiwan and International Commercial Bank of China (ICBC). All these places give you the official rate. Money is difficult to change in rural areas – take care of it in major cities. When you change money, it is essential to save your receipts if you wish to reconvert your excess NT$ when you depart. You *cannot* change South Korean money in Taiwan even though the

Korean Tourist Information Centre says you can.

Exchange Rates

A$1	=	NT$20.5
C$1	=	NT$23.20
HK$1	=	NT$3.40
NZ$1	=	NT$14.80
UK£1	=	NT$46.60
US$1	=	NT$26.25
Y100	=	NT$20.25

Costs

Prices have risen almost to European levels. It's still much cheaper than Japan, but almost every country is. Excluding airfares, you could possibly manage on NT$500 a day if you stay in youth hostels, eat noodles and don't travel around much.

Tipping

Fortunately, tipping is not a custom in Taiwan.

Bargaining

There's some latitude for bargaining in street markets, but not much hope elsewhere. Some small shops will give you a discount on clothing, cameras and a few big-ticket items, but don't expect to knock off more than 10%, or even that.

Consumer Taxes

Taxes are high for some consumer goods but are already added to the price tags. Expensive hotels add a 10% service charge plus a 5% value added tax to the bill, but cheaper hotels include all taxes in the quoted price.

WHAT TO BRING

Pharmaceutical items are very expensive. Panadol is worth its weight in gold – ditto aspirin. Deodorant, mosquito repellent and sunblock (UV) lotion are hard to find and expensive. Dental floss, shaving cream, vitamins and medicines are overpriced in Taiwan. For some strange reason, clothing is ridiculously expensive even though Taiwan exports the stuff.

It's impossible to find an electric immersion heater for making hot water in a teacup, but you can buy small electric teapots at supermarkets and hardware stores.

TOURIST OFFICES

Local Tourist Offices

There is a tourist information counter at CKS International Airport near Taipei, which is where most travellers arrive. You'll see the counter after you clear Customs.

In central Taipei, it's best to visit the Taiwan Tourism Bureau (☎ (02) 7218541), 9th floor, 280 Chunghsiao E Rd, Section 4.

Overseas Reps

Taiwan's visa-issuing offices also dispense tourist information. See the previous section on Visas and Embassies.

USEFUL ORGANISATIONS

The *Kangwen Culture & Education Foundation* (☎ (02) 7554871), Room 9B, No 145 Fuhsing S Rd, Section 2, sells IYHF cards, as well as STA and ISIC cards if you have the right credentials. They can also book discounted air tickets for ISIC members.

An organisation to *avoid* is the *Chinese Taipei Youth Hostel Association*. For years they have been masquerading as an IYHF representative – in fact they are not, and have been charging an NT$1000 membership fee to use their services.

BUSINESS HOURS & HOLIDAYS

These are almost the same as in Western countries – weekdays, from 8 or 8.30 am to 5 or 5.30 pm. On Saturday, most people work a half day until noon. Many offices shut down for lunch from noon until 1.30 pm. Department stores are usually open daily from 11 am to 10 pm. Small shops keep long hours, typically from 6 am to 11 pm. Banks are open from 9 am to 3.30 pm Monday to Friday and from 9 am to noon on Saturday.

There are two types of public holidays – those that go according to the solar calendar and those following the lunar calendar. Solar holidays include: Founding Day, 1 January (few work on 2 January); Youth Day, 29 March; Tomb Sweep Day, 5 April, or 4 April in leap years; Teacher's Day, 28 September; National Day, 10 October; Restoration Day, 25 October; Chiang Kaishek's Birthday, 31 October; Sun Yatsen's Birthday, 12 November; Constitution Day, 25 December.

There are only three lunar public holidays: the Chinese lunar new year, 1st day of 1st moon (see the introductory Facts for the Visitor chapter for dates); the Dragon Boat Festival, 5th day of 5th moon; and the Mid-Autumn Festival, 15th day of 8th moon.

CULTURAL EVENTS

National Day (10 October) is a good time for visiting Taipei – fireworks over the Tanshui River starting around 7 pm, light show around the Presidential Building and special exhibits and discounts at the National Palace Museum.

Taoist temples are at their most active during Kuanyin's Birthday (19th day of 2nd moon) and Matsu's Birthday (23rd day of 3rd moon). Ditto for the 1st and 15th days of the 7th lunar month – the 'Ghost Month'.

The Chinese lunar new year is a cultural event that travellers should avoid! It's a family holiday – businesses shut down while hotels and transport fill to overflowing.

POST & TELECOMMUNICATIONS

Post offices are open from 8 am to 5 pm Monday to Saturday.

Postal Rates

Domestic rates are just NT$3 for regular letters. 'Prompt Delivery' costs NT$8 and should be delivered within 24 hours.

The rates on aerograms and international airmail letters (up to 20 grams) vary according to destination:

Destination	Airmail	Aerogram
Hong Kong & Macau	NT$9	NT$8
Asia & Australia	NT$13	NT$11
South America	NT$17	NT$14
Europe & Africa	NT$17	NT$14
USA & Canada	NT$17	NT$12

Sending Mail

Printed matter is cheap. Besides writing 'printed matter' and 'airmail' on the envelope, it must be stapled shut rather than glued – this way postal inspectors can open it to see you haven't sneaked a letter in. A greeting card can also be printed matter, but you must leave the envelope unsealed – tuck in the flap rather than glueing it shut.

Receiving Mail

Poste restante is available at all main city post offices. At the Taipei office there is a separate window for poste restante – in other cities, check at the information desk.

Telephones

Local calls cost NT$1 for three minutes. Public phones work as expected, but privately owned pay phones found in some hotels and youth hostels are for local calls only. You must pick up the receiver before inserting the coin or else you will lose it – furthermore, after you are connected you must push a button on the phone so the money goes down. If you fail to push the button, you will be able to hear the other party but they will not be able to hear you.

Most convenient are telephone cards (diànhùa kǎ) which can be purchased for NT$100 at 7 Eleven and other stores near where the phones are located. If the tele-phone card runs out of money before you're finished talking, you can insert a new one if you first push the button to the left of the keypad.

It is now possible to dial international calls direct from some card telephones. These phones are marked ISD (international subscriber dialling) and can be found in major bus and railway stations, or at the telephone company. To dial direct, the international prefix is 002, followed by the country code, area code and the number you want to dial. Taiwan's country code is 886. There are significant discounts on international calls from midnight to 7 am.

Some important numbers: English directory assistance – (02) 3116796; Chinese local directory assistance – 104; Chinese long-distance directory assistance – 105; overseas operator – 100. Important area codes include Taipei (02), Taichung (04), Tainan (06) and Kaohsiung (07).

Fax, Telex & Telegraph

Fax, telex and telegraph services are available at the main branches of the telephone company – they charge NT$200 per page for international faxes. Hotels typically charge NT$500 per page for the same service.

TIME

Taiwan does not have daylight-saving time. The time in Taiwan is Greenwich Mean Time plus eight hours. When it is noon in Taiwan it is also noon in Singapore, Hong Kong and Perth; 2 pm in Sydney; 8 pm the previous day in Los Angeles; 11 pm the previous day in New York; and 4 am in London.

LAUNDRY

This is a hassle. Some youth hostels have washing machines – otherwise, use the sink. There are plenty of laundry services, but most are slow, expensive and geared towards ironing and dry cleaning. Fast and cheap laundry services are found near the universities catering to the student population. They charge by the weight of the clothes and some have a four kg minimum.

WEIGHTS & MEASURES

Taiwan uses the international metric system, but ancient Chinese weights and measures still persist. One catty *(jīn)* is 0.6 kg (1.32 pounds). There are 16 taels *(liǎng)* to the catty, so one tael is 37.5 grams (1.32 ounces). Most fruits and vegetables in Taiwan are sold by the catty, while tea and herbal medicine are sold by the tael.

Another unit of measure is the ping – one ping is approximately 1.82 metres square (5.97 feet square). When you buy cloth or carpet, the price will be determined by the number of pings. Ditto for renting an apartment or buying land.

ELECTRICITY

Taiwan uses the American system – AC 60 cycles, 110 V. That having been said, most new apartments have at least one 220-V outlet available solely for the use of air-conditioners – a few travellers have managed to blow up their appliances by plugging into it. To prevent this from happening to you, look at the following diagram:

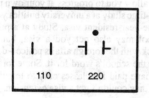

BOOKS & MAPS

Jim Steed's Hidden Treasure Guide of Taipei is an English map of the city showing virtually every place a foreigner would need to find. It costs NT$160 and is available from major Taipei bookstores like Caves and Lucky. It's getting a bit out of date, but hopefully Jim will come out with a new edition soon.

Most maps available in Taiwan are in Chinese only and tend to be out of date and inaccurate.

A good coffee-table book is *Images of Taiwan* by Daniel Reid & Dan Rocovits (Hong Kong Publishing Co Ltd), available in Taiwan for NT$400.

Lonely Planet publishes a comprehensive *Taiwan – a travel survival kit.*

MEDIA

Newspapers & Magazines

Taiwan produces two English-language newspapers, the *China Post* and the *China News*. At NT$12 for 12 pages, they rate as two of the most expensive newspapers in the world, especially when you consider they are mostly devoted to advertising.

Taipei Magazine (☎ (02) 8718923, fax 8719127), 2nd floor, 88 Tienmu E Rd, is probably the most intelligent magazine published in Taiwan. It's printed monthly and costs NT$75.

A few bookshops and some tourist hotels in the main cities sell imported publications.

Radio & TV

Taiwan has one English-language radio station, ICRT, which broadcasts 24 hours on AM 576 and FM 100. There are no English-language TV stations, but some shows shown late at night are in English with Chinese subtitles. The *China Post* and *China News* carry the daily TV programming schedule.

FILM & PHOTOGRAPHY

Cameras are expensive, but certain camera accessories like tripods and electronic flashes are made in Taiwan and are cheap. Film is also cheap, but Kodachrome is not available. The standards of photoprocessing are very high and costs are low. Slide film is readily available in big cities, but scarce in rural areas.

Photography is prohibited around military installations.

HEALTH

Food and water are safe though some travellers get diarrhoea from drinking unboiled tap water. Taiwan's medical care is of a very high standard and surprisingly cheap, but it's best to go to a public hospital rather than a private doctor if you need medical tests.

Taiwan is possibly the best place in Asia to get your teeth fixed.

WOMEN TRAVELLERS

There have been reports of women being raped and/or robbed by taxi drivers, usually at night. If you can't be escorted by a male friend, perhaps the safest thing you can do is call a radio dispatch taxi. There is an English-speaking dispatcher in Taipei (☎ (02) 2821166).

Another common precaution is to have a friend write down the taxi's licence plate number before you enter the vehicle and note the time and location. It should be made clear to the driver that this is being done – they are not likely to take you for a special ride if they know their number has been recorded by someone else. This has become a common practice and drivers are used to it. The licence plate number is displayed on the rear window and should be highly visible. Never get into a taxi if the licence plate number appears to have been obscured.

DANGERS & ANNOYANCES

There is very little violent crime, but motorcycle theft and residential burglaries are a problem.

There is a high noise level in Taiwan's cities. Being deaf can be a virtue, and if you're not deaf now, you may be by the time you leave. Westerners get irritated by all this racket, but the Taiwanese seem to be immune. Much of the noise is generated by vehicles, so when chosing a hotel room try to find one at the back of the building away from the street.

If you do any hiking, be aware that Taiwan has a fine assortment of deadly snakes. One interesting species is the '100 pacer', so called because if it bites, you can expect to walk about 100 paces before dropping dead. Fortunately, most snakes are timid – the most likely way to get bitten is to chase after one with a stick.

WORK

Quite a few foreigners find employment teaching English in Taiwan, mostly illegally. Recently there has been a crackdown on this, but the main problem for travellers is that the police are no longer so easy about giving visa

extensions. This means you can only stay for two months.

Visa extensions are usually granted readily to those studying Chinese at least 10 hours per week at government-approved schools. If you're a serious student of Chinese, there should be no problem with visas and working part-time. If you're just coming to Taiwan to work, visas can be trouble.

ACTIVITIES
Hiking

Taiwan has some outstanding hiking areas. The terrain is extremely mountainous and the subtropical weather permits year-round activities, but be prepared for sudden storms.

Courses

There are a number of language centres where you can study Chinese. The university-run language schools are good but will really push you to study, while private ones will allow you to progress at your own pace. Full-time study at a university entitles you to a one-year resident visa. Study at a private school may also net you a visa, but first check with the foreign affairs police – do not take the school's word for it. Some foreigners have paid for classes only to learn later that they couldn't get a visa extension.

HIGHLIGHTS

If you have a passion for ancient Chinese art, the National Palace Museum in Taipei is unmatched. Taipei also has a rich collection of temples.

Taroko Gorge on the east coast is Taiwan's most famous natural attraction. Alishan offers fine mountain scenery for both hikers and low-energy tourists. So does the Central Cross-Island Highway. Hohuanshan is a fairly easy mountain to climb; more challenging is Yushan, Taiwan's highest peak. Lanyu – an island off the south-east coast – offers a chance to view a unique aboriginal culture and fine scenery.

ACCOMMODATION

Hostels

Taiwan's government operates youth hostels under an organisation called the China Youth Corps (CYC), which is not connected with the International Youth Hostel Federation (IYHF). Therefore you do not need an IYHF card. The cost of a dormitory bed is around NT$100 to NT$200. Most of the hostels are in mountain areas, though there are a couple of urban ones. The mountain hostels get crowded at weekends and on holidays, but some will allow you to camp out – a few even provide tents. For more information, contact CYC at *Taipei International* (☎ (02) 3621770) (TIYAC) (*gúojì húodòng zhōngxīn*), 30 Hsinhai Rd, Section 3, Taipei.

There are some private hostels in Taipei and Kaohsiung, and there are a few teachers' hostels and Catholic hostels. These are listed in the relevant parts of this book.

Cheap Hotels

Older hotels sometimes have very cheap Japanese-style *tatami* rooms. In resort areas, you can sometimes find a dormitory (*tuántifáng*). These are usually meant for large groups, but sometimes you can attach yourself to a group of students. Prices can be as low as NT$100.

Next up the scale is a room with shared bath (*pǔtōngfáng*) – prices start at NT$300. Rooms with private bath (*tàofáng*) start at about NT$500. All resort areas have discounts from Monday to Friday, excluding holidays.

Your best bet for saving money is to travel with a friend – double rooms are usually the same price as singles.

FOOD

Chinese food is so good in Taiwan you'll wonder how it can be so bad in China. Of course, prices are higher in Taiwan – your best bet for keeping costs down is to eat at inexpensive stalls and noodle shops. Cafeterias (*zìzù cān*) offer cheap, good meals for lunch and dinner, but get there either just before noon or around 5.30 pm for the best selection. Western-style fast food is expensive and considered something of a delicacy by the Chinese.

Bread tends to be expensive. Much cheaper is the traditional Chinese breakfast consisting of soybean milk (*dòujiāng*) with steamed buns (*mántóu*), clay-oven rolls (*shāobǐng*) or an egg-and-flour omelette (*dànbǐng*).

An inexpensive treat you shouldn't miss is Chinese dumplings; you dip them in soy sauce as you eat them. These can be boiled dumplings (*shuǐ jiǎo*), fried (*gūo tiē*) or steamed (*zhēng jiǎo*).

Self-Catering

There are numerous shops offering microwave rice dishes, instant noodles and other plastic foods, some of them open late.

DRINKS

Taiwan produces top-grade tea, the best being oolong (*wūlóng chá*) and green tea (*lùchá*). These are both heavy in caffeine and will get your heart pumping – not recommended for cardiac patients. Chinese tea is never served with milk. Sugar is never put in hot tea, but iced tea will normally be very sweet.

ENTERTAINMENT

The Chinese love nightlife and you'll find it in abundance in any large city. Especially in Taipei, there is a well-established pub and disco scene catering for foreigners.

If you like amateur singing contests, visit a Kala OK (from the Japanese word Karaoke). The Taiwanese love to sing, and if you visit a Kala OK you'll certainly be asked to perform. If your singing is truly awful, limit yourself to one song for the sake of international relations.

One of Taiwan's innovations is Music & TV (MTV) clubs offering the chance to see movies on video tapes in either a large group room or in the privacy of your own little cubicle – very popular with foreigners. Then there is KTV – Kala OK and MTV combined. Want to sing along with your own movie? It seems to be popular with the Taiwanese but not many foreigners get into it.

THINGS TO BUY

Overall, there are few bargains in Taiwan – Hong Kong is much better for shopping.

Some good deals in Taiwan include hiking and camping equipment, rain gear and computer hardware. Taiwan is a great place to buy motorcycle accessories, including special security locks, alarm systems and luggage racks.

Check out hardware stores for all sorts of cheap miscellaneous items, including dishes, crockery, electric appliances and tools. Chinese tea sets are an excellent souvenir. Avoid buying these things in large department stores – they tend to be expensive.

Getting There & Away

AIR

Most travellers arrive at CKS International Airport at Taoyuan, near Taipei. There is another international airport at Kaohsiung in the south of the island. Taiwan is well connected to most countries in the region, but there are no direct flights to mainland China.

Taiwan is not the cheapest place to buy air tickets, but travel agents give better deals than buying directly from the airlines.

The cheapest flights out of Taiwan are to Seoul. Taipei to Seoul one-way/return fares are NT$3500/5500; Manila one-way/return is NT$5900/11,000; Tokyo one-way/return costs NT$6200/11,500.

Tickets to Hong Kong are overpriced, but some airlines offer special APEX fares. Korean Air has a round-trip Taipei-Hong Kong ticket for NT$6000, but most airlines charge NT$8300. One-way Taipei-Hong Kong tickets cost NT$5000. Flights from Kaohsiung to Hong Kong are slightly cheaper.

SEA

To/From Macau

A weekly ferry runs between Macau and the port of Kaohsiung in Taiwan. The name of the ship is the *Macmosa*.

From Macau, a one-way 1st-class fare is M$1060; 2nd class is M$860. From Taiwan, one-way 1st-class tickets cost NT$3700, and 2nd class is NT$3000. Round-trip fares are exactly double. There is one boat weekly during the winter, but at least two weekly during the summer months. The journey takes 24 hours. In winter, departures from Macau are at 2 am on Tuesday. From Taiwan, the ship leaves Kaohsiung at 4 pm on Wednesday. Check departure times – they can change.

In Macau tickets are most easily purchased at the ferry pier. In Hong Kong, you can buy tickets at Kwanghwa Tour & Travel Service (☎ 5457071), Room 803, Kai Tak Commercial Building, 317-321 Des Voeux Rd, Central, Hong Kong Island. In Taiwan, you can buy tickets at the pier in Kaohsiung or from the Kwanghwa Tour & Travel Service in Taipei and Kaohsiung. The Taipei office (☎ (02) 5310000) is on the 7th floor, 72 Sungchiang Rd. The Kaohsiung ticket office (☎ (07) 2821166) is on the 6th floor, 79 Chunghua 3rd Rd. In Kaohsiung, the boat departs from Pier 1 on Penglai Rd – take bus No 1 to get there. Taiwan charges a departure tax of NT$200. Macau has no departure tax.

To/From Japan

There is a weekly passenger ferry that operates between Taiwan and the Japanese island of Okinawa. From Okinawa, there are many passenger ferries to Japan's other major port cities.

Student discounts are available. The ship leaves Okinawa and arrives in Taiwan the next day after making brief stops at the islands of Miyako and Ishigaki. The ship alternates between the Taiwanese ports of Keelung and Kaohsiung. The fare to Keelung is Y15,600; to Kaohsiung it's Y18,000.

You can buy tickets from travel agents in the port cities from which the ferries depart. Youth hostels in Japan will often be able to refer you to a local travel agent who can speak English.

In Taiwan, you can buy tickets from Yeong An Maritime Company (☎ (02) 7715911), 11 Jenai Rd, Section 3, Taipei.

From Keelung the fare is NT$2900; from Kaohsiung, it's NT$3949.

LEAVING TAIWAN

Airport departure tax on international flights is NT$300. Departure tax for ships is NT$200. There are no places to change money after you pass immigration so take care of this beforehand.

Getting Around

Taiwan's public transport is very efficient, but buses and taxis move slowly during the rush hour. There are frequent accidents on the North-South Freeway which often result in long delays.

AIR

Due to Taiwan's small size there is little need to fly unless you want to visit some of the smaller islands around Taiwan, like Penghu or Lanyu. For all flights you must carry your passport and arrive at the airport about an hour before departure time. This is especially true during the holidays, when they are quite likely to give away your seat if they need the space.

Buy domestic air tickets directly from the airlines. If you buy directly from the airline, it will be much easier to obtain a refund. Travel agents give discounts only on international tickets.

Taiwan's domestic carriers include Far Eastern Air Transport (FEAT), China Airlines (CAL), Great China, Foshing, Formosa, Makung and Taiwan Airlines.

BUS

There are two basic classes of long-distance government-owned buses – the Kuokuang (gúogūang hào) and the Chunghsing (zhōngxīng hào). The Chunghsing is the cheaper of the two but not by much. The Kuokuang is worth the slight extra cost – it has a toilet in the rear of the bus, a big convenience on long trips.

On all buses you must save your ticket stub. You should turn it in to the driver or conductor when you get off the bus or you will have to pay the full fare again.

There are a number of private bus companies known as 'wild chickens' (yĕjī chē). The wild chickens have been known to use all sorts of methods to attract customers, including the installation of video cassette players on the bus to entertain passengers. The wild chickens are cheaper and sometimes faster. They also allow passengers to smoke – supposedly against the rules. If you don't smoke you'd better avoid these buses, as the air gets as thick as oyster sauce after a few hours.

TRAIN

Service is fast and frequent. There are two major lines, the west coast line and the east coast line, plus a few spur routes like the one to Alishan. Timetables (shí kè biǎo) cost NT$20 but are entirely in Chinese.

Trains are more expensive than the buses. There are five classes – the first three are fast, have air-con and reserved seats. The last two are cheap but very slow. In descending order, they are: Tzuchiang (zìqiáng hào); Chukuang (jǔgūang hào); Fuhsing (fùxīng hào); Pingkuai (píngkùai chē); the 'common train' (pǔtōng chē).

If no seats are available, you are permitted to board but will have to stand. Save your ticket – you must turn it in when you get off. If you want to change your destination after boarding, find the conductor and upgrade your ticket (bǔ piào).

You can receive a 15% discount on round-trip tickets, but the ticket must be used within 15 days of purchase. If necessary, you can get a refund for the unused return trip.

TAXI

Long-distance share taxis are best avoided. They are expensive and many of the drivers are thugs. If you must take one, write down the taxi's licence plate number before you even get in, just in case you have to file a complaint later. Always agree on the fare in advance and don't pay until you arrive at your destination.

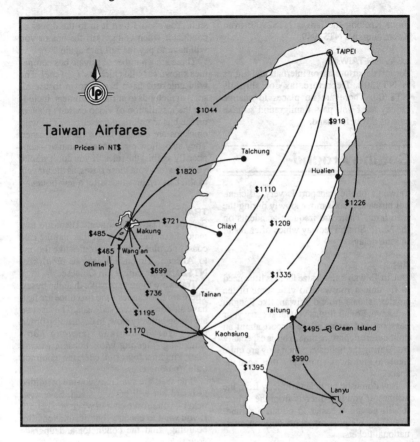

Taiwan Airfares
Prices in NT$

$1044
$919
$1820
$1110
Taichung
Hualien
$1226
$721
Chiayi
$1209
Makung
$485
$1335
$465
Wang an
Chimei
$699
$736
Tainan
Taitung
$1195
$495 — Green Island
$1170
Kaohsiung
$990
$1395
Lanyu

CAR & MOTORBIKE

An International Driving Permit is necessary in Taiwan unless you obtain a Taiwanese driver's licence. If you wish to obtain a local driver's licence be sure to bring along your home country's licence – you can use it to get the Taiwanese licence without taking a written exam or driving test.

Motorcycles can be hired around tourist resorts like Hualien, Lanyu and Penghu. In cities they are very hard to hire – you can sometimes work out a deal where you buy a motorcycle from a shop and sell it back to them a few months later.

Overall, Taiwanese drivers are insane. The traffic rules are also insane – it's often hard to know what is or isn't legal. In Taipei, the police use hidden cameras to catch traffic violators, which means the owner of the vehicle gets the citation, not necessarily the driver. Many car rental agencies are upset about this and will often demand you put up a deposit or sign a blank check to cover the possibility of them receiving a citation after you've departed the country. In general, driving is a big headache in Taiwan, but if you're determined, get a safety helmet (for motorcycles) and have your will updated.

The free-form traffic pattern is unnerving, what with disregard of traffic signals; disregard of life and limb; disregard of common sense; disregard of accepted (Western) vehicle maintenance practices, etc. But myself? Being a desert car and motorcycle racer who kind of thrives on running on the ragged edge, it's OK. Always a challenge. But for others it may not be their cup of oolong.

Anthony H Tellier

LOCAL TRANSPORT
Bus
They're good in Taipei and reasonably OK in Taichung and Kaohsiung, but elsewhere inner city buses are scarce. Cost varies from a low of NT$8 (Taipei – non-aircon) to NT$13 in Taichung.

Underground
Taipei is building an underground system – at present, the whole city is a big mess from the construction. No other city has a subway system, but Kaohsiung plans to begin construction of its underground next year.

Taxi
Taxis were given permission in 1990 to charge NT$5 more than the meter price because of the increased cost of petrol. This was supposed to be temporary, but now appears to have become permanent.

Fares start at NT$40 – this will get you 1500 metres, after which it's NT$5 for every 400 metres. If the taxi gets stuck in traffic, there is an additional NT$5 waiting charge for every five minutes.

Fares are 20% higher during the rush hours from 7 to 9 am and from 5 to 7 pm. The higher charge also applies from 11 pm to 5 am. During these hours the driver is supposed to press the button on the right (usually blue) to start the meter. During regular hours he should use the red light button on the left side of the meter.

TOURS
There are a number of agencies offering guided tours and English-speaking tour guides. Among the selection:

Huei-Fong Travel Service
    4th floor, 50 Nanking E Rd, Section 2, Taipei (☎ (02) 5515805, fax 5611434)
Southeast Travel Service
    60 Chungshan N Rd, Section 2, Taipei (☎ (02) 5517111)

Taipei 台北

The capital and largest city, Taipei *(táiběi)* is home to governmental institutions, universities, booming businesses, wheezing cars, whining motorcycles and some three million Taiwanese. Probably the best word to describe it is 'busy'. It's not a particularly beautiful city, but it's prosperous, the people are friendly, nightlife is plentiful, food is excellent and there are unexpected treasures like Taoist temples and top-notch museums. Most travellers come here first to get their bearings before heading out towards Taiwan's truly scenic spots.

Orientation
There is a logical system to finding addresses, and it applies to other cities besides Taipei. However, Taipei is unique in that it is divided into four compass points. Chunghsiao Rd bisects the city into the north and south sections of the grid. All major roads that cross Chunghsiao Rd are labelled accordingly. Thus, we have Linsen North Rd and Linsen South Rd, Yenping North Rd and Yenping South Rd, etc.

Chungshan Rd bisects the city into the east and west sections of the grid. Roads to the east of Chungshan Rd are labelled east and those to the west are labelled west. Thus, we have Nanking East Rd and Nanking West Rd.

In all of Taiwan's cities, major roads have sections. In Taipei there is Chungshan N Rd, Section 1, Section 2, Section 3 and so on right up to Section 7. Sometimes, instead of writing 'Wufu Rd, Section 3', they might write 'Wufu 3rd Rd', but the meaning is the same. A section is normally about three blocks long. When finding an address you

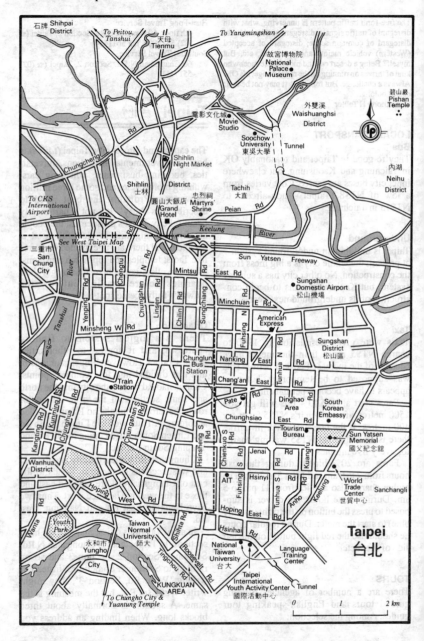

石牌 Shihpai District

To Peitou, Tanshui

天母 Tienmu

To Yangmingshan

故宮博物院 National Palace Museum

碧山巖 Pishan Temple

電影文化城 Movie Studio

外雙溪 Waishuangshi District

內湖 Neihu District

東吳大學 Soochow University

Tunnel

Shihlin Night Market

Chungcheng Rd

Shihlin District

Tachih 大直

To CKS International Airport

圓山大飯店 Grand Hotel

忠烈祠 Martyrs' Shrine

Peian Rd

三重市 San Chung City

See West Taipei Map

Keelung River

Tanshui River

Chengtu Rd

Mintsu Rd

Sun Yatsen Freeway

East Rd

Sungshan Domestic Airport 松山機場

Chungshan N Rd

Linsen Rd

Chilin Rd

Sungchiang Rd

Minchuan E Rd

American Express

Sungshan District 松山區

Minsheng W Rd

Yenping Rd

Fuhsing Rd

Tunhua N Rd

Train Station

Chunglun Bus Station

Nanking East Rd

Chang'an East Rd

Dinghao Area

South Korean Embassy

Kunming Rd

Chunghua Rd

Chungshan S Rd

Hsinsheng S Rd

Chienkuo S Rd

Pate Rd

Chungshiao East Rd

Tourism Bureau

Sun Yatsen Memorial 國父紀念館

Wanhua District

Kanghua Rd

Jenai Rd

Kuanghu Rd

World Trade Center 世貿中心

Sanchangli

Hoping West Rd

AIT

Hsinyi Rd

Tunhua S Rd

Anho Rd

Keelung Rd

Youth Park

Wanta Rd

Taiwan Normal University 師大

Fuhsing S Rd

Hoping East Rd

Hsinhai Rd

Roosevelt Rd

Shihta Rd

Tingchou Rd

永和市 Yungho City

National Taiwan University 台大

Language Training Center

Taipei 台北

KUNGKUAN AREA

To Chungho City & Yuantung Temple

Taipei International Youth Activity Center 國際活動中心

Tunnel

0   1   2 km

really have to pay attention to which section you are in.

All of Taiwan's cities have lanes. A lane, as the name implies, is a small side street and they never have names, just numbers. A typical address might read like this: 16 Lane 20, Chungshan N Rd, Section 2. The 16 simply refers to the house number and Lane 20 is the name of the lane which intersects with Section 2 of Chungshan N Rd. That's not too difficult, but is there an easy way to locate Lane 20?

Fortunately, there is. As you walk along Chungshan N Rd, Section 2, keep your eye on the house numbers. Lane 20 should intersect with Chungshan N Rd just near a building bearing the street address number 20. Once you understand this system, it becomes very easy to find the lane you are looking for.

Occasionally, you'll have to find an alley. An alley is a lane which runs off a lane. Again, the same system is used. Alley 25 will intersect with a lane, and the house at the corner of this intersection should be number 25. A typical address could be 132 Alley 25, Lane 20, Chungshan N Rd, Section 2, Taipei. It may look complicated, but it's very systematic.

Information
Tourist Office The Taiwan Tourism Bureau (☎ (02) 7218541), 9th floor, 280 Chunghsiao E Rd, Section 4, is not far from the Sun Yatsen Memorial and the South Korean Embassy. There is a Tourist Information Hot Line (☎ (02) 7173737), which accepts calls from 8 am to 8 pm, every day of the year.

Travel Agencies Highly recommended is Jenny Su Travel Service (☎ (02) 5951646), 10th floor, 27 Chungshan N Rd, Section 3. Another reputable travel agent is Wing On Travel Service (☎ (02) 7722998), 73-79 Jenai Rd, Section 4.

Money The bank at CKS Airport is supposed to remain open whenever international flights are arriving or departing. In Taipei, the International Bank of China (ICBC) is the best place to change money.

Branch near Train Station
    6 Chunghsiao W Rd, Section 1 (☎ (02) 3118298)
Chungshan Branch
    15 Chungshan N Rd, Section 2 (☎ (02) 5119231)
Nanking Branch
    198 Nanking E Rd, Section 3 (☎ (02) 7516041)
Dinghao District
    233 Chunghsiao E Rd, Section 4 (☎ (02) 7711877)
Shihlin District
    126 Chungshan N Rd, Section 6 (☎ (02) 8345225)
Tienmu District
    193 Chungshan N Rd, Section 7 (☎ (02) 8714125)

The other most likely place to change money is at the Bank of Taiwan:

Main Branch
    120 Chungching S Rd, Section 1 (☎ (02) 3147377)
Chungshan Branch
    150 Chungshan N Rd, Section 1 (☎ (02) 5423434)
Dinghao District
    560 Chunghsiao E Rd, Section 4 (☎ (02) 7073111)
Shihlin District
    248 Chungshan N Rd, Section 6 (☎ (02) 8367080)

Post & Telecommunications The GPO in Taipei is on Chunghsiao W Rd, close to the railway station, and is called the North Gate Post Office. There is a separate window for poste restante.

You can make overseas calls and send fax messages, telegrams and telexes from the main telephone company office (☎ (02) 3443781) at 28 Hangchou S Rd, Section 1 – open 24 hours a day. With a telephone card, you can make international direct-dial phone calls from the Taipei railway station.

Foreign Embassies & 'Trade Offices' These are listed in the Facts for the Visitor section at the beginning of this chapter.

Cultural Centres Within the grounds of the Chiang Kaishek Memorial is the National

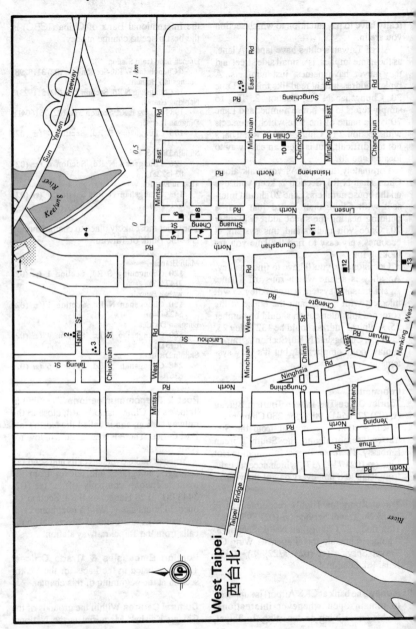

West Taipei
西台北

■ PLACES TO STAY

6 President Hotel
統一大飯店
8 Imperial Hotel
華國大飯店
10 Amigo Hostel
12 Formosa-II Hostel
13 Formosa Hostel
14 Happy Family-II Hostel
16 Happy Family Hostel
19 Hilton Hotel
希爾頓大飯店
20 YMCA
基督教青年會
21 Phoenix Palace Hotel
鳳宮大飯店
23 Taipei Hostel
24 Lai Lai Sheraton Hotel
來來大飯店
27 Friendly House Hostel
37 International House
國際學舍

▼ PLACES TO EAT

5 Pubs
7 Pubs

OTHER

1 Swimming Pool
游泳池
2 Paoan Temple
保安寺

3 Confucius Temple
孔子廟
4 Fine Arts Museum
美術館
9 Hsingtien Temple
行天宮
11 Caves Books
敦煌書局
15 North Bus Station
17 East Bus Station
18 West Bus Station
22 Provincial Police Administration
(Mountain Permits)
25 Taiwan University Hospital
26 GPO
郵政總局
28 Police (Visa Extensions)
外事警察
29 Bank of Taiwan
台灣銀行
30 Presidential Building
總統府
31 Foreign Affairs Ministry
外交部
32 Lungshan Temple
龍山寺
33 National Central Library
中央圖書館
34 Telephone Company Main Office
電信總局
35 National Museum of History
歷史博物館
36 Mandarin Daily News
國語日報
38 Lucky Bookstore
師大書苑

Chiang Kaishek Cultural Center (☎ (02) 3925060), which consists of two buildings: the National Theater *(guójiā jùyùan)* (☎ (02) 3924954) and National Concert Hall *(guójiā yīnyuè tīng)*. A schedule of events is published monthly and is available from the Tourism Bureau.

Cultural events are also staged in the Sun Yatsen Memorial Hall (☎ (02) 7588008) at 505 Jenai Rd, Section 4, near the Tourism Bureau and the South Korean Embassy.

The New Schoolmate Theater (☎ (02) 7049947) is in the basement of the New Schoolmate Bookstore, 501 Tunhua S Rd.

They often have plays, operas and dance troupes.

Chinese operas are performed nightly at 7 pm in the Armed Forces Cultural Activity Center (☎ (02) 3114228) *(guójūn wényì zhōngxīn)*, 69 Chunghua Rd, Section 1.

Bookshops The widest selection is at *Caves Books* (☎ (02) 5371666), 103 Chungshan N Rd, Section 2. Also excellent is *Lucky Bookstore* (☎ (02) 3927111), 129-1 Hoping E Rd, Section 1. A good shop for imported magazines and some books is *New Schoolmate Bookstore* (☎ (02) 7007000) *(xīn xúe yǒu* *shūjú*), though the sign above the store says 'Books Plaza'. It's at 501 Tunhua S Rd. There is another branch (☎ (02) 8735566) in Tienmu at 36 Tienmu E Rd, a short walk from the Taipei American School.

Libraries The American Cultural Center maintains a library at 54 Nanhai Rd (☎ (02) 3075639), across from the Botanical Gardens. Hours are noon to 6 pm Monday to Saturday.

Emergency The Adventist Hospital has English-speaking doctors and caters to foreigners, but is very expensive – if you have health insurance you might be covered. Other hospitals are government-run and high-standard, but can be very crowded. Some hospitals in Taipei include:

Adventist Hospital *(tái ān yīyùan)*
    424 Pate Rd, Section 2 (☎ (02) 7718151)
Chang Gung Memorial Hospital *(cháng gēng yīyùan)*
    199 Tunhua N Rd (☎ (02) 7135211)
Mackay Memorial Hospital *(mǎjiē yīyùan)*
    Chungshan N Rd, Section 2 (☎ (02) 5433535)
Taipei Medical College Hospital *(táiběi yīxúe yùan)*
    252 Wuhsing St (☎ (02) 7372181)
Veterans General Hospital *(róngmín zhōng yīyùan)*
    201 Shihpai Rd, Section 2 (☎ (02) 8712121, English extension 3530)

English-speaking police can be contacted at the city centre office by calling (02) 3119940, or 3119816, ext 264; in the Chungshan area, call (02) 5119564; in Tienmu, call (02) 8714110, 8714440. As elsewhere in Taiwan, the Chinese-speaking emergency numbers are 110 for police and 119 for fire.

For an ambulance, call (02) 7216315. If this doesn't work, call the Tourist Information Hot Line (☎ (02) 7173737).

Things to See

National Palace Museum *(gùgōng bówù yùan)* The museum holds the world's largest collection of Chinese artefacts, over 600,000 items in all. There are so many that they cannot be displayed all at once, so the display is rotated.

There are good English tours of the museum twice daily at 10 am and 3 pm. The tours will run even if only one person shows up.

The museum is open from 9 am to 5 pm every day of the year; admission is NT$30. Buses which go to the museum are Nos 210, 213, 255 and 304. You must pay double fare (NT$20) as it is a long way out.

Martyrs' Shrine *(zhōng liè cí)* The shrine was built to honour those who died fighting for their country. There are two rifle-toting military police who stand guard at the gate in formal dress – absolutely rigid, not moving a muscle or blinking an eye – while tourists harass them. It's a wonder these guys don't run amok and bayonet a few of their camera-clicking tormentors.

The Martyrs' Shrine is less than a 10-minute walk along Peian Rd, due east of the Grand Hotel.

Fine Arts Museum *(měi shù gǔan)* This museum (☎ (02) 5957656), 181 Chungshan N Rd, Section 3, is just south of the Grand Hotel. As art museums go it's OK, but it pales into insignificance when compared to the National Palace Museum. It's open from 9 am to 5 pm daily, except Monday, and from 1 to 9 pm on Wednesday.

Botanical Gardens *(zhíwù yúan)* The Botanical Gardens, on Nanhai Rd, south of the central area and near the American Cultural Center, are a pleasant retreat from the noisy city. There is a beautiful lotus pond in the gardens, adjacent to the National Museum of History, National Science Hall and National Arts Hall – all worth looking into. The National Museum of History is open daily from 9 am to 5 pm, NT$10 admission.

Chiang Kaishek Memorial *(zhōngzhèng jì niàn táng)* This memorial hall is a fantastic piece of architecture. It's enormous and surrounded by a lush garden. You'll find it on Hsinyi Rd, Section 1.

Lungshan Temple *(lóngshān sì)* This is an extremely colourful temple and is packed with worshippers most of the time; the air is heavy with smoke from burning incense and 'ghost money'. Adjacent to the temple is an active market and two blocks away is the famous Snake Alley.

Paoan Temple *(bǎo'ān gōng)* This lovely old Taoist temple is a short walk from the Confucius Temple. The address is 16 Hami St, not far from the Grand Hotel.

Pishan Temple *(bì shān yán)* This is a magnificent temple perched on the side of a mountain, with a breathtaking view of Taipei, but it gets surprisingly few visitors.

The temple is in the Neihu district, which is the high-class north-east part of Taipei. From the Hilton Hotel area (near the railway station) take bus No 247 to the last stop. From there you must walk up the hill, following a paved road. Along the way you will pass the small Golden Dragon Temple *(jīnlóng sì)*.

Night Markets *(yèshì)* The most exotic night market is in the Wanhua area between Chunghua Rd and the river (near the Lungshan Temple). The centre of activities is Snake Alley *(huáxī jiē)*, where you can see snake vendors taunt live cobras before serving them up on the dinner plate (boiled, fried or pickled). The Chinese have long believed that the organs of wild animals serve as aphrodisiacs, especially those which are long and strong. Thus, eating snake, powdered deer antlers or rhinoceros horn is considered a potent cure for those whose virility is on the wane. Another treatment is to drink a potion consisting of wine with drowned bees in it. You'll find all these delicacies for sale in Snake Alley.

The biggest night market of all is the Shihlin Night Market *(shìlín yèshì)*. It's to the north-west of the Grand Hotel, just to the west of Wenlin Rd and starting from the south side of Chungcheng Rd. This market is open in the daytime, but really comes alive

at night. It normally shuts down around 10 to 11 pm – hours are even longer on weekends.

Yangmingshan *(yángmíngshān)* A pleasant mountain park north of Taipei, Yangmingshan has hot springs, peaks to climb, and something else that Taipei lacks – breathable air. The park is noted for its cherry blossoms from February to April. Real estate developers have recently moved onto the lower slopes and have erected some ultra-expensive US-style housing projects with names like 'Taipei California'. Fortunately, most of the mountain is protected as a national park.

If you would like a moderately difficult hike, climb Seven Star Mountain *(qīxīngshān)*. At an elevation of 1120 metres, it is the highest peak in the area. From the summit, you can look down one side of the mountain and see Taipei. In the opposite direction the ocean is visible.

From Taipei you can get to Yangmingshan on bus No 301, which runs along Chungshan N Rd. The trip only takes about 45 minutes. Stay on the bus to the very last stop at the top of the mountain. It's about a 10-minute walk to the park entrance.

Chihnan Temple *(zhǐnán gōng)* One of the largest temples in north Taiwan, the Chihnan Temple is 19 km south-east of Taipei in the suburb of Mucha. As it's perched on a mountainside, there are outstanding views of Taipei when the weather is clear. When the weather is not clear, that's OK too – who wants to see Taipei anyway?

You can get there from Taipei by taking a bus operated by the Chihnan (CN) Bus Company *(zhǐnán kèyùn)*. CN bus No 1 runs along Nanking E Rd, then Sungchiang Rd, Hsinsheng S Rd, Roosevelt Rd and on out to Mucha, ending at the Chihnan Temple. CN bus No 2 runs down Chunghua Rd, Aikuo Rd, Roosevelt Rd and finally terminates in Mucha. Be sure to tell the driver your destination – some of the buses take a different route and terminate at the Taipei Zoo rather than the temple. Alternatively, take bus No

236 or 237 to Chihnan Rd in Mucha, then change to CN bus No 1 or 2.

From where the bus drops you off, you cannot see the temple. Follow the steep steps up and up until you reach a small Taoist temple. The main temple is to your right; to the left are some picnic grounds.

Activities

If you get up at the crack of dawn, you can practise taichichuan at the Chiang Kaishek Memorial, sometimes accompanied by the thump of disco music.

There are numerous clubs sponsoring organised activities. Most of these are announced in *Taipei Magazine*. Aspiring mountaineers might want to contact the ROC Alpine Association (☎ (02) 5942108), 10th floor, 185 Chungshan N Rd. Volleyball, basketball and badminton are offered by the Taipei Youth Program Association (☎ (02) 8739900), 800 Chungshan N Rd, Section 6. You can guess the activities of the ROC Cycling Association (☎ (02) 7210459), 3 Lane 153, Chang'an E Rd, Section 2; ditto for the Photographic Society of China (☎ (02) 3416919), 5th floor, 104 Chinhua St.

Language Courses

There are a number of places in Taipei to study Chinese, including the following:

Taiwan Normal University Mandarin Training Center
129-1 Hoping E Rd, Section 1 (☎ (02) 3639123)
National Taiwan University
Roosevelt Rd, Section 4
Mandarin Daily News
11-1 Fuchou St (☎ (02) 3915134)
Everyday Language Center (ELC)
5th floor, 72 Chunghsiao W Rd, Section 1 (☎ (02) 3114595)
Cathay Language Center
2nd floor, 8 Lane 190, Chungshan N Rd, Section 7, Tienmu, Taipei (☎ (02) 8729165)
Language Testing & Training Center
170 Hsinhai Rd, Section 2 (☎ (02) 3216385)
My Language School
2nd floor, 126-8 Hsinsheng S Rd, Section 1 (☎ (02) 3945400)

Taipei Language Institute (TLI)
7th floor, 104 Hsinyi Rd, Section 2, (☎ (02) 3410022, 3938805)
Shihlin Branch, 2nd floor, 684 Chungshan N Rd, Section 5, Shihlin, Taipei (☎ (02) 8360480/1)
Taichung Center (☎ (04) 2318842)
Kaohsiung Center (☎ (07) 2513638)

Places to Stay

Hostels The *Happy Family Hostel* (☎ (02) 3753443) is on the 4th floor, 16-1 Peiping W Rd, about a stone's throw from the railway station. The position couldn't be better! This very popular place is often full. The friendly management makes an effort to keep it clean in spite of the constant flow of travellers. The cost is NT$160 per night or NT$1000 per week.

Under the same management is the *Happy Family II* (☎ (02) 5810716), 2nd floor, 2 Lane 56, Chungshan N Rd, Section 1; it's a short walk away from the railway station. It's a small but very clean hostel and has a washing machine, kitchen and video tape player – the owner lives on the premises. Ring up first because it's often full. Dorm beds cost NT$180 per night or NT$1100 per week.

Happy Family International (☎ (02) 5633341) is on the 5th floor, 12-5 Lane 77, Chungshan N Rd, Section 2. This is one of the newest and best hostels in Taipei with aircon, kitchen, washing machine, TV, video and good hot showers. The dorm beds cost NT$180.

One of the cleanest and best-run hostels in Taipei is *Formosa-II* (☎ (02) 5116744). The hostel is on the 2nd floor, 5 Lane 62, Chungshan N Rd, Section 2. The price is NT$170 per day or NT$1100 per week.

The nearby *Formosa Hostel* (☎ (02) 5622035), 3rd floor, 16 Lane 20, Section 2, Chungshan N Rd, is under the same management but does not have such a high standard as the Formosa-II. Nevertheless, it's a good place to stay and the location off Chungshan N Rd is convenient. It has a kitchen and washing machine – cost is NT$160 nightly or NT$1000 weekly.

Probably the most popular hostel with travellers is *Amigo Hostel* (☎ (02) 5420292),

4th floor, 286 Chilin Rd. It is clean, has air-conditioning, a video tape player and extremely friendly management. The price is NT$160 daily or NT$1000 weekly. It's not within walking distance of the railway station – take bus No 502 and get off at the corner of Minchuan E Rd and Chilin Rd, opposite the Ritz Hotel.

Also recommended is *ABC Hostel* (☎ (02) 5073397), Flat 3, 14th floor, 226 Fuhsing N Rd. Beds cost NT$180 daily, or NT$150 per day if rented on a weekly basis. Take bus No 25 from the railway station.

Slightly higher priced is the *Friendly House Hostel* (☎ (02) 3818804) 11th floor, 50 Poai Rd. Clean but tiny single rooms cost NT$280. In a double room, it's NT$240 per person.

The *Taipei Hostel* (☎ (02) 3952950), 6th floor, 11 Lane 5, Linsen N Rd, is popular but not terribly clean. The management claims this is the oldest hostel in Taipei – it certainly looks it. The location is very central near the Lai Lai Sheraton Hotel. They charge NT$180 daily, NT$170 for students, or on a weekly basis it's NT$1050 (student or not). Double rooms are NT$400. They have a very good notice board for travellers, a laundry service and a TV set, but no kitchen.

Hotels Huaining St *(húainíng jiē)* is just opposite the railway station and is a hunting ground for relatively cheap hotels in the NT$500 to NT$600 range. Among the choices are the *Paradise Hotel* (☎ (02) 3313311) *(nánguó dàfàndiàn)*, 7 Huaining St, where doubles cost NT$550 to NT$700. Nearby is the *Yon Hong Hotel* (☎ (02) 3611906) *(yǒngfēng bīngǔan)*, 10 Huaining St, where doubles start at NT$500. Also nearby is the plush-looking *Chuan Chia Huam Hotel* (☎ (02) 3814755) *(qúanjiā hūan bīngǔan)*, 4th floor, 6 Huaining St. Doubles cost NT$700.

In the same neighbourhood is the *Phoenix Palace Hotel* (☎ (02) 3713151) *(fènggōng dàfàndiàn)*, 4 Hankou St *(hànkǒu jiē)*, Section 1. Prices are NT$600 to NT$650 for a double – not exactly cheap, but this is

Taipei. The hotel is comfortably air-conditioned and tolerably clean.

Rainbow Hostel (☎ (02) 5965515) *(cǎihóng bīngǔan)*, 91 Chungshan N Rd, Section 3, offers very clean accommodation at NT$880 for a double.

Just to the south of the railway station is the YMCA (☎ (02) 3113201) *(jīdūjiào qīngnián hùi)*, 19 Hsuchang St. Doubles are NT$940 to NT$1050; twins NT$1140 to NT$1250

The *Keyman's Hotel* (☎ (02) 3114811) *(húainíng lǚdiàn)*, 1 Huaining St, is almost as luxurious as the Hilton but a lot cheaper. Singles/doubles are NT$1280/1360.

Places to Eat
Budget eats are found in back alleys or from street vendors.

Grandma Nitti's (☎ (02) 7330449) advertises 'home cookin' – just like Grandma used to make'. It's at 61 Alley 118, Hoping E Rd, Section 2 and open from 7 am to 9 pm – now a popular venue for breakfast with the all-night disco crowd.

You can find excellent Thai food at the *Golden Triangle* (☎ (02) 3632281), 11 Lane 49, Shihta Rd. Dishes cost NT$80 but are very filling and good value.

Highly recommended is *Chalet Swiss* (☎ (02) 7152051), 47 Nanking E Rd. *Jake's Country Kitchen* (☎ (02) 8715289) serves such exotica as blueberry pancakes, tacos, pizza and cheesecake. The address is 705 Chungshan N Rd, Section 6, Shihlin.

McDonald's has apparently lost interest in catering to foreigners. The menus – which used to be bilingual – are now entirely in Chinese.

Entertainment
MTV One of the most popular is *Solar Systems*, 2nd floor, 8 Tunhua N Rd.

Pubs & Discos Highest recommendations go to the *Pig & Whistle* (☎ (02) 8731380) 78 Tienmu E Rd. Congenial atmosphere, good pubgrub and the best live music in Taipei. Take bus No 220 from anywhere on Chungshan N Rd.

Along similar lines *The Farmhouse* (☎ (02) 5951764), 5 Lane 32, Shuang Cheng St. Live music begins nightly at 9 pm.

A good hangout close to Taiwan Normal University is *The Bushiban* (☎ (02) 3949675), 2nd floor, 152 Roosevelt Rd, Section 3.

Small but extremely popular with the foreign crowd is *Barleyfield Pub* (☎ (02) 3923958), 1 Fuchou St, close to the Mandarin Daily News. Beer costs NT$70 and there is no cover charge.

Another place getting rave reviews from travellers is *Whiskey A-Go-Go* (☎ (02) 7375773, 7354715), 65 Hsinhai Rd, Section 3, near National Taiwan University – cover charge is NT$150.

The ever-popular *Roxy III* is a small, jazz-oriented pub with excellent music – it's on the 2nd floor, 300 Roosevelt Rd, Section 3. Rather more expensive is *Roxy IV* at 6-1 Hsinsheng S Rd, Section 3.

Awards for unusual design go to *Indian* (☎ (02) 7410550), 196 Pate Rd, Section 2. It's hard to describe what this place is – a pub and restaurant with a dinosaur skeleton on the roof and dinosaur bones sticking out of the walls and ceiling. The waitresses wear dinosaur bone T-shirts.

One of the slickest discos in town is *Kiss* (☎ (02) 7121201), in the Mandarin Hotel, 166 Tunhua N Rd – admission is NT$350. One of Taipei's newest dancing venues is *Funky Disco & Pub* (☎ (02) 3971003), B-1, 10 Hangchou S Rd, Section 1.

Things to Buy

The Chunghua Bazaar *(zhōnghúa shāngchǎng)* runs along Chunghua Rd from Chunghsiao Rd down to around Chengtu Rd. It's two levels of stores jam-packed with almost everything imaginable, but electronics are particularly plentiful.

The place to go for backpacking gear is Taipei Shanshui, 12 Chungshan N Rd, Section 1. Just a few doors up the street is another good shop, Deng Shan You (☎ (02) 3116027), 18 Chungshan N Rd, Section 1.

The Chinese Handicraft Mart (☎ (02) 3217233), 1 Hsuchou Rd (near the intersec-

tion with Chungshan S Rd), is a nonprofit government-sponsored organisation selling jewellery, furniture, and arts & crafts. It's open every day from 9 am to 5.30 pm.

Underneath the overpass on Hsinsheng S Rd, just north of Pate Rd, is the Kuanghua Bazaar *(gūanghúa shāngchǎng)*, which houses about a dozen small computer shops and stores selling electronic components. Most of the machines are generic. The quality of the computers is questionable, but it's an interesting place to browse.

Getting There & Away

Air CKS International Airport is 40 km from Taipei near the city of Taoyuan. Taipei's domestic airport is Sungshan, almost in the city.

Airline offices in Taipei – both domestic and foreign – are as follows:

Asiana
    5th floor, 65 Chienkuo N Rd, Section 2 (☎ (02) 5081114)
Canadian International
    4th floor, 90 Chienkuo N Rd, Section 2 (☎ (02) 5034111)
Cathay Pacific
    137 Nanking E Rd, Section 2 (☎ (02) 7152333)
China Airlines
    131 Nanking E Rd, Section 3 (☎ (02) 7151212)
Continental
    2nd floor, 150 Fuhsing N Rd (☎ (02) 7195947)
Delta
    3rd floor, 50 Nanking E Rd, Section 2 (☎ (02) 5418681)
Far Eastern
    (☎ (02) 3615431)
Formosa
    (☎ (02) 5074188)
Foshing
    (☎ (02) 5221241)
Garuda Indonesia
    6th floor, 82 Sungchiang Rd (☎ (02) 5612311)
Great China
    (☎ (02) 3568000)
Japan Asia
    2 Tunhua S Rd (☎ (02) 7765151)
KLM Royal Dutch
    1 Nanking E Rd, Section 4 (☎ (02) 7171000)
Korean Air
    53 Nanking E Rd, Section 2 (☎ (02) 5214242)
Makung
    (☎ (02) 7187614)

Malaysian
  2nd floor, 102 Tunhua N Rd (☎ (02) 7168384)
Northwest
  181 Fuhsing N Rd (☎ (02) 7161555)
Philippine
  2nd floor, 90 Chienkuo N Rd, Section 2 (☎ (02) 5053030)
Royal Brunei
  11th floor, 9 Nanking E Rd, Section 3 (☎ (02) 5062331)
Singapore
  148 Sungchiang Rd (☎ (02) 5516655)
South African
  12th floor, 205 Tunhua N Rd (☎ (02) 7136363)
Taiwan
  (☎ (02) 7551772)
Thai
  2nd floor, 150 Fuhsing N Rd (☎ (02) 7152766)
United
  12th floor, 2 Jenai Rd, Section 4 (☎ (02) 3258868)

Bus There are three important bus terminals near the railway station and another about two km to the east. Probably most important is the West Bus Station, where you get highway buses to major cities, including Taichung, Chiayi, Tainan and Kaohsiung. The West Bus Station is on Chunghsiao W Rd, a three-minute walk west of the railway station.

The East Bus Station is almost in front of the railway station. From here you get buses to CKS Airport and to Keelung.

The North Bus Station is on the north side of the railway station. Here you can get buses to Hsinchu and Chungli, as well as to Hualien (transfer in Suao).

The Chunglun Bus Station is on the southwest corner of Pate Rd and Fuhsing Rd, over two km east of the railway station. You can get there by taking city buses Nos 57, 69, 205 or 311. Important destinations from Chunglun Bus Station include Chinshan Beach and Fengyuan.

Getting Around

To/From the Airport It takes nearly an hour to travel between CKS Airport and central Taipei, even longer during the rush hour. There are two classes of airport buses: limousine buses (Chunghsing Line) for NT$73;

and a local bus (not recommended) for NT$34.

Limousine buses run every 15 to 20 minutes, beginning at 6.30 am and ending at 10.30 pm. There are two limousine buses – the more popular one with travellers goes to the Taipei railway station right in the city centre. The other limousine bus goes to Sungshan Domestic Airport in the north-east part of the city. There is only one route for the local bus – it makes a few stops near the city centre and then terminates at Sungshan Domestic Airport.

When heading to the airport from Taipei, you can catch the limousine bus from two locations; the East Bus Station at 173 Chunghsiao W Rd (in front of the main railway station), or from the bus terminal on the western end of Sungshan Domestic Airport.

Bus Nos 23, 262 and 502 connect Sungshan Domestic Airport to the railway station. Other buses going to Sungshan Domestic Airport include Nos 214 and 254.

Bus There is a reasonably good English bus guide available from Caves Books and Lucky Bookstore for NT$100, but it's getting out of date. At the time of this writing, Taipei's bus system was in a state of chaos because many roads are being converted into one-way streets.

Buses without air-conditioning cost NT$8 a ride, but these buses are nearly extinct. Most buses have air-con and cost NT$10 – exact change required. Longer trips can be double or even triple this amount, as the fare is determined by the number of zones you travel through.

Somewhere near the driver should be a sign in Chinese or a red light telling you to pay when you get on *(shāng)* 上 or when you get off *(xià)* 下. Usually you pay when getting off.

Underground This should be nice, if they ever finish building it.

Taxi They're easy to find everywhere except during the rush hour.

Car Driving is not recommended for the city, but a car could be of limited use in the countryside. Taipei has several agencies that can put you in the driver's seat:

Avis Rent-A-Car
   Chienkuo N Rd, Section 2, Taipei (☎ (02) 5006633)
Central Auto Service
   1098 Chengte Rd, Taipei (☎ (02) 8819545, 8821000)
Hertz Rent-A-Car
   642 Minchuan E Rd, Taipei (☎ (02) 7173673)
VIP Rent-A-Car
   606 Minchuan E Rd, Taipei (☎ (02) 7131111)

Around the Country

CENTRAL CROSS-ISLAND HIGHWAY
中部橫貫公路

This spectacular highway *(zhōngbù hénggùan gōnglù)* connects Taroko Gorge on the east side of Taiwan with the city of Taichung on the west, a distance of 195 km. Virtually every km of this highway offers a stunning view of lush forests and towering mountain peaks, and should not be missed if you have the time. The road is occasionally closed due to landslides, especially after a typhoon – which is not surprising considering that in many places the road is carved out of sheer cliffs.

Getting Around
If you want to do this trip nonstop, it takes slightly more than eight hours by bus to travel across the island on this highway. From Hualien, buses depart for Taichung at 7.30, 8 and 11 am. Going in the other direction, buses depart Taichung for Hualien at 7.15, 7.50 and 9.30 am. The fare is NT$300. You can also catch the bus in Tienhsiang. Although the trip can be done in one day, three days would be more reasonable to allow for side trips to Wuling Farm and Hohuanshan.

If you're not headed to south Taiwan, then Fengyuan is an important transit point at the western end of the highway. It's about an hour north of Taichung (see the Central Taiwan map). You can get a train from Taipei to Fengyuan and bypass Taichung completely. This saves nearly two hours on a trip from Taipei to the Central Cross-Island Highway.

TAICHUNG 台中
Taiwan's third largest city, Taichung *(táizhōng)* ('Central Taiwan') is a major transport hub on the western end of the Central Cross-Island Highway. Although the city has a few museums, temples and other places of interest, for most travellers it will just be an overnight stop on the way to somewhere else.

Places to Stay
It's much easier to find good budget accommodation if you are travelling with somebody. There are several hotels with rooms for NT$300 or less. Taichung is difficult for a single budget traveller wanting to pay less than NT$200. The only youth hostel in this city provides accommodation for female students on a monthly basis, which is not much use to travellers.

One of the cheapest places in town is *zhōngzōu lüshè* (☎ (04) 2222711), on the 2nd floor at 129 Chienkuo Rd. They have singles/doubles for NT$200/250. It's on the circle just opposite the railway station behind the bus stop, between Chungcheng Rd and Chungshan Rd. Just to the left of this place is a narrow alley called Lane 125. On this lane you will find the *jiànchéng lüshè* (☎ (04) 2222497), 10 Lane 125, Chienkuo Rd. They have singles/doubles for NT$200/250 with shared bath, or NT$350 with private bath. The *dōngchéng dàlüshè* (☎ (04) 2225001), 14 Chungshan Rd, has doubles starting at NT$250 with shared bath, NT$350 with private bath.

A few blocks from the central area is the *First Hotel* (☎ (04) 2222205) *(dìyī lüshè)*, 51 Chikuang St *(jìguang jiē)*, where singles start at NT$300. It's very close to the classy Taichung Hotel.

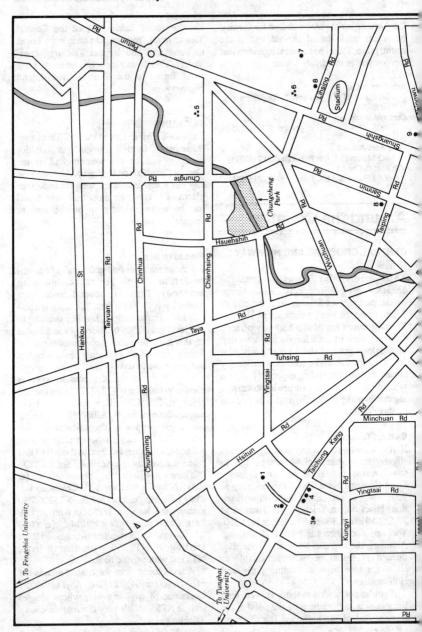

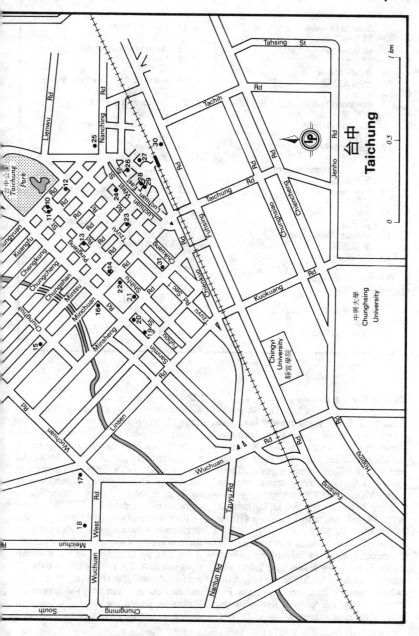

1	Science Museum 科學博物館		17	Cultural Center 文化中心
2	McDonald's 麥當勞		18	Taiwan Museum of Art
3	Hotel National 全國大飯店		19	YMCA 青年會
4	Pubs		20	Police Station (Visa Extensions) 外事警察
5	Paochueh Temple 寶覺寺		21	Telecommunications 電信局
6	Confucius Temple 孔廟		22	Municipal Government 市政府
7	Martyrs' Shrine 忠烈祠		23	First Hotel 第一旅社
8	Lai Lai Department Store 來來百貨		24	Shopping Mall 第一廣場
9	Swimming Pool 游泳池		25	Buses to Sun Moon Lake, Lishan & Hualien 干城車站
10	YMCA 青年會		26	Fengzhong Movie Theater 豐中戲院
11	Haohua Movie Theater 豪華戲院		27	Taipei Buses 台汽總站
12	McDonald's 麥當勞		28	Jiancheng Lüshe 建成旅社
13	Central Bookstore 中央書局		29	Dongcheng Dalüshe 東城大旅社
14	GPO 郵政總局		30	Buses to Hsitou, Chiayi & Kaohsiung 南站
15	ICBC		31	Bank of Taiwan
16	Taichung Hospital			

Getting There & Away

As it's 105 km south of Taipei on the major north-south freeway and railway line, you won't have trouble getting to Taichung. There are also buses coming over the mountains from Hualien on the east coast, via the scenic Central Cross-Island Highway. There are direct buses to many scenic areas in central Taiwan.

From Taipei the bus fare to Taichung is NT$156 and the train fare ranges from NT$188 to NT$259.

There are three major bus terminals in Taichung. The one in front of the railway station is for buses heading for Taipei and other places in the north. The one behind the railway station is for southbound buses. For country buses, the terminal is two blocks north of the railway station.

KUKUAN 谷關

Kukuan (*gŭgūan*) is a small town and hot spring resort towards the western end of the Central Cross-Island Highway, about 1½ hours by bus from Taichung. Being rather close to the city, it gets crowded at weekends, but it is OK at other times. The scenery is certainly good, though not as spectacular as higher up in the mountains. Kukuan has an elevation of 750 metres.

The hot springs are piped into hotel baths; unfortunately there are no outdoor pools. In addition to the hot springs, another attraction is the hike up to Dragon Valley Waterfall (*lónggŭ pùbù*). It's an easy hike – only 3.3 km for the round trip. However, it's in a park and they charge a steep NT$80 admission. Within the park are a zoo and a botanical garden. To find the park, cross the footbridge near the Dragon Valley Hotel and just follow the trail. Bring some junk food to feed the monkeys.

Orientation

The town is divided into two – one half is next to the highway and the other on the north bank of the river. You get to the north side by crossing a footbridge on the eastern (upper) part of the village. The north side is definitely the nicer part of town, since it has no whining motorcycles or cars.

Places to Stay

Kukuan is overrun with tourists at weekends and during holidays, but on weekdays business is very slow and most hotels offer a 20% discount off the rates quoted here.

Many of the hotels have tatami dormitories. If you're a single traveller, you can't be certain that you can stay in them. If the hotel is empty – as it often is on a weekday – they'll usually let you stay by yourself in the dorm.

Across the footbridge on the north bank is the *gūgŭan shān zhūang* (☎ (045) 951126), which costs NT$100 for the dorm and NT$350 for a double. The *dōnggŭan wēnqúan dàfàndiàn* (☎ (045) 951111) has doubles/twins for NT$800/1000. The *dōnggŭ fàndiàn* (☎ (045) 951236) has dorms for NT$150 and doubles for NT$800.

Utopia Holiday Hotel (☎ (045) 951511/5) (*jiàqí dàfàndiàn*) is a great place to stay, and it ought to be for the price – doubles/twins cost NT$1200/1800. It's also on the quiet north bank of the river.

On the busy side of town, the *Dragon Valley Hotel* (☎ (045) 951325, 951365) (*lónggŭ dàfàndiàn*) has doubles/twins for NT$1350/1550.

Getting There & Away

Buses from Taichung are frequent, starting at 6 am. All buses running between Taichung and Lishan stop in Kukuan.

In Kukuan the bus stop is at the east end of town, right in front of the Kukuan Hotel. The buses do not stop in the centre of town.

LISHAN 梨山

Lishan (*líshān*), or 'Pear Mountain', is a small farming community near the middle of the Central Cross-Island Highway. Some 1900 metres above sea level, the area is famous for growing cold-weather fruits which cannot grow in the subtropical lowlands of Taiwan, but is being transformed into a tourist resort. There really isn't that much to do in Lishan itself, but it is a transit point for the trip to Wuling Farm and Hsuehshan.

Hiking opportunities are limited in Lishan because most of the land is occupied by orchards. However, you can hike to Lucky Life Mountain Farm (*fúshòushān nóngchǎng*). Along the way you pass a small villa which once served as a mountain retreat for Chiang Kaishek. The whole hike is only about 10 km. To find the road leading up there, walk out of town on the highway going east (towards Hualien). Less than a km of walking brings you to a church on the left side of the road. On the right side is the road you want. The road passes the elementary school, Chiang Kaishek's villa and the Lishan Culture Museum (*líshān wénwù gǔan*). The museum is good, and the views from the back porch of the surrounding mountains are fantastic.

Places to Stay

So many tour buses arrive in Lishan at weekends and on holidays that it's a wonder the mountain doesn't collapse. Accommodation is very tight at these times, so you're definitely better off arriving on a weekday. The following rates are for weekdays – on Saturday night, the rates will be about 50% higher if you can find a room at all!

Chungcheng Rd is the main road in town; it's actually part of the Cross-Island Highway. It's mostly lined with restaurants, but there are a few hotels including the *líshān lǚshè* (☎ (045) 989261), which charges NT$300 for a double. *Fu Chung Hotel* (☎ (045) 989506) (*fúzhōng dàfàndiàn*), 61 Chungcheng Rd, has singles/doubles for NT$500/600.

One block south of Chungcheng Rd and

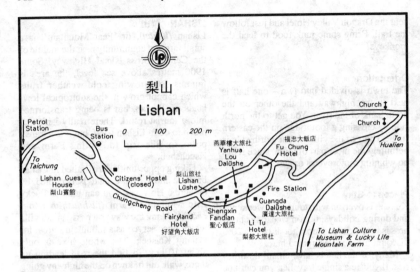

梨山
Lishan

Church
Church

Petrol Station

Bus Station

0   100   200 m

To Taichung

To Hualien

燕華樓大旅社 Yanhua Lou Dalüshè

福忠大旅店 Fu Chung Hotel

Lishan Guest House 梨山賓館

Citizens' Hostel (closed)

梨山旅社 Lishan Lüshè

Fire Station

Chungcheng Road

Shengxin Fandian 聖心飯店

Guangda Dalüshè 廣達大旅社

Fairyland Hotel 好望角大飯店

Li Tu Hotel 梨都大旅社

To Lishan Culture Museum & Lucky Life Mountain Farm

running parallel to it is Mintsu Rd, which is where most of the hotels are. The cheapest is *gǔangdá dàlǔshè* (☎ (045) 989216), 21 Mintsu Rd (next to the fire station), which has doubles with private bath for NT$200. The *yànhúa lóu dàlǔshè* (☎ (045) 989615, 989511) has doubles for NT$300. The *shèngxīn fàndiàn* (☎ (045) 989577) has singles/doubles for NT$400/500. The *Li Tu Hotel* (☎ (045) 989256, 989512) (*lìdū dàlǔshè*) has singles/doubles for NT$400/500. *Fairyland Hotel* (☎ (045) 989256, 989512) (*hǎowàngjiǎo dàfàndiàn*), 52 Mintsu Rd, charges NT$600 for doubles.

Getting There & Away

Lishan is easily reached by any bus going along the Cross-Island Highway between Hualien and Taichung.

From Taichung there are 13 buses daily, with the last bus leaving at 2.30 pm. Most of the buses from Taichung end the trip at Lishan but a few continue to Hualien. The fare is NT$140 and the trip takes 3½ hours. From Hualien, the buses leave at 7.30, 8 and 11 am and take 4½ hours to reach Lishan. The Hualien to Lishan fare ranges from

NT$134 to NT$161, depending on which bus you take.

There are three buses daily going to Lishan from the north-east coastal city of Ilan.

WULING FARM 武陵農場

Wuling Farm (*wǔlíng nóngchǎng*) is a fruit-growing area, but its main attraction is to hikers who want to challenge Taiwan's second highest peak, Hsuehshan (*xǔeshān*), or 'Snow Mountain', which is 3884 metres in elevation.

Hikes

A mountain permit is supposedly required for Hsuehshan, but there is no-one around to check it. It's a 10 to 12-hour climb to the summit. There are two huts along the way where you can spend the night. The first one, Chika Hut (*qīkǎ shān zhūang*), is a two-hour hike from the trailhead and has water. The second one, Three Six Nine Hut (*sān liù jiǔ shān zhūang*), is an additional six-hour climb and has no water. There are no facilities at the huts, so you'll need a sleeping bag, food,

Map: **Wuling Farm 武陵農場**

Labels on map:
- Yensheng Waterfall 烟聲瀑布
- Youth Activity Center (Hostel) 青年活動中心
- To Snow Mountain (Hsuehshan) 往雪山
- Orchards
- No Buses 5 km
- 0   0.5   1 km
- Orchards
- Bus Terminal
- Wuling Rest House 榮民休憩中心
- Orchards
- To Ilan
- Buddha Statue
- Bus Stop
- Pavilion
- Wuling Guest House 武陵國民旅社
- To Lishan

Wuling Rest House (☎ (045) 901259) *(róngmín xiūxí zhōngxīn)* is much cheaper and is right near the bus stop; the dormitory there costs NT$120 and doubles are NT$400.

The *Wuling Youth Activity Center* (☎ (045) 901020) *(qīngnián húodòng zhōngxīn)* is a five-km hike up the valley road from the last bus stop. The dormitory costs NT$132 and doubles are NT$1100.

All these places are practically empty during the week but can fill up on weekends and holidays. Camping is not permitted next to the hostels or in the farming area of the valley. If you want to camp, you'll have to do it in back country.

Getting There & Away

Wuling Farm is 25 km north-east of Lishan, just off the branch highway leading down to the coast at Ilan. It's most easily reached by bus from Lishan. There are six buses daily, departing from Lishan at 8 and 10.10 am, noon, and 1, 3 and 4.50 pm.

The buses going from Ilan to Lishan also stop at Wuling Farm.

HOHUANSHAN 合歡山

Hohuanshan *(héhūanshān)* reaches an elevation of 3416 metres and the summit is above the tree line. At this height it is cool even in summer, but in winter the night temperatures can dip well below freezing and there is sufficient snowfall in January and February to permit skiing. However, the skiing isn't very good – the ski lift broke down years ago and hasn't been repaired.

During the rest of the year it is certainly worth visiting Hohuanshan for the magnificent views. In the morning, you can usually witness that beautiful Taiwanese phenomenon, the 'sea of clouds'.

Hohuanshan is reached by a branch highway that runs off the Central Cross-Island Highway. This narrow road runs between Tayuling and Wushe and it's the highest road in Taiwan.

Hohuanshan is peaceful during the off season, but when it snows everybody converges on the mountain. People in Taiwan

stove and all the other other backpacking paraphernalia.

A much easier hike would be to Yensheng Waterfall *(yānshēng pùbù)*. It's at the top end of the valley past the Youth Activity Center. From there you could also climb Peach Mountain *(táoshān)*, which has an elevation of 3324 metres.

Places to Stay

There are three places to stay in Wuling. The *Wuling Guesthouse* (☎ (045) 901183) *(wǔlíng gúomín lǚshè)* is the classiest, with doubles/triples at NT$1000/1200. The have few opportunities to see snow, so when it falls on Hohuanshan everyone who can makes the pilgrimage there to see the white stuff. The mountain is much better when there is no snow – it's quieter and warmer.

Places to Stay

There is a youth hostel near where the bus drops you off in Tayuling. Take the switchback trail up the hill to reach the hostel. Otherwise, you'll have to walk up a long dirt driveway. Reservations for this hostel are usually made from the Tienhsiang Youth Hostel (☎ (038) 691111/3). The local hostel is called *Tayuling Youth Hostel (dàyùlǐng shān zhǔang)*.

At Hohuanshan there is only one place to stay, *Sung Hsueh Lou (sōng xǔe lóu)* (☎ (049) 802732). In English, Sung Hsueh Lou means 'Pine Snow Hostel'. The tatami dormitory costs NT$130, and doubles are NT$1200 during the peak season (winter) and NT$900 during the off season. There are no shops in or near the hostel, so bring food, film, toilet paper, a torch (flashlight) and plenty of warm clothes. If you don't have a reservation, bring a sleeping bag, because there is only one quilt for every guest and there probably will be no extras. If all the beds are taken, it's almost certain they will allow you to roll out a sleeping bag on the dining room floor when it's time for lights out.

In any event, be prepared for a cold night. At 3400 metres you are no longer in the tropics, so be sure to bring your winter woollies.

Places to Eat

Sung Hsueh Lou is the only place that has food or anything else. Prepared meals are available but only if you made a reservation in advance. You are therefore strongly advised to bring extra food unless you want to forage for nuts and berries.

Getting There & Away

One major tactical problem with visiting Hohuanshan is that there is no bus service along the dirt road that leads to the top of the mountain and the lodge. You have two options, either to go by wild chicken taxi or to walk. Opportunities for hitching are limited because traffic is almost nil. There are two routes – you could go up one way and down the other. Most people approach from the north side because it's shorter. Either route may be closed occasionally due to landslides.

North Side Wild chicken taxis from the base of the mountain will be waiting for you near the bus stop in Tayuling. They charge about NT$250 to NT$400, subject to bargaining. The best way to arrange this is to round up a group of Chinese tourists on the bus to Tayuling so you can split the cost. Let them handle the bargaining.

If you walk from Tayuling, it's a steep but breathtakingly beautiful walk of nine km – four hours uphill or three hours downhill. Certainly the best way to appreciate the scenery is on foot.

South Side From Puli, you can get a bus to Tsuifeng *(cuìfēng)* (elevation 2375 metres) and from there it's 15 km, or about 6½ hours of walking. The bus departs Puli from the Nantou Bus Company Station *(nántóu kèyùn zhàn)*. There are no taxis in Tsuifeng, nor is there a place to stay unless you camp out. The nearest place that has accommodation is Quiet Farm, but Wushe has a youth hostel and is a better option for budget travellers. The bus from Puli passes through Wushe and Quiet Farm, and terminates in Tsuifeng. Start early because the weather is usually clearest in the morning.

TIENHSIANG 天祥

Tienhsiang *(tiānxiáng)* is a resort town nestled between towering cliffs at the upper end of Taroko Gorge *(tàilǔgé)*, Taiwan's top scenic drawcard. The gorge is 19 km long with a rushing white-water river surrounded by sheer cliffs. The road – which is the eastern end of the Central Cross-Island Highway – was carved out of the cliffs at a cost of US$11 million and some 450 lives.

Things to See
Taroko Gorge *(tàilügé)* The best way to see the gorge is to walk down from Tienhsiang to the Eternal Spring Shrine at the bottom of the gorge. The walk takes about four hours and it's best to hike in the morning when rain is least likely. There are no stores in the gorge, so be prepared to be self-sufficient for four hours. It's best not to go on Sundays or holidays, since the number of cars on the road will be much greater at those times.

Eternal Spring Shrine *(cháng chūn cí)* A short distance inside the entrance at the eastern end of the gorge is the Eternal Spring Shrine, which features a pavilion with a waterfall passing through it. The shrine is reached by hiking up a short hill from the highway. It was built in memory of those who lost their lives while constructing the highway.

Tunnel If you walk exactly one km uphill from Tienhsiang on the main highway, on your left you will find a tunnel with a red gate. The gate is too small to permit motor vehicles to enter but a hiker can easily squeeze through. This is your gateway to a really fun hike, but you'll need a torch, mosquito repellent and plastic bag to protect your camera. A raincoat or umbrella wouldn't hurt either because you'll be walking through many tunnels with 'rain' inside. Just follow the road – you can't get lost – and walk for about six km. The destination is an impressive waterfall which cascades over the road.

Up at Tienhsiang, one of the nicer things we did was to just walk upstream along the river. After 100 metres we were completely alone with the beautiful landscape, since nobody else bothered to go this far...On a hot, sunny day, swimming in the cool, crystal-clear water was wonderful – it is not allowed in the centre of Tienhsiang.

Maria Ahlqvist & Staffan Jonsson

Wenshan Hot Springs *(wénshān wēnqúan)* About three km up the main highway is Wenshan Hot Springs, at 575 metres above sea level. You can reach the springs by taking a bus or by hiking. The bus stops in front of a national park police station. Get off there and continue walking up the road for 400 metres. Before you enter the third tunnel up from Tienhsiang, there are some steps leading down to the river. Walk down, then cross the suspension bridge and go down a path on the other side to reach the hot springs.

Places to Stay
This resort is extremely popular, so hotel space can be a problem at times and a reservation is advisable. On weekends or holidays, forget it unless there's a typhoon or an earthquake.

The best bargain in town is the *Catholic Hostel* (☎ (038) 691122) *(tiānzhǔ táng)*, where it is NT$80 in the dormitory and NT$500 for a double. It sits on a hill just above the parking area.

Continuing up the same hill just a little further will bring you to a gleaming white building which is the *Tienhsiang Youth Activity Center* (☎ (038) 691111/3). In spite of the fact that it has over 300 beds it's often full, so call ahead. Dormitory/doubles are NT$120/360.

Getting There & Away
If you're coming from the west side of Taiwan over the Central Cross-Island Highway, you can stop in Tienhsiang.

The local bus between Hualien and Tienhsiang costs NT$44 one way; the express bus costs NT$51. Departures from Hualien are at 8.05, 8.15, 8.55 and 9.40 am, but check since the schedule changes periodically.

There are several tour buses from Hualien going to the gorge, all of which start out in the morning. They stop often so you can admire the scenery while the Chinese tourists take pictures of each other standing in front of the bus. There is a lunch stop before the tour concludes and then they bring you back to Hualien. The total cost is NT$450, lunch included.

HUALIEN 花蓮
The largest city on the east coast, Hualien

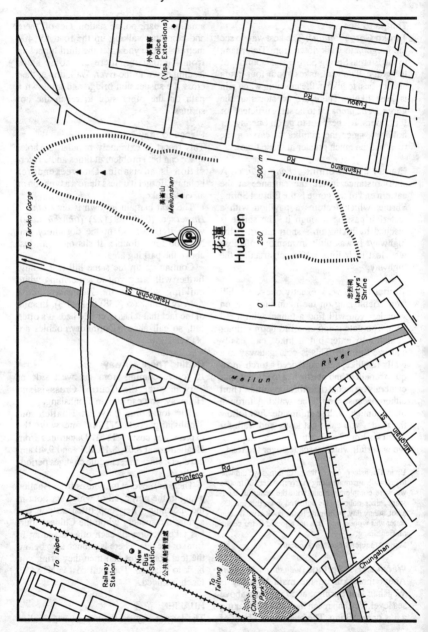

花蓮
Hualien

外事警察
Police
(Visa Extensions)

Fusen Rd

Hsinshing Rd

美崙山
Meilunshan

To Taroko Gorge

忠烈祠
Martyr's Shrine

Hsiangchih St

Meilun River

Meilun St

Chinfeng Rd

Chungshan

Chungshan Park

To Taipei

Railway Station

New Bus Station
公共車船管理處

To Taitung

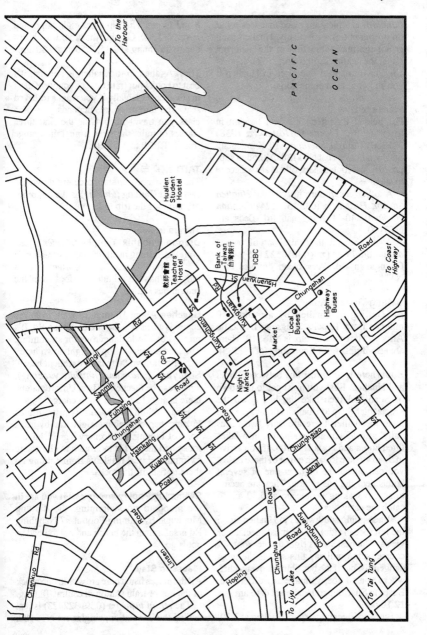

(hūalián) is a pleasant place that sees a fair bit of tourist traffic. Actually, Hualien itself is not the main attraction in the area, but rather the nearby Taroko Gorge. You'll probably have to spend one night in Hualien if you're going to visit the gorge.

Places to Stay

For budget travellers, the best bargain in town is the *Teachers' Hostel* (☎ (038) 325880) *(jiàoshī hùiguǎn)*, 10 Kungcheng St. Dormitories cost NT$130. Although supposedly just for teachers, others are welcome to stay.

Another cheap dormitory is the *Hualien Student Hostel* (☎ (038) 324124) *(hūalián xúeyùan)*, 40-11 Kungyuan Rd. Beds are NT$100.

A good hotel in the central part of town is *dàxìn dàlǚshè* (☎ (038) 322125), 101 Chungshan Rd. Very clean doubles cost NT$500.

Getting There & Away

Air Getting to Hualien by air takes 40 minutes from Taipei's Sungshan Domestic Airport. The one-way fare is NT$919. There are also flights from Kaohsiung (NT$1335).

Bus There is no direct bus between Taipei and Hualien. First you must get to the town of Suao and then take the bus down the spectacular Suao to Hualien Highway. From Suao to Hualien there are only two buses daily, at 6.15 am and noon. The trip takes three hours and costs NT$109. If you arrive in Suao too late to catch either of these buses, you can spend the night at one of several hotels near the bus station. They are accustomed to waking people up at 5.30 am to catch the early bus.

When going southwards to Hualien sit on the left (ocean side) for the most spectacular views. The best seat is right up the front. Of course, some will say this seat is the most dangerous, but if the bus plunges over a cliff, where you sit doesn't make any difference. Buses to Suao depart Hualien at 6.15 am and 12.10 pm.

Buses to Taichung depart Hualien at 7.30,

8 and 11 am. The trip takes eight hours and costs NT$300. Coming the other way, buses depart Taichung at 7.15, 7.50 and 9.30 am.

Train As the trip to Hualien is popular, it's best to book your train ticket a couple of days in advance, especially if you want a reserved seat. The fare of course depends on which class you travel in, but for the first three classes of train, the fares from Taipei range from NT$230 to NT$334.

TAITUNG 台東

The last major population centre down the east coast, Taitung *(táidōng)* is the jumping-off point for the trip to Lanyu.

Things to See

Dragon Phoenix Temple *(lóngfèng fóugōng)* In Taitung itself, the main attraction is the Dragon Phoenix Temple, which is on a hill less than 10 minutes by foot from the central bus station.

Beaches About 10 minutes walk from the centre is a beach at the end of Tatung Rd. It's pretty, but a little dangerous for swimming. The land seems to drop straight down here

North of town there is an excellent beach, Shanyuan *(shānyúan hǎishǔi yùchǎng)*, which can be reached by bus. Unfortunately, there is an NT$20 admission charge.

Hsiao Yehliu *(xiǎo yěliǔ)* is just north of Fukang harbour, about eight km by road north of Taitung. The scenery is great, but it's rocky and the surf is too rough to allow safe swimming. Local residents from Taitung go there to fish off the rocks.

Swimming Pool *(yóuyǒng chí)* If you are in the mood to go swimming, the Taitung Municipal Swimming Pool at 37 Nanching Rd is safer than the beach and not too bad as pools go.

Places to Stay

All the places listed here are within one block of the bus or train station in central Taitung.

The *rén'ài lǚshè* (☎ (089) 322423) is just behind the bus station; singles are NT$180.

The *dōngbīn lǚshè* (☎ (089) 322222), at 536 Chunghua Rd, Section 1, has doubles/triples for NT$250/300. The *quánchéng lǚshè* (☎ (089) 322611), 51 Hsinsheng Rd, is NT$300 for a single.

The *Teachers' Hostel* (☎ (089) 310142) *(jiàoshī hùiguǎn)*, 19 Nanching Rd, is clean, pleasant and popular with foreigners, but not very cheap. Prices for singles/doubles are NT$420/580, NT$630 for twins.

Places to Eat

Chunghua Rd is lined with numerous restaurants. Between Chunghua Rd and Chungshan Rd are many little alleys which become an active market at night. You can find almost anything imaginable to eat there. Chengchi Rd, between Chunghua Rd and Poai Rd, becomes a fruit market at night.

A good but inexpensive dumpling restaurant is *tóngxīn jū* (☎ (089) 323249) on the south-west corner of Chengchi Rd and Chungshan Rd.

Getting There & Away

Air Far Eastern Airlines flies from Taipei to Taitung four times daily. The fare is NT$1226 one way. Other possible destinations include Green Island (NT$495) and Lanyu (NT$990).

Bus It takes about four hours by express bus along the coastal highway to get from Hualien to Taitung.

There are plenty of buses connecting Taitung with Kaohsiung on the west coast, a four-hour journey. This same bus also stops at Fengkang, where you can change buses to go to Kenting.

Train From Taipei there is a frequent train service direct to Taitung via Hualien. The fastest trains take over five hours.

A railway line connecting Taitung to Kaohsiung is under construction and might be open by the time you read this.

LANYU 蘭嶼

Some 62 km south-east of Taiwan proper is the tropical island of Lanyu *(lányǔ)*, which has been designated a national park. The island is known for its unique aboriginal culture and fine scenery. Lanyu means 'Orchid Island', but in fact the orchids are scarce.

Places to Stay

There are two hotels on the island, both charging high prices. Alternatively, you can sleep in a school, but ask first. Camping is another possibility.

The two airlines which fly to the island also operate the two hotels and both hotels offer a free shuttle service to and from the airport. The *Orchid Hotel* (☎ (089) 320033) *(lányǔ dàfàndiàn)*, in Kaiyuan village, is operated by Taiwan Airlines. Dormitory accommodation costs NT$250 and doubles range from NT$700 to NT$900. It is also the closer of the two hotels to the harbour, should you arrive by boat.

The *Lanyu Hotel* (☎ (089) 326111/3) *(lányǔ biéguǎn)*, operated by Formosa Airlines, has dorm accommodation for NT$250, singles for NT$400 to NT$600 and doubles for NT$700 to NT$1500. It's also adjacent to what is probably the best beach on the island, and within walking distance of the airport.

Places to Eat

Food in Lanyu is available at the two hotels but is expensive. There are a couple of cheaper noodle shops near the hotels and some closet-size grocery stores.

Getting There & Away

Air Two airlines, Formosa Airlines and Taiwan Aviation Company (TAC), fly small aircraft from Taitung to Lanyu. From Taitung, a one-way airfare is NT$990, double that for the round trip. You can book these tickets at their offices right next to the Taitung bus station.

Both airlines also operate flights between Kaohsiung and Lanyu once a day. The fare is NT$1395 one way.

Hovercraft The hovercraft *(qìdiàn chúan)* runs a loop route from Taitung to Green

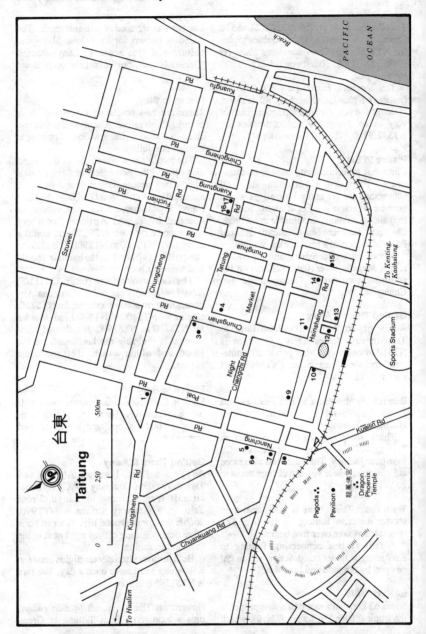

台東

Taitung

PACIFIC OCEAN

Beach

Kuangfu Rd

Chungcheng Rd

Szuwei Rd

Kuangtung Rd

Fuchien Rd

Chungcheng Rd

Chunghua Rd

Tatung Rd

Market

16●17●

Kuangtung Rd

●15

●14

Hsinsheng Rd

Chungshan Rd

●4

●2

●3

●11

Night Market

●12●

●13

Poai Rd

Chengchii Rd

●10

●9

Sports Stadium

To Kenting, Kaohsiung

●1

Kungsheng Rd

Nanching Rd

●5

●6

●7

●8●

Kueilin Rd

Chuankuang Rd

To Hualien

龍鳳佛宮
Dragon Phoenix Temple

Pagoda ●
Pavilion ●

0   250   500m

1 Lanyu Shipping Office
台東縣輪船管理處
2 Police (Visa Extensions)
外事警察
3 City Government Building
市政府
4 Bank of Taiwan
台灣銀行
5 Swimming Pool
游泳池
6 Teachers' Hostel
教師會館
7 Sunshine Man Restaurant
香斯曼
8 Tungnung Supermarket
9 Motorcycle Rental
榮春機車行
10 Hotel Zeus
興東園大飯店
11 Bus To Chihpen Hot Springs
12 Bus Station
13 Lenya Hotel
聯亞大飯店
14 Dongbin Lüshe
東賓旅社
15 Laundry
志倫洗衣店
16 Telephone Company
電信局
17 Post Office
郵局

Island, Green Island to Lanyu, and Lanyu back to Taitung. It takes 35 minutes to reach Green Island, another 75 minutes to Lanyu, and 90 minutes back to Taitung. The place to book tickets is Thankyou Lines (shānjiǔ hángyùn gōngsī) (☎ (089) 320413, 324030), 222 Hsinsheng Rd, near the corner with Poai Rd. A one-way ticket from Taitung to Green Island costs NT$310; Taitung to Lanyu costs NT$832; Green Island to Lanyu is NT$680. Boats normally run twice daily, subject to weather and number of passengers.

You must have your passport for this boat trip. Departures are from the port of Fukang (fúgāng) which you must reach by bus or taxi. Fukang is to the north of Taitung.

Getting Around

Walking is great for those who have the time and energy, but the island really is large and many travellers opt for motorised transport. Motorcycles are available for rent from the hotels for NT$500 per day.

A bus goes around the island four times daily, twice in a clockwise direction and twice anticlockwise. The last bus makes a run between 3.30 and 4.30 pm.

The two hotels occasionally run a touring minibus around the island for NT$280 per person if they can get enough passengers.

KENTING 墾丁

Situated on a bay just a few km from Taiwan's southernmost tip, Kenting (kěndīng) has the best beaches on the island. Although there is a chilly wind in winter, it is just warm enough for year-round bathing. It gets really crowded in summer – avoid Kenting on weekends when jet-ski gorillas take over the beaches. At other times, it's one of the most relaxing places in Taiwan.

Places to Stay

It's easy to find accommodation in Kenting, except at weekends and on holidays. If you arrive during the week you can book into a room, but be warned that some places will ask you to leave on Saturday because another group has booked and paid for all the rooms in advance. Weekend prices may be double, if you can get a room at all. On weekends, you might be forced to stay in Hengchun, a not-very-attractive town nine km to the north.

The *Teachers' Hostel* (☎ (08) 8861241) (jiàoshī huìguǎn) offers good rooms at bargain prices. The dormitory costs NT$100 and doubles cost NT$300 but, unfortunately, it is usually full. Anyway, you are supposed to be a teacher or a student studying at an officially-recognised university in Taiwan. The nearby *Catholic Hostel* (☎ (08) 8861540) (tiānjǔjiào huódòng zhōngxīn) is also cheap but not nearly as attractive as the Teachers' Hostel. The dormitory costs NT$100.

The *Hongbin Hotel* (☎ (08) 8861003)

(hóngbīn lǔshè) in the centre of town is a pleasant place to stay. Singles/doubles cost NT$300/400 during the week, but at weekends prices escalate and rooms are usually not available. Right next door is the *Foremost Hotel* (☎ (08) 8861007) (*fúlè tàofáng*), where singles/doubles cost NT$300/400.

One place has a sign outside which just says 'Motel' but it actually has a dorm. The Chinese name is *yǎkè zhījiā* (☎ (08) 8861272). The dorm costs NT$150 and double rooms are NT$960.

The *Kenting Youth Activity Center* (☎ (08) 8861221) (*kěndīng húodòng zhōngxīn*) is a government-operated place that boasts a unique architecture designed to resemble an ancient Chinese village. On the negative side, it's expensive for a youth hostel with dormitory beds costing NT$250. It is also somewhat isolated from the centre of town, where you will probably want to eat and stroll around at night.

Getting There & Away

Some buses go directly to Kenting, but if you can't catch one of these, then go to Hengchun (*héngchūn*), nine km north of Kenting. Shuttle buses connecting Hengchun with Kenting run about every 40 minutes between 8 am and 6 pm.

To/From Taitung To reach Hengchun from Taitung, buy a ticket to Fengkang (*fēnggǎng*). All buses going to Kaohsiung stop in Fengkang. From Fengkang there are numerous buses heading south to Hengchun and/or Kenting.

To/From Kaohsiung There are frequent buses from the Kaohsiung main bus station to Hengchun and/or Kenting. The fare is NT$140.

To/From Taipei There are a few direct buses from Taipei – fare is NT$558. If you have the money but not much time, you may consider flying to Kaohsiung Airport and catching a bus south to Hengchun or Kenting. Buses go right by the airport entrance and can be

flagged down, so it's not necessary to backtrack into Kaohsiung city.

Getting Around

There is a regular bus service between Hengchun and Oluanpi, stopping at Kenting along the way. Wild chicken taxis also regularly patrol the roads. Hitching is another possibility.

It's a great area for walking or cycling. There are plenty of bicycles for hire in Kenting and you'll have no trouble finding a rental shop. A bike costs about NT$100 for eight hours.

CHIAYI 嘉義

A small city in the centre of Taiwan, Chiayi (*jiāyì*) is the departure point for journeys into Taiwan's high mountains, especially the trip to Alishan.

Places to Stay

The cheapest place in town is the *pénglái lǔshè* (☎ (05) 2272366), 534 Jenai Rd, where singles/doubles cost NT$120/200. The *Hotel North-west* (☎ (05) 2223331) (*xīběi dàlǔshè*), 192 Jenai Rd, has singles/doubles for NT$200/250. The hotel address will probably have changed by the time you read this because the street is being renumbered.

If you'd rather be a little closer to the centre of things, there are numerous moderately priced hotels on Chungshan Rd. A nice, clean-looking place is the *Hotel Shin Kao* (☎ (05) 2272252) (*xīn gāo dàlǔshè*), 581 Chungshan Rd, where doubles are NT$500. You can also try *tián yúan dàlǔshè* (☎ (05) 2222541), 434 Chungshan Rd, where doubles are NT$450.

Chungcheng Rd is also a rich hunting ground for hotels. About the cheapest is *Hotel I-Tong* (☎ (05) 2272250) (*yī tóng dàfàndiàn*), 695 Chungcheng Rd, where doubles are NT$450. Next door is *jiā xīn dàfàndiàn* (☎ (05) 2222280), 687 Chungcheng Rd, with doubles from NT$600 to NT$700. On the other side of the street is *tǒng yī dàfàndiàn* (☎ (05) 2252685), 720 Chungcheng Rd, where doubles are NT$500 to NT$650. The *yì xīng lǔguǎn* (☎ (05)

2279344), 739 Chungcheng Rd, has doubles for NT$500 to NT$700.

Places to Eat

Chungshan Rd is lined with restaurants on both sides, and various noodle and rice shops spill out into the side alleys. The little nameless hole-in-the-wall places are cheapest, but for nicer surroundings try *lǎotáng niúròu miàn* (☎ (05) 2232662) at 504 Chungshan Rd. This place is famous for its beef noodles *(niúròu miàn)* and dumplings *(shuǐjiǎo)*.

Getting There & Away

Bus The north-south freeway passes through Chiayi, and there are frequent transport services from all the major points to the north and south. The bus fare from Taipei is either NT$237 or NT$294 depending on which bus you take.

In Chiayi, there are two bus terminals in front of the train station. The terminal to your left as you leave the train station belongs to the Taiwan Bus Company *(táiqì kèyùn)*. They run buses to major cities in Taiwan such as Taipei, Taichung, Tainan and Kaohsiung. The terminal to your right as you leave the train station is the Chiayi County Bus Company *(jiāyì xiàn gōngchē)*, which serves nearby towns like Alishan, Peikang and Kuantzuling.

Train As it sits right on the north-south railway, Chiayi has train service to Taipei and Kaohsiung about once every 30 minutes.

ALISHAN 阿里山

Ask any resident of Taiwan what is the most beautiful place on the island and the chances are high that he or she will say, Alishan. And no wonder! After the busy cities and the subtropical heat, Alishan is literally a breath of fresh air. At an elevation of 2200 metres, this is one of Taiwan's highest and best-known mountain resorts. Climbing the mountains and breathing the cool air does wonders for your health – a trip to Alishan *(ālǐshān)* could restore a mummy to its former strength and vitality.

The transformation that takes place on

weekends is truly amazing. On Saturday morning, it's so calm and peaceful you could hear a pin drop. Around 2 pm the first tourists start to arrive. By evening it resembles downtown Taipei. Even the trees seem to wilt under the stress. Sunday is also busy, but around 3 or 4 pm the crowds vanish like magic. It's as if a tidal wave rolled in and rolled out again. Serenity returns and Alishan is just a sleepy mountain village once more, at least until the following weekend.

If you come to Alishan, be prepared for the cold. Even in summer it's chilly at night. Fortunately, several hotels rent out jackets – usually bright orange or red, with the hotel's name in big letters on the back – for the day.

Things to See

Alishan Loop Hike The most popular hike is an easy walk going in a loop past the Two Sisters Pond, an elementary school, the Alishan Giant Tree and a museum. You can also stroll up to the summit of Chushan, which is very tranquil at any time other than the dawn rush hour.

You can also walk along the road leading to Yushan, but you cannot go further than the checkpoint without a mountain permit. The checkpoint is about a two-hour hike from Alishan.

Sunrise at Chushan The dawn trek to Celebration Mountain or Chushan is religiously performed by virtually everybody who comes to Alishan. In fact, it's almost mandatory. Hotels typically wake up all their guests around 3 to 4 am so that they can stumble out of bed and begin the hour-long pilgrimage up the mountain. Bring warm clothes and a torch (flashlight). There are minibuses and a train for those who can't handle the hike. The minibuses depart from the main parking area and also from Alishan House. The train departs from the main Alishan station and also makes a stop at the old station near Alishan House. The departure time is about 45 minutes before sunrise – in summer, that's around 4.30 am. The round-trip fare is NT$100 and the trip takes 30 minutes.

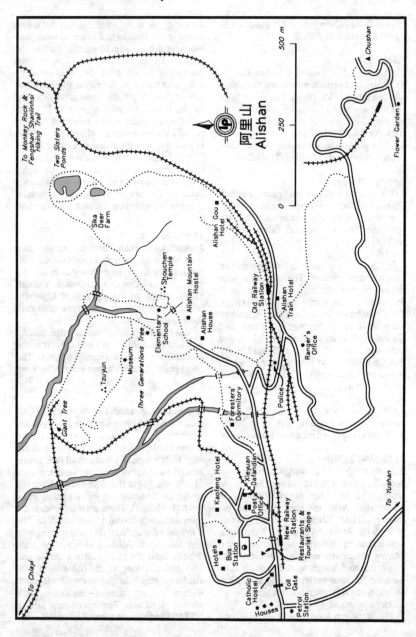

阿里山 Alishan

Monkey Rock After sunrise, the next event of the day is the train ride out to Monkey Rock (shíhóu), eight km further into the mountains. The train goes there twice a day. The first departure is at 7.50 am, the second at 1.30 pm. The train leaves Monkey Rock at 9.55 am and 3.35 pm to return to Alishan.

Monkey Rock itself is just a rock – it's the train ride out there on a steam locomotive that interests the tourists, and the views along the way. It's interesting to take the ride out there and walk back, but bring a torch for the tunnels – it's completely dark (and spooky) inside. The price is rather high for the short distance – NT$120 one way, NT$200 for the round trip, but there is a slight discount for students.

Yushan At 3952 metres, Yushan (Jade Mountain) is Taiwan's highest peak, and the highest peak in North-East Asia outside western China. Unfortunately, a class A mountain permit is required to climb Yushan. This has to be arranged through a mountain club, such as the ROC Alpine Association (☎ (02) 5911498), 10th floor, 185 Chungshan N Rd, Section 2, Taipei.

Places to Stay

The cheapest place in town is the *Alishan Mountain Hostel* (☎ (05) 2240132) (ālǐshān shān zhuāng), where dorm accommodation is NT$130. Unfortunately it's often full. It's next to the expensive Alishan House.

The *Kaofeng Hotel* (☎ (05) 2679739) (gāofēng dàfàndiàn) is a popular place with budget travellers. They have several standards of accommodation. Tatami singles/doubles are NT$150/200; they are closet-size rooms but about the best deal you're going to find in expensive Alishan. Double rooms with shared bath cost from NT$400 to NT$800, or NT$800 to NT$1600 with private bath. It's just down the hill from the bus station, behind the tourist information office. You can also eat there for NT$100.

Many travellers like the *Catholic Hostel* (☎ (05) 2679602) (tiānzhǔ jiào táng), which has dorm beds for NT$200. It's at the lower end of the village, just past the entrance gate on the north side of the road.

The *Foresters' Dormitory (sùshè qū)* is not really a dormitory but rather a collection of houses mostly occupied by government workers and some local people. They have rooms which they rent from around NT$150 to NT$400 per person. The Foresters' Dormitory is also known as *mínfáng*, which means 'people's house'. The standard of accommodation varies but is generally mediocre – it's usually a tatami attic and you'll have to share with several other people on weekends. To get into the Foresters' Dormitory, it's best to inquire first at the tourist information office near the bus station. If your Chinese is good, just ask around for *mínfáng*.

Getting There & Away

Bus The bus from Chiayi costs only NT$76 and takes a little over two hours. Departures from Chiayi are at 6.30, 8 and 9 am, and 12, 1 and 4 pm. On Sundays or holidays there are additional departures at 7 am and 2 pm.

From Taipei, there are two morning express buses to Alishan that depart at 8.30 and 9.30 am. Going the other way, the buses leave Alishan at 9 and 10 am. The fare is NT$321 and the trip takes six hours.

From Kaohsiung there is a daily bus that departs at 7.20 am. An additional bus departs at 11.10 am at weekends and on holidays only. From Alishan, daily buses to Kaohsiung leave at 3.30 pm and the additional weekend bus leaves at 9.20 am. The fare is NT$196 and the travel time is four hours and 40 minutes.

From Taichung, daily departures are at 8 am. An additional bus departs at 11 am on holidays. From Alishan to Taichung, daily departures are at 1 pm and the holiday bus departs at 9.30 am. The fare is NT$174, and the travel time is just under four hours.

There is a NT$65 charge to enter the Alishan Forest Recreation Area.

Train There are three trains daily in each direction. Two are 1st-class trains and one is 2nd class.

If you arrive in Chiayi by train, you can get on the Alishan train and buy your ticket on board. You don't have to go into the Chiayi railway station to buy a ticket, but doing so has one advantage – there is a better chance that you'll get a reserved seat and not have to stand.

The one-way fares are NT$373 for 1st class and NT$346 for 2nd class. When leaving the railway station in Alishan you will be charged NT$65 for admission to the Alishan Forest Recreation Area. They charge half price for people shorter than 145 cm (we're not making this up).

The train schedule at the time of writing was:

Chiayi to Alishan

	depart	arrive
1st class	8.25 am	11.35 am
2nd class	9 am	12.10 pm
1st class	12.50 pm	4.03 pm

Alishan to Chiayi

	depart	arrive
1st class	8.40 am	11.50 am
1st class	12.35 pm	3.45 pm
2nd class	1.05 pm	4.12 pm

Index

Dear traveller

Prices go up, good places go bad, bad places go bankrupt ... and every guidebook is inevitably outdated in places. Fortunately, many travellers write to us about their experiences, telling us when things have changed. If we reprint a book between editions, we try to include as much of this information as possible in a Stop Press section. Most of this information has not been verified by our own writers.

We really enjoy hearing from people out on the road, and apart from guaranteeing that others will benefit from your good and bad experiences, we're prepared to bribe you with the offer of a free book for sending us substantial useful information.

Thank you to everyone who has written and, to those who haven't, I hope you do find this book useful – and that you let us know when it isn't.

Tony Wheeler

The region is buzzing with changes. Mongolia is not only an easier place to travel in, but has had its first free election as a parliamentary democracy, and the communist Mongolian People's Revolutionary Party surprised even itself by the extent of its landslide victory, winning 71 of the 76 parliamentary seats. Japan has alarmed half of its population and most Asian countries, with a decision to send members of its armed forces on missions outside of its national boundaries. China is surging ahead with its market economy drive, and tourism is once again on the upswing.

The information in this Stop Press section was compiled with the help of letters sent to us by these travellers: Dale Bay, Henry & Jo Dodds (UK), John Milanese (Aus), Gayle Parry, Safia Shaw (UK), Douglas Wilkerson & Edward Yersh (C).

CHINA

China is again heading along the road to private enterprise, which has been directed from the top by Deng Xiaoping. Deng has pointed out that these changes are economic and not political, as he and the Communist Party will not be introducing democracy, and will not tolerate any political dissent.

Visas & Permits

Before leaving London, two English travellers obtained bicycle permits from CITS. The permits cost UK£20 each and stipulated that the bearers had to enter China at Guangzhou, via the express train from Hong Kong. Apparently, without this permit, they would not have been allowed to enter China through this border crossing.

Money & Costs

The official current exchange rate is US$1 to Y5.46. The American Express office in Beijing, due to government regulations, cannot provide the Emergency Cheque Cashing service, but it is provided by four Chinese Banks. For this and other enquiries, contact American Express at W115D China World Tower, China World Trade Center, Beijing.

Getting Around

To get a bike on a local train you have to buy a ticket for yourself and your bike. Then go to the rear of the train and throw the bike into the train. This seems to be the acceptable solution – all the locals do it.

Travellers' Tips

We cycled along the Karakoram Highway and it was worth it as the valley is beautiful. You see the many peaks disappear as you ride into the flat desert from the Karakoram range.

You need to get permits as you go, because most of the area is closed to tourists. Normal permits are often not enough for cyclists, as special ones are required from Beijing. The trick is, when you are applying for the permit, not to tell the official that you will be travelling by bicycle. When officials found out that we were on bicycles, they insisted that we take the bus. It took a lot of time trying fruitlessly to persuade them to let us cycle, but in the end we always ended up leaving unnoticed.

We had no problems at police checkpoints along the way, but I think it depends on the police who are there at the time, as other people have had problems. It is advisable to always camp out of sight because passing police patrols can cause problems.

It seems that Trans-Siberian tickets are quite difficult to obtain before Christmas. The people at CITS at the back of the Chang Fu Gong Hotel were useless and directed us to the International Hotel. They had cancellation seats available a couple of days before departure to Moscow for Y800FEC (US$146) on the Trans-Manchurian. Monkey Business seems to have cornered all the seats, but charge US$280 for the Mongolian route and US$250 for the Manchurian one.

Visas are now easy to obtain and it's possible to get all of them in one day (at the right price). You don't need proof of train reservations and the 10-day Soviet transit visa and a three-day Mongolian visa, give you enough time to wait for a cancellation to come through with the International Hotel and get to Western Europe.

Caroline Porter

TIBET

Tibet is not an easy place to visit, and has been virtually closed to independent travellers since the 1987 riots. The Chinese authorities are now only allowing organised tours into Tibet. Meanwhile, any Tibetans who are actively supporting independence for their country are still being imprisoned. Ecologically the country is being ruined at the expense of progress and development.

Visas & Permits

A Chinese visa and a Tibetan permit are required to enter Tibet, but the permit is only given if an organised guided tour is booked. This is the official way of entering Tibet, but strangely enough one person can comprise a tour group. It is quite expensive, as a seven-day tour from Kathmandu or Chengdu to Lhasa costs around US$1000 per person.

Some travellers enter Tibet illegally, and if caught can face fines and in rare cases even deportation from China. The situation at present is not very clear, as some travellers seem to get around the rule of a Tibetan permit and an organised guided tour without any problems, and others can not!

PSB in Shigatse is a good place for getting permits. They don't give permits for the Everest area.

Money & Costs

The bank at the Chinese border with Nepal keeps unreliable opening hours. One traveller reported that he could not exchange any money – as a result he was allowed to take FEC out of the country but not RMB.

Getting Around

If hitchhiking, never pay in advance. The rate is about Y1RMB per 10 km.

Remember that if local truck drivers are caught with 'foreign hitchhikers' in their trucks, they are given heavy fines.

Tingri

There is a new place to stay in Tingri. The *Mt Everest Mountain View Hotel*, is very basic, has no electricity, and costs Y10 per person. The only meals they cook are 'momos' and instant noodle soup.

Travellers' Tips

If you would like to enjoy an extra four to seven days in Tibet, courtesy of CITS, volunteer to give up your seat on your return flight. Confirmed seats on the Lhasa to Kathmandu flight don't always match the number of hopeful travellers, resulting in stranded passengers. If you do stay make sure CITS provides you with a visa extension.

Kay Starr – England

HONG KONG

The Hong Kong Tourist Association has for

a number of years made available a guide booklet for physically handicapped visitors. It is available free of charge, and gives details on transportation, places of worship, shopping centres, restaurants, public facilities and hotels which are accessible to physically handicapped visitors. It is designed to be used in conjunction with visitor guide books and maps.

Money & Costs
The current official exchange rate is US$1 to HK$7.73.

Dangers & Annoyances
Women travelling alone should be very careful where they stay in the Chungking Mansions, on Nathan Road, Kowloon.There have been reports of men hanging about the walkways to the D and E block elevators, where they whistled, groped and offered sums of money to some women. One woman was allegedly physically attacked and chased down the stairs from the seventh floor to the ground floor.

JAPAN
All foreigners visiting Japan need to carry their identification on them at all times – whether it's a passport for tourists or an ARC for foreigners living in Japan. This applies 24 hours a day, every day, everywhere, even at the beach or while taking out the garbage in front of your residence.

Money & Costs
The official current exchange rate is US$1 to Y124.35.

Places to Stay
Very handy accommodation is provided by Weekend Monthly Mansions. These apartments are rented out on a daily/weekly/monthly basis and include a small kitchen. Normal cost is around Y8000 a night with cheaper weekly and monthly rates. The Tourist Office in Tokyo can give you a list of locations. One is located close to Shinjuku in Shimotikaido on the Keio Line at Sky Court (tel 03-3323 4411).

Getting There & Away
Upon leaving Japan from Tokyo's Narita Airport, it's worthwhile considering the option of checking in at Suitengumaie station, which is at the end of the Hanzomon Line. From there, buses take 70 minutes to reach Narita Airport. At Suitengumaie, it is possible to fully complete checking in procedure without the hassle of crowds. Everyone there speaks perfect English, your passport is stamped, and you are treated as if you have already left the country. Another advantage is that if you are asked to pay more for overweight luggage, you can simply tell them you'd rather check in at Narita, giving yourself a second chance not to pay the extra charge.

Travellers' Tips & Comments
Japan is no longer an expensive place to buy airline tickets. If you shop carefully through the places advertising in the English language magazines, like *Kansai Time Out*, you can find tickets cheaper than in any other first world country. The price I got on a round trip Osaka-San Francisco-Osaka ticket couldn't be beaten by a friend scouring the bucket shops of San Francisco, and I have heard similar stories from friends flying to Australia and Europe. The odd thing about Japan is that you will get a better deal than the locals, as many of the discount agencies quote higher prices to the Japanese than to 'gaijin'!

Heather McDougal – USA

TAIWAN
Travellers should try not to overstay their visas. The penalty for a first offence is filling out some forms and paying a small fine. Afterwards, in Taiwan you might be asked each time you hand over your passport to any official, why you overstayed your visa – this will even happen when entering neighbouring countries. If you overstay a second time, for whatever reason, your visa will be cancelled and you will be asked to leave Taiwan as soon as possible.

Money & Costs
The currant official exchange rate is US$1 to NT$24.60.

Lonely Planet Guidebooks

Lonely Planet guidebooks cover every accessible part of Asia as well as Australia, the Pacific, South America, Africa, the Middle East and parts of North America and Europe. There are four series: *travel survival kits*, covering a country for a range of budgets; *shoestring guides* with compact information for low-budget travel in a major region; *walking guides*; and *phrasebooks*.

Mail Order

Lonely Planet guidebooks are distributed worldwide and are sold by good bookshops everywhere. They are also available by mail order from Lonely Planet, so if you have difficulty finding a title please write to us. US and Canadian residents should write to Embarcadero West, 112 Linden St, Oakland CA 94607, USA and residents of other countries to PO Box 617, Hawthorn, Victoria 3122, Australia.

Europe

Eastern Europe on a shoestring
Iceland, Greenland & the Faroe Islands
Trekking in Spain
USSR
Russian phrasebook

Indian Subcontinent

Bangladesh
India
Hindi/Urdu phrasebook
Trekking in the Indian Himalaya
Karakoram Highway
Kashmir, Ladakh & Zanskar
Nepal
Trekking in the Nepal Himalaya
Nepal phrasebook
Pakistan
Sri Lanka
Sri Lanka phrasebook

Africa

Africa on a shoestring
Central Africa
East Africa
Kenya
Swahili phrasebook
Morocco, Algeria & Tunisia
Moroccan Arabic phrasebook
Zimbabwe, Botswana & Namibia
West Africa

North America

Alaska
Canada
Hawaii

Mexico

Baja California
Mexico

South America

Argentina
Bolivia
Brazil
Brazilian phrasebook
Chile & Easter Island
Colombia
Ecuador & the Galápagos Islands
Latin American Spanish phrasebook
Peru
Quechua phrasebook
South America on a shoestring

Central America

Central America on a shoestring
Costa Rica
La Ruta Maya

Middle East

Egypt & the Sudan
Egyptian Arabic phrasebook
Israel
Jordan & Syria
Yemen

The Lonely Planet Story

Lonely Planet published its first book in 1973 in response to the numerous 'How did you do it?' questions Maureen and Tony Wheeler were asked after driving, bussing, hitching, sailing and railing their way from England to Australia.

Written at a kitchen table and hand collated, trimmed and stapled, *Across Asia on the Cheap* became an instant local bestseller, inspiring thoughts of another book.

Eighteen months in South-East Asia resulted in their second guide, *South-East Asia on a shoestring*, which they put together in a backstreet Chinese hotel in Singapore in 1975. The 'yellow bible' as it quickly became known to backpackers around the world, soon became *the* guide to the region. It has sold well over half a million copies and is now in its 7th edition, still retaining its familiar yellow cover.

Today there are over 80 Lonely Planet titles – books that have that same adventurous approach to travel as those early guides; books that 'assume you know how to get your luggage off the carousel' as one reviewer put it.

Although Lonely Planet initially specialised in guides to Asia, they now cover most regions of the world, including the Pacific, South America, Africa, the Middle East and Eastern Europe. The list of *walking guides* and *phrasebooks* (for 'unusual' languages such as Quechua, Swahili, Nepalese and Egyptian Arabic) is also growing rapidly.

The emphasis continues to be on travel for independent travellers. Tony and Maureen still travel for several months of each year and play an active part in the writing, updating and quality control of Lonely Planet's guides.

They have been joined by over 50 authors, 40 staff – mainly editors, cartographers, & designers – at our office in Melbourne, Australia, and another 10 at our US office in Oakland, California. Travellers themselves also make a valuable contribution to the guides through the feedback we receive in thousands of letters each year.

The people at Lonely Planet strongly believe that travellers can make a positive contribution to the countries they visit, both through their appreciation of the countries' culture, wildlife and natural features, and through the money they spend. In addition, the company makes a direct contribution to the countries and regions it covers. Since 1986 a percentage of the income from each book has been donated to ventures such as famine relief in Africa; aid projects in India; agricultural projects in Central America; Greenpeace's efforts to halt French nuclear testing in the Pacific and Amnesty International. In 1991 $68,000 was donated to these causes.

Lonely Planet's basic travel philosophy is summed up in Tony Wheeler's comment, 'Don't worry about whether your trip will work out. Just go!'